THE AMERICAN PEOPLES

ENCYCLOPEDIA YEAR BOOK 1973

Grolier INCORPORATED

ISBN 0-7172-0404-9

Library of Congress Catalog Card Number: 48-171

Copyright © 1973 by  Grolier INCORPORATED

Copyright in Canada © by Grolier Limited

 PRINTED
IN
U.S.A.

Editor in Chief	Edward Humphrey
Managing Editor	John S. Cox
Executive Editor	James E. Churchill, Jr.
Art Director	Frank H. Senyk

Staff

Editors	Hallberg Hallmundsson
	William E. Kennedy
	Susan E. Linder
	Maureen V. O'Sullivan
Editorial Assistants	Mary Cordts
	Ellen R. Jacobs
	Anita L. Pasternak
Indexers	Kathleen Leerburger
	Marilyn J. Walkiewicz
Layout Artist	Charles W. Adams
Photo Researchers	Karen Tobias
	Lenore Weber

Manufacturing

Director	Edward C. McKenna
Assistant Director	Raymond H. Labott

Editorial Director	Wallace S. Murray

Contributors

ALBERT BARHAM is national soccer correspondent of *The Guardian,* Manchester and London.
SPORTS: Soccer

EDWARD BEHR, is chief of the Paris Bureau of *Newsweek.*
FRANCE

CHARLES W. BELL, former manager for Italy of United Press International, is UPI night editor in New York.   CYPRUS; GREECE; ITALY; MALTA; SWITZERLAND; TURKEY

ALTON BLAKESLEE, science editor of The Associated Press, New York City, is the author of *What You Can Do about Dangerous Drugs.*
DRUG ABUSE

GEORGE A. W. BOEHM, a free-lance science writer, is a member of the National Association of Science Writers.   PHYSICAL SCIENCES

ERIKA BOURGUIGNON, chairwoman of the department of anthropology at the Ohio State University, is the editor and coauthor of *Religion, Altered States of Consciousness and Social Change.*   ANTHROPOLOGY

PETER BROCK is news editor of *World Medicine,* published in London, a medical columnist of the *London Evening News* and a BBC contributor.
MEDICINE

BOB BROEG, sports editor of the *St. Louis Post-Dispatch,* is the author of *Super Stars of Baseball.*
SPORTS: Commercialization of Professional Sports; Football

STEPHENS BROENING, is a correspondent for The Associated Press in Moscow.
UNION OF SOVIET SOCIALIST REPUBLICS

LES BROWN, television and radio editor of *Variety* magazine, is the author of *Television: The Business Behind the Box.*
TELEVISION AND RADIO

KEVIN BURKE is visiting professor of geology at the University of Toronto.   GEOLOGY

RICHARD BUTWELL, chairman of the Department of Political Science at the State University of New York at Brockport, is the author of *Southeast Asia Today and Tomorrow.*
PHILIPPINE REPUBLIC; TAIWAN; THAILAND

LEON CARNOVSKY is professor emeritus of the Graduate Library School at the University of Chicago.   LIBRARIES

DINK CARROLL is sports editor of *The Gazette,* Montreal.   SPORTS: Ice Hockey

WILLIAM CEMLYN-JONES is foreign correspondent in Spain for both *The Guardian* and the *Observer,* London.   PORTUGAL; SPAIN

HELMUT A. ABT, astronomer at Kitt Peak National Observatory, Tucson, is managing editor of *The Astrophysical Journal.*   ASTRONOMY

THOMAS ALBRIGHT is art critic of the *San Francisco Chronicle* and a contributing editor of *The Art Gallery* magazine.   ART

HERBERT E. ALEXANDER, director of the Citizens' Research Foundation, Princeton, is the author of *Money in Politics.*
CAMPAIGN SPENDING

DAVID M. ALPERN is an associate editor of *Newsweek.*   CITIES

RICARDO ANZOLA-BETANCOURT is director of the Division of Tourism for the Organization of American States.
TRAVEL: Tourism Year of the Americas

FRANK BALDWIN, a research associate of the East Asian Institute, Columbia University, is spending the 1972–73 academic year in Tokyo on a Fulbright Fellowship.   KOREA

JOHN BALLANTINE is lawn tennis correspondent of the *Sunday Times,* London.
SPORTS: Tennis

DWIGHT CHAPIN is a sportswriter for the Los Angeles *Times*.   SPORTS: Swimming; Track

FRED CHEVALIER is author of the chess column for *The Christian Science Monitor*.   CHESS

MARQUIS CHILDS, awarded a Pulitzer Prize for distinguished commentary, serves as a contributing editor for the *St. Louis Post-Dispatch*.
U.S. ELECTIONS

HAROLD (SPIKE) CLAASSEN is a free-lance sportswriter.   SPORTS: Boxing; Golf

BOB COLLINS is sports editor of *The Indianapolis Star*.   SPORTS: Auto Racing

TAYLOR K. COUSINS is an assistant professor of economics at the College of William and Mary.
CARIBBEAN ISLANDS

WILLIAM A. DAVIS is travel editor of *The Boston Globe*.   TRAVEL

ISTVAN DEAK is a professor of history and director of the Institute on East Central Europe at Columbia University.
ALBANIA; AUSTRIA; HUNGARY; YUGOSLAVIA

A. GIB DeBUSK is a professor of biological science at Florida State University and the author of *Molecular Genetics*.   BIOLOGICAL SCIENCES

PETER DESBARATS is Ottawa editor and political columnist of *The Toronto Star* and frequently comments or writes for the Canadian Broadcasting Corporation.   CANADA

ROBERT W. DIETSCH, business and economics editor of Scripps-Howard Newspapers, is a contributor to *The New Republic* and *Saturday Review*.
SOCIAL SECURITY; STATES, U.S.; WELFARE

DIANE DURYEA, a member of the editorial staff of *Yachting Magazine*, is director of the N.Y. Council of the Navy League of the United States.
SPORTS: Yachting

DEAN EAGLE, sports editor of the *Courier-Journal*, Louisville, Ky., is a former president of the National Turf Writers Association.
SPORTS: Horse Racing

WILLIAM J. EATON, Washington correspondent of the *Chicago Daily News*, won a Pulitzer Prize for national reporting. He is the coauthor of a biography of Walter Reuther.
DEFENSE; DISARMAMENT; FOREIGN AID

JERRY C. EDGERTON, environmental reporter in the Washington bureau of McGraw-Hill Publications, in 1972 took a leave of absence to study at the London School of Economics.
ENVIRONMENT

GEORGE H. FAVRE, assistant chief editorial writer for *The Christian Science Monitor*, is the author of *Can We Survive Our Cities?* HOUSING

HARRY FLEISCHMAN is executive secretary of the National Alliance for Safer Cities.   CRIME

JAMES C. FLETCHER is the administrator of the National Aeronautics and Space Administration.
SPACE: The Space Cooperation Agreement

HAROLD W. FOX, a professor of marketing at DePaul University, is the author of *The Economics of Trading Stamps*.   CONSUMER AFFAIRS

HARVEY L. FRIEDMAN, an associate professor of political science, is the director of the Labor Relations and Research Center at the University of Massachusetts.   POSTAL SERVICE, U.S.

ERIK J. FRIIS is editor of *The American Scandinavian Review*.
DENMARK; FINLAND; NORWAY; SWEDEN

R. H. GARDNER, drama and film critic of *The Baltimore Sun*, is the author of *The Splintered Stage: The Decline of the American Theater*.
MOTION PICTURES

LILLIAN N. GERHARDT is editor in chief of the *School Library Journal*.
LITERATURE, JUVENILE

CHARLES H. GOREN is a world-famous bridge expert.   BRIDGE

CURT GOWDY, sports broadcaster for NBC-TV, is the host of ABC's "American Sportsman."
OLYMPIC GAMES

FRED P. GRAHAM, U.S. Supreme Court correspondent for *The New York Times*, joined CBS in a similar capacity late in 1972. He is the author of *The Self-Inflicted Wound*.   LAW

GEORGE W. GRAYSON, associate professor of government at the College of William and Mary, is also a lecturer at the State Department's Foreign Service Institute.   BOLIVIA; COLOMBIA; ECUADOR; GUYANA, SURINAM AND FRENCH GUIANA; PERU; VENEZUELA

PHILIP GREER, New York financial correspondent of *The Washington Post*, won the G. H. Loeb Award in 1971.
ECONOMIC AFFAIRS: U.S. Economy

MEL GUSSOW, drama critic for *The New York Times*, is the author of a biography of Darryl Zanuck.   THEATER

JAMES J. HAGGERTY, former editor of *Aerospace Year Book*, has written numerous books on aerospace; among the most recent is *Apollo Lunar Landing*.   SPACE

JOSEPH W. HALL, JR., is a member of the U.S. Senate staff in the Washington bureau of The Associated Press. TAXATION

SYBIL E. HAMLET is public information officer for the National Zoological Park, Washington, D.C. ZOOS: Panda-Musk Oxen Exchange

NORMAN HAMMOND, a practicing archeologist, is archeological correspondent of *The Times,* London. ARCHEOLOGY

EARL O. HEADY, professor of economics at Iowa State University and executive director of the Center for Agricultural and Economic Development, has written numerous books on agriculture. AGRICULTURE

FRED M. HECHINGER, a member of the editorial board and former education editor of *The New York Times,* has served as president of the Education Writers' Association. EDUCATION

WALTER B. HERBERT, fellow of the Royal Society of Arts, is a self-employed consultant on Canadian cultural matters. CANADA: Arts and Letters

DORIS HERING, critic-at-large for *Dance Magazine* and executive director of the National Association for Regional Ballet, is the author of *Twenty-Five Years of American Dance.* DANCE

RONALD HILTON is a professor at Stanford University and the executive director of the California Institute of International Studies. BRAZIL; CENTRAL AMERICA; MEXICO

STEPHEN HOLDEN is record reviewer of *Rolling Stone* magazine. MUSIC, POPULAR

FREDERIC H. HUNTER, stationed in Nairobi, Kenya, is Africa correspondent of *The Christian Science Monitor.* AFRICA

CHUCK JOHNSON is sports editor of *The Milwaukee Journal* and president of the Milwaukee Press Club. SPORTS: Basketball

STEPHEN W. KANN is the editor and publisher of *Industrial World* magazine. INDUSTRIAL PRODUCTION

CARROLL KILPATRICK is White House correspondent of *The Washington Post* and winner of the 1971 Merriman Smith award for distinguished White House coverage. UNITED STATES

BERNARD KRISHER is Tokyo bureau chief of *Newsweek.* JAPAN

RUBEN LEVIN is editor and manager of *Labor,* a weekly newspaper published by the Labor Cooperative Educational and Publishing Society. LABOR

DAVID LIDMAN, stamp news editor of *The New York Times,* is author of *The New York Times Guide to Collecting Stamps.* HOBBIES: Stamps and Stamp Collecting

BARBARA LOBRON, a free-lance photographer, is a senior editor of *Camera35.* PHOTOGRAPHY

WELLINGTON LONG, chief correspondent in Germany for United Press International, is the author of *The New Nazis of Germany.* GERMANY

WILLIAM R. MacKAYE is the religion editor of *The Washington Post.* RELIGION

SIGURDUR A. MAGNUSSON is the editor of *Samvinnan,* published by the Federation of Iceland Co-operative Societies. ICELAND

JOHN ALLAN MAY is chief of the London news bureau of *The Christian Science Monitor* and a member of the Economic Research Council of Great Britain. IRELAND, REPUBLIC OF; UNITED KINGDOM

DAVID A. McGILL is professor of ocean science at the U.S. Coast Guard Academy, New London, Conn. OCEANOGRAPHY

PATRICIA A. MILGRAM is fashion and pattern editor of *Woman's Day* magazine. FASHION

ARTHUR C. MILLER is senior editor of *The Asia Letter,* an authoritative newsletter on Asian affairs published in Hong Kong. AFGHANISTAN; BURMA; CEYLON; MONGOLIAN PEOPLE'S REPUBLIC

CHARLES W. MOORE, a consultant for the National Endowment for the Arts, is professor of architecture at Yale University. ARCHITECTURE

ROGERS C. B. MORTON has been U.S. Secretary of the Interior since January 1971. PARKS: Yellowstone Centennial

DANIEL B. MOSKOWITZ, a correspondent for the McGraw-Hill Washington news bureau, specializes in economics. ENERGY

BRUCE W. MUNN has been chief United Nations correspondent for United Press International since 1949. UNITED NATIONS

VICTOR S. NAVASKY, formerly an editor of *The New York Times Magazine,* is the author of *Kennedy Justice.* FEDERAL BUREAU OF INVESTIGATION

LEE C. NEHRT, professor of international business at Indiana University, is the author of several books on business and finance. ECONOMIC AFFAIRS: International Trade and Finance; FOREIGN AID: International Development Assistance

RICHARD NORTON-TAYLOR, is foreign correspondent in Brussels of *The Guardian,* Manchester and London.
BELGIUM; LUXEMBOURG; NETHERLANDS

JAMES O'GARA is editor-at-large of *Advertising Age.* ADVERTISING

TAKASHI OKA is chief Paris correspondent for *The Christian Science Monitor.*
EUROPEAN ECONOMIC COMMUNITY

MARVIN C. OTT is assistant professor of political science at Mount Holyoke College specializing in Far Eastern affairs.
HONG KONG; INDONESIA, MALAYSIA; SINGAPORE

W. DONALD POINTER is associate executive director of the American Correctional Association.
PRISONS

SHIRLEY POVICH is sports editor of *The Washington Post* and a former president of the Baseball Writers of America. SPORTS: Baseball

PETER S. PRESCOTT is book review editor of *Newsweek* and author of *Soundings: Encounters with Contemporary Books.*
LITERATURE, ADULT

GEORGE E. REEDY, dean of the college of journalism at Marquette University, was press secretary to President Lyndon B. Johnson.
INDOCHINA WAR: RETROSPECTIVE—1965–72

EDWARD C. ROCHETTE, editor of *The Numismatist,* is executive director of the American Numismatic Association.
HOBBIES: Coins and Coin Collecting

JOHN RODERICK, foreign correspondent of the Associated Press stationed in Tokyo, was assigned to China before the Communist takeover. He is the author of *What Everyone Should Know About China.* CHINA

EDGAR B. SCHICK is vice-president for academic affairs and dean of St. John Fisher College, Rochester, N.Y. YOUTH

GUNTHER SCHULLER, a composer and writer, is president of the New England Conservatory and author of *Early Jazz.* MUSIC, CLASSICAL

E. PRESTON SHARP is executive director of the American Correctional Association and correspondent of the United States to the United Nations in the field of social defense. PRISONS

JEANNETTE SMYTH is a reporter for *The Washington Post.* WOMEN

WILLIAM SPENCER, professor of history at Florida State University, has traveled extensively in and written about North Africa and the Middle East. ARAB STATES; IRAN; ISRAEL

BRIAN SULLIVAN is a writer for the science department of The Associated Press and coauthor of *What You Should Know About VD.* HEALTH

WILLIAM H. TAFT, professor of journalism at the University of Missouri, has written extensively about his field. Among his most recent works is *Newspapers as Tools for Historians.*
PUBLISHING

PHILLIPS TALBOT, formerly U.S. ambassador to Greece and Assistant Secretary of State for Near Eastern and South Asian Affairs, is president of The Asia Society.
BANGLADESH; INDIA; PAKISTAN

MICHAEL S. TEITELBAUM is assistant professor of sociology at Princeton University and an associate of the Office of Population Research.
POPULATION

JACK C. THOMPSON is professor of meteorology at California State University at San Jose and coauthor of *Elements of Meteorology.*
METEOROLOGY

RAYMOND F. VALENTI is professor of finance and insurance at the School of Management, Syracuse University. INSURANCE

CRAIG R. WHITNEY is chief of the Saigon bureau of *The New York Times.*
INDOCHINA WAR: A DECISIVE YEAR

RICHARD WIGG was Latin America correspondent of *The Times,* London, until late 1972 when he was transferred to *The Times'* Paris bureau.
ARGENTINA; CHILE; PARAGUAY; URUGUAY

ERNEST W. WILLIAMS, JR., is professor of transportation at the Graduate School of Business, Columbia University, and the author of several books on transportation. TRANSPORTATION

J. TUZO WILSON, professor of geophysics and principal of Erindale College of the University of Toronto, is coauthor of *Physics and Geology.*
GEOLOGY

R. M. YOUNGER, former director of the Australian News and Information Bureau in New York City, is the author of *Australia and the Australians.*
AUSTRALIA; NEW ZEALAND; OCEANIA

JOSEPH FREDERICK ZACEK is professor of history at the State University of New York at Albany and the author of several books on Central and Eastern Europe.
BULGARIA; CZECHOSLOVAKIA; POLAND; RUMANIA

ILLUSTRATION JOHN A. LIND

TABLE OF CONTENTS

Pages 64-480 Alphabetical Section (partial listing)

U.S. ELECTIONS:
PRESIDENT OF ALL THE PEOPLE

by Marquis Childs

Contributing Editor

St. Louis Post-Dispatch

The winner, President Nixon, with his wife, acknowledging his landslide triumph in November, declared the result a "victory for America."

J. P. Laffont, Gamma

Vice-President Agnew, on the campaign trail, avoided the harsh invective that characterized his activities in the 1970 Congressional heat.

Doug Bruce, Camera5

In a newspaper interview released just after the U.S. election of 1972, President Richard Nixon said that the outcome was determined on the day that Sen. George McGovern was nominated on the Democratic ticket. His assertion may have been a slight exaggeration, yet as one of the keenest political analysts, with an intimate and extraordinary knowledge of the political map of the United States, state by state and district by district, Mr. Nixon spoke with uncommon authority. In retrospect, it appeared that he had fashioned his entire campaign on just that judgment.

The campaign of 1972 was in many ways unique. What happened before the nominating conventions of the two parties in Miami Beach had far more significance than the contest that began in September. In primaries in 21 states and delegate election contests that followed the pattern of nominating choice in two others, the Democrats proceeded to cut each other to pieces. There were two centrist candidates, Sen. Edmund Muskie and Sen. Hubert Humphrey. Humphrey had initially indicated he would not run again, following his narrow defeat in 1968, but he threw himself into the race with all of his characteristic vigor and intensity.

The two men at the center obviously were destined to divide the vote of the moderates. To the right of them was Sen. Henry M. Jackson, whose strong card was his stand for a firm defense posture. At the outset, in the New Hampshire primary, marginal candidates, such as Rep. Wilbur Mills of Arkansas, further divided the vote. Although he had the backing of many Democratic leaders, Muskie did not long stay the course. The episode of his weeping outside the offices of the Manchester (N.H.) *Union-Leader,* which had reprinted an attack on his wife, harmed him greatly. Television viewers would remember the Senator from Maine standing on a flatbed truck as the snow fell on his bare head and tears welled in his eyes.

Muskie's departure in effect left the race to Humphrey and McGovern. Increasingly McGovern made the war in Vietnam central to his campaign. The young, the doves and others, did not need to be reminded that Humphrey had been Lyndon Johnson's vice president and that as such he had supported the Johnson policy of escalating the war. These same young worked tirelessly by the thousands for their candidate. In state after state, McGovern was the victor,

Packed with new faces conspicuously representative of youth, women and minorities, the Democratic Convention was a creature of the party's McGovern-drawn delegate selection rules. Many key regulars were missing.

In striking contrast to the Democrats', the Republicans' convention was a celebration of near-unanimity by mostly well-heeled party stalwarts.

Fred Ward, Black Star

Symbolic of the new forces pressing for representation in Democratic party decisions in 1972 was this delegate from Senator McGovern's home state of South Dakota.

Dennis Brack, Black Star

13

Following the debacle of Sen. Thomas F. Eagleton's withdrawal, McGovern chose and the Democratic committee endorsed R. Sargent Shriver as running mate.

Campaigning in California, McGovern succeeded, as elsewhere, in drawing enthusiastic crowds, but the polls consistently showed him far behind his elusive rival.

although in some states—Pennsylvania was one—Humphrey, with the backing of organized labor and the blacks, managed temporarily to oppose the tide.

The climax came in California's winner-take-all primary with its reward of 271 delegates. Traveling up and down the big state, Humphrey attacked McGovern vigorously. He charged that McGovern's proposed cut of $30,000,-000,000 in the defense budget over a period of three years would cost thousands of jobs in defense and aerospace industry. With unemployment already substantial in those industries in California, the point was telling. He attacked McGovern's welfare proposal of $1,000 for every American.

At the start of the California campaign the Field poll had forecast victory for McGovern by at least 15 points. At the polls, McGovern claimed the victory by fewer than 5 points. After the primary, Humphrey filed a claim in Federal court, charging that the winner-take-all formula had deprived him of his proportionate share of the delegates based on the votes cast and was therefore unconstitutional. If anything had been needed to widen the breach in the party, that was it. The McGovern camp was furious even though the claim was finally rejected. McGovern prepared for the convention at Miami Beach with a total of 1,383 delegates, and the general expectation was that he would acquire either before or just on the eve of the convention the requisite 1,509 to nominate.

Meanwhile, throughout the primary season, as the Democrats were engaged in their bruising internecine war, the Republicans were carefully abjuring partisan politics. The President was scoring diplomatic triumphs with National Security Adviser Henry Kissinger at his side in Peking and Moscow. Out of the Moscow meeting came a whole series of agreements, foremost among them an historic limitation on defensive nuclear missiles. Mr. Nixon was establishing his bona fides as President of all the people.

He had opposition in the Republican primaries, but it was hardly more than token opposition. Rep Paul N. (Pete) McCloskey of California opposed him in several states on the war issue, demanding an immediate pullout from Vietnam. On the other side, Rep. John Ashbrook of Ohio charged the President with departing from the ways of orthodox conservatism. They received no more than splinters of the vote.

As the Republican primaries had been carefully stage-managed, so was the Republican convention in Miami Beach. From first to last it was a controlled and orderly celebration of the renomination of the President and his vice president, Spiro Agnew. The GOP faithful in their best bib and tucker followed a script prepared long in advance. The President was put in nomination by his one-time rival, Gov. Nelson Rockefeller of New York, whose speech was received with less enthusiasm than that of Gov. Ronald Reagan of California, who turned the fire of his rhetoric on Democratic sins. Vice President Agnew emerged as a moderate, mild in speech, readying himself, so many believed, to be the presidential nominee in 1976 with the blessing of the President. Outside the convention hall and the hotel that was convention headquarters, the Fontainebleau, long haired protesters, held in bounds by the police, screamed imprecations at the delegates as they passed by. The contrast on the television screens between the shouting demonstrators and the well dressed delegates could only have enhanced the Republican appeal to the great silent majority.

Gravely wounded by a would-be assassin, George Wallace (left) abandoned active campaigning and, despite his appearance at the Democratic Convention, declined to support McGovern.

The Democratic convention also had been orderly; orderly at any rate in comparison with the riotous condition that prevailed four years before in Chicago. But it was a minority of the party that convened in Miami Beach, as it had been a minority, often a small minority, that had given McGovern the victory in so many states. Under the rules of the reform commission that had been headed by Senator McGovern himself, minorities—blacks, women, the young—were represented as never before. Mayor Richard Daley of Chicago and his delegates were excluded in spite of the suit in the courts to claim places for them. W. Averell Harriman, a former governor of New York and a mainstay of U.S. diplomacy for a generation, was denied a seat when he was defeated in the New York State delegation contest by a young woman backed by the McGovernites. After a long night's session that lost much of the television audience on the Eastern seaboard, McGovern was nominated to the cheers of his admirers.

The presidential campaign that followed came almost as an anticlimax, and that was particularly true after the disaster that befell the Democrats at the outset. McGovern had persisted almost to the moment of his nomination in believing that he could persuade Sen. Edward M. Kennedy to take the number two place on the ticket. The polls had shown that Kennedy would make a difference of more than 15 points with the voters, while other possible vice presidents would have provided little or no additional margin for the Democratic ticket. As he had said earlier with respect to the presidential nomination, Kennedy repeatedly rejected McGovern's pleas, insisting that he would have no place on the national ticket in 1972.

Canvassing a list of three or four candidates, after several other leading Democrats had declined to take the second place, McGovern and his staff

selected the name of Sen. Thomas Eagleton of Missouri. Informed of his choice on the telephone and asked if he had any skeletons in his closet, Eagleton replied that he did not. His nomination quickly followed, after the delegates in a frivolous mood had put in nomination a number of irrelevant candidates, including Martha Mitchell and Roger Mudd of CBS.

What followed was a disaster comparable with the riots in Chicago that had dimmed Humphrey's chances of winning in 1968. Whispers soon arose that Eagleton had been hospitalized for psychiatric treatment and during that hospitalization had undergone shock therapy. Although not documented by medical records, a report to that effect was in the hands of at least one newspaper bureau. Before it could be made public, McGovern, with Eagleton at his side in Rapid City, S.D., where the candidate was theoretically taking a rest before the beginning of the campaign, disclosed that he had learned of Eagleton's illness and that it made no difference in his choice of a vice presidential candidate. The controversy grew more intense as reporters pressed McGovern and, more particularly, Eagleton about the details of his illness. At one point, McGovern said he stood behind Eagleton 1000 percent, which was to haunt him, as a week later he announced that Eagleton had agreed to leave the ticket. Taken as a sign of indecision, McGovern's about-face was to plague him in the weeks that followed. Moreover, Democrats had lost from three to four weeks of organization, planning and effort to unite the major elements of the party.

With a highly professional staff using new techniques, employing the computer and massive telephone banks, the Republicans prepared a low key campaign. There could be no doubt that President Nixon himself was the architect of the campaign. It took a leaf from the book of Franklin D. Roosevelt's successful campaign in 1936, when the Democrats won every state but Maine and Vermont. President Nixon was never to mention the name of his opponent. That was left, when it seemed essential, to surrogates—members of his family, his Cabinet and leading Republicans in the Congress, who did far more actual stumping than the President himself.

Under the direction of former Secretary of Commerce Maurice Stans a highly successful fund raising drive brought in an estimated $47,000,000, most of it in large gifts and most of it unattributed because the big spenders had been urged to make their contributions prior to the April 7 cut off set by the Campaign Election Law for public disclosure of contributions. The fund raising was done under the skilled direction of the Committee to Re–elect the President, which was as carefully monitored as the campaign of the President himself.

On June 17 five men wearing rubber gloves and equipped with the tools of electronic espionage were arrested in the Democratic national headquarters. It soon developed that two of the men had previously been employed by the Committee to Re–elect the President, and two of them had been at one time White House consultants. Ultimately seven men were indicted in connection with the break-in. It appeared that in a trial and also perhaps in a Congressional investigation the details of this mysterious and unprecedented act would come to light, and the Democrats would reap the benefits.

That never happened, and McGovern's repeated efforts to focus attention on what he said was the criminal act of the Watergate affair, together with later

Tricia Nixon Cox enjoys a GOP picnic. Members of the first family and the administration did much of Mr. Nixon's campaigning.

charges of Republican sabotage in the Democratic primaries, failed to arouse any widespread public concern. On one of his last paid half-hour television appearances, McGovern vigorously attacked the Nixon administration for sanctioning such acts. As for Nixon, he said at a rare press conference that no one then employed in the White House had had any part in the Watergate break-in. The denial was repeated when *The Washington Post,* the newspaper that had most strenuously pushed the charges, published the names of various White House aides alleged to have had a connection with the indicted men.

Day after day, McGovern criss-crossed the country in his chartered plane, the Dakota Queen II, speaking often four or five times a day in widely separated centers. The crowds turned out; they cheered him. But were they the same minority, for the most part the young, who had given him the nomination in the primaries? When he met with reporters, they almost invariably asked him about the polls, which consistently showed a 26 point spread in President Nixon's favor. McGovern insisted that he would win and prove the polls false. The Democratic candidate was haunted, too, by reports on every side of the apathy that prevailed with respect to the election. His vice presidential candidate, Sargent Shriver, nominated at a hastily called meeting of the Democratic National Committee after Eagleton's withdrawal, campaigned with equal zeal. As the campaign wore on, McGovern resorted to charges that seemed to many voters, including even many Democrats, both reckless and unwarranted. He called the Nixon administration the most corrupt in America's

history. He even suggested an analogy with Hitler in the tactics used by the Republicans.

For the Democrats everything seemed to go wrong. McGovern sought to make his peace with Daley and the other regulars who had been alienated by the convention and the tactics pursued in the primaries. This disillusioned many of the newly franchised voters, the 18- to 25-year-olds, who felt that their champion had compromised with the old politics. The candidate backed away from his $1,000 per person proposal and modified other stands that had seemed to make him a radical.

Yet the radical label stuck. He never escaped the overtones of the primaries, in which his youthful followers had talked about legalizing marijuana, abortion, and even, in the Minnesota state-wide convention made up of ardent Mc-Governites, legalizing homosexual marriage. As the primary campaign developed, the issue of amnesty was raised, McGovern promising forgiveness for young Americans who had fled the country rather than accept conscription into the Army. The President at his press conference and repeatedly during the campaign, on the other hand, stated that he would never grant amnesty to men who had deserted their country, that to do so would impugn the valor of 2,500,000 Americans who had served with the armed forces in Vietnam.

Throughout, the President asserted what he said were the fundamental values of the American people. He made most of his paid political addresses on radio because, as he has frequently observed, he finds the techniques of television—especially lighting and makeup—not only distracting but also time consuming as against those of the microphone in the quiet of his study. On Oct. 21 he made a significant radio address in which he declared that he would defend the basic human values of good, decent people, who should stop "letting themselves be bulldozed by anybody that presumes to be the self-righteous moral judge of our society." He alluded to those who resist higher taxes and "income

PERCENTAGE OF POPULAR VOTE

NIXON   McGOVERN

70-79%

60-69%   D.C. 79%

50-59%   MASS. 55%

redistribution," one of McGovern's repeated stands in his determination to reform the tax system; who object to the busing of their children from neighborhood schools to other schools; and oppose employment quotas for the benefit of disadvantaged minorities. Their values, said the President, were ones to be proud of, "values that I shall always stand up for when they come under attack."

Thereafter in what seemed to be a chart for the four years ahead he declared: "The rights of each minority must be virorously defended—and each minority must be protected in the opportunity to have its opinion become accepted as the majority view. But on these basic concerns [busing, higher taxes, the work ethic] the majority view must prevail. . . . You can be sure of this: on matters affecting basic human values—on the way Americans live their lives and bring up their children—I am going to respect and reflect the opinion of the people themselves."

The statement revealed Mr. Nixon's conviction that most Americans were resistant to change—they might not like things exactly as they were, but after the upheavals of recent years they were not prepared to accept the kind of drastic changes McGovern seemed to be proposing.

Carefully controlled as was his campaign, the President did go into 17 states, and in three of them, Kentucky, Rhode Island and North Carolina, he cam-

RICHARD M. NIXON

On Nov. 7, Richard Nixon was reelected President by the widest popular vote margin in U.S. history. Running against maverick Democrat George McGovern, he captured more than 60 percent of the vote.

Nixon was born in Yorba Linda, Calif., on Jan. 9, 1913. After graduating from college and law school, he saw wartime service in the Navy and in 1946 launched his political career. Conducting a series of tireless and, some felt, ruthless campaigns on the theme of anti-Communism, he was elected to Congress in 1946 and 1948 and to the Senate in 1950.

As Vice-President, under Eisenhower (1953–61), Nixon was more active than most of his predecessors. He traveled widely, and attacks directed at him overseas merely increased his prestige at home.

In 1960 he was narrowly defeated for the presidency by John F. Kennedy, and two years later, for the governorship of California by incumbent Pat Brown. Chosen overwhelmingly as the Republican Presidential nominee in 1968, he won by an eyelash.

SPIRO T. AGNEW

From having been almost completely unknown in 1968, Spiro Agnew had emerged by November 1972 as a well known if controversial Vice-President.

The son of a Greek immigrant, he was born on Nov. 9, 1918, in Baltimore, Md. He studied law there and served in the Army in World War II and the Korean war. After cutting his political teeth as Baltimore County's executive (1962–66), he was elected governor of Maryland with liberal support, which he later lost. His lack of a clear political identity may have recommended him to Richard Nixon, who chose him as his running mate in 1968.

In the ensuing campaign and throughout his first term, Agnew proved to be an energetic speechmaker whose blunt, if elaborate, turn of phrase—"an effete corps of impudent snobs"—attracted heavy publicity, enraged liberals and delighted conservatives.

After much speculation as to whether Nixon would bypass Agnew in favor of former Secretary of the Treasury Connally, Nixon decided not to "break up a winning team."

paigned for Senatorial candidates who seemed to be in trouble. His appearances were without the hoopla of 1968, the Nixonettes, the flood of balloons, the organized cheering squads. Indeed, the reporters traveling with him complained that he was so secluded, so surrounded by his own people and by the Secret Service, that he was hardly visible. At a big fund raising dinner early in the campaign in the Century Plaza hotel in Los Angeles, at which $1,400,000 was raised, reporters were not allowed in the dining hall and witnessed the proceedings only on closed circuit television.

The Democrats tried harder, but to no avail. The press reported disagreements and even quarrels among McGovern's campaign staff. Most of the staff members had no acquaintance with national campaigning, and scheduling often went wrong. The Democratic candidate frequently complained that the press was unfair. He did succeed, however, in raising an estimated $34,000,000 —at least four times the amount Humphrey had raised in the course of the 1968 campaign—and most of it came from small contributors.

For the Republicans, or at least the incumbent in the White House, everything went right. Grain sales to the U.S.S.R. and China, although they were assailed by the Democrats in terms of prices and subsidies to the grain dealers and the farmers, had a marked effect on the farm vote, promising as they did that surpluses would be reduced or eliminated. Although unemployment re-

GEORGE S. McGOVERN

Conceding defeat to incumbent Richard Nixon in the November election, George McGovern brought to an end a 22-month campaign for the presidency which had aroused the fervent support of millions of Americans and the disdain of centrist voters of both major parties.

From the start his candidacy attracted thousands of young volunteers, but it failed to get more than tacit support from Democratic regulars and labor chiefs. It faltered when the candidate failed to improve his standing in the polls after the convention, foundered with the disclosure that vice-presidential running mate Eagleton had been hospitalized for depression and ended in crushing defeat.

McGovern was born in Avon, S.D., on July 19, 1922, the son of a Methodist minister. After distinguished service as a bomber pilot in Europe in World War II, he completed graduate studies in history and political science and, abjuring an earlier commitment to the ministry, taught college in South Dakota. Largely responsible for reviving Democratic politics in the state, he was elected to Congress in 1956 and to the Senate in 1962.

R. SARGENT SHRIVER

On Aug. 5, some three weeks after his own nomination, Democratic candidate George McGovern announced that Sargent Shriver would be his vice-presidential running mate. The circumstances surrounding the choice were unique in American history, the original nominee, Sen. Thomas F. Eagleton, having withdrawn.

Shriver was born on Nov. 9, 1915, in Westminster, Md. He served in the Navy in World War II and in 1946 began a long association with the Kennedy family. He subsequently managed the Chicago Merchandise Mart, the world's largest office building, owned by Joseph P. Kennedy, and in 1953 married Eunice Kennedy.

Shriver joined the Kennedy administration as director of the Peace Corps and remained in that post and simultaneously was director of the new Office of Economic Opportunity under President Johnson. Named ambassador to France by Johnson, he retained the post under Nixon until 1970. As McGovern's running mate, Shriver was an enthusiastic and articulate candidate.

Anti-Nixon protesters blocked the sidewalks before the Fontainebleau Hotel in Miami Beach during GOP Platform Committee hearings. Some 1,000 demonstrators were arrested during the convention.

mained at 5.5 percent of the work force, most of the indicators showed a marked economic upturn and the possibility of a boom in 1973. Moreover, when Henry Kissinger gave a "peace is at hand" press conference on Oct. 26, the war seemed finally to have faded from the campaign. (The polls had previously indicated, however, that the President already enjoyed the support of 58 percent of the people on the war issue.) With peace at hand, even though it was not promised before election day, the torpid stock market took off, and prices on the Exchange began to climb.

One important factor was missing. In 1968, Gov. George Wallace had retained 13 percent of the total vote and carried five Southern states. In 1972, running in the Democratic primaries, Wallace had obtained a plurality in Florida and more than 50 percent of the Democratic vote in Michigan. Whether, failing to get the nomination, which seemed a virtual certainty, he would run on a third party ticket in the fall was conjectural. Many observers thought it unlikely. But the question was settled when he was struck down and grievously wounded by an assassin's bullet after speaking at a shopping center rally in Maryland.

During his long convalescence, confined to a wheelchair with little hope that he could ever overcome the paralysis he had suffered, Wallace kept his preferences strictly to himself. McGovern later revealed that he had appealed directly and repeatedly to Wallace for support on the ground that their populist approaches contained common views on wealth, the working man and the farmer, although emphatically not on busing and other Wallace positions that seemed to have racial overtones.

Observers around the country reported a general indifference among the people, even as McGovern made his more extreme charges. The preacher's son from South Dakota could not reach the mass of the American people. The McGovern camp had believed that in the last two or three weeks of the campaign the polls would show him narrowing the gap. But up to the very last day the spread was nearly as wide—perhaps one or two points narrower—as

it had been at the beginning. Gloom pervaded the McGovern camp; only the candidate himself insisted that a miracle would come to pass on polling day. In a last 24-hour surge he sped across the continent, speaking in New York, Pennsylvania and California—and finally back to his home state of South Dakota to await the returns.

Every headline had reinforced the hold of the incumbent on the office. In California for some last rallies the President proceeded to his handsome estate at San Clemente to rest, go early on election morning to cast his vote and then fly to Washington for the triumph that he and all of those around him were confident was theirs. He acknowledged it, one of the greatest landslides in history, with a calm, almost matter-of-fact television appearance shortly before midnight.

The victory was essentially Nixon's. Confronted with massive ticket splitting, the Republicans lost two seats in the Senate, giving the Democrats a majority of 57–43, and gained only 12 seats in the House, 25 fewer than needed to control. The Democrats had carried one state, Massachusetts, and the District of Columbia. Before a loyal, cheering crowd in Mitchell, S.D., McGovern put a brave face on his overwhelming defeat and read a telegram promising to cooperate with the victor.

Thus ended one of the strangest elections in American history. The outcome, given the improved and scientific nature of polling and the very large spread, had never been in doubt. Apathy persisted to the end. Many voters apparently felt that the election was a choice of evils. Others appeared so confident of Nixon's victory that they took little interest in the proceedings. As a result, one prediction could be made with confidence—that fewer eligible voters would go to the polls than at any time in recent years. And that was the way it turned out—with only 55 percent of the potential vote cast.

Michael Lloyd Carlebach

Eleanor McGovern, the attractive and articulate wife of the Democratic presidential nominee, traveled extensively on her own in behalf of the Senator.

THE INDOCHINA WAR

A DECISIVE YEAR:

by Craig R. Whitney

Saigon Bureau Chief, *The New York Times*

RETROSPECTIVE:

by George E. Reedy

Dean, College of Journalism, Marquette University

Former Press Secretary of President Johnson

A DECISIVE YEAR

To the North Vietnamese—the principal external motive force behind the decade-long "War of National Liberation" in South Vietnam—1972 was to be a "decisive year," as they heralded it to friends and enemies alike before the year began. To the United States—the chief external motive force resisting the revolutionary movement—1972 was to be a decisive year as well. The year set the stage for complete American troop withdrawal and the end of a long and costly military involvement.

It is a war that has cost a million lives, only 55,000 of them American ones. It is a local war that grew and spread to the neighboring states of Laos and Cambodia, and it is a war that nobody has won. But at the end of 1972, North Vietnam and its allies or clients, the Pathet Lao in Laos, Khmer Communists in Cambodia and the "Vietcong"—the National Liberation Front and the Provisional Revolutionary Government in South Vietnam—were in a position of greater strength than at any time since before American intervention began in earnest in the mid-1960's.

The position was reached at the cost of a bloody offensive that took at least 100,000 North Vietnamese lives, left that country's roads, bridges and factories ruined by American bombing and tore much of South Vietnam apart. One million South Vietnamese refugees were driven from their homes; 40,000 soldiers of Saigon's army (ARVN, the Army of the Republic of Vietnam) died, and double or triple that number were injured or disabled. Cambodia, drawn into the war after the overthrow of Prince Norodom Sihanouk in 1970, was riven asunder and overwhelmed by forces beyond its control. Laos was partitioned.

The provincial capital, An Loc, was reduced to ruins by Communist artillery and U.S. bombs.

A Hanoi street, after the May decision to resume bombing increased the war's devastation.

Bombs released by a B-52 carpet bomber will cut a path of destruction one-half mile wide and one and one-half miles long.

But the American bombing and mining of North Vietnam's harbors, and the tenacity of Saigon's army kept the Communists from achieving total victory. What the Communists did achieve was the reestablishment of their claim to be a significant political force in the South, and the destruction of the myth that they had been erased.

Having achieved that much—not as much as they had hoped to attain when they launched their 1972 offensive in the spring—the North Vietnamese offered a peace settlement that compromised in important ways. The offer separated the military aspects from the political problems and gave the United States the opportunity to withdraw all its forces from Indochina, recover its prisoners of war from Hanoi and leave the Vietnamese to work out their political future themselves. It was a compromise, and the Americans, if not their South Vietnamese allies, appeared willing to take it. If so, would the fighting really stop for good?

Some thought it had stopped by the end of 1971. But what was happening then was more ominous. North Vietnam's army was arming and concentrating for large-scale, intense military activity as it had never waged it before in the 20 years of the French and American Indochina wars.

In northern Laos the 312th and 316th North Vietnamese Army divisions were probing westward onto the Plain of Jars, the high, barren plateau just north of the Laotian capital of Vientiane. In the southern part of the country the Ho Chi Minh Trail—a complex network of dirt roads, paths, bridges and hidden supply lines under the canopy of the jungles—was busy with trucks,

tanks and ammunition moving south into North Vietnamese base areas along the South Vietnamese border in Laos and Cambodia.

American fighter-bombers and B-52 strategic bombers ran intensive interdiction missions on these trails in early 1972 as they had been doing since the mid-1960's, but how many military supplies were still getting through no one knew. What the pilots did know was that they were being shot at more intensively in early 1972 than in the past—an indication that the North Vietnamese needed their trail and were protecting it with batteries of heavy antiaircraft guns and even SAM-2 surface-to-air missiles.

At the southern outlet of the trail, in eastern Cambodia, North Vietnamese troops concentrated in the mountains just west of Pleiku, and in rubber plantations 75 miles to the northwest of Saigon other troops were also getting ready for heavy action. But rubber plantations and highland jungles are hard to see into from the air, and the details of the military preparations going on below were a secret to the Americans, who depended heavily on air reconnaissance for their intelligence information.

American and South Vietnamese troops had invaded the jungle "sanctuaries" that the North Vietnamese and the Vietcong had used in Cambodia in the

North Vietnamese rockets, deployed around Hanoi targets, downed 15 B-52's in December.

Mark Riboud, Magnum

U.S. bombers operating from Seventh Fleet carriers fly pinpoint missions.

spring of 1970 (after the pressure had become too great for Prince Sihanouk and war had broken out there between the Communists and his own army, which then overthrew him). But in early 1972 there were only 150,000 American troops left; Cambodia was off limits to them, and the South Vietnamese were too preoccupied with problems at home to chase their enemies in the Cambodian jungles.

The 1972 offensive began in Laos and Cambodia in early December 1971—the beginning of the dry season there, when the dirt roads dry out from the rains and military movement is easier. The North Vietnamese quickly drove the Royal Laotian Army and General Vang Pao's tired and decimated CIA-supported irregular Laotian troops off the Plain of Jars, besieged their rear base at Long Cheng and simultaneously drove the Laotian forces off the Bolovens Plateau in Southern Laos, apparently to widen the trail system.

Then they drove at the Cambodian government troops who were attacking their western flanks in Cambodia, sending whole battalions of Marshal Lon Nol's fledgling American-supported army reeling down Highway 6 north of Phnom Penh in early December. It was a heavy psychological blow from which the Cambodians never recovered, for they made no other offensive thrust against the Vietnamese Communists.

Thus, at the outset the North Vietnamese had established relative security on their flanks. They were free in 1972 to concentrate on their main objective—reestablishing the guerrilla and political movement in South Vietnam, weakened

While South Vietnamese troops struggle for An Loc, B-52's blast the terrain.

by years of heavy fighting with American troops and by pacification programs that had deprived the Communists of much of their manpower base in the South.

The way the North Vietnamese set about their task was direct military intervention, brutal and massive, and less concealed than in the past, when they had refused even to admit that they had troops in South Vietnam.

The first big attacks came on Easter weekend, at the end of March, with artillery barrages of thousands of rounds from long-range 130 mm guns inside and across the Demilitarized Zone that had separated North and South Vietnam since 1954. At the beginning of April a push of North Vietnamese tanks, troops and more guns moved directly through the DMZ into Quang Tri Province, and the ARVN forces fell back under heavy pressure. After a month, on May 1, Quang Tri city, the province capital, fell; South Vietnam's Third Infantry Division collapsed and was routed, and the defenders fell back down Highway 1 into Thua Thien province near the central Vietnamese capital of Hue. Thousands of troops and hundreds of civilians were killed by the Communist artillery barrage in what was probably the biggest single South Vietnamese defeat of the war. The collapse left Hue open to attack by four enemy divisions from the north as well as from the hills to the southwest, where at least two North Vietnamese divisions also were attacking. Half of Hue's population fled to Da Nang in terror, not to return until the gravest threat had passed and South Vietnamese marines had succeeded in retaking Quang Tri city, a bombed ruin, on Sept. 15.

The second major front opened, quite unexpectedly, in Binh Long province on the Cambodian border north of Saigon on April 5. The North Vietnamese attackers, from three divisions—the 5th, 7th and 9th—quickly swept past the border town of Loc Ninh and encircled the province capital, a small rubber-processing center, An Loc. Then, on April 7, began a siege that lasted for months and took a terrible toll. One whole South Vietnamese division, the 21st, was brought up from the Mekong Delta to try to open Highway 13 to An Loc in early April, but it failed and was withdrawn at the end of May. An Loc was reduced to rubble by a massive North Vietnamese artillery bombardment and American bombing in retaliation. A hundred tanks that Allied intelligence did not know the Communists possessed thrust out of the rubber plantations to batter the South Vietnamese defenders, but ARVN held at An Loc. The town never fell. But the road was never reopened either, and a tenuous stalemate prevailed in Binh Long at the end of the year, as it did in Quang Tri.

The third major front was in the central highlands provinces of Kontum and Pleiku, where intelligence reports had predicted the enemy would make his biggest and first push. It opened, dramatically, on April 24, when troops of Hanoi's 320th division and local units drove the South Vietnamese of the 42nd Regiment out of their headquarters at Tan Canh just north of Kontum. Long-

Scenes of despair were legion in a year which saw more than 1,000,000 uprooted.

Despite official U.S. disclaimers, pictures and eyewitness reports indicated that North Vietnam's dikes were damaged by bombs. Humanitarians deplored this risk of flood and famine.

entrenched guerrilla units also attacked in the coastal provinces of Quang Ngai and Binh Dinh to the east, and though the fighting in the highlands was not as intense as at Quang Tri or An Loc, the Communists scored impressive territorial gains and by the end of the year controlled a substantial part of the rural population in the highlands in a dramatic reversal of the pacification program.

Washington's reaction, in the spring, was equally dramatic. President Nixon, acknowledging that the "specter of defeat" was in the air, ordered full-scale resumption of the bombing of North Vietnam, suspended since November 1968, and B-52's obliterated parts of Haiphong harbor itself on April 16, while fighter-bombers raided Hanoi.

On May 8, Nixon gambled that the Soviet Union and the People's Republic of China would not risk a direct confrontation with the United States and ordered the mining of all the principal North Vietnamese harbors, to prevent new Soviet and Chinese war supplies from reaching the attackers.

His assumption held, and under the pressure of unprecedented American air and naval bombardment—a task force of 35 Navy cruisers and destroyers combined with seven aircraft carriers, 150 to 200 B-52's and more than 600 Air Force jets based in Thailand—there were no more spectacular South Vietnamese defeats. And as the offensive lost momentum, the bombing of North Vietnam was cut back in mid-October to targets south of the 20th parallel.

The North Vietnamese offensive, however, was the opening wedge for a series of smaller, more widespread guerrilla attacks countrywide. By the end of the year there were daily battles 10 miles outside Saigon, in long-peaceful areas of the Mekong Delta, where most of the South Vietnamese people live, and in most of the country's five northern provinces.

By the end of 1972 all except one of the principal North Vietnamese divisions had been committed to the fighting in the South; the North Vietnamese had nearly exhausted their supplies and manpower and had taken heavy losses from the sustained bombing. The choice then lay between maintaining smaller scale mobile warfare in a military stalemate situation in which Saigon would have the advantage in supply and reinforcement, or trying for a cease-fire to exploit the gains achieved in the offensive. Hanoi's leaders chose the latter course, in a proposal for a cease-fire and "National Council of Reconciliation and Concord," first advanced to the American negotiator Henry A. Kissinger in Paris on Oct. 8. Agreement in principle was reached between the Americans and the North Vietnamese but was not quickly followed by anything more definite, or by an end to the fighting. The warring factions in Laos also began direct negotiations between themselves at about the same time. In Cambodia the official attitude was one of helpless resignation to forces beyond the Khmers' control.

Hanoi had never waged war for purely military objectives but rather for political goals—the establishment of political conditions in the South that would eventually lead to a Communist or coalition government there and the creation of neutral, buffer-state regimes between Vietnam and Thailand in Laos and

Desolation marked the headlong South Vietnamese retreat from Quang Tri during the first days of the North's spring offensive.

Cambodia. Whether the North Vietnamese were to enjoy at least the possibility of working openly for their political goal in South Vietnam remained unclear at the year's end. Henry Kissinger had asserted on Oct. 26 that "peace is at hand" and later had added, "What we have done is give South Vietnam an opportunity to survive in conditions that are, today, political rather than military." Despite Kissinger's pronouncements, no cease-fire agreement had been signed by the end of 1972, and the heaviest bombing of the entire war had been unleashed on North Vietnam.

CRAIG R. WHITNEY

RETROSPECTIVE: 1965–1972

In many respects the American military intervention in Vietnam was the best-planned military operation in history. The individual soldier was equipped with devastating firepower and shielded by virtually unchallenged air supremacy. The logistics were close to perfection—all the way from a steady supply of high-nutrition rations to helicopters that could whisk the wounded to field hospitals within minutes after they fell. Electronic—and presumably infallible —brains had computed the "kill ratio" that meant success and the munitions that would produce the ratio.

Only one factor had been left out of the equation—the willingness of the American people to sustain a conflict in which the objectives were unclear and about which they had not been consulted. The missing ingredient turned out to be crucial. The war in Vietnam, whatever its impact on the balances of world power, evolved as an inconclusive struggle that damaged the fabric of national unity in the United States as though there had been a conclusive defeat.

From the beginning it had been apparent that this was not the kind of war that would inspire civilians to rush into combat. Historically, men have fought for God, for national honor, for survival, for justice, for liberation, for loot or for sheer lust of conquest. The conflict in Vietnam did not provide the United States with any of those goals, noble or ignoble. The sole objective of the American forces was to push the North Vietnamese and the Vietcong back across a geographical line and restore the *status quo ante*. Only professional soldiers will battle for such ends, and there were not enough professionals in the United States to man an operation of the size required.

Even the line and the status quo ante were nebulous concepts. The Vietcong enemy forces were as indigenous to the south as they were to the north, and the status quo ante could only mean the temporary division of Vietnam that was imposed at a conference in Geneva after the French withdrew as a colonial power. It could not be said with confidence that the forces of the south were united in their opposition to the forces of the north, as apparently had been the case in Korea.

In its totality, the situation raised an issue that was not taken into account until it was too late. It was whether a democracy has the will to sustain a major war whose sole purpose is to put pressure on an alien ideological bloc and induce its leaders to sign an agreement that leaves the world power balance unchanged. Whatever may be the verdict of history on the motivations of the American effort, the obvious answer is that the strains on national unity were far too great.

THE INDOCHINA WAR

U.S. TROOPS CAPTURED AND MISSING

Captured: 473 in North Vietnam
108 in South Vietnam
6 in Laos
587

CASUALTIES

U.S.
Dead: 45,933
Seriously Wounded: 153,300

Missing: 515 in North Vietnam
505 in South Vietnam
315 in Laos
1,335

South Vietnamese
Military Dead: 183,528
Seriously Wounded: 499,026
Civilian Dead: 415,000
Seriously Wounded: 935,000

North Vietnamese and Vietcong
Dead: 924,048

U.S. MILITARY SPENDING

1965	$	103,000,000
1966	$	5,800,000,000
1967	$	18,400,000,000
1968	$	20,000,000,000
1969	$	21,500,000,000
1970	$	17,400,000,000
1971	$	11,400,000,000
1972	$	7,300,000,000
1965-1972:	$101,903,000,000	

Source: "The New York Times," 25 Jan. 1973

The problem stems from the close relationship between war and governmental secrecy. No one contends that military operations can be, or even should be, conducted in an atmosphere of open debate. The purpose of fighting is to inflict casualties on the enemy—to kill or maim enough of his soldiers that he no longer has the strength to resist. Such purposes are inseparable from stealth and surprise, plans that are kept hidden and clandestine efforts to learn the other side's plans. The philosophy is summed up in a line referring to "the enemy" in *Rule Britannia:* "Confound his politics; frustrate his knavish tricks."

History suggests that a democracy can engage successfully in such an enterprise and emerge relatively intact, although battered. The United States has fought many wars without seriously disrupting the national will. In the past, however—with the sole exception of the Korean war, in which the fighting began with a clearcut act of aggression by one country against another—the wars were preceded by national debates. Generally speaking, the American people were not asked to accept the conditions of warfare until they had been afforded an opportunity to "have their say" about accepting those conditions.

No such opportunity was afforded in respect to Vietnam, nor was there any dramatic event of the kind that mobilizes men and women for sacrifice. The war came on imperceptibly, and, in retrospect, it seems quite possible that the American people may have been "nickled and dimed" into it. The beginning was the shipment of a few supplies to the South Vietnamese government, then a trickle of advisers, then a few thousand troops to protect the advisers, then several thousand troops to protect the few thousand. Suddenly, or so it seemed, half a million Americans were fighting and taking heavy casualties in what had been considered, at most, a "brush-fire" war.

Had those 500,000 men been able to register a quick and decisive success, dissension most probably would not have followed. Human beings rarely argue with anything that can be presented as "victory," regardless of the methods by

which it is attained. But there was no definable "success"—only a monotonous stream of "kill" statistics, which were soon drained of their horror because they took on an air of unreality in the face of the obvious lack of progress in achieving American goals, whatever they might be.

This impasse left the American people with no reserves of willpower to sustain them through the strains of a war that was essentially political. Conservatives did not have the promise of "victory" that appeals so strongly to those who base their world outlook on the simple symbols of national unity. Liberals did not have the slogans of high moral purpose (such as "the war to end wars" or "the four freedoms") that appeal so strongly to those who have an emotional need for lofty goals. And the pragmatic majority did not have a simple blueprint of exits from an intolerable situation.

Even more important was the fact that none of these groups, on any significant scale, really knew there was anything to quarrel about until the nation actually had been committed to the operation. At that point, with men shooting and being shot at in Vietnam, a widespread public debate took on the coloration of sabotage. For it is one thing to question whether one's nation should enter a shooting war and quite another to question whether soldiers in the line of fire should be there at all. The denial of an opportunity to ask the first question makes asking the second extremely difficult.

Whether the leaders of the United States intended to bring the country into the war under a blanket of secrecy probably will be open to question for decades. Any valid judgment will take time and a careful sifting of the evidence by dispassionate men and women (it is not possible for the present generation to be dispassionate). My own impression, from observing those who participated in the basic decisions, was that they no more anticipated the magnitude of the crisis they were precipitating than did the totally uninformed "man in the street." Even at the very highest levels of government there is no guarantee of omniscience. And the conditions were such that a genuine national debate was virtually impossible.

In the first place, very few Americans knew enough about the area to understand what little information was available. To most citizens, Vietnam did not exist until 1964 or 1965. Some had a dim awareness of a place called Indochina, but until 1954 it "belonged" to the French and was as remote from the stream of American consciousness as Outer Mongolia.

In the second place, no American foreign policy leader had served a tour of duty in Vietnam prior to the war. The policy-making establishment had men in high positions who were intimately acquainted with Europe, men who knew something about China, men who had been intimate with India, even a few who had been in Africa. Kremlinologists and Arabic scholars were readily available. But Southeast Asia had been considered the realm of the French and the British. There were no authoritative voices to spark a debate.

When the debate began, it was confined to small groups in the State and Defense Departments. Moreover, both those who approved and those who had doubts found that they were arguing solely for the benefit of one man—the President—and they kept their arguments within official channels. The resulting disputation found no outlet in terms of national debate. The latter requires leaders of authority if it is to have any tinge of legitimacy, and the authoritative

leaders, such as they were, addressed their memoranda to the White House rather than to the citizens as a whole.

This situation was highlighted by the publication of the Pentagon Papers in the summer of 1971. Whether the papers really shed clear light on how the nation got into the war is problematical. No one can be certain which of the documents actually got to the President, which actually caught his attention, which served as a basis for action. But those considerations are irrelevant when placed within a much larger issue. The papers, under any circumstances, revealed that a heated debate was going on within the government but that it was unknown to the public at large and unknown within most of the government itself. Even in the White House most of the assistants were under the impression that the Administration's Vietnam policy enjoyed the solid backing of all experienced officials within the State and Defense departments and the Central Intelligence Agency. Undersecretary of State George Ball was known to have some reservations, but they were considered to be vague.

No purpose can yet be served by speculating on whether the United States was deliberately misled into the war under a cover of secrecy. The objective, observable fact is that most Americans found their country at war without having had an opportunity to see that it was coming. The war, therefore, became a major test of the degree to which secrecy in crucial areas of national policy can be tolerated in a democratic society. The test results suggest that the tolerance is not very great.

Aside from a handful of intellectuals, the first adverse reaction came from the young people in the colleges. They, of course, were the first to feel the brunt. Until 1964 the fighting had been conducted entirely by professionals, who could not very well complain about the vicissitudes of a career they had adopted voluntarily. From 1965, however, the situation called for more and more men, and draftees were demanded. Selective Service had been in effect since the beginning of World War II, but, except for Korea, very few men had been drafted, and college was a safe haven. With very little warning, college graduates who had been comtemplating careers found themselves confronted by the possibility of conscription.

The reaction was unmistakable. Those most intimately involved felt that they wanted no part of it. Draft dodging became a major preoccupation on every college campus, and students developed an incredible expertise in probing the weak spots of the Selective Service system. The demand for a volunteer army arose at meetings throughout the country—and it was clear that what was meant was an army in which the leaders of the movement did not have to volunteer.

The unrest spread—a sit-down in the White House, sit-downs at draft boards, raids on draft board records and finally huge demonstrations in Washington. At first only the college students were involved, and the initial reaction from the rest of the country was that they were spoiled brats. Thereafter their parents took up the cudgels, and the polls began to reflect a change in American attitudes. More and more citizens registered the opinion that the war was useless and that the only sensible course was to find an honorable way out. The Tet offensive in the spring of 1968, which American military leaders considered a Vietcong defeat but which toppled an American government, was the last

straw. After that, there was no question of the United States' winning, only a question of how to get out.

The continuation of the war for four years after Richard M. Nixon was elected President seems at first glance a modern miracle. The reality, however, is that the rapid withdrawal of ground units and the consequent lowering of American casualties created the widespread feeling that the country was getting out with honor. The replacement of ground power with air power did little to shatter this feeling, as the latter involved only a comparative handful of casualties, and somehow air strikes do not carry the same emotional connotation as hand-to-hand combat.

The lessening of tensions, however, did not restore vibrant confidence in the government or in the country's institutions. The polls disclosed little faith in political leaders of both parties, and despite the lopsided result, the presidential election of 1972 was an exercise in apathy. Moreover, any college professor can testify to the cynicism of those whom he is teaching—supposedly the leaders of the coming generation. The disaffection in the armed forces can no longer be denied, and the campuses are kept quiet only by the promise of a total end to the draft in June 1973.

Although I personally believe that Vietnam was a tragic mistake, I am willing to concede that history may render a different verdict. However, the impact of the war on national unity and national morale is incontrovertible. The war has conclusively demonstrated that a democratic society and secrecy in government are incompatible and that Americans must rethink some of their attitudes toward government secrets. It may well be that there is no advantage to national secrecy that can offset its potential for disruption and that an "open society" is not just an idealistic goal but a fundamental necessity.

In the past, secrecy in government has been regarded as a necessary evil—a requirement for maintaining the nation's security in a hostile world. This attitude was fostered by the Cold War, with its clandestine intelligence operations and its races to be first to the hydrogen bomb, first to put a man in space and first to put a man on the moon. Thoughtful Americans recognized that secrecy involved a risk because if some things can be legally and properly classified there is no way of knowing whether other things are being illegally and improperly classified. The country did not, however, recognize the greater risk: that all such practices can inhibit national debate over vital issues and leave the people drained of confidence in their nation.

Whether the lesson will strike home is questionable. There is a tendency on the part of government leaders to regard the people's business as too important and too difficult to be confided to them. Secret diplomacy was the watchword of the Cold War, and it remains such in the remote reaches of the National Security Council. The illusion still prevails that cool planning by experts who are free from the pressures of domestic politics is the path to national success. Perhaps some day the thought will penetrate that planning free of domestic political pressures is also free of any assurance of the people's backing.

A popular catchword among the college youth of today is: "Suppose some day they give a war and nobody comes." Much more secret diplomacy and it just might happen.

GEORGE E. REEDY

THE 1972 OLYMPICS

by Curt Gowdy

Television Sportscaster

Until 1972 the Olympic Games, with their emphasis on international goodwill, brotherhood and idealism, were athletics' purest expression. The quintessence of the best that largely amateur athletics can achieve, the games were a great common denominator in bringing together the peoples of divergent races and political persuasions. Many of sports' most dazzling achievements—by such immortals as Jim Thorpe, Johnny Weissmuller, Jesse Owens, Bob Mathias, Al Oerter, Don Schollander, Bob Hayes, Bill Toomey and countless others— occurred in Olympic competition. When the Olympic flame was extinguished at Munich on Sept. 11, 1972, however, a day later than planned, a dark cloud had descended on all that went before and, perhaps, even on the future of the games themselves.

The Germans initially had titled the 1972 events "the happy games," in an effort to erase the memory of Germany's last Olympiad, in 1936 Berlin. The happy games, nevertheless, ended in confusion, terror and death—when Palestinian guerrillas stormed the Israeli living complex. The guerrillas killed one team member and mortally wounded another at the outset and took nine others hostage. Some 18 hours later, at an airport shootout north of Munich, the remaining Israeli athletes and coaches were killed as a worldwide television audience watched in horror and disbelief. The Olympics were exempt no longer from the political violence of everyday life.

The Winter Games. The 1972 quadrennial opened with the 11th Winter Games in Sapporo, Japan, in which 1,300 athletes from 35 nations competed. The event marked the first time that the winter competition had been held in an Asian country. (Sapporo had been slated to host the 1940 Winter Games, but World War II intervened.)

The first note of trouble sounded when the bickering over professionalism and commercialism resulted in famed Austrian skier Karl Schranz' being banned from competition. In addition, French skier Annie Famose was suspended five days after finishing eighth in the women's downhill because of involvement with a European television network. Retaliating, the athletes contended that "Russian athletes are subsidized by their government and all international athletes get help from one source or another." The question of whether to open the Olympics to the world's best athletes, pro or amateur, reached a peak at Sapporo and carried over to Munich.

The brightest star of the Winter Games was Ard Schenk, a 6 foot-3 inch, 200-pound Dutchman who swept the 5,000 meter, 1,500 meter and 10,000 meter speed-skating titles. Although his events were not so glamorous as the alpine skiing races that showcased Jean-Claude Killy in 1968, Schenk's long, powerful, rhythmic strides put him in a class by himself.

The highlight of the Winter Olympics for the United States was the performance of the American girls, who won three gold medals, a silver and a bronze. Barbara Ann Cochran, 21-year-old member of Vermont's famed skiing Cochrans (sister Marilyn and brother Bob were U.S. team members), fought her way through thick clouds and a swirling, driving snowstorm on Mt. Teine to win America's first gold medal in women's alpine skiing in 20 years.

Northbrook, Ill., a small Chicago suburb, became the speed-skating capital of the United States when two of its hometown girls, 20-year-old Dianne Holum, in the 1,500 meters, and Ann Henning, 19, in the 500-meter spring, raced to gold medals, the first ever by U.S. women in that event. Miss Holum finished second in the 3,000 meters, and Miss Henning picked up a bronze in the 1,000 meter race. Bronze medals went to two other U.S. stars—Susan Corrock, in alpine skiing, and blond, petite Janet Lynn, in figure skating. The lone bright spot for U.S. men was the lightly regarded hockey team, which finished a surprising second to the Soviet Union's.

The Summer Games. The quarrel over commercialism at Sapporo was only a minor prelude to the turmoil, political controversy and tragedy that surrounded

In Olympic Stadium, Munich, Sept. 6, a crowd of more than 80,000 persons attend a memorial service for 11 Israeli athletes killed in an attack by Arab terrorists.

the Summer Games in Munich. On a site that once contained rubble from World War II bombings, just a short distance from the Dachau concentration camp where thousands of Jews had died, the Germans had erected a $650,000,000 athletic extravaganza calculated to disperse by sheer virtuosity any lingering aura of death. And until the nightmarish events of Sept. 5, it appeared that the Germans had succeeded.

Prior to the opening of the games athletes from the black African nations and many American black athletes vowed to boycott the Olympics if Rhodesia, whose government exercises white supremacy, was allowed to compete. In a move that Avery Brundage, president of the International Olympic Committee, termed "political blackmail," Rhodesia was expelled, and the games began on schedule.

Politics moved to the forefront again during the actual competition—particularly in the team and judgment sports such as boxing, diving and basketball. Such trouble first appeared in wrestling, when U.S. heavyweight Chris Taylor lost to the favored Soviet athlete by a disputed decision. Thereafter in boxing, American Reggie Jones, who dominated his Soviet opponent throughout most of the three round bout, lost the decision. Several other boxers also were deprived of deserved victories because of slanted officiating, and a tug of war soon broke out between judges from Communist and free world countries.

Similarly, the basketball outcome will be discussed for years to come. With three seconds of play remaining and the United States leading the U.S.S.R., 50–49 (thanks to two pressure free throws by Doug Collins), the U.S. record of never having lost an Olympic basketball game seemed secure. The Soviets, having frantically tried to call time out as the buzzer sounded, were given another chance, but a desperation pass bounced off the backboard, giving the jubilant Americans an apparent victory. Then an I.O.C. official sitting at the head table held up three fingers, and, notwithstanding the objections of the timekeepers and a referee, the Soviets were given an additional three seconds to play. Thereafter they sank a single basket and were awarded a gold medal for a 51–50 victory. After several protests went unheard, Henry Iba's U.S. team declined to accept the silver medal.

Track and field had its mishaps too. When U.S. coach Stan Wright failed to get two of his fastest sprinters—Eddie Hart and Rey Robinson—to the starting block in time, Valery Borzov of the U.S.S.R. swept the 100-meter dash with little competition.

Controversy also surrounded the 400-meter run, won by Vince Matthews, with Wayne Collett second. After declining to stand at attention and face the American flag during the awards ceremony, an obvious protest, the two U.S. runners were banned for life from Olympic participation. Thus the United States was unable to field a team for the 1,600-meter relay.

There were other mishaps in track and field, notably in the pole vault. The United States lost the event for the first time since 1908, when favored Bob Seagren was ordered to use an unfamiliar pole. Jim Ryun, his four-year prospective comeback on the threshold of a celebrated rematch with Kip Keino of Kenya, tripped and sprawled to the track while trying to qualify in the 1,500 meters. U.S. athletes won only six gold medals in men's track and field, an all-time low.

Olga Korbut, 17-year-old Soviet gymnast, won the hearts of Olympic fans everywhere as she captured two gold medals.

Amid the rancor, political rhubarbs and ultimate tragedy at the 1972 Olympics, there were nevertheless moments of beauty and greatness to be remembered. The U.S.S.R.'s Olga Korbut, the tiniest Olympian, practically revolutionized gymnastics as she captured the world's fancy. U.S. Air Force Captain Micki King, 28, came from behind to win the springboard dive. (In 1968 at Mexico City she had hit the board and broken her arm.) The U.S. wrestlers, led by the fiercely dedicated Dan Gable, pulled upset after upset. Many others will be particularly remembered: Dave Wottle in his golf cap, turning on his patented kick to win the 800 meters; Frank Shorter, slender and mustashioed, jogging through the city where he was born to a grueling marathon victory; Australia's Shane Gould, winning three gold medals in swimming; and the most memorable one of all, Mark Spitz, churning his way through the choppy Olympic pool to an incredible seven gold medals. Spitz' performance was by far the most impressive individual effort in Olympic history.

The Future. Whatever intrusions politics may make in future games—none, it is to be hoped, in any way comparable to those that disrupted the events in 1972—Olympic officials must reevaluate the overall purpose and scope of the games. Must $700,000,000 be spent in preparation? Are so many events necessary? Should team sports be trimmed from the program? Can the judges ever do a proper job? Are the flag-waving awards ceremonies appropriate? These are some of the questions that the new IOC president, Lord Killanin of Ireland, and his various committees must answer by 1976.

The XX Olympiad complex consisted of an 80,000-seat stadium (center), large gymnasium, swimming hall and living quarters for the athletes.

SUMMER GAMES

Gold Medal Winners

Archery

Men's Individual: J. Williams, U.S.A.
Women's Individual: D. Wilber, U.S.A.

Basketball

Team: U.S.S.R.

Boxing

Light Flyweight: G. Gedo, Hungary
Flyweight: G. Kostadinov, Bulgaria
Bantamweight: O. Martinez, Cuba
Featherweight: B. Kousnetsov, U.S.S.R.
Lightweight: J. Szczepanski, Poland
Light Welterweight: R. Seales, U.S.A.
Welterweight: E. Correa, Cuba
Light Middleweight: D. Kottysch, West Germany
Middleweight: V. Lemechev, U.S.S.R.
Light Heavyweight: M. Parlov, Yugoslavia
Heavyweight: T. Stevenson, Cuba

Canoeing

Men's Kayak Singles Slalom: S. Horn, East Germany
Canadian Singles Slalom: R. Eiben, East Germany
Canadian Doubles Slalom: East Germany
Men's Kayak Singles: A. Shaparenko, U.S.S.R.
Men's Kayak Pairs: U.S.S.R.
Men's Kayak Fours: U.S.S.R.
Men's Canadian Singles: I. Patzaichin, Rumania
Men's Canadian Pairs: U.S.S.R.
Women's Singles Kayak Slalom: A. Bahmann, East Germany
Women's Kayak Singles: Y. Ryabchinskaya, U.S.S.R.
Women's Kayak Pairs: U.S.S.R.

Cycling

1,000 m. Time Trial: N. Fredborg, Denmark
Sprint: D. Morelon, France
Tandem: U.S.S.R.
Individual Pursuit: K. Knudsen, Norway
Team Pursuit: West Germany
Individual Road Race: H. Kuiper, Netherlands
100-km. Time Trial: U.S.S.R.

Equestrian

Individual Three-Day Event: R. Meade, England
Team Three-Day Event: England
Dressage: L. Linsenhoff, West Germany
Dressage Team: U.S.S.R.
Individual Jumping: G. Mancinelli, Italy
Team Jumping: West Germany

Fencing

Men's Foil: W. Woyda, Poland
Men's Foil Team: Poland
Men's Saber: V. Sidiak, U.S.S.R.
Men's Saber Team: Italy
Men's Individual Epee: C. Fenyvesi, Hungary
Men's Épée Team: Hungary
Women's Foil: A. Rogno, Italy
Women's Team Foil: U.S.S.R.

Field Hockey

Team: West Germany

Gymnastics

Men's Team: Japan
Men's All-Around: S. Kato, Japan
Men's Floor Exercises: N. Andrianov, U.S.S.R.
Men's Side Horse: V. Klimenko, U.S.S.R.
Men's Rings: A. Nakayama, Japan

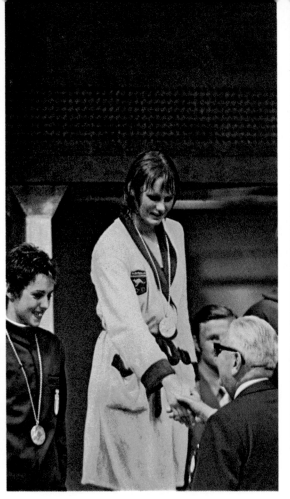

Australian swimmer Shane Gould went to the circle for gold medalists on three occasions.

Mark Spitz made Olympic history by returning to his U.S. home with seven gold medals.

Men's Long Horse: K. Koeste, East Germany
Men's Parallel Bars: S. Kato
Men's Horizontal Bar: M. Tsukahara, Japan
Women's Team: U.S.S.R.
Women's All-Around: L. Tourischeva, U.S.S.R.
Women's Long Horse Vault: K. Janz, East Germany
Women's Uneven Parallel Bars: K. Janz
Women's Balance Beam: O. Korbut, U.S.S.R.
Women's Floor Exercises: O. Korbut

Handball

Team: Yugoslavia

Judo

Lightweight: T. Kawaguchi, Japan
Welterweight: T. Nomura, Japan
Middleweight: S. Sekine, Japan
Light Heavyweight: S. Chochoshvili, U.S.S.R.
Heavyweight: W. Ruska, Netherlands
Open: W. Ruska

Modern Pentathlon

Individual: A. Balczo, Hungary
Team: U.S.S.R.

Rowing

Single Sculls: Y. Malishev, U.S.S.R.
Double Sculls: U.S.S.R.
Pairs: East Germany
Coxed Pairs: East Germany
Fours: East Germany
Coxed Fours: West Germany
Eights: New Zealand

Shooting

Free Rifle: L. Wigger, U.S.A.
Small Bore Three Position: J. Writer, U.S.A.

Small Bore Prone: H. Li, North Korea
Free Pistol: R. Skanaker, Sweden
Rapid-Fire Pistol: J. Zapedzki, Poland
Moving Target: L. Zhelezniak, U.S.S.R.
Trap: A. Scalzone, Italy
Skeet: K. Wirnhier, West Germany

Soccer

Team: Poland

Swimming

Men's 100-m. Freestyle: M. Spitz, U.S.A.
Men's 200-m. Freestyle: M. Spitz
Men's 400-m. Freestyle: B. Cooper, Australia
Men's 1,500-m. Freestyle: M. Burton, U.S.A.
Men's 100-m. Breaststroke: N. Taguchi, Japan
Men's 200-m. Breaststroke: J. Hencken, U.S.A.

MARK ANDREW SPITZ

Mark Spitz was born on Feb. 10, 1950, in Modesto, Calif. Introduced to swimming at age two, Mark was coached by Sherman Chavoor and George Haines. A pre-dental student at the University of Indiana (1969–72), he led its swim team to consecutive NCAA titles and set several individual records.

Frank Shorter became the first American in 64 years to win the 26 mi.-385 yd. marathon.

Nikolai Avilov, 181-pound Ukrainian, established a world record in the decathlon event.

Men's 100-m. Butterfly: M. Spitz
Men's 200-m. Butterfly: M. Spitz
Men's 100-m. Backstroke: R. Matthes, East Germany
Men's 200-m. Backstroke: R. Matthes
Men's 200-m. Individual Medley: G. Larsson, Sweden
Men's 400-m. Individual Medley: G. Larsson
Men's 400-m. Freestyle Relay: U.S.A.
Men's 800-m. Freestyle Relay: U.S.A.
Men's 400-m. Medley Relay: U.S.A.
Men's Springboard Dive: V. Vasin, U.S.S.R.
Men's Platform Dive: K. DiBlasi, Italy
Women's 100-m. Freestyle: S. Neilson, U.S.A.
Women's 200-m. Freestyle: S. Gould, Australia
Women's 400-m. Freestyle: S. Gould
Women's 800-m. Freestyle: K. Rothhammer, U.S.A.
Women's 100-m. Breaststroke: C. Carr, U.S.A.
Women's 200-m. Breaststroke: B. Whitfield, Australia
Women's 100-m. Butterfly: M. Aoki, Japan
Women's 200-m. Butterfly: K. Moe, U.S.A.
Women's 100-m. Backstroke: M. Belote, U.S.A.
Women's 200-m. Backstroke: M. Belote
Women's 200-m. Individual Medley: S. Gould
Women's 200-m. Individual Medley: G. Neall, Australia
Women's 400-m. Freestyle Relay: U.S.A.
Women's 400-m. Medley Relay: U.S.A.
Women's Springboard Dive: M. King, U.S.A.
Women's Platform Dive: U. Knape, Sweden

Track and Field

Men's 100-m. Dash: V. Borzov, U.S.S.R.
Men's 200-m. Dash: V. Borzov
Men's 400-m. Relay: U.S.A.
Men's 400-m. Run: V. Matthews, U.S.A.
Men's 1,600 m. Relay: Kenya
Men's 800-m. Run: D. Wottle, U.S.A.

Men's 1,500-m. Run: P. Vasala, Finland
Men's 5,000-m. Run: L. Viren, Finland
Men's 10,000-m. Run: L. Viren
Men's Marathon: F. Shorter, U.S.A.
Men's Steeplechase: K. Keino, Kenya
Men's 110-m. Hurdles: R. Milburn, U.S.A.
Men's 400-m. Hurdles: J. Akii-Bua, Uganda
Men's High Jump: J. Tarmak, U.S.S.R.
Men's Long Jump: R. Williams, U.S.A.
Men's Triple Jump: V. Saneyev, U.S.S.R.
Men's Pole Vault: W. Nordwig, East Germany
Men's Shotput: W. Komar, Poland
Men's Discus Throw: L. Danek, Czechoslovakia
Men's Hammer Throw: A. Bondarchuk, U.S.S.R.
Men's Javelin Throw: K. Wolfermann, West Germany
Men's Decathlon: N. Avilov, U.S.S.R.
Men's 20-km. Walk: P. Frenkel, East Germany
Men's 50-km. Walk: B. Kannenberg, West Germany
Women's 100-m. Dash: R. Stecher, East Germany
Women's 200-m. Dash: R. Stecher
Women's 400-m. Relay: West Germany
Women's 400-m. Dash: M. Zehrt, East Germany
Women's 1,600-m. Relay: East Germany
Women's 800-m. Run: H. Falck, West Germany
Women's 1,500-m. Run: L. Bragina, U.S.S.R.
Women's 100-m. Hurdles: A. Ehrhardt, East Germany
Women's High Jump: U. Meyfarth, West Germany
Women's Long Jump: H. Rosendahl, West Germany
Women's Shotput: N. Chizhova, U.S.S.R.
Women's Discus Throw: F. Melnik, U.S.S.R.
Women's Javelin Throw: R. Fuchs, East Germany
Women's Pentathlon: M. Peters, England

Volleyball

Men's Team: Japan
Women's Team: U.S.S.R.

For a few seconds, the U.S. basketball team celebrated victory over the Soviets. In a disputed decision, the game was resumed and the Soviets got a gold medal.

Water Polo

Team: U.S.S.R.

Weight Lifting

Flyweight: Z. Smalcerz, Poland
Bantamweight: I. Foeldi, Hungary
Featherweight: N. Nourikian, Bulgaria
Lightweight: M. Kirzhinov, U.S.S.R.
Middleweight: Y. Bikov, Bulgaria
Light Heavyweight: L. Jenssen, Norway
Middle Heavyweight: A. Nikolv, Bulgaria
Heavyweight: Y. Talts, U.S.S.R.
Super Heavyweight: V. Alexeyev, U.S.S.R.

Wrestling, Freestyle

Paperweight: R. Dmitriev, U.S.S.R.
Flyweight: K. Kato, Japan
Bantamweight: H. Yanagida, Japan
Featherweight: Z. Abdulbekov, U.S.S.R.
Lightweight: D. Gable, U.S.A.
Welterweight: W. Wells, U.S.A.
Middleweight: L. Tediashvil, U.S.S.R.
Light Heavyweight: B. Peterson, U.S.A.
Heavyweight: I. Yarygin, U.S.S.R.
Super Heavyweight: A. Medved, U.S.S.R.

Wrestling, Greco-Roman

Paperweight: G. Berceanu, Rumania
Flyweight: P. Kirov, Bulgaria
Bantamweight: R. Kazakov, U.S.S.R.
Featherweight: G. Markov, Bulgaria
Lightweight: S. Khisamutdinov, U.S.S.R.
Welterweight: V. Macha, Czechoslovakia
Middleweight: C. Hegebus, Hungary
Light Heavyweight: V. Rezantsev, U.S.S.R.
Heavyweight: N. Martinescu, Rumania
Super Heavyweight: A. Roshin, U.S.S.R.

Yachting

Soling: H. Melges, U.S.A.
Tempest: V. Mankin, U.S.S.R.
Dragon: J. Cueno, Australia
Star: D. Forbes, Australia
Flying Dutchman: R. Pattison, England
Finn: S. Maury, France

WINTER GAMES

Gold Medal Winners

Alpine Skiing

Men's Downhill: B. Russi, Switzerland
Men's Giant Slalom: G. Thoeni, Italy
Men's Special Slalom: F. Fernandez, Spain
Women's Downhill: M. Nadig, Switzerland
Women's Giant Slalom: M. Nadig
Women's Special Slalom: B. Cochran, U.S.A.

Nordic Skiing

Men's 15-km. Cross Country: S. Lundback, Sweden
Men's 30-km. Cross Country: V. Vedenin, U.S.S.R.
Men's 40-km. Relay: U.S.S.R.
Men's 50-km. Cross Country: P. Tyldum, Norway
Men's Combined (70-m. jump, 15-km. cross country): U. Wehling, East Germany
Men's 70-m. Special Jump: Y. Kasaya, Japan
Men's 90-m. Jump: W. Fortuna, Poland
Women's 5-km. Cross Country: G. Koulakov, U.S.S.R.
Women's 10-km. Cross Country: G. Koulakov
Women's 15-km. Cross Country Relay: U.S.S.R.

Biathlon

Individual: M. Solberg, Norway
Relay: U.S.S.R.

Some 1,300 athletes from 35 nations participated at Sapporo in the 11th Winter Games.

Yukio Kasaya became the first Japanese athlete to win a gold medal in the Winter Games as he smoothly captured the 70-meter ski jump.

Luge
Men's Singles: W. Scheidel, East Germany
Men's Doubles: Italy, East Germany (tie)
Women's Singles: A. Muller, East Germany

Bobsled
Two Man: West Germany
Four Man: Switzerland

Figure Skating
Men's: O. Nepela, Czechoslovakia
Women's: T. Schuba, Austria
Pairs: I. Rodnina, A. Ulanov, U.S.S.R.

Speed Skating
Men's 500 meters: E. Keller, West Germany
Men's 1,500 meters: A. Schenk, Netherlands
Men's 5,000 meters: A. Schenk
Men's 10,000 meters: A. Schenk
Women's 500 meters: A. Henning, U.S.A.
Women's 1,000 meters: M. Pflug, West Germany
Women's 1,500 meters: D. Holum, U.S.A.
Women's 3,000 meters: S. Baas-Kaiser, Netherlands

Hockey
Championship: U.S.S.R.

LORD MICHAEL JOHN KILLANIN

After taking over as president of the International Olympic Committee on Sept. 12, 1972, Lord Michael John Killanin of Ireland said that he would aim to "deflate the ultranationalism" that has marred recent Olympics. A journalist, author, movie producer and businessman, Lord Killanin was born in London in 1914. The former athlete was president of Ireland's Olympic Council, a member of the IOC from 1952 and chief deputy to Avery Brundage from 1968.

47

Janet Lynn, a petite 18-year old from Rockford, Ill., delighted the figure-skating audiences and won a bronze medal.

Charles Moore, Black Star

Final Medal Standings

	Gold	Silver	Bronze
U.S.S.R.	50	27	22
United States	33	31	30
East Germany	20	23	23
West Germany	13	11	16
Japan	13	8	8
Australia	8	7	2
Poland	7	5	9
Hungary	6	13	16
Bulgaria	6	10	5
Italy	5	3	10
Sweden	4	6	6
Britain	4	5	9
Rumania	3	6	7
Cuba	3	1	4
Finland	3	1	4
Netherlands	3	1	1
France	2	4	7
Czechoslovakia	2	4	2
Kenya	2	3	4
Yugoslavia	2	1	2
Norway	2	1	1
North Korea	1	1	3
New Zealand	1	1	1
Uganda	1	1	0
Denmark	1	0	0
Switzerland	0	3	0
Canada	0	2	3
Belgium	0	2	1
Iran	0	2	1
Greece	0	2	0
Mongolia	0	2	0
Austria	0	1	2
Colombia	0	1	2
Argentina	0	1	0
Lebanon	0	1	0
Mexico	0	1	0
Pakistan	0	1	0
South Korea	0	1	0
Tunisia	0	1	0
Turkey	0	1	0
Brazil	0	0	2
Ethiopia	0	0	2
Spain	0	0	2
Ghana	0	0	1
India	0	0	1
Jamaica	0	0	1
Niger	0	0	1
Nigeria	0	0	1

Final Medal Standings*

	Gold	Silver	Bronze
U.S.S.R.	8	5	3
East Germany	4	3	7
Switzerland	4	3	3
Netherlands	4	3	2
United States	3	2	3
West Germany	3	1	1
Norway	2	5	5
Italy	2	2	1
Austria	1	2	2
Sweden	1	1	2
Japan	1	1	1
Czechoslovakia	1	0	2
Poland	1	0	0
Spain	1	0	0
Finland	0	4	1
France	0	1	2
Canada	0	1	0

* Owing to a first-place tie, an extra gold medal was presented in lieu of a silver one.

48

Photoreporters

THE TRUMAN LIBRARY, DEC. 27.

DIARY OF
EVENTS
1972

Jan. 10: Mujibur Rahman of Bangladesh is a free man.

JANUARY

Londonderry, Northern Ireland, Jan. 30. Below: A strike closes Ottawa's airport.

5 U.S. President Richard M. Nixon gives the go-ahead for the development of a space shuttle system.

7 President Nixon and Japan's Prime Minister Eisaku Sato conclude two days of talks in San Clemente, Calif.

Communist China conducts a nuclear test in the atmosphere at its Lop Nor test site.

10 Sheikh Mujibur Rahman, the leader of Bangladesh, imprisoned in West Pakistan since March 1971, is repatriated.

Pakistan's President Zulfikar Ali Bhutto orders former President Agha Mohammad Yahya Khan placed under house arrest.

Israeli forces cross into Lebanon and stage retaliatory raids against Palestinian commandos.

12 Sheikh Mujibur Rahman changes his title from president to prime minister of Bangladesh, adopts a provisional constitution and names a cabinet.

13 Ghana's Prime Minister Kofi A. Busia is overthrown in a bloodless military coup led by Col. Ignatius Kutu Acheampong.

President Nixon announces that 70,000 additional U.S. troops will be withdrawn from South Vietnam by May 1.

15 Following the death of Denmark's King Frederik on Jan. 14, Princess Margrethe is proclaimed queen.

16 Egypt's President Anwar el-Sadat appoints Aziz Sidky premier.

19 In Rhodesia, violent protests by blacks against the 1971 British-Rhodesian political agreement spread to Salisbury, the capital. (Demonstrations had begun in Gwelo on Jan. 16.)

20 President Nixon delivers annual State of the Union address.

Gaston Eyskens, who resigned as premier of Belgium following November 1971 general elections, forms a new coalition government.

22 Representatives of ten Western European nations sign the Treaty of Accession in Brussels, enlarging the European Economic Community from six to ten members. Enlargement requires ratification by the four new members—Great Britain, Denmark, Ireland and Norway.

24 The Soviet Union grants diplomatic recognition to Bangladesh.

25 President Nixon discloses a plan to end the Indochina war which was secretly presented to the North Vietnamese in October 1971.

27 Maurice H. Stans resigns (effective in mid-February) as U.S. secretary of commerce; Peter G. Peterson is named to the post.

28 In Canada, air-traffic controllers begin returning to work following a ten-day strike. Differences in wage-contract negotiations are to be submitted to binding arbitration.

30 Thirteen persons are killed by British troops in Londonderry, Northern Ireland, as rioting erupts following a civil-rights march. The British Government had banned the march.

31 North Vietnam reveals a nine-point peace program, which was secretly presented to the United States in June 1971.

2 The British embassy in Dublin is destroyed by fire bombing, set by demonstrators protesting the killing of 13 persons in Londonderry on Jan. 30.

Sir Keith Holyoake resigns as prime minister of New Zealand. Deputy Prime Minister John Marshall is chosen as leader of the National Party and prime minister.

4 A joint communiqué, issued after two days of talks between Egypt's President Sadat and Soviet leaders in Moscow, states that the United Nations "should immediately resume" negotiations with Israel and Egypt to seek a Middle East peace settlement.

7 President Nixon signs legislation requiring the "full reporting of both the sources and uses of campaign funds," and limiting a candidate's personal investment as well as the amount spent on the media in Federal elections.

14 The White House orders further relaxation in U.S. trade policy with Peking, placing Communist China under same restrictions as the Soviet Union.

In Patchogue, N.Y., Valery I. Markelov, a Russian translator for the UN Secretariat, is arrested and charged with espionage.

15 U.S. Attorney General John N. Mitchell resigns (effective Mar. 1) to direct President Nixon's reelection campaign. Deputy Attorney General Richard G. Kleindienst is named as Mitchell's successor.

16 Following the ouster of Ecuador's President Jose Maria Velasco Ibarra in a bloodless military coup on Feb. 15, junta leader Brig. Gen. Guillermo Rodriguez Lara proclaims a "revolutionary and nationalist government."

19 Leaders of Britain's striking coal miners' union agree to a settlement proposed by a three-man board of inquiry.

21 President Nixon, who arrived in Peking on Feb. 20 for an eight-day visit, and China's Chairman Mao Tse-tung hold a one-hour "frank and serious" talk.

22 Seven persons, including a Roman Catholic priest and five women, are killed when Irish Republican Army terrorists blow up an officers' mess at the Aldershot (England) military base.

In a bloodless military coup, Sheikh Khalifa bin Hamad al-Thani replaces Sheikh Ahmed bin al-Thani as ruler of Qatar, the Persian Gulf emirate.

23 In Finland, a coalition government, headed by Social Democratic party leader Rafael Paasio, is sworn in.

25 John Taylor, Northern Ireland's minister of state for foreign affairs, is shot and seriously wounded in Armagh, about 40 miles southwest of Belfast. He is the first member of Northern Ireland's government to be a victim of an attempted assassination.

27 President Nixon and China's Premier Chou En-lai conclude a week of discussions with a joint communiqué. The United States promises gradually to reduce its military forces on Taiwan; both nations pledge to increase U.S.–Chinese contacts and exchanges.

28 UN Security Council demands that Israel cease all military action against Lebanon and "forthwith withdraw all its military forces from Lebanese territory."

UPI

To the French nation, Premier Chaban-Delmas denies having avoided income tax payments.

An historic meeting, Feb. 21.

The White House

FEBRUARY

As the month ends, West Virginia suffers severe flooding.

UPI

Voters in India speak: Congress Party scores a victory.

The 1972 presidential election campaign begins; Muskie wins New Hampshire primary.

MARCH

From a hospital bed, ITT lobbyist Dita Beard denies link between ITT contributions to GOP and the "favorable settlement" of ITT's antitrust cases.

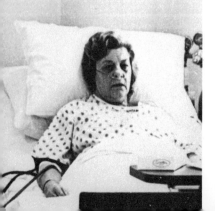

2 Pioneer 10, an unmanned U.S. spacecraft which is to explore the planet Jupiter, is launched from Cape Kennedy.

Michael Manley, leader of Jamaica's People's National Party, is sworn in as prime minister. (The party had won a majority in the Feb. 29 legislative elections.)

3 Pakistan President Bhutto dismisses Lt. Gen. Abdul Gul Hasan, acting commander in chief, and Air Marshal Abdul Rahim Khan, commander of the Air Force.

4 The Soviet government announces that it has signed a pact with Libya calling for the joint production and refining of Libyan oil.

6 Rep. William M. Colmer (D-Miss.), 82-year-old chairman of the Rules Committee of the U.S. House of Representatives, announces that he will not seek reelection in November.

10 Cambodia's Premier Lon Nol assumes complete governmental power. (Earlier, Cheng Heng had resigned as chief of state.)

13 Britain agrees to establish full diplomatic relations with China.

14 Results of India's assembly elections held Mar. 5–12 become known; Prime Minister Gandhi's ruling Congress Party wins absolute majorities in 14 of 16 states and in 1 of 2 union territories.

19 India's Prime Minister Gandhi and Bangladesh's Prime Minister Mujibur sign a 25-year friendship and mutual-defense agreement.

20 A large time bomb explodes in a crowded Belfast, Northern Ireland, street, killing six persons and injuring 146.

21 To stimulate the British economy, the government announces immediate tax cuts totaling $3,140,000,000.

Taiwan's National Assembly elects Chiang Kai-shek to a fifth six-year presidential term.

23 Leonard Woodcock, president of the United Automobile Workers, resigns from the Federal Pay Board; President Nixon reorganizes the tripartite board into a seven-member public group. AFL-CIO leaders George Meany, I. W. Abel and Floyd Smith had resigned from the board on Mar. 22.)

25 In El Salvador, more than 100 soldiers and civilians are killed in an unsuccessful antigovernment uprising.

26 Representatives of Britain and Malta sign a seven-year agreement granting the British continued use of Malta's military bases.

27 In Addis Ababa, Ethiopia, an agreement is signed ending a 16-year-old Sudanese civil war.

28 Poland's Parliament elects Henryk Jablonski as the nation's president.

29 The Bolivian government orders 119 members of the Soviet embassy in La Paz to leave the country within a week. According to Bolivia's foreign minister, the expulsion involves a "question of sovereignty."

30 The British government suspends the provincial government and parliament of Northern Ireland and imposes direct rule from London for one year.

1 U.S. military souces in Danang report that thousands of North Vietnamese and Vietcong troops have swept across the demilitarized zone and are pushing South Vietnamese forces toward their southern bases.

4 President Nixon orders 10 to 20 additional B-52 bombers dispatched to South Vietnam.

The United States extends diplomatic recognition to Bangladesh.

5 UN Secretary-General Kurt Waldheim appoints Tang Ming-chao, U.S. educated Chinese diplomat, as undersecretary general for political affairs and decolonization.

6 Charging that King Hussein's proposal for a federation of Jordanians and Palestinians would legitimize Israel's position in the Arab world, Egypt "severs all relations" with Jordan.

7 Sheikh Abeid Amani Karume, first vice president of Tanzania and president of Zanzibar before its merger with Tanganyika, is assassinated on the island of Zanzibar.

9 The Soviet Union and Iraq sign a 15-year treaty of friendship and cooperation.

10 The United States, the Soviet Union and Britain are among some 70 nations to sign a convention outlawing biological weapons and requiring states to destroy their stockpiles of such weapons.

Gen. Juan Carlos Sanchez, commander of Argentina's second Army Corps, and Oberdan Sallustro, director of Argentina's Fiat subsidiary who was kidnapped on Mar. 21, are murdered by a group of political extremists.

Roy Jenkins, a supporter of Britain's entry into the EEC, resigns as deputy leader of the Labor Party. (Party leader Harold Wilson opposses entry.)

16 For the first time since the U.S. bombing of North Vietnam was curtailed in March 1968, U.S. planes bomb in the vicinity of the port city of Haiphong.

Concluding two days of talks in Ottawa, Canada's Prime Minister Pierre Elliott Trudeau and President Nixon sign a joint agreement to combat pollution in the Great Lakes.

17 The Soviet Union publishes a report accusing the United States of damaging four Soviet merchant vessels during bombing raids on Haiphong.

20 In Burma, Ne Win becomes premier of the nation's first civilian government in ten years.

21 Two Apollo 16 astronauts, Navy Capt. John W. Young and Air Force Col. Charles M. Duke, Jr., explore the surface of the lunar highlands.

22 An 11-day strike involving approximately 200,000 Quebec teachers and civil servants ends.

26 President Nixon announces that 20,000 additional troops will be withdrawn from South Vietnam by July 1.

27 The opposition party in West Germany's Bundestag (lower house of parliament) fails in its attempt to replace Willy Brandt as chancellor. A no-confidence motion was two votes short.

UPI

The United States renews bombing of North Vietnam.

APRIL

Information Canada Photothèque

Apr. 16: the Great Lakes Water Agreement is signed in Ottawa.

John Young and the lunar roving vehicle explore the moon.

NASA

The United States formally returns Okinawa to Japan.

MAY

The Kremlin, May 26: President Nixon and Chairman Brezhnev agree to limit offensive and defensive weapons.

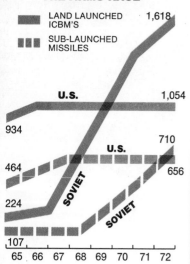

THE ARMS RACE

▬ LAND LAUNCHED ICBM'S

▪▪▪ SUB-LAUNCHED MISSILES

1,618

U.S. 1,054

934

710

U.S.

464 656

224

107

65 66 67 68 69 70 71 72

WARHEADS

U.S.

SOVIET

3,000 6,000

1 The U.S. Cost of Living Council announces that all businesses or government units employing 60 persons or less are no longer subject to wage and price controls.

3 Following the death of J. Edgar Hoover on May 2, President Nixon names Assistant Attorney General L. Patrick Gray 3d as acting director of the Federal Bureau of Investigation. Gray is to serve until after the November presidential elections.

8 In a nationwide radio and television address, President Nixon announces that all North Vietnamese ports will be mined and that all rail supply routes to North Vietnam will be bombed. The moves are to prevent the flow of military supplies to North Vietnam.

10 President Nguyen Van Thieu imposes martial law throughout South Vietnam.

13 U.S. Secretary of Defense Melvin R. Laird announces that no more than 50,000 men will be drafted in 1972.

15 The island of Okinawa, under U.S. rule since 1945, is returned to Japan.

Alabama Gov. George C. Wallace is shot and critically wounded while campaigning for the presidency in a Laurel, Md., shopping center. Arthur H. Bremer, a 21-year-old white man, is arrested as the assailant.

16 The resignation of the only Democrat in President Nixon's Cabinet, Secretary of the Treasury John B. Connally, is announced at the White House. George P. Schultz is named to the post; Caspar W. Weinberger is named to succeed Schultz as director of the Office of Management and the Budget.

17 West Germany's Bundestag approves treaties of friendship with Poland and the Soviet Union.

The government of Peru issues new standards restricting television and radio programming and advertising.

18 Following several weeks of violence in the Malagasy Republic, President Philibert Tsiranana gives full governmental power to Gen. Gabriel Ramanantsoa, Army chief of staff.

22 President Nixon arrives in Moscow on the first U.S. presidential visit to the Soviet capital.

Ceylon becomes the independent socialist republic of Sri Lanka.

24 Soviet Premier Kosygin and President Nixon sign a space cooperation agreement, providing for a joint Soviet–U.S. space flight with linked spacecraft in 1975.

26 President Nixon and Soviet Party Chairman Brezhnev sign two agreements, limiting antiballistic missile (ABM) systems and offensive missile launchers.

30 The Burundi Government radio reports that at least 50,000 people have been killed since an abortive coup d'etat in late April. The slaughter was caused by struggles between the ruling Tutsi and the majority Hutu tribesmen.

Twenty-four persons are killed and 76 others are wounded as three Japanese gunmen, hired by a Palestinian commando group, fire into a crowd at the international airport near Tel Aviv, Israel.

1 Following stopovers in Iran and Poland, President Nixon returns to Washington and addresses a joint session of Congress on his Moscow trip.

The Government of Iraq nationalizes the Iraq Petroleum Company, a Western-owned consortium which has produced and marketed Iraq's oil for almost 50 years.

Chile becomes the first South American nation to grant diplomatic recognition to North Korea and North Vietnam.

5 Twelve-hundred delegates from 112 nations attend opening session of the United Nations Conference on the Human Environment in Stockholm, Sweden.

After winning a vote of confidence in Turkey's National Assembly, the government of Premier Ferit Melen is installed.

8 By a 64–19 vote, the U.S. Senate approves the nomination of Richard G. Kleindienst as attorney general.

12 Before the U.S. House of Representatives Armed Services Committee, Gen. John D. Lavelle acknowledges that he was dismissed in March as commander of U.S. Air Force units in Southeast Asia after ordering some 20 unauthorized bombing raids on North Vietnam.

13 Israeli and Egyptian planes engage in the first air battle since a Middle East cease-fire went into effect in August 1970.

14 William D. Ruckelshaus, administrator of the U.S. Environmental Protection Agency, orders the toxic pesticide DDT banned (except for reasons of health) effective Dec. 31, 1972.

17 Five men, possessing sophisticated eavesdropping and photographic equipment, are arrested for breaking into the headquarters of the Democratic National Committee in Washington, D.C.

20 Gen. Creighton W. Abrams, commander of U.S. forces in Vietnam, is named Chief of Staff, U.S. Army.

21 An Israeli armored force strikes into southern Lebanon, capturing five Syrian officers, a Lebanese officer and three Lebanese military policemen; simultaneously, Israeli jets attack a Palestinian guerrilla area in southeastern Lebanon.

23 The British Treasury announces that it will permit the British pound to float in value for an indefinite period.

26 In Italy, a center coalition government, with Giulio Andreotti as premier, is sworn in.

The U.S. military command in Saigon reports that more than 2,000 pilots and some 150 planes have been transferred to Thailand from the Danang air base, South Vietnam.

27 In South Vietnam, pro-government senators pass a bill giving President Thieu authority to rule by decree on defense and economic matters for six months.

28 Agence France-Press reports that France has resumed nuclear atmospheric testing in the South Pacific.

29 The U.S. Supreme Court rules that capital punishment, as imposed under present statutes, is "cruel and unusual punishment" and unconstitutional.

UPI

Angela Davis is all smiles following her June 4 acquittal.

Giulio Andreotti heads new coalition government in Italy.

Keystone

JUNE

An auto smashes into a jet preventing skyjack attempt. Skyjackings increased in June.

UPI

India's Gandhi and Pakistan's Bhutto hold summit talks.

JULY

Egypt's President Sadat orders Soviet military withdrawal.

Senators McGovern and Eagleton announce a change.

1 President Nixon signs into law a bill extending the $450,000,000,000 debt ceiling until Oct. 31 and increasing Social Security benefits by 20 per cent.

Citing family responsibility, John N. Mitchell resigns as President Nixon's campaign manager. Clark MacGregor, presidential adviser on congressional relations, is named to the post.

3 Following five days of meetings, India's Prime Minister Gandhi and Pakistan's President Bhutto sign an agreement to withdraw all forces from their mutual borders, to freeze present troop positions in Kashmir pending further discussions and to go about a "step-by-step" normalization of their relations.

4 North and South Korea issue a joint communiqué announcing that during secret talks in Seoul and Pyongyang the two nations renounced the use of force and agreed on principles to reunify the divided nation peacefully and independently.

5 After accepting the resignation of Premier Jacques Chaban-Delmas, President Pompidou selects Pierre Messmer, a 56-year-old Gaullist, as France's new premier.

6 Japan's Diet (parliament) confirms the election of Kakuei Tanaka as premier. The new premier and Liberal-Democratic Party president succeeds Eisaku Sato, who retired.

8 The White House announces that the United States will sell the U.S.S.R. at least $750,000,000 of U.S. wheat, corn and other grain during a three-year period.

9 The militant Provisional wing of the Irish Republican Army ends its two-week cease-fire on offensive operations.

14 Sen. George McGovern (S.D.) and Sen. Thomas F. Eagleton (Mo.) accept the nominations of the Democratic Party as its presidential and vice-presidential candidates, respectively.

18 Egypt's President Sadat announces that he has ordered the immediate withdrawal of Soviet "military advisers and experts" from his nation.

19 The Executive Council of the AFL-CIO votes to remain neutral and not endorse President Nixon or Senator McGovern in the 1972 presidential campaign.

Presidential adviser Henry Kissinger confers secretly for six and a half hours with North Vietnam's chief negotiator at the Paris peace talks.

22 White House Press Secretary Ronald L. Ziegler reveals that President Nixon has chosen Vice-President Spiro T. Agnew as his running mate on the 1972 Republican Party ticket.

24 Crown Prince Jigme Singye Wangchuk is inaugurated king of the Himalayan nation of Bhutan, succeeding his father King Jigme Dorji Wangchuk, who died July 21.

28 Sen. James O. Eastland (D-Miss). succeeds the late Sen. Allen J. Ellender (D-La.) as president pro tempore of the U.S. Senate.

31 Senator Eagleton announces that he is withdrawing as the Democratic Party's nominee for vice-president. (On July 25, the Senator had disclosed that he had been hospitalized three times for "nervous exhaustion and fatigue" and had undergone psychiatric treatment.)

2 Following three days of talks in Tobruk and Benghazi, Libya, Egypt's President Sadat and Col. Muammar al-Qaddafi of Libya agree to set up by Sept. 1, 1973, a "unified political leadership" to work toward the unification of the two nations in such areas as education, economics, and political and constitutional organization.

4 A jury of six men and six women finds Arthur Bremer guilty of the shooting of Gov. George C. Wallace (D-Ala.) and three other persons on May 15. The 21-year-old itinerant jobholder is sentenced to 63 years in prison.

7 According to the third annual report of the U.S. Council on Environmental Quality, the nation's air is getting cleaner while its water is becoming dirtier.

8 The Democratic National Committee nominates R. Sargent Shriver, former director of the Peace Corps and ambassador to France, to replace Senator Eagleton as the Democratic Party's vice-presidential candidate.

11 The last U.S. ground combat unit in Vietnam is deactivated.

13 Former U.S. Attorney General Ramsey Clark returns to the United States after spending two weeks in North Vietnam.

15 UN Secretary General Waldheim concludes a four-day trip to Communist China.

16 Morocco's King Hassan is unhurt as Moroccan Air Force jets strafe the commercial airliner carrying the King to Rabat from Paris.

The U.S. House of Representatives votes to sustain the presidential veto of a $30,500,000,000 health, education, welfare, and labor appropriations bill.

The Rev. Philip A. Potter, a 50-year-old Methodist pastor from the British West Indies, is elected general secretary of the World Council of Churches.

18 In Saigon, South Vietnam President Thieu and U.S. presidential adviser Kissinger confer for more than two hours.

21 Britain's dock workers return to work, ending a four-week strike. (On Aug. 3, the nationwide strike had forced the British government to declare a state of emergency.)

23 In Miami Beach, Fla., the 30th Republican National Convention comes to a close after President Nixon and Vice-President Agnew accept nomination for second terms; some 1,100 antiwar demonstrators are arrested.

25 Casting its first veto in the UN Security Council, Communist China bars Bangladesh from UN membership.

26 The XX Olympic Games open in Munich, West Germany. (Earlier, protests against the racial policy of Rhodesia led the International Olympic Committee to vote that nation out of the Games.)

29 The White House announces that U.S. troop strength in South Vietnam will drop from 39,000 on Sept. 1 to 27,000 on Dec. 1.

31 In the Canadian province of British Columbia, David Barrett, a 41-year-old former social worker, is elected premier. The New Democratic Party leader defeated W. A. C. Bennett who had held the office for 20 years.

UPI

The last U.S. combat battalion in Vietnam is deactivated.

AUGUST

Stephen Shames, Black Star

Ramsey Clark discusses his Vietnam trip with newsmen.

A four-week strike by British dockworkers ends, Aug. 21.

Photo Trends

Airport near Munich the day after Sept. 5 tragedy.

SEPTEMBER

Philippine President Marcos declares martial law.

U.S. prisoners of war (l-r) Charles, Elias and Gartley arrive in Denmark following their release by Hanoi.

Photos UPI

1 Concluding a two-day conference in Hawaii, President Nixon and Japan's Premier Tanaka agree that Japan will purchase about $1,100,000,000 worth of U.S. goods over the next two years in an effort to reduce a predicted $3,800,000,000 U.S. trade deficit with Japan in 1972.

Canada's Premier Trudeau calls a general election for Oct. 30.

In Montevideo, Uruguay, Paul Sendic, founder of the Tupamaro guerrilla movement, is shot and captured by police.

Bobby Fischer becomes the first American to win the world's chess championship.

5 At an airport near Munich, West Germany, nine Israeli athletes, five Arab terrorists and a German policeman are killed in a shootout between Arab commandos and German police and soldiers. Earlier the Arabs, armed with automatic rifles and demanding the release of Arab terrorists imprisoned in Israel, had entered the Israeli quarters of Olympic Village, killed two members of the Israeli team and seized the nine Israelis as hostages.

In a Federal District Court in Harrisburg, Pa., the Rev. Philip Berrigan is sentenced to four concurrent two-year prison terms for smuggling letters at the Lewisburg (Pa.) Penitentiary. (The conspiracy case that has been brought against Berrigan had ended in a mistrial on April 5.)

6 By executive decree, the South Vietnamese government abolishes popular democratic elections in the country's 10,775 hamlets. Nearly all of the nation's administrative officials are to be appointed by President Thieu.

8 In reprisal for the shooting of 11 Israelis at Munich, Israeli Air Force planes attack ten Arab guerrilla bases and naval installations in Syria and Lebanon.

Residents of Pnompenh, Cambodia, stage a protest against the acute shortage of rice.

9 Israeli and Syrian warplanes do battle, ending a truce of more than two years.

10 The United States vetoes a UN Security Council resolution calling for an immediate halt to military operations in the Middle East but failing to condemn terrorism.

19 Stanislaw Trepczynski of Poland is elected president of the 27th session of the UN General Assembly.

23 President Ferdinand Marcos declares martial law throughout the Philippines. The action follows an unsuccessful assassination attempt against the nation's defense secretary and a series of bomb explosions.

24 In a two-day referendum, Norwegians vote against membership in the European Economic Community.

26 Addressing the annual meeting of the International Monetary Fund, U.S. Secretary of the Treasury George P. Shultz proposes a new international monetary system, including wider fluctuation in exchange rates.

29 In Peking, Premier Chou En-lai and Premier Tanaka sign a joint communiqué establishing diplomatic relations between China and Japan.

5 The foreign ministers of Tanzania and Uganda sign an agreement ending hostilities which had broken out between the two nations in September.

Anker Henrik Jorgenson takes office as premier of Denmark. (Jens Otto Krag had resigned on Oct. 3 after the Danish electorate overwhelmingly endorsed his plan to join the European Economic Community.)

6 France and Poland sign a "friendship and cooperation" treaty.

11 The buildings of the French diplomatic mission in North Vietnam are damaged during a U.S. bombing raid. Pierre Susini, France's chief diplomat in Hanoi, is fatally injured; five persons are killed.

16 A two-engine plane carrying U.S. Rep. Hale Boggs (D-La.), the House majority leader, Rep. Nick Begich (D-Alaska) and two other persons is reported missing in southern Alaska.

17 In South Korea, President Chung Hee Park proclaims martial law, suspends part of the constitution and all political activity, dissolves the National Assembly, imposes press censorship and closes all colleges and universities.

A minority coalition government, headed by Lars Korvald, takes the oath of office in Norway. (Premier Trygve Bratteli had resigned on Oct. 6 after Norwegians rejected EEC membership.)

18 After overriding a Presidential veto of a $24,600,000,000 water pollution bill, the second session of the 92nd Congress adjourns.

Representatives of the Soviet Union and the United States sign a three-year trade agreement, which includes settlement of the Soviet's World War II lend-lease debt.

21 Leaders of the nine EEC nations conclude a two-day summit conference in Paris.

24 Nixon administration sources disclose that the White House has ordered a halt of all U.S. bombing north of the 20th parallel in North Vietnam.

26 In an hour long briefing of the press, presidential adviser Kissinger declares that "peace is at hand" in Indochina.

Dahomey's ruling Presidential Council and the National Consultative Assembly are dissolved as the Army takes command of the African nation.

27 President Nixon announces the sale of 300,000 tons (12,000,000 bushels) of corn to Communist China.

President Nixon vetoes nine spending bills which he claims would "breach the budget" by some $750,000,000 in fiscal 1973 and by nearly $2,000,000,000 in fiscal 1974.

28 Ending several weeks of heavy border fighting, the nations of Yemen and Southern Yemen agree to merge.

29 Palestinian guerrillas hijack a West German jetliner over Turkey and obtain the release of three Arab commandos accused of involvement in the slaying of 11 Israelis at the Olympic Games.

30 National elections are held in Canada; the Liberal Party of Prime Minister Trudeau loses its Parliamentary majority.

UPI

Danish Premier Krag votes in Oct. 2 EEC referendum.

OCTOBER

Dr. Kissinger tells newsmen Vietnam peace is at hand.

Wide World

Election results incomplete, Trudeau remains smiling.

The Canadian Press

President Nixon leaves San Clemente voting booth.

West German Chancellor Brandt wins a second term.

NOVEMBER

Norman Kirk leads New Zealand Labour party to victory.

2 Canada's Prime Minister Trudeau announces that despite election setbacks which reduced his party's parliamentary majority to a minority his government will remain in power.

Protesting injustices, about 500 American Indians seize control of the U.S. Bureau of Indian Affairs building in Washington, D.C.

4 Representatives of North Korea and South Korea sign agreement calling for broader economic and political cooperation leading to eventual reunification.

6 Britain's Prime Minister Heath imposes a 90-day freeze on wages, prices, rents and dividends.

West Germany and East Germany complete negotiations on a draft treaty to establish formal diplomatic relations.

7 In U.S. elections, President Richard M. Nixon wins a second term; the Democratic party retains control of both houses of Congress.

8 Pakistan withdraws from the Southeast Asia Treaty Organization.

15 A spokesman for the U.S. State Department announces that Canada, Hungary, Indonesia and Poland have agreed in principle to serve on an international commission to supervise a Vietnam cease-fire once it becomes effective.

16 Two black students are killed and one is wounded during a day of violence and confrontation on the campus of Southern University, Baton Rouge, La.

The White House announces the resignation of the Rev. Theodore M. Hesburgh as chairman of the U.S. Commission on Civil Rights.

17 Juan D. Peron returns to Argentina following 17 years of exile. (He was president of the South American nation from 1946 to 1955.)

19 In West Germany, voters by a substantial margin give the coalition government of Chancellor Willy Brandt a second term.

21 Heavy fighting erupts between Israel and Syria on the Israeli-occupied Golan heights.

22 President Nixon lifts a 22-year-old ban on travel to China by U.S. ships and airplanes.

23 Bolivia's President Hugo Banzer Suarez declares a state of siege (semimartial law) after factory workers in La Paz call a 24-hour antigovernment strike.

25 The New Zealand Labour Party of Norman E. Kirk is victorious in national elections.

27 Pakistan President Bhutto orders released all 617 Indian prisoners of war held in Pakistan since December 1971 war.

28 President Nixon nominates Elliot L. Richardson, Caspar W. Weinberger and Roy L. Ash as secretary of defense, secretary of health, education and welfare and director of the White House Office of Management and Budget, respectively.

29 Peter J. Brennan is named U.S. secretary of labor.

The Rev. Philip F. Berrigan, after serving 38 months in prison for antiwar activity, is granted parole effective Dec. 20.

2 The Australian Labor party of Edward Gough Whitlam wins a majority in parliamentary elections.

5 U.S. Undersecretary of Commerce James T. Lynn is named secretary of housing and urban development.

The U.S. Supreme Court rules that a state can deprive a nightclub of its liquor license for permitting acts of "gross sexuality" among its entertainers, other employees and customers.

6 A South Carolina textile manufacturer, Frederick B. Dent, is appointed secretary of commerce.

7 To help combat inflation, the French government announces a major cut in its national sales tax and a $1,000,000,000 bond issue which will mature in 15 years.

Claude S. Brinegar, a California oil executive, is named secretary of transportation.

8 In the Republic of Ireland, voters decide to abolish the special constitutional position of the Roman Catholic Church.

9 Robert Strauss, a Dallas, Tex., lawyer, is named to succeed Mrs. Jean Westwood as chairman of the Democratic party.

10 In elections for Japan's lower house of parliament, the Liberal-Democratic party of Premier Tanaka is returned to power, but the Socialist and Communist parties gain additional seats.

13 The UN General Assembly adopts its Finance Committee's recommendation that the U.S. contribution to the UN budget be reduced from 31.5 percent to 25 percent "as soon as practicable."

15 White House spokesmen announce that John A. Scali, presidential consultant and former newsman, will succeed Geoorge Bush as U.S. representative to the UN. (Bush has been designated chairman of the Republican party.)

19 Apollo 17, carrying Capt. Eugene Cernan, Comdr. Ronald Evans and Dr. Harrison Schmitt, splashes down in Pacific Ocean. During the 12½-day mission, last of the Apollo series, Cernan and Schmitt explored moon surface for 22 hours 5 minutes.

21 President Nixon announces the appointment of James R. Schlesinger, chairman of the Atomic Energy Commission, as director of the Central Intelligence Agency.

22 The new governments of Australia and New Zealand grant diplomatic recognition to Communist China.

23 Thousands of persons are killed as a series of earthquakes destroys much of Managua, Nicaragua's capital.

26 Harry S. Truman, 33rd President of the United States, dies in Kansas City, Mo.

29 Four members of the Israeli Embassy staff in Bangkok, Thailand, and the wives of two of them are released unharmed after being held hostage by four Palestinian guerrillas for nearly 19 hours.

30 President Nixon orders a halt of all U.S. bombing of North Vietnam north of the 20th Parallel. (Full-scale U.S. bombing of North Vietnam had been resumed Dec. 18 after the United States and North Vietnam had failed to reach "a just and fair agreement" in Paris.)

Australian Labor Party leader Whitlam meets press for first time as prime minister.

DECEMBER

"Life" ceases publication with its year-end issue.

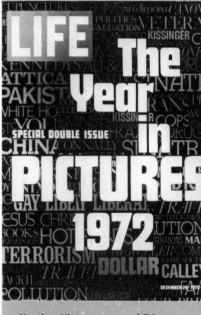

North Vietnamese children wave from the wing of one of the 15 U.S. B-52's downed by Hanoi during December.

Photos UPI

Steve Northrup Camera 5

the year 1972

ADVERTISING

Expectations were that U.S. advertising expenditures would reach record levels in 1972—a total of between $22,500,000,000 and $22,800,000,000, up from $20,600,000,000 in 1971. A Department of Commerce projection indicated that advertising outlays would rise to $26,000,000,000 in 1975 and to $36,000,000,000 in 1980. Meanwhile, a joint study by the International Advertising Association and International Research Associates reported that advertising expenditures were up in 75 countries, amounting to a combined $33,000,000,000 in 1970. The United States, West Germany, Japan, the United Kingdom, Canada and France accounted for 83 percent of the 1970 total.

In the United States in 1971 the 100 leading national advertisers increased their promotional spending to $4,600,000,000, an advance of 6 percent over 1970. The leading advertisers were Procter & Gamble, with an investment of $275,000,000; Sears, Roebuck & Co., $200,000,000; General Foods, $160,000,000; General Motors, $140,377,000; and Warner-Lambert, $128,000,000. Advertising agency billings advanced to a new high of $10,500,000,000. About 88 percent of that total was handled by 66 agencies. The largest agencies were the J. Walter Thompson Co., with $774,000,000 in billings; McCann-Erikson, $593,900,000; Young & Rubicam, $503,500,000; Ted Bates & Co., $434,800,000; and the Leo Burnett Co., $422,700,000. Outside the United States the biggest agencies were Japan's Dentsu, $565,300,000, and Hakuhodo, $192,000,000.

To reduce U.S. Postal Service deficit, a Cincinnati ad agency man suggested that the service sell advertising space on its stamps.

UPI

But while advertising in the United States seemed to be at the start of a five- to ten-year boom period in 1972, its regulators and critics rained attacks on it. Perhaps the most significant move of the year came when the Federal Trade Commission (FTC) singled out breakfast cereal manufacturers for an historic test of advertising and marketing as antitrust factors. The FTC leveled a "shared monopoly" charge against Kellogg, General Mills, General Foods and Quaker Oats. The FTC claimed, not that the companies conspired in the classic sense, but that they achieved a monopoly effect through brand proliferation, intensive trademark promotions, artificial product differentiation, restrictive allocation of store shelf space, restrictive trade and consumer promotions and misleading advertising.

Among other actions, the FTC called for the proof behind advertising claims for cough and cold remedies, and for electric shavers and air conditioners. (One company protested that the mere fact the Federal agency publicized its demands for such information inevitably caused people to think that something was wrong and that the company's advertising claims were being challenged as false and misleading.) The FTC ruled that Ocean Spray cranberries must run "corrective" advertising in one of every four of its advertisements for a year to make clear that in discussing "food energy" it referred to calories and not to vitamins and minerals.

The FTC was embarrassed in a challenge of a "stop-leak" television commercial by DuPont's Zerex antifreeze. The challenge was dropped when the FTC decided it did not have enough information about DuPont's side of the issue when it first made the complaint.

The government agency also charged Coca-Cola with misrepresenting the nutritional merits of its Hi-C drink and said it should be required to run corrective advertising. Later, an FTC administrative judge praised Hi-C as an "excellent" source of vitamin C for children and said FTC attorneys had failed to establish that the advertising misled or deceived regarding nutritional values.

The FTC dropped a two-year-old case against Pfizer's Unburn that charged false and misleading advertising. One observer commented that the FTC was not questioning the product but testing a theory about the kinds of proof an advertisement should have before the advertiser made a claim. Advertising industry executives later raised the question: How is Pfizer to win back the confidence of consumers?

Meanwhile, the Federal Communications Commission (FCC) began studying the possible effects of counter-advertising on television.

During 1972 many residents of Afghanistan suffered from severe famine, the result of more than two years of drought and exceptionally severe winters.

Some experts warned the FCC that many advertisers would leave the airways rather than face an order demanding such advertising. And in response to a petition calling for a ban against advertising on children's television programs, the FCC started a study of that situation too.

One of the largest advertising agencies in the United States, Lennen & Newell, which reached a billings high of $160,000,000 in 1970, went into bankruptcy in 1972.

JAMES V. O'GARA
Editor-at-Large, *Advertising Age*

AFGHANISTAN

Afghanistan was still struggling with the threat of famine in 1972, the result of more than two years of serious drought and exceptionally severe winters. But the mountainous, landlocked kingdom was beginning to lift itself from its misery, largely as the result of stepped up aid from the United States, the U.S.S.R., China and U.N. agencies.

Nevertheless, five of the 28 provinces in the country continued to suffer serious shortages of wheat, the country's principal food. Despite substantial donations of both food and clothing to Afghanistan's nearly 18,000,000 people, inefficient distribution by the government, illegal hoarding and blocked roads due to heavy snowfalls ensured that much of the relief supplies would not reach the worst-hit areas. But relief efforts continued to develop and improve throughout the year. The government initiated a "wheat for work" program in eight provinces which gave employment to nearly 60,000 people in 173 projects ranging from road building to irrigation. Unfortunately, wheat prices soared to a level 450 percent higher than at the end of 1971.

The effects of the bad weather on Afghanistan's large and important livestock industry also began to be tackled. Replacement stock for animals lost to the drought and severe winters began to arrive during the year. More important, the United Nations Food and Agriculture Organization launched a program to set up centers to diagnose animal diseases, manufacture vaccines and generally boost livestock production. Disease even in good years normally kills 20 percent of the country's 40,000,000 head of livestock.

The dismal outlook of the previous two years was somewhat brightened by new foreign assistance from Afghanistan's major donors. China offered $2,470,000 in commodities for projects it is supporting, including irrigation projects, poultry and silk farming and the expansion of the Bagrami Textile Mills. U.S. economic assistance for the year amounted to $7,000,000, mainly for irrigation and farming projects already underway. And the Soviet Union committed at least another $1,000,000 for farm machinery and other equipment to be used on a 90,000-acre agricultural project it is supporting.

Politically, the year was a quiet one with most attention focused on the country's economic troubles. King Mohammad Zahir Shan, in any case, did not feel moved to do anything about the long-awaited legislation to legalize political parties, which continues to be the most important political issue in the country.

ARTHUR C. MILLER
Senior Editor, *The Asia Letter*

AFRICA

The following summary pertains to events in sub-Saharan Africa. The Arab countries of North Africa are covered in the article ARAB STATES.

A widening of the gulf that separates black-ruled and white-ruled African states characterized events in sub-Saharan Africa in 1972. Events in Uganda and Burundi demonstrated the virulence of tribalism and racism in black Africa, and a mild mirror image of this situation appeared in the rightward trends evident during the year in southern Africa's white-minority regimes.

Sudan. In a year in which events did not in general encourage optimism about Africa's future, one event raised considerable hopes. In late February peaceful negotiations ended 17 years of sporadic warfare in southern Sudan. The warfare had pitted the Arabicized Muslims of the north against the black animist Christian Nilotes of the remote, undeveloped south. The three-day ouster from power of Sudanese head of state Gen. Gaafar al-Nimeiry, in July 1971, seemed to have convinced him that his retention of power depended on resolving the hitherto insoluble "southern question." Canon Burgess Carr, the Liberian secretary-general of the All-Africa Conference of Churches, was instrumental in mediating the dispute.

The settlement provided for a cease-fire and a transitional period of refugee repatriation and granted considerable autonomy to the south. Its terms provided that southerners should have a regional governmental unit with its own representative assembly; direction over their own economic development and public services; representation in the National Assembly; official recognition of English as their working language; and, for a period of five years, a guarantee that half the army personnel stationed in the south would come from the ranks of former Anyanya guerrillas. Even so, the existing peace would remain fragile until the difficult rehabilitation process showed signs of progress.

The peace settlement exerted beneficial effects on neighboring states with similar patterns of conflict between Arabicized Muslims and Christian animist blacks. This was especially true in Ethiopia where the momentum of the developing secessionist movement in Eritrea was undercut. However, by requiring the Khartoum government to focus its attention on black Africa, the settlement also caused strains in Sudan's relations with its Arab neighbors. It forced the postponement—possibly the abandonment—of Sudanese membership in the Libyan-Egyptian-Syrian Federation of Arab states.

Burundi. Hardly had peace been initiated in Sudan when tribal massacres in Burundi provoked the continent's most agonizing situation of 1972. One of Africa's tiniest nations, poor and very populous, Burundi is a 400-year-old state periodically torn by conflict engendered by tensions that exist between its feudal traditions and its quest for modernity.

On its simplest level, the conflict sets the traditional ruling minority, the tall, elegant Tutsis (less than 15 percent of the population), against the Hutus, Bantu agriculturists and traditional serfs (85 percent of the population). The Tutsis are themselves divided, royalists opposing commoners, traditionalists opposing modernizers. Nonetheless, fearing extermination, the Tutsis unite when faced by a Hutu threat.

Such a threat occurred in late April when Hutu nationalists, seeking to exploit Tutsi divisions exacerbated by the return of the exiled king, launched simultaneous attacks on several towns. Dominating the government and the army, the Tutsis soon mastered the situation. Thereafter, in order to prevent Hutu uprisings in the foreseeable future, the ruling Tutsis initiated systematic massacres designed to eliminate virtually all Hutus capable of playing leadership roles. Many observers believe that the Hutu death toll exceeded 150,000 persons.

The Burundi massacres will retard the country's development, probably for a generation. They had the immediate effect of perpetuating Tutsi domination of Burundi's affairs, but they also virtually guaranteed that eventually the Hutus will rise, probably with equal bloodthirstiness, to throw off Tutsi overlordship. Although little reported, the massacres constituted a major tragedy for Africa, illustrating the ferocity of unchecked tribalism.

Another facet of the tragedy was the fact that no black African state effectively raised its voice to curb the slaughter.

Uganda. Events in Uganda, which dominated the year's news from black Africa, had less alarming human consequences, but immense geopolitical significance. Three basic events emerged: a mass expulsion of Asians; an invasion by exiles from Tanzania; and Uganda's realignment of its foreign relations.

In early August, Gen. Idi Amin announced his determination to expel all noncitizen Asians from Uganda within 90 days. The announced policy produced initial disbelief; some 55,000 to 65,000 noncitizen Asians were thought to live in Uganda. Other aspects of the move also occasioned incredulity: its gratuitous harsh-

ness, the inevitable administrative difficulties, its blatantly racial motivation, the uncertain behavior of an undisciplined and violence-prone army, the apparent disregard for the expellees' rights of compensation for confiscated property and, not the least, the economic consequences of the action for Uganda.

General Amin, however, quickly proved that his policy was not negotiable. In the event, the expulsion exercise took place more smoothly than most observers thought possible. Britain accepted responsibility for its citizens, who made up the vast majority of the expellees, and the noncitizen Asian population fortunately proved to be only about half its previously estimated size. While Ugandan soldiers subjected Asians to considerable intimidation, indignities and sporadic violence, the expellees suffered comparatively little loss of life.

Relations with Britain grew extremely strained. They worsened in mid-December when Uganda nationalized 41 firms and tea estates, all but seven of them wholly or partly British-owned, and increased pressures against British aid personnel.

By year's end there appeared little likelihood that the expelled Asians would ever re-

Asian exodus from Uganda, decreed by President Idi Amin (right), made Kampala merchants and 50,000 other British subjects destitute.

Both photos, Camera Press from Pictorial

Cars and buildings in the Tanzanian town of Mwanza stand gutted after attack by the Uganda Air Force in October.

ceive just compensation for their abandoned property. This hardship was partly mitigated by the fact that many had already deposited money abroad.

During the expulsion exercise it became clear that General Amin had actually intended to rid Uganda of all of its Asians. A late August announcement that citizen Asians would also be expelled was subsequently rescinded. Nevertheless, in nationwide document examinations officials deprived about half the citizen Asians of their Ugandan nationality.

General Amin later announced that any remaining citizen Asians would be resettled in villages. This policy, added to the general uncertainty, seemed likely to cause the eventual departure of the estimated 2,000 citizen Asians who remained after the Nov. 8 deadline.

On Sept. 17, in the midst of the expulsion confusion, Ugandan exiles invaded Uganda from Tanzania. Virtually all of the invaders were supporters of Milton Obote, whom General Amin had ousted in January 1971. Hailing from northern Uganda and bent on restoring Dr. Obote to power, the invaders found little support for their insurrection in the country's southwest and were quickly routed.

The invasion hurled Uganda and Tanzania, whose government had significantly supported the exiles, to the brink of war for several days. Ugandan planes bombed two Tanzanian towns, Mwanza and Bukoba, but without inflicting significant damage. Eventually the Somali government arranged a truce. During much of the year law and order in Uganda appeared on the verge of collapse. Indications of impending breakdown were the disappearances of Benedicto Kiwanuka, the country's chief justice; of Frank Kalimuzo, vice chancellor of Makerere University; and of other prominent Ugandans, the presumed victims of government assassination squads. Christian leaders were harassed as General Amin tried to extend Muslim influence into all spheres of Ugandan life.

The government's actions significantly affected Uganda's foreign relations. The Asians' expulsion seemed certain to trigger serious economic retrogression and the curtailment of aid.

General Amin's manifest racism, as well as the harshness of his expulsion policy and its disregard of compensation, strengthened the position of southern Africa's white-minority regimes, bolstering credibility of their propaganda.

Continuing instability loomed over East Africa. The Uganda-Tanzania truce resolved none of the two countries' basic differences. Uganda's Asian expulsions were likely to adversely affect Kenya's economy and the position of its Asians. The East African Community's future seemed increasingly problematic.

Meanwhile, in April, General Amin had expelled all Israelis residing in Uganda and increased efforts to align Uganda with the Arab world. Apparently, he expelled the Israelis in order to escape repaying develop-

ment loans, to eliminate Israeli influence in a restive army and to bolster his Muslim credentials sufficiently to win Arab monies.

The Israelis' expulsion constituted a major blow to their country's African policy. Libya's Col. Muammar al-Qaddafi and Saudi Arabia's King Faisal sought, with grants of financial and military aid, to exploit a major opportunity for increasing Arab influence in black Africa. But given General Amin's erratic nature, his record of perfidy and his country's poverty, Uganda would seem to represent a questionable cornerstone for the Arab states' African policy.

Coups. During 1972 black Africa saw the military assume power in three countries. In the Malagasy Republic longtime President Philibert Tsiranana's fall from power in May contrasted sharply with his overwhelming electoral victory in January, in which he captured a third term unopposed. Besides corrupting the island's electoral process, the physically ailing president had grown dictatorial, removed from the people and too allied with French interests. When student-worker strikes revealed the weakness of his government, he invited the military to assume power. An October referendum gave the military a mandate to rule the island for five years and forced President Tsiranana's resignation.

Coups also occurred in the states of Ghana and Dahomey. They dramatized military impatience with politicians' failures to solve such basic problems as corruption, tribal and regional rivalries, lack of economic progress and the proclivity of ruling elites to live beyond their countries' means.

Ghanaian coup leader Col. Ignatius Acheampong seized power in mid-January, ousting Kofi Busia, a former sociology professor. Maj. Mathieu Kerekou's late-October coup, Dahomey's sixth in its 12 years of independence, ended a two and one-half year experiment in government by a triumvirate of regional leaders.

In what resembled a governmental coup against the electorate, President Kenneth Kaunda virtually ended multiparty democracy in Zambia. Despite clear evidence that substantial, if minority, support existed for two opposition parties, the Kaunda government introduced legislation to make Zambia a one-party state. The move appeared partly designed to maintain the control of the United National Independence party—and some of its stalwarts —over patronage, perquisites and payoffs.

Rhodesia. Meanwhile the white-ruled governments' oppressive stability prevented similar upheavals, although events in southern Africa underlined the extent to which such stability depended on the use of force for its maintenance.

Rhodesian whites began the year with unbridled optimism, feeling that the long-anticipated settlement with Britain was finally within reach. The settlement, on favorable terms negotiated in November 1971, would have guaranteed international recognition for Rhodesia, ended most aspects of economic sanctions, provided access to development capital and left Rhodesian social practices basically unchanged. The only remaining obstacle to adoption was the forthcoming Pearce Commission's test of the proposal's acceptability to the population as a whole.

Apparently as secure on his throne as ever, Haile Selassie greets a West African diplomat at the Ethiopian emperor's 80th birthday ceremony.

Ray Ellis from Rapho Guillumette

Both photos, John McGeorge, Gamma

John Burges (top), envoy of the Pearce Commission, declares the 1971 Anglo-Rhodesian accord unacceptable. Black Rhodesians hailed the news.

The British commissioners had no sooner arrived in Rhodesia than African riots erupted in several towns. The riots illustrated African excitement at their having once again a voice in their political destiny. The riots also suggested that most Africans opposed the settlement terms and doubted that the white government would implement them fairly. Whites clung to the conviction that fear of intimidation had silenced the African majority and that government-paid chiefs, who initially supported the settlement, truly represented African opinion.

When announced in late May, therefore, the Pearce Commission's finding that the terms were not acceptable to the majority of Rhodesians came as no surprise. Nevertheless, the Ian Smith government rejected the commission's conclusions.

The Pearce Commission's rejection opened a new era in Rhodesian politics. The acceptability test showed that African nationalist leaders possessed a broad, nationwide constituency. The commission's findings established the credibility of the African National Council (ANC), a body formed by former African

political detainees and led by Methodist Bishop Abel Muzorewa which had organized African opposition sentiment. The findings also called into question the assumption that the tribal chiefs were authentic representatives of African opinion and labeled distrust of the white government as the basic motivation for African rejection of the settlement.

Although it dashed white Rhodesian hopes for immediate recognition, the Pearce Commission's work created basic conditions for workable solutions. It provided an outside analysis of what ailed Rhodesian society; it defined the real dispute preventing settlement as between Rhodesia's black and white communities. It implied a strategy—dialogue—for solving this dispute and offered a visible reward —British recognition—once measurable progress had been made.

Prime Minister Smith found himself caught between the pro-apartheid views of his all-white Rhodesian Front party's restive right wing and the sentiments of Africans who could veto the settlement. The Smith government's willingness to negotiate terms with Britain constituted an acknowledgment that it could never fully overcome the problems created by its exclusion from development capital. Thus, eventually, it would have to negotiate with the ANC, regardless of right-wing white opinion. Indeed, late in the year, while officially denying that formal talks were being held, the Smith government entered such negotiations.

No clear pattern, however, emerged in the country's race relations. At a September Rhodesian Front party congress, Mr. Smith outflanked his right-wing opponents, winning their grudging agreement that they would not implement apartheid-style discriminatory measures lest they jeopardize settlement efforts. He stressed the fact that the deteriorating security situation in neighboring Mozambique had added greater urgency to the quest for international recognition.

Nevertheless, the government did impose further restrictions on Africans. Those further limiting their patronage of multiracial bars were nullified by the high court. But the government also went ahead with a "provincialization" scheme, which many considered a thinly disguised form of apartheid, and held in reserve proposed legislation requiring all Africans to carry identity cards, a move with obvious security implications.

Despite the thwarted settlement, there was little evidence to suggest that white voters wanted to abandon the Rhodesian Front, which ruled the country as a one-party state. At its October congress, for instance, the moderate Centre party attracted only 80 supporters. The Rhodesia party emerged late in the year. Formed with the support of white farmers, a group badly hit by economic sanctions, the party had uncertain long-term prospects.

Guerrilla Movements. In late 1972 it became increasingly clear that the Mozambique Liberation Front (Frelimo) was extending its operations ever deeper into Portuguese territory, moving into Manica and Sofala province, which provides Rhodesia's road and rail links to the sea. Frelimo confined its activities to small-scale ambushes and mining operations, but even these activities significantly disrupted free movement. The 60,000-man Portuguese armed forces in Mozambique proved unable to contain the guerrillas. Work on the giant Cabora Bassa hydroelectric scheme continued on schedule, however.

Clearly concerned, the Rhodesian prime minister visited Marcello Caetano, his Portuguese counterpart, in early October. Rhodesian officials also visited Malawi, whose moderate black government seemed incapable—and possibly undesirous—of interdicting Frelimo sanctuaries in its territory. The Rhodesian and South African defense ministers conferred in late October. While Portugal did not publicly accept offers of military assistance, Rhodesian military officers admitted that Rhodesian forces had fought secretly against the guerrillas on Portuguese territory.

It remained impossible accurately to assess the progress of the African party for the Independence of Portuguese Guinea and Cape Verde (PAIGC). (Cape Verde refers to the Cape Verde Islands in the Atlantic Ocean, an overseas Portuguese territory.) The movement's longtime leader, Amilcar Cabral, was granted observer status at the United Nations, a signal diplomatic victory. He claimed that PAIGC had established a functioning government administration in "liberated" Guinea and stated that it would soon make a unilateral "African" declaration of independence.

Meanwhile, the Southwest Africa People's Organization continued to harass South African troops with land mines, largely concentrated in the Caprivi Strip.

South Africa. During the year the South African government veered sharply to the right. The swing appeared to stem from a growing awareness that the grand design of separate development was not offering viable solutions to the country's racial problems. As a result, a crunch seemed necessary to reassure whites, especially the Dutch-descended Afrikaners, that their interests would remain paramount whatever the failings of ideology.

After 24 years in power, the (Afrikaner) Nationalist government based its appeal to the all-white electorate on three fundamentals: the separate development ideology by which it promised just solutions to South Africa's racial dilemma; its ability to maintain law and order; and its position as the executive of the political will of the Afrikaner—and, by extension, all white—people in South Africa.

During the year Africans challenged apartheid in several areas. Although their efforts brought little prospect of immediate change, the challenge suggested a declining willingness to acquiesce in an exploitive system. Black ferment challenged the basis of the Nationalists' grand design and their long-term capacity to maintain economic order.

Three work stoppages were significant because Africans in South Africa have no legal right to strike, cannot belong to registered trade unions and generally face harsh police measures, including imprisonment, if they organize strikes or refuse to work.

January saw continued striking in South West Africa, where some 13,000 contract laborers of the northern Ovambos, the territory's most populous tribe, refused to work at mines, ports, farms and construction sites. Some workers are paid less than 50 cents a day.

Although the government blamed the strike on foreign agitators and meddling clerics, some officials acknowledged that the workers' living conditions were below acceptable standards.

Underlining South West Africa's dependence on Ovambo labor, the strike led to some improvements in the contract labor system, demonstrating that work stoppages could win concessions. But the strike also provoked strong government reaction. In February the government placed the Ovambo bantustan—semi-autonomous areas under black control—under emergency regulations, curtailed political activity and sent white police reinforcements into the area.

In early June some 300 African bus drivers, striking for higher pay, were arrested in Johannesburg. Another 100 drivers stopped work to support the strike, hampering access of some 80,000 African workers to the city. In October, Zulu stevedores at Durban port, some of them earning only about $12 per 60-hour workweek, struck briefly for higher pay and better working conditions. Their action collapsed, however, in the face of police intervention and the threat of repatriation to their impoverished homeland.

The strikes showed that South Africa's economy, although rigidly stratified, was also highly

Laborers return to their Ovambo compound near Windhoek, South West Africa. Ovambo tribesmen struck nearby mines and ports in January.

Frederic Hunter

Adults attend school in a black guerrilla-controlled area of Portuguese Mozambique, where the anticolonial struggle continued through the year.

integrated. A growing realization of this fact led to some improvements in African wages in industry. Some "non-whites" were also granted equal pay for equal work (for example, doctors employed by the Johannesburg City Council and tellers employed in certain banks). However, such instances of salary equalization remained isolated.

The emerging "black consciousness" movement also illustrated the "non-white" mood of independence. The South African Students Organization, a black consciousness pioneer, sought to overcome "resignation consciousness" through leadership training and community projects designed to instill a group confidence and black pride. The Black People's Convention, a political movement, also emerged in 1972. While black consciousness appears to fit into the ideology of separate development, movement leaders stressed the ever-present threat of political detention.

In early June, Cape Town University students supported black consciousness by demonstrating against the expulsion of black students from an ethnic university. The protest led to student-police violence, which most news dispatches reported as instigated by the police. Police entered St. George's Cathedral, where they beat students, forcibly dragging some of the protesters outside. The government blamed the protest on foreign agitators. Late in the year, Cape Town and Johannesburg courts dismissed charges against students who had participated in the protest. Government ministers reacted to the rulings by demanding changes in the law.

In another manifestation of black independence, bantustan leaders, especially Kwa Zulu's Gatsha Buthelezi and Transkei's Kaiser Matanzima, made increasing demands for more land and a fairer division of wealth and opportunity. Because the doctrine of separate development legitimated the positions of these men, it seemed doubtful that such demands could be indefinitely ignored.

Early in the year Nationalist politicians grew seriously worried about reduced majorities in by-elections and defections from their party. To recoup the losses, prominent party spokesmen accused the opposition United party of "boerehaat," Afrikaner hatred, an ethnic appeal which produced an increased majority in the crucial Oudtshoorn by-election but damaged white solidarity. Prime Minister Vorster also reshuffled his cabinet, but without appointing any prominent liberal.

French President Georges Pompidou and his wife read about their visit to Niger while awaiting the start of a revue with Niger's President Diori Hamani (in cap) in January.

Trying to modernize, the United party introduced a new federal policy designed eventually to give all South Africa's racial groups a voice in running the country. While the policy sought to provide more realistic solutions to existing problems than those provided by separate development ideology, November by-elections offered scant evidence that white voters really wanted new ideas.

South West Africa. During 1972 the United Nations and South Africa made important progress in tackling their long-standing dispute over the status and independence prospects of South West Africa, or Namibia. UN Secretary-General Kurt Waldheim visited the territory in March; his personal representative, Alfred Escher, a former Swiss diplomat, toured it extensively in October. While Escher's contacts proved controversial, the Security Council nevertheless extended Dr. Waldheim's mandate until April 30, 1973. The UN Council on Namibia also was expanded from 11 to 18 members.

Dialogue. The quest for black-white dialogue was one of the year's main casualties. Varied factors contributed to its virtual demise: the uncertainty of political arrangements in Rhodesia; renewed black African enthusiasm about guerrilla prospects; the loss of forward momentum, especially after the Malagasy Republic changed governments; the basic incompatibility of black and white goals; South Africa's general intransigence and its movement to the right.

International Events. During the year the Organization of African Unity held its first All-Africa Trade Fair in Nairobi, Kenya, an event which constituted an important first step in stimulating inter-African trade. Work also continued on the Trans-Africa Highway, a project designed to link the Indian and Atlantic Oceans via Kenya, Uganda, Zaire, Central African Republic, Cameroun and Nigeria.

Two UN conferences—one on trade and development (UNCTAD) held in Santiago, Chile, in May and the June Stockholm meeting on the environment—dramatized the differences in perspective between the rich nations and those of Africa and the developing world. African leaders resented the way in which the rich manipulated and exploited the poor at UNCTAD, refusing to negotiate trade terms until exchange rates were fixed and ignoring the stake of the poorer countries in rich-nation monetary talks.

While they hoped that the rich nations would help them avoid environmental mistakes, they feared that the rich intended to penalize them because of—or make them pay for—the developed world's pollution. Without minimizing environmental concerns, they saw growth—in terms of industrialization, expanded trade, better living conditions, full employment—as their prime objective.

Despite these basic differences of viewpoint, vigorous lobbying by the African nations succeeded in getting the UN Environment Agency sited in Nairobi.

FREDERIC HUNTER
African Correspondent
The Christian Science Monitor

AGRICULTURE

Major developments for agriculture and food in 1972 were related to changed international relationships and general conditions of domestic economies.

At the level of international relationships the civil war between Pakistan and Bangladesh in late 1971 caused a shortfall of crops in the latter country and created an extended period of extreme hunger. The politics of the conflict, plus national pride, caused India to restrict the amount of aid and number of agricultural improvement teams from the United States serving in the country.

Following President Nixon's precedent-setting trip to China, the Chinese placed the first large grain order (20,000,000 bushels of wheat and some soybeans) with the private U.S. grain trade in nearly 25 years. Also, following his trip to the U.S.S.R., and subsequent visits by Secretary of Agriculture Earl Butz, the Soviets contracted for very large grain deliveries.

The European Economic Community (EEC) accentuated its agricultural policy reforms in member countries as a means to improve the Community's competitive position, reduce its dependence on costly farm programs, restrain consumer food costs and prepare for active membership of Britain, Ireland and Denmark.

Crop Production, Sales and Income. Weather was favorable for crop production in North America, and the United States escaped damage from corn blight for the second successive year. While cold, damp weather delayed spring plantings, ample moisture and favorable temperatures during the summer resulted in a U.S. corn crop of 5,266,000,000 bushels, second in size only to the record 1971 crop. (A small reduction in the feed grain crop was due mainly to a smaller acreage induced by larger government payments to farmers for not planting their land.) The large 1971 crop had depressed corn prices to the lowest levels since the early 1940's. Hence, to hold plantings and production below 1971, the government's greater supply control payments caused the total cost of farm programs to approach $7,000,000,000. The 1972 soybean crop was 1,317,000,000 bushels, the largest on record. The wheat crop was 1,559,000,000 bushels, the third largest on record and only slightly below 1971. Under market circumstances of recent years the large 1972 crops, following the bumper yields of 1971 and large carry-over stocks, would have seriously depressed grain prices. The large sales of grain to the Soviets, however, counteracted the large supplies from 1972 and caused grain prices to rise sharply in early fall. For example, the wheat futures prices rose by about 50 cents or by a third of the level prevailing a year earlier.

Weather for crop production was unfavorable in Eastern Europe, especially in the Soviet Union, where 1972 grain production was about 15 percent less than planned. The Soviet contract called for purchase of $900,000,000 to $1,000,000,000 of U.S. farm products made up mostly of wheat, feed grains and soybeans. The $750,000,000 worth of grains is to be delivered over a three year period.

The wheat order alone was for nearly 500,-000,000 bushels, a third of total U.S. production in 1972. The Soviet purchase was at world market prices prevailing at the time of the contract. Following the contract, as word of the large sale spread throughout the market, wheat prices increased sharply. After the price increase, the U.S. government withdrew the subsidy that it had been paying grain exporters at the time of the Soviet contract and which applied to it accordingly. Hence, after the Soviet contract had been reflected in the market and the subsidy withdrawn, other importers of U.S. wheat caused an increase of about 50 percent in purchase price. The Soviet contract pushed U.S. agricultural commercial exports to record levels. For the 12 months following July 1, 1972, projected U.S. wheat exports were 1,000,000,000 bushels, as compared with a total production in 1972 of 1,600,000,000 bushels.

While grain sales to the Soviets had beneficial effects on U.S. farm prices and income, they became a major political issue in the 1972 presidential campaign. Senator McGovern accused the Nixon administration of rigging the grain sales so that the gains went to grain exporting firms at the expense of the public and to the disadvantage of farmers. He charged, and the administration denied, that word of the Soviet contract was leaked to grain exporters, who then could buy supplies before the prices rose. Because of the timing of the announcement and the activation of grain purchases to meet the export contracts, farmers who harvested and sold wheat early in the summer gained little from the Soviet sales. Those who harvested and sold later realized an increase of around 45 cents per bushel. This differential did not occur among corn producers, who harvested their crop later in the year, after the large grain sale was reflected in the market.

Improved grain and livestock prices raised U.S. net farm income to a record level. Realized net income was slightly more than $18,000,000,000 in 1972. The previous high was $17,000,000,000 in 1947.

The M-V "Kasimov" arrived in Houston Dec. 4 to commence loading the U.S. grain for which the U.S.S.R. had contracted earlier in the year.

The U.S. grain contract superseded some Canadian wheat sales in Eastern Europe. However, it was not fully competitive with them because the magnitude of the contract exceeded the amount which Canada could supply, and

On July 8 U.S. and U.S.S.R. representatives signed an agreement under which the U.S.S.R. will buy $750,000,000 in grain over three years.

Canadian farmers realized some gains through an improved international market.

Owing to the sharp increase in wheat prices, U.S. bakers proposed to increase the price of bread from two to three cents per loaf. They were denied the increase by the Federal Price Commission. Nevertheless, prices continued to be the basis of heated debate between farmers and consumers during the year. The debate centered on the price of beef, following the rise of cattle prices to levels not experienced since 1952. Secretary Butz came to the vigorous defense of farmers and the level of beef prices, indicating that it was "only right" for farmers to receive prices as high as those prevailing in 1952 because the price level for other commodities, materials and labor had risen considerably throughout the entire economy during the 20 year period.

Adding fuel to the debate was a Food and Drug Administration ban on the use of stilbestrol in cattle feed. Stilbestrol, a hormone incorporated with feed to speed and cheapen cattle gains, may cause cancer in consumers if deposited in the tissue of animals in sufficient quantities.

Technological Change. At the time of his nomination in the fall of 1971, Earl Butz was

accused of having primary interest in large agribusiness firms and serving as a proponent for elimination of family farms. However, once confirmed as secretary of agriculture, he became an active spokesman for all farmers and their need for higher prices and income following depressed earnings of previous years.

Debate over the continued trend toward large-scale, corporate and integrated farms intensified in the United States during the year. Several bills were introduced in Congress to restrain the trend, but none became law. Other countries followed diverse paths with respect to farm size. The U.S.S.R., for instance, planned to use part of its U.S. grain purchases to further develop large-scale, specialized poultry and livestock farms. In the 1971–75 five-year plan, the Soviets planned to upgrade consumer diets by increasing meat and egg production by 27 percent, mainly on large-scale, specialized farms.

In contrast, Rumania decided to restrict specialized swine farms to 30,000 hogs per year. Previously, it had developed the largest swine farms in the world—up to 300,000 head per year. Officials stated that very large units were not efficient because of intensified disease and management problems. During the autumn emergency declared by President Ferdinand Marcos the Philippine government announced a national land reform program to break up large land holdings and turn tenant farmers into owners.

Underdeveloped World. Considerable progress toward improved farming was made in the less developed countries during the year, although the potential for long-run food shortages remained very real. Further adoption of the short-stemmed, high-yielding wheat and rice varieties occurred in the region embracing Southeast Asia and the Middle East. However, increases in rice demand outran production during the year. The Philippines, an exporter in 1970, became a net importer again. Japan, Burma and Thailand, previously bothered with large stocks, were able to reduce their reserves.

The cereals crop in India, while somewhat smaller than in the previous year, was still favorable and allowed the country to continue its policy of reducing dependence on imports representing international food aid. Projections indicate that India should be able to produce 144,000,000 tons of cereals by 1980. A crop of that size, nearly a third larger than the record 1971–72 crop of just over 100,000,000 tons, would still require some imports because of population growth.

A number of large-scale research programs was initiated or extended in South America, directed toward improving agriculture in those countries of rapidly growing populations. The multiple-country programs deal with soil classification and fertility, irrigation, crop variety improvements and improved livestock nutrition. A multi-country team perfected a system to control bats, which prey on cattle and either kill them or greatly reduce their productivity in most countries of South America.

The supply and price of beef, as in the United States, was the basis of continued controversy between consumers, ranchers and the government in Argentina. Beef is an extremely important component of consumer diets in Argentina. Also, it is an equally important commodity in the country's foreign exchange earnings. To protect its balance of payments position, through enlarged beef exports, the government instituted a program of restricted domestic consumption—an action not favored by consumers.

Brazil and Argentina continued some emphasis on improvement of field crop production. Both have favorable soils and climate but have not been able to parallel Mexico and the United States in improvement of grain production. This was especially true in Argentina, where, aside from beef production, agricultural productivity has been stagnant for several decades.

While it already has several large-scale irrigation projects underway, Mexico applied to the United Nations Development Program during the year for a loan to study further the efficient development and allocation of its very scarce water sources. Complete socialization of farmland was one step taken in Chile during the year in attempts to bolster sagging production. The country also initiated two new farm credit programs in this attempt. However, total imports of farm products still doubled over the previous year.

Displacement of Farm Labor. Of growing concern around the world during the year was the distribution of benefits from agricultural development. The new and high-yielding crop varieties do best when grown with appropriate applications of fertilizer and irrigation water. Generally it is the larger farmers who can combine optimally the new varieties, fertilizer and water. Not only do they have more capital; their farms also tend to be large enough to make a tube well or other water system profitable. In contrast, the small farmer, with too little land for a well and lacking funds for fertilizer and insecticides and the equipment to apply them, gains little or nothing from new farm technologies. The problem is intensified— a definite trend is underway—when the grow-

ing profits of the large farmers allow them to buy tractors and hire less labor from the families of the small farmers.

These problems are becoming intense in Southeast Asia and South America, where the large cities are surrounded by rapidly growing slums fed from the migration of unemployed families from rural areas. A special study initiated in 1972 for Eastern Africa, with emphasis on Nigeria and Zambia, has the objective of determining methods of agricultural improvement that can absorb labor in countries of rapidly growing populations, rather than replace it.

Technical advance and mechanization of agriculture continued to create complex problems in the rural areas of developed countries. The growing size and commercialization of farms has reduced greatly the work force of agriculture. With a smaller farm population, the volume of business and employment in rural towns has dropped sharply. This has been especially true in countries, such as the United States, Canada and Sweden, that have broad expanses of land and a widely dispersed farming industry.

The exodus from farms and rural towns has helped concentrate populations at urban centers, causing problems of traffic congestion, environmental pollution and social disfiguration. The problem has been less severe in Japan, although that country has an advancing and efficient agriculture, because a more uniform dispersion of industry throughout rural areas there has provided employment for persons displaced from farming.

The Netherlands has developed efficient plans to accommodate displaced farm labor in new towns on reclaimed land in the farm polders created by dikes to wall off North Sea waters and through training programs and compensation for persons who transfer from agriculture to industrial employment in conventional farming areas. Both Hungary and Yugoslavia have active programs for spreading new industry to rural areas and absorbing displaced farm workers.

With the problem centering on displacement and underemployment of farmers and workers in small towns, Canada initiated some new features in its rural development program. The revitalized program not only encourages industrial development in the countryside, the amalgamation of small farms and retraining of migrating farm workers but also provides for compensation of businesses in small towns where economic opportunity has become depressed because of the continued commercialization and mechanization of agriculture.

The problem of depressed farm communities linked with congested urban centers has prevailed in the United States for some time. However, the complex problem received unprecedented attention from Federal administrators, legislators and politicians in 1972. As a result, Congress passed the Rural Development Act of 1972 by large majorities in both houses, and the package was signed into law in August by President Nixon. The act includes numerous provisions to create employment, improve the quality of living and partially subsidize the retention in or return of population to the countryside. An important provision of the act relates to facilities for small farms.

EARL O. HEADY
Executive Director, Center for Agricultural
and Economic Development
Iowa State University

ALBANIA

The prevailing themes for 1972 in Albania were the Communist leadership's continued drive to improve relations between the party and the people and the further expansion of Albania's diplomatic activity. Talking to the district party committee in Mati in February, the first secretary of the ruling Albanian Party of Labor (APL), Enver Hoxha, called for more popular participation in the administration of the country. This and similar appeals on other occasions were aimed at lessening apathy and skepticism toward the party.

In foreign affairs, Albania continued to improve relations with its Balkan neighbors, especially through increased contacts with the Yugoslav autonomous republic of Kosovo, which has a large Albanian population. The effort was only partly overshadowed by Albania's sharp anti-Soviet and anti-Yugoslav attacks during the Yugoslav president's June visit to Moscow. The Sino-Albanian alliance remained firm despite Albanian criticism of President Nixon's visit to Peking.

At the Second Plenum of the Central Committee of the APL it was decided to establish an Academy of Sciences. The decision marked the country's second most important step in higher education since the founding of the national university in Tiranë in 1957.

In economic affairs, the current five-year plan continued attempts to diminish the urban-rural gap with a more rapid rate of agricultural growth. This is to be achieved through heavy Chinese financing.

ISTVAN DEAK, Director
Institute on East Central Europe
Columbia University

AMBASSADORS AND ENVOYS[a]

FROM U.S.	COUNTRIES	TO U.S.	FROM U.S.	COUNTRIES	TO U.S.
Robert G. Neumann	AFGHANISTAN	Abdullah Malikyar	G. McMurtrie Godley	LAOS	Pheng Norindr
John Davis Lodge	ARGENTINA	Carlos M. Muñiz	William B. Buffum	LEBANON	Najati Kabbani
Walter L. Rice	AUSTRALIA	James Plimsoll	Charles J. Nelson	LESOTHO	Mothusi T.
John P. Humes	AUSTRIA	Arno Halusa			Mashologu
William A.	BAHRAIN	(Vacant)	Melvin L. Manfull[c]	LIBERIA	S. Edward Peal
Stoltzfus, Jr.			Joseph Palmer 2d	LIBYA	Abdalla Suwesi
Herman F. Eilts	BANGLADESH	S. K. Karim[b]	(Vacant)	LUXEMBOURG	Jean Wagner
Eileen R. Donovan	BARBADOS	Valerie T. McComie	Joseph A. Mendenhall	MALAGASY	Henri Raharijaona
Robert Strausz-Hupé	BELGIUM	Walter Loridan		REP.	
Ernest V. Siracusa	BOLIVIA	Edmundo Valencia-	William C. Burdett	MALAWI	Nyemba W. Mbekeani
		Ibáñez	Jack W. Lydman	MALAYSIA	Tan Sri Yoke
Charles J. Nelson	BOTSWANA	Amos M. Dambe			Lin Ong
William M. Rountree	BRAZIL	J. A. de Araujo	Christopher	MALDIVE IS.	(Vacant)
		Castro	Van Hollen		
Horace G.	BULGARIA	Khristo Delchev	Robert O. Blake	MALI	Seydou Traoré
Torbert, Jr.		Zdravchev	John I. Getz	MALTA	Joseph Attard-
Edwin W. Martin	BURMA	U Lwin			Kingswell
Robert L. Yost	BURUNDI	Terence Nsanze	Richard W. Murphy	MAURITANIA	Moulaye El Hassen
Emory C. Swank	CAMBODIA	Sonn Voeunsai	William D. Brewer	MAURITIUS	Pierre G. G. Balancy
	(KHMER REP.)		Robert H. McBride	MEXICO	José Juan de
C. Robert Moore	CAMEROON	François-Xavier			Olloqui
		Tchoungui	Stuart W. Rockwell	MOROCCO	Badreddine Senoussi
Adolph W. Schmidt	CANADA	Marcel Cadieux	Carol C. Laise	NEPAL	Kul S. Sharma
(Vacant)	CENTRAL AFR.	Christophe Maidou	J. W. Middendorf 2d	NETHERLANDS	R. B. van Lynden
	REP.		Kenneth Franzheim 2d	NEW ZEALAND	Lloyd White
Christopher	CEYLON	Neville Kanakaratne	Turner B. Shelton	NICARAGUA	Guillermo Sevilla-
Van Hollen	(SRI LANKA)				Sacasa
Edward W. Mulcahy	CHAD	Lazare Massibe	Roswell D. Mc	NIGER	Abdoulaye Diallo
Nathaniel Davis	CHILE	Orlando Letelier	Clelland		
Walter P. McConaughy	CHINA (TAIWAN)	James C. H. Shen	John E. Reinhardt	NIGERIA	John M. Garba
Leonard J. Saccio	COLOMBIA	Douglas Botero-	Philip K. Crowe	NORWAY	Arne Gunneng
		Boshell	(Vacant)	PAKISTAN	Sultan M. Khan
Viron P. Vaky	COSTA RICA	Rafael A. Zuniga	Frank T. Bow	PANAMA	Nicolas Gonzalez
David H. Popper	CYPRUS	Zenon Rossides			Revilla
Albert W. Sherer, Jr.	CZECHOSLO-	Dusan Spacil	George W. Landau	PARAGUAY	Roque J. Avila
	VAKIA		Taylor G. Belcher	PERU	Fernando Berckemeyer
Robert Anderson	DAHOMEY	Wilfrid de Souza	Henry A. Byroade	PHILIPPINES	Eduardo Z. Romualdez
(Vacant)	DENMARK	Eyvind Bartels	Richard T. Davies[c]	POLAND	Witold Trampczynski
Francis E. Meloy, Jr.	DOMINICAN	S. Salvador Ortiz	Ridgway B. Knight	PORTUGAL	Joaõ Hall Themido
	REP.		William A.	QATAR	Abdullah S. Al-Mania
Findley Burns, Jr.	ECUADOR	Alberto Quevedo Toro	Stoltzfus, Jr.		
Henry E. Catto, Jr.	EL SALVADOR	Julio A. Rivera	Leonard C. Meeker	RUMANIA	Corneliu Bogdan
C. Robert Moore	EQUATORIAL	(Vacant)	Robert F. Corrigan	RWANDA	F. Nkundabagenzi
	GUINEA		Nicholas G. Thacher	SAUDI ARABIA	Ibraham Al-Sowayel
E. Ross Adair	ETHIOPIA	Kifle Wodajo	G. Edward Clark	SENEGAL	André Coulbary
Kenneth Franzheim 2d	FIJI	S. K. Sikivou	Clinton L. Olson	SIERRA LEONE	Philip Jonathan
Val Peterson	FINLAND	Leo O. Tuominen			Gbagu Palmer
John N. Irwin 2d[c]	FRANCE	Jacques Kosciusko-	Edwin M. Cronk	SINGAPORE	Ernest S. Monteiro
		Morizet	Matthew J.	SOMALI DEM.	Abdullahi A. Addou
John A. McKesson 3d	GABON	Gaston-Robert Boucat-	Looran, Jr.	REP.	
		Bou-Nziengui	John G. Hurd	SOUTH AFRICA	Johan S. F. Botha
G. Edward Clark	GAMBIA	(Vacant)	Horacio Rivero	SPAIN	Angel Sagaz
Martin J.	GERMANY (W)	Rolf Pauls	Cleo A. Noel, Jr.[c]	SUDAN	Abdel Aziz Hamza[b]
Hillenbrand			Charles J. Nelson	SWAZILAND	S. T. Msindazwe
Fred L. Hadsel	GHANA	Henry R. Amonoo			Sukati
Walter H. Annenberg	GREAT BRITAIN	Earl of Cromer	(Vacant)	SWEDEN	Yngve Möller
Henry J. Tasca	GREECE	John A. Sorokos	Shelby C. Davis	SWITZERLAND	Felix Schnyder
William G. Bowdler	GUATEMALA	Julio Asensio-	W. Beverly	TANZANIA	Paul L. Bomani
		Wunderlich	Carter, Jr.		
Terence A. Todman	GUINEA	Sadan Moussa Touré	Leonard Unger	THAILAND	Anand Panyarachun
Spencer M. King	GUYANA	Rahman B. Gajraj	Dwight Dickinson	TOGO	E. A. Mawussi
Clinton E. Knox	HAITI	René Chalmers[b]	Kenneth Franzheim 2d	TONGA	(Vacant)
Hewson A. Ryan	HONDURAS	Roberto Galvez Barnes	Anthony D. Marshall	TRINIDAD AND	Ellis E. I. Clarke
Alfred Puhan	HUNGARY	Károly Szabó		TOBAGO	
Frederick Irving	ICELAND	Haraldur Kroyer	Talcott W. Seelye	TUNISIA	Slaheddine El-Goulli
Daniel Moynihan[c]	INDIA	Lakshmi Kant Jha	William J. Handley	TURKEY	Melih Esenbel
Francis J. Galbraith	INDONESIA	Sjarif Thajeb	Thomas P. Melady	UGANDA	Mustapha Ramathan
Richard Helms[c]	IRAN	Amir-Aslan Afshar	Jacob D. Beam	U.S.S.R.	Anatoliy F. Dobrynin
John D. J. Moore	IRELAND	William Warnock	Donald B. Easum	UPPER VOLTA	Télésphore Yaguibou
Walworth Barbour	ISRAEL	Yitzhak Rabin	Charles W. Adair Jr.	URUGUAY	Hector Luisi
John A. Volpe[c]	ITALY	Egidio Ortona	Robert McClintock	VENEZUELA	Andres Aguilar
John F. Root	IVORY COAST	Timothee N'Guetta	Ellsworth Bunker	VIETNAM (S.)	Tran Kim Phuong
		Ahoua	Kenneth Franzheim 2d	WESTERN SAMOA	(Vacant)
Vincent de Roulet	JAMAICA	Douglas V. Fletcher	William R.	YEMEN	Ahmad Ali Zabarah[b]
Robert S. Ingersoll	JAPAN	Nobuhiko Ushiba	Crawford, Jr.		
Lewis Dean Brown	JORDAN	Zuhayr Muftri	Malcolm Toon	YUGOSLAVIA	Toma Granfil
Robinson McIlvaine	KENYA	Leonard O. Kibinge	Sheldon B. Vance	ZAIRE	Lombo Lo
Philip C. Habib	KOREA (S.)	Dong Jo Kim			Mangamanga
William A.	KUWAIT	Salem S. Al-Sabah	Jean M. Wilkowski	ZAMBIA	Unia G. Mwila
Stoltzfus, Jr.					

[a] As of Jan. 15, 1973
[b] Chargé d'affaires
[c] Nominated but not confirmed by Congress

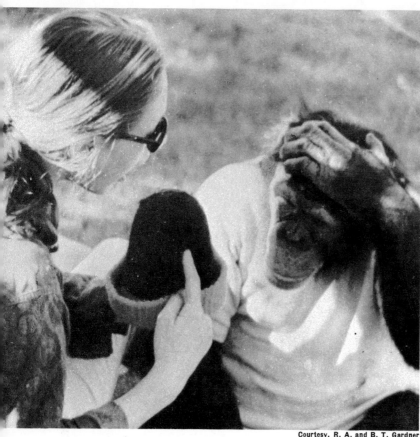

Two University of New Mexico psychologists have taught the chimpanzee Washoe the American sign language of the deaf. The research represents a major breakthrough in discovering the learning capacity of chimps.

Courtesy, R. A. and B. T. Gardner

ANTHROPOLOGY

Amidst the contemporary world crisis precipitated by an expanding population, pollution and rapid culture change, anthropologists find themselves just as concerned with man's present and future as with his past. The record of the past, however, remains a key to all three. The most important find of 1972 and perhaps of the decade was announced by Richard Leakey, following several years of exploration near Lake Rudolph in Kenya. The find comprised portions of a skull and leg bones 2,500,000 years old which appeared to be those of a form of man much more advanced than any previously known to exist in the remote past.

The most important focus of research in 1972 was the enlargement of man's fossil record, with the earliest finds continuing to come from East Africa and Ethiopia. These fossil discoveries proceed so rapidly that their detailed description and analysis necessarily lags far behind.

While the date of the earliest man is being extended backward in time by new discoveries, two Australian scholars have found evidence which, they believe, indicates a survival into more recent times of some ancient forms of man. A. G. Thorne and P. G. Macumber published in *Nature* information on the discovery of the mineralized bones of some 40 individuals found in the state of Victoria. These skulls and skeletal bones show a number of features that link them to *Homo erectus* (Java man) as well as to modern *Homo sapiens*. The bones are only about 10,000 years old, while modern man is known to have existed in Australia for some 25,000 years.

Behavioral Studies. Scholars are becoming increasingly interested in the evolution of behavior as well as in the evolution of man's physical structure, as recorded in fossil bones, skulls and teeth. Several new techniques are being developed in an attempt to generate data in this field. Thus, a linguist, P. Lieberman of the University of Connecticut, together with an anatomist, E. S. Crelin of Yale, and a computer specialist, D. H. Klatt of M.I.T., announced in 1972 that the linguistic ability of Neanderthal man was probably inferior to that of modern man. They arrived at this startling conclusion through studies in comparative anatomy and computer simulation of the functions of the

vocal tract area assumed to be characteristic of Neanderthal man. These findings will undoubtedly stir much discussion among specialists, because they have far-reaching implications about the relationship between Neanderthal man and modern man.

These behavioral studies come at a time when, on the one hand, the age of Neanderthal man in Europe has been extended back to the middle of the Pleistocene epoch, and when, on the other, the results of important behavioral work with chimpanzees and other primates are being reported. In particular, two psychologists, R. A. Gardner and B. T. Gardner, have taught the American sign language for the deaf to a chimpanzee, Washoe, who has learned to communicate in brief sentences. As all previous attempts at teaching chimpanzees to articulate language had failed, this research represents a major breakthrough toward discovering the potential learning capacity of chimpanzees. Much new behavioral data has also been generated by field observations of primates in their native habitat, as documented, for example, by Jane van Lawick-Goodall in the important book *Shadow of Man*.

Evolution of Agriculture. Exciting work in prehistoric archeology continued in several major areas. W. G. Solheim II, an archeologist at the University of Hawaii, for example, proposed a revision of our present timetable for the development of agriculture. He produced evidence for the development of agriculture in the Northern rim of mainland Southeast Asia (Thailand, North Vietnam) which would date the origins of agriculture at 13,000 B.C., about 5,000 years prior to the first evidence of plant and animal domestication in the Middle East.

D. R. Harris sees this innovation in Southeast Asia as one feature of the worldwide development of tropical agriculture, based on root crops as opposed to seed crops. He finds such a zone of tropical swidden agriculture in South America and Africa as well. Thus, in prehistoric archeology as well as in physical anthropology, "firsts" are being pushed further and further into the past as new finds emerge and dating methods are improved.

Contemporary Concerns. Cultural anthropologists have become increasingly concerned with a variety of urgent contemporary problems. For example, in 1972 *Current Anthropology*, a world journal of anthropology, published a major series of articles on anthropology and population problems. These included a discussion of variations in human fertility observed in different nonindustrial areas and attempts to understand these variations in light of relevant social, economic, ecological and religious factors. Certain policy recommendations, as formulated by Professor S. Polgar, involve encouragement of socio-economic advancement for women, a development which would hopefully contribute to a reduction in the birth rate.

Anthropologists also continued to examine the ethical implications of research in their particular world areas and the responsibilities implied by such research. While much of the discussion has concerned U.S. government–sponsored anthropological studies in Thailand, the implications of the problems raised by this involvement are of a much broader scope. The executive Committee of the American Anthropological Association established a standing committee on "potentially harmful effects of anthropological research," to develop information on this controversial subject.

The International Union of Anthropological and Ethnological Sciences founded a special commission on ethnocide, genocide and forced acculturation (cultural extinction through forced migration or resettlement). The commission is to investigate instances of such abuse and to "apply all means at its disposal to the arrest of these inhuman acts." The major impetus for this extraordinary action by the Union appears to have been continuing massacre of Brazilian Indians, which has belatedly attracted worldwide attention.

Isolated Tribes. While such atrocities continue under the cloak of legality, much attention has also been devoted to the discovery in the Philippines of an isolated tribe of 27 persons, the Tasaday. Apparently, the tribe was isolated for a long time because its members possess no metal tools, do not use salt and have no knowledge of many of the other practices common among peoples of the area. Contact with modern civilization is hazardous to isolated peoples because it not only disrupts their traditional way of life but also exposes them to diseases against which they have not developed resistance. The periodic discovery of such isolated peoples arouses public curiosity, while the gradual disappearance of traditional peoples with simple technologies generally goes unheeded.

Thus, in 1972, a combined French and Chilean expedition reported in the French museum journal *Objets et Mondes* that of the 11,000 Indians that inhabited Tierra del Fuego at the Southern tip of South America in 1850, barely 50 individuals remained in 1971. The remaining population will probably die out or be absorbed into the Chilean population.

ERIKA BOURGUIGNON
Chairman, Department of Anthropology
The Ohio State University

Student demonstrations in Cairo highlight widespread discontent over President Anwar el-Sadat's "no war, no peace" policy toward Israel.

ARAB STATES

The continuing military stalemate with Israel and the inability of the Arab States either to marshal effective international support for their cause or to exert pressure on the Israelis toward a settlement on favorable terms or, at the very least, withdrawal from occupied territories precluded any serious steps on their part toward peace in the Middle East. After a brief resumption in January the mission of UN Special Representative Gunnar Jarring to mediate on the basis of UN Resolution 242 (of November 1967) was abandoned permanently; Jarring could find no leader on either side who was willing to talk peace. Israeli intransigence on the question of withdrawal without Arab recognition of its independence and the Arabs' insistence on withdrawal before recognition apparently doomed all efforts at third-party mediation.

The frustration of "no war, no peace" with Israel weighed heavily on Arabs everywhere and at all levels, but nowhere more heavily than in Egypt. Massive Soviet arms deliveries had restored the Egyptian army and air force to their pre-1967 capabilities, but the officer corps in particular chafed under the truce restraints and the refusal of President Sadat to

order at least punitive raids into Israeli-occupied Sinai. Egyptian students, later joined by industrial workers, were equally vocal in demanding action. Impelled by these pressures as well as by the widespread anti-Soviet feeling in Egypt, Sadat was forced to act. On July 18 he ordered the withdrawal of all Russian military advisers. The U.S.S.R., although taken by surprise, complied, and within two weeks some 15,000 advisers had been airlifted home. The only Russians left in Egypt were 500 technicians working on industrial projects.

The expulsions gave Sadat's government a reprieve and restored some of the popularity he had lost by his failure to carry out repeated pledges to invade Israel. Sadat commented that Soviet refusal to supply Egypt with Mig-23 aircraft and offensive weapons was the main cause of this failure. But more important reasons for the ouster than the denial of weapons were the highhanded attitude of Soviet advisers toward Egyptian officers, their refusal to allow Egyptian entry into certain missile bases and derogatory comments by Soviet officials about Islam.

A factor in Sadat's thinking was that the lessening of Egypt's dependence on the U.S.S.R. might result in increased U.S. support, if not outright aid. But this was not forthcoming.

Neither President Nixon nor Senator McGovern made any formal comment supporting the Arabs during the 1972 presidential campaign, nor did the United States seek to reopen diplomatic relations with Egypt. Meanwhile, the Egyptian war machine began to run down owing to lack of spare parts and replacement equipment. In October, Sadat dismissed War Minister Gen. Mohammed Sadek, an outspoken anti-Communist, and Prime Minister Sidky went to Moscow to obtain, reportedly, a pledge to resume Soviet spare parts deliveries.

With the strongest Arab army facing Israel essentially immobilized and no other Arab state capable of more than vocal action, the Palestinian guerrilla organizations supplied what leverage there was available to Arab hands in the endless struggle against their common enemy. Early in the year the guerrillas were able to mount effective attacks against Israel from bases in southern Lebanon. However, massive Israeli retaliatory raids, which caused heavy civilian casualties and property damage, deterred the guerrillas and caused the Lebanese government to rethink its policy toward their presence in Lebanon. On June 27 the government reached an agreement with the Palestine Liberation Organization (PLO), the principal guerrilla group, that the PLO would withdraw from most of its bases and limit its actions to defensive operations.

Thus deprived of their last convenient base from which to launch attacks against Israel, the guerrilla organizations formed rival blocs which increasingly feuded among themselves rather than developing a common policy. Several guerrilla leaders in Beirut were murdered or badly injured by letter bombs or cut down by gunfire in broad daylight as the feuding reached a peak in mid-summer. The lack of guerrilla organizational unity was a further deterrent to the movement; although all Arab leaders gave lip service to the Palestinian cause, none was willing to recognize a Palestine government-in-exile.

In the absence of unity some of the smaller guerrilla groups turned to global terrorism to dramatize their cause. Ignoring the PLO directives, the Popular Front for the Liberation of Palestine (PFLP) hijacked airplanes and recruited foreign militants to carry out their objectives. On May 6 three Japanese terrorists, members of Sekigunha (United Red Army), shot up the passenger terminal at Lydda Airport in Tel Aviv, killing 25 persons, including 16 Puerto Ricans on a pilgrimage to the Holy Land. The surviving Japanese (two were killed) declared that the Palestine revolution was theirs, as a necessary part of the world

Jacques Haillot, Gamma

Gaping ruins in Lebanon bear witness to the ferocity of Israeli reprisals after Munich.

revolution. The PFLP claimed credit for the action as well as for numerous bombings of targets within Israel.

In September a worldwide television audience watched with horror as Arab commandos killed two and kidnapped nine members of the Israeli Olympic team from their dormitory in Munich; all were killed in the course of a shootout with West German police. The commandos had held their victims as hostages for the release of Palestinian Arabs held in Israeli jails. Three guerrillas were captured, but were later released and flown to Libya aboard a chartered West German plane after yet another airliner had been hijacked by members of the same guerrilla organization, the "Black September Movement" (so called from the September 1970 crushing of guerrilla forces in Jordan by the Jordanian army).

International condemnation of the Munich massacre had no effect on the guerrillas; they equated their action with the 1948 Deir Yassin slaughter of Arab villagers by Israeli irregular troops. Large-scale Israeli raids into Lebanon and aerial attacks on Syria followed as angry Israelis sought to gain revenge. Lebanon complained to the UN Security Council, but a resolution of censure was vetoed by the United States—its second veto in UN history—because it mentioned only military operations in the Middle East and did not refer to terrorism.

Although the Arab States could neither entirely ignore the Palestinians, albeit they refused to extend formal recognition, nor bring themselves to accept the existence of Israel, several positive inter-Arab developments suggested that Israel was in fact the window-dressing for a more profound concern with Arab unity and appropriate forms of Arab political activity. The Federation of Arab Republics of Egypt, Libya and Syria formalized its overall administration with a Presidential Council of the (three) Heads of State, a federal supreme court, a unified trade union council and three holidays

Israeli authorities begin trial in August of two young Palestinian women guerrillas accused of hijacking a Belgian jetliner.

Gamma

President Sadat of Egypt (left) and Col. Muammar Qaddafi, ruler of Libya, announce in August the merger of their two countries.

Remolvile, Gamma

corresponding to the "independence days" of the three member states. On Aug. 2, Sadat and Libya's President Muammar Qaddafi announced the merger of Egypt and Libya into a single state within the federation, to take place within a year. The merger, if consummated, would create the largest and most powerful state in Africa in terms of wealth and manpower.

In October another long-standing inter-Arab dispute was settled when Yemen and its neighbor, the Peoples' Democratic Republic of Yemen, which together make up the southwestern corner of the Arabian Peninsula, agreed to a cease-fire along their common border. The policies of the Peoples' Republic of instigating "socialist revolutions" throughout the peninsula had drawn it into hostilities with Yemen, Saudi Arabia and the sultanate of Oman; its capital city of Aden had provided a home for various Arab nationalist groups pledged to overthrow the regimes of these three states. The Aden government agreed to

cut off support to all such rebel groups and to unite with Yemen in a single state on the Egypt-Libya model.

Another federated Arab state composed of several members added a seventh, when the Sheikhdom of Ras al-Khaimah joined the Union of Arab Emirates. Ras al-Khaimah previously had demanded equal representation and veto rights in the union assembly with Abu Dhabi and Dubai, the largest and richest members, as its price for adhesion; its ruler dropped these demands and in return was given six assembly seats and three cabinet posts in the union government.

The last unsettled civil conflict in the Arab world ended on March 6 with a cease-fire and peace settlement between the Sudan government and rebels in the southern Sudan (*see* Africa).

Elsewhere in the Arab world border agreements and joint exploitation of oil and mineral resources characterized the growing accord among Algeria, Morocco and Tunisia. The

Algerian-Moroccan border pact settled an issue which had produced a brief war between the two states in 1963. Algerian President Houari Boumedienne visited Tunisia for the first time and agreed with President Bourguiba, fully recovered after a series of illnesses which had cast doubt on the stability of the Tunisian one-party system, on joint development of the El Borma oil and gas fields, which straddle the border.

Internal political problems continued to plague the Arab states, or at least some of them. There were at least two confirmed attempts to overthrow President Sadat, both related to military dissatisfaction over the lack of positive moves against Israel. In November, Sadat purged the armed forces, arresting some 100 officers, including three generals. About the same time an attempt was made by Palestinian sympathizers and army officers to overthrow King Hussein of Jordan. The king in March had presented a proposal before a group of Jordanian notables for a United Arab Kingdom which would incorporate the Israeli-occupied West Bank and Jordan itself into a unitary state. The proposal was denounced by other Arab states as a sellout of Arab interests, and Egypt freed the Palestinian assassins of Jordanian Prime Minister Wasfi al-Tal as a gesture of protest.

Yet the uneasiest head among Arab leaders clearly belonged to Hassan II of Morocco. On Aug. 16, just over a year after an army revolt against him, Morrocan air force jets strafed the king's private plane as it returned from a visit to France. Hassan's luck held; he escaped uninjured, and support for the mutineers did not materialize. The plot was traced to Gen. Mohammed Oufkir, minister of de-

fense and the official thought to be Hassan's most loyal supporter, who had been instrumental in stopping the July 1971 rebellion. Oufkir committed suicide prior to arrest. The irony of the Moroccan coup was that Hassan had seemed not only to have the situation in hand but had made major concessions toward the return of representative government. An amnesty was issued to political prisoners, and the cadet corps was acquitted of involvement in the 1971 uprising. The king issued a new constitution, which was approved by 98 percent of the voters in a March 1 referendum despite a call for a boycott by the opposition National Front, composed of the two major parties still permitted to function outside the government. But continuing army instability and the absence of dialogue on any level between Hassan and his political opponents left his future as a constitutional monarch very much in doubt.

Regarding Arab economic development, a major step forward was taken with the conclusion of new arrangements with the Western oil companies that manage Arab oil interests. In January five Arab oil-producing countries, Saudi Arabia, Kuwait, Bahrain, Qatar and Abu Dhabi, formed the Organization of Arab Petroleum-Exporting Countries (OAPEC). Led by Saudi Minister of Oil Sheikh Ahmed Zaki Yamini, OAPEC negotiated in October "participation" agreements with the oil companies calling for a 25 percent interest for each country in the management of oil operations, along with marketing, sales and distribution. The interest would rise in annual stages to 51 percent majority control by 1983, remaining at that level until all current oil concessions expire early in the 21st century. The Saudi agreement with Aramco provided the model for the

King Hussein of Jordan, shown at a press conference in March, withstood another year of incessant intrigues against him.

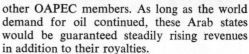
Henri Bureau, Gamma

The damage inflicted by strafing air force officers on his jet airliner (right) did not prevent King Hassan II (below) from landing safely in Morocco.

Ch. Simonpietri, Gamma

other OAPEC members. As long as the world demand for oil continued, these Arab states would be guaranteed steadily rising revenues in addition to their royalties.

The participation formula in the long run held out better prospects for both the companies and the Arab oil-producing states than outright nationalization. Arab states which followed the latter procedure found themselves in difficulties. Iraq nationalized the Iraq Petroleum Company on June 1 after years of bickering which had led the company to cut back its production steadily. The impact of a shutdown in operations and loss of revenues forced Iraq to borrow $129,000,000 from OAPEC and $21,000,000 from Libya. Only France among Iraq's Western customers continued to buy Iraqi oil, and only 23.75 percent of the total output at that. Libya nationalized British Petroleum Company facilities and promptly faced a court action prohibiting the Libyan National Oil Company from selling BP oil abroad. However, Libya won an 8.4 percent price increase from the numerous other companies that manage its oil production and was not seriously affected by the stoppage of BP shipments.

Thus the Arab states continued to chart an uneven course toward full development, some, like Saudi Arabia, making good use of their resources and politically stable, others, like Egypt and Morocco, hampered by political unrest and unfulfilled social aspirations.

WILLIAM SPENCER
Professor of Middle Eastern History
The Florida State University

Marc Riboud from Magnum

An eerily futuristic glow emanates from the meticulously-crafted jade burial shroud of a Han Dynasty prince entombed over 2,000 years ago.

ARCHEOLOGY

The most startling archeological revelation of 1972 was in fact a discovery unearthed four years earlier. In June 1968 a company of soldiers on night duty near Man-ch'eng, a town in Hopei province, China, discovered two tombs hewn out of a limestone cliff in the foothills of the Lingshan Mountains. The tombs proved to be those of Liu Sheng, prince of Chung-shan (modern Chengting), who died in 113 B.C., and his wife Tu Wan, who died in 104 B.C. Liu Sheng's tomb was 155 feet long and more than 20 feet high, his wife's tomb was shorter but extended 192 feet in width. Both tombs were cruciform in shape and con-

tained a number of separate chambers. One side chamber of each tomb was a stable, supplied with carriages and horses, while the main chambers held an elaborate array of grave-goods—more than 1,500 separate objects in the prince's tomb and 1,200 in that of his wife.

The most spectacular objects to be excavated were the jade suits in which the bodies were garbed, each fashioned of more than 2,000 polished nephrite plaques sewn together with gold wire. Each suit represented at least 10 years' work by a skilled lapidary. The jade-clothed bodies were enclosed in wheeled coffins resting on white marble bases and were accompanied by perforated jade discs, *pi*, which were symbols of heaven.

Liu Sheng was the ninth son of the Emperor Ching-ti, and the tombs contained several objects that evinced a connection with the Imperial court. Such objects included a gilded bronze figure of a kneeling girl holding a lamp. This artifact came from the Imperial Bath in the palace of the Dowager Empress Tu, the prince's grandmother. Another spectacular find was a *Po-Shan-lu* incense burner of cast bronze inlaid with gold and silver, which depicted in relief a mountainous landscape.

The importance of the Man-ch'eng tombs is still not fully realized; apart from the value implicit in the association of so many closely dated objects and the fact of their sheer aesthetic importance, this discovery will also exert a profound effect on studies of the development and diffusion of Chinese art in the Han period.

At sites in both South America and Palestine important discoveries dating back even further in time were made. At Sechin, in the Casma Valley on the north coast of Peru, excavations begun in 1971 continued well into 1972 under the direction of Lorenzo Samaniego. On this site, in 1937, Julio Tello discovered 90 incised monoliths depicting victorious soldiers and their dismembered enemies. The assembled monoliths formed a wall in front of an earlier mud-brick temple platform. Excavation of the site showed that the monoliths occupy their original location, forming the front wall of a square platform, each of whose sides extends 170 feet in length. An estimated 500 incised stones adorn the four platform walls. In layers overlaying that of the temple, pottery of the Chavin style of 850–500 B.C. was found, indicating that the temple had in fact been constructed prior to this date, perhaps as early as 1500 B.C.

At Tel Beer-sheba in southern Israel three seasons of excavation under Dr. Yohanan Aharoni determined that the original town was

protected by a 20 foot-high artificial rampart of gravel and earth flanked by a deep outer ditch. This is the first such major fortification of the Israelite period to be excavated. Two successive walls surrounded the city, an earlier solid Solomonic one of the 10th century B.C., and a chambered casemate wall of the 9th–8th centuries. This wall, and the town itself, were destroyed at the end of the 8th century, probably by forces under the Assyrian king Sennacherib. The sequence of solid to casemate walls found on this site is the opposite of that found on the contemporaneous site of Hazor, demonstrating that both types of wall were in use throughout the period of the Israelite monarchy.

Inside the city walls, the later Roman fort that occupied the site has been excavated, revealing beneath its structure a planned town of the 9th–8th centuries B.C. An intramural ring road ran from the gate on the south side of the town, which was flanked by towers. Within the city, the administrative buildings were located to the left of the gate, and to the right were three royal stores containing pottery vessels used for storing grain, wine and oil. In the middle of the town stood a pagan shrine, on the site of which was found a group of cult objects exhibiting a strong Egyptian influence.

In Mexico two interesting projects were conducted in 1972. At Chalcacingo in Morelos, in the highlands south of Mexico City, Dr. David C. Grove of the University of Illinois discovered a number of new Olmec sculptures, and also evidence confirming the theory that Olmec culture was based in the lowlands of the Gulf Coast. On the island of Cozumel, off the coast of Yucatan, a joint Harvard-University of Arizona project began a major investigation into the nature and role of trade among the Pre-Columbian Maya. Finds during the 1972 season showed that during the Postclassic period, extending from the 10th to 15th centuries A.D., a planned grid of low walls covered the entire island, dividing it into small plots. At the center of the island was found a large site, named San Gervasio, covering about 250 acres, which seems to have functioned as the "capital" at that period. The pottery found on this site in 1972 revealed a strong connection in the Early Postclassic between Cozumel and the city of Mayapan in the northwest part of the Yucatan Peninsula.

In Britain the excavation of three Roman cemeteries produced a wealth of important data on the burial habits of Roman Britons. One cemetery, at Puckeridge in Hertfordshire, dating from the 2nd and 3rd centuries A.D., yielded the ashes from a number of cremations enclosed in bronze-bound boxes. At a Dorchester cemetery of the 3rd or 4th centuries the Christian and pagan sections were separated by a fence. Some evidence indicated the existence of family plots in the Christian section, and it has been conjectured that a number of mausolea may contain the remains of the bishops of Roman *Durnovaria* (now Dorchester). Evidence for the existence of family plots was again forthcoming from the Lankhills cemetery at Winchester, dating from the 4th and 5th centuries A.D. This site also demonstrated how burial practices changed over time, and that Germanic mercenary soldiers entered the local population, married local women and were thereby absorbed into the British community.

Two other sites have provided glimpses of conditions in Saxon Britain. At Chalton, in Hampshire, part of a 7th century A.D. village was uncovered, revealing the presence of substantial timber houses 40 feet in length grouped around what may be England's earliest known village green; while at Spong Hill in Norfolk some 200 cremation burials depict the Saxons in death. The ashes were enclosed in black pottery urns, often highly decorated, and accompanied by domestic and personal possessions such as tweezers, shears, brooches, combs and gaming counters.

At the Iron Age site of Gussage All Saints in Dorset, dating to the first century A.D., recovered artifacts revealed that the inhabitants practiced bronze-casting by the lost-wax process. The artifacts—relief-ornamented horse and chariot gear—indicated that the owner of the three-acre enclosure was of a sufficiently high social status to possess a chariot.

One of the most encouraging developments in 1972 was the growing realization on the part of the public that our past is fragile, and that centuries of human history can be obliterated in a matter of hours. In Britain this realization prompted the founding of *Rescue: a Trust for British Archaeology,* and the establishment of full-time research units in the important Roman towns of Lincoln and York. In the United States representatives of several major museums and of Harvard spoke out against the purchase of stolen and smuggled antiquities. But as 1972 ended, the rape of archeological sites continued—more Maya steles have been smashed for removal; an Olmec rock-carving at Xoc in Mexico has been stolen; and a band of looters chased from Peru resumed work in Ecuador.

NORMAN HAMMOND
Archeology Correspondent
The Times, London

Gleaning some of the finest surviving architecture of 18th century Boston from the decay of Scolay Square, urban redevelopers produced a brilliant fusion of styles in the Faneuil Hall—Quincy Market lee of Beacon Hill. City Hall is in the foreground, Faneuil Hall beyond.

ARCHITECTURE

The new buildings that caught the public imagination in 1972 were mostly grand or fancy ones. There was little news about planning and technological developments, which might reduce the cost of building, but much excitement about commercial wonderlands and fantastic environments for leisure and shopping. Perhaps the most sophisticated and serious innovations derived from a growing concern for improving relations with the past and with the landscape.

Blend of Old and New. A particularly successful example of the increasingly close and comfortable entente between new buildings and old was the New York Bar Center in Albany, N.Y., for which James Stewart Polshek and Associates were architects. The design preserved the front parts of three fine 19th century row houses, behind which an elegantly contemporary new building, scaled to the old, was erected. The old buildings, which face an important park, were approached with familiarity and love, reflecting a confidence new in American architecture.

The same sort of easy familiarity with the recent past was evident in the new academic wing of the University Museum at the University of Pennsylvania, in Philadelphia, by Mitchell/Giurgola Associates. The original 1890 building, in the Lombard Renaissance style, which would have elicited scorn not many years ago, prompted the architects to note that the original architects had "designed a structure of tremendous scope, still operable today" and to key their new work closely to it, even in such details as brick color, roof slopes and tile.

Projects blending old structures into an elegant new commercial world, following on the successes of Ghirardelli Square and the Cannery in San Francisco, included in 1972 the Faneuil Hall—Quincy Market area of Boston, planned by Ben Thompson to offer shops, cafes, restaurants, theaters, covered arcades, street vendors boutiques and night clubs, all in the cradle of the American Revolution.

Different use of history found National Homes commissioning the Frank Lloyd Wright Foundation to design, in the "organic" way so

passionately espoused by the late dean of American architects, a full collection of dwellings from mobile homes, garden apartments, town houses and cluster developments to $200,000 residences.

Indulging Nature and Fancy. A phenomenon parallel to the growing relation to the past was a developing concern for and sophistication in relation to the natural environment. The prestigious First Design Award of *Progressive Architecture* magazine went to the projected South Dearborn Community High School in Aurora, Ind., by James Associates. The building is designed to cling to a hillside in a geometry imitating the natural landscape. Slices taken from the descending form will admit natural light where it is most desirable.

Meanwhile, in Virginia Beach, Va., where no natural hill exists, construction workers began development on an apotheosis of the sanitary land fill, nicknamed Mt. Trashmore, and 85 percent garbage. The site eventually will contain a new recreation park with a 10,000-seat amphitheater, soapbox derby, tennis courts, baseball diamonds, picnic areas and an artificial lake.

In the realm of leisure fantasy nothing in 1972 quite rivaled the abandon of Walt Disney World in Florida, opened in 1971, but similar projects were developing apace. A new ski resort at Avoriaz, France, will accommodate 15,000 persons in hotels, condominia, chalets and hostels tightly clustered to recreate the ambiance of a village. New Franconia, a projected new town south of Washington, D.C., is planned for a population of 39,000 and will feature a "horizontal elevator" tied into the D.C. Metro transit system.

Urban Malls and Mirrors. Elsewhere, concentrated urban malls were attracting attention. Lancaster, Pa., and Niagara Falls, N.Y., were planning new downtown centers with malls designed by Gruen Associates. Louisville, Ky., commissioned Ryan Associated Architects to design a downtown mall, and Philip Johnson was planning for a $400,000,000 new community in central Philadelphia. In Nashville, Tenn., a "new town in town" by Hart, Krivatsy and Stubee was scheduled to cost $650,000,000, and Yonkers, N.Y., was reported ready to receive a "heart transplant." Trenton, N.J., and Tel Aviv also were developing downtown shopping centers.

High rise buildings too reflected a new urban style, in some cases literally from walls of reflecting glass. They are bronze colored at the splendid Regency Hyatt House at Chicago's O'Hare Airport, a John Portman and Associ-

Guests' rooms surround the indoor garden of a ten-story atrium in the sumptuous Regency Hyatt House at Chicago's O'Hare International Airport. The luxury hotel was designed by John Portman & Associates in Atlanta.

ates design, most striking on the inside, where an enclosed ten-story atrium is filled with glass elevators, plants and dazzled guests. Rising above Copley Square in Boston, the John Hancock Building by I. M. Pei and Partners is situated to reflect H. H. Richardson's Trinity Church in its 60-story gray mirrored walls. In Boston, as in San Francisco, the hilly horizon was becoming obscured under sky-bound towers.

Technical Developments. Although research and development in structural systems for large new buildings produced few new forms during the year, the scale of parts and scope of applications exploded, stretching the uses of three-dimensional trusses and space frames. Chicago's new convention center, McCormick Place, by C. F. Murphy Associates, replacing a burned down predecessor, employs a 15-foot deep two-way truss to cover approximately 20 acres, with a 75-foot cantilever around the perimeter.

The winning scheme in the year's most important international architectural competition, for a cultural center at the Plateau Beaubourg in Paris, was conceived as an enormous loft made of trusses strapped to pylons and able to be hydraulically raised and lowered. Its designers, Renzo Piano and Richard Rogers, planned the whole building as a billboard, with rear projection within plastic facades.

Withal, the most exciting new technical developments were tools for imagining the third and fourth dimensions. There was increasing use of computers for graphics, including perspective drawings and simulation of movement through a space. And perhaps the most exciting resource, holograms—plates from which a three-dimensional image can be projected into space—suggests that architecture may be on the threshold of an entirely new visual world.

CHARLES W. MOORE, Professor, and
ROBERT J. YUDELL, Graduate Student
Yale School of Architecture

A stunning innovation in animated architecture, designed by Renzo Piano and Richard Rogers, will house the Plateau Beaubourg arts center, Paris.

French Embassy Press & Information Division

Argentina's president, Gen. Alejandro Lanusse (center), is flanked by the heads of the country's Navy (right) and Air Force as he views the national Independence Day parade in Buenos Aires.

UPI

ARGENTINA

The decision by Argentina's armed services to restore civilian government to their 23,500,000 countrymen dominated the nation's confused political life during 1972.

Six years after the army coup d'etat that eventually put him into the president's chair, Gen. Alejandro Lanusse, the army's commander-in-chief, decreed it an overriding priority that the country be steered toward "institutional normalcy," and he scheduled presidential as well as congressional elections to take place on March 25, 1973. Many Argentines realized that the military were virtually admitting the failure of their "Argentine Revolution." Inspired by the Brazilian model, it had been launched in 1966 in an effort to cure the country's enduring economic malaise by authoritarian methods.

The tacit admission of failure was accompanied by another even more dramatic reversal: President Lanusse also began actively to seek an agreement with Gen. Juan Domingo Peron, the 77-year-old former dictator who was ousted in an army-led national revolt in 1955. In the last analysis there was no getting around the fact that the Peronist myth still held sway over nearly one-third of the electorate. Long after the lean years for the masses that followed Peron's downfall, his adherents remained the largest political force in the country. President Lanusse, a member of a

rich anti-Peronist landowning family, had become convinced that a "national reconciliation" between the former dictator's followers, whose strength was concentrated in the working and lower middle classes, and the upper-class anti-Peronists was a dire necessity. Such a rapprochement, he hoped, would provide the basis for a return to viable constitutional government, end 40 years of recurring intervention in the country's politics by the armed forces, and banish the specter of civil war.

General Lanusse's strategy for incorporating the *Justicialistas* (the Peronist movement) into the political life of the country was disclosed to a big gathering of service leaders in February. The President then began touring the country, advocating a "Grand National Agreement" (GAN). But he immediately aroused suspicions in the Peronist camp by obliquely hinting that he himself might want to run as the GAN presidential candidate and letting it be known that the armed forces would insist on reforming the constitution before any elections in order to strengthen the presidency. And so they did. Amid opposition from all the country's political parties the constitution was amended in October.

In the meantime, President Lanusse had been secretly negotiating with General Peron through emissaries sent to his exile home in Madrid. The wily veteran populist, however, rejected any agreement and repeatedly casti-

gated the regime in left-wing nationalist tones, which especially roused Argentine youth. In June, the *Justicialistas* declared Peron their candidate for the presidency. After the announcement had been made, army pressure obliged President Lanusse to decree that General Peron must either take up residence in Argentina by August or be disqualified from running. The former dictator retorted that he would come home when he chose. President Lanusse saw himself outsmarted and buried his hopes for a personal candidacy.

Peron took his time. He did not leave Spain until Nov. 14 and then he went to Italy. Rebuffed in his efforts to obtain a private audience with the Pope, however, the once ex-

Thousands of General Peron's supporters (below) acclaim the former Argentinian dictator who had just returned to his homeland after 17 years in exile. Peron appears with his wife at center window of his suburban residence (left), to acknowledge the crowd's thunderous welcome.

Photo Atlantida, Gamma (both)

communicated leader turned homeward, arriving in Buenos Aires on Nov. 17 under the grudging gaze of the regime.

Security measures by the government were tight and effective. Labor unions had called for a general strike that day in order to enable workers to greet their hero at the airport, but the government had defused a potentially explosive situation by declaring instead a "paid holiday." In addition, the airport was surrounded with tanks and troops, while the former dictator himself was hurriedly whisked away for an overnight stay at an airport hotel —ostensibly for his own protection.

As it happened, the homecoming itself proved to be the most dramatic consequence of Peron's decision to return to his country. Although intense political maneuvering between him and other Argentine politicians during the first week of his stay resulted in a broad alliance of political groupings, Peron's physical presence in the country never became acutely felt. For one thing, his public appearances were few and mostly restricted to the windows of the upper-class suburban house that his followers had bought for him. For another, all the political wheeling and dealing looked disappointingly "bourgeois" to many among the radical youth who previously had seen in him a revolutionary leader. In live proximity to its believers, the myth of Juan Peron seemed to fade. Cracks began to show in the political alliance, through which its internal tensions and rivalries were clearly visible. During early December, the front fell apart.

All through these developments, President Lanusse firmly adhered to his earlier pronouncements on Peron's ineligibility to run; he had arrived too late to take up residency, and that was that. On Dec. 14, then, leaving behind him a written statement in which he rejected the Peronist movement's presidential nomination, Juan Domingo Peron departed his homeland in much the same way as he had in 1955—flying first to Paraguay and later back to Spain. It was a singularly anticlimactic end to nearly a year of anticipation.

While the political maneuvering was taking place, the Argentine economy steadily deteriorated. Many ordinary citizens felt that the military regime, amid empty calls for national discipline, had benefited only the privileged minorities, sold out Argentine firms to foreign investors, and proved unable to create new opportunities for employment. By May, the value of the Argentine peso had sunk to a mere 10 U.S. cents—a fall by more than half since a year earlier. Well-to-do Argentines showed no confidence in their country, adding eagerly to the estimated $8,000,000,000 already deposited abroad. Alternate beefless weeks, to permit continued exports of Argentina's best foreign-exchange earner, underlined the basic failure to reorganize the old-fashioned meat industry, which, if properly directed, might enable the country to rebound economically in a world of increasing meat consumption.

As the year wore on, Argentina reached a 60 percent rate of inflation, topping its world lead of just under 40 percent in the previous year. President Lanusse was pledged to a maximum 25 percent inflation rate for 1972. Under pressure from the trade unions that were obeying the Peronist line, the regime was forced to concede three—still inadequate—wage increases between January and September.

A second problem was the attempts by tiny, embittered, left-wing guerrilla groups to exploit the frustration and sullen disillusionment of the masses. To provoke the military, who ruled under continuous state-of-siege provisions, to greater repression, all the guerrilla movements struck. For ideological reasons they opposed elections, alleging that elections were a "bourgeois trick" to prolong the imperialist exploitation" of the country. The guerrillas' victims, consistent with their line of reasoning, were often prominent foreign businessmen. These included Dr. Oberdan Sallustro, managing director of the Argentine subsidiary of Fiat, who was kidnapped by the Trotskyite People's Revolutionary Army (ERP) in Buenos Aires in March and assassinated on April 10. On the same day, the neo-Peronist *Montoneros* combined with ERP to murder the commander of Rosario's army garrison, who had been accused by the guerrillas of allowing torture of young detained opponents of the regime. Complaints of torture by the security forces persisted during the year, and in June a "day of protest" was organized by Argentine counselors-at-law.

The guerrillas staged their most daring exploit in August, when they broke out of an army-run top security prison in Patagonia, and some of them managed to hijack a commercial plane and escape to Chile. Naval marines later shot 16 recaptured young guerrillas, men and women. That episode caused serious doubts in Argentina whether the security apparatus had not gotten out of control only six months before popular elections.

RICHARD WIGG
Latin-American Correspondent
The Times, London

Intricacy and finish, achieved through utter fidelity to visual events, recommended Richard Estes' "Store Fronts" to viewers and buyers alike.

ART

In contrast to the rapid proliferation of new concepts, attitudes and styles which have swept the contemporary art world in recent years, 1972 seemed to signal a breathing spell in the pace of developments, if not a retreat.

Festivals. To be sure, the 36th Venice *Biennale* opened with the release of an immense cloud of butterflies, and similarly far-out artistic productions liberally spiced many of the pavilions at the normally staid international showplace, under the theme "Work or Behavior." Even more unusual forms of expression were everywhere in Kassel, Germany's, *Documenta*, which has superseded the *Biennale* as the Western world's most prestigious (and controversial) art fest, and customarily serves as a reliable barometer of avant-garde activity. The quadrennial exhibition's fifth edition, with the ambitious theme "Inquiry into Reality," charted a course midway between painting and sculpture that projected images of photographic or wax-museum literalism and experimental works and performances wherein the emphasis was on raw processes and ideas rather than objects. The ideas at *Documenta* often were expressed in terms more commonly associated with theater,

literature and science and group dynamics than with art.

Nevertheless, the experiments primarily involved elaborations of ideas that had arisen in recent years from "conceptual art" and related movements. Sympathetic critics generally agreed that such manifestations reflected a desire for an art of greater intellectual and social substance, but that this desire had yet to be realized. Thus, it appeared that further refinement and development might replace rampant innovation as the keynote theme for the immediate future.

Regarding the "new," or "sharp focus," realism at the other extreme at *Documenta,* the work displayed also carried forward a style the basic ground rules of which had been established in the late 1960's. Nevertheless, it formed the year's most popular and coherent trend in painting and most successful one in the market place. The style was exemplified with particular authority in the paintings of Chuck Close and Richard Estes and in the sculpture of Duane Hanson.

Significantly, Americans formed the largest national group among the more than 200 artists represented at Kassel, indicating the decisive

position of the United States as the center of gravity of the contemporary art world.

Exhibitions. Seeking an alternative to the "new realism," some American painters took up the banner of "lyrical abstraction," working in a style that generally combined the improvisatory freedom of abstract expressionism with the more rigorous approach of subsequent color field painting. Notable among this group was the New York artist David Diao.

All things considered, the prevailing atmosphere seemed to be one of relaxed eclecticism in which painters and sculptors felt free to follow any one of several styles with an equal chance of critical recognition and/or commercial success. The situation provided an opportunity to assess recent movements with a degree of perspective and tended to give renewed emphasis to work of solid achievement. Attention focused on artists who have remained independent of passing fads and fancies or who have developed what may have appeared originally as an ephemeral fashion into a mature personal expression.

Among the former, several were honored with exhibitions. Robert Motherwell was represented at Minneapolis' Walker Art Center in a masterful series of recent abstract paintings that pitted sensuous color against an austere geometric structure. Richard Diebenkorn's "Ocean Park" series, presented at the San

O. K. Harris Gallery

Subject matter and treatment in Duane Hanson's "Policeman and Rioter" ensure visual impact.

"Lyrical abstraction," as opposed to "new realism," recalls the freedom of abstract expressionism. David Diao's "Possibilities" is an example.

Cunningham Ward Gallery

In a year in which artists and critics seemed to pause and reflect, attention focused on mature artists whose independence of past trends was seen in retrospect as a virtue. The painter Robert Motherwell, whose "At Five in the Afternoon" is shown above, and the kinetic sculptor George Rickey, whose massive "Unstable Cube" appears at left, were both honored with retrospectives during the year.

Among the practitioners of pop art, Claes Oldenburg may be both the most endearing and enduring. The Pasadena Art Museum's touring retrospective of his "soft sculptures" and drawings was a treat of craftsmanship and wit. "Three-Way Plug," shown here, was in the bag of tricks taken on tour.

Francisco Museum of Art, used somewhat parallel means to arrive at ends that were quite different, but equally authoritative. George Rickey, the kinetic sculptor, was given a retrospective of his delicately balanced, wind-propelled metal constructions by the galleries of the University of California at Los Angeles. "Chicago Imagest Art," organized by the Chicago Art Institute and later seen in New York, brought forth a large and diverse group of artists who have worked for years with a zealous oblivion to mainstream trends and whose fantastic, wildly idiosyncratic expression was a far remove from the "imagest art" of the new realists. The death of the Dutch print-maker and master of visual paradox M. C. Escher was followed by a flurry of exhibitions of his work in a number of American museums and galleries.

Prominent members of the latter group also were honored. James Rosenquist was given a retrospective exhibition by the Whitney Museum in New York in which the evolution of his billboard-inspired Kandy Apple-colored pop art was delineated. A touring exhibition of Class Oldenburg, organized by the Pasadena Art Museum, traced the recent development of his work from drooping "soft sculptures" of grossly enlarged common objects to designs for colossal pop "monuments."

UPI

Christo Javacheff's quarter-mile "Valley Curtain" cost some $750,000 and survived 27 hours.

A traveling show of constructions and water-colors by William T. Wiley, originated by the University of California in Berkeley, exemplified a quizzical, crochety, sardonic form of gently mystical expression that has grown out of the West Coast "funk art" movement. In a class by itself was the gigantic, orange nylon "curtain" suspended by the artist Christo across, a 1,350-foot wide valley near Rifle, Colorado. The culmination of a $750,000 project which aborted in initial attempts to put the curtain in place in 1971, the installation survived for only 27 hours before the giant tissue was ripped to shreds by winds of 60 miles an hour. During its brief life, however, it formed the most monumental expression yet attained by the new, anti-object movement in contemporary art.

Nostalgia remained a strong mood in American life, and it was a prominent ingredient in several unusual exhibitions, some of them firmly grounded on historical scholarship, others emphasizing the charm and innocence of bygone traditions and ways of life and others reflecting the current concern for preserving the natural environment. One of the most remarkable, "The Hand and the Spirit," formed the first survey ever presented of the religious impulse in historic American art; displayed at the University Art Museum in Berkeley, it represented the 18th and 19th centuries with rarely-exhibited examples by "naive" artists as

well as work by painters and sculptors of more familiar reputation. "The American West," organized by the Los Angeles County Museum, brought together paintings by the artists who recorded the American frontier between 1820 and 1900. The same museum presented major displays of antique American quilts and of Navajo blankets. The latter was only one example among many of a growing interest in the art—both traditional and contemporary—of American Indians.

The Whitney Museum assembled a large show of paintings by the 19th century American genre artist Eastman Johnson, and the California Palace of the Legion of Honor in San Francisco mounted a survey of turn-of-the-century American "Tonalism" as exemplified both in painting and photography. The University of Maryland circulated an immensely popular traveling show that traced the history of the newspaper comic strip.

Inevitably, some of these shows offered nostalgia and little else of value. Such was the impression of a large exhibition of Pre-Raphaelite paintings at the University of Miami.

The year was conspicuously lacking in spectacular anniversary celebrations on the order of recent homages to Dürer and Rembrandt, but it provided several exhibitions of older masters of major importance. *L'Orangerie* in Paris assembled the first comprehensive collection of paintings by the 17th century French master Georges de la Tour. In Florence a mammoth retrospective of sculpture and other works by Henry Moore inaugurated the old *Forte di Belvedere* as an exhibition place. Moore's was the largest of many shows devoted to earlier

This and other Navajo blankets constituted the whole of a hit Los Angeles County Museum show.

Los Angeles County Museum of Art

20th century masters. Others included a major survey of paintings by Kandinsky at the Guggenheim Museum in New York, drawn from its collection; retrospective shows of sculpture by Jacques Lipchitz, at the Metropolitan in New York, and by Wilhelm Lehmbruck, at the National Gallery in Washington; bronze sculptures by Matisse at the Museum of Modern Art; selections of Kurt Schwitters collages, also at MOMA, and of paintings by Georges Braque at the Chicago Art Institute.

One of the more unusual modern master shows was a retrospective of Giorgio de Chirico at the New York Cultural Center which included his rarely displayed work of the past 50 years as well as the celebrated "metaphysical" paintings with which he anticipated surrealism earlier in the century. The exhibition dramatically demonstrated the decline and fall of Chirico's once extraordinary talent.

A cultural exchange traveling exhibit of the Soviet Union's "Arts and Crafts in Ancient Times and Today" was one of the year's most popular displays in six American cities. In London, a display of treasures from the tomb of King Tutankhamen, presented for the first time outside of the Cairo Museum, drew more than 1,000,000 visitors to the British Museum.

Sales and Patronage. The art market, in the United States and elsewhere, paralleled the curious state of the U.S. economy, wherein high taxes, interest rates and other forces conspired to give most people less money to spend at the same time that prices steadily increased. Thus, the market generally was depressed, while auction prices still managed to set new records. These included the highest prices ever paid for a sculpture by a living artist ($260,000 for a Henry Moore figure), for an English work of art ($700,000 for a recently discovered Gainsborough portrait), for a Japanese print ($18,-000 for an 18th century work by Haranobu) and for an art work other than a painting ($573,000 for a 14th century Chinese wine jar). The purchase by the Norton Simon Foundation of a painting by Zurbarán for $3,000,-000 was the third highest price ever paid for any art work.

Important accessions to American museum collections included a Goya portrait of *Pepito Costa y Bonells,* by the Metropolitan, and Géricault's *Trumpeters of Napoleon's Imperial Guard* by the National Gallery, Washington. In Britain, the National Gallery raised $4,500,000 to secure Titian's *Death of Actaeon* and prevent its sale to an American buyer, thanks in part to a year-long public fund drive.

The big news of the year, however, was not accessions but "de-accession," or the sale of "lesser" or "redundant" works from a museum's permanent collection. Announcement that the Metropolitan Museum had thus disposed of valuable paintings by Van Gogh and Henri Rousseau in an unpublicized sale to a private dealer provoked a storm of controversy about the ligitimacy and wisdom of this rather traditional museum practice.

"De-accession" was only one symptom of the continuing financial bind in which many of the largest American museums remained caught. Others included the imposition or increasing of admission charges, reduction of hours, curtailment of exhibition schedules and abbreviation of the intinerary for many traveling shows.

Within this generally gloomy picture were a few bright spots. Grants totaling more than $1,000,000 were announced by the National Endowment for the Arts for a two-year pilot program of museum conservation and renovation efforts; the Endowment itself received an appropriation of $39,000,000 for the 1972–73 fiscal year, an increase of $9,000,000 over its previous year's budget. The new Kimbell museum opened in an impressive $6,500,000 building in Fort Worth, Tex., and a smaller Museum of South Texas opened in Corpus Christi.

Women's Lib and Other Problems. On the other hand, museums were confronted with many problems and pressures of a nonfinancial nature. A growing number of women joined other groups which in recent years have protested a lack of proportionate representation in exhibitions and other museum programs; for the most part, their complaints were expressed by quietly conducted statistical surveys rather than militant demonstrations, and they were coupled with a number of exhibitions designed to define a "feminine sensibility."

Air pollution was identified as a critical threat to art works housed in many American and European museums alike. Art thefts continued to increase in number, value and audacity, culminating in thefts of four paintings valued at $1,000,000 from the Worcester Art Museum in Massachusetts (the works were later recovered) and of $2,000,000 worth of paintings from the Montreal Museum of Fine Arts.

Finally, in addition to many lesser instances, the year recorded the most shocking occurrence of art vandalism in recent history when a visitor to the Vatican suddenly took a hammer to Michelangelo's *Pietà* and managed to sheer off the Virgin's nose and left arm before anyone could stop him.

THOMAS ALBRIGHT
Art Critic, San Francisco Chronicle

ASTRONOMY

Expansion of the Universe. Distant galaxies invariably show spectral red shifts that are usually attributed to the Doppler shift in the wavelength of light emitted by objects in motion away from some center. It has been observed that the farther away a galaxy is from the earth, the faster it is receding. The measurement of the velocities of distant galaxies by this method has led to the concept of a universe expanding outward from an initial explosion that occurred many billions of years ago. How fast is the universe expanding and when did the initial "big bang" occur? Although it is possible to determine relatively directly the speed of recession of a distant galaxy, it is more difficult to determine accurately its absolute distance. Since 1936 when Edwin Hubble first estimated the distance of various galaxies and the rate of expansion of the universe, determinations of astronomical distances have gradually increased by a factor of ten.

In 1972 astronomers Allan Sandage and Gustav Tammann determined the age of the universe as about 18,000,000,000 years, although this figure is still indefinite owing to an uncertainty as to the extent of deceleration that has occurred as the components of the universe have moved outward. With continued deceleration, the universe will eventually stop expanding and may start to contract. It is possible that the universe pulsates, alternately expanding and contracting. The new research by Sandage and Tammann was performed mainly with the Palomar 200-inch telescope.

Quasars. Quasars, or quasi-stellar radio sources, are energetic distant objects that may represent galaxies in early stages of formation. They are very small in size—too small to permit precise diameter measurements with even our largest radio telescopes. It is very difficult to understand how the large quantities of energy released by quasars can be produced by such a small volume. The existing radio telescopes are sufficiently large to detect the radio noise from quasars, but much larger telescopes would normally be needed to resolve their diameters. However, observations made simultaneously with two telescopes that have been accurately timed to within a billionth of a second (as determined by atomic clocks) can be combined. This technique will provide the same resolution as could be obtained from a single telescope having a diameter equal to the distance between the pair of telescopes.

Experiments with telescope pairs in the United States, Canada, Sweden and Australia have determined that some quasars are smaller than 0.001 second of arc (one second of arc is 1/3600 of a degree). The limit of resolution by this technique is obtained by using telescopes separated by a distance equal to the diameter of the earth. Such experiments have been conducted in recent years with radio telescopes in the U.S.S.R. and the United States. Such a technique is complicated by the need to transport the delicate atomic clocks between the two observatories without losing a billionth of a second during the transport. The results of these measurements are then recorded on magnetic tapes and combined in computers. These experiments have shown that some quasars are smaller than one millionth of a second of arc in diameter, or the diameter of a pin-point as observed at a distance of 5,000 miles. Thus, some individual quasars produce more radio energy, in a volume comparable to that of our solar system, than does our entire galaxy of 10,000,000,000 stars.

Radio Pictures. The spectacular photographs taken with optical telescopes have for many years provided detailed views of distant objects that can be seen only dimly with the naked eye. The information obtained by radio telescopes has, however, taken a different form: radio telescopes resemble photographers' exposure meters in that they simply measure the total amount of radiation in a particular frequency range that is being received from a large area of the sky. The reason for the difference in representation is that there exists no radio equivalent of the photographic film— that is, a two-dimensional detector sensitive to radio waves. Recently, however, a technique has been developed for scanning a region of the sky with a radio telescope and reconstructing a radio "picture," somewhat as a television receiver constructs a picture as the incoming electron beam scans the front surface of an oscilloscope tube. These radio pictures can show graphically where the radio waves originate in a particular galaxy, for instance, and they can then be compared with optical pictures showing the origins of light waves. If, for example, the telescope measures the radio frequency emitted by neutral hydrogen gas, the picture will show where the interstellar clouds of this gas are located, and this radio picture can then be compared with optical photographs showing the locations of the surrounding stars.

Radio Stars. Our galaxy (the Milky Way) contains billions of normal stars, but until recently none of these stars was known to radiate significant amounts of radio waves. The celestial radio noise measured by radio telescopes is usually produced by clouds of gas, interstellar molecules, distant galaxies and peculiar objects such as pulsars, X-ray sources, novae and the

solar corona. Now three normal stars in our galaxy have been found to emit weak sporadic radio noise. Two are well-known eclipsing double stars: Beta Lyrae and Algol. The third is Antares' companion star, of which little is known other than the fact that it is surrounded by a cloud of gas. It seems likely that in some closely-spaced double stars a hot plasma surrounding the stars emits radio radiation in some yet undefined manner.

Solar Neutrinos. The sun produces light and heat by nuclear reactions in its central core where the temperature reaches about 10,000,-000 degrees C°. Fusion reactions in the nuclear core convert hydrogen atoms into helium atoms, releasing in the process neutrinos and other elementary particles. However, the end products of these reactions weigh less than the original ones, and the decrease in mass appears as energy in amounts revealed by the equation, $E = mc^2$ (c being the velocity of light). The neutrinos are neutral energetic particles possessing no rest mass. They interact so little with other matter that they can pass virtually uninhibited through the outer layers of the sun. Since the total energy produced by the sun is a known quantity, one can predict the number of neutrinos that should reach the earth daily.

Experiments designed to detect these solar neutrinos have been conducted for five years by Brookhaven National Laboratory physicist Raymond Davis, Jr. To prevent contamination of the results by cosmic rays, the experiments are conducted 4,850 feet underground in the Homestake gold mine in South Dakota, where a tank containing 100,000 gallons of tetrachloroethylene (cleaning fluid) is emplaced. The solar neutrinos convert chlorine atoms to radioactive argon atoms in a predictable way that can be detected with Geiger or other counters. But the observed rate of arrival of solar neutrinos has been ten times slower than was predicted by theory. The solar interior calculations were then refined, but this only increased the discrepancy in the results. Scientists are now reexamining data on the basic physical properties of neutrinos and conjecturing that the sun may "turn off" its nuclear reactor occasionally and adjust to a new interior configuration. Even if the central solar reactor should become inactive for several thousand years, a slight contraction of the sun would keep the earth's temperature constant within a few degrees. The problem of the discrepancy in the number of emitted solar

Detectable alterations of the fluid in this tank, positioned deep in the earth's interior, are used to gauge the influx of solar neutrinos.

neutrinos is currently one of the major unsolved problems of astronomy.

Milky Way Explosions. In September 1972 four unusually violent explosions were recorded within the Milky Way. Although events of such a magnitude had been observed in distant parts of the universe, this represented the first time, except for supernovae, that such explosions have been observed in our own galaxy. The character of the radio emissions indicated that they originated in a gas cloud expanding at about half the speed of light. The explosions, which occurred beyond a dust-filled spiral arm of our galaxy in the constellation Cygnus, were not those of a supernova. The Mount Palomar telescope also detected an object radiating in the infrared that subsequently was identified with the radio source. Emissions in the X-ray portion of the spectrum also were detected from an object known as Cygnus X-3, in the same region of the sky as the source of the radio waves, but by the end of 1972 it had not been determined conclusively if the two sources are identical.

Future Plans for Astronomy. Where is astronomy heading, and what are its greatest needs?

To help answer these questions for the next ten years, the National Academy of Sciences supervised a study conducted by a group of astronomers under the leadership of Caltech's Jesse L. Greenstein. The committee urgently recommended construction of the proposed VLA ("Very Large Antenna"), which would consist of twenty-seven 85-foot radio telescopes distributed in a Y-shaped array over a distance of 26 miles.

The $62,000,000 project would be operated by the National Radio Astronomy Observatory at a proposed high-altitude site west of Socorro, N.M. Second priority is assigned to developing more sensitive electronic auxiliary instruments that would increase the effectiveness of existing telescopes. The committee also recommended the early launching of a satellite with equipment designed to measure high-energy radiation and particles (X-rays, gamma rays, cosmic rays) and suggested planning for a large optical telescope in space, probably in the 1980's.

HELMUT A. ABT
Astronomer
Kitt Peak National Observatory

A cone-shaped shadow raced from west to east across the earth's surface during July's total solar eclipse. In the New York City area, 79.5 percent of the solar disc was obscured at eclipse's maximum extent (r.).

"The New York Times"

Australia's mineral sands industry, important in exports, is bound by law to restore the land.

AUSTRALIA

After a year in which Australia continued to suffer severe inflation and a stagnant economy, the voters in December replaced the Liberal-Country party coalition government with a Labor party one, setting the nation on a new course in domestic and international affairs. Labor gained a majority of nine in the 125-seat House of Representatives, bringing to power 56-year-old Edward Gough Whitlam, the first nonunionist Labor prime minister in Australia's history. The vote confirmed an electoral reaction both to a lackluster performance by a jaded coalition 23 years in office and to Prime Minister William McMahon's uninspired leadership. It represented a 3 percent swing to Labor from the 1969 poll.

In spite of a buoyant stock market and improved wool prices, the economy caused concern throughout the year. Business was slack, and unemployment rose to more than 1.5 percent. Some of the economic troubles were attributable to the revaluing of the Australian dollar in December 1971; this reduced Australia's competitive position on key exports.

With economic sluggishness unrelieved, manufacturing interests were harshly critical of the McMahon government. Criticizing its piecemeal approach, manufacturers called for a "comprehensive coordination of the efforts of government and industry" in common pursuit of national objectives for industrial growth. Other sections of the community appeared equally disenchanted with the government's performance. Labor, besides being finally free from its long-crippling factional disputes, promised more dynamic policies.

Labor's platform included a proposal to provide funds for better education, higher social-welfare payments, a government-run health plan, housing aid for low-income families, free university tuition, a new drive to develop the "empty north" and measures to help Australians buy back overseas-controlled companies.

EDWARD GOUGH WHITLAM

The career of Gough Whitlam, Australia's first Labor party prime minister in 23 years, began inauspiciously and progressed uncertainly. Twice defeated for public office before his election to the House of Representatives in 1952, he battled repeatedly with the Labor leadership before supplanting it in 1967. Born on July 11, 1916, the son of a future solicitor general of Australia, Whitlam practiced law before entering politics.

On immigration, a scaling-down was proposed, with emphasis on bringing in members of recent newcomers' families.

Labor's major pledges included an undertaking to put an end to the draft. Among the first administrative acts of the new government were the release of young men jailed for noncompliance with the draft law and abolition of the law itself.

In defense and foreign affairs, Labor favored immediate recognition of China and a softening of the military stance expressed through SEATO and the five-power ANZUK defense arrangement established with New Zealand and the United Kingdom in 1971 for Malaysia-Singapore. (These policies coincided with the views of New Zealand's newly elected Labour party government). On assuming office, Prime Minister Whitlam, acting as his own foreign minister, confirmed that Australia would move toward "a more independent stance in international affairs." He supported a proposal put before the United Nations that a "peace zone" be created in the Indian Ocean.

While the ANZUS Treaty with New Zealand and the United States was considered basic to Australia's defense, Whitlam foreshadowed changes to reduce the pact's military emphasis and to make it more an instrument "for justice and peace and political, social and economic advancement in the Pacific area." He reaffirmed a pledge, given by McMahon in November, to grant internal self-government to Papua and New Guinea in 1973, with full independence to follow as soon as the government and people of the territories indicate they want it.

It was a year of gains for aboriginal rights. In January a new type of general-purpose lease for federal land was created to give aborigines on reservations land tenure for 50 years wherever "reasonable economic and social use" would be made of the land. In addition, substantial sums were made available to buy land outside reservations for aboriginal enterprises.

Mining had another good year despite some adverse effects of international currency problems. In February, Australia signed an agreement with Japan on future sales of large quantities of uranium ore.

President Suharto of Indonesia made a five-day official visit to Canberra, Sydney and Melbourne in February, and in June, Prime Minister McMahon visited Indonesia. A three-year, $83,000,000 economic aid program for Indonesia was signed.

R. M. YOUNGER
Author, *Australia and the Australians*

AUSTRIA

Economics occupied center stage in Austria in 1972. A special trade agreement between Austria and the European Economic Community (EEC), mutually reducing tariff barriers, was signed. Production continued to increase at a high rate, as did prices and wages. Politically, the year saw only one provincial election, which was won by the incumbent Socialist party. Austria continued to expand its relations with both Western and Eastern Europe.

On Sept. 14 the National Assembly voted unanimously to enact the interim agreement recently concluded between Austria and the EEC. The understanding secured for Austria, as the only EFTA member state, the benefit of a 30 percent mutual tariff reduction. Federal Chancellor Bruno Kreisky termed the agreement the most important treaty in the history of the Second Republic since the state treaty of 1955 ending Allied occupation.

On Oct. 8 the governing Socialist party, led by Chancellor Kreisky, won the elections to the Diet of Burgenland province, slightly increasing its share to 50.5 percent of the popular vote. The conservative People's party, the major opposition, secured 45.7 percent, a decrease of one percent, and the right-wing Freedom party, previously unable to capture a seat, obtained 3.1 percent and one seat. The election, the first test for the Socialists since they had gained a clear majority in the general elections of October 1971, showed continued popular support for the government. Following an uninterrupted period of coalition governments since World War II, the Socialists are the first party to govern Austria alone.

The Austrian economy continued its steady growth at a rate slightly exceeding five percent, with particular increases in construction and the production of consumer goods. The expansion followed employment of additional foreign labor, which exceeded 200,000 in mid-August (130,000 from neighboring Yugoslavia), raising the quota of foreign labor to eight percent of the national labor force. In tourism the comparative rise in net receipts was 22 percent over the record of the previous year. Exports surpassed the record high of 1971 by nine percent (for the January–July period); imports increased by 11 percent. Consumer prices rose by six percent, prices in industry by six percent and the level of standard wages by five percent, all for the period January to August.

ISTVAN DEAK, Director
Institute on East Central Europe
Columbia University

BANGLADESH

In this article, Phillips Talbot, president of The Asia Society and a former U.S. Assistant Secretary of State for Near Eastern and South Asian Affairs, examines the nation state of Bangladesh, born in the Pakistani civil war of 1971. The article is intended to serve not only as a review of events in 1972 but also as an introduction to the world's eighth most populous country.

It is man's dreams, so it is said, that make the realities of life bearable. Fortunately for the people of Bangladesh, battered and bloodied in 1971 in the process of gaining independence and almost impossibly burdened in 1972 by the early tasks of reconstruction and nation-building, they have such a dream. Nourished from the roots of a rich and ancient culture and expressed in the verses of the Nobel Prize-winning poet Rabindranath Tagore, it is the dream of *amar sonor Bangla,* "my golden Bengal."

The question is how far the dream can carry them.

When in early 1972 the new state of Bangladesh chose Tagore's moving poem as its national anthem (thus making Tagore probably the only author of two nations' official anthems; India's *Jana-gana-mana,* "Morning Song of India," is also a Tagore poem), its leaders

Flags of Bangladesh appear in profusion in the market in Dacca following Sheikh Mujibur Rahman's return from captivity.

Dacca, looking toward the Federal Reserve Bank of Pakistan down Motijeel Road, shows little of the ravages of the nation's civil war.

could have been looking both forward and backward. On some future day, they seemed to be saying, their densely crowded districts may again be as golden as they were when Tagore knew them in the early 20th century. The rich earth is still there, the sun and the water, the shaded hills for cultivating tea and the flat deltaland where the tall jute and the rice grow green and golden as the fields flood and dry. Given a respite from tragedy, perhaps the dream of Bangladesh might not be impossible of achievement.

Unhappily, such modest good fortune has escaped east Bengal for an entire generation. Time and again the region has been struck by natural of man-made disasters—a devastating famine in 1943; Hindu-Muslim massacres in 1946; the economically-disruptive partition of 1947 that, in placing east Bengal in Pakistan, separated it from its natural market center in Calcutta; increasingly bitter confrontation with the weighty west wing of Pakistan; a 1970 cyclone that appears to have caused the greatest known loss from any natural disaster.

Yet none of the upheavals matched the catastrophic effects of events in 1971. It had been evident for years that differences between east Bengal and west Pakistan were deepening. Ironically, it was Pakistan President Yahya Khan's decision to return the country to parliamentary government after a dozen years of authoritarian rule that permitted Sheikh Mujibur Rahman's Awami League party in east Bengal to transform itself in 1970 elections into a national legislative majority—a contingency that had never previously confronted the west Pakistanis. Months of bargaining and negotiation between political forces in the west and east wings broke down in March 1971 when President Yahya ordered the Pakistani military forces in east Bengal to take charge of the province and suppress the Awami League on the ground it had become secessionist in character.

Reconstruction of East Bengal's shattered transport system was a critical challenge facing Mujibur's government in the aftermath of the war.

Routed West Pakistani soldiers, shown surrendering their arms in the newly independent East, were interned in India, where some 90,000 remained in captivity at the end of the year.

The rest became common knowledge. As outsiders from the distant Indus valley region, the Pakistani troops failed to break Bengali resistance. Local guerrillas, hastily trained and equipped with some help from neighboring India, put the government's troops on the defensive. In the terror that ensued millions of Bengalis fled their homes and crossed the frontier into India, where for months they lived in refugee camps, an international issue. Dissidence in east Bengal became rebellion and subsequently an independence movement. Increasing Indian assistance and involvement, which the Pakistani troops tried to counter, precipitated a two-week war in December 1971 that ended in total Pakistani capitulation in east Bengal. Thus was set the stage for the creation of Bangladesh.

The campaigns from March onward through the war had taken a heavy toll of life and had caused severe damage to ports, shipping, railways, roads, bridges, factories, telephonic and telegraphic communications and other essential facilities and services. Food shortages became desperate in some areas; export crops could not be shipped; the economy was shat-

tered. Many of the most promising potential leaders had been killed during the fighting or in late purges, and Sheikh Mujibur Rahman was still imprisoned in West Pakistan. The birth of Bangladesh was a joyful event for the east Bengalis, but the omens were not auspicious.

The Bengali nation that emerged on the international scene at the beginning of 1972 is the eighth most populous state in the world. Its 70,000,000 to 75,000,000 people, 85 percent of them Muslims and the remainder mostly Hindus, live in are area about the size of Wisconsin. It is the second largest Muslim state, after Indonesia (and before India and Pakistan, which now rank third and fourth, respectively, in Muslim population). But Bangladesh, like India, has declared itself to be a secular state and turned its back on the Pakistani doctrine of religious nationalism.

Shortly after the new year began, President Zulfikar Ali Bhutto of Pakistan, who had replaced the discredited President Yahya Khan, released Sheikh Mujibur from detention and permitted him to return home. After a joyous welcome there, and upon becoming prime min-

Bodies of Bengali intellectuals murdered in the last days of fighting were found in a Dacca kiln.

Flanked by elated supporters, Sheikh Mujibur enters Dacca atop a flower-strewn truck.

SHEIKH MUJIBUR RAHMAN

For Sheikh Mujibur Rahman, as for many other leaders of newly independent nations, the road to power lay through his oppressors' jails. Born on March 17, 1920, he was educated at Dacca University. First imprisoned for resisting British rule and subsequently for opposing that of West Pakistan, he was jailed a third time at the outbreak of civil war in 1971. He became premier of Bangladesh on his release in January 1972.

ister, the national leader of Bangladesh assumed all-but-overwhelming tasks of relief and rehabilitation, building an administration, setting a political course and opening international contacts. He found ports choked, transport blocked, food and supplies marooned, industries idle, the treasury empty, the civil services disrupted, police and military cadres immobilized, large stores of arms in the hands of former guerrillas and youth bands and smoldering antagonisms ready to break into conflict between members of the Bengali majority community and the minority Biharis, many of whom had sided with Pakistan in 1971.

Yet he also found a people exuberant in its independence, responsive to his leadership and better disciplined than might have been expected in the circumstances. In mood, at least, the early days were ones in which, despite all the problems, the joy and excitement of self-rule by Bengali Muslims for the first time since the 18th century evoked the idea of golden Bengal.

In its first year of independence, Bangladesh received recognition from many countries, a number of which showed their concern for its difficulties by contributing—along with official international agencies and many voluntary agencies—to what in total became a massive international program of relief and rehabilitation assistance. China and several other states, particularly among the Arabs, however, held back after having supported Pakistan's stand in 1971. Because Bangladesh and Pakistan did not manage to settle their differences in the months following independence, China went so far in September as to veto Bangladesh's application for membership in the United Nations.

On the other hand, the United States, which officially had also not favored the Bangladesh cause in 1971, began providing very substantial economic assistance through United Nations channels early in 1972, and in April recognized Bangladesh as a sovereign state. The Soviet

Union had supported India's position on Bangladesh throughout 1971. When independence came, the Soviets moved promptly to develop a visible diplomatic and aid presence in the new state.

India also, and very naturally, quickly entered into close working cooperation with the state for whose creation it had assumed major responsibility. In aid, trade and political relations—including a 25-year treaty of friendship, which also provides for mutual defense consultations in case of need—India can be expected to maintain a leading position in Bangladesh provided their links are handled with delicacy to avoid serious bilateral strains. Much as it needs support and assistance, Bangladesh has made clear its determination to protect its newly won sovereignty.

Gradually relief and rehabilitation efforts have begun to take hold. As 1972 wore on, bridges were repaired and roads made serviceable. Getting the ports back into full operation proved slow work. The important jute mills, which had been nationalized after their former West Pakistani owners had departed, got back into partial production. Yet the economic disarray continued, particularly because the food supply in some areas remained excessively tight. As in India, the 1972 monsoons were deficient. This raised the specter of having to import perhaps 2,500,000 tons of foodgrains in 1973. Moreover, farmers and traders near the Indian border found it advantageous to sell their goods and buy consumer items in India for the black market in Bangladesh, causing a further drain on the economy.

Especially during the latter months of 1972 political stress in the country brought fresh anxieties to leaders of the government and the rulers of the Awami League party. Opposition, especially from the left, became more vocal, and Awami League candidates, who had been unchallengeable in 1970, began losing local and special-constituency elections. Yet the prime minister obtained agreement on a new constitution built on democratic principles and announced that fresh elections would be held in the spring of 1973.

For Bangladesh, 1972 was not a year of taking the rough with the smooth; once independence had been obtained, there was little enough of the smooth anywhere. Nevertheless, the people of Bangladesh had endured the catastrophes of earlier years, including 1971, and their survival potential still seemed strong after a year of self-rule. With all their difficulties, indeed, Tagore's dream had not lost its appeal. They still sang of "my golden Bengal."

Jason Lauré, Rapho Guillumette

An artisan of the Moch tribe of the aboriginal Chittagong hill people works at her hand loom. Such textiles are an important export item.

During the summer, the councilmen of Brussels prohibited private-car parking in Grand'Place. Heavy traffic and pollution had caused tourists to avoid the well-known square in the heart of Belgium's capital.

BELGIUM

Owing to the resilience and pragmatism of Prime Minister Gaston Eyskens, it seemed for a while in 1972 that Belgium would at last achieve a respite from the long-standing Flemish-Walloon language dispute, which has poisoned the country's economic, social and political life for years.

Returned to office at the head of another Social Christian–Socialist coalition government (his fourth and the country's 19th government since World War II) following general elections in November 1971, Eyskens proceeded to tackle the problem along the lines set forth in 1970 constitutional reforms. These provided for the country to be divided into Flemish- and French-speaking regions, as well as a bilingual one around Brussels, each with limited autonomy.

The language rivalry, however, in the end proved tougher than Eyskens. Its intensity was well illustrated by the case of the Fourons, on which the government finally fell. The Fourons is a small group of villages (about 4,500 inhabitants) in eastern Belgium. Although many of the people there speak a kind of German patois, they are passionately attached to Wallonia. In 1963 the Fourons had been given to the Flemish province of Limbourg. In 1972, however, the central government proposed that the area should be directly administered from Brussels, officially a bilingual island in the country, but in fact dominated by French-speakers. The Flemish demanded concessions in return, specifically the end of "encroachment" by Brussels, an expanding city, on the "Flemish soil" surrounding it. By Nov. 22, Eyskens had decided that the problem was insoluble, and he resigned, declaring that he would retire from politics. By the end of the year no new cabinet had been formed.

Despite its tradition of weak coalition governments nervously held together by lack of alternatives and spending a great deal of energy trying to pacify the two language communities, Belgium recorded the highest increase in industrial production of all the Common Market countries. It also had a lower rate of consumer price increases than all but Luxembourg.

A separate French-speaking section of the University of Louvain, the country's oldest university, founded in 1425, opened its doors for the first time.

In October some 700,000 cafe-owners and shopkeepers—representatives of the self-employed Belgian middle class—staged a two-day strike in protest against the complicated value-added tax system and discrimination over pensions.

RICHARD NORTON-TAYLOR
Foreign Correspondent
The Guardian, Manchester and London

BIOLOGICAL SCIENCES

The Environment. The attention of the public as well as that of the U.S. Congress was focused on issues linked to "the environment" in 1972. As a result, the environmental biologist has been required to spend an increasing amount of his time and energy documenting for many unfamiliar groups, such as politicians, industrialists, and members of state and national agencies, the fact that problems do indeed exist. He is urgently seeking ways of measuring quantitatively with a test organism, in a short period of time, how and to what degree pollution is contributing to the increase in the number of endangered species, including possibly man.

The role of apologist for the environment is a very uncomfortable and unfamiliar one for the ecologist, who in the past has concerned himself solely with examining the relationship of organisms to their environment, without making any attempt to influence the outcome of this interaction. If one species "won" over another in its struggle for survival, the ecologist described the event, documented the factors involved, and sometimes made predictions about other interacting systems. Gradually he formulated theories which were tested by his fellow biologists, and which were then either accepted or rejected. No one outside of science took much notice of these efforts. Perhaps the new public support for environmental research will produce some "good science" if the biologist can reclaim sufficient time for well-considered ecological studies.

Molecular Biology. While attention remained riveted on environmental matters, the field of molecular biology began its third decade of highly imaginative, productive and top-quality research. A slight change in emphasis in molecular biology studies was evident, partly because of funds provided through the various (and often conflicting) "cure cancer" crusades. There was an evident shift toward the more "applied" research, a development which was to be expected as molecular theory based on experiments with simple systems evolved.

Until 1972 molecular biology had largely drawn its data from studies conducted with bacteria and bacterial viruses. The techniques employed in these studies are now being applied to cells, particularly tissue culture cells, of man and other higher organisms. Such cells are now being manipulated and analyzed in the same way as were the microorganisms. At the same time researchers are seeking an "advanced" microorganism that, in terms of complexity, lies between bacteria and man and which can be grown and handled more easily than cells from the latter.

The advanced microorganism must be subject to both genetic and biochemical analysis and possess some degree of developmental complexity. The two organisms which appear most suited to fill this role are yeast (*Saccharomyces*) and the mold *Neurospora crassa*. Yeast has long been used by the baking and brewing industry and thus a base of well-developed practical knowledge already has been developed about this organism. *Neurospora* was the organism which in the 1950's provided the biochemical basis for molecular biology.

Cancer. Recent studies support the concept that vertebrates contain the genetic information necessary to produce an RNA (Ribonucleic acid) tumor virus. Dr. Robert Huebner and Dr. George Todaro (both of the National Cancer Institute) have suggested that this information has formed part of the genomes of vertebrates since early in their evolution. Either virus or tumor production may be induced sometime during the life of these animals as a function of the particular genetic makeup of the individual or as a result of the action of various environmental agents or conditions.

Thus, genetic material (virogenes) that exists within and is part of the DNA of the animal may be converted into a virus and ultimately a tumor. According to this hypothesis part of the virogene is unique in terms of its control by the host cell and that portion of the DNA is called the viral oncogene. Normal cells prevent the expression of the oncogene by the action of special repressor molecules. Agents such as radiation and chemical carcinogens may, however, allow the oncogene to be "switched on," resulting in virus production even in normal cells.

The striking and sobering aspect of the oncogene hypothesis is the suggestion that cancer is built into, and has long formed a part of, the genetic apparatus (DNA) of animal cells. If this is true, scientists must tamper with man's genetic system when attempting to "control cancer." Certainly some tumor viruses are transmitted from parent to offspring in a "vertical" fashion. The question remains as to the possible transmission of tumor viruses between unrelated individuals in a "horizontal" fashion (infection). The identification of a human milk virus associated with breast cancer suggests that "horizontal transmission" may occur during breast feeding.

Studies of the so-called reverse transcriptase enzyme, originally observed by Howard Temin (University of Wisconsin), have suggested mechanisms for the transmission of horizontal infection between individuals. Reverse transcriptase is an enzyme that uses RNA (the

virus) to make DNA (the host genetic material). Thus, the infective virus could be converted into DNA which could be integrated into the host cell DNA and would thereby be similar in character to the oncogene. Much current work involves experimentation with this new and exciting enzyme system.

The Membrane Era in Biology. A number of biologists have suggested that biological membranes will assume a prominence in the research of the 1970's and 1980's similar to that held by the nucleic acids in the 1950's and 1960's. Indeed the emphasis on membranes appeared simultaneously on almost all fronts; almost no biologist can overlook the possible relevance of membranes to his specialty.

Since the early 1930's membranes have been viewed as lipid bilayers with the hydrophobic "tails" of the lipid molecules pointing inward while the hydrophilic polar "heads" faced outward toward the aqueous environment. After a long period of debate this bilayer model, first suggested by James Danielli, has been confirmed, the latest evidence being provided by Nobel laureate M. H. F. Wilkins and colleagues through the analysis of the X-ray diffraction patterns produced by cell membranes (a technique which also led to an understanding of the structure of DNA).

The unique feature of the bilayer is the fact it need not be continuous and may contain "patches" of other specialized components which may themselves form the crucial entities of functional membranes. For example, membrane proteins which were once thought to form a "sandwich" cover over the lipid molecules are now believed to occur in patches. The membrane model envisioned by most workers in the field today is that of a lipid "sea" interspersed with "icebergs" of protein that sometimes may extend completely through the lipid bilayer. Such protein (or glycoprotein) "icebergs" may be free to rotate within this "sea" (just as might a cube of ice) without disrupting the continuity of the lipid layer. Thus, the lipid bilayer serves as a structural backbone for the membrane and as a primary permeability barrier. It acts as a molecular insulator in which the molecules that account for the dynamic role of membranes—the proteins and glycoproteins—are immersed.

The central role of membranes is to serve as very selective permeability barriers. Active transport of molecules, such as sugars and amino acids, across the cell membrane occurs by means of carrier systems called "permeases." The analysis of the genetic and biochemical control of "permeases" is presently the subject of intensive investigation. It appears that in higher organisms the role of carrier molecules may be filled by glycoproteins rather than simple proteins, as is the case with bacteria. Glycoproteins are molecules that consist of a protein core with attached carbohydrate side chains; both components may vary enormously in both size and complexity.

The transmission of all chemical and electrical information to the cell's interior and the regulation of all information flow between cells involve membranes. Hormones, for example, appear to exert their effects by means of receptor molecules in the cell membrane which, through a series of subsequent steps, elicit the characteristic cell response to the hormone.

Many molecules are synthesized on cell membranes, sometimes on the membranes that interlace the interior of the cell. In 1972 it was shown that the "granddaddy" of all informational macromolecules, DNA, is synthesized on a membrane site. Protein synthesis occurs on ribosomes, which are also often associated with membranes. Many enzymes involved in syntheses function sequentially as steps in a "production line" on membrane surfaces. Cancer cells have been shown to be cells that are altered in one normal membrane characteristic. A phenomenon called contact inhibition restricts cell growth when the membranes of two separate cells come into contact. Cancer cells have lost the ability to undergo contact inhibition and such cells continue to proliferate and pile up to form a tumor.

There is every indication that biological membranes will become increasingly important as ongoing research identifies additional membrane-bound compartments within cells in which certain specialized functions occur. The interrelationship between such compartments is only now being traced by direct experimentation.

Molecular Biology of Aging. Two alternate theories have been developed to account for cellular aspects of the aging process. One theory suggests that it is a "programmed process" and represents only the end product of differentiation. The other theory suggests that aging is an "error accumulation" process.

During 1972 experiments carried out with microorganisms as well as with human tissue cultures supported the error accumulation theory. According to this theory, a modification of enzymes through errors in protein synthesis leads to the production of still more macromolecular errors and ultimately to what has been called "error catastrophe."

A. GIB DEBUSK
Professor of Biological Science
The Florida State University

BOLIVIA

Political consolidation and moderate economic progress characterized Bolivia in 1972 as the military government of Gen. Hugo Banzer Suarez, which seized power in August 1971, forged a governing coalition and placed its opponents on the defensive. Legislation introduced in April enabled Banzer to form a National Popular Front, which, like the Institutionalized Revolutionary Party in Mexico, appeared aimed at channeling political participation through officially designated structures.

The president invited supporters to join the cabinet, awarding portfolios to the National Revolutionary Movement of Victor Paz Estenssoro, the right-wing Bolivian Socialist Falange and representatives of business and the armed forces. Prospects for the government brightened as Banzer rotated commands, purged dissidents and promoted allies to gain broad support within the army.

Although the most firmly entrenched chief executive since Rene Barrientos, Banzer still met opposition from disgruntled union members, students, guerrillas, supporters of former president Torres and leaders of the Roman Catholic Church. The Church's opposition diminished somewhat when nuns were discovered sheltering militants of the National Liberation Army, the nation's principal guerrilla force, which the government subsequently claimed to have infiltrated and destroyed.

Political stability appeared to favor economic growth in this Andean nation of 5,300,000 persons. During 1972 the economy expanded even more than in 1971, when national income rose 3.8 percent and per capita income increased 1.2 percent. A new industrial investment law, promulgated in December 1971, offered tax incentives to foreign investors entering joint ventures with Bolivian entrepreneurs, while the state petroleum corporation contracted with private companies to undertake explorations to bolster Bolivia's dwindling oil reserves.

In addition, a new tin smelter opened near Oruro; the Soviet Union granted a loan to construct a tin-ore volatilization plant in Potosi; and a gas pipeline linking Santa Cruz and Yacuiba was opened after a two year delay.

Austerity measures, including a 66.6 percent devaluation of the peso, brought massive opposition from workers in November. However, the government restored order by imposing a state of siege.

GEORGE W. GRAYSON
Associate Professor of Government
College of William and Mary

An Indian family mines the incredibly rich soil near Potosi on a small scale for traces of silver, tin, or semi-precious stones.

Keystone

The traditional customs of the Indians who inhabit Brazil's Mato Grosso region face imminent extinction as the government presses for a sweeping development of the Amazonian interior which will permanently disrupt the Indians' ties to their native lands.

BRAZIL

In 1972, Brazil celebrated the eighth anniversary of the 1964 revolution. The army continued to run the country, and politics were virtually taboo. Some politicians, such as former President João Goulart, remained in exile, but most, like Juscelino Kubitschek, the last president to complete his term (1956–61), simply devoted themselves to business activities, even though they had been stripped officially of their political rights.

Nominally, President Emilio Garrastazu Medici ruled through the government party, the National Renovating Alliance (ARENA), but the party was little more than a rubber stamp. It protested mildly when the military government began to talk about agrarian reform in the states of Rio de Janeiro and São Paulo. Hitherto, agrarian reform had been confined to the Northeast. The government forbade any discussion of its activities and even moved against the famous conservative newspaper *O Estado de São Paulo*.

The President made it clear that he rejected suggestions that the dictatorship should begin to restore constitutional order. Even discussions of who would succeed Medici in 1974 were forbidden. He began issuing decrees, allegedly relating only to national security, of which the titles alone were published. When the official opposition party, the Brazilian Democratic Movement (MDB), protested, the government warned that the party was permitted to exist only on sufferance.

As leftist violence was brought under control, the right-wing "death squad," which had taken the law into its own hands, faded away. The junta's suppression of terrorism was appreciated generally, but the opposition remained, albeit muted. Liberal churchmen defied the government. Eleven members of the West German Bundestag (parliament) unsuccessfully proposed the name of Dom Helder Camara, archbishop of Recife, for the Nobel Peace Prize for his opposition to the dictatorship. The National Conference of Bishops charged that torture and illegal arrests were continuing.

There also were serious charges against the regime for its neglect of social services. Real government spending on public health has declined in the last four years. Brazil still has the highest tuberculosis rate in the Western Hemisphere, the Northeast being especially affected. Economists claimed that the real income of the poorer half of the population had not changed since 1960, while that of the top 10 percent had increased by 61 percent. The government continued to defend itself against accusations that the Indians were being attacked by settlers; the Indian population was estimated to be 130,000.

Brazil is always thought of as a coffee country, but its economy is being diversified, not only by the growth of industry but also by the increased production of sugar, which in 1972 totaled slightly more than 5,000,000 tons —second in Latin America to Cuba's 8,000,000 tons. Brazil even sold 180,000 tons of sugar to China, to the dismay of Cuba. The Soviet Union, which refrains from criticizing the Brazilian dictatorship because it would like to make a deal with it, reportedly bought $32,-000,000 worth of Brazilian sugar at higher than market prices.

The Northeast has been the most impoverished area of Brazil and the center of serious unrest. Thanks to tax incentives, the superintendency of the Northeast has stimulated a remarkable growth of industry in cities like Recife. The "land statute" of 1964 laid down the principles for agrarian reform in the Northeast; in 1972, at long last, the administration responsible for such reform began to implement it in the states of Pernambuco, Paraiba and Ceara.

The building of the 3,500-mile Trans-Amazon highway continued, and the National Colonization and Agrarian Reform Institute (INCRA) initiated a gigantic homesteading program to settle Amazonia. The construction of a new supersonic airport began at Manaus.

While the military regime vigorously suppressed student unrest, it encouraged technical and elementary education. A literacy program known as MOBRAL aims at the virtual elimination of illiteracy by 1980.

Brazil followed the example of most of the Spanish-American countries and claimed sovereignty over a 200-mile-wide band of territorial waters. But unlike Ecuador, which has had a running argument with the United States over fishing vessels, Brazil signed an agreement which permitted fishing (especially shrimp) by U.S. ships without implying U.S. recognition of the Brazilian claims.

Brazil declared its role as a world power and made manifest its dislike of being labeled a Latin-American country. It celebrated the 150th anniversary of its independence, and its close relations with Portugal, the mother country from which it separated without war, were stressed. President Americo Thomaz of Portugal accompanied to Brazil the remains of Emperor Pedro I, who had proclaimed Brazilian independence—a sesquicentennial gift from the Portuguese government. They were carried solemnly through the major Brazilian cities and then interred in the independence monument in São Paulo. Brazil also recalled its historic ties with black Africa, and, as Portugal and Brazil had adopted virtually common citizenship, the triangle Portugal-Angola-Brazil established a kind of South-Atlantic alliance.

During most of the year relations between Brazil and Argentina were tense. Argentina resented the development of a Brazilian hegemony over South America, and the two countries feuded over Brazil's right to build a series of dams on the upper Parana River. Finally, however, they reached an agreement by which Brazil would go ahead with the building of the world's largest dam, 50 percent bigger than Egypt's Aswan High Dam. Argentina's chaotic situation was viewed with apprehension in Brazil, as was the revolutionary turmoil in Chile, where Brazilian revolutionaries have found a refuge. Paradoxically, Brazilian tourists flooded Argentina, attracted by the favorable exchange rate resulting from the weakness of the Argentine peso.

The fate of South America was largely in Brazilian hands. The "Peruvian model" was closely studied in Brazil; the Peruvian army, traditionally allied with conservatives and big business, had followed the example of the late Gamal Abdel Nasser of Egypt and was using its power to impose social reforms which the conservatives denounced as leading to communism.

RONALD HILTON
Executive Director
California Institute of International Studies

The projected 3,500-mi. Trans-Amazon highway will cut a deep swath through Brazil's interior.

Charles Trainor, Rapho Guillumette

BRIDGE

The highlight of 1972 in bridge competition was the reemergence of the famed Italian Blue Team at the Fourth World Bridge Team Olympiad, played in Miami Beach in June. The team came out of retirement to defend the title it had won in the Third Olympiad in Deauville, France, in 1968. As expected, its most serious challenge was posed by the U.S. team, the reigning world champion Aces.

Both teams qualified for the Olympiad final with consummate ease—the Blue Team by beating France and the Aces by defeating Canada in the semifinals. In the finals, Italy took the lead from the start and, despite a brief rally by the United States in the later stages of the contest, went on to win convincingly.

An international ranking system was adopted by the World Bridge Federation for the first time in 1972. There are three ranking categories: grand master, world master and international master. Italian Blue Team stars Giorgio Belladonna and Pietro Forquet topped the rankings, but the United States had more ranked players than any other country.

Evidence of growing interest in bridge was provided by a record booking of 365 passengers on a Travel With Goren Caribbean Bridge Cruise.

Winners of 1972 U.S. national championships were as follows:

Spingold Teams: B. Jay Becker, Michael Becker, Andrew Bernstein and Jeff Rubens.

Vanderbilt Teams: Steve Altman, Gene Neiger, Tom Smith, Alan Sontag, Joel Stuart and Peter Weichsel.

Blue Ribbon Pairs: Warren Kornfeld and Richard Khautin.

Life Masters Pairs: Alvin Roth and Barbara Rappaport.

Life Masters Men's Pairs: Marc Jacobus and Les Bart.

Life Masters Women's Pairs: Rhoda Walsh and Amalya Kearse.

Mixed Teams: William and Marietta Passell, Michael and Gail Moss.

Reisinger Teams: Steve Goldberg, Steve Robinson, Steve Parker and Lou Bluhm.

CHARLES H. GOREN
Bridge Authority

BULGARIA

Of major significance in 1972 was the sharp about-face in Bulgaria's traditionally hostile relations with Yugoslavia. Steady improvement, probably reflecting the desire of the Soviet Union to better its own relations with the Yugoslavs, has been evident since the visit of Soviet leader Leonid Brezhnev to Belgrade in September 1971.

Bulgaria and Yugoslavia agreed to strengthen their collaboration on health questions and to simplify the formalities and conditions governing reciprocal visits by their nationals living near the common border. Anti-Macedonian and anti-Yugoslav polemics largely disappeared from the Bulgarian mass media, and there was renewed talk of a summit meeting between Bulgarian Communist party leader Todor Zhivkov and Yugoslav President Tito to focus on the crucial Macedonian questions.

In contrast to the regime's eased handling of foreign affairs was its apparent determination to tighten domestic ideological conformity. In July the party central committee held a special conference to sharpen the ideological struggle against bourgeois-imperialist anticommunism and all deviations from true Marxism-Leninism, whether Western or Eastern. In an attempt to gain greater control over culture, especially

Eastfoto

Tano Tzolov (r), vice-president of the council of ministers of Bulgaria, and his North Vietnamese counterpart Lai Than Ngui signed a treaty under which Bulgaria granted North Vietnam increased economic assistance.

literature, the party also took steps to subordinate the relatively independent Bulgarian Writers' Union to its own Committee on Art and Culture, removing the union's president, Georgi Dzhagorov, and reshuffling its ruling personnel.

In March the Seventh Congress of Bulgarian Trade Unions called for continued emphasis on labor discipline and "socialist competition." In the field of education, the Council of Ministers again threatened to take drastic steps to stem the chronic shortage of teachers in the country, particularly in "undesirable areas." As part of the long-term overhaul of the Bulgarian educational system begun in 1968, the council also approved a new, comparatively flexible model for secondary education and advanced professional training.

JOSEPH F. ZACEK
Professor of History
State University of New York, Albany

BURMA
Progress in moving Burma from rule by a military junta to a more representative form of government highlighted developments in that Southeast Asian country in 1972. The government of Gen. Ne Win began the long process of shedding its military cloak by scrapping the old administrative system and drafting a new constitution. At the same time, Ne Win discharged himself and several other ranking Burmese leaders from the army in order to give the government a more civilian look. He also adopted the title prime minister, replacing that of chairman of the revolutionary council.

The new constitution was by far the year's most important development, for when it is sanctioned by an elected People's Congress of more than 600 members in March 1974, it will spell the end of a rule by military fiat that has existed since 1962. The draft of the new constitution calls for creation of a "Socialist Republic of the Union of Burma" in which there will be one-party rule (that of Ne Win's Burma Socialist Program party) and a popularly-elected unicameral People's Congress. Moreover, the instrument provides that all major means of production will be nationalized or turned into cooperatives.

In 1972, Burma's fragile economy was plagued by shortages of rice and cooking oil, the country's two most important commodities, which spawned a new round of inflation. Rice prices rose more than 150 percent, and the cost of cooking oil soared more than 325 percent. Hopes for some economic advance from successful offshore oil exploration received a set-back, at least temporarily, when a rig exploded and collapsed.

The country's economic troubles were reflected in a $76,800,000 deficit expected in the fiscal 1972–73 budget (despite foreign loans of nearly $100,000,000), a substantial increase over the $57,600,000 deficit of the previous fiscal year. The only bright spots in the economic forecast were good prospects for future oil and mineral development and continued foreign assistance.

ARTHUR C. MILLER
Senior Editor, *The Asia Letter*

CAMPAIGN SPENDING
While U.S. candidates and parties were spending record amounts—about $400,000,000—on political activity at all levels in 1972, political finance, or the ways in which money is raised and spent for the nomination and election of individual candidates as well as for the year-round maintenance of party organizations, emerged as an issue of consequence. The issue arose partly in response to new Federal legislation regulating political finance, partly as a result of the manner in which money was raised, handled and spent, and partly because of the efforts of the media and citizens' organizations to monitor campaign funding.

The record $400,000,000 in spending represented a 33 percent increase over the $300,-000,000 spent in 1968, and was almost triple the $140,000,000 spent 20 years earlier, in 1952. Roughly equal amounts, about $100,-000,000, were spent in four areas: (1) to elect a President, including prenomination campaigns; (2) to nominate candidates and elect a Congress; (3) to nominate candidates and elect governors, other statewide officials and state legislators and to campaign for or against state ballot issues and constitutional amendments; and (4) to nominate candidates and elect the hundreds of thousands of county and local public officials.

Of the $100,000,000 spent in the presidential nomination and election processes the largest amount—$47,000,000, an all-time high—was spent in the reelection of President Richard M. Nixon. Little more than $1,000,000 was spent by Nixon's ideological Republican prenomination challengers; on the left, Rep. Paul N. McCloskey, Jr., spent $750,000, and on the right, Rep. John M. Ashbrook spent $250,000. Numerous candidates sought the Democratic nomination for President, spending an aggregate of $20,000,000. Some Democratic candidates incurred their expenses throughout very long campaigns, dating from late 1970 for

The Other Side of the Tracks

Bruce Shanks in "Buffalo Evening News"

Sen. Edmund Muskie and from early 1971 for Sen. George McGovern. Spending ranged from the high of $7,000,000 for McGovern to a low of $135,000 for Rep. Shirley Chisholm.

The Democratic nominee, Senator McGovern, spent little more than half the amount spent by Nixon in the general election period, or $27,000,000. Nevertheless, it was a Democratic record, not matched by the costs of the Kennedy, Johnson, or Humphrey campaigns. As McGovern's campaign was funded in large measure by small contributions from 600,000 contributors, it was a financial success if an electoral failure.

About $5,000,000 in presidential campaign costs was used to cover party and delegate expenses related to the national nominating conventions, minor party costs and direct out-of-pocket costs of politically active individuals not accounted for by candidate or organizational spending.

Years of effort directed at reforming the antiquated Federal system of regulating political finance came to a sudden climax in late 1971 and early 1972 when Congress passed two measures that may prove to be pivotal. One

enactment, the Federal Election Campaign Act of 1972, had considerable impact on events and on the raising and spending of money in the 1972 campaigns. The other law, the Revenue Act of 1971, had a less-immediate impact but major long-range implications.

The Federal Election Campaign Act provides for comprehensive disclosure of political receipts and expenditures and represents a notable improvement over the corresponding provisions of its predecessor, the Federal Corrupt Practices Act. It requires candidates for nomination or election to Federal office and political committees raising or spending in excess of $1,000 on their behalf to file periodic reports disclosing all receipts and expenditures, itemizing the full name and address, occupation and principal place of business, date and amount of contribution of each person contributing in excess of $100, and including information about any lender or endorser of a loan and about any transfers of funds between committees. The appropriate Federal supervisory officer receives the reports, which he is required to make available to the public. He must also compile totals for each candidate and

for various receipt and expenditure categories. Auditing of the reports is discretionary, but all violations must be referred to law-enforcement authorities.

A major restriction in the Federal Election Campaign Act limits the amounts candidates for nomination and for election to Federal office can spend in the communications media to 10 cents per person of voting age, subject to changes in the Consumer Price Index. The limits apply separately to campaigns for nomination and campaigns for election. Communications media subject to these limits are television, radio, newspaper and magazine advertising; outdoor advertising facilities; and certain uses of telephones, such as paid telephonists and automatic telephone equipment used to communicate with voters. Not more than 60 percent of the amounts allowed for communications may be used for broadcast purposes; production costs of broadcasts or other materials employed in the communications media are not included within these limits. For a period of 45 days before a primary and 60 days before a general election, broadcasters' charges for time cannot exceed the lowest unit rate charged other advertisers for the same class and amount of time. At other times, and for newspaper advertising, charges must be levied at the same rates as those levied for comparable use by other customers.

The Federal Election Campaign Act has other provisions, including amendments to existing prohibitions on corporate, labor union and government contractor contributions, and limitations on the amounts candidates and their immediate families can contribute to or spend on their own campaigns.

The Federal Election Campaign Act was instrumental in producing certain revelations about the financing of American politics. First, in line with the spirit of the new law which was soon to take effect, certain presidential candidates in both major parties, following the lead of Senator McGovern, voluntarily disclosed those contributors who gave $1,000 or more to their campaigns, revealing some very large contributions, some in the hundreds of thousands of dollars. Some candidates refused to make voluntary disclosures of contributors, among them President Nixon. A suit by Common Cause, the citizens' lobby, to require disclosure resulted, in part for technical and legal reasons, in a consent decree which stipulated that a partial listing of large contributors be made public. This list revealed the two largest contributions in U.S. history, one of $1,000,000 and another of $800,000; it later developed that both donors had given additional sums.

The voluntary and consent decree listings were made public because the Federal Election Campaign Act became law in mid-campaign, raising questions about financing prior to its taking effect. In the case of President Nixon's reelection campaign, the first disclosure required under the new law showed that his campaign organization had in excess of $10,000,000 in cash on hand when the law became effective on April 7, 1972. This large unaccounted-for fund triggered the Common Cause suit and became a campaign issue. Moreover, this particular fund was implicated in a dubious undertaking when an investigation of wiretapping and illegal entry at the Washington headquarters of the Democratic National Committee revealed that money found on an agent entering the headquarters had previously been contributed, in a manner possibly in violation of the new law, to the Nixon reelection campaign. The subject of political finance became an issue because these and related events focused attention on the question at the same time that public organizations, particularly Common Cause, undertook programs to monitor the operation of the new law.

The Revenue Act of 1971 provides for tax credits or deductions for political contributions, effective for the first time in 1972. The purpose of this provision is to encourage more donations by small contributors by granting limited tax incentives for political contributions, thus in effect bringing the Federal government to share some of the costs of political activity. The act also provides for a tax checkoff, effective in 1973, whereby taxpayers can direct that $1 of the tax paid on a single return or $2 on a joint return be placed in a fund for distribution to nominated candidates for President who want the funds, who meet requirements of sufficient popular support and who agree not to raise funds privately. The long-range implications of this provision are that the Federal government is assuming direct responsibility for the campaigns of certain candidates for the Presidency by subsidizing the general election campaign.

The high cost of political activity in 1972 and the public disillusionment with certain aspects of private financing are certain to prompt many legislative proposals for extending government subsidy programs to prenomination campaigns and to candidates for other Federal offices. Undoubtedly many legislative proposals designed to modify the Federal Election Campaign Act, based on the experience in its first year of operation, will be submitted.

HERBERT E. ALEXANDER
Director, Citizens' Research Foundation

CANADA

Canadians were in a critical and conservative but indecisive mood in their election on Oct. 30, 1972. They voted to end more than four years of majority government under Prime Minister Pierre Trudeau but failed to give any of the four parties a clear majority in the 264-seat House of Commons.

When the national television networks went off the air early the next morning, Trudeau's Liberal party and the Progressive Conservative party, led by Robert Stanfield, each held 108 seats, the first dead heat between two major parties in Canadian history. Vote recounts later gave the Liberals two more seats than the Conservatives, helping to justify Prime Minister Trudeau's decision to remain in office and to lead a minority government in the new session of Parliament in January.

The result of the election caused less surprise in Canada than in other countries. Since he won his first election as Prime Minister in 1968, leading his party to 155 seats in the House of Commons, Trudeau had been more visible on the world scene than any of his predecessors, with the exception of Lester B.

Pearson, his immediate predecessor and winner of the Nobel Peace Prize. Trudeau traveled widely during the first part of his term, blazing a trail to Moscow and Peking that created new diplomatic, scientific and commercial contacts for Canada before President Richard Nixon of the United States followed the same course.

At home, his administration consolidated and expanded the progressive social programs that had been put in place during the previous decade, attempted without success to obtain the agreement of the ten Canadian provinces on a new constitution and took steps to ensure that French-speaking Canadians would participate fully in the economic and political life of the nation.

In 1968, Canadians had voted for the bilingual Trudeau as the "swinging bachelor" from Montreal who knew how to deal politically with those of his French-speaking compatriots in Quebec who want to transform that province into an independent French-language state.

By 1972, the marriage of the Prime Minister, the birth of his son and an unusually private domestic and social life in Ottawa had

A large crowd greeted Prime Minister Trudeau as he campaigned for reelection in La Tuque, Que.

Opposition leader Stanfield voted in Halifax. The former premier of Nova Scotia traveled some 50,000 miles during the campaign.

economic relations with other countries, particularly the United States.

Leaders of the three opposition parties drew attention to the failure of the government to limit unemployment and inflation in an expanding economy.

Conservative Leader Robert Stanfield, 58, a former premier of the province of Nova Scotia waging his second national campaign against Trudeau, promised "a job for Canadians" as he traveled more than 50,000 miles within all the provinces and the northern territories during September and October. His campaign was helped in the final month by government statistics showing that the seasonally adjusted unemployment rate in September had been 7.1 percent, the highest since 1961. The percentage represented more than 459,000 Canadians unemployed. In the same month, the consumer price index was 9.7 percent higher than a year earlier.

made him a less exciting public figure. Opinion polls during his term showed that he had gradually acquired a reputation for being not only remote from the concerns of Canadians but intellectually arrogant in his response to their problems.

This feeling was aggravated by the Prime Minister's decision to base his 1972 campaign on "the integrity of Canada" rather than specific issues. He assured Canadians that many of the traditional divisions between various language, ethnic and regional groups in Canada had been overcome during the previous decade. He maintained that Canadians could move confidently toward the solution of more practical problems caused by industrial and resource development and by changing

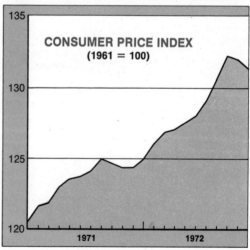

Lester Pearson, the former premier and Nobelist who died Dec. 27, was buried in Wakefield, Que.

The government contended that unemployment was caused by abnormally large increases in the Canadian labor force, the result of a high national birth rate after the Second World War and immigration during the same period. International studies of the Canadian economy tended to confirm this. In July the 23-member Organization for Economic Cooperation and Development, based in Paris, had forecast that Canada would be one of the leaders of the world's seven major industrial nations in growth in the next 12 months, exceeded only by Japan. It predicted that unemployment in Canada would decrease to 5.5 percent in 1973.

High unemployment and increases in wages and the cost of living boosted total benefits paid by the federal Unemployment Insurance program to more than $2,000,000,000 by the end of 1972. This was more than double the amount predicted by the government in the previous year, when it had increased benefits and extended coverage under the program. The plan is financed by government and employer-employee contributions, with the government's share increasing as the unemployment rate rises. The taxpayers' share of the cost in 1972 was estimated at $890,000,000.

The program was attacked during the campaign on the premise that its maximum benefit of $100 a week discouraged workers from taking low-paying jobs. Conservative leader Stanfield accused the Trudeau government of making "sort of a chicken-hearted effort to revise the work ethic," and he coined the term "chicken socialism" to describe the government's philosophy.

The campaign of the socialist New Democratic party attacked the government for favoring big business through low taxes and high incentive grants. NDP Leader David Lewis, a 63-year-old former labor lawyer in his first campaign as party leader, published tax and grant statistics on 115 corporations that he had designated as "corporate welfare bums." A majority of the corporations were foreign-owned; companies engaged in resource development and export formed the largest single group.

Despite only token support for the party in French-speaking Quebec, the NDP won 31 seats on Oct. 30 compared with 22 seats in the 1968 election.

Social Credit, a party of monetary reform led by Réal Caouette, a 54-year-old automobile dealer from northern Quebec, won 15 seats, one more than in 1968. All of the Social Credit victories were in rural or working-class Quebec ridings, where the party promised a guaranteed annual income of $1,800 for every Canadian over 18 years of age.

Secondary issues in the campaign appeared to reveal a growing spirit of conservatism in the Canadian electorate. In addition to the "welfare backlash," focused on the Unemployment Insurance program, there was an undercurrent of feeling in some parts of English-speaking Canada, particularly on the prairies and the West Coast, against pressures from

External Affairs Minister Mitchell Sharp (r) officially opened Canada's trade fair in Peking in August. The exhibit was the largest one ever held abroad by Canada.

French-speaking Canadians in recent years for greater influence in Federal decision-making. This was reflected after the election in cabinet changes that provided more important roles for a number of English-speaking cabinet ministers from Ontario.

Criticism of immigration policy also persuaded the government, after the election, to cancel a regulation that had permitted tourists to apply for landed immigrant status after their arrival in Canada. The regulation was being employed by an increasing number of tourists from the Caribbean and Asia. There was also criticism during the campaign of the government's new and relatively liberal parole system in federal prisons, as well as demands for the reintroduction of capital punishment in 1973 at the end of an experimental five-year period in which hanging has been almost completely abolished in law and, in fact, not employed.

Although domestic issues dominated the election campaign, Canadians continued to show concern in 1972 about their relations with the United States. During a 40-hour visit to Ottawa in April, President Nixon spoke to a joint sitting of the Canadian Commons and Senate, calling for a new era in U.S.–Canadian relations that spurns "sentimental rhetoric" and recognizes separate identities and significant differences between the two countries.

At the end of his visit on April 15, President Nixon signed with Prime Minister Trudeau an agreement committing both countries to a Great Lakes pollution cleanup. It will cost the United States about $2,000,000,000 and Canada $250,000,000 over a five-year period.

During the Nixon visit the Canadian–American Committee, a private organization made up of prominent businessmen and labor, agricultural and professional leaders on both sides of the border, published a report suggesting that more systematic consultations are needed between the two countries to expose differences "before they had become hardened into irrevocable positions." The proposal was made in the context of trade discussions between Ottawa and Washington that broke down early in 1972 when Canada resisted U.S. requests to reduce its favorable trade balance.

On May 2 the federal government published draft legislation to control foreign ownership of Canadian industry. The legislation emerged from cabinet discussions of a federal task force report under preparation since the spring of 1970. It would have created a screening organization to review foreign takeovers of companies in Canada with assets of more than $250,000 or gross annual revenue of more than $3,000,000. The legislation remained on the order paper at the dissolution of Parliament, but the government was committed to introducing it again, with some changes.

On May 25 the government of Ontario, Canada's most populous and productive prov-

ince, suspended the granting of performance or forgiveable loans to foreign-owned companies by the state-owned Ontario Development Corporation. About half of the $33,000,-000 in performance loans granted by the ODC since its inception in the early 1960's had gone to foreign-owned companies.

Canadian ownership of a proposed Mackenzie Valley pipeline to carry gas from the Arctic to consumers in southern Canada and the United States was advocated during the election campaign by both major parties. The New Democratic party opposed the pipeline because of its impact on the northern environment and native peoples.

Despite uncertainty about the pipeline, work started during the summer on a 1,050-mile all-weather highway from Alberta in western Canada to the Arctic Ocean. Announcing the project in Edmonton on April 28, Prime Minister Trudeau said that it will cost up to $100,000,000 and will form part of an oil-gas–highway corridor along the Mackenzie Valley.

A minor but symbolic and widely reported flare-up of nationalist sentiment was triggered when the police commission in Calgary, Alberta, hired Chief Charles R. Gain of Oakland, Calif., to head Calgary's 700-man force. On Aug. 8, eight days after the controversial appointment, Gain withdrew his application for the post "because of the intense nationalistic feeling he has experienced," according to Calgary police commission chairman J. E. Prothroe.

Earlier visits by Prime Minister Trudeau to the U.S.S.R. and China were followed in 1972 by an agreement for cultural and scientific exchanges signed by Canada and the Soviet Union on July 6 and a visit to China by External Affairs Minister Mitchell Sharp to open a Canadian trade fair in Peking in August. More than 500 representatives of 200 companies participated in the trade fair, which was the largest exhibit Canada had ever staged abroad.

Two weeks later, China's Minister of Foreign Trade Pai Hsiang-kuo opened a Chinese exhibit at the Canadian National Exhibition in Toronto. Pai later visited Gravenhurst, Ontario, birthplace of Dr. Norman Bethune, a surgeon who died in 1939 while serving with the Chinese liberation forces. Little known in Canada until recently, Bethune is a national hero in China. He was officially declared to be "a Canadian of national historic significance" by the Canadian government when Pai visited his birthplace on Aug. 17.

Canada and China concluded a civil air agreement on Oct. 13. Direct flights between

An official of the Montreal Museum of Fine Arts showed newsmen photos of 18 paintings stolen Sept. 4 by three knowledgeable art thieves.

the two countries were expected to begin in 1973.

Although more than 70 percent of Canada's international trade is with the United States, there was concern in 1972 about the economic effects in Canada of Britain's entry into the European Economic Community on Jan. 1, 1973. More than half of Canada's $1,300,000,-000 annual export trade with Britain benefited in 1972 from preferential tariffs for Commonwealth countries that will disappear during the next five years. Prime Minister Trudeau made his only overseas trip of the year on Dec. 2 when he flew to London to receive assurances from Prime Minister Edward Heath that Britain will favor "outward-looking" trade policies as a member of the European Community.

Trudeau also announced in London that Queen Elizabeth will visit Canada in 1973. She is expected to attend the first conference of Commonwealth heads of government to be held in Ottawa.

Britain's entry into the EEC reminded Canadians that half of their exports outside North America now go to the European Community but that their share of this market has not kept pace in recent years with total EEC imports. Discussions in Ottawa and at EEC headquarters in Brussels during the year explored the possibility of a bilateral trade agreement between Canada and the EEC.

Long-term European interest in Canadian resources was illustrated by reports in September of talks between Canadian and West German concerns about development of iron ore deposits at Mary River on the north coast of Baffin Island in the Eastern Canadian Arctic. A subsidiary of the Krupp steel interests was reported to be studying the construction of heavy icebreaking freighters capable of moving the ore from Baffin Island to Germany on a year-round schedule.

Canada's traditional enthusiasm for ice hockey, considered by most Canadians to be the national game, reached unprecedented heights in September during an eight-game series between an all-star team from the Soviet Union and Canadian stars of the National Hockey League. It was the first time that a team of Canadian professional hockey players had faced a Russian team.

Despite demands from many Canadians, led by Prime Minister Trudeau, that Team Canada should also include players from the rival World Hockey Association, the National Hockey League refused to allow Bobby Hull, Derek Sanderson and other WHA players to participate in the series.

After losing two of their four games in Canada, and tying a third, the Canadians achieved a one-game margin in the series by winning their final three games in Moscow. By scoring three consecutive game-winning goals in Moscow, Paul Henderson of the Toronto Maple Leafs was Canada's 1972 sports hero.

Other significant events in 1972 included the following:

All-star hockey teams from Canada and the U.S.S.R. met for the first time in September. The Canadians captured the eight-game series.

The Canadian Radio-Television Commission gave permission on July 21 to Global Communications Ltd. of Toronto to create a six-station television network in Ontario. It could become the nucleus of a third national network, alongside the state-owned and privately owned networks now in operation. The new network will help overcome the influence in Canada of U.S. television networks, which, according to CRTC Chairman Pierre Juneau, operate in the rich Ontario industrial heartland "as if they were licensed." Canadian advertisers, for example, purchase about $15,-000,000 worth of television time annually from stations in Buffalo, N.Y., which are capable of reaching large audiences in Toronto. Global was given permission to establish the new network partly on the basis of a commitment to spend at least $8,000,000 a year on Canadian programming.

After 20 years in office the Social Credit government of 71-year-old Premier W. A. C. Bennett in British Columbia was defeated on Aug. 30, exactly one year after the defeat of a Social Credit government in the neighboring province of Alberta. The monetary-reform party had taken root in Canada during the Great Depression of the 1930's. Bennett was defeated in British Columbia by a 41-year-old social worker, David Barrett, at the head of the socialist New Democratic party. The NDP won 38 of the 55 seats in British Columbia's legislature. During the campaign, Bennett warned voters about the economic intentions of "the socialist hordes at the gates" of the province, but the NDP campaigned successfully on promises of better employment opportunities, high old-age pensions and a pragmatic policy on nationalization of private business.

Montreal's Mayor Jean Drapeau unveiled plans on April 6 for a 50,000-seat stadium for the 1976 Olympic Games to be held in the city. During the year there was increasing local opposition to the games from Montrealers concerned about the city's ability to finance them. Mayor Drapeau, who was mainly responsible for bringing the successful Expo 67 world's fair to Montreal in 1967, rejected a request by citizens' associations for a local referendum on the games.

The mightiest single-site hydroelectric power development in the non-Communist world was opened on June 16 in central Labrador by Prime Minister Trudeau. The $950,000,000 project at Churchill Falls will produce about 34,500,000,000 kilowatt hours a year, equivalent to more than 11 percent of Canada's forecast 1976 electrical energy requirement.

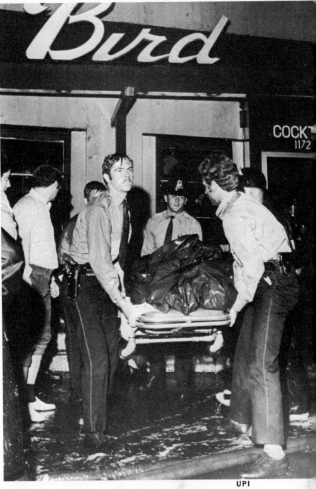

UPI

Thirty-seven persons were killed and more than 50 were injured in the fire-bombing of a nightclub in Montreal, Sept. 1.

Emergency legislation passed by the Quebec legislature on April 21 ended an 11-day public service strike of 200,000 teachers, civil servants and workers in public utilities in that province. At the end of the year the three principal leaders of the strike were appealing one-year jail sentences for contempt of court as a result of their actions during the strike.

On March 30, aboard the destroyer *HMCS Kootenay* anchored at Halifax, Rear Admiral R. W. Timbrell gave the order to "splice the main brace" and shots of two and a half ounces of dark rum, the traditional daily naval ration, were drawn for the last time. Facilities for the sale of wine, spirits and beer aboard vessels replaced the old custom.

PETER DESBARATS
Ottawa Editor, *The Toronto Star*

"Sculpture of the Inuit," a major exhibition of Eskimo art at the Vancouver Art Gallery (above) included "Howling Spirit and its Young" (left).

Painting and Sculpture. As a show stopper, nothing in the year's events rivaled the Sept. 4 robbery, by three armed bandits, of the museum in Montreal. The loot, valued at $2,000,-000, included a Rembrandt oil landscape worth $1,000,000 and noted canvases by Courbet, Daumier and Gainsborough. Also included were 40 pieces of 17th, 18th and 19th century jewelry.

Speculation as to motive was rife inasmuch as no dealer or gallery would try to handle such well known works and museums have maintained a policy of not paying ransoms. An international search was launched.

Less spectacular but as exceptional in its way was the traveling show of stone and whalebone carvings by Canadian Eskimos. In a standard, ski-equipped air freighter, its interior transformed into a 32-foot long art gallery with draperies, carpet and fluorescent lighting, a collection of 80 prize-winning carvings visited 18 remote settlements. The exhibition was the first of any kind in the Canadian Arctic and truly a gala occasion for the resident Eskimos, civil servants, construction workers, and Royal Canadian Mounted Police who saw it. Meanwhile, a 400-piece masterworks exhibition of Canadian Eskimo work, "Sculpture of the Inuit," which opened in Vancouver in 1971, toured Paris, Copenhagen, Leningrad and London to critical acclaim.

The National Gallery of Canada in Ottawa mounted a major and unique exhibition in the summer titled "Art and the Courts . . .

CANADA: Cultural Affairs

A multimillion-dollar heist from the collection of the Montreal Museum of Fine Arts and the tour of an airborne sculpture gallery designed to acquaint Eskimo audiences with Eskimo art were noteworthy events in a generally unexciting cultural year in Canada. Although substantial achievement marked the work of Canadian artists and performers in 1972, it generated on the whole less enthusiasm than usual —probably owing to a national gloom that fed daily on front page reports of unemployment, inflation and bad luck. Paradoxically, the Canadian economy had already emerged robustly from recession, and patronage of the arts flourished. But the spirited support of the young in particular, so apparent in 1971, had mysteriously disappeared.

in confilio impiorum: & in uia pcc
catorum non ftetit: & in cathedra pe
ftilentie non fedit.
Sed in lege domini uoluntas eius:
& in lege eius meditabit dic ac noctc.
Et erit tanquam lignum qd plan
tatum eft fecus decurfus aquarum:

A superb illuminated manuscript page, M-102, Folio 2, from the Windmill Psalter.

Gilded marble statue of the Virgin by a 14th century French master.

Cantor's staff from Limoges Cathedral by a 13th century French goldsmith.

ART AND THE COURTS

A cultural event of international importance in Canada in 1972 was the National Gallery of Canada's exhibition "Art and the Courts . . . France and England . . . 1259–1328." Drawn from collections in Europe and America, it received world-wide notice.

Celebrating its 20th anniversary with a production of "La Sylphide," among others, the National Ballet Company made a European tour.

France and England . . . 1259–1328." It contained 105 precious items borrowed from world-famous collections—among them, gold and silver chalices, illuminated manuscripts, enameled cases, embroidered robes and purses, stained-glass pieces, ivory chessmen and small sculptures of alabaster. The show attracted art scholars from numerous institutions overseas, but the ordinary public, including thousands of routine visitors to the national capital, also was appreciative.

Dance. A worldwide surge of public interest in dance as popular entertainment was reflected in Canadian enthusiasm, and financial support, for the country's ballet companies. The Royal Winnipeg Ballet, Canada's oldest and most traveled company, took its lively repertoire to Australia and New Zealand for ten weeks. Toronto's National Ballet Company observed its 20th anniversary year with a European tour, its first—35 performances in seven countries in eight weeks. In September the company undertook a Sol Hurok tour of North American cities with Rudolf Nureyev as guest star.

Les Feux Follets, a French-Canadian folk dance group which had delighted audiences in many countries for two decades, seemed on the verge of bankruptcy and oblivion in the spring. Canadians rejoiced when the company was later "reborn" as a basic element of the permanent Charlottetown (P.E.I.) Festival Centre. In mid-August, *Les Grands Ballets Canadiens* put "Tommy" to rest, reluctantly. The rock ballet which had played 220 exciting performances during two years, including three visits to Broadway, was a genuine money maker; but the Montreal-based company preferred to return to its normal programming.

Music. Every year seems to be a good music year in Canada; traditionally the emphasis has been on conservative and proven forms and styles. In June 1972, however, the officially styled "Maple Leaf Music Junket" let itself go. The Junket was a $100,000 commercial promotion, underwritten jointly by the Canadian music industry and the federal government, which brought 100 music-journalists from 14 European countries for a four-day visit to Montreal. The aim of the exercise was to promote European interest in Canadian perform-

Extraordinary success attended the National Arts Centre Orchestra, directed by Mario Bernardi.

ers and Canadian music. Concerts, rock sessions, lectures, workshops, seminars, tours, personal appearances and lots of cocktail parties made it a strenuous work-fun session for everyone concerned; and everyone seemed to believe it was worthwhile.

The major Canadian orchestras prospered financially and artistically in 1972. The extraordinary rise of the fledgling National Arts Centre Orchestra (Ottawa) to front-rank status was a matter of importance. The 44-piece ensemble enjoyed what must be termed brilliant success with its home audience and in other Canadian and U.S. cities. Its New York debut in Alice Tully Hall in February, an event nervously anticipated, was carried out with éclat.

The old, established Toronto Symphony Orchestra, a major group by any measurement, added extra punch to its 1972 season with a May-June "Brahms Festival and Bash," featuring Maureen Forrester, Isaac Stern and John Browning in solo performances. The Winnipeg Symphony celebrated its 25th anniversary with a fine season, and in October it enjoyed the honor of opening the Chester Fritz Concert Hall at the University of North Dakota.

Early in 1972, at the end of an everything-went-wrong season, Montreal's symphony orchestra had accumulated a $300,000 deficit. Six months later its new season was an 80 percent subscription sellout, and the year ended in artistic and financial success. The Western Canada symphonies all had good seasons; they were helped by generous financial support from federal and provincial governments, the pull of big-name guest artists and excellent receipts at the box offices.

The second annual Montreal International Music Competition, devoted in 1972 to a violin competition, heard 25 brilliant young virtuosi from 12 countries. The $10,000 first prize went to Ruban Agaronian of the U.S.S.R., while second and third place awards went to competitors from the U.S.S.R. and France. Another item that caught the fancy of the wire services, and thus of the whole country, was a trip by Indian war-canoe of 35 members of the Ontario Youth Orchestra to perform for the 700 residents of Moose Factory, a community at the south end of Hudson Bay.

During 1972 opera also enjoyed strong public support. The Toronto-based Canadian Opera Company sold 11,000 subscriptions for its September-October home season—a substantial increase over the 1971 record figure. Many Canadians, and visitors, were delighted by the renewed interest in opera shown by the Stratford Festival's spirited production of Brecht's *Threepenny Opera*.

Literature. The Canadian literary scene, in upheaval in recent years, was surprisingly quiet and correct in 1972. The Governor General's Awards (see also Prizes and Awards), to six books out of 300 nominated, were distributed without protest parades, sit-ins, threats of libel suits or charges of pornography and treason.

The Canadian book publishing industry, which had complained bitterly for many years about "unfair competition from south of the border," received a big uplift in February when the federal government announced the award of $2,000,000 in new subsidies to encourage domestic publishers. The provincial governments of Ontario and Quebec also substantially increased their assistance to textbook and nonfiction publishers. North America's first international book fair, held in Quebec City in May, exhibited more than 70,000 titles in

In its 20th season the Stratford Festival branched out from Shakespeare into Musset, Goldsmith and the Brecht-Weill "Threepenny Opera."

Stratford Festival, Stratford, Ontario

Lorenzo Michaud

North America's first international book fair drew thousands of foreign visitors to Quebec.

French, English, German and Spanish and drew thousands of visitors.

Theater. Substantial government support was a major factor in making 1972 a successful year for theater production in Canada. The Canada Council granted $435,000 to the Stratford Festival, $430,000 to the National Theatre School, $225,000 to *Le Théâtre du nouveau monde,* $209,000 to Toronto's St. Lawrence Centre Theatre and $205,000 to the Holiday Theatre in Vancouver. Virtually every smaller professional theater group benefited from the Council's largess. A new federal government grant program (Local Initiatives Projects) and special grants from the federal cultural affairs branch added to the psychological well-being of the theater people.

The Stratford Festival Theatre, directed by Quebec's Jean Gascon, observed its 20th anniversary with well attended productions of *King Lear, As You Like It,* Goldsmith's *She Stoops to Conquer* and Musset's *Lorenzaccio.* Ottawa's National Arts Centre Theatre presented its repertory in both English, to a 97

percent box office, and French, to a 94 percent box office.

In June an exciting international conference on children's theater was held in Montreal. Delegates from many countries and demonstration companies from Moscow, Bucharest, Warsaw and London attended.

Personalities. Among several appointments to key posts in Canadian cultural institutions in 1972, the most noteworthy was that of André Fortier, 44-year-old career public servant, to the prestigious post of director of the Canada Council. Maureen Forrester was named president of *Jeunesses Musicales du Canada.* Gerry Aldred moved from the director's job at Manitoba Theatre Centre to become general manager of Toronto's National Ballet Company.

A new appointee as president of the Canadian Broadcasting Corporation was Laurent Picard; he succeeded George Davidson, who moved to the United Nations secretariat in New York. Two other assignments to the United States involved Leopold Simoneau, who exchanged the directorship of the Quebec Opera for that of the San Francisco Conservatory of Music, and Mario Amaya, who left the curatorship of the Art Gallery of Ontario to join the New York Cultural Center.

Canada's highest civilian honor, membership of the official Order of Canada, was accorded in 1972 to a number of eminent arts people, including Mario Bernardi (conductor), Marie-Claire Blais (novelist), Oscar Peterson (jazz pianist), Robert Lapalme (cartoonist) and Jack Shadbolt (painter).

WALTER B. HERBERT
Consultant on Canadian Cultural Matters

André Fortier assumed direction of the Canada Council, overseer of Canadian cultural affairs.

The Canada Council

CANADA: Provinces and Territories

ALBERTA

Proceedings in the provincial legislature were televised live for the first time March 15. Members took advantage of the free publicity by questioning cabinet officers with unprecedented thoroughness. ● The completion of a $30,000,000 federal arrangement to rehabilitate southern Alberta's irrigation works was announced July 7. ● Alberta became the first province to sign an agreement to enter the federal small farms development program. ● The federal government turned down plans to develop a $30,000,000 resort in the Banff National Park. The provincial government had previously declined to support the project.

BRITISH COLUMBIA

U.S. billionaire recluse Howard R. Hughes took up residence in a Vancouver hotel March 14. ● Some $500,000,000 worth of construction came to a halt April 28, when 840 contractors locked out 30,000 members of 18 building unions. ● The provincial supreme court upheld the 1971 legislation banning advertisement of liquor and tobacco in the province. ● Thirty-one Vancouver policemen were injured June 3, as they tried to contain a mob of 2,500 rock-hurling youths attempting to crash a concert by the Rolling Stones. ● The 20-year tenure as provincial premier of W. A. C. Bennett was ended when his Social Credit party went down to a crushing defeat in Aug. 30 elections. Bennett himself won reelection as a legislator, but later resigned. Most of his cabinet members were defeated. David Barrett, leader of the New Democratic party, became the new premier.

MANITOBA

Manitoba's first winery was officially opened at Gimli March 3. ● The provincial legislature July 20 rejected a proposal by Premier Edward Schreyer that a special commission to study grants of financial aid to private and parochial schools be established. The same day the legislature approved a new provincial labor code, under which policemen and employees of government corporations are granted the right to strike. The code also facilitates the formation of labor unions and provides for a compulsory withholding of dues. The new law, held to be the most progressive labor code in Canada, became effective Jan. 1, 1973.

NEW BRUNSWICK

Premier Richard Hatfield disclosed Jan. 13 that $10,000,000 would be spent to create some 3,000 temporary jobs in the northeastern part of the province, adversely affected by shrinkage of forest and mining industries. ● A conference of French-speaking New Brunswickers May 20–22 voted to establish a new francophone association and made demands for extended French-language services in the province. Nearly 40 percent of the provincial population is French-speaking.

NEWFOUNDLAND

Liberal Joseph Smallwood, premier since 1949, stepped down Jan. 18, following a court ruling that gave a pivotal seat in the legislature to the Progressive Conservative party. Frank Moores was sworn in as the new premier the same day. On Feb. 5, Edward M. Roberts was elected leader of the opposition Liberal party, succeeding Smallwood. New elections March 24 gave

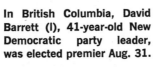

In British Columbia, David Barrett (l), 41-year-old New Democratic party leader, was elected premier Aug. 31.

In Newfoundland, Edward M. Robert (r), 31-year-old former provincial health minister, became leader of opposition Liberal party.

A ski-equipped air freighter, transformed into an art gallery, visited remote settlements in 1972.

the Progressive Conservative party 33 out of 42 seats in the legislature. ● Prime Minister Trudeau June 16 inaugurated a $950,000,000 hydroelectric project at Churchill Falls. Scheduled for completion in 1975, it will have a capacity of 5,225,000 kw.

NORTHWEST TERRITORIES

The establishment of two new national parks, the Baffin Island (8,200 sq. mi.) and the South Nahanni (1,840 sq. mi.), was announced Feb. 22. ● An oil strike on Ellesmere Island, 700 mi. from the North Pole, was disclosed Feb. 24; the commercial value of the find was not immediately determined. ● About 50 infants were affected—three of them fatally—by a respiratory disease in Igloolik and Cape Dorset. The Frobisher Bay hospital was converted into a children's ward to cope with the epidemic. ● The Eskimo Brotherhood *Inuit Tapirisat* held its first annual conference at Pangnirtung, Baffin Island, Aug. 17–27. The meeting was attended by 60 delegates from 34 communities.

NOVA SCOTIA

The provincial legislature ended its session—the longest since 1914—on May 15, having approved some 130 bills. Opposition Leader John Buchanan (Progressive Conservative) nevertheless termed the session the "most nonproductive" in recent years. ● Nurses at St. Rita Hospital, Sydney, struck June 15 for parity in job classification. The strike, Canada's first by nurses, ended July 14. Patients of the hospital had been either transferred or released.

ONTARIO

Premier William G. Davis reorganized the provincial government, reducing the number of ministries from 24 to 21. ● Canada's first commercial power plant fueled by a nuclear reactor was dedicated Feb. 25 at Pickering. ● Dissident students occupied Simco Hall of the University of Toronto March 10–13, demanding that freshmen and the general public be allowed use of a new research library, scheduled to open in 1973. ● A bomb explosion in Toronto March

Nurses from St. Rita Hospital in Sydney, N.S., join the picket lines during their month-long summer strike.

The control room of Canada's first commercial nuclear generating station in Pickering, Ont.

18 killed two persons and destroyed a supermarket and a travel agency. ● Darcy Mc-Keough, provincial minister of finance, resigned Aug. 31, after disclosure that he had approved land subdivision by a development company in which he had financial interest. A code of rules governing the financial holdings of cabinet members was subsequently published. ● David Crombie was elected mayor of Ottawa.

PRINCE EDWARD ISLAND

A total of $826,000 was allotted by the federal government for public works in the province during 1972. ● The legislature adjourned April 14, having passed some 65 bills, including the Succession Duties Act, which gave the province authority to collect inheritance taxes retroactively to Jan. 1, 1972. ● The provincial government ruled that any proposed sale of more than 10 acres, or 330 ft., of shoreline to a nonresident must be approved by the cabinet. The regulation was intended to check the alarming rate at which nonresidents—U.S. nationals in particular—have been buying up shoreline property and other potential recreational land.

QUEBEC

A massive power failure, the fourth in less than a year, blacked out most of the province March 2. ● Two plastic bombs wrecked the Cuban Trade Commission offices in Montreal April 2, killing a Cuban security guard. ● A general strike by public service workers began April 11, after the provincial government refused to negotiate their wage demands. The strike ended April 22, a day after the legislature passed a tough emergency law. When three union officials drew one-year prison terms for defiance of the law, walkouts and wildcat strikes followed, resulting in violence. Talks on labor's

demands resumed June 6. The provincial assembly later established Sept. 15 as a deadline for imposed settlement by the government. ● Thirty-seven people were killed and more than 50 injured as a result of the fire-bombing Sept. 1 of a Montreal nightclub. ● Three armed robbers looted the Museum of Fine Arts in Montreal of art works valued at $2,000,000 Sept. 4.

SASKATCHEWAN

Woodrow S. Lloyd, provincial premier from 1961 to 1964, died April 8 in Seoul, South Korea; he was 58 years old. ● A record 158 bills were passed by the legislature during its 51-day session ending May 5. The major piece of legislation was the so-called Land Bank Act, which permits farmers to sell their land to the government for renting or reselling. ● A federal-provincial board completed a five-year, $4,800,000 study of the Saskatchewan and Nelson rivers. Measurement of water resources was the main purpose of the study.

YUKON TERRITORY

The establishment of Kluane National Park, with an area of 8,500 sq. mi., including Canada's highest peak, Mt. Logan, was announced Feb. 22. ● Yukon Territory narrowly won the 1972 Arctic Winter Games, held March 6–11 in Whitehorse. Alaska was second by half a point. ● Self-government and provincial status for Yukon was recommended in a report, released March 16, of a special parliamentary committee on a new Canadian constitution. ● The federal government put an embargo on explorative oil drilling in the territory March 21. It was to be effective until new regulations could be formulated.

See also Canada Census (p. 482–83).

CARIBBEAN ISLANDS

The economy of the Caribbean area was plagued by continued decline in the tourist trade in 1972, and the various islands increased efforts at economic cooperation in order to combat unemployment and discontent.

Important political elections occurred during the year, bringing into office many more liberal candidates. Violent outbreaks were few; all the islands took pains to present a friendly and alluring image in order to attract more tourists. Agricultural production improved, and there was growing interest among investors in many parts of the world in developing Caribbean industries. On the whole, the year brought many changes, the full effects of which cannot be assessed until later.

Jamaica. Jamaica became the first of the newly independent members of the Commonwealth of Nations to achieve a peaceful change of national leadership. The People's National Party (PNP), headed by Michael Manley, soundly defeated the Jamaican Labor Party (JLP) and projected Manley to the prime minister's post. He replaced Hugh Shearer, whose party had governed Jamaica since independence in 1962. As a result of the elections the PNP held a clear majority of parliamentary seats—53 compared with the 36 retained by the JLP. Manley had campaigned on the issues of favoritism, corruption, unemployment, violence and neglect of youth.

On March 5 the new prime minister said that the most pressing task was to find a way "to put together an economic strategy which will provide jobs and happiness." Less than six months later Manley was finding the task difficult. The downward trend of the economic growth rate had continued, and the state of chronic unemployment had not been altered. Controls on exchange and on ownership of land and businesses by nonresidents, a general price freeze and a ban on car imports were imposed by the new administration to help solve the island's economic problems.

The major industries continued to be tourism and bauxite mining, both of which the new prime minister wished to see expanded, but with an emphasis on Jamaican welfare rather than that of foreign investors. The major foreign policy shift of the new administration was toward a friendlier attitude to Caribbean economic integration.

Haiti. During his first full year as president, "Papa Doc's" son, Jean-Claude Duvalier, attempted to strengthen his position primarily by means of renewed military aid from the United States. An eight-man U.S. military fact-finding mission, visiting Port-au-Prince in late July, represented the first U.S. military team in Haiti since 1964. (At that time, "Papa Doc" had expelled the U.S. marine unit that had trained his palace army, the *Tontons Macoutes*.) Informal U.S. military aid reached Haiti via a Miami-based firm named Aero-Trade. The firm supervised both personnel training and armament delivery.

The internal struggle, evident within the Duvalist regime since "Papa Doc's" death, continued. Victims during the year appeared to be "Papa Doc's" daughter, Marie-Denise, and her husband, Max Dominique, who was fired by Jean-Claude from his post of ambassador to France. Interior and Defense Minister Luckner Cambronne had vowed earlier never to allow the two back into the country. But the situation changed, and Cambronne, a de facto prime minister, not only saw a return visit by Marie-Denise, but suffered a general decline in political power.

"Papa Doc's" widow, Simone, continued to have the last word in all affairs of state. It seemed likely that she would back Roger la Fontant, Haiti's consul general in New York City for prime minister, a position that will be created with the formation of a proposed parliamentary regime. Late in the year, Defense Minister Cambronne was stripped of his position and went into exile.

On June 8, Venezuela and Haiti resumed diplomatic relations, which had been severed in May 1963.

The Dominican Republic. The National Congress passed President Joaquín Balaguer's agrarian reform program which, if truly carried out, will have the effect of reducing the land holdings of the rich and the military. All publicly irrigated land used to grow rice will be distributed to small farmers. In addition, at least 200,000 acres of public land will be divided, in small parcels, among the peasantry. President Balaguer further planned government purchase of uncultivated land for redistribution.

Balaguer's position appeared strong, as the leaders of the left continued to disagree and fight among themselves. An example of the heavy hand with which his Reformist Party continued to rule was the dismissal on Apr. 27 of Manuel Jiménez Rodríguez, mayor of Santo Domingo, who was a member of the party. Ordered to stand trial for subversion, Jiménez Rodríguez took refuge in the Mexican embassy and later left the country.

At least twice during the year police and soldiers combatted students sympathetic to guerrilla leaders who oppose Balaguer. On April 4, government forces searching for Tacito

Prime Minister Lynden Pindling of the Bahamas greets supporters on election day. Pindling won a second term when his Progressive Liberal party polled a majority.

World Wide Photos

Perdomo Robles, leader of the Dominican Popular Movement, occupied the autonomous University of Santo Domingo, arresting some 150 people and killing a female student.

On the surface, Dominican-Haitian relations were improving. However, the Dominicans feared Haiti's rearmament and were wary of excess Haitian labor, spilling over onto Dominican soil. A visit to the Dominican Republic by Luckner Cambronne made public the fact that the Haitian government was exporting cane cutters to the Dominican Republic, thus embarrassing the government of Balaguer, who had denied that Haitian labor was being used. The Dominican sugar industry, unlike that of some other Caribbean countries, prospered during the year. Exports to the United States were particularly favorable.

The Bahamas. Prime Minister Lynden Pindling won reelection, as his Progressive Liberal Party defeated the Free National Movement, a coalition of right-wing groups. The movement included the predominantly white United Bahamian Party (sometimes called the Bay Street Boys), which formerly ruled the country.

Pindling is believed to be moving the Bahamas toward independence from Britain. Once independent, the Bahamas could remain within the Commonwealth of Nations and also become eligible for membership, and therefore aid, in the Organization of American States, the Inter-American Development Bank and the Caribbean Free Trade Association.

Trinidad and Tobago. Two members of the People's National Movement, which, unopposed, won all 36 seats in the House of Representatives, left the party and began sitting on the opposition benches—J. R. F. Richardson, deputy speaker and parliamentary secretary, and Dr. H. Charles. Richardson resigned from the party in opposition to Prime Minister Williams' industrial relations bill; Charles was expelled for voting against it.

The new act was passed before June 16, when the state of emergency, lasting since October 1971, was lifted. It was the last in a series of moves on the part of Williams to silence dissent. Strikes by workers in the country's two main industries, oil and sugar, are forbidden, and so are strikes by prison officers, dock and electricity workers and others employed in fields defined as "essential industries." Leaders of the 1971 "black power" rebellion and army mutiny were freed when the state of emergency, caused by the rebellion, was ended.

Cuba. The slow emergence of the country out of hemispherical isolation and the strengthening of ties with Communist and other friendly governments were the most notable developments in Cuban foreign relations. Premier Fidel Castro toured African and East European countries from May to July—visiting Guinea, Sierra Leone, Algeria, Bulgaria, Rumania, Hungary, Poland, East Germany, Czechoslovakia and the Soviet Union. A joint Soviet-Cuban communiqué on July 6 stressed con-

Ch. Simonpietri, Gamma

Seeking better relations, Premier Fidel Castro of Cuba parades with President Boumedienne of Algeria after receiving the keys to Algiers.

Prensa Latina

A skyjacked Southern Airways jet landed safely at Havana in spite of ruined landing gear.

tinued Soviet support of Cuba and expansion of economic and technological cooperation. A few days later Cuba was formally admitted as a member of COMECON, the common market of the eastern block.

Peru and Cuba resumed diplomatic relations, suspended since 1964. The Peruvian move contravened a vote in the Organization of American States to continue sanctions against Cuba. The vote seemed to portend the demise of the U.S.-inspired isolation policy. Later Barbados, Guyana, Jamaica and Trinidad and Tobago established diplomatic ties with the island.

Economically, the year was less favorable. The government admitted in February that sugar production had suffered severe setbacks, and individual sugar rations were reduced in order to fulfill export commitments. The sugar harvest ending in mid-July was also termed "bad" by President Osvaldo Dorticos. The tobacco crop, on the other hand, showed a sizable increase.

Puerto Rico. The question of Puerto Rico's political status was the issue at an Aug. 18 meeting in New York of the U.N. Special Committee on Colonization. While a Cuban proposal that the island be classified as a U.S. colony was not approved, the committee on Aug. 28 declared "self-determination and independence" to be the "inalienable right of the people of Puerto Rico."

The people expressed their preference in the Nov. 7 elections by sweeping the Popular Democratic Party, which favors continued commonwealth status, back into power. The party captured not only the governorship for 36-year-old Rafael Hernández Colón, but also both houses of the legislature and 72 out of 78 municipalities. The Puerto Rican Independence Party did not draw enough votes to win a legislative seat.

Antigua. During most of the year, two of Antigua's leading newspapers were inoperative as a consequence of the 1971 Newspaper Registration Act and the Newspaper Security Act. *The Antigua Star* and *The Worker's Voice,* however, resumed publication when Justice Allen Louisy declared the acts "repugnant to the . . . Antigua constitution," which guarantees freedom of opinion and expression. The acts provided for payment by all newspapers of a $600 license fee and a deposit of $10,000 against possible libel suits. Prime Minister George Walter announced during the year that he would seek independence from Britain for Antigua.

TAYLOR K. COUSINS
Assistant Professor of Economics
College of William and Mary

CENTRAL AMERICA

The 1971 Honduras-El Salvador war was a major force in influencing events in Central America during 1972. In fact, as a result of the war, the Central-American Common Market virtually ceased to function in 1972. Although Mexican President Luis Echeverria had attempted in 1971 to demonstrate interest in Central America by meeting with all but one of the six Central-American presidents, there were complaints that visits alone meant nothing. In response, the Mexican government in 1972 opened its borders to more Central-American products.

Guatemala. Political violence in Guatemala, which in 1971, according to the censored press, had resulted in 959 deaths, 171 kidnappings and 194 disappearances, continued throughout 1972. President Carlos Arana Osorio, however, claimed that terrorism was being controlled. The country moved toward a one-party system, with the rightist Movement of National Liberation holding all power. As a British land, sea and air force held training exercises in British Honduras, there were rumors that it was doing so because Guatemala was massing forces along the border for an invasion. The Guatemalan government denied the allegation, saying that its troops were merely chasing guerrillas.

British Honduras. With a grant of more than $12,000,000 from Britain, British Honduras proceeded to build its new capital, Belmopan. Fifty miles inland, the city will be relatively free from the hurricanes that ravage Belize.

El Salvador. The February elections in El Salvador featured a whole spectrum of parties. The candidate of the extreme-right Independent Democratic United Front, representing large landowners, was Gen. Jose Alberto Medrano. A lawyer, Jose Antonio Rodriguez, was the choice of the conservative Salvadorean Popular party, controlled by industrialists. Col. Arturo Armando Molina represented the moderately conservative National Coalition party, which has held the presidency since 1962. Jose Napoleon Duarte of the Christian Democratic party was the candidate of the leftist coalition, the National Union of Opposition, which had the support of the illegal Communist party. Thanks to the support of President Sanchez Hernandez, Molina won by a slim margin. As no candidate had an absolute majority, however, congress had to choose; it selected Molina. Duarte charged that the elections were fraudulent. He staged a bloody but unsuccessful uprising; about a hundred soldiers and civilians were killed. Duarte escaped to Guatemala.

Honduras. Honduran President Ramon Ernesto Cruz said there could be no peace with El Salvador unless that country signed a general accord to resolve pending problems. Honduras signed bilateral pacts with Costa Rica, Nicaragua and Guatemala, to replace the former Central-American agreements. While the country maintained a hostile attitude toward El Salvador, it sought closer relations with Nicaragua, with which it signed trade and other treaties. The two countries agreed to exchange electrical energy. President Cruz opposed the establishment of Soviet embassies in Central America on the ground that students who had gone to the Patrice Lumumba University in Moscow had returned as agitators.

Although the Honduran strongman, Gen. Oswaldo Lopez Arellano, who had been in power since 1963, had formally relinquished the presidency after the elections of 1971, there was constant fear that, from his position as chief of the armed forces, he might again take over the government. That fear proved well-founded; General Lopez overthrew President Cruz on Dec. 4 and had himself installed as president for the remainder of the elective term, which expires in 1977.

Nicaragua. Early in 1972, Nicaragua's governing Liberal party, headed by President Anastasio Somoza Debayle, formed a coalition with the Conservative party of Fernando Aguero Rocha. Under their agreement, the two parties would govern the country, with the Somozas, who have controlled it for more than 30 years, remaining effectively in power. Many Liberals and Conservatives were dismayed by this opportunism, and even Archbishop Miguel Obando y Bravo of Managua denounced the subsequent elections as a farce. Held in February, the elections gave an overwhelming victory to the Liberals, but a third of the electorate abstained from voting. The assembly, which was to draft a new constitution, opened in April; by agreement, 60 members were Liberals and 40 Conservatives. President Somoza's term ended in May. The assembly elected a triumvirate to preside over a provisional government until December 1974; Somoza could then again be a candidate for the presidency. The triumvirate consisted of two Liberals, Gen. Roberto Martinez Lacayo and Alfonso Lovo Cordero, and one Conservative, Fernando Aguero Rocha.

In late December a major earthquake destroyed much of the capital, Managua, causing thousands of deaths.

Costa Rica. Costa Rica's main problem in 1972 was a serious trade deficit and diminishing foreign reserves. President Jose Figueres sought to remedy the situation by virtually withdrawing from the Central-American Common Mar-

Some intimation of the impact of the Dec. 23 earthquake on the Nicaraguan capital of Managua can be had from this view of the city's shattered landscape. The second quake to strike Managua in this century, it killed over 10,000 persons and caused the evacuation of all survivors to outlying villages.

UPI

ket, which he held largely responsible for Costa Rica's adverse trade balance, and by promoting exports, especially coffee, to countries such as the Soviet Union and Japan.

The Soviet Union showed a special interest in Costa Rica. It proposed to build a 500-megawatt hydroelectric plant in Guanacaste to supply power to the southeast, where Alcoa is beginning to exploit large bauxite deposits. In late 1971, Costa Rica had become the first Central-American country to establish diplomatic relations with the Soviet Union. There was widespread criticism of President Figueres for doing so without informing congress or the public; he justified the move on the ground that Costa Rica needed new markets for its coffee. Throughout 1972 there were charges that the Soviet embassy in San Jose was a center of subversion.

Costa Rica, which abolished its army in 1948, was uneasy because the other isthmian countries were virtual military dictatorships. It refused to join CONDECA (Central American Defense Council) and denounced an alleged plot by Central-American military elements to overthrow its government and help reactionary groups to establish a military dictatorship. Although leftists continued to attack the United Fruit Company, it saved Costa Rica from financial disaster, because bananas overtook coffee as the country's leading export and dollar earner.

Panama. There were reports that the U.S. government had agreed to relinquish sovereignty over the Panama Canal Zone. A U.S. House subcommittee, headed by Rep. John Murphy (D-N.Y.), held hearings in Washington and Panama on the proposed new canal treaty. The American Society of Panama opposed any concessions. There were also protests in Congress from Sen. Strom Thurmond (R-S.C.) and Rep. Robert Price (R-Texas), who urged the United States not to relinquish its sovereignty over the zone, as the Panamanian government demanded. Panama's strongman, Gen. Omar Torrijos Herrera, insisted that unless the colonial enclave were removed, Panamanians would march on the canal. To underscore its point, the government refused to accept the $1,900,000 annual annuity payment which the United States has made to Panama for the use of the Canal Zone since 1955. The National Assembly declared that acceptance of the annuity implied approval of the 1903 treaty and was an insult to the nation. Canal tolls climbed to a record $101,600,000 in fiscal 1972.

Torrijos, who is not president, legalized his authority by having the National Assembly approve a new constitution giving almost full powers to "a maximum revolutionary leader." This will allow Torrijos to rule the nation for six years. Demetrio B. Lakas and his deputy, Arturo Sucre, who had been serving on a provisional basis, were formally appointed president and vice president for a six-year term. The new assembly, known formally as the Assembly of Community Representatives, is not like the old one, which had close ties with international circles. Its nationalistic attitude was shown in the proviso of the new constitution that executive positions in private business must be held by Panamanian citizens.

RONALD HILTON
Executive Director
California Institute of International Studies

Prime Minister Bandaranaike raises new national flag as the Asian nation of Ceylon officially becomes the Republic of Sri Lanka.

CEYLON (SRI LANKA)

On May 22, 1972, Ceylon became the Republic of Sri Lanka. The date of the changeover was carefully selected by Ceylon's best astrologers as the most auspicious for beginning a new form of government. But judging by developments throughout the remainder of the year, Sri Lanka can hardly be said to have gotten off to a promising start. For the government of Prime Minister Sirimavo Bandaranaike continued to face serious political unrest and to wrestle with an economy on the brink of bankruptcy.

Part of the problem was the nation's heavy social welfare burden—including free education, free rice allowances and heavily subsidized medical and health care. These services cost the government more than $260,000,000 annually, nearly half of all state revenue. Moreover indications of the economic morass were inescapable. Gross National Product in 1971 fell by 1.1 percent, and the downward trend continued in 1972. Export earnings from tea, rubber and coconuts (the main export items) declined during the year because of adverse weather and falling world market prices. Payments on foreign debts consumed 40 percent of the country's foreign exchange earnings.

To meet Sri Lanka's immediate money needs, Finance Minister N. M. Perera went to the International Monetary Fund (IMF) for a $25,000,000 standby arrangement. But the IMF demanded a change of the Ceylon rupee's exchange rate, which Mr. Perera steadfastly refused to yield.

On the political front, the government encountered strenuous opposition to its increasingly repressive measures. An uproar followed announcement of a projected government Press Council which, in effect, would have censored the nation's independent and outspoken news media. The government retreated. Unrest, however, continued. Late in the year more than a million workers of the Ceylon Workers Congress and the Ceylon Mercantile Union joined in a one day hunger strike to protest the attack on the press and the government's Criminal Justice Commission Act, under which youths allegedly involved in the 1971 "Che Guevarist" uprising can be tried in absentia. Meanwhile, discontent among Ceylon's youth continued to seethe, and reports circulated of new strength among the "Che Guevarist" revolutionary forces.

The only relief from all the discord and trouble came in mid-year when Mrs. Bandaranaike made a successful state visit to China and returned with a $56,000,000, 30-year, no-interest loan. Without doubt, that aid helped meet immediate problems. But the underlying causes of social, economic and political tension in Sri Lanka remained undisturbed.

ARTHUR C. MILLER
Senior Editor, *The Asia Letter*

CHESS

Held July 11-Sept. 1 in Reykjavik, Iceland, the Fischer-Spassky world-championship match with all its attendant problems, generated mainly by Fischer, was the major chess event of 1972.

Newspapers that previously had scarcely mentioned chess, even when Bobby Fischer and, before him, Samuel Reshevsky, had consistently won the U.S. championship, now awarded the game front-page prominence, even supplying the scores of the games. Television news shows described Fischer's successes and detailed the problems relating to television cameras, lighting, noise, and so on, that seemed to disturb the challenger. Although the patience of Icelandic authorities was sorely tried by Fischer's numerous demands, the match was finally concluded, and Fischer, who had forfeited the second game by refusing to appear, rebounded to convincingly defeat Boris Spassky, the incumbent titleholder.

The Soviets had held the title since 1948, when Mikhail Botvinnik won the tournament arranged by the International Chess Federation to fill the title vacant since the death of Alexander Alekhine in 1946.

In Reykjavik, Iceland, Sept. 1, Bobby Fischer became the first American to win the world's chess title. He defeated Boris Spassky.

Leslie Howard, Photoreporters

The final score, 12½–8½, entitled Fischer to claim 60 percent of the $250,000 purse, half of which had been contributed by an English businessman, James D. Slater, in order to induce Fischer to compete.

Although the Soviets relinquished the individual world chess title, they continued to dominate the Olympiad, played in Yugoslavia in the fall. Hungary placed second in the tournament, 1½ points behind the U.S.S.R., with Yugoslavia third. The United States, without Fischer, who had demanded too much money to play in the tournament, tied for eighth with the Netherlands. The Soviets also won the world student team championship.

The U.S. championship tournament, which qualifies the two top players to compete in the first stage of the international competition that eventually produces an official challenger for the world championship, ended in a three-way tie for top honors: Samuel Reshevsky, who was a pre-Fischer champion on several occasions, Robert Byrne and Lubomil Kavaleck, the former Czech grand master. A play-off to determine which two of the three finalists would compete in the 1973 Interzonal was being arranged at the year's end.

One of the strongest tournaments of the year, with 16 masters and grand masters in competition, began in San Antonio on Nov. 18. Fischer and Spassky were invited to play but both declined. Fischer refused to play presumably because he was not offered a satisfactory appearance fee. Spassky declined perhaps because of Soviet displeasure at his loss of the world title. The event was sponsored by Church's Fried Chicken, the first such sponsorship of a chess event in the United States. The $7,000 first prize was divided equally among Anatoly Karpov and Tigran Petrosian, both of the Soviet Union, and Lajos Portisch of Hungary. Each scored 10½ points.

FREDERICK R. CHEVALIER
Chess Columnist
The Christian Science Monitor

ROBERT JAMES (BOBBY) FISCHER

Bobby Fischer, the first American to win the world chess championship, was born in Chicago, Ill., on March 9, 1943. He learned the basics of chess at the age of 6 and won his first U.S. championship eight years later. At 15 he was a grand master—the youngest in history. In 1959 the future champion dropped out of high school to concentrate on the game that would later dominate his life.

Belying the economic disruption resulting from half a revolution in Chile, construction continues on Santiago's new subway system.

CHILE

Chile's "Socialist Experiment," a unique attempt at a Marxist social revolution through Western democratic means, ran into mounting unpopularity and economic difficulties during 1972. President Salvador Allende, a 64-year-old parliamentarian, celebrated his second anniversary in power, having just installed three ministers from the armed forces in order to shore up his faltering administration.

The year began ominously for the government, with two by-election defeats in January. The opposition Christian Democrats, who control Congress jointly with the right-wing Nationalists, picked up a valuable senate seat in a rural area. The result showed owners of small and medium-sized farms deeply worried that the government's agrarian reform would engulf them after the big landowners had been eliminated under the 200-acre limit imposed on holdings of irrigated lands.

In the first 21 months of Dr. Allende's "Popular Unity" coalition, formed by Socialists, Moscow-line Communists, Radicals and left-

wing Catholics, some 22,230,000 acres were expropriated by the state, affecting more than 3,000 larger estates. Peasant cooperatives were set up in their place, with "centers of agrarian reform" substituted where the peasants were judged more disposed to stricter Marxist ideas of communally held property. The minister of agriculture, Dr. Jacques Chonchol, a left-wing Catholic land-reform expert, was under continuous attack from the opposition for acting too fast and even illegally. At the same time, the pro-Castroite Revolutionary Left Movement (MIR) aroused many of the 500,000 surviving Araucanian Indians, whose ancestors lost their lands to white settlers in southern Chile during the 19th century.

Disputes over the pace for implementing the Allende program, designed to take Chile "on the road to socialism," persistently troubled the government. In March the Radical party broke up, a powerful faction of it joining the opposition after correctly sensing that their lower middle-class voters were bitterly inimical to the regime. The Communists, who favored a

less rapid approach, arguing that an electoral majority was essential to putting through a revolution "by bourgeois means," tried to moderate the more leftist Socialists but failed. Taking issue with the theoreticians, the Communist party leader, Sen. Luis Corvalan, pleaded for temporary concessions in order to assuage small farmers and shopkeepers. He publicly criticized agrarian reform bureaucrats for neglecting to stimulate the peasants to increase agricultural production, which alone could stave off town dwellers' disillusionment over food shortages and lengthening queues.

In June, Dr. Allende attempted a rapprochement with the Christian Democrats. The purpose was to reach a compromise in congress on the nationalization of 90 major industrial concerns, which would give the Marxists control over the "commanding heights" of the economy. Dr. Pedro Vuskovic, who functioned—until finally dropped in June—as Dr. Allende's all-powerful "economic czar," had ruthlessly used a series of administrative "emergency" decrees to obtain outright control of more than 200 enterprises.

But even though the Chilean economy had been subjected to considerable state intervention since the late 1930's, the economic issue in June proved an ideological chasm too wide to bridge. The Christian Democrats, representing the interests of private enterprise, big and small, subsequently overrode President Allende's veto of a constitutional amendment proposed by the opposition to restrict nationalizations. This had the effect of blocking the government's program indefinitely. The president shied away from seeking a plebiscite, and the opposition lacked a two-thirds majority to impeach him.

September and October brought a crescendo of protests, with strikes and street demonstrations against the government from schoolchildren, students, shopkeepers, housewives and truckowners. The working class stood by Dr. Allende, who declared repeated states of emergency and called out the troops.

The national situation was bleak. Chile was stuck, halfway on the road to socialism, with serious economic dislocations. The escudo had been devalued again in August, as the country's trade deficit for 1972 passed $300,000,000. Diminished production by Chile's nationalized copper mines, traditionally the source of 80 percent of its foreign earnings, forced cutbacks of essential imports, including raw materials and foodstuffs. By November inflation had reached a Chilean record of 130 percent for a 12-month period, nullifying the 100 percent wage increase just granted.

As the crisis mounted, Gen. Carlos Prats, the army's commander-in-chief, repeatedly declared that the military would not permit a coup d'état to "rescue" the country from chaos. A continent accustomed to military coups listened awestruck as General Prats told Chileans that the armed forces refused to consider "spurious initiatives which would lead us to sully our arms and our uniforms with the blood of thousands of fellow citizens."

On Nov. 2, Dr. Allende announced the only viable alternative: he had persuaded a representative of each of the armed services to take a seat in his cabinet. Included was General Prats, who replaced a Socialist in the key post of minister of the interior. Three other ministers, among them Dr. Chonchol, facing the third impeachment proceedings of the year, left the government.

An army general and more than 30 colonels had at that time just been retired, but Chile's traditionally professional armed forces nevertheless assumed the unusual task of upholding constitutional authority until the March 1973 congressional elections. The elections will enable the Chilean people to pronounce on Dr. Allende's experiment in socialism. The presence of the armed forces reassured the opposition.

Throughout the year the government's legal wrangle with three U.S. copper companies further troubled Chile's relations with Washington, already involved with the renegotiation of Chile's heavy national debts. After a 1971 expropriation of their mines, the companies had received inadequate compensation. In September a Chilean special tribunal rejected the companies' final appeal. At about the same time the country's crucial trading credits in the United States had dwindled to zero.

In March, shortly before Santiago, the Chilean capital, hosted the third UN Conference on Trade and Development, a Washington newspaper columnist revealed alleged attempts by the International Telephone and Telegraph Corporation to prevent Dr. Allende from assuming the presidency in 1970. The disclosure helped the Chilean government to rally third world countries against "economic imperialism." Not surprisingly, the multinational concern denied the allegations. In December, however, Dr. Allende repeated the charges, with a ringing condemnation of all "economic aggression," before the UN General Assembly in New York. Thereafter—following a stopover in Algeria—the president paid a three-day visit to Moscow, seeking Soviet financial aid.

RICHARD WIGG
Latin-American Correspondent
The Times, London

Guards secure the gates to the Forbidden City while the Nixons view its treasures.

CHINA

Much heralded, long awaited and seen on live television by hundreds of millions of persons, President Richard M. Nixon's state visit to Peking in February, the first such visit by an American president, proved to be not only the China event of the year but also an occasion of historic importance.

The trip was the fulfillment of a prediction, made by Premier Chou En-lai ten months earlier to American ping-pong players and newsmen on their breakthrough visit to the mainland, that Sino-American relations would enter a new, warmer phase.

For the People's Republic, however, the year 1972 was not only one of quickening exchanges

White House Photo

Premier Chou En-lai welcomes President Nixon and Mrs. Nixon at Peking airport at the start of their historic meeting in February.

Magnum Photos Inc.

Premier Chou and President Nixon enjoy a feast of food and friendship at a state dinner marking the start of talks.

Sightseeing in Peking, Mrs. Nixon attracts a retinue of curious onlookers. The First Lady also visited school and hospital facilities.

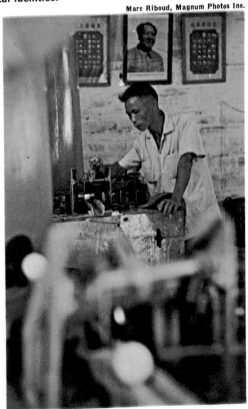

with the United States. It witnessed the formal establishment of relations with Japan, as well as with the Federal Republic of Germany. It also marked an upturn in long-cool relations with Britain.

The year likewise inaugurated full Chinese involvement in the affairs of the United Nations, often constructively. But it was the year of the first Chinese veto, cast to bar Bangladesh from membership in the world organization.

Domestic Affairs. Domestically, China continued to consolidate its economic gains, with emphasis on agriculture and light industry. Grain production for 1971 reached an all-time high of 246,000,000 tons. With this as a foundation, heavy industry also moved forward. Steel production totaled 21,000,000 tons, seventh in world output.

Foreign trade reflected Chinese determination to keep imports and exports close to the balancing point. Total trade of $4,611,000,000 was 9 percent more than in 1970. Exports were 15 percent greater at $2,364,000,000, and imports a scant three percent greater, at $2,247,-000,000.

Under the omnipresent poster likeness of Chairman Mao a Chinese machine tool operator produces Ping-Pong balls.

Politically, the surviving leadership pressed its efforts to tighten control over the army, a source of disaffection not only in the 1966–69 Cultural Revolution but in the aftermath.

As 1972 drew to a close, China had no president (chief of state Liu Shao-chi was purged in the Cultural Revolution), no defense minister and no chief of the army general staff. The five man standing committee of the party politburo, the most powerful organ in the country, had been whittled down to two—Chairman Mao Tse-tung and Chou. One of the members, Kang Sheng, was ill. The other two, Defense Minister Lin Piao and Mao's old secretary, Chen Po-ta, had been purged.

The leadership elite consisted of a handful of men and one woman: Mao, Chou, former marshal Yeh Chien-ying, Vice Premier Li Hsien-nien, Chiang Ching (Mao's wife) and Yao Wen-yuan, Madame Mao's associate in the Cultural Revolution.

The death of Lin Piao, Mao's designated successor, had been rumored for months. It was confirmed in July. The official version as told by Mao and Chou to visiting foreign dignitaries, was that Lin aspired to immediate power, even though the party's revised 1969 constitution named him as Mao's heir. He plotted to overthrow his aged (79 on Dec. 26, 1972) chief. When the conspiracy was discovered in mid-September, 1971, so the story went, Lin's son commandeered an airliner, which headed for Moscow via Mongolia. Out of fuel, it crashed deep inside Mongolia, and all aboard, including Lin, his wife, Yeh Chun (a member of the politburo), and his son (a military officer) died.

For some observers, the explanation sounded thin. Lin was the man who had everything; all he needed to do was wait for the plum of power to fall into his lap. Another explanation offered itself: that Lin opposed the Mao-Chou policy

Foreign and domestic craft crowd the port of Shanghai, China's largest. Limited trade between China and the United States resumed in 1972.

Marc Riboud, Magnum Photos Inc.

Chinese heavy industry relies on domestic steel production, such as that shown at right, for all its needs.

Marc Riboud, Magnum Photos Inc.

Produce in Chinese markets is plentiful, varied, cheap.
UPI

Peking workers begin the day with fresh air and exercise.

A city of bicyclists, Peking is air-pollution free.

of rapprochement with the United States and wished instead to put the Chinese eggs in the Soviet basket. Because Chou bore the main burden of the new policy, the dispute was, essentially, one between Lin and Chou. Lin, seeking support, may then have turned to his men in the armed forces, among them Chief of the General Staff Huang Yung-sheng. But Chou also had important backers in the military—the older officers who had been his students in the 1920's when he was political commissar of the Whampoa Military Academy. In any case, in a showdown, Chou won. How Lin Piao was eliminated may never be known.

Equally mysterious was the disappearance of Chen Po-ta, the firebrand of the Cultural Revolution who counted Madame Mao as his ally. Party officials in Shanghai reported in October that in some unspecified way he was associated with the Lin Piao plot.

Notwithstanding the threats to their leadership, or perhaps because of them, Mao and Chou decreed greater relaxation at home. Party members, military men and cadres who had erred in the Cultural Revolution were restored to their jobs after periods of reindoctrination in "May 7" schools. By the time Nixon arrived in Peking, the situation appeared to have been stabilized.

Nixon Visit. The President's visit had been arranged by Washington for maximum effect. A U.S. press corps of 87 newsmen, photographers and radio and television reporters gave it saturation coverage.

Hours after the restrained welcome at the airport the atmosphere gave way to one of warmth. An hour's audience with Chairman Mao broke the ice. The Nixon-Mao discussions were described as "serious and frank." In the week that followed, Nixon and Chou held seven rounds of talks. In between, the President toured the Ming Tombs, the Forbidden City and the Great Wall of China.

The Wall reminded him, Nixon said at his farewell Peking banquet, "that for almost a generation there has been a wall between the People's Republic of China and the United States of America." The process of removing that wall, he said, had begun.

In the joint communiqué signed in Shanghai on Feb. 27, Nixon and Chou took note of their differences but said these should not prevent normalization of Sino-American relationships. The document stopped short of diplomatic recognition but solemnized agreements usually concluded between allies—among them, acceptance of the principles of peaceful coexistence, renunciation of the use of force and refusal to seek domination of the Pacific area.

The communiqué also went far toward drawing the fangs of the Taiwan problem. Nixon acknowledged that the Nationalist-held island is part of China and recognized that its future is for the Chinese themselves to settle. He said the U.S. objective was to withdraw all U.S. military men (about 9,000) from the island. With an eye to continued de-escalation of the Vietnam war, he went further and said that he would "progressively reduce" American forces "as the tension in the area diminishes."

People to people exchanges, stepped up trade and periodic consultations at a high level also were spelled out in the agreement. The preeminent exchange took place in June, when presidential adviser Henry Kissinger returned to Peking for five days of talks with Chou.

The exchanges markedly increased in the months following the summit meeting. By November more than 500 Americans—journalists, physicians, scientists, scholars and "friendly personages"—had made the journey to the mainland.

Chinese visits to the United States were less frequent. But by year's end, following a successful tour by the Chinese ping-pong team, others had made the trans-Pacific hop. Among them were Chinese scientists, physicians and acrobats.

Although no one foresaw that U.S.-China trade would be substantial at the outset, the first hesitant steps were promising. Americans appeared for the first time at the Canton Trade Fair. And in September, U.S. officials announced the first sale of American wheat to China in 22 years—a total of 15,000,000 bushels, a figure increased in November to 18,700,000 bushels.

Also in the autumn, unofficial indications that China anticipated a two-year boom in construction and air transportation were borne out by a flurry of Chinese buying in the United States and the United Kingdom. Purchases included ten Boeing 707's, valued at $125,000,000, and $25,000,000 worth of Pratt and Whitney engines. Britain's Hawker-Siddeley group sold the Chinese 20 Trident jets, valued at approximately $159,800,000. The advent of Chinese participation in international air transport seemed imminent.

On Nov. 22, Nixon cleared away another important barrier to Sino-American trade and travel when he lifted U.S.-imposed restrictions that for more than two decades had barred U.S. planes and ships from visiting the mainland. It was the start of a process of establishing regular air and sea service between the United States and China. Major U.S. airlines quickly expressed interest.

Other Foreign Affairs. Nixon's China visit, formalizing as it did a dramatic about-face in U.S. policy toward the People's Republic, had a domino effect on America's Asian allies. For Japan, long a loyal follower of U.S. efforts to bolster Taiwan and deny Peking a seat in the United Nations, the effect was close to trauma. Prime Minister Eisaku Sato belatedly tried to clamber aboard the China bandwagon, only to be rebuffed by Peking. By July his popularity among Japanese who favored a China rapprochement had nose-dived. In subsequent party elections, Sato was succeeded by a pro-China coalition led by the Minister of International Trade and Industry, Kakuei Tanaka.

Tanaka made the desired journey to Peking late in September. After five days of talks with Chou and an audience with Mao, he signed a communiqué establishing diplomatic relations. Preparations soon were launched for the conclusion of a peace treaty and for trade, commerce and air agreements. Although diplomatic ties with Taiwan, with which it had done an annual trade in excess of $1,000,000,000, were broken, Japan sought to keep economic and cultural ties with Taipei alive.

Meanwhile and thereafter, more than 20 other countries recognized the People's Republic as the only legitimate government of China. Shortly after Tanaka's successful visit, West German Foreign Minister Walter Scheel visited Peking, where he formalized Bonn's diplomatic recognition, leaving the United States alone among the major world powers in recognizing the Republic of China on Taiwan.

In October the Chinese took a long step toward improving their frayed relations with Britain. The process of rapprochement had begun with the elevation of the two countries' respective diplomatic missions from chargé d'affaires status (existing since 1949) to full ambassadorial level. A visit by Foreign Secretary Sir Alec Douglas-Home produced public expressions of friendship and hopes for more rewarding exchanges.

Winds of Change. On a less tangible level changes of still another kind seemed to be in process in China. To one observer, seeing Canton, Shanghai and Peking for the second time in 18 months, the changes seemed less material than of the spirit. Physically, these great cities appeared much the same as before. There were no important new buildings, no noticeable improvements in air, rail or road transportation. The streets, as before, were clean, and there were no beggars in evidence. Although the Chinese had more goods to choose from in the shops and a greater variety in their diet, they continued to dress in drab Mao jackets and trousers. Cosmetics, jewelry and dresses still were luxuries quite alien to Chinese women.

But in subtle ways, the mood appeared to have altered. Whereas in 1971 the Chinese were hesitantly friendly, somewhat on the defensive, in 1972 they carried themselves with greater confidence, a reflection perhaps of a more secure standard of living, relaxed restrictions on their personal lives and greater familiarity with the visiting foreigner. There was also a greater awareness of the international role China had begun to play, an unconcealed pride in China's ability to host successfully two major summit conferences.

Moreover, the cult of Maoism—stressed repeatedly during the Cultural Revolution—had abated. The process of restoring Mao to a symbol rather than glorifying him as a proletarian saint had begun in the spring of 1971. It was far advanced in the autumn of 1972, when fewer Mao portraits, statues and quotations were in evidence. For the first time, it also was possible to see Chinese just standing around, loafing. The urgency and busyness of 1971 were less apparent.

In 1972 ordinary Chinese talked more freely to foreigners, and without signs of uneasiness. A more relaxed relationship prevailed between lower party officials, guides and interpreters and their foreign guests. Whereas previously they had spoken of China in stilted, Marxist terms, in 1972 they talked freely of themselves and exhibited curiosity about people, places and political events in the United States.

How long the new mood would continue was a matter of conjecture. The Chinese leadership was an aged one. The purges of the Cultural Revolution and its aftermath had created undeniable stresses within the party, the government and the army. Instead of having to cope only with disgruntled supporters of cashiered President Liu Shao-chi—a considerable body if the official reports were to be believed—the Mao-Chou leadership had to be on the alert against the dispossessed followers of Lin Piao.

In short, the political balance was a delicate one. Another plot and another purge could conceivably upset it. The possibility existed that the "rightists" of the Cultural Revolution might eventually make common cause with the "leftists" of the Lin Piao challenge, battering against the Mao-Chou center. No evidence of impending turmoil was apparent. However, events in China seldom are preceded by discernible warnings.

JOHN RODERICK
Foreign Correspondent, Tokyo Bureau
The Associated Press

CITIES

Pollution. Congestion. Crime. An epidemic of narcotics addiction. The steady flight of the middle class. For the cities in 1972 the problems were all terribly familiar and seemingly as resistant as ever to any quick and clear-cut solutions. Perhaps that was one reason for the increased attention that was paid during the year to the form of urban government itself.

The debate among theoreticians, social activists and ordinary city dwellers was often spirited. On one hand there were increased calls for broad regional planning and control to permit more effective handling of the complex U.S. growth patterns. From the opposite direction came demands for decentralization—more power to the neighborhoods and greater involvement of city dwellers themselves in the attempts to solve their problems.

Revenue Sharing. Following expenditure of nearly $160,000,000,000 in Federal aid on urban problems since 1960, it was obvious that money alone was no answer. Nevertheless, financial aid remained the central issue on the urban frontier. The biggest battle was over revenue sharing—direct grants from the Federal treasury—and while the big cities won in principle, they paid a price in hard cash.

In October, Congress enacted a compromise five-year, $30,200,000,000 plan—considerably short of the sum the nations mayors had hoped for. A third of the money was earmarked for state governments. The rest was to go directly to cities, counties and towns for public safety, environmental protection, public transportation, health, recreation and libraries (but not for education or general administration). There were early indications that many communities planned to use the funds not to increase services but to take the burden off local budgets and thereby provide local tax relief. The formula for distribution involved population, local tax effort and relative poverty and therefore favored poorer urban and rural areas over well-to-do suburbs and some smaller cities. For most major cities revenue-sharing funds were expected to amount to between 5 percent and 8 percent of the municipal budget.

But what Congress gives it can also take away, and the revenue-sharing act also included a new $2,500,000,000 annual ceiling on the Department of Health, Education and Welfare's previously unlimited "social services" program, designed to help people get off welfare—a program that had been expected to approach $5,000,000,000 in 1973.

Regional Planning Proposed. One of those who felt most deeply about the plight of the cities and the possibilities for greater Federal assistance was the man largely in charge of that assistance—Secretary of Housing and Urban Development George Romney. After years of trying to stimulate greater concern on the part of the administration, Romney threw in the towel and indicated at mid-year that he would not serve in a second Nixon administration.

Throughout the year, Romney had admitted that the Federal government would not foot the bill for restoring the central cities, and he made a final desperate appeal for other solutions. "It is time to determine whether state, suburban and private leadership are willing to recognize that if the central cities continue to rot it will gradually spread throughout the area," Romney said. "I believe that it is absolutely essential that metropolitan–wide problems be dealt with on a metropolitan–wide basis."

Similar emphasis on a broader view of city problems cropped up again and again during the year. In April, Sol M. Linowitz, chairman of the national Urban Coalition, proposed a comprehensive new Federal approach based on a network of "metropolitan development agencies," which would be able to acquire land (through the power of eminent domain, if necessary), develop it, preempt local zoning and building codes, provide social services and tap private capital through the issuance of federally guaranteed bonds.

The next month, at a seminar entitled "New Government for New York City," jointly sponsored by Columbia University and City College, urban experts agreed that such a metropolitan approach—politically welding the city to its suburbs—was an essential part of the city's salvation. Speaking to the group, Dr. Annmarie Hauck Walsh, an urban expert from the Institute of Public Administration, reported that, outside of Southeast Asia, the United States was the only nation in the world in which big cities were not governed regionally.

Other Proposals. A somewhat grander strategy for urban recovery and revival was put forward in June by Paul R. Porter, who had served as a special U.S. representative in Europe for regional supervision of the Marshall Plan. Porter proposed an up-to-date urban equivalent of the 1862 Homestead Act, which opened up the U.S. frontier to settlers. According to Porter's proposal, the area for development—through Federal and state land use policies, job programs and metropolitan planning—would be wholly new communities or revived small cities. In both cases the goal would be to combine new housing with sufficient concentrations of industry and other job opportunities to approach economic self-sufficiency. Moreover, as the urban poor moved in to take advantage of

the opportunities in these new areas, Porter suggested, middle class suburbanites could be lured back into newly refurbished central cities, where they would provide the tax base and talent that had been slipping away for years. (In Porter's view, well known "new towns," such as Reston, Va., and Columbia, Md., were little more than exceptionally self-sufficient bedroom suburbs that only exacerbated big city problems. However, an all-black project in North Carolina known as Soul City was moving slowly toward eventual balance between residential and industrial use and, consequently, a more heterogeneous population.)

According to one Federal study, however, even metropolitan-wide approaches may be too narrow for the problems ahead. The report, prepared for the President's Commission on Population Growth and the American Future, urged creation of broad regional governments to handle the frantic pace of urbanization. By the year 2000, the study said, more than eight of every ten Americans will live in one of 28 "urban regions"—each with a population of more than a million people. The largest would lie along the Atlantic seaboard and would include 57,000,000 inhabitants.

"By the time we have achieved metropolitan government of some sort, we will long since have desperately needed regional governmental bodies to deal with the structure and development of urban regions," predicted Jerome P. Pickard, a leading authority on metropolitan growth and the author of the Federal study. He cited particularly the problem areas of water pollution, highway congestion and the cost of public services.

Planning Assailed. Predictably, the increasing emphasis on regional direction appeared to produce a counterreaction. Well-to-do suburbanites, for their part, seemed increasingly worried that their interest would be sacrificed by pointy-headed planners trying to break down the barriers of poverty and discrimination. A case in point was the pitched battle that developed in New York State's Westchester County when the powerful, quasi-governmental state Urban Development Corporation announced plans to put moderately priced housing projects into nine Westchester towns.

New York's projected World Trade Center and planned commercial-residential development saw completion of the trade center's "twin towers."

Acknowledging a disastrous failure in inner city public housing planning, St. Louis undertook the partial demolition of its once-heralded Pruitt-Igoe project in March. Redevelopment will entail complete removal of some buildings and dismantling upper stories of others.

Even more interesting was the fact that the poor themselves were beginning to show signs of being fed up with having their destinies mapped out by social planners and giant institutions. In March some 1,600 representatives of black, Spanish-speaking and white ethnic communities met in Chicago to protest against those institutions they held responsible for systematic destruction of the central cities—beginning with the Federal Housing Administration and including real estate interests, banks and insurance companies throughout the country.

The fallibility of urban planning was illustrated as perhaps never before at the Pruitt-Igoe development in St. Louis. A complex of 43 giant buildings erected in 1954 at a cost of $36,000,000, it was designed to provide decent housing and a chance for upward mobility for the city's poor. Instead, it was eventually transformed into an urban jungle and by 1971 only 600 of its 2,800 housing units were occupied. Indeed, the city decided to spend an additional $39,000,000 to tear down two of the monoliths, slice the top half dozen stories off all the others and generally redesign the project through the addition of parks, playgrounds, stores and factories.

As some urban thinkers viewed the problem, however, it was more than simply a matter of faulty planning or administration. In a book entitled *Playing Urban Games*, Martin Kuenzlen declared: "The decline of the cities derives not from technological problems but from the antagonistic contradictions within the structure of society itself . . . like those in feudal times where a few kings and lords used their political and economic power to make people dependent on them." The obvious solution, in Kuenzlen's view, was a redistribution of power to the neighborhoods—decentralization. That approach had also been proposed by the Kerner Commission, originally appointed by President Lyndon Johnson to study the time bomb ticking away in the nation's ghettos in the 1960's. Reappraising the situation in 1972, the commission found things generally worse than ever. Its conclusion: "The problems of each city, perhaps of each neighborhood, are as unique as the people who live in them and require solutions that can only be worked out in detail in the places and by the people concerned."

Debate over Decentralization. Ironically, one of the coauthors of the Kerner followup study was New York City Mayor John V. Lindsay, who found himself embroiled during the year in a battle against what appeared to be just the kind of urban decentralization that he had been heralding. There was more than a little partisan politics involved in the much-publicized investigation of Lindsay's Liberal-Democratic administration by a state study commission appointed by Republican Gov. Nelson Rockefeller. And Lindsay's earlier creation of a giant web of super-agencies to administer city services did provide a tempting bureaucratic target.

Nevertheless, the criticisms made could have been applied to many of the nation's other

major cities. "New York City's present structure is incapable of delivering local services efficiently and effectively," said the study commission's Task Force on Jurisdiction and Structure. "The hierarchies of the city Departments which direct the delivery of local services are too large and cumbersome to permit effective management of basic functions such as street cleaning, street repairs, housing code enforcement, local park maintenance and personal social services."

In place of New York's single bureaucracy, the task force proposed creation of 30 to 35 local districts—each with a population of 200,000 to 300,000 people and its own locally elected district council that would administer local services within guidelines set down by a city Policy Board made up of the mayor, the controller and five county executives. Cited most often as a model for this kind of decentralization was the city of London, where 32 separate, self-governing boroughs operate under the overall authority of the Greater London Council.

Given all the obvious problems of big city government and the rising tide of neighborhood consciousness—both among the privileged and underprivileged—decentralization was a delicate subject to deal with. Yet, there were dedicated urbanists who were certain that it simply would not work. London, they said, was a bad example for American cities because it does not have the same kind of deeply rooted ethnic divisions and because many of London's expenses, such as welfare, are funded largely by the national government. (They also noted that in 1963, London actually "centralized" by reducing its complement of boroughs from 102.)

But the real question was whether decentralization in the United States would actually stimulate greater citizen participation and effectiveness. "The mythology is, the more localized it is, the more people participate but all the data in terms of electoral data indicate the opposite," reported Dr. Frank Smith of Dartmouth College at a seminar on decentralization at New York's Hunter College. Others pointed to the lower voter turnouts in elections for the city's antipoverty councils and local school boards. "Small constituencies," said Wallace S. Sayre, late Eaton professor of public administration at Columbia, "also display unstable, highly factionalized, personalized politics or tight oligarchical control. . . ."

In the end, Governor Rockefeller decided that the plan for breaking up New York's City Hall was too primitive to be put before the voters in November, and he tabled it. But clearly the debate over decentralization—and regionalization—was destined to continue in New York and the rest of the cities of the nation, along with the rest of their problems, for some time to come.

See also Architecture; Crime; Housing; Transportation.

DAVID M. ALPERN
Associate Editor, *Newsweek*

REVENUE SHARING

50 Largest U.S. Cities	Actual Amount Received Autumn 1972
1. New York, N.Y.	$100,847,538
2. Chicago, Ill.	31,185,549
3. Los Angeles, Cal.	15,781,264
4. Philadelphia, Pa.	21,981,080
5. Detroit, Mich.	18,302,265
6. Houston, Tex.	7,433,362
7. Baltimore, Md.	11,831,968
8. Dallas, Tex.	5,795,317
9. Washington, D.C.	11,834,502
10. Cleveland, Ohio	7,214,134
11. Indianapolis, Ind.	5,482,887
12. Milwaukee, Wis.	5,539,902
13. San Francisco, Cal.	8,833,517
14. San Diego, Cal.	3,132,436
15. San Antonio, Tex.	4,242,612
16. Boston, Mass.	8,904,129
17. Honolulu, Hawaii	5,933,488
18. Memphis,Tenn.	4,411,281
19. St. Louis, Mo.	6,251,132
20. New Orleans, La.	8,448,471
21. Phoenix, Ariz.	3,785,490
22. Columbus, Ohio	3,267,245
23. Seattle, Wash.	4,152,054
24. Jacksonville, Fla.	4,014,785
25. Pittsburgh, Pa.	5,862,953
26. Denver, Colo.	5,915,173
27. Kansas City, Mo.	4,603,544
28. Atlanta, Ga.	3,042,473
29. Buffalo, N.Y.	3,348,729
30. Cincinnati, Ohio	4,132,782
31. San Jose, Cal.	2,084,882
32. Minneapolis, Minn.	2,792,508
33. Nashville-Davidson, Tenn.	3,534,501
34. Fort Worth, Tex.	2,277,266
35. Toledo, Ohio	2,293,844
36. Portland, Oregon	4,169,841
37. Newark, N.J.	4,246,878
38. Oklahoma City, Okla.	2,731,487
39. Louisville, Ky.	4,674,030
40. Oakland, Cal.	2,304,155
41. Long Beach, Cal.	1,517,152
42. Omaha, Nebr.	2,036,844
43. Miami, Fla.	3,289,574
44. Tulsa, Okla.	2,129,832
45. El Paso, Tex.	2,711,743
46. St. Paul, Minn.	2,122,552
47. Norfolk, Va.	3,368,770
48. Birmingham, Ala.	2,486,792
49. Rochester, N.Y.	1,145,117
50. Tampa, Fla.	2,618,590

An apartment building complex (foreground) is the attractive keystone of the international center of Bogota, Colombia's capital. The project was financed by the Banco Central Hipotecario.

COLOMBIA

Although two years remained before Colombians would choose a president, parties began preparing their campaigns after the April 16, 1972, municipal and departmental elections. From these contests the Liberals—under sole leadership of former president Carlos Lleras Restrepo—emerged as the majority party. Their victory sparked a reappraisal of the National Front, an electoral agreement whereby the Liberals and Conservatives have alternated in the presidency while sharing key positions in the cabinet and administration.

At first it appeared that the Liberal landslide would sound the death knell of the 15-year-old bilateral accord as Liberals joined with Communists and members of the Popular National Alliance (ANAPO) to elect congressional officers. However, in October, Lleras Restrepo unexpectedly agreed with President Misael Pastrana Borrero, a Conservative, to extend the National Front for eight more years—a move aimed at gaining Conservative party support for a Liberal candidate.

Meanwhile, two Conservatives—former Sen. Alvaro Gomez Hurtado and Agriculture Minister Hernan Jaramillo Ocampo—cast their hats into the presidential ring, while former dictator Gen. Gustavo Rojas Pinilla proclaimed his candidacy under the rabble-rousing ANAPO's banner. However, his party suffered severe setbacks both in the April elections and in mid-August, when 25 legislators resigned in reaction to their leader's alleged "dictatorial" style.

Uncertain of the future, President Pastrana sought to broaden his political base by encouraging independent workers to apply for social security, raising interest rates on accounts of small savers and encouraging the establishment of retail stores in the shantytowns that gird the major cities of this coffee-producing republic of 23,000,000 persons.

Pastrana's government suffered protracted opposition in 1972. Many universities remained closed throughout much of the academic year because of student violence, which forced the dismissal of the education minister. Peasant invasions of large farms reached unprecedented proportions. Bogota slum dwellers reacted against the deletion from a newly-enacted urban reform law of a provision allowing tenants to become owners after five years of occupancy. More than 100,000 teachers struck in protest against low wages and a proposed education act. Despite the military's rout of a vast guerrilla network, pro-Moscow, Maoist and Castroite insurgents continued to operate. And, finally, Catholic priests in Colombia's increasingly more liberal Church excoriated arbitrary arrests by the army.

Because of alleged Soviet aid to leftist guerrillas, the foreign ministry in August announced the expulsion of eight Soviet diplomats. At the same time, Colombian-American relations improved as the United States recognized as Colombian the controversial islet of Quitasueno and the keys of Roncador and Serrana. Moreover, the Agency for International Development announced that in the 1973 fiscal year it would lend Colombia $78,600,000 and a subsidiary of Kennecott Copper pledged $120,000,000 to develop coal deposits.

The outcome of the local elections and prolongation of the National Front pleased Colombia's business community, whose confidence, enhanced by a boom in coffee sales, stimulated an increase in real national income surpassing 6 percent, while inflation hovered around 13.5 percent. Apparently safe from the populist ANAPO, Colombia's Athenian democracy enjoyed modest but steady economic growth.

GEORGE W. GRAYSON
Associate Professor of Government
College of William and Mary

Anthony Wolff

Leisure time development projects, many in the Southwest, often contrasted with advertising claims.

CONSUMER AFFAIRS

Confronted with the most varied choice of goods and services ever offered to any people, consumers in the United States spent a record $750,000,000,000 in 1972 for their personal use—$11,500 for every household in the land. Preliminary statistics indicated that personal expenditures in the United States, including $18,000,000,000 for interest payments, far exceeded such expenditures in any other country in the world. Moreover, because of continuing technological progress and governmental surveillance, much of what they purchased with their dollars was safer and more serviceable than its equivalent in the past.

From many a consumer's standpoint, however, the conditions of purchasing and using household products still were unsatisfactory. Despite the burgeoning consumer protection movement of recent years, consumers encountered problems at every stage. Among the most frequent complaints received by state and local consumer agencies in 1972 were: misleading and deceptive advertising, fraudulent selling tactics, unfair credit and collection practices, nondelivery of merchandise, mal-

functioning products, sellers' evasions of warranty responsibilities and faulty repairs or excessive charges for repairs. On the other hand, environmentalists charged that manufacturers and consumers alike still were not reckoning sufficiently with the cost of post-consumption disposal that inflicts damage on the natural environment.

Creation of Wants. In striving to attract customers, businesses continued to use many questionable methods. For example, in proceedings before the Federal Trade Commission a key question was: do advertisements compel persons to buy things they do not want? Some behavioral scientists thought they did.

Another important issue was the effect of television advertising on children. Consumer protection activists maintained that, by means of trick photography and clever commentary, commercials for cereals, snacks, candy, toys, toothpaste and other products advertised on children's programs motivated viewers to pressure their parents into buying the advertised items. The same critics argued that when the items failed to meet expectations, cynicism followed.

Meanwhile, at the other end of the age spectrum, elderly consumers complained of being victimized by unscrupulous promoters. They cited retirement dream houses that lacked essential facilities, dancing lessons they could not use, home improvement swindles and injurious prosthetic devices. Other offerings pandered to the fantasies of middle age.

Truth in Packaging. The welter of manufacturers' special interest pleadings and the superabundance of offerings compounded the consumer's difficulties in the marketplace. Some remedies were forthcoming. In 1972 several more retail chains, responding to consumer pressures and local statutes in several cities, instituted unit pricing, which supplements the stamped cost per package with information on the cost per some measure of comparison, such as ounce, pound or gallon. Many stores also priced each item individually, so that a hurried shopper would not need to check whether a special offer of four cans for $1.19, for instance, is a better buy than one can for 29 cents. (Often the special offer is no bargain.)

Another time-honored business practice, the dating of perishable goods in codes that consumers cannot decipher, increasingly gave way during the year to "open dating" with straightforward, readable numbers. See-through trays—permitting products, especially meats, to be seen from all sides—were another concession to the demands of consumerists.

Virginia H. Knauer, President Nixon's Special Assistant for Consumer Affairs, prodded the cosmetics industry to list its traditionally secret ingredients for the benefit of allergic consumers. "If the consumer movement has a cardinal theme," she declared, "it is its demand for the right to know about a product before it is purchased."

Several other Federal agencies took specific action during the year. The Food and Drug Administration of the Department of Health, Education and Welfare insisted on nutritional labeling of foods. The Federal Trade Commission required gasoline service stations to post minimum octane numbers on their dispensing pumps, and the same agency pressed a campaign to make advertisers document their claims. The Commission hopes that adverse publicity about unsubstantiated claims will help consumers to make a rational choice.

In March the U.S. Supreme Court ruled that the Federal Trade Commission possesses broad powers, beyond those in the letter or spirit of the antitrust laws, to prohibit business practices that are unfair to consumers. In April, however, a lower court held that the FTC had no authority to issue trade regulation rules. The decision set aside the Commission's order to gasoline stations to post octane ratings. The FTC filed an appeal.

Retail Practices and Consumer Grievances. The very act of purchasing often is a struggle. Perhaps the advertised bargain is not available. Or a promise of something free may be encumbered with previously undisclosed conditions. Another deception, called "bait and switch," entails two steps. First, an offering turns out to be a piece of junk which, the confidence-inspiring salesman readily agrees, is useless. Second, the salesman offers a substitute at a very high price. The tactic has been used in the sale of clothing, furniture, used cars and many other goods and services, including funerals.

Poor people who must rely on neighborhood stores continued in many instances to pay exorbitant prices for inferior merchandise. In 1972, however, luxury stores in wealthy neighborhoods for the first time also came under heavy criticism. Middle class women customers testified that their credit cards and charge accounts had been discontinued solely because they got married. Other consumers complained about retailers' refusals to straighten out billing errors. With all available evidence indicating that the small claims courts by and large are failing consumers, pressure mounted for a Federal consumer credit law.

The nub of consumer problems was "products that don't perform as represented," a national consumer referendum by the Council of

HOW THE U. S. CONSUMER SPENT HIS DOLLAR IN 1972

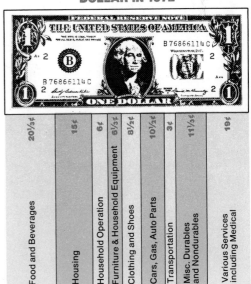

Food and Beverages	Housing	Household Operation	Furniture & Household Equipment	Clothing and Shoes	Cars, Gas, Auto Parts	Transportation	Misc. Durables and Nondurables	Various Services including Medical
20⅓¢	15¢	6¢	6⅓¢	8⅓¢	10½¢	3¢	11⅓¢	19¢

Better Business Bureaus found in 1972. Many consumer goods were found to be dangerous or defective. The recall by manufacturers during the year of millions of automobiles, food products, medicinal drugs and other goods indicated the broad scope of the problem.

A compilation by the Federal-State Relations Division of the Office of Consumer Affairs pinpointed the leading consumer grievances. Among the products causing the most frequent dissatisfaction were automobiles, magazines and books, home improvements, mobile homes, housing and real estate, furniture and home furnishings, vocation and trade schools and repairs. Repair services appeared near the top of other survey lists as well. "Too many consumers have paid for unnecessary repairs, and too many consumers have had repairs made with unsatisfactory results," Mrs. Knauer said.

Legislative Proposals. Despite the continuing tide of criticism by consumer advocates and demands by the Federal government for legislative action to alleviate the consumer's travails, no new relief was afforded in 1972. In March the Senate Commerce Committee voted, 17–1, to dismantle the Food and Drug Administration in favor of an independent consumer agency. But lack of House action and administration opposition stymied the proposal.

Also, in June the Senate approved, 69–10, proposed legislation to create an independent Federal agency to establish and enforce mandatory safety standards for consumer products. Prospects for enactment, however, were clouded by opposition from the Nixon administration, which favored creating the authority within the Department of Health, Education and Welfare.

Finally, the Democratic Party's platform, adopted in July, favored creation of a new consumer advocacy unit to present the consumer's case in deliberations of all three branches of the Federal government. However, the Democrats also stopped short of proposing a super-governmental, independent *ombudsman* to act on consumer complaints. In August the Republicans likewise adopted a plank favoring creation of an independent consumer agency within the executive branch.

HAROLD W. FOX
Professor of Marketing, DePaul University

Protesting the high cost of beef, consumers in Keene, N.H., mount a determined selective boycott.

UPI

CRIME

Crime continued to rise in 1972, but at a lower rate than in immediately preceding years. The Federal Bureau of Investigation said that reported serious crime in the United States during the first six months of 1972 rose only 1 percent above that of the same period in 1971. The Crime Index offenses (murder, forcible rape, robbery, aggravated assault, burglary, larceny of $50 and over and auto theft) were 7 percent greater in 1971 than in the previous year, compared with an 11 percent growth in 1970, 12 percent in 1969 and 17 percent in 1968.

During the first half of 1972, the murder rate was 1 percent greater than in the first half of 1971, whereas it had risen 11 percent in 1971. Robbery decreased 4 percent, compared with a rise of 11 percent in 1971. Aggravated assault, usually accompanied by use of a weapon, increased 6 percent in the first half of 1972, compared with a 10 percent growth in 1971. But forcible rape rose 14 percent in the first half of 1972, while the increase was 11 percent in 1971. Auto theft dropped 4 percent in the first half of 1972, compared with a growth of 2 percent in 1971.

Armed robbery, which makes up about two-thirds of all robbery offenses, declined 2 percent from January through March 1972, while aggravated assaults committed with firearms increased 5 percent. In 1971, armed robbery had risen 16 percent, and aggravated assault with firearms 12 percent. Burglary rose 6 percent in the first half of 1972, compared to 9 percent in 1971.

Policemen paid a heavy toll in 1971, the FBI reported, when 126 were killed "due to felonious criminal action," compared with 100 killed in the line of duty in 1970. In all but five of the killings, the FBI said, criminals used firearms, usually handguns. During the 10-year period ending in 1971 some 722 policemen were killed, with the annual toll zooming from 48 in 1962 to 126 in 1971. Twenty policemen were slain in ambush in 1971, more than in any other year. In the ten-year period, 119 were slain in the Northeastern states, 131 in the West, 185 in the North Central states and 287 in the South.

Most crimes continue to go unsolved, according to the FBI. In 1971 law officials "cleared" 20 percent of reported serious crimes. They solved 84 percent of the murders, 55 percent of forcible rapes, 66 percent of aggravated assaults and 27 percent of robberies. In the area of property crimes, police cleared 19 percent of burglaries and larcenies. Interestingly, while police cleared only 16 percent of auto thefts, they were successful in recovering about 82 percent of all stolen vehicles, more than half of them within 48 hours.

In all, nearly 6,000,000 serious crimes were reported throughout the nation in 1971. Property crimes accounted for 5,185,000 of the number, violent crimes for 810,000. For each 100,000 persons in the United States, said the FBI report, 393 were victims of violent crimes in 1971, while 2,514 suffered property-crime loss.

Crimes in suburban and rural areas again increased, while crime in the cities dropped. Suburban law enforcement agencies reported a 5 percent increase in serious crimes, and crime in rural areas was up 7 percent in the first half of 1972. Meanwhile cities with 100,-000 or more people reported a 2 percent decrease. For all of 1971, serious suburban crime rose 11 percent, rural crime 6 percent, and city crime 5.6 percent.

Women continued to gain in another area in which male supremacy had traditionally held sway—crime. FBI figures revealed that the increase in violent crime arrests of men in 1971 was 10 percent, while female arrests rose 14 percent. Comparative arrest trends for major crimes from 1960 to 1971 showed that male arrests went up 83 percent in that period, while female arrests jumped 219 percent. The female rate of gain in major crime during that period was most pronounced in robbery, burglary, larceny and auto theft.

Crime by children and juveniles also increased rapidly. From 1960 to 1971, according to the FBI, police arrests for all criminal acts except traffic violations rose 34 percent, while arrests of those under 18 years of age rose 124 percent. In 1971 some 45 percent of all arrests for major crimes were of offenders under 18, while 66.6 percent of all arrests for major crimes were of offenders 21 years old or younger.

A comprehensive study by three University of Pennsylvania criminologists indicated that one of three boys born in Philadelphia in 1945 was arrested at least once before he was 19 years old. The statistics also showed that the ratio of arrests for black youths was even higher—one in every two. However, a "hard core" of only 627 boys, or 6 percent of the total of 9,945 boys studied, accounted for 53 percent of the 10,214 juvenile crimes committed by the entire group in the final year studied. The study showed that the criminal-justice system tended to deal more severely with nonwhite boys than with white boys. White boys in lower socioeconomic status groups had greater chances for disposition of

Street-gang warfare erupted during the year, with youthful assassins in three cities—Los Angeles, Philadelphia and New York—committing more than 100 murders in what some police officials feared was a resurgence of the street-gang warfare that swept urban America in the 1950's.

A summary of 68,914 offenders in the FBI's Computerized Criminal History file who were arrested during 1971 showed that 47,197 (68 percent) were repeat offenders. Repeaters ranged from 33 percent for embezzlers to 77 percent for murderers. Predatory crime offenders had high repeat rates, with 75 percent of robbers and auto thieves and 73 percent of burglars arrested in 1971 being repeat offenders. Among narcotics offenders, 63 percent were repeaters.

The Careers in Crime study for the Uniform Crime Reporting Program, says the FBI report, has "consistently documented the fact that the younger age group shows a greater frequency of repeating." Repeat offenders under 20 were rearrested more frequently than any other age group, with an average of one arrest every four months per offender. Arrest rates for other age groups were: 20–24 years, every nine months; 25–29 years, every 14 months; 30–34 years, every 18 months; 35–39 years, every 22 months; 40–49 years, every 28 months; and over 50 years, once every 38 months.

These facts, the FBI asserts, call "for greater rehabilitation efforts directed at the younger offender, if hardened criminal careers are to be aborted." However, in the initial two-year period in which Federal appropriations for the Nixon administration's Law Enforcement Assistance Administration (LEAA) increased from $270,000,000 to $699,000,000, funds for the Federal juvenile delinquency programs were cut from $15,000,000 to $10,000,000.

Fear of Crime. Nearly six of every 10 women (58 percent) interviewed in a Gallup Poll in April 1972 said they were afraid to go out alone at night in their own neighborhoods, an increase of 14 percent since the same question was asked in 1968. Nationally, 41 percent of men and women combined said they were afraid to do so, an increase of 10 percent.

Those living in communities with populations of 2,500 to 50,000 showed the greatest fear percentage increase—up 19 percent from 1968, compared with increases of 11 percent

their cases without arrest than did nonwhite boys of higher status groups. Only 48 percent of white boys who committed serious crimes were arrested, as against 68 percent of nonwhite boys.

in cities with populations of 50,000 to 500,000 and 9 percent in cities over 500,000.

The survey also revealed that 35 percent of interviewees believed there was more crime in their communities than there had been a year earlier. Those who believed there was "about the same" amount of crime numbered 42 percent, while 11 percent believed there was "less crime."

To help reduce both crime and fear of crime, the National Alliance for Safer Cities, a coalition of 68 national and regional citizen groups, published *Twenty-Two Steps to Safer Neighborhoods,* which outlined citizen action in such areas as improved street lighting, buzzer systems, burglar alarms linked to police, auto theft, crime-watch programs, block mothers, tenant and street patrols, police-community relations and auxiliary police. More than 2,000,000 copies were distributed by the Alliance and its member organizations.

Anticrime Drive. Attorney General Richard G. Kleindienst's first annual report (Sept. 1, 1972) on Federal law enforcement and criminal justice assistance activities itemized massive increases in funds for state and local crime reduction programs. For instance, there was a rise in funding for the LEAA from $63,000,-000 in fiscal year 1969 to $699,000,000 in fiscal 1972. Among "encouraging signs of progress," Kleindienst noted that 54 of the nation's major cities reported in 1971 that their rates of serious crime had dropped from the prior year, and that 80 of the largest cities reported an "actual reduction of serious crime in the first three months of 1972." Moreover, he reported, "six cities with populations of more than one million" reduced the number of serious crimes "by 6 percent in comparison with the same period in 1971." Another sign of progress was "the steep rise in indictments of narcotics traffickers and organized crime figures," which included "about 2,400 arrests and about 1,600 indictments of organized crime figures," including "at least one-half of the so-called leadership of the crime organizations."

Critics, such as the National Urban Coalition, charged that the government's program to make American streets safe from crime had failed to improve understanding of the problem or promote better ways of dealing with it. A

draft of a study prepared for the Coalition by the Lawyers Committee for Civil Rights Under Law said that the Justice Department's LEAA generally "has neither led the way for the states nor held the states to strict performance standards." The study charged that most of the money distributed to states by LEAA had been used for computerized data banks, police hardware and other equipment. It said that LEAA had failed to emphasize innovative projects to

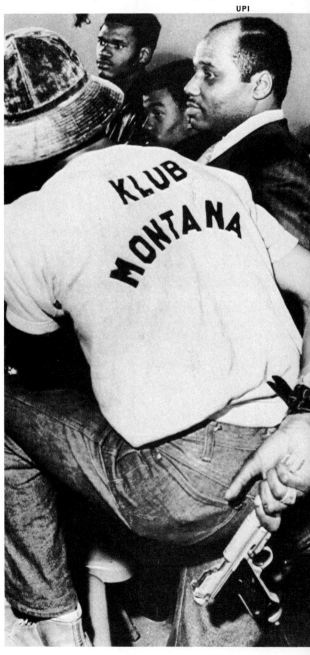

UPI

In a movement reminiscent of the 1950's, street-gang warfare erupted in several U.S. cities. A Philadelphia gang member (r) voluntarily gave his weapon to the police.

reform police, courts and corrections systems, as called for in legislation creating the agency.

Another study, by the administrative branch of the Federal courts, on "Federal Crimes and Sentences," revealed that the conviction rate for Federal felony defendants had dropped during the previous four years. Since the beginning of 1968, the study concluded, there had been a decline of 20 percent in the conviction rate for violators of narcotics laws; bank-robbery convictions had fallen 14.6 percent; convictions for assaults were down 12 percent; and postal-theft convictions were off 10 percent.

The Senate Judiciary subcommittee, which drafted the original LEAA legislation, will hold hearings on renewing the program, which expires on July 1, 1973. Other hearings will be held by the House Judiciary Committee and other Congressional bodies. LEAA Administrator Jerris Leonard resigned.

Crime Costs Against Business. Hijackers, burglars, thieves and other criminals cost U.S. business nearly $16,000,000,000 a year, according to the Federal Bureau of Domestic Commerce. The bureau limited its study to seven "ordinary" crimes against business—burglary, robbery, shoplifting, vandalism, employee theft, bad checks and arson. Retail stores reportedly lose $4,800,000,000 annually. Service establishments—restaurants, hotels and hospitals—lose more than $2,700,000,000 a year to employees who carry off food, liquor, silver and table linens. The transportation industry's direct loss of $1,500,000,000 is laid in large part to organized crime. Manufacturing loses $1,800,000,000, and wholesaling $1,400,-000,000 yearly. In addition, business spends about $3,300,000,000 a year in equipment, services and other crime-prevention measures.

Moreover, these figures represent only direct costs. The Library of Congress research service told a Senate committee that the $1,500,000,-000 theft in the transportation industry was only the tip of an iceberg. "Additional direct costs," it said, "costs of processing claims, costs of lost business and profits—raised the estimate to $8,000,000,000 to $10,000,000,000."

Victimless Crimes. The Uniform Alcoholism and Intoxication Treatment Act, drafted by the National Conference of Commissioners on Uniform State Laws, has been enacted by the District of Columbia, Alaska, Arizona, Florida, Hawaii, Maryland, Massachusetts, Minnesota, Oregon and Washington. The act declares that "it is the policy of this state that alcoholics and intoxicated persons may not be subjected to criminal prosecution because of their consumption of alcoholic beverages but rather should be afforded a continuum of treatment in order that they may lead normal lives as productive members of society."

In a far-reaching unanimous decision the Supreme Court ruled invalid a Jacksonville, Fla., ordinance barring from public places all "common night walkers" and "persons able to work but habitually living upon the earnings of their wives and children." In November the Wisconsin Supreme Court ruled that it is unconstitutional for judges to order an indigent person jailed when he has not been able to pay a fine.

The prestigious nonpartisan Committee for Economic Development called for repeal of laws against casual gambling such as bingo in church basements, plus a government take-over of all organized gambling. It also urged abandonment of criminal penalties for the use of marijuana. Similarly, a study by the Fund for the City of New York reported that one out of four New Yorkers plays the numbers game, and called for its legalization to drive organized crime out of this field and to reduce corruption.

Pennsylvania voted to legalize premarital and extramarital sex. The law prohibiting adultery and fornication was deleted from the revised criminal code. Rep. Robert C. Wise said that the old law had been used mainly to blackmail persons in property settlement suits.

Organized Crime. Brooklyn, N.Y., District Attorney Eugene Gold led a special force of 1,200 policemen who in 1972 served grand jury subpoenas on more than 600 members of the metropolitan area's five alleged organized crime families. Electronic surveillance of a headquarters in a Canarsie junkyard, said Gold, turned up the names of 200 New York businesses infiltrated or dominated by organized crime. Also subpoenaed for questioning were 100 policemen, ranging in rank from patrolman to lieutenant, who were suspected of having protected organized crime operations.

Meanwhile, the Justice Department distributed 230,000 copies of a pocket-sized handbook, *Police Guide on Organized Crime,* to help policemen on the beat recognize organized crime and learn what to do about it.

Corruption. Police corruption, including charges of selling heroin, accepting payoffs from gamblers and procuring prostitutes, was uncovered in at least 23 states and the District of Columbia, according to an article by David Burnham in *The New York Times.*

See also Drug Abuse; Federal Bureau of Investigation.

HARRY FLEISCHMAN
Executive Director
National Alliance for Safer Cities, Inc.

CYPRUS

Archbishop Makarios III, the bearded patriarch president of Cyprus, survived 1972 by actions that some critics called surrender but others termed necessary to prevent bloodshed and chaos.

At the end of the year, a permanent solution to the strained—and potentially explosive—relationship between the majority Greek and minority Turkish communities still seemed far off. The largest peace-keeping force in the world, the 3,100-man U.N. Force in Cyprus (UNFICYP), continued to maintain order.

On Jan. 10 a Greek Cypriot national guardsman was shot dead near a line dividing the two ethnic communities in Nicosia—the first such fatality in two years. Within a month, Athens sent Makarios a diplomatic note, demanding that he surrender some 15,000 small arms he had imported secretly from Czechoslovakia at a cost of $2,500,000, reorganize his government to rid it of "anti-Greek" elements and publicly acknowledge greater influence in Cypriot affairs by Athens. Makarios rejected the note as unacceptable, but Turkey supported Athens in demanding surrender of the Czech weapons.

In mid-March Makarios finally agreed to place the guns under UN control. He also announced that he was trying to purchase more guns from Syria. Diplomats said he apparently wanted to enlarge his own police force to guard himself against any major move to unseat him as political and spiritual ruler.

Three fellow bishops on the governing board (synod) of the Orthodox Church of Cyprus twice publicly demanded that Makarios resign the presidency, claiming that his temporal duties conflicted with his spiritual ones. Makarios refused.

In May, Spyros Kyprianou, foreign minister since independence (1960), resigned, declaring he was doing so under pressure from Athens. It appeared only a matter of time until Makarios would shake up his entire ten-member cabinet. On June 16, Makarios dropped seven ministers and shifted the eighth one to another ministry. His new foreign minister was Ioannis Christohides.

At about the same time, under pressure from UN Secretary General Kurt Waldheim, envoys of the island's Turkish and Greek communities resumed their long-lapsed peace talks. During a visit, June 6–8, Waldheim also arranged the first meeting in nine years between Makarios and his former vice president, Fazil Kutchuk, leader of the 120,000 Turkish Cypriots. The negotiations continued on and off for several weeks without any concrete results.

The United Nations agreed to prolong its peacekeeping presence on Cyprus after Waldheim issued a pessimistic report.

CHARLES W. BELL
Former Manager for Italy
United Press International

CZECHOSLOVAKIA

The political trials begun in Czechoslovakia in 1971 by the regime of Gustav Husak, aimed at solidifying its own power and "normalizing" conditions within the country, moved into high gear in 1972. Early in the year about 200 persons were arrested. In July and August 46 supporters of former Communist party First Secretary Alexander Dubcek were tried, found guilty and sentenced to terms of imprisonment ranging from nine months to six-and-one-half years.

The defendants were convicted of subversion, distributing antigovernment leaflets prior to the 1971 general election, forming organizations to slander and overthrow the socialist state system and maintaining contacts with hostile emigre groups. The trials evoked protests and charges of illegality and judicial persecution from many foreign quarters, including the French and Italian Communist parties, the French socialists and the International Commission of Jurists. A petition for pardon of the defendants came from 38 dissident Soviet intellectuals.

The Husak regime vigorously pursued its antirevisionist ideological campaign in many domestic areas. In mid-April a plenary session of the party's Central Committee reaffirmed the importance of central economic planning and control, and the need to make all future economic decisions primarily with Comecon integration and cooperation with the Soviet Union in mind. At the June congress of Czechoslovak trade unions more stringent measures were demanded against the lingering revisionist influences of 1968 that were still present in workers' ranks. The party also continued to harass artists, writers, journalists and other intellectuals known to be in sympathy with the 1968 liberalization program, closing theaters, censoring publishing houses and forcing retirements and dismissals. In the educational system, class-political criteria were reinstated for the selection of candidates for entrance into schools of higher learning. There was also renewed pressure against religion, particularly the Roman Catholic Church, in Czechoslovakia.

JOSEPH F. ZACEK
Professor of History
State University of New York at Albany

New York City Ballet's Stravinsky Festival: Jerome Robbins and George Balanchine perform in their jointly choreographed "Pulcinella."

DANCE

In the annals of the dance, the 19th century is termed the "Age of the Ballerina," for in it the prestige of female dancing stars superseded that of the choreographers who created roles for them and the male dancers who partnered them.

The decade of the 1970's—certainly the year 1972—in contrast has projected the male star, with Russian-born Rudolf Nureyev and American-born Edward Villella receiving almost constant exposure in a variety of contexts. Nureyev completed the year with a British-made film, *I Am a Dancer,* which, although showing him with ballerinas Carla Fracci, Lynn Seymour, Deanne Bergsma and Margot Fonteyn, was centered on his own highly idiosyncratic performing and life style. The year also finished with extensive National Educational Television exposure of Nureyev's restaging of the full length *Sleeping Beauty* produced by the National Ballet of Canada with Nureyev and Veronica Tennant in the principal roles. Although *Sleeping Beauty* has traditionally been considered a ballerina vehicle (it introduced Dame Margot Fonteyn to the United States in 1949), the Nureyev version placed emphasis on the *premier danseur.*

The pinnacle for Edward Villella of the New York City Ballet was his performance of the principal role in Jerome Robbins' *Watermill,* premiered on Jan. 20. Instead of relying on Villella's virtuoso attainments, Robbins created a thoughtful, ruminative vehicle in which a mature man looked back on the phases of his life. Both choreographer and dancer sought to join man and nature in a philosophical whole, a moment suspended in time and yet encompassing all of time. The result was profoundly moving.

Villella appeared also as guest with a variety of American resident dance companies, among them the New Jersey Ballet Company, the Boston Ballet and the Pittsburgh Ballet. New York's Mayor John V. Lindsay, joining in the critical acclaim, presented to Villella the city's Physical Fitness Award.

Nevertheless, notwithstanding the accelerated interest in male dancers, choreographers dominated the art. The greatest tour de force in the New York City Ballet's 25-year history was its June 18–25 Stravinsky Festival, in which the company's artistic director, George Balanchine, honored the late composer (from 1928, beginning with *Apollo,* one of Balanchine's closest artistic collaborators) with a burst of 30 ballets,

20 of them premieres. On the very first program, Balanchine realized two masterpieces—the vivid *Violin Concerto* for 20 dancers and *Symphony in Three Movements*, which sped along with the kind of relentless energy of which only the Balanchine-trained New York City Ballet dancers are capable. Other choreographers represented in the monumental event, which attracted international critical acclaim, were Jerome Robbins, Lorca Massine, John Clifford, Todd Bolender, John Taras and Richard Tanner. Only Robbins, however, approached the composer's music with a freedom and confidence akin to Balanchine's. The others often were too literal in their musical interpretations. Although the festival took place little more than a year after Stravinsky's death, Balanchine and Robbins forswore solemnity and performed rollicking high camp roles in their jointly choreographed *Pulcinella,* and Robbins played ringmaster to a host of little girls in his *Circus Polka.*

Modern, or concert, dance witnessed during the year two rather daring projects, both produced by Charles Reinhart, who manages the Coordinated Residency Touring Program of the Federal government's National Endowment for the Arts. The first was the American Dance Festival Repertory Company, assembled to perform during the opening and closing events of the Connecticut College American Dance Festival's 25th season in New London. The purpose was to form a modern dance repertory company, as distinguished from the one-choreographer company. The company's repertory, underwritten by the Rockefeller Foundation, the Ford Foundation and the National Endowment, consisted of revivals of Martha Graham's *El Penitente,* Charles Weidman's *Flickers,* Doris Humphrey's *New Dance* and *With My Red Fires,* and Jose Limon's *Emperor Jones.* Rudy Perez was accorded the only premiere, *Asparagus Beach,* which provided a spirited and structurally succinct contrast to the more traditional works. The company was unfortunately disbanded at summer's end.

Subsequently Reinhart and Norman Singer, executive director of the New York City Center organization, reverted to the individual company format to assemble 20 modern dance groups for an Oct. 2–Nov. 11 American Dance Marathon at New York's ANTA Theatre. Here, too, the National Endowment played a financial role, hoping that the theater in New York's Broadway district could eventually be developed as a permanent home for dance.

The programming of the marathon, however, was weak, and the box office results were remarkably poor. Nevertheless, some fine choreography showed among the dross. Paul Sanasardo, Erick Hawkins and Jose Limon all contributed substantial new works. The Limon works, *Orfeo* and *Carlota,* were triumphs of creative will, for on Dec. 2 this major artist died after a protracted illness.

The ANTA marathon also included five black companies, with the Alvin Ailey City Center Dance Theatre by far the most sophisticated both technically and choreographically. Donald McKayle's relatively new Inner City Repertory Company of Los Angeles had more spirit than polish, and McKayle's newest choreography was somewhat blighted by the routines he turns out for the CBS-TV weekly *Bill Cosby Show.* Other black groups represented were the militant Eleo Pomare Company, the somewhat less intense Rod Rodgers Dance Company and the Dance Theatre of Harlem, whose director, Arthur Mitchell, is principally concerned with developing black classical dancers.

The major ballet companies were finding national touring so prohibitively expensive that they have been forming small ensembles of young dancers to absorb the shorter engagements. Thus, Joffrey II, a branch of the City Center Joffrey Ballet, was kept busy all year. And by autumn the American Ballet Theatre had formed the Ballet Repertory Company to be its junior representative.

The other side of the picture was the increased activity of the country's resident dance companies in virtually every state of the union. In four regions of the country they have been banding together in spring festivals. A fifth region, the Mid-States, was added in April in Kansas City. Of 19 companies evaluated for possible inclusion, 12 appeared, thus introducing a plethora of choreographers scarcely seen before outside of their own communities. Among them were Loyce Houlton of the Minnesota Dance Theatre (Minneapolis), Tibor Zana of the Wisconsin Ballet Company, Valerie Roche of the Omaha Ballet, David Howard of the Kansas City Ballet and Michael Simms of the St. Louis Dance Theatre.

The trend toward regional collaboration is important. For dancers are as interesting as the choreography given to them. New, progressive choreographic names mean new possibilities for dancers, new visions for audiences. In addition to those choreographers already mentioned, Gene Marinaccio of Los Angeles, Bess Saylor of Dayton, Heinz Poll of Akron, Dom Orejudos of Chicago and Norbert Vesak of San Rafael were importantly represented outside of their communities in 1972.

DORIS HERING
Critic-at-Large, *Dance Magazine*

HARRY S. TRUMAN
(1884–1972)
Thirty-third President
of the United States

On Dec. 26, 1972, 22 days after entering a Kansas City, Mo., hospital for treatment of lung congestion and circulatory difficulties, Harry S. Truman, a one-time Missouri farm boy, unsuccessful businessman, organization politician, U.S. Senator from Missouri and President of his country during one of the most trying periods of its existence, succumbed to the infirmities of old age. He was 88 years old and had served as Chief Executive from April 1945, when he succeeded to the office on the death of President Franklin D. Roosevelt, until January 1953 when he was succeeded by Gen. Dwight D. Eisenhower.

Leading tributes throughout the nation and the world, President Nixon declared: "Harry S. Truman will be remembered as one of the most courageous Presidents in our history, who led the nation and the world through a critical period with exceptional vision and determination. Our hopes today for a generation of peace rest in large measure on the firm foundation that he laid."

Truman was suddenly elevated from the Vice-Presidency at a time when the imminent collapse of Nazi Germany in World War II portended a period of dangerous rivalry with Soviet Russia in Europe and when the war effort against Japan was approaching what many planners feared would be its costliest phase—invasion of the enemy's homeland. Largely excluded from administration councils while Roosevelt was alive and wholly unaware of the existence of the Manhattan Project, which was to yield the first atomic bomb explosion near Los Alamos, N.M., three months later, Truman was confronted from the very outset of his term in office with agonizing decisions. That he acted on them courageously and decisively is generally accepted; that he acted on them wisely in the circumstances also is widely believed.

Roosevelt had chosen Truman as his running mate in 1944 largely for domestic political reasons. Ironically, Truman's successes were almost entirely in foreign affairs. His apprehension of the Cold War, for the initiation of which some analysts have held him partly responsible, produced perhaps the most creative and innovative designs of U.S. foreign policy: the so-called Marshall Plan for the reconstruction of Western Europe, the Truman Doctrine for containment of Communism by means of U.S. aid and the North Atlantic alliance. Truman's support of Israel, his judicious but firm handling of a dangerous confrontation at the time of the Berlin Airlift, his decision to intervene in the Korean war—all reflected a firm assertion of the power which had been thrust on the country in wartime, and which some would have liked to relinquish in peacetime. Truman's Presidency was a decisive turning point from American isolationism.

In domestic affairs, the man from Independence was a man before his time. His advocacy of broadened civil rights, national health insurance programs and Federal aid to education, among other moderate proposals, was frustrated by Congress, but vindicated under subsequent Presidents and Congresses.

On Jan. 22, 1973, 17 years after a severe heart attack appeared to have foreclosed any chance he might become President, Lyndon Baines Johnson, hand-picked candidate of the Texas Democratic establishment, Congressman, Senator, Senate majority leader and President of the United States, died suddenly at his ranch on the Pedernales river in Johnson City, Tex. Death followed several months of congestive cardiac failure.

President Nixon, in a statement immediately following news of the only living former President's death, declared: "To President Johnson, the 'American Dream' was not a catch phrase—it was a reality of his own life. He believed in America, in what America could mean to all its citizens and what America could mean to the world. In the service of that faith, he gave himself completely."

Noting that Johnson "knew times of triumph and times of despair," the President observed: "Yet, no matter what the mood of the moment, at the center of his public life—and at the center of his spirit—was an unshakable conviction in the essential rightness of the American experience."

Like Truman, who predeceased him by less than a month, Johnson was elevated to the Presidency by the death in office of another man. Denied the Presidential nomination by the Democratic Convention of 1960, the one-time school teacher and legislative aide surprised many of his Senate colleagues by accepting second place on the ticket headed by John F. Kennedy. It was a fateful decision—for the ticket, which carried Texas and, thereby, narrowly, the nation, and for Johnson, whose succession after Kennedy's death by assassination on Nov. 22, 1963, heralded far-reaching action on the slain President's stalled legislative program.

The ensuing "Great Society" enactments—among them the most substantial civil rights legislation in a century, provision for the first time of medical care under Social Security, massive Federal aid to education, a liberalized Federal minimum wage and a major new housing program—while conceived by others and borne on a wave of sympathy for Kennedy, were substantially the product of Johnson's conviction of their rightness and of his astute stewardship of their passage through Congress.

Returned to office in 1964 as the peace candidate amid signs of a deteriorating anti-Communist position in South Vietnam, Johnson immediately confronted a critical situation there. His subsequent piecemeal commitment of more than half a million U.S. forces to a war which became the longest in the country's history undid the purpose of much of his domestic program, profoundly distorted the U.S. economy, bitterly divided the American people and ultimately persuaded him to retire from the scene without seeking reelection.

Embittered and withdrawn in his last years, Johnson died on the eve of a North Vietnam-U.S. cease-fire accord. He was buried at his ranch.

In the words of columnist James Reston, Johnson was "a little nearer to the old spirit... of the American frontier than most of his fellow countrymen, but also a little nearer to the folks who had been left behind when the frontier and battle moved to the cities."

Wide World

LYNDON BAINES JOHNSON
(1908-1973)
Thirty-sixth President
of the United States

JOHN EDGAR HOOVER
1895–1972

On May 2, J. Edgar Hoover, director of the Federal Bureau of Investigation for 48 years, died in Washington, D.C. On hearing of his death, President Nixon called him "a legend in his own lifetime," praising his "courage, patriotism . . . and granite-like honesty and integrity."

Presiding over the FBI from May 1924, Hoover molded the small, politics-ridden Bureau into one of the world's most efficient detective agencies. Under his leadership the Bureau's agents killed or apprehended several notorious gangsters in the 1930's and captured a number of German spies during World War II. Later, however, Hoover was criticized as authoritarian and out of step with a changing world. Nevertheless, thousands mourned him at the Capitol, where he lay in state, the first civil servant to be given the honor.

Dr. Hy Simon from Pictorial

LESTER B. PEARSON
1897–1972

Lester Pearson, Canadian premier and Nobel laureate, died in his home in Ottawa on Dec. 27. Pearson's overwhelming interest throughout most of his career was to see Canada take a responsible role in world affairs. He joined the foreign service in 1928 and in 1945 was appointed ambassador to the United States. As secretary of state for external affairs (1946–57) he represented Canada at the United Nations; he was president of the General Assembly in 1952–53. Toward the end of his tenure at the UN, in 1956, he proposed the UN emergency force that obtained a Suez truce. The following year he was awarded the Nobel Peace Prize. As prime minister of Canada (1963–68), Pearson instituted many domestic reforms. Symbolic of his attempt to unify French and English factions was his decision to adopt a new national flag.

UPI

EZRA POUND
1885–1972

Ezra Pound, 87, died on Nov. 1 in his adopted home of Italy. A scholar of disparate languages and periods of literature, Pound tried to revitalize poetry, calling for compactness and a musical use of rhythm. An example of his imagery is contained in the poem "In a Station of the Metro": "The apparition of these faces in the crowd;/ Petals on a wet, black bough." His work, *Cantos,* begun in 1915, occupied him for the rest of his life. Modeled after Dante's *Divine Comedy,* it showed the progress of man's spirit through history toward a new social and metaphysical order.

During World War II, Pound espoused fascism, and in 1945 he was arrested as a traitor. Judged unfit to stand trial, he was confined to a mental institution in Washington, D.C., until 1958, when he returned to Italy.

"Paris Match," Pictorial

JACKIE ROBINSON
1919–1972

Jackie Robinson, the first black baseball player in the major leagues, died of a heart attack at the age of 53 in Stamford, Conn., on Oct. 24. At his death, Robinson was praised for his courage as a trail-blazer for all black athletes.

In 1946 the Brooklyn Dodgers signed Robinson for the 1947 season—and thereby provoked outcries and an attempted strike by a rival club. Known for his daring plays, he stole a career total of 197 bases, including an unprecedented 11 steals of home. His lifetime batting average was .311. In 1962 he became the first black member of baseball's Hall of Fame. After his retirement from baseball in 1956, he held executive posts in several business firms. His biography, *I Never Had It Made,* was published after his death.

Pictorial Parade

EDMUND WILSON
1895–1972

Generally acknowledged to be the dean of American literary critics, Edmund Wilson died on June 12 at his 172-year-old family home in Talcottville, N.Y.

Wilson's writings embraced such dissimilar works as *Axel's Castle,* a systematic study of symbolist literature; *To The Finland Station,* a polemic on the revolutionary tradition in Europe; *The Scrolls from the Dead Sea,* his presentation in English of a rich Near Eastern archeological find; and *Patriotic Gore,* a study of the literature of the American Civil War. His best known work of fiction is *Memoirs of Hecate County,* a collection of stories satirizing suburban mores. In 1963, Wilson received the Presidential Medal of Freedom, praising him as "a critic and historian [who] has converted criticism itself into a creative art." He was later awarded the National Medal for Literature.

The Oxford University Press

DUKE OF WINDSOR
1894–1972

The Duke of Windsor, who ruled Britain briefly as Edward VIII until his abdication in December 1936, died on May 27 at his home in Paris. The oldest son of George V, Edward ascended the throne on Jan. 20, 1936. He had hoped to bring the public image of the monarchy into accord with changing social attitudes. Eleven months later, however, he resigned the throne to marry "the woman I love," the twice-divorced American, Wallis Simpson.

Thereafter the duke and his duchess lived abroad, estranged from the royal family until 1965, when Queen Elizabeth II made overtures toward reconciliation. On his death she wrote: "I know that my people will always remember him with gratitude and great affection." The duke was buried in England at the royal burial ground at Frogmore.

UPI

Hubert Henrotte, Gamma

Robert Casadesus, 73, popular French pianist and composer (1917–72); Paris, Sept. 19.

Oscar Levant, 65, pianist, composer, actor and wit; Beverly Hills, Calif., Aug. 14.

UPI

James F. Byrnes, 92, U.S. Congressman (D-S.C., 1911–25), Senator (1931–41), Justice, U.S. Supreme Court (1941–42), Secretary of State (1945–47), Governor (S.C., 1951–55); Columbia, S.C., April 9.

Marti Cole, Photo Trends

UPI

Mahalia Jackson, 60, gospel singer ("Move Up A Little Higher"); Evergreen Park, Ill., Jan. 27.

Saul Alinsky, 63, community organizer, poverty fighter, author of *Rules for Radicals* (1971); Carmel, Calif., June 12.

Athenagoras I, 86, patriarch of the Eastern Orthodox Church; Istanbul, Turkey, July 7.

Charles Atlas, 79, founder of the mail-order muscle-building business; Long Beach, N.Y., Dec. 23.

Victor Babin, 63, Russian-born pianist, director, Cleveland Institute of Music; Cleveland, Ohio, March 1.

Cristobal Balenciaga, 77, Spanish-born fashion designer whose clothes were known for their classic elegance; Valencia, Spain, March 23.

George M. Bell, 59, Canadian newspaper publisher, controlled the *Toronto Globe and Mail* and the Calgary *Albertan;* Montreal, July 20.

John Berryman, 57, U.S. poet; winner of Pulitzer Prize and National Book Award; Minneapolis, Jan. 7.

Warren K. Billings, 79, labor organizer, imprisoned for a 1916 bombing in San Francisco during a patriotic parade, but formally pardoned in 1961; Redwood City, Calif., Sept. 4.

Dan Blocker, 43, television actor, created Hoss in the *Bonanza* series; Inglewood, Calif., May 13.

Thomas Hale Boggs, 58, U.S. Congressman (D-La., 1941–43, 1947–72), Democratic whip (1966–71), Majority Leader (1971–72); missing and presumed · dead in Alaska air crash, Oct. 16.

Frank T. Bow, 71, U.S. Congressman (R-Ohio, 1952–72); Bethesda, Md., Nov. 13.

William Boyd, 74, film actor, portrayed · Hopalong Cassidy; South Laguna Beach, Sept 12.

Prescott Bush, 77, U.S. Senator (R.-Conn., 1952–63); New York City, Oct. 8.

Bruce Cabot, 67, film actor, starred in *King Kong;* Hollywood, May 3.

James Gordon Canfield, 74, U.S. Congressman (R-N.J., 1941–61); Hawthorne, N.J., June 20.

Leo G. Carroll, 80, British-born stage and television actor; New York City, Oct. 16.

Hodding Carter, 65, winner of 1946 Pulitzer Prize for newspaper editorials criticizing Southern segregation; Greenville, Miss., April 4.

Americo Castro, 87, Spanish writer who helped initiate the Spanish cultural renaissance; Spain, July 25.

C. W. Ceram, 57, German author and expert on archeology (*Gods, Graves, and Scholars*); Bonn, Germany, April 12.

Chen Yi, 70, Chinese Communist military leader and foreign minister (1958–68); Peking, Jan. 6.

Sir Francis Chichester, 70, British adventurer who in 1966–67 made a solo trip around the world in a 53-foot yacht; Plymouth, England, Aug. 26.

Roberto Clemente, 38, baseball player for Pittsburgh Pirates; near San Juan, P.R., Dec. 31.

Padraic Colum, 90, Irish poet, playwright, folklorist, a founder of Abbey Theater; Enfield, Conn., Jan. 11.

Charles Correll, 82, vaudevillian, voice of Andy on *Amos 'n' Andy* radio show; Chicago, Sept. 26.

Richard Crooks, 72, tenor, sang with Metropolitan Opera Company and on the *Voice of Firestone* radio show; Portola Valley, Calif., Oct. 1.

Cecil Day-Lewis, 68, mystery writer, poet laureate of Britain (1968–72); London, May 22.

Brandon de Wilde, 30, actor, remembered for his childhood roles in *Member of the Wedding* and *Shane;* Lakewood, Colo., July 6.

Martin Dies, 71, U.S. Congressman (D-Tex., 1931–45), chairman of the House Committee on Un-American Activities (1938–45); Lufkin, Tex., Nov. 11.

Henry Dreyfuss, 68, industrial designer; South Pasadena, Calif., Oct. 5.

Philip Drinker, 77, pioneer in industrial hygiene, co-inventor of the iron lung; Fitzwilliam, N.H., Oct. 19.

Allen J. Ellender, 81, U.S. Senator (D.-La., 1937–72); president pro tempore of the Senate (1971–72); Bethesda, Md., July 27.

Herbert Feis, 78, economist, author of books on U.S. foreign policy, awarded Pulitzer Prize in history (1961); Winter Park, Fla., March 2.

Lord Fisher of Lambeth, 85, Archbishop of Canterbury and Primate of All England (1945–61); Sherborne, England, Sept. 15.

Frederik IX, 72, king of Denmark (1947–72); Copenhagen, Jan. 14.

Goeran Gentele, 54, Swedish opera director, was to become manager of the Metropolitan Opera in the fall of 1972; Porto Cervo, Sardinia, July 18.

Philip B. Gove, 70, editor, *Webster's New International Dictionary* (3rd edition); Warren, Mass., Nov. 15.

Frank P. Graham, 85, Southern civil rights leader; president of University of North Carolina (1930–49); Chapel Hill, N.C., Feb. 16.

William T. Grant, 96, founder, W. T. Grant department store chain; Greenwich, Conn., Aug. 6.

Ferde Grofé, 80, composer (*Grand Canyon Suite*); Santa Monica, Calif., April 3.

Nubar Gulbenkian, 75, Armenian-born financier, eccentric oil millionaire; Cannes, France, Jan. 10.

Carl T. Hayden, 94, U.S. Senator (D-Ariz., 1927–69), president pro tempore of the Senate (1957–69); Mesa, Ariz., Jan. 25.

Gabriel Heatter, 82, radio news commentator; Miami Beach, Fla., March 30.

Gil Hodges, 47, first baseman of the Brooklyn and Los Angeles Dodgers, manager of New York Mets (1968–72); West Palm Beach, Fla., April 2.

Miriam Hopkins, 69, movie actress (*Becky Sharp* and *Old Acquaintance*); New York City, Oct. 9.

Howard D. Johnson, 75, founder, Howard Johnson restaurant-motel chain; New York City, June 20.

Yasunari Kawabata, 72, only Japanese novelist to win a Nobel Prize (1968); Zushi, Japan, April 16.

Edward C. Kendall, 86, physiologist, winner of Nobel Prize (1950); Princeton, N.J., May 4.

Louis S. B. Leakey, 69, British anthropologist; London, Oct. 1.

Violette Leduc, 65, French existentialist novelist (*La Bâtarde*); Faucon, France, May 28.

Jose Limon, 64, Mexican-born, U.S. modern dancer and choreographer (*The Moor's Pavane*); Flemington, N.J., Dec. 2.

Edward V. Long, 64, U.S. Senator (D-Mo., 1961–69); Brookhill, Mo., Nov. 7.

Heinrich Luebke, 77, second president of West Germany (1959–69); Bonn, April 6.

Neil H. McElroy, 68, U.S. secretary of defense (1957–59); Cincinnati, Ohio, Nov. 30.

Ruth McKenney, 60, author (*My Sister Eileen*); New York City, July 25.

Compton Mackenzie, 89, British novelist, playwright and biographer (*The Four Winds of Change* and *Whisky Galore*); Edinburgh, Nov. 30.

R. Samuel McLaughlin, 100, Canadian automotive pioneer; Oshawa, Ontario, Jan. 6.

Marilyn Maxwell, 49, Hollywood actress and singer; Beverly Hills, Calif., March 20.

Maria Goeppert Mayer, 65, U.S. physicist, first woman since Marie Curie to win Nobel Prize in Physics (1963); San Diego, Calif., Feb. 20.

Bronislava Nijinska, 81, Russian-born choreographer and dancer; Pacific Palisades, Calif., Feb. 21.

Norman Norell, 72, U.S. fashion designer; New York City, Oct. 25.

Basil O'Connor, 80, medical philanthropist, first president, National Foundation of March of Dimes; Phoenix, Ariz., March 9.

Maurice Chevalier, 83, French singer and film actor ("Gigi," "Love in the Afternoon"); Paris, Jan. 1.

UPI

Jules Romains, 86, French novelist ("Men of Good Will"), dramatist, poet; Paris, Aug. 14.

Rapho Guillumette

Kwame Nkrumah, 62, president of Ghana (1957–66); Bucharest, April 27.

Central Press from Pictorial

Marianne Moore, 84, poet, Pulitzer Prize and National Book Award winner; N.Y.C., Feb. 5.

"A" from Pictorial

Edgar Snow, 66, American journalist, sinologist ("Red Star Over China"); Eysins, Switzerland, Feb. 15.

Nils-Gunnar Nilsson, Random House

"Paris Match," from Pictorial

Paul-Henri Spaak, 73, Belgian diplomat, architect of European unity; Brussels, July 31.

Syndication International, Photo Trends

Dame Margaret Rutherford, 80, English actress known for comic stage and screen roles, Chalfont St. Peter, Buckinghamshire, May 22.

Nathan Orbach, 87, founder and director, Orbach chain of department stores; New York City, Nov. 19.

Kenneth Patchen, 60, poet, one of the first to read his poetry to jazz accompaniment; Palo Alto, Calif., Jan. 8.

Rudolf Petrak, 54, Czechoslovakian opera singer and tenor with the New York City Opera Company (1948–56); Greenwich, Conn., March 4.

Philip J. Philbin, 74, U.S. Congressman (R-Mass., 1941–71); Bolton, Mass., June 14.

Adam Clayton Powell, 63, Baptist minister, controversial 11-term U.S. Congressman (D-N.Y.), chairman, House Committee on Education and Labor; Miami, Fla., April 4.

Michael Rabin, 35, violinist; New York City, Jan. 19.

Chakravarti Rajagopalachari, 94, governor-general of India (1948–50), leader of India's fight for independence; Madras, India, Dec. 25.

William F. Ryan, 50, U.S. Congressman (D-N.Y., 1961–72); New York City, Sept. 17.

Aline Saarinen, 58, art critic and television commentator; New York City, July 14.

Marquess of Salisbury, 78, British Conservative party leader; Hertfordshire, England, Feb. 23.

George Sanders, 65, film actor, known for his portrayals of the cynic or villain (All About Eve and Rebecca); Barcelona, April 25.

Harlow Shapley, 86, U.S. astronomer, proved that the solar system is located at the galaxy's edge; Boulder, Colo., Oct. 20.

Ted Shawn, 80, the "father of modern dance"; Orlando, Fla., Jan. 9.

Igor I. Sikorsky, 83, U.S. aviator, developed first practical helicopter (1939); Easton, Conn., Oct. 26.

Betty Smith, 75, author of best-selling novel A Tree Grows in Brooklyn; Shelton, Conn., Jan. 17.

Joseph Fielding Smith, 95, tenth president Church of Latter-Day Saints; Salt Lake City, July 2.

Akim Tamiroff, 72, Russian-born character actor (For Whom the Bell Tolls); Palm Springs, Calif., Sept. 17.

Max Theiler, 73, developed yellow fever vaccine, Nobel Prize winner (1951); New Haven, Conn., Aug. 11.

Llewellyn E. Thompson, 67, U.S. diplomat, ambassador to U.S.S.R. (1957–62, 1967–68); Bethesda, Md., Feb. 6.

Eugene Cardinal Tisserant, 87, dean of the Roman Catholic College of Cardinals (1951–72); Albano, Italy, Feb. 21.

Helen Traubel, 69, Wagnerian soprano; Santa Monica, Calif., July 28.

Paul Howard (Dizzy) Trout, 56, Detroit Tigers' baseball pitcher; Chicago, Ill., Feb. 28.

Mark Van Doren, 78, poet, critic and professor, author of Introduction to Poetry; Torrington, Conn., Dec. 10.

John Carter Vincent, 72, China specialist, director, U.S. State Department's Office of Far Eastern Affairs (1945); Cambridge, Mass., Dec. 3.

Georg von Bekesy, 73, Hungarian-born scientist, Nobel Prize winner for human ear research (1961); Honolulu, Hawaii, June 13.

Margaret Webster, 67, British actress and director; London, Nov. 13.

Sinclair Weeks, 78, secretary of commerce (1953–58); Concord, Mass., Feb. 7.

George Weiss, 78, baseball executive, general manager, New York Yankees (1947–60), president, New York Mets (1961–66); Greenwich, Conn., Aug. 13.

Charles E. Wilson, 85, president, General Electric Co., (1940–42; 1944–50); Scarsdale, N.Y., Jan. 3.

Walter Winchell, 74, radio commentator and newspaper columnist; Los Angeles, Calif., Feb. 20.

DEFENSE

Anticipating disengagement from seven years of war in Vietnam, the United States defense establishment placed new emphasis in 1972 on modernizing its nuclear force and converting to a smaller, all-volunteer Army.

National security became a major issue in the U.S. presidential campaign as the Democratic candidate for the White House, Sen. George S. McGovern, advocated a three-year, $30,000,000,000 reduction in defense spending. President Nixon warned of cuts that would, he said, make the United States a second-rate world power, and the President's supporters went further to charge that Senator McGovern's defense budget would raise a "white flag of surrender" to American adversaries.

Congress approved a $74,300,000,000 military appropriations bill, the largest since the end of World War II, but about $5,000,000,000 less than the administration requested in its budget for fiscal year 1973. In a separate action, Congress cut $2,300,000,000 from the President's proposals before approving a $20,900,000,000 military procurement bill.

Although the totals were large, the figures concealed some significant trends. Since President Nixon took office and began withdrawing U.S. troops from Vietnam, military manpower has been reduced by one-third and purchases from military contractors have been lowered by one-fourth.

Major salary increases—including a 100 percent increase in pay for the lower ranks of officers and enlisted men—accounted for much of the higher defense outlays. Inflation, which was triggered by the Vietnam buildup in 1965 and later years, also swelled the Pentagon budget.

With Vietnam spending down from a peak of $28,000,000,000 to about $6,000,000,000 in 1972, President Nixon decided to seek funds for a new nuclear submarine, the Trident, and the development of the B-1 bomber, a supersonic replacement for the B-52 nuclear fleet. Some analysts predicted a defense budget of $100,000,000,000 by 1980.

Defense Secretary Melvin R. Laird, completing a four-year term in the cabinet post, said he believed the historic arms reduction agreements negotiated with the Soviet Union in 1971–72 should be scrapped if Congress refused to provide money for the Trident and the B-1. Critics objected to the cost of the new weapons systems. The Pentagon estimated each Trident submarine would cost $1,200,000,000 and the B-1 could cost $80,000,000 per plane. Senator McGovern contended that existing Polaris and Poseidon submarines are adequate to serve as the U.S. undersea nuclear deterrent and regarded a manned bomber as a wasteful investment in the Missile Era. Together, the Trident and B-1 would cost $25,000,000,000 over the next decade.

The differences between the administration and Senator McGovern also involved the number of troops required in Europe as part of the U.S. commitment to the North Atlantic Treaty Organization (NATO). Early in his campaign, Senator McGovern said he favored withdrawal of half of the 300,000 U.S. servicemen assigned to NATO nations. Later he said he favored consultation with allies before reducing troop levels and wanted to keep enough military strength in Europe and the Mediterranean to aid Israel in case Soviet forces were increased in the Middle East. "What is essential in our relations with other NATO nations is not a particular troop level but our continued commitment to collective defense," the Democratic party platform said.

In contrast, President Nixon pledged to strengthen the Atlantic alliance and supported mutual, balanced reduction of military forces in Europe in negotiations with the Soviet-backed Warsaw Pact countries. The groundwork for such talks was laid and preparatory meetings begun in Helsinki for a European Security Conference early in 1973. The United States, Canada and 32 European countries—Communist, non-Communist and neutral—were invited to discuss troop reductions.

As part of his program to end U.S. involvement in Vietnam, President Nixon ordered that draftees not be assigned to the Indochina war area against their will. Moreover, the reduction of U.S. forces in Vietnam to fewer than 35,000 by the end of 1972 made it possible to reduce draft calls to 50,000 for the year. Mr. Nixon set a target date of July 1, 1973, to end reliance on the draft entirely and urged Congress to approve special reenlistment bonuses for Army specialists and National Guard and Army reserve troops to assure combat readiness.

In submitting his budget, the President projected a decrease in military manpower to 2,358,000 by mid-1973. This would represent a decline of 1,189,000 from peak strength at the height of U.S. fighting in Vietnam in 1968. Under Mr. Nixon's plan, the Army would have a strength of 841,000; Air Force, 717,000; Navy, 602,000; and Marines, 198,000. The figures included cuts of 20,000 for the Army and 13,000 for the Air Force. Congress, however, cut still further and established a troop ceiling of 2,342,000 for the year ending June 30, 1973.

A member of the new civilian corps of cooks and dishwashers authorized by the U.S. Congress in 1972 attends to the "KP" duty formerly assigned to enlisted men.

U.S. Army Photo

A larger role for women in the Army was expected with the advent of an all-volunteer force. The size of the Women's Army Corps was scheduled to double in five years, from its 1972 level of 13,000. All but 48 combat-related jobs of the 484 military specialties were declared open for women applicants. In the Navy, precedent was shattered when women were assigned to general sea duty for the first time and billets traditionally assigned only to men opened to Navy women.

In another history-making development, Congress ended the widely unpopular duty of "kitchen police" or "KP" for enlisted men and women. It allocated $60,000,000 to enable the Army to hire civilian cooks and dishwashers. President Nixon opted for continuity in another major respect, however, by appointing Adm. Thomas D. Moorer to a second two-year term as chairman of the Joint Chiefs of Staff.

The most serious blow to the Pentagon's high command during 1972 was a Senate investigation of charges that, from late 1971 to early 1972, Air Force Gen. John D. Lavelle conducted 28 bombing raids on targets in North Vietnam without authorization. Lavelle was relieved of command and retired at two-star rank, a symbolic reprimand that did not reduce his $27,000 annual pension. Although the Senate Armed Services Committee concluded that Lavelle alone was responsible for the unauthorized raids from Udorn Air Base in Thailand, the general said he had had assurances that his military superiors would not question the covert violation of standing orders.

The Lavelle case raised the issue of civilian control over military commanders in the field inasmuch as it was not disputed that the bombing raids broke the "rules of engagement" in effect at the time. The rules did not permit bombing in North Vietnam unless U.S. planes

were fired on from the ground or unless enemy radar had fixed their location and speed, preparatory to firing.

An Air Force intelligence sergeant, Lonnie D. Franks, testified that more than 200 officers and men were involved in falsifying reports to justify "protective reaction" raids that otherwise would not have been allowed. Moorer and Gen. Creighton W. Abrams, who was U.S. commander in Vietnam when Lavelle headed the 7th Air Force, both denied any knowledge of the unauthorized attacks.

In a letter to the committee, Lavelle said his staff was told that the Joint Chiefs of Staff would provide "full backing" in case of adverse publicity from the raids directed against North Vietnamese airfields and antiaircraft installations. "It seemed clear to me that higher authorities had recommended, encouraged and commended an extremely liberal policy, well beyond the literal language of the rules of engagement," Lavelle said.

President Nixon's resumption of bombing of North Vietnam on May 8, designed to halt the Communist invasion of South Vietnam, took some of the steam out of the charges against the Air Force general. In a related development, five Navy pilots said they also had made bombing raids from their carrier which violated the rules of aerial warfare.

Hearings into Lavelle's actions, triggered by the sergeant's letter to Sen. Harold Hughes (D-Iowa), delayed confirmations of Abrams' nomination to be Army Chief of Staff for more than five weeks. He was approved on an 84–2 vote.

The Pentagon also was rocked by a report from the General Accounting Office declaring that three of the four Army divisions in a Strategic Armed Force were not "combat ready" because of defective tanks, radars and

rifles. Only the 82nd Airborne division, stationed at Ft. Bragg, N.C., was thought to be ready for instant mobilization.

In a little-noticed aftermath to the controversy over disclosure of the secret Pentagon Papers dealing with U.S. involvement in Vietnam, the Federal government sharply reduced the number of persons authorized to wield secrecy stamps. The number of persons who can restrict public access to documents was reduced from 43,586 to 16,238 with the largest decline occurring in the Pentagon, where the stamp-wielders were reduced from 30,542 to 8,809. Daniel Ellsberg, the former Rand Corporation consultant accused of leaking the documents to *The New York Times* and other publications, won a delay in his Federal trial until the Supreme Court decides if the Justice Department must disclose wiretapped conversations involving a defense lawyer.

WILLIAM J. EATON
Washington Correspondent, *Chicago Daily News*

DENMARK

King Frederick IX of Denmark, who had reigned since 1947, died on Jan. 14. His death was attributed to an attack of Asiatic flu and subsequent heart failure. He was buried in the Cathedral of Roskilde, the traditional place of interment for Danish monarchs. His oldest daughter, who became Queen Margrethe II, succeeded him on the throne. (The first Margrethe was a Danish queen who also ruled Norway and Sweden in the late 14th century.) Queen Margrethe II, who was born in 1940 and educated both in England and France, has a keen interest in archeology. Her husband, Prince Henrik, is a former French diplomat, Count Henri de Laborde de Monpezat. The couple has two children.

The year 1972 was a year of decision for Denmark as well as Norway. The issue of whether Denmark should join the European Economic Community (EEC) had been hotly debated for years, by the press, the politicians and the general public. Because Britain and West Germany form the two largest markets for Danish exports, it was felt that EEC membership would greatly aid an economy being threatened by inflation and a faltering balance of payments. Opponents of membership pointed to a possible loss of sovereignty and autonomy by Denmark and also expressed fear that membership would promote the influx of international conglomerates. The final decision on membership was left to the people, in an Oct. 2 plebiscite whose outcome was binding on the Folketing (Parliament). Although Norway had rejected EEC membership the previous week, the Danish voters rolled up a solid majority favoring membership; the final result was 1,955,932 in favor and 1,124,106 opposed.

On Oct. 3, Prime Minister Jens Otto Krag announced unexpectedly that he would resign, wishing to return to private life. The ruling Social Democratic party selected Anker Jorgen-

Queen Margrethe II, who succeeded her father King Frederick IX upon his death Jan. 14, presides over her first Council of Ministers.

Henri Bureau-Gamma

sen, 50, a labor union leader and member of the Folketing, as his successor, but no other change was made in the cabinet.

In April, Denmark inaugurated its fourth university, located in the city of Roskilde on the island of Zealand. The student body of 700 will receive a rather unorthodox education, their six years of study being divided into three two-year periods, devoted successively to the study of political and social science, natural science and the humanities.

In August the first oil was brought ashore from the Danish sector of the apparently oil-rich bottom of the North Sea. Drilling had taken place in an area lying about 125 miles west of the city of Esbjerg, and the oil was removed in large tankers. The area is also expected to yield large quantities of natural gas.

ERIK J. FRIIS
Editor, *The American-Scandinavian Review*

DISARMAMENT

The United States and the Soviet Union, antagonists for nearly a quarter of a century following World War II, took an initial, historic step away from nuclear catastrophe in 1972.

President Nixon signed an agreement in the Kremlin with Soviet Communist Party Secretary Leonid I. Brezhnev to place the first limit on strategic weapons in each nation's nuclear arsenal. Moreover, they agreed to seek a further slowdown in the arms race in a second round of Strategic Arms Limitation Talks (SALT), which holds the key to lasting disarmament.

Mr. Nixon, whose accomplishments in Moscow contributed to his landslide reelection victory on Nov. 7, received overwhelming Congressional approval for the accords. Congress instructed him, however, not to limit the United States to "levels of intercontinental strategic forces inferior to the limits provided for the Soviet Union" in any future agreement.

In requesting endorsement of the first-round results, the President urged Congress to approve his plans for a new and faster bomber, the B-1, and a longer-range nuclear submarine, the Trident, to provide "bargaining chips" for SALT II. He said the "supreme interests" of the nation could be jeopardized if there was not agreement on more comprehensive arms reduction within the next five years.

The accord reached in Moscow has two parts. The first part limits each nation to two antiballistic missile (ABM) systems. One must be centered on the national capitals—Moscow and Washington. The other may be placed to defend a part of either the Soviet or U.S.

attacking missile force—the dreaded Intercontinental Ballistic Missiles (ICBMs). Under the terms of the agreement, no ABM site may have more than 100 antimissile missiles; its radar also is limited.

The understanding will be enforced by U.S. and Soviet camera-carrying satellites, the spy-in-the-sky satellites long used by both nations for intelligence gathering. These aerial observers were termed "national technical means of verification" in the diplomatic language of the formal documents. A standing consultative commission, composed of Soviet and American officials, was established to carry out the agreement and discuss possible revisions.

The second part of the agreement dealt with offensive nuclear weapons—the ICBMs and missiles fired from submarines known as SLBMs (for submarine-launched ballistic missiles). Both countries agreed not to start construction of more land-based ICBMs after July 1, 1972. Modern submarines and SLBMs were to be limited to those at sea or under construction on May 26, 1972, when the agreement was signed. The limitations were to expire in five years unless reconfirmed or extended before 1977.

Henry A. Kissinger, assistant to President Nixon for national security affairs, said the Soviet Union had a total of 2,328 missiles—1,618 ICBMs and 710 SLBMs—when the accord was signed. The United States, he said, had a total of 1,710, composed of 1,054 ICBMs and 656 SLBMs.

But the United States, because of multiple warheads on many of its missiles, has a total of 5,900 nuclear warheads compared with the 2,200 in the Soviet Union. U.S. bombers capable of carrying nuclear weapons total 531, compared with 140 such planes in the Soviet air force. The Soviets, however, have bigger payloads, among them the giant SS-9 missile with the destructive power of 25 megatons.

As Kissinger explained the agreement to American newspapermen in the garish nightclub of Moscow's Intourist hotel: "If you compare megatonnage, the Soviets have about three times as much. If you count warheads, we have about three times as much."

Critics such as Sen. Henry Jackson (D-Wash.) noted that the protocol which was made a part of the agreement on offensive weapons would allow the Soviets to have 62 modern nuclear submarines, compared with 44 for the United States. Jackson also said the Soviets would be free to place multiple warheads on their missiles once they had mastered the technology to do so. "In no area covered by the agreement is the United States permitted to

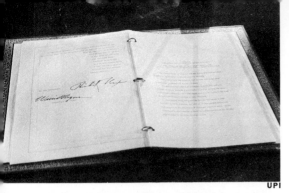

President Nixon and Communist Party Secretary Brezhnev sign the Strategic Arms Limitation agreement (above) restricting the nuclear capabilities of their countries.

maintain parity with the Soviet Union," Jackson told the Senate even before President Nixon had returned from his journey to Moscow.

Joseph Alsop, a columnist, said Nixon had accepted an agreement that would allow the Soviet Union to have a 3–2 lead in nuclear strategic power for some years to come. Alsop termed this "a calculated risk of the most hair-raising character."

Supporters of the accord said it was designed to assure that both the Soviets and the United States would be equally vulnerable to mass destruction in the event of nuclear war, leading each side to pull back from a potential disaster. Secretary of State William P. Rogers said the agreement represented "the most important step in arms limitation ever taken by this country." Gerard C. Smith, the U.S. diplomat who was a chief negotiator at Helsinki and Vienna during the first SALT talks, said the ABM treaty was "of tremendous psychological importance, a recognition that the deterrence (attacking) force of either side is not going to be challenged." Kissinger added: "The future will record that both sides won."

The President, appearing before a joint session of Congress on June 1, said the agreements would block a "major spiraling of the arms race." He also assured the lawmakers that no power on earth was stronger than the United States and that he would preserve that strength.

Explaining his request for new weapons systems on the heels of the step taken to limit nuclear arms, the President later told Congressional leaders: "Since they (the Soviets) will be going ahead with their programs, for the United States not to go ahead with its programs would mean that any incentive the Soviets had to negotiate the follow-on agreement would be removed." And he said the United States was going to benefit from a freeze on missile deployment because it has no current building program under way for the categories of weapons which were limited by the agreement.

Despite the assurances, Senator Jackson successfully fought for an amendment directing the President not to accept "inferiority" in future negotiations with the Soviet Union. The Nixon administration supported Jackson's position, but the debate delayed approval for five weeks.

Sen. J. William Fulbright, chairman of the Senate Foreign Relations Committee, unsuccessfully argued that Jackson really favored superiority in view of the American advantage in warheads, accuracy and nuclear weapons deployed in Europe. The Senate rejected, 48–38, Fulbright's proposal to require the United States to seek only "overall equality, parity and sufficiency" in arms reduction talks in the future. The Senate then approved the agreement by an 88–2 vote, and the House by a vote of 306–4.

With success in Moscow behind them, the United States and the Soviet Union scheduled intensive negotiations in 1973 on SALT II. A conference on European Security was on the agenda also, along with the start of talks on Mutual and Balanced Force Reductions in Europe in what could become a turning point toward wide-scale disarmament.

WILLIAM J. EATON
Washington Correspondent
Chicago Daily News

DISARMAMENT   181

DISASTERS

January 7   Spain: An Iberian Airlines jet crashes into a mountainside on the Spanish island of Ibiza; 104 persons die.

26   Colombia: Torrential rains trigger a landslide in the Bogota village of San Josecito, killing some 70 people.

February 18   Egypt: A bus traveling from Port Said to Cairo veers into a bridge wall and plunges into a Nile River canal; 77 persons die.

26   United States: Torrential rains cause a makeshift dam of coal mine wastes to burst and flood a valley in Logan County, W. Va.; 118 persons die.

March 11   U.S.S.R.: A fire and/or explosion at a radio engineering plant at Minsk takes about 100 lives.

14   Union of Arab Emirates: A Danish charter plane returning from Ceylon crashes near Kalba; 112 persons killed.

April 10   Iran: A major earthquake, registering 7 on the Richter scale, strikes southern Iran, devastating the villages of Ghir and Karzin; about 5,000 people are killed.

May 2   United States: A smoldering fire erupts at the 3,700-ft. level of the Sunshine Silver Mine in Kellogg, Idaho; 91 killed.

6   Italy: An Alitalia DC-8 jetliner strikes a mountainside near the Palermo airport, killing all 115 aboard.

11   Uruguay: A Liberian oil tanker, the *Tien Chee*, and a British cargo ship, the *Royston Grange*, collide at entrance to River Plate channel; 83 die.

13   Japan: A fire erupts in a nightclub atop a department store in Osaka; at least 115 persons die.

18   U.S.S.R.: A Soviet Antonov 10 airliner bound from Moscow to Kharkov crashes on its landing approach to Kharkov airport; 108 are killed.

June 4   Bangladesh: A crowded passenger train is directed to the wrong track upon entering the station at Jessore and strikes a stopped train; 76 die, over 500 injured.

6   Rhodesia: An explosion at the Wankie Colliery in northwestern Rhodesia traps workers in the underground coal mine; 427 miners die.

10   United States: Flash floods, the result of thunderstorms over the Black Hills, collapse two dams and inundate Rapid City, S.D.; 235 die, some 2,000 are left homeless.

14   India: A Japan Air Lines DC-8 jet crashes as it prepares to land at an airport near New Delhi; 85 die.

15   South Vietnam: A Cathay Pacific Airlines flight bound for Hong Kong crashes in South Vietnam's Central Highlands; 81 persons die.

16   France: Two trains derail and collide in a tunnel near Soissons; 107 persons die, some 90 are injured.

18   England: A British European Airways jet crashes into a field after taking off from Heathrow airport in London; 118 persons die.

   Hong Kong: Three days of tumultuous rains start massive landslides and the collapse of large apartment buildings; over 100 die.

19–24   United States: Hurricane Agnes sweeps north from Gulf of Mexico and during its week-long journey up the Eastern Coast deluges sections of Florida, Virginia, West Virginia, Maryland and New York; 134 persons die; some 500,000 left homeless.

25   Philippines: Typhoon Ora strikes central and southern Luzon, Eastern Visayas and the Bicol region, killing over 100 persons; some 26,000 families homeless.

July 17   Japan: Floods and landslides follow two weeks of heavy rains in many areas of Japan; at least 370 persons are killed, 67 are missing.

21   Spain: A holiday express train and a local passenger train crash head-on in southern Spain; 76 persons die; 103 are injured.

August 6   Philippines: Month-old floodwaters that collapsed dams and caused landslides begin to recede, leaving an estimated 250 dead.

9   Nepal: Over a two-week period, landslides and monsoon floods claim at least 105 lives.

14   East Germany: A Soviet-built Ilyushin 62 explodes in the air and crashes minutes after take-off from East Berlin's Schönefeld airport, killing all 156 persons aboard.

20   South Korea: Extremely heavy rains produce flooding that destroys an estimated $17,000,000 of property in the northern sector of the nation; at least 368 deaths, 326,000 homeless.

September 16   Philippines: A wooden bridge, thronged with worshippers during a religious festival in Naga city, collapses and plunges into the Bicol River; at least 100 die.

October 4   U.S.S.R.: A Soviet Ilyushin-18 crashes near the Black Sea resort of Sochi; 100 are killed.

5   Mexico: A speeding train carrying passengers from a religious fiesta jumps the tracks near Saltillo, killing 208 persons.

13   U.S.S.R.: A Soviet Ilyushin 62 passenger jet crashes and explodes near Moscow's Sheremetevo airport, killing 176 persons.

December 3   Canary Islands: A chartered Spanish Convair 990-A Coronado crashes shortly after takeoff from Santa Cruz de Tenerife, killing 155 persons.

21   Ceylon: A landslide caused by heavy rains in the central section of the nation kills 50 persons.

23   Nicaragua: A major earthquake strikes Managua, the nation's capital, destroying most of the city's buildings, leaving over 10,000 persons dead and an estimated 200,000 homeless.

29   United States: An Eastern Airlines TriStar jumbo jet crashes in an Everglades swamp on its approach to Miami International Airport, killing 100 of the 176 persons on board.

In Congers, N.Y., March 24, a freight train ripped through a school bus at a crossing, killing five high-school students and injuring 45 others.

Despite a devastating earthquake that left 10,000 Nicaraguans dead and 90 percent of the population of Managua without shelter, the city's cathedral escaped serious damage.

Rescue workers combed the wreckage of a jumbo jet that crashed in the Florida Everglades on Dec. 29. One hundred lives were lost in the crash.

DRUG ABUSE

Cruel and ruinous, the heroin epidemic continued its sweep across the United States in 1972. Unofficial estimates indicated that as many as 650,000 Americans were addicted. The figure was 10 times that for the country's total addict population in the mid-1960's.

While there were some signs that the tide might be stemmed, or eventually reversed, the unabated spread of heroin was the harshest fact of the changing drug scene. It was not simply a big city crisis, either. "Horse" or "smack" was becoming popular in small towns as well, partly seeded by returning Vietnam servicemen, some authorities complained.

Heroin continued to reach into the middle class and blue collar youth, and to the very young. In one area of New York City youth workers told of 9 and 10 year olds working as "pushers" in their neighborhoods. In that same metropolis estimates of the addicted population ranged up to 400,000, with 1,000 persons reported dying of overdoses of heroin a year, and about 1,000 babies being born a year addicted from their mothers' habit, and having to undergo withdrawal.

Marijuana was still popular, and apparently increasingly so on college campuses. The National Commission on Marijuana and Drug Abuse estimated that 24,600,000 Americans have tried "pot," with 8,300,000 currently using it. Stating that there might be some risk from heavy, long-term use of marijuana, the commission opposed its legalization, but also opposed criminal penalties for private possession. (Similarly, the Canadian government eased its marijuana laws, but rejected recommendations aimed at legalizing possession.)

The American Bar Association called for reducing criminal penalties for possession and use of marijuana. And the American Medical Association recommended that personal possession of "insignificant" amounts of marijuana be considered at most a misdemeanor (which is what Federal law now calls for) with commensurate penalties to be applied.

The liberalization of laws and a trend to decriminalize personal possession stirred concern for persons imprisoned under earlier laws that made possession of pot a felony. In at least four states numerous prisoners were freed, with other states considering similar steps. In Michigan one of 128 persons freed by a state Supreme Court order was a radical poet who had been sentenced in 1969 to nine and a half to ten years for possession of two marijuana cigarettes.

Some authorities reported increased consumption of cocaine. The flow of cocaine smuggled from Chile was said to be at record levels.

In the treatment of heroin addiction, programs utilizing methadone—a synthetic, addictive narcotic that eliminates some of the craving for heroin—continued to expand. In August the White House Special Action Office for Drug Abuse Prevention estimated that methadone was being dispensed to some 85,000 addicts in about 450 programs throughout the United States.

Methadone maintenance had its critics. Some opposed it on ethical grounds—substituting one addictive drug for another, they said. And the drug was frequently diverted to illegal use. Deaths occurred among persons who took strong doses to which they had not acquired a tolerance. Some critics said that the programs should be accompanied by efforts at social rehabilitation of addicts.

Proponents credited methadone with having helped many addicts lead useful, constructive lives. A study by New York City's Health Services Administration in cooperation with the Police Department reported that arrest rates of drug addicts enrolled in the city's methadone treatment programs had dropped as much as 82 percent. The study involved 333 addicts arrested for crimes and drug use.

Dr. Jerome H. Jaffe, head of the White House office, said that the true addiction rate among servicemen leaving Vietnam was down to 1.1 percent to 1.5 percent of all men returning, compared with about 5.5 percent to 6 percent when a program to detect and treat drug abusers was instituted in June 1971.

Forms of methadone that would be effective for longer than one day continued to be tested, and the White House announced a new $2,000,000 intensified program to perfect safe, long lasting and nonaddictive drugs to treat

WHO USES MARIJUANA?		
	YOUTHS (age 12-17)	ADULTS (18 and over)
Have used marijuana but no longer use it	45%	41%
Use it once a month or less	15%	9%
Use it 2-3 times a month	10%	8%
Use it once a week	9%	4%
Use it several times a week	4%	5%
Use it once a day	1%	1%
Use it more than once a day	4%	2%
No answer in survey	12%	30%

National Commission on Marijuana and Drug Abuse

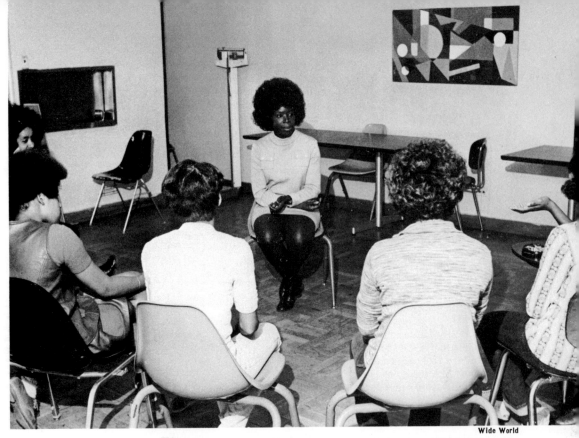

Some experts believe that the best treatment for drug addicts is to group them with counselors and reformed addicts in a family atmosphere.

and prevent heroin addiction. Part of the effort seeks chemicals that would block the effects of heroin, possibly for several weeks. Experts were also looking for a vaccine that might prevent heroin addiction permanently.

In another direction, the National Institute of Mental Health announced that it was exploring psychological substitutes for drug addiction. "We hope," said Dr. Bertram S. Brown, NIMH director, "to focus the skills, energy and ideas of people all over the country on discovering innovative pursuits and resources to meet human needs and make life more rewarding. . . . Drug abuse basically springs from boredom, alienation, and a sense of inability to cope with life. It is obvious that efforts to combat drug abuse are futile unless we expand opportunities for young people and adults to find satisfaction and meaning in today's world."

In February four leading U.S. foundations created the National Drug Abuse Council, calling it a major effort to evaluate and coordinate drug treatment programs. The Ford and Kaiser foundations, Carnegie Corporation and Commonwealth Fund were to donate $5,000,000 to $10,000,000 by 1977 for the proj-

ect. And in New York City some 75 labor and business organizations formed PACT (Provide Addict Care Today) with the goal of placing every heroin addict in the city under treatment by the end of 1974. Helping to provide jobs for former addicts is also a target. The organizations will contribute $500,000 a year to PACT.

Agents of the Bureau of Narcotics and Dangerous Drugs and U.S. Customs intercepted and seized increasing amounts of heroin, but the demand was still huge and the supplies kept coming into the United States. In fact, the U.S. government, in a 111-page report prepared by the Cabinet Committee on International Narcotics Control, revealed that despite increased enforcement efforts the United States and other nations seized only a "small fraction" of the total illegal heroin flow.

Some experts predicted that the war on heroin would end only if the addicts' desire could be controlled or eliminated. But not even the most optimistic experts on drug abuse could predict how or when that might be achieved.

ALTON BLAKESLEE
Science Editor, The Associated Press

ECONOMIC AFFAIRS

U.S. ECONOMY

The United States' economy surged ahead strongly in 1972, building up a head of steam that was expected to produce even more growth in 1973 as it made the transition from a mere recession rebound to a full-fledged expansion. The first full year of peacetime wage and price controls in the country's history saw many economic indicators reach new records, although some serious trouble spots remained.

The wage-price control system created by President Nixon in late 1971—the so-called "Phase Two" that followed a 90-day freeze on wages and prices—continued through the year, with plans underway to shift into Phase Three early in 1973.

Under Phase Three, announced on Jan. 11, 1973, all mandatory wage and price controls, except those involving food, health care and construction industries, as well as all Federal rent controls, were ended. In addition, the Federal Price Commission and Pay Board were abolished and the controls were replaced with a system based on "voluntary cooperation." The President did, however, ask Congress to extend until April 30, 1974, his authority to control wages and prices.

Whether the growth of 1972 was due to the imposition of controls, which lent an air of stability and encouraged business executives to expand and consumers to spend, or developed simply because all the economic factors were in place was a subject of frequent debate. But that the economy recorded one of its best all-time performances was undeniable.

The broadest gauge of all, the gross national product—the total value of all the goods and services produced in the country—rose to $1,152,000,000,000 (or $1.152 trillion), a gain of about 10 percent over the year–end 1971. One of the most encouraging aspects of the increase, moreover, was the fact that price inflation accounted for only about 3.5 percent, while "real" growth made up 6.5 percent.

The 3.5 percent inflation rate was still above the 3 percent level named as the administration's target when the inflation-fighting plan was inaugurated, but it was a sharp drop from the 6 percent annual rate of price hikes registered before controls.

Throughout most sectors of the economy the story was much the same: strong growth. Personal income climbed to about $972,000,000,-000, a gain of about 11 percent. Disposable income—that part left after taxes—was up 6.5 percent, to $793,500,000,000. Corporate profits after taxes soared 15 percent, to $53,900,000,-000 (although dividends paid by those corporations climbed only slightly, to $26,500,000,000, because corporations were anxious to increase their liquidity—holdings of cash—and the wage-price control guidelines limited dividend increases to 4.5 percent a year).

As noted, however, there were some important areas in which the government's planning did not pay off. Although the overall inflation rate declined, food prices continued to rise sharply. In November alone food prices rose at an annual rate of 13.2 percent. (Agricultural goods were not subject to controls.)

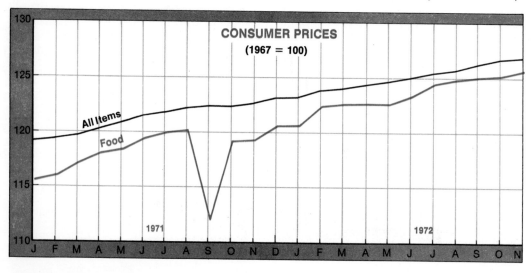

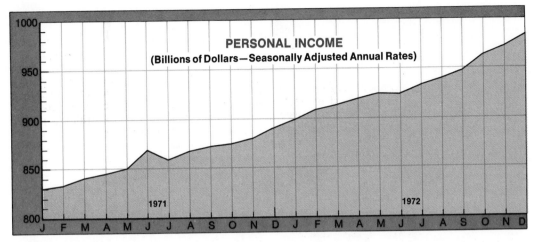

PERSONAL INCOME
(Billions of Dollars—Seasonally Adjusted Annual Rates)

One of the prime targets of Federal economic policy was to reduce the unemployment rate to no more than 5 percent by year end, from the 5.9 percent level of 1971. Throughout most of 1972 the unemployment rate held just under the 6 percent figure, with four one-month declines to 5.5 percent. Not until November did unemployment really fall, but that month showed a rate of 5.2 percent, the lowest since August 1970. For the year as a whole unemployment averaged about 5.5 per-

cent of the work force. At the end of November some 82,700,000 Americans were at work, an increase of 2,000,000 over 1971, while 4,300,000 were still looking for jobs.

American trade with foreign countries also did not respond to government efforts. In 1971 the country had experienced its first balance-of-trade deficit since 1893, and the situation worsened appreciably in 1972. The balance of trade measures the flow of goods in and out of the country. It is a prime component of the balance of payments (BOP), which also includes such factors as tourist spending overseas, government military and economic aid and business investment abroad. In the years since World War II the BOP had almost always been in deficit, but surpluses in the balance of trade kept the red ink from getting too far out of hand.

Through the first 11 months of 1972, however, the balance of trade posted a deficit of $5,800,000,000 on an annual basis, compared with $2,000,000,000 in 1971. Clearly new efforts would have to be made to bolster American exports, and, in fact, President Nixon

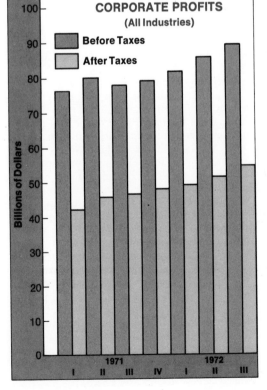

CORPORATE PROFITS
(All Industries)

Before Taxes
After Taxes

Billions of Dollars

1971 — I II III IV
1972 — I II III

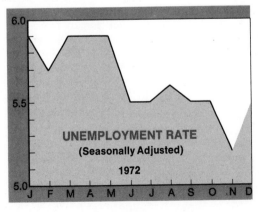

UNEMPLOYMENT RATE
(Seasonally Adjusted)
1972

SEC Chairman William J. Casey was named undersecretary of state for economic affairs.

named William J. Casey, chairman of the Securities and Exchange Commission, to be undersecretary of state for economic affairs, a post that had been vacant for years, to concentrate on that probem.

The currency revaluations of 1971 and stronger government efforts to expand American markets overseas nevertheless brought a marked improvement in the BOP figures. For the year, the deficit was estimated at about $10,000,000,000, and further improvement was expected in the near future.

The year itself produced no major economic event in the United States. Instead, the economy seemed just to keep building momentum. There was some uneasiness among businessmen when Sen. George McGovern of South Dakota was nominated for President by the Democratic party inasmuch as part of Senator McGovern's platform included proposals for revamping the country's tax structure and closing loopholes, such as the oil depletion allowance and capital gains treatment for investments held more than six months. The concern, however, was reflected more in heavy business contributions to President Nixon's reelection campaign than in any slackening in the business growth rate. Fairly early in the campaign, President Nixon took a commanding lead in the polls, and Senator McGovern's candidacy stopped having much effect on business psychology.

Throughout the second half of the year an undercover battle raged between the government and the nation's banks. As the business recovery gained momentum, demands for loans increased. Bankers, who had seen their chief loan rate decline from a high of 8.5 percent in 1968 to 5 percent, began to move rates higher again. Their action ran into heated government opposition because administration experts were afraid that rising interest charges would put a damper on the recovery before it could gather real strength. (In tandem with the increasing loan demand, the Federal Reserve Board cut back the rate of increase in the money supply—to keep the expansion from moving too rapidly—and put further pressure on the banks.)

As interest rates edged upward, Federal Reserve Board chairman Arthur Burns began a personal campaign to keep rates in line. The administration did not want to impose ceilings on interest charges, he said, but it might if the rates went up too fast.

For most of the six months, Burns' tactics worked, as banks resisted the lingering pressures to raise rates. In the last week of the year, however, the dam broke, and the prime rate—the charge banks make to their biggest and best customers, virtually all large corporations—was posted at 6 percent. As expected, the administration, this time in the person of Treasury Secretary George Schultz, hinted strongly that the administration would investigate the feasibility of imposing controls on interest rates. Nevertheless, most economists expected rates to move even higher as the business expansion continued.

Longer-term interest rates did not fluctuate very much. Home mortgage charges, for example, fell a fraction to an average of 7 percent and then edged up slightly late in the year.

One of the features of the business growth was a sharp increase in consumer spending. Consumers, a necessary bulwark of any expansion, had been hoarding their money—increasing savings accounts, for instance—for several years. In 1972, however, they began to loosen the purse-strings. Retail sales were an estimated 12.9 percent greater than in the previous year. In addition, the Christmas shopping season turned out to be a bonanza. Estimates late in the year put sales in the week before the holiday a whopping 26 percent ahead of those of the same period of 1971. Sales of durable goods—washing machines, refrigerators and television sets, for example—were 30 percent ahead of sales in the previous year, while nondurables—such as clothing—were up 25 percent.

The increase in consumer credit was another indicator of a more confident public. In October alone consumer credit rose a record $1,600,000,000 to a total of $150,580,000,000, which was 11 percent higher than at the end of October 1971. The total was expected to rise to $155,500,000,000 by year-end.

Automobile sales climbed steeply, as might be expected when consumers became more confident. By the end of November the year appeared headed for a new record in sales of domestic and foreign cars, with 10,800,000 units the estimate used by most observers. The earlier record was set in 1971, when 10,200,-000 units were sold.

Domestic auto production for the year was put at 8,800,000 cars, or 200,000 more than in 1971. Auto makers were planning record production of 2,617,000 cars in the first three months of 1973.

Capital spending by business—outlays for new plants and machinery—did not keep pace with the business expansion. In the third quarter of the year spending rose only 0.6 percent on an annual basis (the Commerce Department had forecast a 4 percent boost). For the year as a whole, plant and equipment outlays were estimated at $88,500,000,000, which would be an increase of 9 percent over 1971, but below administration forecasts that businessmen would spend 10.5 percent more than in the previous year.

Inventory buildup was quite slow, barely keeping up with the rise in sales. That was taken as another indication that businessmen were hedging their bets on the near future. Business inventories rose only 7 percent in 1972, to an estimated $195,000,000,000—and most of that increase came late in the year.

The consumer savings rate declined to 6.4 percent of disposable—after tax—income from the more than 8 percent of the two previous years. Most observers, however, attributed the decline to the over-withholding of Federal income taxes through a miscalculation by the Internal Revenue Service. In 1973, when the extra taxes are rebated, the savings rate is expected to return to 7.5 to 8 percent. (The decline in savings had one notable exception. The Treasury reported that purchases of government savings bonds set new records in ten of the first 11 months of the year. At the end of November total holdings of series E and H bonds stood at a record $57,300,000,000, and monthly sales were the highest since the end of World War II.)

A substantial increase in 1972 Christmas-shopping sales compared with 1971 helped boost total retail sales by an estimated 12.9 percent.

"U.S. News & World Report"

Broad economic indicators showed a nearly unanimous upward climb. Machine tool orders, a key indicator of manufacturers' future plans, rose markedly toward the end of the year. In November orders were nearly 16 percent greater than in October and more than double those of November 1971. Durable goods orders increased to a seasonally adjusted $37,810,-000,000 in November from $31,210,000,000 a year earlier. By the end of November the Federal Reserve Board's index of industrial production stood at 118.5 percent of the 1967 average, a mark 10.3 percent above the same month in 1971.

Construction, one of the few areas of the economy which withstood the recession of 1970, continued to rise, although there was at least one dark cloud on the horizon. Through most of 1972 private residential housing starts were running at an annual rate of 2,400,000 units, with the largest increase in multi-family dwellings and a continued slackening in one-family housing.

Near the end of the year, however, President Nixon indicated that the administration would cut back sharply on Federal-assisted housing programs. The move would primarily affect low- and moderate-income housing and could cut sharply into the totals of new residential construction in 1973.

In Wall Street, the stock market was slow to recognize the budding boom. In the first quarter of the year the market was extremely active and moved generally higher. Traders and investors were buoyed by the Nixon administration's change of economic signals in 1971, a change which conceded what most economists had felt right along—that the former policies of fighting inflation had taken the life out of the economy without slowing the wage-price spiral. Through the first part of the year, Wall Street was still cautiously optimistic, wondering

UPI

Wall Street, Nov. 14: For the first time, the Dow Jones Industrial Average, a key N.Y. Stock Exchange index, closed above 1,000.

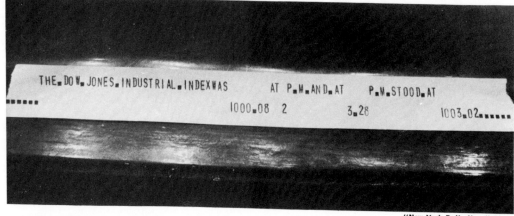

THE DOW JONES INDUSTRIAL INDEX WAS AT P.M. AND AT P.M. STOOD AT 1000.08 2 3.28 1003.02

"New York Daily News" Photo

whether the recovery would carry over to the second half of the year.

Just as indications began to grow that business would expand even faster in the latter part of 1972, the stock market seemed to run out of steam. Sen. George McGovern's economic and tax proposals hit the street harder than they did the rest of the business community, and brokers and their customers also were concerned about rising interest rates and the seemingly endless Vietnam war.

In early October, as indications appeared of some movement in settling the war, the market picked up excitement. At the end of the month, when presidential adviser Henry Kissinger said peace was "at hand," the market took off on a spree. On Nov. 10—after President Nixon was reelected—the Dow Jones Industrial Average edged over the 1,000 mark for the second time in its history and the first time in more than six years. Prices fell back before the end of trading, but on Nov. 14 the historic breakthrough was finally accomplished, with the Dow closing at 1,003.16, the first time it had ever finished a trading session above the 1,000 level.

Investors and traders seemed to gain encouragement from the breakthrough and pushed the averages to the year's high of 1,036.27 on Dec. 11. Thereafter the Vietnam truce talks bogged down, and investor enthusiasm waned accordingly.

At the end of the year the Dow Industrials stood at 1,020.02—thanks to a jump of more than 12 points on the final day of the year—for a gain of 129.82 points for the year as a whole. The Dow Transportation average, on the other hand, lost 16.55 points during the year, finishing at 227.17. The slight decline was a reflection of the profit problems that beset airlines through most of the year.

Volume on the New York Stock Exchange climbed to a new record of 4,138,187,706 shares, eclipsing the old mark of 3,890,000,000 set in 1971. Among broader market indicators, the NYSE's own index chalked up a gain of 8.05 points to 64.48. The NYSE index measures virtually all the stocks on the exchange.

The American Stock Exchange missed most of the action. The smaller board registered turnover of 1,110,000,000 shares, a slight increase over the 1,070,000,000 traded in the previous year. The Amex's market average edged ahead 0.77 points to 26.36.

Mutual funds continued to lose favor in 1972. In 1971 the funds had paid out to redeeming shareholders more money than they took in from new buyers, for the first time in history. In 1972 the outflow swelled.

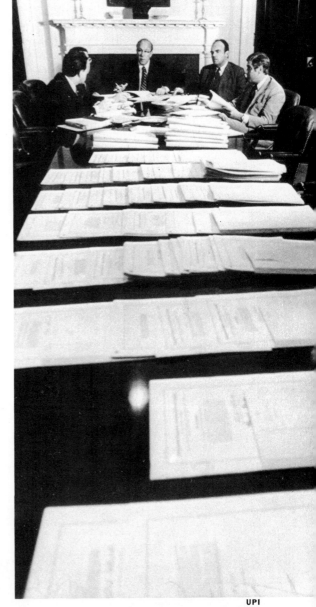

On Oct. 19, the President's top economic advisers discussed the financial ramifications of more than 100 bills enacted by Congress.

As the year ended, the American economy was barreling along, apparently headed for even greater heights. There were some potential problem areas, but nothing that seemed likely to prevent even more records in 1973.

PHILIP GREER
New York Financial Correspondent
The Washington Post

INTERNATIONAL TRADE AND FINANCE

Despite far-reaching measures taken by the United States in 1971 to correct its unfavorable balance of trade, the U.S. trade deficit for the first half of 1972 totaled $3,600,000,000, compared with a 1971 full-year deficit of $2,000,-000,000, the country's first since 1893. Although the unfavorable trend moderated slightly in the second half of the year, partly owing to implementation of restraints on textile and steel imports, it was clear that international trade and monetary reforms, slated for negotiation in 1973, would be needed if protectionist pressures were to be held in check. The United States' trade deficit for the entire year 1972 was an estimated $5,800,000,000, according to government economists.

World Trade. That patterns of longstanding in world trade were changing can be demonstrated by comparing recent year-end figures. Total world exports grew from $273,000,000,-000 in 1969 to $312,000,000,000 in 1970 and $346,000,000,000 in 1971—a 14.3 percent growth during 1970 and a 10.9 percent growth in 1971. The figures, however, represent a significant falling off in the rate of increase. Moreover, the developing countries and the Communist countries of Eastern Europe maintained their previous rates of increase, so the contraction was primarily in exports from the industrialized countries. This, in turn, may be attributed largely to a relative stagnation of exports from the United States, which had an increase of 14 percent in 1970 but one of only 2 percent in 1971.

While the United States maintained an export surplus with Western Europe, the surplus decreased from $2,900,000,000 in 1970 to $800,000,000 in 1971. The usual (since 1965) deficit with Japan increased from $1,200,000,-000 in 1970 to an estimated $4,000,000,000 in 1972. The deficit with Canada remained at almost $2,000,000,000 in 1971, while the surplus with the rest of the world decreased from $2,200,000,000 to $1,400,000,000.

U.S. Balance of Payments. The unfavorable U.S. trade balance in 1971 was partly offset by a favorable shift in investment income, which rose 18 percent over the 1970 figure to $9,300,-000,000. The resultant balance of all goods and services yielded a surplus of $760,000,000. Large outflows for remittances and U.S. government grants, however, caused a current account deficit of more than $2,700,000,000. In the capital account, there was a significant increase over 1970 in private foreign long-term investment.

However, the outstanding feature in the year was the unprecedented outflow of more than $10,800,000,000 in unrecorded transactions. This huge "errors and omissions" figure reflected the sale of U.S. dollars, in exchange for foreign currencies, by individuals, business firms and other nonbanking institutions. Finally, an increase of recorded short-term private capital outflows, to almost $7,800,000,000, resulted in an official reserve transactions deficit of $29,700,000,000, compared with $9,800,000,000 in 1970.

A close look at total outstanding U.S. foreign private investments at the end of 1971 shows that $86,000,000,000 was direct investment, while $21,700,000,000 was ownership of foreign stocks and bonds. While direct foreign investment had increased throughout the world

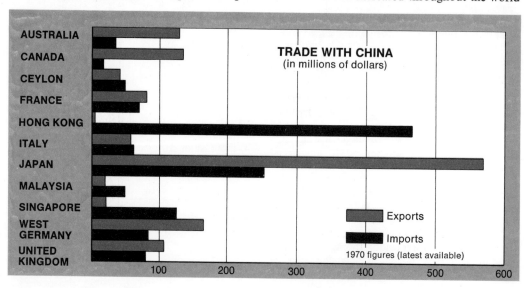

TRADE WITH CHINA
(in millions of dollars)

AUSTRALIA
CANADA
CEYLON
FRANCE
HONG KONG
ITALY
JAPAN
MALAYSIA
SINGAPORE
WEST GERMANY
UNITED KINGDOM

Exports
Imports
1970 figures (latest available)

100   200   300   400   500   600

during the year, the pattern of outflow nevertheless disclosed continuation of a disturbing long-term trend—namely, the increasing inability of the developing countries to attract private investment. In 1961, for example, 27 percent of new U.S. private investment went to the developing world. In 1971 the percentage fell to 20. Canada and Western Europe, particularly the expanded European Economic Community, continued to be the primary targets for U.S. private direct investments.

European Economic Community. The outstanding development in the European Economic Community (EEC) in 1972 was its enlargement to include the United Kingdom, Ireland and Denmark. These countries, along with Norway, had officially applied for admission to the community in 1967. Formal negotiations on the applications were opened on June 30, 1970, and the treaty permitting them accession (with various terms and conditions) was signed on Jan. 22, 1972—the enlarged community to become a reality on Jan. 1, 1973. It was agreed that the integration of the four new countries would be gradual, and in steps, with full alignment for most rules and regulations to be achieved by 1977.

In September 1972 the Norwegian government held a plebiscite on its entry into the EEC and the popular vote was against entry into the economic unit.

U.S. Trade with China and the USSR. During President Nixon's February visit to China for discussions with Premier Chou En-lai and Chairman Mao Tse-tung, trade was discussed and limited agreement reached. China agreed that U.S. companies could be represented at China's semiannual trade fairs, and the United States agreed in return to eliminate its embargo on trade with China, except for goods of "strategic" importance. Although in October China purchased some 12,000,000 bushels of U.S. corn, no one anticipated that the accord would result in any large increases of exports to or imports from China in the near future.

During President Nixon's Moscow summit meeting with Soviet Party Leader Leonid Brezhnev in May, trade again was discussed. Historically, U.S. purchases from the Soviet Union have been dominated by a few commodities, primarily furs and metals, such as manganese and chromium. Expansion of U.S. purchases has been impeded by a lack of Soviet goods of interest to U.S. importers. Moreover, U.S. government restrictions on exports of "strategic" goods have been broadly applied and prevented the export of the types of advanced-technology goods which the Soviet Union would like to import.

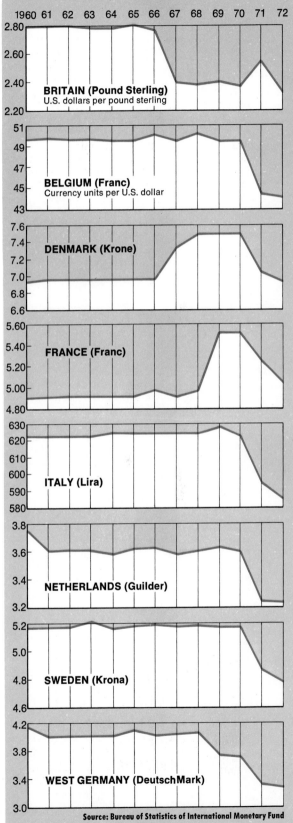

FOREIGN EXCHANGE RATES
(thru October 1972)

BRITAIN (Pound Sterling)
U.S. dollars per pound sterling

BELGIUM (Franc)
Currency units per U.S. dollar

DENMARK (Krone)

FRANCE (Franc)

ITALY (Lira)

NETHERLANDS (Guilder)

SWEDEN (Krona)

WEST GERMANY (DeutschMark)

Source: Bureau of Statistics of International Monetary Fund

Photos United Nations

President Salvador Allende of Chile addressed the inaugural meeting of the third session of the UN Conference on Trade and Development. Some 1,500 delegates from 141 nations attended the session.

While a definitive trade pact was not achieved, the tone of the discussions promised significant future increases in Soviet-American trade, which would go well above the $200,-000,000 total of exports plus imports between the two countries in 1971. The first big step was taken on July 8, 1972, when President Nixon announced that an agreement had been signed whereby the Soviet Union would purchase $750,000,000 of feed grains from the United States over a period of three years. Meanwhile, hopes increased that U.S. companies might participate in the development of timber, mineral, gas and oil resources in Siberia, and that imports of these would eventually balance Soviet imports of grains and high technology goods.

UNCTAD. The third session of the United Nations Conference on Trade and Development (UNCTAD) was held in Santiago, Chile, from April 13 to May 21. (The first session was held in Geneva in 1964 and the second in New Delhi in 1968.) The 1972 session yielded three major resolutions. The first was a key one regarding the international monetary system, asking that special drawing rights (SDR's) be linked to development financing. The second was designed to ensure that the developing countries would have effective participation in the coming 1973 GATT (General Agreement on Tariffs and Trade) negotiations, and the third contained assurance that industrialized countries would recognize the heterogeneous nature of the developing countries and would follow "special measures" (increased aid with easier and more flexible terms) for the 25 countries recognized as the "least advanced."

Smithsonian Agreement. The finance ministers of the Group of Ten countries met at the Smithsonian Institute in Washington, D.C., the weekend of Dec. 17–18, 1971. The conference resulted in the Smithsonian Agreement, whereby the United States agreed to devalue the dollar by 7.89 percent to a new value of $38 per

ounce of gold. The United States also agreed to eliminate the 10 percent surtax on imports which it had instituted in August. In return, other countries agreed to revalue their currencies by varying amounts.

The largest revaluation was by Japan (11 percent), with West Germany second (5.5 percent) and Switzerland third (4 percent). The British and French essentially kept their gold par value, which left them about 8 percent higher in relation to the dollar than under their previous dollar exchange rates. The Canadians decided to continue to let their dollar float. By May 1972 the effective exchange rates, compared with those of a year earlier, had risen and fallen as follows: United States, −10 percent; Japan, +12.5 percent; West Germany, +6.5 percent; Switzerland, +2.5 percent; Britain and France, no change; and Canada, −3 percent.

The U.S. government left unchanged its August 1971 decision no longer to allow foreign governments to convert dollars into gold. This, it appeared, might only be changed in some future, sweeping reform of the international monetary system.

Revising the Monetary System. The annual meeting of members of the International Monetary Fund was held in Washington, D.C., on Sept. 26. No firm decisions were taken, but George Shultz, U.S. secretary of the treasury, presented a plan which will be the major working paper for the new powerful Committee of Twenty, which is to draw up a detailed proposal for reform of the international monetary system prior to the 1973 annual meeting.

The essence of the Shultz Plan is as follows: (1) Each currency should have a par value and be allowed to fluctuate 2.25 percent on either side of par. (2) Special drawing rights (SDR's), rather than the U.S. dollar, should become the basic *numéraire* (specie) of the system. (3) A country in basic deficit should devalue. If it does not, sanctions against it might be withholding of borrowing rights or SDR allocations. (4) A country in basic surplus should revalue. If it does not, sanctions may include the loss of the right to demand conversions or, alternatively, other countries should be free to impose a surcharge on imports from the country in surplus.

Gold. From the 1930's the official price of gold was pegged at $35 per ounce, and dollars were freely convertible into gold by foreign central banks. But a free market for gold existed and was formalized in 1961 when eight major countries formed the London Gold Pool. The free market gold prices tended to stay near $35 per ounce until the sterling crisis of 1967, which forced the disbanding of the Pool and the establishment of a two-tier gold price system. Under this new structure central banks continued to exchange gold at the official price but did not engage in any transactions in the private market, where the price would fluctuate in response to supply and demand factors. The freemarket price gradually returned to $35 per ounce, in early 1970, and stayed near that price for most of the year. In the latter part of 1970, however, the free market price began to rise at an increasing rate, reaching $45 per ounce by the end of 1971 and $70 near mid-1972.

LEE C. NEHRT
Professor of International Business
Indiana University

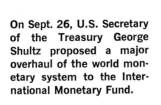

On Sept. 26, U.S. Secretary of the Treasury George Shultz proposed a major overhaul of the world monetary system to the International Monetary Fund.

ECUADOR

On Feb. 15, 1972, the armed forces of Ecuador overthrew Dr. Jose Maria Velasco Ibarra, five times president of the country, bringing to power a junta headed by Gen. Guillermo Rodriguez Lara. The military action sprang from fear that Assad Bucaram, a populist former governor of Guayas Province, would win the presidential election scheduled for June 1972.

Proclaiming itself "nationalist and revolutionary," the new regime at first emulated the socially progressive officers who run Peru; it reaffirmed support for the concept of sovereignty over 200 miles of territorial waters, advocated a progressive tax system and called for agrarian reform.

But advocacy of reform turned to arid rhetoric as the military showed interest in determining how oil revenues would be spent rather than in reshaping Ecuador's pyramidal social structure. Significant revenues are anticipated, as a major oil strike in the Oriente region promised to make Ecuador, the world's leading banana producer, South America's second largest petroleum exporter. Moreover, work was completed on a pipeline to carry 250,000 barrels per day to the port of Esmeraldas. It appeared that the monies earned would be used to purchase arms and line the pockets of the wealthy rather than bring about the social reforms so desperately needed in this Pacific nation of 6,500,000 persons where per capita income averages only $250 per year.

Ecuador also enjoyed a construction boom in 1972, while an industrial development law helped increase manufacturing output. This expansion—stimulated in part by the country's

Workers clear dense vegetation to open a road to recently discovered Oriente oil fields.

Gulf Oil Co.

membership of the Andean Common Market—may be limited because of insufficient supplies of electric energy.

The oil fever partly diverted attention from the "tuna war" with the United States, which still raged as Ecuadorean naval vessels seized unlicensed tuna clippers within 200 miles of shore. Action by the U.S. Congress to cut aid to Ecuador was decried in Quito as an "undeniably interventionist policy." Nevertheless, as long as major U.S. oil firms remain heavily involved in the Oriente, the State Department will doubtless find ways to reach accommodation with the new Ecuadorean regime.

GEORGE W. GRAYSON
Associate Professor of Government
College of William and Mary

EDUCATION

Retrenchment was the order of the day on all levels of education in 1972. Two decades of expansion and growth had come to an end. Instead of planning how best to meet the increased demand, institutions were beginning to worry about productivity—how to operate more economically, without reducing quality. In Detroit, the teachers' union, which in past years had developed a reputation for militancy, agreed to extend its contract for one year without an increase in the scale, as the city ordered a general belt-tightening. Throughout the United States, a record 53 percent of all school bond issues was turned down.

Colleges and universities tried to reduce the size of their teaching staffs or increase their enrollments in order to eliminate rising deficits. New York University, one of the country's largest private institutions, laid off 217 faculty members, either by non-renewal of contract or through retirement. Cornell University considered admitting more than 1,000 more students without increasing faculty.

The Carnegie Commission on Higher Education, which earlier had warned that two-thirds of the nation's 2,400 institutions of higher learning either were in financial trouble or heading for it, issued a projection of future campus costs. Urging universities to trim their budgets, it estimated that in order to function effectively, they would have to reduce their expenditures by $10,000,000,000 annually by 1980, while at the same time seeking $16,000,-000,000 in "new" funding, probably from the Federal government.

On the positive side, the atmosphere on the campuses was calm. Protests and violence had once again given way to concern about academic work. Some observers saw in this a re-

turn to apathy, but others felt that the students, having attained the right to vote at age 18, were more likely to work within the normal system of the political parties, particularly during a Presidential election year.

The public reaction toward education turned increasingly conservative. A special Gallup Poll reported that discipline had once again become the number one concern in the majority's view of the schools. Alarm over drug abuse in the schools, on the other hand, had declined, perhaps indicating a reduction in incidents.

The Roman Catholic parochial schools, caught in a particularly tight squeeze between inflation and the need to replace increasing numbers of nuns and priests with lay teachers, were reported to be closing at a rate of one school a day. Proposals for aid to these hard-pressed institutions included the possibility of income tax credits for parents paying non-public school tuition. Such credits would make it easier for schools to increase their tuition, thus reducing their deficits. The U.S. House Ways and Means Committee approved a tax credit bill, but also suggested that the provision, if eventually passed, would have to undergo an early test by the Supreme Court to determine its constitutionality.

The rise of college tuition, which in recent years had averaged 7 percent annually, seemed to be leveling off. Public universities reported that the increases in 1972 ranged between 2.5 percent and 4.9 percent in different types of institutions.

Enrollments. Total U.S. enrollments in 1972, public and pri ate, from kindergarten through graduate school, stood at 60,390,000, thus registering an increase for the 28th consecutive year. In 1971 the total was 60,060,000, according to estimates by the U.S. Office of Education. With an increase of half of 1 percent, the rate of growth had almost come to a halt; indeed it was only in higher education that substantial increases continued for the time being.

The elementary schools (kindergarten through grade 8), which had shown their first actual decline in 1970, were down from 36,-360,000 to 35,900,000. The decline was a continuing reflection of the lower birthrate of the 1960's. Of the 1972 total, 3,800,000 were enrolled in nonpublic schools, the overwhelming majority in Roman Catholic parochial schools, but the nonpublic enrollment was also down 100,000.

The largest percentage increase, a 6 percent gain, about equal to that of the previous year, was in higher education enrollment. But as a result of overexpansion, the colleges reported approximately 500,000 vacant places, a dra-

UPI

A November U.S. Court of Appeals decision upheld a teacher's right to remain silent during recitation of the Pledge of Allegiance.

matic change from the years of extreme admissions pressure.

In the secondary schools (grades 9 through 12) enrollment stood at 15,510,000 compared with 15,230,000 in 1971. The growth was entirely confined to the public sector. The non-public schools, with an enrollment of 1,300,-000, remained unchanged.

Colleges and universities estimated that their total fall 1972 enrollment was 8,980,000, compared with 8,470,000 in 1971. The total excludes about 730,000 undergraduates enrolled in occupational programs not eligible for credit toward degrees. Graduate enrollment was estimated at about 1,040,000, compared with 970,000 the year before. The proportion of students enrolled in private higher education continued to decline, with the total number at 2,230,000.

Teacher Supply. The total number of employed teachers was estimated at 2,982,000, about 55,000 more than in 1971. Of the total, 664,000 were in higher education. The ratio of pupils per teacher remained at slightly more than 22. There was a substantial oversupply of teachers, estimates by the National Education Association running as high as 111,000. The only fields in which a low supply of applicants was still reported were: trade, industrial, vocational and technical education; industrial arts; specialists in remedial reading and speech correction as well as those trained for teaching disadvantaged children; librarians; and mathematics teachers.

Teachers' salaries, which had been rising at a rate of about 6 percent a year during the 1960's, rose only 5 percent to 5.5 percent in 1971–1972.

Increasing militancy is evident as striking Indianapolis teachers picket Marion County jail to protest the jailing of over 100 fellow teachers.

The national average in 1972 was estimated at $9,690, compared with $9,269 the year before.

Graduates and Degrees Granted. Approximately 3,100,000 students were expected to be graduated from high school in 1973, the largest class in U.S. history. For persons in the 16–17 year age group, the official survey predicted that more than three-fourths, or about 78 percent, will be graduated from high school; 48 percent will enter a college or university; one-fourth will earn a bachelor's degree; 8 percent, a master's degree; and 1.5 percent, a doctorate.

In the 1972–73 academic year, the following numbers of degrees were expected to be conferred by U.S. colleges and universities: bachelor's and first professional—up 55,000 to 958,000; master's—up 18,000 to 256,000; doctorates—up 3,000 to 38,000. Since the beginning of the 1960's the number of bachelor's degrees conferred annually had doubled and that of graduate degrees more than tripled.

Expenditures and Costs. The total (fiscal 1972–73) expenditure for education in the United States at all levels, public and private, was estimated at $90,500,000,000. The overall sum—$55,800,000,000, for the elementary and secondary schools and $34,700,000,000, for higher education—represented about 8 percent of the gross national product. Approximately $79,200,000,000 was used for operating budgets, an increase of almost $5,000,000,000. Capital construction accounted for $11,300,000,000. The total expenditure for the nonpublic sector stood at $16,600,000,000.

The Federal government's role in the support of education continued to grow at all levels. The subsidies rose from $3,400,000,000 in 1965 to $11,600,000,000 in 1972 and were expected to total $12,800,000,000 for the fiscal year ending June 30, 1973.

The per pupil expenditure in 1972 averaged $929, compared with $858 the previous year, and about $450 a decade ago. These figures, do not reflect the impact of inflation.

Parochial Schools. President Nixon said that parochial schools were closing at the rate of one a day, largely as a result of financial pressures and rising tuition costs. He warned that the disappearance of these schools would add approximately $3,000,000,000 annually to public school operating costs, plus about $10,000,000,000 in school construction.

Legislation. A far-reaching higher education bill was enacted by Congress. If fully funded, which was not considered likely, the measure could provide more than $16,000,000,000 in new aid in the next five years. Two aspects of the new law are particularly significant.

In the first place, colleges and universities would be given unrestricted aid tabulated on the basis of the number of Federally supported scholarship students enrolled. Thus, the colleges would be rewarded for the service they render to needy students.

The second innovation would be the allocation of up to $1,400 annually to every college-age student, minus the amount his family can, according to their income status, be reasonably expected to contribute. The so-called entitlement grant would gradually be decreased, until it would completely disappear as family income reached approximately the $13,000 level.

The bill also provides: additional aid to the universities prorated on the basis of the number of graduate students enrolled; and a special fund at the disposal of the U.S. commissioner of education to aid colleges facing bankruptcy.

Job Outlook. According to the Bureau of Labor Statistics, the decade 1970–1980 will see the entry into the job market of approximately 9,200,000 young college graduates, plus 600,000 older ones—women and immigrants who either graduated earlier or abroad. This, it is estimated, will add up to 200,000 more college-qualified job seekers than openings, in contrast to the situation during the 1960's when industrial recruiters were unable to find enough such applicants for the jobs that needed to be filled.

Busing. President Nixon called for a temporary moratorium on busing for purposes of school desegregation. Congress passed a relatively mild measure, as a rider to the higher education act, which prohibits new busing for purposes of creating "racial balance." A tougher anti-busing law which would have allowed the reopening of previously court-settled desegregation issues was passed by the House but deferred by the Senate.

Despite the political debate over the issue, there seemed to be little additional busing at the start of the new school year, and in some communities, among them Nashville and San Francisco, there was actually less. According to government statistics, nearly 20,000,000 pupils were transported to school by bus at public expense (estimated at about $1,000,000,000), but desegregation was a factor in only about 3 percent of all the busing. More than 15 states also permitted the transportation of pupils to nonpublic schools at public expense.

School Financing. The Commission on School Finance recommended that the states take over a major part of the burden of financing the public schools. This appeared to be a response to recent court tests in which it was held that the extreme disparities in the expenditure per pupil between affluent and poor communities denies children "equal protection," thus violating the Constitution. In order to achieve such a shift by the states, the commission estimated, the Federal government would have to offer the states up to $7,800,000,000 annually, as an incentive to lift the burden from the 17,500 local school districts. No action was taken during the year.

However, it was expected that one of several tests, notably in California, Texas and New Jersey, would soon reach the U.S. Supreme Court. The most widely discussed case was California's *Serrano v. Priest,* testing the difference in per pupil school expenditure in Baldwin Park ($577) and Beverly Hills ($1,232). The California Supreme Court, ruling such a difference to be in violation of the Baldwin Park children's rights, asked the localities and the state to come up with a more equitable formula.

"The New York Times"

Canarsie residents, who oppose the busing of black students from a neighboring district, regard the demonstration from their porches. Maintaining that any further integration of JHS 211 would irrevocably tip the school's racial balance, they temporarily boycotted the school.

Campus Mood. The mood of campus protest and violence continued to give way to a more peaceful one, with political action largely confined to student participation in the regular election campaigns. At Yale University, President Kingman Brewster, Jr., in welcoming the new freshmen said: "The demand for relevance, the glorification of the happening, the resort to violence all had one thing in common. They were all short cuts. They were doomed to frustration and letdown."

Negro Colleges. The Federal government, responding to pleas from the nation's 115 predominantly black colleges, increased its aid to these institutions from $108,000,000 in fiscal year 1969 to $171,000,000 in fiscal 1971.

Union Merger. The United Federation of Teachers, New York City's flagship local of the AFL-CIO-affiliated American Federation of Teachers, after consolidating all the state's locals, merged with the New York State Teachers Association, an affiliate of the once anti-union National Education Association, creating the United Teachers of New York, the first such statewide merger and, in the view of some observers, a forerunner of a national merger.

Language Study. After a short period of revival, following the infusion of government money in 1958 after the panic over the Soviet achievements in space, foreign language study has once again gone into decline. Since 1968, the percentage of high school students enrolled in modern language classes has declined by 2 percent, the first downturn in ten years. High school enrollment in Russian stood at 32,027 in 1965, but had gone down to 22,984 by the time of the last count in 1970, despite an overall increase in high school enrollment. In the same period, Latin enrollment had declined from 626,199 in the public high schools to only 271,469. A mere 186 students were enrolled in ancient Greek.

The situation also was worse in the less commonly taught modern languages in the colleges. According to the census of 1970, only 5,319 undergraduates and 769 graduate students were studying Chinese; 59 undergraduates and 8 graduate students were learning Thai, and only 12 and 6 respectively, Vietnamese. Only Spanish and Italian, among modern languages, were registering absolute gains.

Technology. The Carnegie Commission on Higher Education, predicting that a technological revolution on the nation's campuses was imminent, said that within the next three decades between 10 percent and 20 percent of the on-campus instruction and 80 percent of off-campus education would be carried out by means of computers, television, cassettes and other electronic devices. It recommended an initial Federal investment of $100,000,000 in 1973, to be gradually increased until it reaches 1 percent of the annual expenditure for higher education.

See also Youth.

FRED M. HECHINGER
Member of the Editorial Board
(Former Education Editor)
The New York Times

Tom Madden, "The New York Times"

Many U.S. colleges now require students and any other authorized personnel to carry identification cards and are employing increasingly rigid security measures in order to thwart any outbreaks of campus violence.

An encircling perforated breakwater will protect the central oil storage tank against the lashes of the North Sea when it is installed in Norway's rich Ekofisk Field. Presently under construction in a majestic fjord, the floating tank will, when completed, have facilities for tanker moorings and living quarters.

Christian Simonpietri-Gamma

ENERGY

The debate over whether the United States is facing a serious energy crisis emerged as one of the prime public policy questions of 1972. The controversy reached far beyond national boundaries, however, for the ever diminishing world fuel supply is a basic consideration of all energy planners, and the U.S. response to the problems will have worldwide ramifications.

"All the evidence now shows that we are going to have a major energy crisis in this country in the 1980's," President Richard Nixon said in backing further tax incentives to stimulate resource exploration. Assistant Secretary of the Interior Hollis M. Dole speculated that the inevitable crunch might come even sooner. He told Congress that the country already "is beginning to feel the pinch on energy in certain forms," and saw signs that the United States might face a deficiency in petroleum refining capacity by 1975. Lawrence Rocks and Richard P. Runyon, in their book *The Energy Crisis,* published late in the year, envisioned a scenario for the future that would entail enforced cutbacks in power for heating and air conditioning units by 1975 and would ultimately proceed to a Great Depression and "serious world conflict over existing energy sources" by the mid-1980's.

However, other participants in the debate have been more sanguine, finding evidence to support the assertion that ample energy sources for the foreseeable future are available on earth. Former Interior Secretary Walter Hickel argued this position, stating that, "I do not agree that there is a world energy crisis. We are not running out of resources." The Federal Power Commission, once worried about U.S. electrical generating capacity a decade hence, announced in 1972 that a resurvey of utility companies had disclosed that they planned to add more than 1,200 new generating units with the ability to produce close to 450,000 additional megawatts—quite enough to keep up with demand.

A major point of divergence between the optimists and pessimists lies in their basic assumptions about future demand and existing supply. The energy consumption of all the richer nations has skyrocketed in recent years, with the United States in the lead. Interior Secretary Rogers Morton announced in 1972 that national consumption of energy for the previous year totaled 69,010,000,000,000,000 BTU's-a per capita figure some six times the world average and more than double the per capita consumption of such an industrialized country as Britain. Standard economic fore-

casts for the United States chart the growth in energy consumption at 4.3 percent a year for the next 15 years. And development of traditional domestic sources of fuel are simply not keeping pace with this increasing demand. The number of new oil wells completed in the country 1972, for instance, barely kept pace with the 11,804 recorded for 1971, and that figure represented a steep decline from earlier years. The American Gas Association announced that during the previous four years the nation had been delivering more natural gas than it was discovering.

But increasingly, in 1972, emerging signs indicated that more efficient use of available resources could trim per capita energy consumption without depriving individuals of light, heat or transportation. Large corporations increasingly sought new approaches to reduce their energy consumption. U.S. Steel found it could substantially cut heating costs at its new Pittsburgh headquarters building by taking into consideration such previously ignored factors as the body heat of the workers. When Eastman Kodak examined the utility of illuminating its facilities, it found it could reduce wattage by as much as 80 percent in some storage areas. In 1972 Combustion Equipment Associates started to market a closed-loop incineration system that powers manufacturing installations with steam generated by the combustion of industrial waste.

Such efficiencies can add up. The U.S. Office of Emergency Preparedness estimated that with proper tax and regulatory policies to goad business into maximum energy conservation, total energy demands could eventually be reduced by between 10 and 15 percent without invoking austerity measures. As a powerful incentive to such conservation, the Federal Power Commission obtained from the Supreme Court in 1972 the authority to allocate fuel supplies so that if shortages did occur, homes, hospitals and schools would receive their energy supplies before the big factories.

On the supply side, Washington varied national policy to permit the importation of more foreign oil, and there were indications that the administration would also approve imports of Algerian liquefied natural gas. Edward E. David, Jr., director of the President's Office of Science and Technology, revealed that his department is funding research into ways of increasing the efficiency of the energy-generating process, which as presently operating, dissipates almost twice as much potential power as it captures.

New Energy Sources. The best hope of filling the world's long-term energy needs lies in re-search into novel means of generating power. Three public utilities conducted a joint test using an alcohol, methanol, as a fuel in a commercial boiler, and pronounced the experiment a success. Chemical companies were planning to construct at least a score of major conversion factories to produce a synthetic equivalent of natural gas from such naturally abundant organic resources as naphtha, ethane, and propane; deliveries to the first commercial customers were expected to begin in 1973. The Bureau of Mines announced plans to test in Wyoming a process for the artificial production of gas underground: a coal seam 400 feet below the surface will be broken up with chemical explosives, burned and the resulting gas pumped to the surface. The National Petroleum Council predicted that by 1985 a significant nine percent of the total electric generating capacity of booming California and Nevada would be extracted from heat naturally trapped underground in geysers and springs. Brooklyn Union Gas Co., adapting a technique developed for the Apollo space capsules, provided all the needed power for three Prospect Place houses with a rooftop fuel cell; Commerce Secretary Peter G. Peterson announced that the test showed that "the idea of the fuel cell as a competitor of the 'neighborhood' power plant is not fanciful."

Not all technological innovations, of course, perform at their expected level. One reminder of this cautionary note appeared in 1972: the Atomic Energy Commission (AEC) moved to close down the country's first breeder nuclear power plant, built nine years previously on Michigan's Detroit River. In its total life span the reactor managed to run at full power for no more than 30 days.

Environmental Considerations. All new moves to meet consumers' energy needs had to contend with intensified demands from environmentalists that the new facilities not contribute to the degradation of existing air and water purity levels. Sen. Henry Jackson (D-Wash.) led a fight against new power plants in the Four Corners region of the Southwest, for instance, because the coal-burning installations would "be major sources of man-made air pollution" in the area. He also backed government research into new energy processes because "advanced power cycles which combine coal gasification with advanced gas and steam turbine technologies in an integrated system offer the potential for a better atmospheric environment and a reduction of the thermal pollution of our waterways."

Ecological considerations prompted the signing of the first contract for an offshore nuclear

power plant, designed to deliver a total of 2,300,000 kilowatts of power from a plant situated three miles off the New Jersey coast. Such considerations also led the AEC to insist that another nuclear installation planned for Indian Point, on the Hudson River, be redesigned to incorporate a more efficient cooling system so that heated effluent from the plant would not injure the fish when it was discharged.

Additional costs for such unorthodox measures have started to appear in the bills of power buyers. Artificially manufactured gas, for instance, will apparently cost close to 90 cents per 1,000 cubic feet—double the average delivered cost of natural gas. The Federal Power Commission (FPC) predicted that electricity costs, after exhibiting a downward trend for more than 40 years, will soon start to undergo an annual increase, largely owing to the extra expense entailed in curbing the environmental impact of energy production. In a 1972 study the FPC found that, on the average, utilities were charging six percent more per kilowatt-hour of delivered power than they had the year before. The "fuel and utilities" component of the government's Consumer Price Index—covering all power sources at retail cost—rose 4.3 percent during 1972.

Government antitrust lawyers, however, think that part of the higher cost of energy results from lack of sufficient competition within the power industry. The economic unit of the Federal Trade Commission released a report suggesting that, increasingly, one fuel can be substituted for another and, thus, the various fuels should be sold against each other. However, the fact that coal, oil, uranium and natural gas assets are often in the hands of the the same company reduces the vigor of such inter-fuel competition. They concluded that new mergers which extend the control of a single corporation into several different energy fields may be unlawful, and that some past mergers should be dissolved.

U.S. energy production statistics for the year showed that electricity production by utilities was running 8.5 percent ahead of the total for 1971, indicating a 1972 total of 1,900,000,-000,000 kilowatt-hours. Bituminous coal production trended downward from the amount mined the previous year, heading for a total of approximately 521,000,000 short tons. And the data for new oil supplies—domestic production plus imports—showed that the figures were ranging 4.65 percent ahead of those for 1971, leading to an estimated 1972 total of 2,600,-000,000 barrels.

DANIEL B. MOSKOWITZ
Correspondent, Washington News Bureau
McGraw-Hill Publications

Strip mining of Arizona's abundant coal alters the land's natural contours while emissions from coal-fueled plants degrade the atmosphere.

Shelly Grossman, Woodfin Camp & Assoc.

Problems affecting the global environment were discussed at UN conference held in Stockholm.

ENVIRONMENT

International concern about pollution of the planet brought representatives of most of the world's nations together in Stockholm in June 1972. In a year of warnings that continued rapid growth could exhaust resources and threaten man's survival, the United Nations Conference on the Human Environment was in itself evidence that environmental protection had become a global issue. But the chaotic, two-week meeting also demonstrated that most nations were unwilling to sacrifice national sovereignty or continued economic growth to protect themselves against a remote future environmental disaster.

Stockholm Conference. The U.N. conference registered some achievements. It voted to establish an environmental secretariat within the United Nations. Various countries pledged a total of $100,000,000 to support the unit for five years (the largest shares were expected to be $40,000,000 from the United States, $15,-000,000 from Japan and $10,000,000 from West Germany). An "Earthwatch" system of monitoring stations around the world to keep track of pollution levels also was endorsed. Among the resolutions passed were a condemnation of nuclear weapons testing and a call for efforts to reduce the damage caused by pesticides and other agricultural chemicals.

But long-standing political and economic differences proved as hostile to the environmental as to other world issues. A dispute over whether East Germany should be admitted to the conference led to a Soviet boycott when its German ally was excluded. The Soviet Union did, however, reach a historic agreement with the United States in 1972 for cooperation on environmental research. The mutual program will include exchange of information on pollution control technology—especially for air pollutants, sulfur oxides and dust—on oil pollution and on wildlife conservation. An experiment in computer modeling of air pollution patterns in St. Louis and Leningrad will be done.

Among the 114 nations that did show up in Stockholm, the biggest source of conflict was the economic gap between the rich nations and the poor. The rich, industrialized nations tend to have the strictest anti-pollution laws—such as the United States' projected controls on auto exhaust and Britain's smoke control regulations. Accordingly, it was the rich nations that were calling in Stockholm for strong worldwide action and for pollution controls in any industrial development of the poorer nations—many of which still have relatively pure air and water.

The less developed nations, on the other hand, took pains to remind the rich nations

that they are the greatest polluters and consumers of resources. The average citizen in the host country, Sweden, for example, uses eight times as much energy as his counterpart in India—with all the attendant air and water pollution and radioactive waste that level of consumption implies. Although the United States possesses only about five percent of the world's population, it consumes 25 percent of the world output of fertilizer and steel, 40 percent of the wood pulp and 36 percent of fossil fuels, such as coal and oil.

The poorer nations, striving for economic growth and a higher standard of living, were skeptical about spending part of their foreign aid funds on pollution control devices rather than on more factories. Some of them also resented the fact that the rich countries, while urging clean-up operations in the Third World, apparently showed no willingness to help pay the bill. As a result, certain developing countries made it clear that they, not some international body, would decide their own environmental policies. The quintessence of the Third World position came from growth-minded Brazil, whose delegation warned that "develop-

Photos NASA

Photos obtained by the first Earth Resources Technology Satellite, launched in July, provide information about geological features, water resources, vegetation, and the extent of pollution. Light from green, red and infrared spectral bands is recorded separately by a multispectral sensor and combined to produce these photos. Above, plumes in upper right reveal an Alaskan forest fire while bands of dense vegetation appear as darker shades of red. Black spots in vegetation signal ponds of deep, clear water while bluer shade of rivers indicates sedimentation. Below, healthy plant life in the New York-New Jersey area appears bright red while cities are colored green or dark gray. An oil slick east of Sandy Hook is revealed as a white squiggle against the blue ocean.

ment should not be negatively affected by a sometimes exaggerated concern for the preservation of the environment."

The one point on which rich and poor nations did manage to agree in Stockholm was that slowing or stopping economic growth was not an acceptable answer to environmental problems. In early 1972 scientists and environmental activists in the United States, Britain and Western Europe warned that at the current rate of growth of consumption of raw materials the world economic system would collapse within 100 years because of resource shortages. These documents—the British "Blueprint for Survival" and a computerized study done for a group of economists and scientists known as the Club of Rome—say the only hope is sharply to limit economic growth. "Blueprint," for example, argues that with world petroleum reserves currently estimated at 2,100,000,000 barrels and consumption increasing 6.9 percent yearly petroleum demand would exhaust the reserves by the year 2000.

While citizens in industrialized nations have indicated a willingness to pay higher prices or more taxes for a cleaner environment, they have not demonstrated support for a remedy as drastic as slowing economic growth and, in some instances, thereby reducing standards of living. The delegates in Stockholm seemed to agree with the British and U.S. economists who have counterattacked against the predictions of imminent ecological disaster. The consensus was that when a certain resource becomes scarce higher prices will limit its use, or substitutes will be found. A resolution asserting that "economic and social development is essential for ensuring a favorable living and working environment," was adopted without debate.

Population control was the most conspicuous issue missing from the agenda at Stockholm. With world population expected to go from 3,600,000,000 in 1972 to 6,500,000,000 by the year 2000 and possibly as high as 14,000,000,-000 by 2020, population growth clearly is a major environmental problem. But emotion on the issue ran so high that conference organizers postponed any full-scale population debate until a 1974 U.N. population conference.

However, population control definitely was debated in unofficial forums during the conference, spokesmen from poor countries generally differing from those from wealthy countries on the need for all to curtail population growth. Conceding that population is growing at an average yearly rate of more than 2.5 percent in the Third World—a third to a half higher than the rate in the developed lands—they observed nevertheless that every infant born in the

The relentless pounding of the surf, intensified by severe storms, is eroding Long Island's barrier beaches and threatening dune-line houses.

Ruth Block

United States will use up 500 times as much of the world's resources in his lifetime as a baby born in Pakistan, Chad or Peru.

Another topic skirted in official discussions at the U.N. meeting but vigorously debated elsewhere in Stockholm was environmental destruction in Vietnam. The U.S. delegation maintained that the question was a purely "military" one—despite allegations of herbicide destruction of more than 4,000,000 acres, stripping more than one-third of the Vietnamese jungle, and evidence that more than 2,500,000 bombs, leaving craters as deep as 30 feet, had permanently altered the landscape. China, attending its first U.N. conference since its admission to the world organization, attacked the United States for "ecocide."

The effects of environmental considerations on world trade were hotly debated in Stockholm. For instance, limits on leaded gasoline going into effect in West Germany, the United States and the United Kingdom will mean economic losses to lesser-developed lead-producing nations. The resource-exporting countries viewed with special alarm campaigns in industrialized nations to recycle raw materials from wastes. If successful, such recycling programs could substantially reduce markets for raw materials. Moreover, the richer nations, led by the United States, resisted all suggestions that the poor countries should be compensated for resulting losses.

Environmental restrictions which affect the trade of manufacturing nations trying to sell in export markets also were discussed. The United Nations Committee for Trade and Development (UNCTAD) estimates that complying with environmental regulations will mean an average increase of five percent to ten percent in capital investment and an equal amount in production costs. Auto makers in West Germany, Japan and Italy already face problems with pending U.S. limits on auto emissions, because the necessary control devices are less easily fitted on their smaller cars. Furthermore, they face the problem of meeting one standard for the U.S. export market and another, less stringent one in their home markets. Exporters of agricultural products, moreover, faced similar problems. For example farmers whose home countries allow the use of DDT have found their products barred from several Western European countries by restrictions against pesticide residues on foodstuffs.

The most serious environmental problem common to almost all nations—pollution of the oceans—was not dealt with by the U.N. conference at all. A hoped-for international convention on ocean dumping of pollutants was reached late in the year.

Crater-riddled South Vietnamese paddies, no longer suitable for rice cultivation, testify to the war's massive environmental destruction.

Gordon Orions

tons of oil enter the oceans each year from accidental spills and intentional flushing of tanks by oil tankers.

Perhaps the major value of the Stockholm conference was educational. Officials used to dealing with environmental problems in a national framework were forced to see them in an international light for two weeks. "We're used to thinking it's a good thing for everybody if you clean up the environment," said one U.S. delegate, referring to purely domestic efforts. "I'd never really thought much before about the hardship there can be for other countries." **Pollution Control.** Economic considerations were

Acidic pollutants in the enveloping fog are ravaging the statuary of Milan's Cathedral.

A new concrete wastebasket may alleviate one facet of the urban dilemma posed by a high concentration of cars, people and pets.

Meanwhile, the condition of the oceans—a vital source of the world's oxygen—deteriorated. Small craft sailors unofficially reported finding polluted water in the middle of the Atlantic. Oil spills from offshore petroleum drilling posed a growing threat. Although only 17 percent of the world's oil supply came from offshore sources in 1972, some 50 percent is expected to come from such sources by 1980. And tankers add to the problem. A U.N. committee of experts estimated that 2,000,000

a problem for the Stockholm conference, but they were an incentive for those producing pollution control equipment in 1972. Although Wall Street investors backed away slightly from a rush to the pollution control industry as a "glamor" stock, analysts agreed that the long-range picture was still bright. An estimated $1,000,000,000 a year is expended on such equipment in the United States, and Japanese industrialists predicted that pollution control equipment sales in Japan would grow to $1,300,000,000 by 1975. Japan reported a 54 percent increase in the production of air pollution control equipment in 1970–71.

Economic prospects for the British-French supersonic aircraft Concorde brightened in 1972 with the announcement that China was considering buying some of the planes. But environmentalists continued to warn that a full fleet of supersonic aircraft could pollute the upper atmosphere. And questions were raised in Britain whether the low fuel capacity of the plane would permit it to make money on the projected trans-Atlantic runs. Despite rejection of the SST by the U.S. Congress, reports that the Nixon administration was still interested in building the plane persisted. However, no direct action was taken during 1972.

The U.S. Environmental Protection Agency continued to project a tough image in its second year of existence. Following lengthy hearings, EPA Administrator William D. Ruckelshaus canceled all remaining U.S. uses of the pesticide DDT, chiefly for cotton and some food crops. "I am convinced that, once used, DDT is an uncontrollable, durable chemical that persists in the aquatic and terrestrial environments," Ruckelshaus said. The ban will not affect sales of DDT in other countries, where it is sometimes needed for malaria control.

The EPA also denied a request by auto companies for a one-year stay of the law requiring exhaust emission controls on 1976 model cars. The agency said the companies had not produced sufficient evidence that they were unable to meet the requirement for a 90 percent reduction in the carbon monoxide and hydrocarbons coming out of the tailpipe. In the fall the largest U.S. car maker, General Motors, changed tactics and conceded it believed it could meet the 1976 standards.

Energy. Construction of the Alaska oil pipeline, long delayed because of environmental dangers, seemed likely to proceed. The U.S. Interior Department completed a court-required statement on possible environmental impact of the pipeline and then gave departmental approval to the project. Final delaying tactics in the courts were expected to fail.

With nuclear power seen as the hope of the future to meet energy requirements, a debate over safety precautions was in full flower. The U.S. Atomic Energy Commission, after protests from the state of Kansas, scrapped plans to store radioactive wastes in abandoned salt mines at Lyons, Kansas. Safe waste disposal remains a major problem. Questions also were raised as to whether emergency systems function adequately to prevent accidents and explosions which could spew radiation from the nuclear power plants themselves.

Clean Waters. In the U.S. Congress a new $24,000,000,000 water pollution bill substantially raising Federal outlays for metropolitan sewage treatment plants and setting tough new standards for both municipalities and industry was passed over a presidential veto. The bill required cities to effect at least "secondary" treatment (that in which biological organisms are used to convert sewage to harmless effluent) by 1977 and more sophisticated treatment by 1983 and to eliminate all discharge of pollutants by 1985.

Congress also passed an ocean dumping bill, placing Federal controls on all dumping for the first time.

Politics and the Environment. The environment did not develop into a major issue in the U.S. presidential campaign as had been expected, partly because of the Democrats' choice of candidate. Sen. George McGovern, the Democratic nominee, did occasionally attack the Nixon anti-pollution record. But the subject had not been a special interest of Senator McGovern—as it had been of Senator Edmund S. Muskie (D-Maine), once considered the likely nominee. Thus, specifics of legislation and administrative action were not raised as often as they might have been.

In the year of the first worldwide meeting to combat pollution, apparently national governments saw environmental degradation as a problem but not a crisis. Growing population and pollution, however, and dwindling resources may force action in the not-too-distant future. As eminent microbiologist René Dubos and economist Barbara Ward cautioned in their book *Only One Earth*, "If all man can offer to the decades ahead is the same combination of scientific drive, economic cupidity and national arrogance, then we cannot rate very highly the chances of reaching the year 2000 with our planet still functioning safely and our humanity securely preserved."

JERRY C. EDGERTON
Washington Environmental Correspondent
(on leave)
McGraw-Hill Publications

EUROPEAN ECONOMIC COMMUNITY

Enlarged from six members to nine, the European Economic Community (popularly known as the Common Market) began 1973 in a make-or-break mood. There were relief and exaltation over the admission of Britain, which —after a decade of negotiations—joined the community on Jan. 1, 1973, along with Ireland and Denmark, and there was hope that the enlargement would give new vitality to community institutions.

At the same time, there was disappointment that the Norwegian voters had rejected membership. This conjured up fears that time might be running out on the postwar dream of a United States of Europe; that the man in the street no longer saw the community as a fulfillment of that dream but rather as merely another layer of bureaucracy superimposed on his own national bureaucracy.

The enlarged community is one of the world's three economic giants. To cite a few key indicators, it outranks both the United States and the Soviet Union in population, steel production, automobile output and merchant shipping. Its population in 1970 was more than 250,000,000; its gross product, $626,000,000,-000 (compared with the $991,000,000,000 of the United States and the $288,000,000,000 of the Soviet Union). It accounts for more than 40 percent of world trade.

But these impressive statistics have not been translated into commensurate political power. President Nixon has flown to Peking and Moscow in search of a stable world peace; he has not found it necessary to go to Paris, Brussels or Bonn since early in 1969. In the 1950's, the United States paid lip service to the idea that a summit meeting required the presence of the Big Four—Britain, France, the United States and the Soviet Union. Today, Moscow is Washington's only partner in talks that directly affect the security of every European nation. Even on such matters as the international monetary crisis of 1971 the United States acted unilaterally. President Nixon cut the U.S. dollar loose from gold without a word of warning to his European allies.

Furthermore, there is ample evidence that the ordinary European is indifferent, if not hostile, to the community and its executive branch, the European Commission. Two-thirds of French voters either abstained or said "no" in a nonbinding referendum Apr. 23, 1972, on enlargement of the community. Nearly 54 percent of Norwegian voters rejected community membership on Sept. 26. Almost every observer is convinced that, if British Prime Minister Heath had agreed to the referendum on British entry that the Labour party demanded, the "noes" would have gained a majority.

The European Economic Community was inspired by two tough-minded French visionaries, Robert Schuman and Jean Monnet, who felt that the most practical way of realizing the dream of a united Europe would be to forge ties of economic interests between countries that previously had fought each other. On May 9, 1950, Schuman, then foreign minister of France, made the historic proposal that French and German production of coal and steel be placed under a single authority. A treaty to this effect, binding six nations, was signed in Paris on Apr. 18, 1951, and the European Coal and Steel High Authority started work in Luxembourg the following year, with Monnet as its first president. The six countries which thus surrendered a portion of their sovereignty to a common authority were France, West Germany, Italy, Belgium, the Netherlands and Luxembourg.

The next step was the Treaty of Rome of 1957. The treaty, or rather treaties, which came into effect on Jan. 1, 1958, established two organizations, the European Economic Community, or Common Market, and the European Atomic Energy Community, or EURATOM. The purpose of the first, besides being a customs union, was to put into practice common rules of competition and to evolve common policies on agriculture, foreign trade and transport; that of the second, to help develop a civil nuclear industry.

These three institutions—the Coal and Steel Community, the Common Market and EURATOM—were combined on July 1, 1967, under a single commission and council of ministers. The combined institution is known as the European Communities (EC). Until Jan. 1, 1973, its executive body, the European Commission, had nine members—two each from France, West Germany and Italy, and one each from Belgium, the Netherlands and Luxembourg. With the enlargement of the EC, the commission was expanded to 13 members, two coming from Britain and one each from Ireland and Denmark.

The European Commission, however, cannot make policy decisions. It can draft policies and execute them, but the decision-making rests with the Council of Ministers, which alone is empowered to represent and commit the member states. A veto by one member can, and has, killed decisions favored by all the other members. The EC also has a Court of Justice which adjudicates disputes arising from the treaties establishing the communities.

Brussels, Jan. 22: Britain's Foreign Secretary Sir Alec Douglas-Home (l) and Common Market negotiator Geoffrey Rippon watch as Prime Minister Edward Heath signs treaty admitting Britain to EEC.

During the 1960's, President Charles de Gaulle of France had twice vetoed Britain's application for community membership: first in 1963, then in 1967. It was only in December 1969, after Georges Pompidou had become president of France, that the heads of government of the six member nations agreed to enlarge the community. Membership negotiations with Britain, Ireland, Denmark and Norway were begun the following year and completed late in 1971. On Jan. 22, 1972, ten nations—the original six and the four applicants—signed the accession treaty, providing for the new members to enter the community as of Jan. 1, 1973. (Norway, however, withdrew after the Sept. 26 referendum.)

The year 1972, therefore, began with éclat for the new community. On the practical side, the idea of monetary and economic union, launched in February 1971, but sidetracked first by the floating of the West German mark and then by the cutting loose of the U.S. dollar from gold, was put back on course in the wake of the Smithsonian agreement of Dec. 18, 1971, in Washington. This agreement resulted in the devaluation of the dollar and the revaluation of the principal European currencies. The dollar remained inconvertible.

Europe, however, was still inundated by unwanted dollars and a threat from the United States that the convertibility of its currency would not be restored until the U.S. balance of trade turned favorable. The finance ministers, both of the original six and the candidate four, felt more keenly than before the need of uniting for their own protection. On Mar. 21, 1972, the finance ministers of the six agreed to relaunch the idea of economic and monetary union, proposing as a first step to narrow the fluctuation band between their currencies from the 4.5 percent stipulated in the Smithsonian agreement to 2.25 percent.

The following month, on Apr. 23, French President Georges Pompidou held a referendum on the treaties bringing Britain, Ireland, Denmark and Norway into the community. Behind this move, political commentators said, was the President's ambition to play a leading role at a European summit meeting he intended to convene in the fall. President Pompidou also proposed that a political secretariat be established for the community—not at its Brussels headquarters but in Paris.

Technically, the referendum was a success; the majority of those voting approved the treaties. But for President Pompidou personally and for the cause of Europe it was a dismal failure. The Socialists campaigned for abstention, the Communists for outright rejection. The result: two-fifths of the electorate abstained and another 7 percent spoiled their ballots. Some 5,000,000—one-sixth of the eligible

voters—said "no," while 10,000,000—only one-third of the electorate—said "yes." Fearful that many of the abstentions and spoiled ballots came, not from the left, but from disgruntled Gaullists, President Pompidou began to take a tougher attitude toward European union. A summit conference would be useless, he said, unless agreements were reached, especially regarding economic and monetary union.

On May 10, Ireland held a referendum on the community. The results were convincingly positive: out of 1,783,604 eligible voters, 1,041,890 voted "yes" and only 211,891 "no."

The following month, a new speculative crisis hit the British pound and, to a lesser degree, the Italian lira. Britain, which originally had associated itself with the Mar. 21 decision to narrow fluctuation bands, ignored the agreement and floated the pound. To the French, who in 1971 had argued against the West Germans floating the mark, the British move was a step backward from the economic and monetary union they envisaged for Europe. All through the summer, the foreign and finance ministers of the community-to-be (all 10 nations) argued the problem of economic and monetary union. Finally, on Sept. 10–11, in Rome, they reached a measure of agreement. The narrow fluctuation bands of Mar. 21 would be retained, and a European monetary cooperation fund would be set up to help central banks which had difficulty maintaining these bands. Britain promised to return to a nonfloating pound, without specifiying a date. President Pompidou decided that enough progress had been made on the subject for him to go ahead with plans for a European summit.

Then came the Norwegian referendum of Sept. 26. The vote was 53.9 percent against membership, 46.1 percent for it. Community officials in Brussels were stunned by the way in which Norwegian opponents of membership equated the community with the ills of modern industrialized society—urban blight, pollution and helter-skelter growth.

The Danish referendum the following week (Oct. 2), in which 63.5 percent voted "yes" and 36.5 percent "no," somewhat alleviated the shock. But it was noted that Copenhagen, the nation's capital and largest city, had given a majority of the "noes" and that large numbers of young workers and students had voted against membership.

These results gave credence to the contention that the community had to lift its sights above technical discussions about rates of exchange or prices of agricultural products if it was to recapture the "European dream" that had inspired its founders.

The summit meeting, held Oct. 19–20 in Paris, heard some splendid oratory about Europe's future, but also came to the sober realization that the nations making up the enlarged community faced important and basic decisions. The heads of government—President Georges Pompidou of France, Prime Minister Edward Heath of Britain, Chancellor Willy Brandt of West Germany and Prime Ministers Giulio Andreotti of Italy, Jack Lynch of Ireland, Gaston Eyskens of Belgium, Pierre Werner of Luxembourg, Anker Jørgensen of Denmark and Barend Biesheuvel of the Netherlands—affirmed their "intention to transform, before the end of this decade, the whole of their relations in a European Union."

They confirmed their finance ministers' decision to establish a European monetary cooperation fund, specified that it be created by Apr. 1, 1973, and called for reports by the end of that year on steps to pool central bank reserves. They also decided to set up, by Dec. 31, 1973, a regional development fund, financed from community resources and not from those of individual nations. The purpose of the fund, strongly advocated by Britain and Italy, would be to correct regional imbalances by aiding distressed areas, such as Italy's depressed rural south and Britain's industrially declining Scotland and Wales.

There was a long debate on community institutions, especially on strengthening the powers of the European Parliament. Dutch Prime Minister Biesheuvel spoke up for direct election of the parliament, while French President Pompidou said this was a matter for the later years of the decade rather than the present. In the end, a vague general declaration was adopted, permitting the Dutch to bring up the question again. The heads of government also called for reports on environmental problems and on social policy by specified dates in 1973. It remained to be seen how the declarations of principles, enunciated at the meeting, would be translated into action.

As a customs union, as an organization to harmonize agricultural policy and to achieve a measure of agreement on economic and monetary policies, the community has been a success. Whether it can develop into something more, whether it will realize the original vision of a United States of Europe, depends on the extent to which Europe—as distinct from the nation states making it up—can kindle a political life of its own, firing the imagination and attracting the loyalty of ordinary citizens.

TAKASHI OKA
Paris Bureau Chief
The Christian Science Monitor

FASHION

Discipline and form once again became the guiding force behind women's clothes in 1972. A decade of fashion had passed which seemed at times desperate in its pursuit of iconoclasm and radical individuality, where dresses seemed mere costume. Mink-lined denim, Army surplus, see-through blouses and velvet knickers had all been part of the general masquerade. Hot pants were still a sweet or sour memory depending on one's age; the mini was relegated to the young, where it had belonged all along; and the midi, which nobody, young or old, had wanted in the first place, was dead. Hemlines stabilized at the knee. A new appreciation of quality and workmanship returned. The well-groomed look was in.

Designers whose talents lay in making things that were beautifully tailored within a traditional framework were the first to proclaim the 1972 philosophy: clothes were to be classic and natural. They would move through contemporary life effortlessly, presenting the kind of elegant solution architects arrived at—stripped down, uncluttered, clean, basic—sleek as a skyscraper. And as feminists sought equality with men in business, politics and academic fields, the new liberated clothes made sense. They were relevant.

Approximately half of the women in the United States held jobs outside the home. The other half were spending more and more time out of the kitchen participating in the community. Trend-setters promulgated a new fash-

Imposing a new look of form on feminine substance, fashions in 1972 returned to first principles after a decade of frantic experimentation.

The color-coordinated, multi-layered ensemble offered the promise of enduring another season, but getting it all together was another thing.

ion image: the cool young couple, pedaling around town on their ten-speed bicycles, free, knowing, clad in deceptively simple clothes which in fact were scrupulously cut, honed to perfection. Pants were basic and very much alive; a feeble effort by a handful of French designers had failed to stifle their immense vitality. Even blue jeans had become Establishment. As a way of life they inspired a fresh outburst of creativity—dashing trench coats, bush jackets, safari suits.

Perhaps the greatest single fashion influence of the year was the sweater. With clothes more natural, concentrating on soft supple lines, the sweater moved into big-time fashion. Of course, it was rediscovered, reinterpreted and updated by two of Paris' *prêt-à-porter* (ready-to-wear) designers, Kenzo and Sonia Rykiel. Sleeves were raglan, dolman, cap, puffed, rolled-up. Necklines were turtleneck, V, scoop or halter. Some sweaters looked like smocks, others like surplice blouses. They were patterned, ribbed, plain. Done in cuddly textures like angora, fleece, cashmere, mohair, and fur blends, sweaters also appeared as coats, dresses and pantsuits. The new sweater look—not to be confused with the old doubleknit look—was looser, softer, gentler.

As sportswear swept the field, the layered look was born. It was a highly calculated assemblage—a mixture of color tones, related patterns and textures. The look consisted of a shirt, a little sweater, pants, topped with either a cardigan or blazer. The effect was unpretentious, but getting it together required a considerable feeling for color and design.

The blazer, a libertarian notion that went equally well with dresses and pants, came into its own. In dressy velvets and velveteens it was paired with long skirts for evening. Stylish toppers were a spring favorite. Paris loved them, and so did the United States. They looked good with pants, and best of all they were comfortable and easy to wear.

Toward fall the dressy coat that stopped at the knee showed up. Women felt they could safely buy one without risking instant obsolescence.

The emphasis on a casual life-style in no way diminished fashion's slow but definite drift toward elegance. Shoulders and backs were exposed for evening, usually in matte jersey dresses with halter necklines and yards of fabric that nevertheless clung to every curve.

Together with ease and comfort the egalitarian principle seemed safely established in women's fashions for years to come. The two-sweater ensemble can be worn with either skirt or slacks.

Feather boas came back. Halter tops, on the whole, remained the domain of the young, who wore them nonchalantly with jeans on Fifth Avenue or the Via Veneto, often braless. Being bare was part of the unstructured and simplified look.

There seemed to be no limit to what fabric designers and the new technology could do. Sportswear was being done in a new fabric that looked and felt just like—and was just as expensive as—suede, but was machine washable. Some top designers responded to the cries of the ecologists and came out with fake furs.

Spring had ushered in bright ginghams, checks, brilliant seersucker plaids, polished cottons, twills, baby prints. Fall presented conservative menswear fabrics—tweeds, flannels, mohair, velveteen, cashmere. Plaid was ubiquitous.

Even though restraint had supplanted frivolousness as the impetus behind fashion, there was still room for fun, invention and improvisation. Clogs were the big 1972 shoe. More than a fad they went straight through the year. Most often thick cork soles were exposed for day and covered with suede or leather for night. Accessories reflected the move toward sobriety—no more cartridge belts slung around lanky middles, but discrete bands of leather or metal.

The return of glamorous necklines and bare backs signaled a marked trend away from radical chic toward frank femininity in evening wear.

A demand for feather boas and fur trim was supplied mostly by various synthetics, some of which cost even more than the real thing.

Art Deco was much talked about. The shoulder bag remained the important handbag. And although the move throughout the year was toward the tailored and the classic, a few designers still came out with oddities like ruffles and coy childlike clothes. However, teetering platform shoes worn with striped knee socks and rolled-up jeans were street shockers flaunted only by a few of the very young. On the whole the new generation seemed less interested in green fingernails and wigs than in acquiring pretty, feminine clothes that looked classy, expensive and as if they might be around for awhile.

Although the swing from campiness and wild abandon to a confident, assured, more contained fashion image was not complete as 1972 ended, the pendulum was clearly moving in that direction.

PATRICIA A. MILGRAM
Fashion and Pattern Editor, *Woman's Day*

Paul Conklin

Acting FBI Director L. Patrick Gray (left), in one of several moves designed to give the agency a new, more egalitarian image, appointed Barbara Herwig (above) to be his special assistant.

FEDERAL BUREAU OF INVESTIGATION (FBI)

The Federal Bureau of Investigation reached a watershed in 1972 owing to the death of its 77-year-old director, J. Edgar Hoover, who for 48 years, serving under eight Presidents, had incarnated the agency he headed. Mr. Hoover had converted a previously demoralized and corrupt organization into a scandal-free intelligence agency with a reputation for ferreting out kidnappers and bankrobbers in the 1930's, Nazi spies in the 1940's, Communists in the 1950's and, despite a late start, Ku Klux Klanners in the 1960's.

In the last years of his life, Mr. Hoover and his agency had been harshly criticized on several grounds—his public squabbles with two former U.S. attorneys general (Robert F. Kennedy and Ramsey Clark), his unproven charge that the Rev. Philip F. Berrigan had conspired to kidnap presidential adviser Henry Kissinger, his role in the electronic surveillance of the late Dr. Martin Luther King, Jr., and revelations in early 1972 by a number of self-styled FBI informants that they had served also as agents provocateurs.

Nevertheless, until Mr. Hoover's death the words spoken in 1962 by Rep. John Rooney, chairman of the House Appropriations Committee, still applied: "The confidence which the committee has in the Federal Bureau of Investigation under the highly capable and efficient leadership of Director J. Edgar Hoover is best illustrated by the fact that this is the tenth consecutive year that not one penny of the funds he has requested of the Committee has been denied. . . ."

Mr. Hoover died of natural causes on May 2. On May 3, Acting Attorney General Richard G. Kleindienst appointed L. Patrick Gray, III, a 55-year-old assistant attorney general and political associate of President Nixon, as acting director of the FBI. Immediately following the announcement of Gray's appointment, Presidential Press Secretary Ronald L. Ziegler said that President Nixon would wait until after the Nov. 7 elections to nominate a full-time FBI director. The President did not "want the matter of nomination to be considered in the middle of an election year," Ziegler said.

Gray was in office less than two weeks when he began a series of highly publicized reforms. He pointed to his colored shirts as proof that special agents of the FBI would no longer be expected to wear the stereotypical white–shirted agents' "uniform," and he pointed to the mod haircut of a young assistant as proof

that the crew-cut G-man was an image of the past. He announced that he had appointed as his personal assistant a 27-year-old woman (who described her new job as "groovy") and that the Bureau would henceforth make an active effort to recruit women and minority group members (it had a handful of women agents by year's end.)

The new acting director moved organized crime and narcotics up in the Bureau's list of priorities and showed a new openness toward the press, holding news conferences and granting interviews. He even received representatives of the Committee for Public Justice, whose conference on the FBI at Princeton in the autumn of 1971 had resulted in some severe criticisms of the Bureau.

Part of Hoover's inner-circle (including Clyde Tolson, John Mohr, Alex Rosen and Tom Bishop) resigned, and Gray did not hesitate to initiate disciplinary transfers to make his point. He transferred and demoted the head of the FBI's Los Angeles office (Wesley Grapp, who retired). He sent Robert Kunkel from Washington to St. Louis for covering up the fact that an agent had been overpowered during a peace demonstration. He transferred Richard Rogge from Honolulu to Richmond for keeping his men on night guard-duty and for publicly reprimanding them. He personally visited more than 50 field offices and generally behaved in a way which led one Federal official to observe, "The agents talk about Gray being the FBI's Pope John."

Before the year was over, however, Gray (who lacked Hoover's nonpartisan tradition and image) and the Bureau were deeply enmeshed in a number of hot political issues.

Possible White House involvement in the bugging of the Watergate headquarters of the Democratic party caused critics to maintain that an investigation should have been conducted by a specially appointed prosecutor rather than by the FBI. Charges of Republican fund-raising irregularities and the possibility that some friends of the administration had made an illicit killing on the sale of $750,000,000 in grains to the Soviet Union raised similar criticisms. Director Gray himself made a number of political speeches in which he called for deemphasizing the significance of crime statistics (a position congenial to President Nixon's election-year needs), asserted that the Federal government was not spending too much on defense as opposed to domestic programs, and asked for relaxation of the Supreme Court's rule excluding illegally seized evidence.

Time magazine revealed that a White House memo requesting election year political advice on "substantive issues in the criminal justice field" was actually circulated to FBI offices throughout the United States. The administration's defense—that the memo was intended for Justice Department action, not FBI action—did not change the fact that it never could or would have happened under J. Edgar Hoover. The new director also came in for some criticism for personally ordering the shooting of tires on a hijacked airplane and thereby provoking one of three heavily armed hijackers into wounding the plane's copilot.

Although President Nixon had not revealed by year's end whether he intended to ask Congress to confirm Mr. Gray as permanent director or to find a replacement, Gray himself continued to behave as an exceedingly active

Newly commissioned special agents, shown at the FBI academy in Quantico, Va., reflect the bureau's liberalized recruiting practices.

acting director. Despite his assurance in May that "You're not going to believe this but there are no secret files," in October he revealed that for 22 years the FBI had been compiling "biographical data" on major Congressional candidates, and he said he was ending the practice immediately.

The Hoover era had come to a close, but the important questions still loomed: Were Gray's changes really substance or style? To what extent were FBI critics justified in charging that the agency had invaded the civil rights and liberties of the citizenry, especially in matters relating to national security and internal subversion? Now that Mr. Hoover, who had the power, authority and status to insist on freedom from political pressure, was out, what assurance was there that the new director would be able to operate independently of partisan politics? What procedures by way of audit might be devised to guarantee that the Bureau not abuse its power? Would Congress, at long last, take the occasion of the confirmation hearings on Mr. Hoover's successor, to conduct a searching inquiry into the FBI, its practices and its potential for good and evil?

VICTOR S. NAVASKY
Author
Kennedy Justice

FINLAND

Finnish parliamentary elections were held on Jan. 2 and 3, but no significant change was effected in the relative positions of the various parties. The non-socialist parties continued to retain a slim majority, holding 108 out of a total of 200 seats, although the leftist groups, including the Social Democrats, made minor advances. The main result of the elections was the formation, on Feb. 23, of a new Social-Democratic cabinet under the leadership of Rafael Paasio. As prime minister, Paasio succeeded Teuva Aura, who had headed a caretaker cabinet since the resignation of Ahti Karjalainen, the former premier, in the autumn of 1971.

In July, Mr. Paasio's cabinet tendered its resignation, responding in part to a widely expressed desire that the base of the cabinet be broadened. Four parties—the Center party (Agrarians), the Social Democrats, the Liberal party and the Swedish party—participated in the formation of a new cabinet headed by Kalevi Sorsa, a Social Democrat. At 42, Mr. Sorsa, who had served as foreign minister in the Paasio cabinet, is the youngest premier in Finland's history and the 56th prime minister in the 55 years of Finland's independence.

Anxious to tread a neutral course and not to antagonize the U.S.S.R., its powerful eastern neighbor, Finland declared that it did not wish to become a member of the European Economic Community (EEC). This action, however, did not preclude Finland's signing a trade agreement with the nations of the EEC. Following many weeks of negotiations, Finland signed a draft for such a trade agreement in Brussels in the summer.

Finland and the German Democratic Republic (DDR) approved the draft of a non-aggression treaty and also of a treaty by which the DDR recognized Finnish neutrality and agreed to settle claims for damage inflicted on Finland by German troops in 1944–45. Finland had intended to sign parallel treaties with the German Federal Republic, but draft treaties had not been approved by the end of 1972.

Local elections were held in cities and townships throughout Finland in October. Except for slight advances achieved by the Social Democrats and the Center party, the relative strengths of the various parties remained fairly constant.

The advisory Nordic Council held its 20th annual meeting in Helsinki in February and passed numerous resolutions designed to facilitate inter-Scandinavian cooperation.

ERIK J. FRIIS
Editor, *The American-Scandinavian Review*

Kalevi Sorsa, at 42 the youngest premier in Finland's history, formed a government in July.

Consulate General of Finland

FOREIGN AID

U.S. PROGRAM

Again in 1972 foreign aid legislation became a battleground on which Congressional opponents of the Vietnam war tried to reduce U.S. military involvement in Southeast Asia and other parts of the world. The Nixon administration successfully resisted further restrictions on its global policy, but Congress cut more than $1,500,000,000 from the President's foreign aid request during the struggle.

Congress had placed a limit on military aid to Cambodia and restricted U.S. payments to mercenary troops in Laos and Thailand as part of the aid bill for the 1972 fiscal year. The amount of military aid was reduced by $529,-000,000 when the appropriations measure was approved belatedly on March 2, 1972. President Nixon, in urging Congress not to cut his aid request for fiscal 1973, warned that such restrictions and reductions "will call into serious question the firmness of our commitments abroad."

Foreign military aid, begun in 1947 when President Harry S. Truman won Congressional backing to help Communist-threatened Greece and Turkey, had come under increasing criticism since the Vietnam stalemate. Rep. Clarence Long (D-Md.) summed up one view in House debate, saying: "You cannot give people the will to fight by pouring dollars onto them." A Senate Appropriations Committee report said U.S. aid often bolstered "oppressive and brutal regimes which represent the exact opposite of every principle we hold dear."

Senate Republican Leader Hugh Scott, however, termed military aid the "linchpin" of the new Nixon Doctrine. The doctrine won support from Rep. Otto Passman (D-La.), once an arch-critic of the program, who said: "We are going to furnish military assistance but we are not going to provide the men . . . and this is a good proposition."

Foes of the Vietnam war tried, but failed, to attach to foreign aid legislation amendments providing for withdrawal of all U.S. troops from the war zone following release of U.S. prisoners. The Senate adopted an end-the-war amendment by a vote of 50–45 on July 24, overriding presidential protests. However, the President's supporters quickly rallied and killed the entire bill by a 48–42 vote. Two months later the Senate voted down an end-the-war provision, 45–42. In the House, which traditionally supports the President on foreign policy, a similar amendment was defeated by a vote of 228–178 on Aug. 10. For the first time, however, the end-the-war rider had the backing of the House Foreign Affairs Committee and the Democratic Caucus, although the party's top leadership still opposed it.

Efforts to curb the President and give Congress a greater voice in foreign policy were reflected in other Senate actions concerning aid. Aroused by the President's failure to submit a 1971 agreement relating to a U.S. air base in the Azores for ratification as a treaty, the Senate voted to bar spending on any overseas bases unless agreements concerning them were presented for approval. The House successfully resisted the Senate move, and the provision was dropped during conference.

Both houses of Congress asserted Congressional priorities on another issue, however, earmarking $350,000,000 of aid funds for Israel. Such agreement was rare, however, and Senate-House efforts at compromise on the overall aid package collapsed on the eve of adjournment. Thereafter, Congress passed a stopgap measure to continue spending for bilateral aid programs until Feb. 28, 1973, at an annual rate of $3,650,000,000. The measure provided for a slight increase in military aid and a slight cut in economic aid. Overall, the total was $1,510,-000,000 below the President's request but $461,000,000 above the previous year's level.

WILLIAM J. EATON
Washington Correspondent
Chicago Daily News

INTERNATIONAL DEVELOPMENT ASSISTANCE

The total flow of financial resources to developing countries from the 16 member states of the Development Assistance Committee (DAC) continued to climb in 1972, as it had in previous years. Rising from $13,800,000,000 in 1969 to $15,900,000,000 in 1970, it increased to $18,300,000,000 in 1971. Each category of aid increased, but the largest increases took place in the private sector—direct investment plus export credits.

The United Nations and the DAC had previously set a target for each donor country: to provide total capital flows to the developing countries equal to 1 percent of the gross national product (GNP) of the donor country. Although that goal had been achieved by seven of the donor countries as of 1972, it had nevertheless lost much of its meaning because higher percentages of total flows were made up of high-cost private credits plus private investments. Consequently, in early 1972 the UN set a target, accepted by most of the member states of DAC, that each provide Official Development Assistance (ODA)—grants plus low-cost, long-maturity government loans—at a level of 0.7 percent of GNP. Only Portugal

Assistance by the United Nations Development Program was directed in 1972 toward improving this and similar tin ore plants in Indonesia.

and France had achieved that goal, although Belgium, the Netherlands and Sweden were expected to attain it by 1975. Denmark hoped to reach it by 1977, and Norway planned to achieve 1 percent by 1978.

In 1971 the total ODA contribution of all DAC countries not only increased by $850,-000,000 in dollar terms but also increased in real terms (taking account of price increases and exchange rate increases) by about 5 percent. It was the largest real rise since 1967 and the second largest in ten years. As a result, the total ODA as a percentage of total GNP rose slightly, to 0.35 percent. While the increase reversed a previous three-year decline, it was still only half of the UN target of 0.7 percent.

At the same time, several non-DAC Western countries also were providing foreign aid to developing countries. These donors included Finland, New Zealand and South Africa. In addition, a number of developing countries were themselves donors. The most important of these were the Middle East oil-producing countries, which provide funds for the Kuwait Fund for Arab Economic Development (KFAED) and for the Arab Fund for Economic and Social Development. In 1970–71 the KFAED provided $27,000,000 in development loans—about average for the nine years of the fund's existence. Finally, Spain and Brazil in recent years have become donors of some significance.

Aid from the Communist countries—in the past generally measured only in terms of disbursements to non-Communist countries—also was substantial. Including aid given to underdeveloped Communist countries, the total for the U.S.S.R. in each of the last several years was about $1,100,000,000 (0.25 percent of its GNP), while that of the other East European countries was about $300,000,000 (0.2 percent of their combined GNP).

Aid from the U.S.S.R. to non-Communist countries took the form, mainly, of long-term loans (12 to 14 years) at about 2.5 percent interest. About three-quarters of the aid went to Cuba, North Korea, North Vietnam, Mongolia and Albania and tended to be in the form of grants. Cuba was the major recipient among Communist countries, while India and Egypt were the major recipients among non-Communist countries.

An important part of the Soviet bloc aid was in the form of technical assistance. Soviet experts in non-Communist countries totaled 9,900 in 1969, 10,000 in 1970 and 11,000 in 1971, while those from East European countries totaled 7,200 in 1968 and 1969 but dropped to 5,400 in 1970 and 1971. Data on the number of such experts assigned to Communist countries are not available.

Soviet bloc and Chinese aid was almost entirely bilateral. It was tied to purchases from the donor country and was strongly project

oriented—concentrated mainly on industry, energy and transport.

China (like Bulgaria and Rumania) still is classified as an underdeveloped country, having a per capita income of about $95 a year. Nevertheless, it has been extending significant amounts of aid to other countries. China does not publish data on its aid, so the DAC has had to use secondary data and some estimates to arrive at the following figures.

From 1953 to the end of 1971, China had committed more than $4,600,000,000 in economic aid. During the first half of the 1960's commitments averaged about $200,000,000 per year, with non-Communist countries receiving almost twice as much as Communist ones (limited primarily to North Vietnam and Albania). The latter part of the 1960's saw a pronounced contraction, owing to the cultural revolution in China. Thereafter, a tremendous resurgence took place, with commitments of $1,079,000,000 in 1970 and $600,000,000 in 1971, apparently indicating a new outward-looking foreign policy. Actual disbursements, however, reached only $340,000,000 and $420,000,000 respectively—about 0.5 percent of China's GNP.

The financial conditions of Chinese assistance were generous. Grants accounted for more than one-third of the total; the remainder consisted of interest-free loans of 20 to 25 years.

The net flow of funds to developing countries from multilateral agencies has grown much more rapidly than the general level of aid. From 1960 to 1970 total net flow of aid from all DAC countries rose by nearly 100 percent (from $8,100,000,000 to $15,900,000,-000), while aid from multilateral sources increased by 400 percent (from $300,000,000 to $1,500,000,000).

By 1970 the World Bank group had become the largest single source of funds for the developing countries—even larger than the U.S. foreign aid agency. In 1970–71 the World Bank group's commitments totaled $2,600,000,-000, and in 1971–72 it increased to $2,800,-000,000, which is twice as much as all the other multilateral agencies combined. The Inter-American Development Bank is lending at a rate of about $650,000,000 per year; the United Nation's Development Program disburses about $280,000,000 per year; the Asian Development Bank spends about $250,000,-000; the European Development Fund (of the European Common Market) commits about $220,000,000; and the African Development Bank, lends about $25,000,000.

Within the World Bank group, in 1970–71, hard loans from the International Bank for Reconstruction and Development (IBRD) totaled $1,896,000,000; the very soft loans from the International Development Association (IDA) amounted to $584,000,000; while the International Finance Corporation (IFC) invested and loaned $101,000,000.

LEE C. NEHRT
Professor of International Business,
Indiana University

Signing a **$64,500,000** World Bank development loan to Brazil's largest steel company in February is bank president Robert S. McNamara, flanked on the left by Brazilian Finance Minister Antonio Delfim Netto.

UPI

Pierre Messmer (left) receives President Georges Pompidou in Moselle, Messmer's home.

FRANCE

Experiencing a continuing economic growth rate of 5.8 percent a year (exceeded only by that of Japan), France in 1972 established itself as one of the world's most prosperous, dynamic nations. But this prosperity occasioned an unprecedented French interest in ecology, the state of the environment and the attendant problems of industrial growth, inducing also an exceedingly sharp public outcry against the burgeoning skyscrapers that are intruding on the Paris skyline.

As the pace of French urban life grew increasingly hectic, political tempers became frayed. Indeed, there was evidence of even more public "moroseness" in 1972 than in 1971, without, on the face of it, sufficient cause. The proximity of the 1973 general elections and the continuing disclosures of a number of scandals within the Gaullist establishment contributed to the weakening of the Gaullist Union of Democrats for the Republic (UDR) party and instilled in many Frenchmen a feeling of indifference, if not disgust, toward the parliamentary process.

The major domestic political event of 1972 was the replacement, on July 5, of Jacques Chaban-Delmas as premier by Pierre Messmer. The switch in prime ministers, accomplished solely at the behest of President Georges Pom-

pidou shortly after Chaban-Delmas had obtained a massive vote of confidence in the National Assembly, emphasized the essentially presidential nature of the French regime—but the roots of this apparently abrupt change actually extended back several months to early 1972. Since February a progressive deterioration of relations between Pompidou and Chaban-Delmas had occurred as a result of a series of conflicts of authority. Pompidou had originally realized that Chaban-Delmas was far less conservative and far more disposed to support drastic social change than Pompidou deemed acceptable. This was followed by the revelation in February, in the weekly journal *Le Canard Enchaîné,* that Chaban-Delmas had taken advantage of existing French tax laws to pay no income tax whatever in 1967 and 1968 and only token sums in 1969 and 1970. Chaban-Delmas' somewhat clumsy defense of his financial activities, and his failure to clear up, for the public record, the origin and extent of his income, deemed considerable by the opposition, made him, in Pompidou's eyes, a growing liability and an unsuitable figure to face the hurdle of the 1973 elections as premier.

The new premier, Pierre Messmer, 56, a former colonel in the Foreign Legion, a war hero and an ardent Gaullist, proved to be a political lightweight who was considered—even by members of his own government—as a man so completely under the control of Pompidou as to be more of an aide than an independent prime minister.

In August, only a month after Messmer's appointment, a new scandal broke involving a former aide of former Public Works Minister Albin Chalandon and a former journalist named Gabriel Aranda. In a series of "revelations" to the French press, Aranda made public a number of letters from Gaullists to Chalandon, all asking favors for businessmen. The fact that none of those soliciting such favors had obtained satisfaction greatly reduced the substance of the corruption charges, but the smear stood the French opposition parties in good stead. Also in August, a major police scandal broke in Lyons with the discovery that some senior French police officials enjoyed cozy and remunerative relations with members of the underworld engaged in prostitution. The disclosure produced a widespread purge of police officials, resulting in at least one court case, and the entire affair was adroitly exploited by the opposition press.

All such scandals were accorded additional prominence because of the proximity of the general elections of March 1973. Ever since the

"backlash" elections of July 1968 (after the failure of the May 1968 "revolution") the Gaullists had enjoyed a strong majority in parliament—but their strength in 1972 was undergoing visible erosion.

The defection was evident in a swing away from the UDR to the growing, conservative "Independent Republican" party within the Gaullist coalition led by Finance Minister Valéry Giscard d'Estaing, and in the growing popularity of the latter. The Gaullists were also shocked in November by the desertion to the opposition ranks of former Gaullist minister Jean-Marcel Jeanneney.

Meanwhile, left-wing leader François Mitterand, the secretary general of the French socialist party, had sealed a somewhat uneasy electoral alliance with the French Communist party in order to present a "common front" in the 1973 elections. There was little likelihood, however, that a left-wing "popular front" would gain control in 1973, and President Pompidou himself openly stated in a press conference on Sept. 21 that if such a coalition were to gain the majority, he would continue to exercise his pre-rogative by calling on the Gaullists to form a government.

As a would-be leader of Europe, Pompidou suffered a setback on April 23 when the French people responded by a large abstention rate (39.6 percent) from a referendum calling for ratification of Britain's entry into the Common Market. Choosing to regard the result as indicating coolness toward the concept of a united Europe, Pompidou originally contemplated canceling the European summit conference, which ultimately took place on Oct. 19–20 in Paris.

At the summit conference Pompidou correctly emphasized the dangers of inflation—and France, of all European Economic Community (EEC) member countries, seemed to be most affected by an inflationary spiral, officially estimated at 6 percent per annum but, in fact, nearer to 8 percent. The inflation rate cut substantially into wages, particularly at the lower income levels, and even a minimum wage proposal of 1,000 francs monthly (about $200) failed to satisfy workers, with the result that from September onward a number of transport

President Pompidou welcomes chiefs of state and foreign and finance ministers of the enlarged European Community at Paris summit.

Henri Bureau, Gamma

Alain Nogues, Gamma

Traffic gluts, such as this one in Paris, attended autumn transport strikes in several French cities.

workers struck repeatedly for higher wages. A new phenomenon in France, in union terms, was the multinational company strike. For example, a strike at the Michelin tire works in Clermont-Ferrand in October succeeded in impeding Michelin operations all over Western

Europe until the French workers obtained their wage settlement.

Despite inflation fears, the French stock market rose in 1972 in a manner unprecedented for 14 years. The main reasons for the sharp upsurge were massive investment (mainly

Alain Nogues, Gamma

Renault workers expel radical leftists from their plant in confrontation after a Maoist agitator was killed there in February.

in real estate, frozen food and clothing industries) by British financial groups preparing for full British membership in the EEC and the recognition, by West German and Swiss bankers, that French blue chip stocks were underpriced and undervalued. The French armaments industry continued to expand, ranking in the non-Communist world in 1972 second only to the United States and displacing Britain to third place. But "black spots" remained on the French economic horizon—the dubious government investment in the controversial supersonic "Concorde" airplane, especially after United Airlines canceled its option to purchase, and the antiquated state of the government-operated telephone communications system (by the end of 1972 there were more that 500,000 unsuccessful phone applicants in France).

In a different field, France's bad wine harvest in 1972 was expected to produce increases averaging 20 percent in the prices of high-quality French wines.

The year also witnessed these developments:

* the most spectacular postwar French holdup, a carefully planned assault on the Mulhouse post office strongroom in which the thieves seized $2,000,000 after opening the safe with keys of a postal employee.

* the first full-scale Kinsey-type report on French sexual habits, revealing that France, far from being the world center of sophisticated sex, was in fact just as conservative in its attitudes, perhaps even more so, as the United States. (Most French people, the report noted, prefer to make love in the dark, and according to those questioned, 78 percent of all French women and 59 percent of the men had never been unfaithful to their spouses.)

* renewed debate over whether capital punishment should be banned as the first condemned men to be executed in France in more than three years went to the guillotine.

* one of the worst French athletic showings in history at the 1972 Winter Olympic Games, with France obtaining only one silver and two bronze medals and no award whatever in its former specialty, skiing.

* the beginning of the end of the "French connection," thanks to such developments as closer cooperation with the U.S. Bureau of Narcotics and Dangerous Drugs, the spectacular discovery of several clandestine laboratories near Marseilles engaged in heroin manufacture and the seizure in the Mediterranean, on March 1, of a shrimp trawler carrying 200 kilos (444 pounds) of U.S.-bound heroin.

* a resumption of gang warfare on the French Riviera, leading to the destruction of at least 12 nightclubs, and a spate of unsolved minor gangland murders—a somber reminder that in France, as in the rest of Western Europe, crime is increasing at the alarming rate of 10 percent yearly.

EDWARD BEHR
Paris Bureau Chief, *Newsweek*

Claude Wherlé, Gamma

A closet containing 200 pounds of pure heroin is uncovered in raid on secret drug laboratory near Marseilles in March.

GEOLOGY

International Geological Congress. In August 1972, Montréal was the host city for the 24th International Geological Congress. More than 4,300 scientists attended the conference and presented various papers which were subsequently published. Guidebooks for excursions to every part of Canada, issued by the congress, provided an unrivaled account of the geology of that country.

Among the significant findings unveiled at the meeting were those reported by Clifford Frondel of Harvard, who said that analysis of the Apollo 11, 12, 14 and 15 lunar samples had yielded 55 minerals, including three new mineral species. He noted that the absence of oxygen and water in the lunar environment at the time when the rocks had crystallized had tended to limit the diversity of minerals on the moon. Brian Mason of the Smithsonian Institution reported that during the past decade the number of minerals identified in meteorites had risen from 40 to a total of about 80. Most of the new discoveries are present in tiny quantities and have been detected only since the development of the electron-beam microscope made improved microanalysis possible.

Mars. Although interest in the moon continued unabated, the year's most exciting new planetary geology was displayed on photographs telemetered from the Mariner 9 satellite in orbit around Mars. When the satellite first entered its orbit, the surface of the planet was obscured by a vast dust storm. As the dust settled, the peaks of four giant volcanoes, the largest nearly 375 miles in diameter, came into view. Later pictures revealed the existence of a rift structure on the Martian surface about 1,100 miles long, and landforms suggestive of glaciation, dune phenomena and possibly running water. By the end of 1972 analyses indicated that Mars has a unique geological landscape and that it is in a state of crustal evolution intermediate between those characteristic of the dynamic earth and the geologically dead moon.

Good photographs of the two tiny moons of Mars were also taken for the first time. Both are quite irregular in shape and are pitted with numerous meteorite impact craters.

Environmental Geology. At the opening ceremonies of the Geological Congress, Maurice Strong emphasized the importance of environmental geology, an area which had also constituted a major topic of the United Nations Stockholm Conference on the Human Environment, of which he was chairman.

Today many geologists are employed in such environmental studies as searching for sources of pure water, investigating sites of potential earthquakes or floods, halting erosion, seeking means of disposing safely of radioactive wastes and of garbage, and assisting in many other attempts to preserve or improve the environment.

Low surface gravity on Mars' tiny moons, Phobos (l) and Deimos (r), permits retention of asymmetrical contours revealed by Mariner 9.

Photos NASA

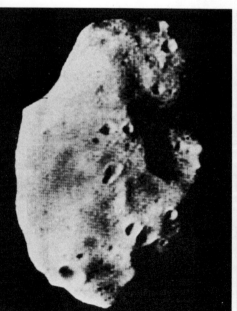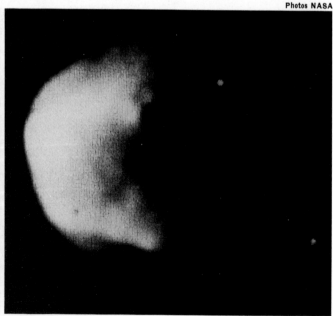

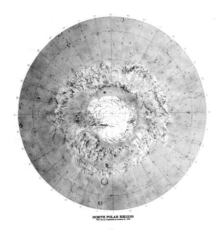

NORTH POLAR REGION

SOUTH POLAR REGION

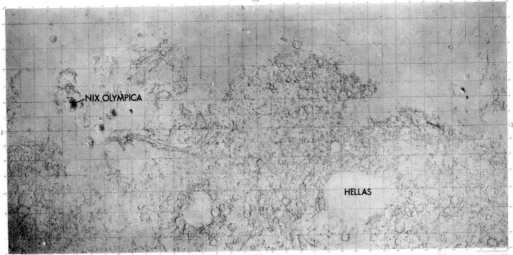

NIX OLYMPICA

HELLAS

U.S. Geological Survey

Martian topographic map displays such distinctive geologic features as Nix Olympica, a volcanic mountain, and Hellas, a vast circular basin.

Modern cities are ill-adapted to cope with such geological hazards as earthquakes and floods. During 1972, for example, the remnants of an Atlantic hurricane swept through several Eastern states of the United States, causing unprecedented flood damage. The Susquehanna River rose more than 30 feet, flooding several cities and much valuable land. Geologists are only now accepting the responsibilities implied by their position as the members of the community best informed about the incidence of such hazards.

U.S. geophysicist M. K. Hubbert correctly predicted ten years ago that U.S. petroleum production would peak around 1970 and that world supplies of fluid petroleum would barely last into the next century. Management of this rapidly dwindling resource is another sphere in which geologists are finding that they can play an important role. In 1972 some geologists expressed reservations about the method proposed for developing the petroleum resources of Alaska and Arctic Canada, but investigations using an experimental length of pipeline indicate that such pipelines can be built over permanently frozen ground without inflicting irreparable damage. Offshore drilling operations in the Arctic must combat the additional hazard posed by floating ice, a consideration which is also currently under study. Some 50 American and Canadian scientists cooperated in one such research project in the Beaufort Sea, a portion of the Arctic Ocean. They camped on the sea ice and investigated the

ocean floor, its waters, the ice and the atmosphere. In spite of the difficulties involved, it appears that reserves located in the Arctic and at offshore sites will be needed if future petroleum quotas are to be met. The problem is how safely to exploit the resources of increasingly difficult locations.

Plate Tectonics. In 1967 scientists first developed the concept of an earth covered by a few rigid lithospheric plates in continuous slow motion over its surface. It is now seen that all active geologic processes including those that produce earthquakes, mountain building, ocean opening and ocean closing are concentrated at the points where the edges of these large plates come into contact. Plates separate under mid-ocean ridges and the ocean bodies widen as the sea-floor moves outward from this point. Plates move together and overlap under deep ocean trenches and active mountains. Plates scrape past one another along faults like the San Andreas fault, occasionally jerking ahead abruptly to shake the vicinity with an earthquake.

An insight provided by this new theory has proved economically beneficial. It has been realized that the distribution of a series of giant ore deposits called porphyry coppers, which ring the Pacific Ocean, is correlated with their location over descending crustal plates. Where one plate has been forced down beneath another, as in Chile, the western United States and Bougainville in the Solomon Islands solutions have emerged to concentrate copper ores.

Oil geologists recently have focused their attention on the sediments which pile up off the shores of recent continental ruptures, such as that represented by the Red Sea. Whether much oil will be found in the sediments that line the coasts of the Red Sea may have been determined by the rate at which the young ocean has opened. If the opening has proceeded too swiftly the sediments may have been heated so much that the petroleum component has been driven off. On the other hand, if the opening has proceeded too slowly plant and animal debris in the sediments may not have been heated sufficiently to be converted into petroleum. Thus, there exists an optimum rate of opening.

Increasingly refined analyses of the ocean floor and of the magnetic pattern produced as new crust is added at mid-ocean ridges are providing detailed histories of the development of the world's ocean during the last 200,000,000 years. The detailed account of the opening of the North Atlantic in the interval since Africa lay against the eastern seaboard of North America, since Greenland adjoined Labrador and since Europe bordered Greenland has been worked out. The complex history of the opening of the Indian Ocean has been analyzed as far back as 75,000,000 years, but doubts still exist as to the exact positioning of India, Antarctica, Australia, Malagasy Republic and continental Africa at the time of the breakup of the great supercontinent, called Gondwanaland, about 200,000,000 years ago.

As geologists have grown increasingly familiar with plate tectonic processes, they have detected mounting evidence of the operation of plate mechanisms through much of the 3,700,000,000 years of earth history that is recorded in terrestrial rocks. About 2,500,000,000 years ago a major geologic change appears to have occurred, because evidence for the existence of continents before that time is lacking, although the very oldest rocks found on earth were apparently deposited in the ocean.

Naturally, as this new theory has been developed, many have speculated as to the mechanism that produces crustal movement. One theory which attracted interest in 1972 was that heated columns of rock rise like plumes at a few places within the earth in rather the same way that bubbles of gas rise in the form of a column in a pan of boiling water. These plumes of solid rock are thought to measure about 100 miles across and to rise a few feet per year. At the points where they occur, they uplift the overlying surface, often producing volcanoes. Thus it has been suggested that such a series of plumes has risen in East Africa, uplifting Ethiopia and parts of Kenya, Uganda and Tanzania. The uplifts are thought to have broken open to produce rift valleys and active volcanoes such as Kilimanjaro.

It is also thought that because the interior of the earth is white hot, the rigid external crust is able to flow easily, if only slowly, over the interior. If this is so, uplifts such as those in Ethiopia, Yemen and southern Arabia may have provided the impetus for the further widening of the existing rifts and the opening of the Red Sea and the Gulf of Aden as the African and Eurasian plates slid apart. Ocean bodies begun in this manner may later undergo still further widening. Thus it is considered that plumes under such active volcanic islands as Iceland, the Azores, Ascension and Tristan da Cunha have uplifted the mid-Atlantic Ridge and caused the subsequent separation of the African and American plates as they slipped off the uplifts. This motion, averaging less than 1 inch a year, has created the Atlantic Ocean.

J. TUZO WILSON
Professor of Geophysics and Principal
Erindale College, University of Toronto

Representatives of East and West Germany exchange draft copies of a transport treaty on May 15.

GERMANY

After almost a quarter-century of hostility the two German states created in the ruins of Hitler's Third Reich formally declared in late 1972 their intention to be good neighbors.

For Chancellor Willy Brandt, who had asked for and got a mandate from the people of West Germany to sign the good-neighbor treaty, the pact was "an important stage on the way towards normalization of relations between the two German states."

For Erich Honecker, first secretary of East Germany's Socialist Unity (Communist) party, the contract signed in East Berlin on Dec. 21 merely confirmed the division of the nation and stabilized the demarcation line between the rival states. "The frontier and the (Berlin) wall remain as existing realities," Honecker told C. L. Sulzberger of *The New York Times* in a rare interview with a Western journalist. "Stabilized borders constitute an aid to peace."

"The wall and the demarcation line remain, and they remain painful," West Germany's Brandt admitted. "But we can now hope that the conditions of life in our divided land will become more tolerable and that the danger of conflict is reduced."

TREATY OF FRIENDSHIP

Terms. Article 1 of the treaty declared that the two German states "will develop normal good-neighborly relations towards one another on a basis of equality." Article 3 said that "they confirm the inviolability of the border existing between them, now and in the future, and pledge

their unconditional respect for territorial integrity." Thus, West Germany recognized East Germany's status as a sovereign state, opening the door to its membership in the United Nations and a host of other international organizations from which non-Communist majorities had excluded it, year after year, with monotonous regularity.

In return for this long-sought prize, Honecker agreed to open some cracks in the walls and death strips with which the Communists had sealed out the West since 1949.

The two German states, said Article 7 of their treaty, "express their readiness, in the course of the normalization of their relations, to regulate practical and humanitarian questions. Thus, they will conclude agreements in order, on the basis of this treaty and for their mutual benefit, to develop and promote cooperation in the fields of economics, science and technology, transportation, judicial affairs, postal and telecommunications, public health, culture, sports, protection of the environment and other areas."

Honecker agreed that under the terms of the treaty millions of West Germans and West Berliners for the first time will be allowed to visit East Germany, at the invitation of their relatives in most cases, but even as tourists in some. Even those who had fled from East to West Germany—almost 3,000,000 since 1949 —thus making themselves liable to criminal prosecution by the Communist regime in the east, were made subject to an amnesty and told they could visit without risk.

Before a packed gallery the foreign ministers of the four nations responsible for Berlin sign the agreement affecting the divided city.

Background and Importance. To grasp the importance of the understanding one must recall that Communist controls had made the East-West demarcation line in Germany the most impenetrable in Europe. Millions of West Germans traveled freely every year throughout Western Europe and to other continents. But because of Communist restrictions few ever had been next door to see the other half of their own nation. West Germans could direct dial telephone numbers anywhere in Western Europe or the United States, but suffered delays of up to 24 hours on calls to relatives in the east. The barrier had an authorized crossing point (for those with permission to cross) only every 70 miles, whereas authorized crossing points were situated every five miles on West Germany's borders with other countries. The Communists permitted only couples both members of which had reached retirement age to make private visits to West Germany.

When he took office in Bonn in late 1969, Social Democrat Brandt set out to change this, to make the Communist wall porous, by announcing and subsequently proving that he was prepared to sign nonaggression treaties with the Soviet Union and Poland based on recognition of the borders drawn across Europe by the Allies after World War II.

Brandt's predecessors in Bonn had refused to take such a step, contending that it would foreclose chances for reunification. Brandt argued on the contrary that the Soviet Union, its armed forces deployed at the Elbe, never would permit reunification. Hence, he said, negotiation of some easing of the suffering caused by the division of the nation must begin with recognition of the reality of the division.

The West German leader, together with his American, British and French allies, however, insisted that part of European reality also was recognition of the existence of a free West Berlin linked to West Germany. Until the U.S.S.R. dropped its challenge to West Berlin and its lifelines, Brandt and his allies insisted, there was no point in holding the European Security Conference that Moscow desired.

Moscow bowed to the pressure, negotiating a new Berlin agreement in 1971, but refusing to sign it and put it into effect unless and until the West German parliament ratified the pre-existing nonaggression pacts, which Brandt had signed in Moscow and Warsaw in 1970.

Suddenly, Brandt confronted serious resistance. Under the heat of what he termed his "Ostpolitik" (Eastern Policy), his parliamentary majority melted, and a half-dozen of his supporters defected to the opposition.

Thereupon an alarmed Moscow brought pressure to bear. Leonid I. Brezhnev, general secretary of the Soviet Communist party, told an interviewer that the choice Bonn faced was one "between a policy of peace or war." Pravda echoed the party line, warning of "irreparable damage" if the West German parliament rejected the treaties.

While Brezhnev wielded the stick, Honecker dangled a carrot. To demonstrate the benefits

Approaching the Warschauer gate in March, two West Germans, carrying gifts, will see their children for the first time in more than six years.

that might flow from West German ratification, Honecker permitted about 1,000,000 West Berliners to visit East Berlin and East Germany at Easter and Whitsun. It was the first time the wall had been opened to West Berliners for years.

Brandt brought the treaties before parliament on May 10. A procedural vote showed the house evenly divided. For a week the struggle raged. First, the opposition said it would vote against the pacts, which, in the circumstances, meant that the pacts would fail of ratification. Later, after Brandt agreed to an accompanying draft resolution stating the treaties did not bind the hands of a future all-German government, the opposition said it would vote for the pacts. However, a strong right-wing block within the Christian Democratic Union rebelled. To preserve a semblance of unity, opposition leaders finally agreed to abstain. When the final division was called on May 17, the treaties were ratified by a vote of 248, with 10 against and 238 abstentions.

Ratification came just in time to smooth President Nixon's trip to Moscow. The weekend after Nixon's talks in the Soviet capital, the

Traffic at the Invalidenstrasse checkpoint in Berlin awaits clearance during momentous East-West reunion in early April.

Anne Marie Renger, first woman president of the Bundestag, is very much at ease behind her lectern.

U.S., British, French and Soviet foreign ministers met in West Berlin and signed the Berlin agreement. Recalling 27 years of West-East struggle in and around the city, U.S. Secretary of State William P. Rogers declared: "For those who live here, Berlin no longer is an isolated island. For the peoples of Europe, this agreement is a step toward dismantling the barriers, barriers which have divided this city and this continent for too long."

DOMESTIC AFFAIRS

West Germany. While Brandt made good progress on the international front, he experienced unusual domestic difficulties. Despite the global readjustment of currency exchange rates at the start of the year, a move the government hoped would ease inflationary pressures, prices continued to rise at an annual rate of 6–7 percent, low by the standards of most other European countries but alarmingly high in

West Germany's third ground station for television satellite transmissions nears completion in northern Bavaria.

West Germany, where price stability had been maintained for years.

Karl Schiller, the professor of economics who had led West Germany out of an economic slump at the end of the 1960's and become the Social Democrats' biggest drawing card next to Brandt himself, resigned from the government in midsummer. He said that Brandt had refused to heed his advice on ways to deal with inflation and that the government as a whole had tended too far left. He campaigned against the government in the election.

Brandt should have had parliamentary approval of his 1972 budget before Christmas of 1971. But by May he still lacked such approval. Therefore, when parliament deadlocked over the nonaggression treaties, he had no choice but to call an early election.

The signs looked promising. The government was convinced that a majority of the people approved of the treaties, and, despite rising prices, the working man was better off than ever before. At the same time, the government swept up the gang of bank robbers, bombers and self-styled revolutionaries led by Ulrike Meinhof and Andreas Baader that had terrorized the republic for a year. On the eve of the Olympic Games in Munich—the first German Games since 1936—West Germany's image as a peaceful, peace-loving state shone.

Arab terrorists tarnished it.

At about dawn on Sept. 5, eight armed men from the Palestinian Black September guerrilla organization invaded the Israeli male athletes' living quarters in Olympic Village, killing two as they went in and holding nine others hostage. The terrorists demanded release of 200 Palestinian guerrillas held prisoner in Israel, which Israel refused. German officials argued with the Arabs all day, finally agreeing after dark to fly them and their Israeli hostages in two helicopters to Fuerstenfeldbruck military airfield, where they would board a larger plane to fly out of the country.

But the Germans had laid a trap at the airfield. As soon as four Arabs left the helicopters, five German sharpshooters opened fire. The Palestinians returned the fire, and one threw a grenade into a helicopter in which some of the Israeli hostages were sitting. The aircraft exploded and burned. When fighting finally ended half an hour later, all nine Israelis, five of the Arabs and one German policeman were dead. German police captured three of the Arabs.

A storm of criticism broke over the government. Some critics complained that the government had failed to give the Israeli athletes adequate protection. Others blamed the Germans as much as or more than the Arabs for the Israeli deaths. Moreover, two months later, another group of Arab guerrillas hijacked a West German airliner and, using it for ransom, extorted the release of the three surviving Arabs awaiting trial in Munich.

The election campaign began in the aftermath of Munich and was intense. Brandt made more than 120 speeches, Christian Democrat Rainer Barzel about 100, and the rivals confronted each other in three televised debates as well. Prices and the treaty negotiated but not

D.P.A.-Pictorial

Contending forces in West Germany's November election erected a forest of posters along the streets in Frankfurt.

yet signed with East Germany were the main issues. Much was at stake, but the campaign was peaceful, lacking the street fighting that had marred the campaign of 1969, when ultras of both left and right still fielded large forces.

An unprecedented 91.2 percent of the eligible voters turned out on Sunday, Nov. 19, a record for any Western democracy. When their ballots had been counted, the result showed Brandt's Social Democrats had won 45.9 percent, and his coalition partners, the Free Democratic (liberal) party, 8.4 percent, giving the government parties a total of 54.3 percent, compared with 44.8 percent for the opposition Christian Democrats. For the first time since the republic's creation in 1949, the Social Democrats controlled the largest bloc of seats in parliament. With a majority of 48 seats in the Bundestag, the 496-member lower house of parliament, Brandt and his government seemed assured of clear sailing for the next four years.

The campaign nevertheless had taken its toll. Right after the election, Brandt was admitted to a hospital for treatment of an infection of his vocal cords, and Barzel went to bed with grippe for a week.

East Germany. The Volkskammer, East Germany's parliament, made history of its own on March 9, when, for the first time, a vote was less than unanimous. At question was a bill to permit any woman to have an abortion during the first three months of any pregnancy. Four-teen Volkskammer deputies voted nay, and eight abstained.

To seal the improvement of relations with West Germany, Honecker released about 25,000 political prisoners. But at the same time he stepped up a campaign to eliminate the last vestiges of capitalism in East Germany. In May officials announced that the last 5,000 wholly or partly privately owned enterprises had been nationalized. Moreover, Honecker's Communist party agitators moved through East German factories urging the workers to sign petitions pledging that they would not invite any West German relatives to visit. Brandt's government protested, saying the petitions ran counter to the good-neighbor treaty.

More such Communist attempts to frustrate the spirit of the pact could be expected, although perhaps not until after the United Nations accepts East Germany as a member, probably at the 1973 General Assembly, and the United States, Britain and France have established embassies in East Berlin, also probably in 1973.

In the meantime, the two German states at long last could begin cooperating on such vital matters as environmental protection. First priority might go to saving the Baltic Sea from total pollution, a matter of immediate interest to millions of persons outside Germany.

WELLINGTON LONG
Chief Correspondent for Germany
United Press International

D.P.A.-Pictorial

West German Chancellor Willy Brandt and his Norwegian-born wife, Rut, enjoy a respite from campaigning in their garden near Bonn.

GREECE

Premier George Papadopoulos, though indicating that he was ready to tolerate a limited and closely watched return of democracy, actually tightened his grip on the levers of power during 1972. As head of both state and government, he assumed more personal and direct authority than anyone in Greece has held since the 1930's. His position of strength derives from such key posts as those of premier, regent, foreign minister and defense minister—and it has begun to inspire jokes about "papadocracy."

The stocky, 54-year-old former tank commander and chief strategist of the 1967 coup began consolidating his political hold on Mar. 21. He dismissed Gen. George Zoitakis and took over his duties as regent, which allowed him to act in the name of the self-exiled King Constantine. Papadopoulos moved again on July 31 by ordering his entire 37-man government to resign. In the fifth major shakeup of its kind since the military takeover, he then named a cabinet of 42 members, including 12

former army officers who had helped him in 1967. The cabinet changes came only two weeks after U.S. Secretary of State William P. Rogers ended a 24-hour visit to Athens, during which he twice met with Papadopoulos. Diplomats said Rogers had urged the premier to hasten the return of democracy. Nevertheless, in September Papadopoulos made public a 15-year development program, an 800-page document, which some Greeks interpreted to mean that the premier intended to remain in power until 1987.

While there was no sign that full democracy was contemplated, the government in November allowed university students to elect their own leaders. It was the first such voting since the military assumed power. Until the elections, all student leaders had been appointed by the government. More important, in mid-November the premier's aides disclosed that Greeks would elect more than 100 members of an advisory body in 1973. The Consultative Committee ("mini-parliament") will have no lawmaking powers but will be permitted to

Sailors' families arrive in the Athens area, where home-port facilities are being established for U.S. 6th Fleet ships in Piraeus.

U.S. Navy Photo

criticize proposed legislation. In 1972 the committee numbered 75, with 60 of its members chosen by 10,670 carefully screened voters, mostly mayors and leaders of approved professional organizations.

Papadopoulos negotiated an agreement with the United States. Announced May 14, it allows sailors of the U.S. Sixth Fleet to settle their wives and children in Athens. The arrangement grants the servicemen and their families judicial immunity, tax exemptions and the same sort of rights as are already enjoyed by 7,000 other U.S. military personnel, most of them present under various NATO agreements. Opponents of the regime said the accord was one more proof that Washington is instrumental in maintaining Papadopoulos in power and once again pointed to the sizable amount of U.S. arms aid granted Greece.

Early in the year the government increased its security vigilance by introducing a loyalty-oath questionnaire designed to prevent the employment of any security suspects by the civil service, banks, public utilities or other government-controlled bodies. Later, the oath was extended to include Greek Orthodox priests because the state pays their salaries.

Dozens of security trials took place during the year. In August a military tribunal sentenced two persons and freed six after weighing evidence of a plot which involved kidnaping the son of the late President John F. Kennedy and other notables as a political gesture. On Feb. 8 an appeals court had dismissed sedition charges against four persons. It was the first time in five years that a court refused to convict persons accused of sedition under laws dealing with anti-regime activities.

Economically, there seemed to be some general improvement, despite the continued failure of the government to attract sizable amounts of foreign investment. The major growth industry was tourism. The 1971 figure for tourists was 2,257,000, with spending set at $307,-000,000, and officials said visitors in 1972 would exceed 3,000,000. But the economy was again blighted by rising costs and a large trade deficit. On the bright side were a good credit line with Western nations and improving trade connections with the East. Papadopoulos negotiated diplomatic ties with China and in November signed an $89,000,000 electric power pact with the Soviet Union.

Exports during the first eight months of the year totaled $517,000,000, a 38 percent increase over the same period in 1971. The Greek balance of trade is traditionally unfavorable, but the difference is made up by such "invisibles" as earnings from tourism, receipts from shipping and money sent home by Greeks working outside the country. ("Invisible" income had totaled $914,000,000 in 1971.) Foreign reserves were up to $800,000,000 in mid-September—a healthy sign, as the balance of payments in 1971 showed a deficit of only $310,000,000. The rate of economic growth was 7.3 percent, slightly lower than the growth rate achieved in 1971.

CHARLES W. BELL
Former Manager for Italy
United Press International

GUYANA, SURINAM AND FRENCH GUIANA

Activities in the international field distinguished the government of Guyana in 1972. Most important was Prime Minister Forbes Burnham's decision to exchange ambassadors with mainland China—a move which came on the heels of a $26,000,000 long-term, interest-free loan from Peking.

Guyana's demonstration of independence from the West, following its 1971 nationalization of foreign bauxite mines, raised Georgetown's political capital within the context of the Caribbean's generally conservative, pro-U.S. nations, which both Brazil and Venezuela have courted.

Nevertheless, the country's economic problems persisted throughout the year. Savings were low. Unemployment was high. Quantities of aluminum ore remained unsold, and per capita income increased only 3 percent. Despite these concerns, however, Burnham solidified his position, as anticolonialist policies further undercut Cheddi Jagan, the pro-Moscow Communist who heads the opposition.

Questions of colonialism concurrently beset Surinam, for reports from Amsterdam implied that ties with its Caribbean colonies might be attenuated to aid Dutch penetration of markets in third world countries, which resent dealing with a colonial power.

Although the Paramaribo government announced a $25,000,000 budget deficit, work proceeded on road building, housing construction and development of forestry and energy resources.

Meanwhile, in French Guiana—once known only as the site of the "Devil's Island" colony—the Soviets in 1972 began using the French space center at Kouru, an excellent launching site for rockets because of the high velocity of the earth's surface at that location.

GEORGE W. GRAYSON
Associate Professor of Government
College of William and Mary

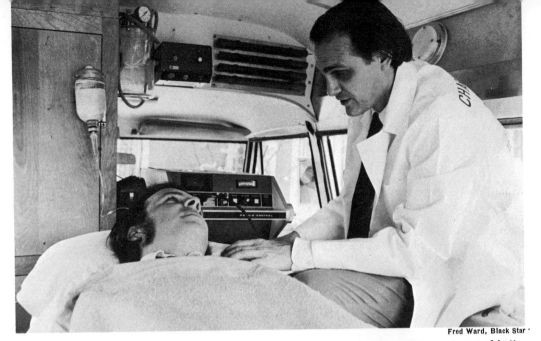

Fred Ward, Black Star

Increasingly doctors are becoming convinced of the importance of better equipped ambulances and more plentiful mobile coronary care units.

HEALTH

Health Care Cost. Following years of talk about rising medical care costs—from total national spending estimates beyond comprehension to hospital room charges all too easily understood —perhaps the most shocking example of the system's exorbitant price was brought to light in 1972: The case of Harold E. Wagner, Ohio machinist.

The 52-year old Wagner entered a Detroit hospital in November, 1971, for treatment of an eye problem but his heart, damaged by an earlier attack, began to fail while he was there. For long hours, doctors undertook heroic efforts to save his life, but they could not, and he died, less than 30 hours after he was admitted to the hospital. The bill was $7,311.

Wagner's tragedy became known in May 1972 at U.S. Senate hearings on health insurance. At the hearings, Leonard Woodcock, president of the United Automobile Workers and a proponent of a national health insurance system, termed the cost "scandalous."

The case symbolized the seemingly endless spiral of the costs of modern, highly skilled, highly technological medicine. And it dramatized for supporters of a national health insurance system the compelling need to do something to remove the threat of bankruptcy to so many families who could not meet the catastrophic health care costs.

But the year passed, and Congress adjourned without any final action on the various proposals, all complex and controversial. In the face of

this inaction, Sen. Edward M. Kennedy, a backer of the broadest insurance plan, offered what appeared to some observers as a peace gesture to organized medicine. Long at war with the American Medical Association, Senator Kennedy said he believed that the principles of free enterprise can be maintained in any new U.S. health insurance system. Speaking to the American Academy of Family Physicians, the Massachusetts Democrat said: "I believe in maintaining the free enterprise system in this country and in American medicine. I would like to see even more variety and competition in the health care system between different forms of care—solo practice, prepaid groups, medical foundations and any other way that is efficient and beneficial to the patients and doctors, too."

Organized medicine will not forget these words when the national health insurance debate begins again in 1973 and it attempts to limit the Kennedy plan, which has the backing of labor. All indications pointed to an early legislative battle. Rep. Wilbur D. Mills (D.-Ark.), chairman of the powerful Ways and Means Committee, told newsmen in April 1972, at a medical meeting in Atlantic City, N.J., that the various national health insurance proposals would be given priority attention in the opening sessions of his committee in 1973. "It could be the first thing on the agenda next year," Mills said. The legislators and witnesses will consider the following cost figures.

The average medical bill for a person 65 or older was $861 during the fiscal year 1971. For

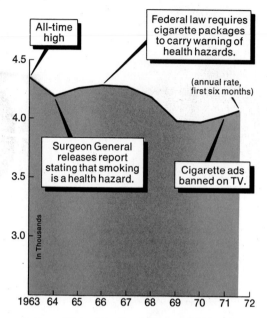

CIGARETTE CONSUMPTION

**Number of Cigarettes Smoked Per Person
(18 years and over)**

All-time high

Federal law requires cigarette packages to carry warning of health hazards.

4.5

(annual rate, first six months)

4.0

Surgeon General releases report stating that smoking is a health hazard.

Cigarette ads banned on TV.

3.5

3.0

In Thousands

1963 64 65 66 67 68 69 70 71 72

uses the services. The key is "prepaid fee," rather than the traditional "fee-for-service" method so cherished by organized medicine.

Both the Nixon administration and Senator Kennedy looked favorably on prepaid group practices in differing degrees. The AMA, however, suggested caution. "Considering all the unknowns related to the HMO concept," the AMA said, "a period of experience-gathering and experimentation would seem very prudent indeed."

The Department of Health, Education and Welfare nevertheless made 110 grants to HMO applicants, including hospitals, group practices and others, for planning and development. A Kennedy bill on funding HMOs was passed by the Senate, 60–14, but it was too late in the session for final Congressional action. This delay conceivably could stall the eventual widespread adoption of the HMO concept.

Physicians' Assistants (PAs). Physicians' assistants would be trained to take over some of the health care functions traditionally performed by physicians. It is envisioned that PAs would perform examinations, make diagnoses and prescribe treatment. Although doctors would not necessarily be physically present, they would supervise. The PA concept grew out of the widespread need to relieve a shortage of physicians.

"In many respects," said a Yale Medical School research team, "the birth and development of the physician's assistant is the most exciting health manpower innovation in several decades. It has highlighted the established belief that many tasks performed only by physicians can be carried out by specially trained health professionals." Despite this enthusiasm, the Yale team expressed its own caution, saying that much nationwide experimentation must take place before the best methods of training and usage of PAs can be agreed on. The team —consisting of a doctor, lawyer and nurse— called for creation of a new professional discipline to insure against serious mistakes.

Emergency Care. While the issue was joined in public debate, many doctors privately agreed that ambulance and emergency room care in the United States is inadequate. The doctors charged that as a result of poor emergency room care thousands of Americans die unnecessarily each year. Following a major study of emergency care, the National Academy of Science reported: "Thousands of lives are lost through lack of systematic application of established principles of emergency care."

Other physicians noted that nationwide use of mobile coronary care units, specially equipped to handle the person suddenly seized with

a person 19 to 64, the bill was $323. For a person under 19, the average was $140, according to the Social Security Administration. Public funds, mainly Medicare and Medicaid, covered two-thirds of the costs for the aged.

The Federal budget estimated that the government's spending on health in 1972 would total $17,000,000,000. A study by the American Medical Association put that figure at $27,000,000,000.

The average cost of one day's care for a hospital patient was $92.31 in 1971, the American Hospital Association reported. This was a 13.9 percent increase over the 1970 average cost of $81.01.

In response to these rising costs, the national health insurance proposals held center stage in most discussions of reforms in health care and cost in 1972. But there were also two relatively new factors in the picture—health maintenance organizations (HMOs) and physicians' assistants (PAs). In the long run, these two factors may have a profound effect on how and where the American people get their health care, both in terms of treatment and prevention.

Health Maintenance Organizations (HMOs). A general definition of HMO is a group of physicians that provides all of an individual's or a family's basic medical services for a set annual fee, regardless of how much the subscriber

a heart attack, could save the lives of perhaps 100,000 heart attack victims yearly. Many medical groups were working to stimulate community interest in developing qualified emergency medical care, and the Department of Health, Education and Welfare was taking steps to provide national leadership.

Flu Epidemic. In 1968 and 1969 a flu pandemic —a worldwide flu epidemic—claimed a stunning 27,900 lives in the United States alone. It was named the Hong Kong flu, a variation of an earlier Asian flu. Late in 1972, there were warnings from public health officials and organizations, including the World Health Organization, of another flu variant, discovered in London. This strain began to appear throughout the world at year's end. The Center for Disease Control in Atlanta, Ga., part of the U.S. Public Health Services, offered a hopeful note, however. The change in the virus discovered in London was apparently not so great a change as the one that produced Hong Kong flu.

PCB, DDT and Hexachlorophene. The names PCB (polychlorinated biphenyl) and hexachlorophene (HCP) joined DDT as household terms in 1972. PCB is a widely used industrial chemical favored in manufacturing because of its high resistance to heat. It is also closely related structurally to DDT and has been found widely in the environment.

At a meeting of the American Chemical Society, an Environmental Protection Agency spokesman reported that PCB had been found in human tissue samples taken in 18 states and the District of Columbia. "These materials are

Monkmeyer

Crops are sprayed with DDT. In 1972 the United States banned the pesticide almost completely.

A French babies' talcum manufacturer used too much hexachlorophene, killing several infants and paralyzing many, including Yannick, below.

Henri Bureau, Gamma

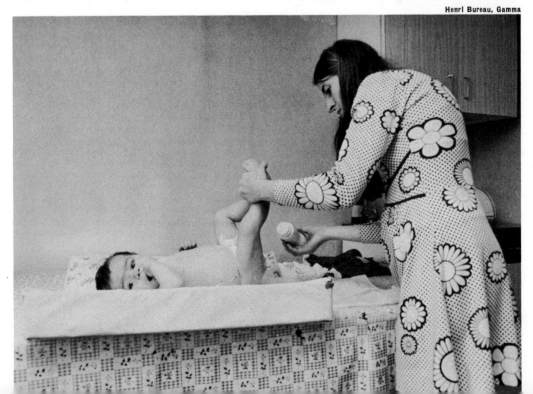

widely found in the population," the spokesman warned. "Positive samples came from every hospital, city and state sampled." PCB was found in drinking water supplies in New York State and in polar bears in the Arctic. Unacceptable levels were found in some chickens, eggs, turkeys and fish. The precise threat to health was not clear, but there was concern over controlling PCB's use in industry.

At the same time, DDT was back in the news, and a long battle seemed over. William D. Ruckelshaus, administrator of the Environmental Protection Agency, issued a nearly total ban on the use of DDT in the United States, a move some saw as certain to influence many other nations, except where DDT was deemed vital in combatting malaria. The DDT ban evoked loud protests from the manufacturer of the chemical, but at year's end there appeared to be no chance of any major change in the ban, effective Jan. 1, 1973.

Hexachlorophene, a chemical used in disinfectants, also joined the out of favor list. The Food and Drug Administration announced in September a ban on non-prescription sales of medicines containing more than 0.75 percent HCP. Laboratory studies had shown that brain damage had developed in baby monkeys scrubbed with HCP.

The controversy over HCP created a dilemma for hospitals that had counted on it to prevent staph outbreaks in nurseries. And the manufacturer of one HCP preparation argued that the FDA's action was precipitate inasmuch as its product was safe and effective when used as directed. The drug company indicated that it would fight the FDA ruling.

Red Tide. Perhaps the most unusual threat to the public's health appeared off the coast of Massachusetts in the fall—the red tide. The ominously-named ocean scourge of tiny organisms bloomed and proliferated, for largely unknown reasons, adding a reddish element to the offshore waters of New England and dealing a serious blow to the shellfish industry. Clams, mussels and scallops, feeding on the organisms, were not adversely affected, but it soon became apparent that the shellfish themselves were toxic to anyone who ate them.

The red tide invasion forced the Massachusetts Department of Public Health to ban the importation, sale and harvesting of soft-shelled clams and mussels as well as the harvesting of cherrystone clams, sea scallops and oysters. By the end of October the red tide appeared to be leaving the Massachusetts coast. As it takes from two to six weeks for the contaminated shellfish to lose the toxin, the crisis appeared over as the year ended. Twenty-five cases of poisoning had been reported officially, and two persons had been hospitalized. There was a suggestion that pollution of the ocean may have contributed to the blooming red tide, but the question of when and if red tide would strike again remained unanswered.

Dr. Bruce W. Halstead, chief of the biotoxicological center of the World Life Research Institute in Colton, Calif., told *Medical World News* that pollution could have contributed to the tide by either providing food or eliminating predators. Dr. Halstead said the offending plankton species is Gonyaulax tamerensis. It bloomed off Britain's Northumberland coast near the Farne Islands on May 30, 1968, poisoning 80 persons. The Pacific Ocean's *G. catenella,* Dr. Halstead said, has been forming red tides off Alaska for years and has hurt the shellfish industry there.

See Also Drug Abuse; Environment; Medicine.

BRIAN SULLIVAN
Science Writer, The Associated Press

UPI

A Massachusetts public health commissioner used charts to point out actions being taken to combat red tide off the state's coast.

HOBBIES: Coin Collecting

The United States' forthcoming bicentennial of its independence and the Eisenhower dollar shared the numismatic spotlight for another year. The controversy continued concerning commemorative coins or medals to mark America's 200th birth-date in 1976. However, both these issues received only secondary attention for a few weeks in July when the first major die error in more than a decade was discovered.

The 1972 double die cent was struck at the Philadelphia mint and is easily recognizable by the doubling of the letters in the motto "In God We Trust." The error was caused by a fault in the production die used for striking the coins.

Mint officials acknowledged the error and estimated that between 20,000 and 100,000 had been released into circulation. The 1972 market price for the penny was in excess of $100. In acknowledging the error, officials indicated that steps would be taken to correct the faulty hub in 1973, but that the die would not be replaced in 1972, because that would create two one-cent varieties for the year.

Within 30 days of this announcement, however, the mint announced a mid-year change in the dies used to strike the Eisenhower dollar. The change resulted from a decision "to take advantage of a technological advancement in die steels," which improved the design's relief.

In addition to the change in the circulating Eisenhower dollar, the Mint announced that copper-nickel specimens would be added to proof sets available to collectors for 1973. In addition to the clad proof, which will be available in complete proof sets only, collectors will still be able to purchase, at a premium, the 40 percent silver proofs and uncirculating specimens. This will make three different Eisenhower dollars, plus the regular issues of the Philadelphia and Denver mints, that the collector will need to complete the new dollar series that began in 1971.

On July 4, the U.S. Mint, the U.S. Postal Service and the American Revolution Bicentennial Commission (ARBC) joined in producing the first in a series of bicentennial numismatic and philatelic issues. This combination piece, comprising a first day cover, a special cancellation and a congressionally-approved national commemorative medal, was issued along with the 1972 set of bicentennial commemorative stamps. The original issue price was $5.00.

Although many members of the coins and medals advisory committee of the ARBC favor a set of commemorative coins to mark the bicentennial, the government leans toward medallic issues that have no monetary face value. The first of the government-issued official medals was contained in the special numismatic-philatelic issue of July 4. One side of the bronze medal depicts a bust of George Washington taken from a medal authorized by Congress in 1776. The reverse side recalls events which precipitated the Revolutionary War with representations of the Sons of Liberty tree in the center, flanked by a replica of the stamp of the hated Stamp Act and a "Join or Die" cartoon originated by Benjamin Franklin.

The greatest problem faced by collectors in 1972 was the growing demand for older choice coins being met by unscrupulous dealers who buffed, "whizzed," or treated coins chemically to make them look in premium, uncirculated condition. The problem became so acute that the American Numismatic Association initiated action to expel dealers caught "whizzing."

The largest coin show of the year was the ANA convention held in August in New Orleans. During the convention one of the five known 1894-S dimes was sold for a reported $50,000. Although mint records note that 24 of these dimes were issued, only five are known to be in collections.

Foreign Coins. West Germany issued a series of commemorative coins to mark and help finance the 1972 Olympics. Panama briefly held the record for the largest silver coin issued for circulation, a 20 Balboas struck in 1971 to mark the 150th anniversary of Central American independence. It was equivalent to $20 in U.S. money. The Cayman Islands, in the Caribbean, topped this with a $25 issue in both gold and silver to mark the 25th wedding anniversary of Queen Elizabeth II and Prince Philip. Current gold laws prohibit U.S. citizens from owning certain gold coins, but the government has eased its stand on some post-dated 1933 foreign gold coins and many uncollectible issues can now be held in U.S. collections.

EDWARD C. ROCHETTE
Editor, *The Numismatist*

Stamps and Stamp Collecting

Spurred by the quadrennial occasion of the Olympic Games, some 200 stamp-issuing countries released approximately 6,000 new stamps in 1972, expanding stamp catalogs to the bursting point.

Countries participating in the games marked the occasion as usual with an array of colorful stamps of a kind particularly prized by collectors. For the first time, however, several non-participating countries, attracted by the scent of profit, issued Olympic commemoratives of

their own—and almost inevitably turned a profit.

Collectors in the United States experienced a companion boon when President Nixon, shortly before his departure for Peking in February, relaxed trading restrictions with Communist China. Previously stamps of the People's Republic had fallen under "trading with the enemy" restrictions and accordingly had been banned from U.S. catalogs. Minkus World Wide Stamp Catalog and the Scott Standard Catalog included Mainland Chinese stamps for the first time in their 1973 editions. China, it should be noted, made no apparent effort to supply the new demand, the Cultural Revolution having discouraged stamp collecting at home. However, entrepreneurs in Hong Kong seemed to have magical sources of supply.

Stamps of many nations called attention to International Book Year, sponsored by the United Nations Educational and Scientific Organization. . . . Britain, its colonies and members of the British Commonwealth issued stamps in honor of the silver wedding anniversary of Queen Elizabeth and Prince Philip. . . . The creation (in 1971) of the United Arab Emirates, a union of Persian Gulf states, increased the flood of postal paper from the area—a fact which bore no direct relation to the requirements of its mostly illiterate citizens.

DAVID LIDMAN
Stamp News Editor, *The New York Times*

HONG KONG

The performance in 1972 of the Hong Kong economy continued to be impressive as evidenced by balance-of-payments and budget surpluses contributing to already substantial reserves. There were, however, reasons for caution.

The 10 percent growth in national income during the 1972 fiscal year was less than that of previous years. The unilateral imposition of quotas on imported textiles by the United States caused anxiety. Hong Kong lives by trade, and textiles comprise 42 percent of its exports, for which the United States is the major market. There was also a recognized need to improve productivity in order to maintain the colony's competitive position in world trade, while meeting urgent domestic demands for wage increases. Consequently, the government tried to encourage more investment in plant and equipment and inaugurated a pilot loan program for small industries.

The government was under increasing pressure to confront various social ills evident in the colony—some of them the consequence of rapid economic growth under laissez-faire conditions. The most notable responses were efforts to combat serious environmental pollution and a commitment "in principle" to build an underground mass transit system. Other innovations included a cash grant welfare program and compulsory primary education (as yet unenforced).

Hong Kong's purchases from mainland China continued to rise. On Feb. 29, 1972, the Chinese ambassador to the United Nations indicated that Peking regarded Hong Kong and Macao as Chinese territory occupied by Britain and Portugal under unequal treaties and that their status should be settled at an appropriate future time.

MARVIN C. OTT
Assistant Professor of Political Science
Mount Holyoke College

UPI

The Queen Elizabeth, in Hong Kong to undergo conversion to a "floating university," lies smoldering in the South China Sea. While firemen fought to extinguish a blaze of undetermined origin, the former luxury liner capsized.

"Operation Breakthrough" funds seeded this development in Macon, Ga. The Federal experiment with prefabricated housing had mixed results.

HOUSING

In purely quantitative terms, the United States in 1972 moved decisively toward the goal set by Congress in the Housing Act of 1968 of 16,000,000 new or rehabilitated housing units by 1978. With the total number of housing units produced exceeding 2,000,000 for the second year in succession, and mobile home production likewise exceeding an additional 500,000 units, the United States had at last reason to hope it could achieve the average annual total of 2,600,000 units needed to meet the goal. And all indications were that this productive capacity would continue.

But if 1972 was to set another record in the quantity of housing units built, there were other, far less favorable indications on the housing scene that revealed deep qualitative flaws.

For those Americans who could afford to buy new houses or to rehabilitate existing ones, the costs in 1972 were higher than ever. Despite President Nixon's wage-price freeze of August 1971 and the subsequent imposition of wage-price controls, construction wages rose from 10 to 12 percent during the year. Building materials also reflected an upward surge, particularly lumber, which accounts for 20 percent of the cost of building a single-family house. From January 1971 to January 1972 lumber prices shot up 36 percent, adding $500 to the cost of a $25,000 house.

From the prospective buyer's standpoint, only mortgage interest rates declined. Federal Housing Agency new home mortgage rates, for example, had come down to 7.54 percent in July from the postwar record high of 9.05 percent in 1970.

More than rising costs, however, troubled the nation's housing program. Following a prolonged series of Congressional investigations, a sordid tale of graft, corruption and racketeering in the low- and moderate-income housing field began to make headlines. Government

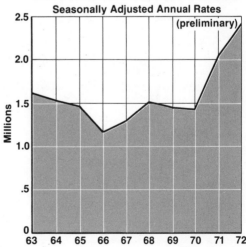

U.S. PRIVATE HOUSING STARTS
Seasonally Adjusted Annual Rates

(preliminary)

Millions

2.5
2.0
1.5
1.0
.5
0

63 64 65 66 67 68 69 70 71 72

employees at the Federal, state and local levels were implicated, along with real estate dealers, lending institutions, lawyers and credit firms— including the nationally respected house of Dun & Bradstreet—in a series of scandals involving the nation's subsidized and public housing programs. Most of the scandals, to make matters worse, centered on the large central cities, where the poorest nonwhite minorities are concentrated.

In New York City a 500-count indictment against a group of alleged conspirators included charges that a fraud of at least $200,-000,000 had been perpetrated against the government. In a blockbusting scheme that involved buying decrepit houses at low cost, giving them "cosmetic" refinishing and selling them to poor families who could not afford to maintain them even with low-interest government loans, developers and others handed to the government the ownership by default of thousands of slum houses. Similar frauds took place in major cities across the country.

Equally disturbing scandals were revealed in the field of new low-income apartment projects supported under Section 236 provisions of the Federal housing laws. From 1968, when the provisions were enacted, to March 1972 some 1,200 Section 236 apartment projects had been built at a cost of $2,200,000,000, with rents subsidized according to a prescribed formula by the Federal Government. During that brief period, 26 percent of the projects had fallen into default. Federal examiners found projects, many of them both poorly constructed and mismanaged, that had earned speculators huge profits with the connivance of Federal officials who overestimated land costs by as much as 221 percent.

Moreover, as housing experts studied trends and patterns in the period since the Federal housing programs were begun in the 1960's,

Partial clearing, construction and preservation of selected older housing are combined in a residential development in downtown Manchester, N.H.

they discovered that, contrary to the intent of Congress, the programs had favored suburbs at the expense of cities. The outflow of blue collar workers from city to suburb had exhausted most of the Section 235 funds for single-family suburban housing, thereby contributing to urban sprawl. And of the Section 235 funds directed to the central cities—for nonprofit apartment housing—a substantial portion had produced the same kind of defaults as those occasioned by Section 236.

Perhaps the most troublesome aspect of the situation was the fact that, while scandal touched only a small part of the total Federal housing effort, its grossness tended to put the whole Federal subsidy program in disrepute. And it did so at a time when Federal programs were essential if low-income housing was to be built. In both 1971 and 1972, for example, more than 500,000 units of housing—about 25 percent of total annual production—were

A Federally financed Affirmative Action project in San Francisco employs 50 percent minorities.

Sam Falk from Monkmeyer

"The New York Times"

Charges of corruption followed abandonment of Brooklyn houses improved at Federal expense.

built with Federal subsidies. If America's poor families are to be decently housed, Federal support cannot be curtailed.

While certain programs were beset by troubles, however, others continued to match expectations, some very successfully, a few with great promise. One of the most promising new experiments was a Department of Housing and Urban Development test program conducted in Pittsburgh and Springfield, Mass., in which 2,000 poor families were given direct subsidies (grants) to pay for all housing costs exceeding 25 percent of income. The grants can be applied to either rent or mortgage payments, and the families may choose their own domiciles, in city or suburb. The grant program, in particular, seemed to promise the poor nonwhite family a chance to escape from the inner-city ghetto.

GEORGE H. FAVRE
Assistant Chief Editorial Writer
The Christian Science Monitor

HUNGARY

While Hungarian tourists flocked abroad and the number of foreigners visiting the country increased in 1972, the party and government experienced mounting criticism from Moscow for their liberal policies.

Serious difficulties in economic and political relations between Hungary and the Soviet Union emerged during a state visit by Premier Jeno Fock to Moscow. Fock was seeking Soviet long-term deliveries of raw materials and fuels, of which Hungary is chronically short. Moscow, on the other hand, pressed for closer integration of Hungary into the Eastern European economic community, Comecon, and accused Budapest of "bourgeois nationalism." At the root of Moscow's reluctance lay ideological problems arising from Hungary's economic experiments (NEM, the New Economic Mechanism, initiated in 1968) stressing autonomy and maneuverability.

Under Soviet pressure, Hungary introduced minor restrictions in cultural life and reduced East-West cultural contacts but apparently refused to change its general economic policy. The aftermath of the economic crisis of 1971, however, forced the government to reduce state subsidies and investment outlays to industry and to restrict labor mobility in order to fight a chronic labor shortage. Available data for 1972 indicated that the restrictions had been only partially effective.

In foreign trade, the year saw an improvement in Hungary's balance of payments, which had shown a record deficit of $232,000,000 in 1971. During the first eight months of 1972 imports decreased by ten percent, while exports rose 24 percent. Hungary signed substantial trade agreements with Italy, Spain and Yugoslavia. In July, during Secretary of State William P. Rogers' visit to Budapest, the United States and Hungary signed a consular convention and a scientific and technical agreement.

In domestic affairs, a revision of Hungary's 1949 constitution was enacted by the National Assembly in April somewhat widening citizens' rights. In the first public unrest since 1956, youths demonstrated in Budapest in March, partly in defense of national values, and partly to protest the high life of Communist functionaries and profiteers of the new economic policy.

ISTVAN DEAK, Director
Institute on East Central Europe
Columbia University

ICELAND

Iceland made more international headlines in 1972 than in any previous year owing to saturation publicity given to the World Chess Championship Match between U.S. Grandmaster Robert ("Bobby") Fischer and Soviet World Champion Boris Spassky (*see also* Chess).

On Sept. 1, Iceland extended its fishing limits from 12 to 50 nautical miles. The extension had been approved unanimously by the 60-member Althing (parliament) on Feb. 15, and a regulation based on a 1948 law concerning the scientific protection of fish stocks on the continental shelf was issued by the minister of fisheries on July 14. After the effective date, agreements were reached with the Faeroe Islands and Belgium about limited temporary fishing by these nations within the new limits. But repeated attempts at similar accords with Britain and West Germany, both of which refused to acknowledge Iceland's right to a unilateral extension, were fruitless. At the end of the year, however, there were hopes of an interim agreement.

The president of Iceland, Kristjan Eldjarn, who has held office since 1968, was returned unopposed for a second four-year term.

SIGURDUR A. MAGNUSSON
Editor, *Samvinnan*

Goess, Gamma

In a demonstration of solidarity, Soviet Communist Party Leader Leonid Brezhnev (saluting) is met at the Budapest airport by his Hungarian counterpart, Janos Kadar (black hat), in November. Earlier friction between the two apparently was overcome.

Prime Minister Indira Gandhi stands before an assembly of India's Congress party as the party convenes to formulate future economic policy.

INDIA

Jubilation marked the mood of India at the beginning of 1972. Having just won a decisive victory in East Bengal, Indians hailed the creation of Bangladesh as a friendly neighbor, the humbling of Pakistan and the enhancement of their own country's primacy in the subcontinent. Domestically, the economy was buoyed by new records in food production. In March, Prime Minister Indira Gandhi, at the peak of her popularity, led her party to impressive victories in state elections.

These cheering developments did not, however, erase the perennial difficulties in India's struggles toward modernization. As the year wore on, confidence eroded in the face of scarcities and rising prices—intensified by a deficient southwest monsoon in the summer—along with seemingly intractable industrial and employment difficulties. Negotiation of issues left over from the 1971 war bogged down. Costs of rehabilitation in Bangladesh weighed heavily. Indians grew anxious about unsympathetic postures displayed by two major powers, China and the United States, as well as by Pakistan. The year ended on a much more sober note than it had started.

The Bangladesh victory was a great event for India. Memories of lackluster performances against Pakistan and China in earlier years were wiped out by the precision and élan with which the Indian military forces conducted the two-week campaign in December 1971. Cooperating with the Bengali *Mukhti Bahini* guerrillas, the Indian units had seized the former East Pakistan, taken the surrender of all Pakistani troops there and helped establish in Dacca the provisional Bangladesh government which had been organized on Indian territory.

In early 1972, India consolidated its relationship with independent Bangladesh. Working closely with Sheikh Mujibur Rahman, the Bangladeshi leader who was released in January after nearly nine months of detention in West Pakistan, Mrs. Gandhi's government moved promptly to repatriate the millions of refugees who had fled to India during the 1971 troubles. The last refugee camp in India was declared closed in March.

In the same month the government announced the return home of the last of the Indian troops who had stayed on in Bangladesh to help administer law and order until the new government could get on its feet. India then signed a 25-year treaty of friendship with Bangladesh. Providing for mutual defense consultations in case of need, it was modeled on the treaty India had signed with the Soviet Union in August 1971.

Prime Minister Indira Gandhi exudes a spirit of friendship as she bids farewell in Dacca to Sheik Mujibur Rahman of Bangladesh, whose nation was launched with Indian assistance in the aftermath of the 1971 India-Pakistan war.

Since artificial irrigation is lacking, a severe drought in India's Nalgonda District has denied the farmer his millet crop. He uses his immature water buffalo to replow the land so that it will be ready to sow again in the event of rain.

On the economic front, India was already providing large amounts of relief supplies and reconstruction assistance to Bangladesh. By this and by the reopening of trade, which had been closed during the Pakistan period, India acknowledged the importance it attached to stability in Bangladesh. The geographic propinquity of the two countries and the ethnic ties between the residents of India's West Bengal and of Bangladesh make Indo-Bangladeshi links inescapably close and sensitive, as developments in either region can readily affect the other.

Sorting out with Pakistan the consequences of the 1971 war proved more difficult. India naturally welcomed the fall of Pakistan's military leader, President Yahya Khan, who had directed the 1971 campaign of oppression in Bengal, and the assumption of power by a civilian president, Zulfikar Ali Bhutto. Nevertheless, although proposals for a meeting between Mrs. Gandhi and Bhutto were made early in the year, intervening difficulties forestalled a face-to-face conference between them until the end of June, six months after the end of the war.

India took the position that the war settlement should include the basic issues that had set the two countries against each other since their independence in 1947, as well as immediate questions. These included Pakistan's recognizing the independence of Bangladesh, the disposition of some 90,000 Pakistani prisoners of war held by India, restoration of the international boundary between India and Pakistan and resolution of the basic Indo-Pakistan dispute over Kashmir.

When Prime Minister Gandhi and President Bhutto met in Simla at the end of June for "unconditional" peace talks, they hammered out a six-point agreement that was taken in both countries as the start toward a final settlement. However, progress in the ensuing months was disappointing; none of the major issues was resolved until December, when both sides repatriated the hundreds of prisoners who had been captured on the western front (but not the tens of thousands of prisoners captured in Bengal). The two sides agreed on a "line of control" in Kashmir, after which Indian forces withdrew from about 5,000 square miles of Pakistan territory they had occupied since the 1971 war, and Pakistani troops were pulled back from the bits of Indian territory they had seized.

Before these agreements had been reached, a clash between Indian and Pakistani troops along the Kashmir cease-fire line and the shooting of six Pakistani prisoners in a disturbance in one of the camps had highlighted the dangers remaining in the situation. As the year drew to its close, India and Pakistan were still deadlocked over the larger issues between them.

Meanwhile, India had a full plate at home. Following her party's successes in the general parliamentary elections in 1971, Mrs. Gandhi's 1972 victories in the state elections put her in a commanding political position. As one journal observed, she had acquired "about as much power as any national leader can have in a

The state sponsors road mending projects as a form of famine relief for farm workers.

Jehangir Gazdar, Woodfin Camp and Assoc.

Two contrasting modes of locomotion symbolize the current stage in India's transition to a modern society. Bullock carts haul kerosene from tank farm to customers in Bombay.

Nevertheless, the party's election pledge—*"gharibi hatao"* ("banish poverty")—soon ran into fresh difficulties. The first poor monsoon in several years caused a disturbing drop in output of food grains, which in turn brought not only scarcities but sharp increases in the prices of basic commodities. Pervasive unemployment, especially among educated persons, grew into a troublesome political as well as economic problem. Power shortages occasioned by increased demand together with production shortfalls became intense. An acute shortage of steel created negative ripple effects in steel-using industries. The government took up the problem of overhauling its entire industrial policy, which instead of stimulating additional production had in some respects become stultifying.

Such economic difficulties as these encouraged a fresh upsurge of opposition to Mrs. Gandhi's leadership in the central government but more particularly in some of the states, where local interests also tried to block the leadership's efforts to legislate land ceilings and other reform measures. Even so, and despite uncertainties about foreign aid, the government reaffirmed late in the year that the next five year plan, its fifth, would start in 1974 at projected record levels of investment.

The year 1972 also brought administrative changes and successes in the government's long-term campaign to eliminate revolutionary

democracy." The question often asked was what she would do with it. The answer, basically, was to continue with the slow, arduous task of building a modern society. During the year a number of key indices—rural electrification, school facilities, health and social welfare programs, even jobs—continued to rise.

pockets in the northeastern zone. In January a former substate of Assam and two former union territories—Meghalaya, Tripura and Manipur—were raised to full statehood and two new union territories were created from the former Northeast Frontier Agency (which became Arunachal Pradesh) and Mizoram. Authorities dealt possibly crippling blows to the extreme Maoist Naxalite movement with the capture of its top leader, who subsequently died of a cardiac ailment, and several of his close associates. The government also undertook a fresh campaign against Naga rebels after several years of truce.

In its relations with the rest of the world, India, like many other nations, was affected by the intense diplomatic maneuvering involving the United States, China, the Soviet Union and Japan during 1972. Following the events of 1971, Indian politicians and newspapers showed anxiety in 1972 that China and the United States were joining in policies unfriendly to India. The government received no response from China to overtures to negotiate the boundary disputes that remained from the 1962 Sino-Indian war. Indians were shocked at China's veto in September of Bangladesh's application for membership in the United Nations. In contrast, relations with the Soviet Union continued warm. India also raised its relations with North Vietnam to embassy level and opened diplomatic relations with East Germany. Mrs. Gandhi made clear, however, India's continuing commitment to nonalignment as a general policy. Both Indian and Soviet officials denied reports that India might provide naval bases to the Soviets in the wake of the 1971 treaty between the two countries.

India's relations with the United States during 1972 continued at the low ebb that had been reached in the preceding year, when India regarded the U.S. official posture on the Bangladesh issue as hostile. Publication by a Washington columnist of purported records of a White House decision to "tilt" United States policy actions against India intensified Indian resentment, as did the impression that the United States government was not eager to take steps that could repair relationships. U.S. development assistance, suspended during the December fighting, was not resumed in ensuing months even though such other countries as Japan promptly resumed their suspended contributions. Bitter Indian criticism of U.S. policies became common, with governmental and Congress party spokesmen from the Prime Minister down even accusing the Central Intelligence Agency of interfering with Indian

domestic affairs—a charge in support of which no proof was offered and which led some Indian newspapers to chide the Indian leaders for going to extremes. In December, however, the Indian foreign minister declared India's desire to strengthen its relations with the United States. Washington welcomed the statement, and President Nixon selected Daniel Patrick Moynihan as U.S. ambassador to India.

PHILLIPS TALBOT
President, The Asia Society

INDONESIA

Throughout 1972, Indonesia continued the generally impressive economic progress that had marked the five years since the final demise of the Sukarno regime. Favorable indicators were numerous: (1) a 1972–73 development budget, based on earnings, which exceeded that of 1971–72 and the original projections of the five-year plan by 28 percent; (2) increased government savings; (3) a rate of inflation of less than one percent—compared with 650 percent in 1966; (4) a 40 percent growth of export earnings over 1971; (5) an estimated 7–9 percent increase of the gross national product; and (6) a rise in foreign assistance ($720,000,000) pledged through the 11-nation Intergovernmental Group on Indonesia (IGGI).

Nevertheless, the progress was not entirely satisfactory. The spectacular flowering of exports was due largely to two commodities, timber and petroleum. Oil alone accounted for more than 50 percent of Indonesia's export earnings, and oil, timber and rubber together for more than 80 percent. This heavy dependence on two or three commodities made Indonesia peculiarly vulnerable to fluctuations in the international market price for these products, and the situation was—at least potentially—aggravated by the fact that 40 percent of Indonesia's 1972 exports went to one country, Japan. In the case of timber, Japan took 80 percent.

More traditional exports, such as tea, coffee, copra, palm oil and pepper, contributed a declining percentage to the total export earnings but continued to be the source of livelihood for 65–70 percent of the population. The consequence could be an unemployment problem of serious proportions, exacerbated by an annual population increase of 2.7 percent. The government gave every indication that it would continue to rely heavily on private capital, including foreign investment.

The military retained its control of the political process, but steps were taken to reorganize and streamline the house of represent-

atives, presumably in preparation for an eventual return to civilian democratic rule. After discussions initiated by President (General) Suharto with the various political parties, the following groupings emerged in the house: (1) Sekber Golkar (functional groups); (2) Armed Forces representatives (appointed); (3) a "Material-Spiritual" group, consisting of the four Muslim parties (Nahdatul Ulama, PSII, Parmusi and Perti); and (4) a "Development-Democracy" group, comprising the two Christian parties, Parkindo and Partai Katolik, and the Partai Nasional Indonesia. Henceforth the parties would not campaign separately but only under the symbols of their group. The result would be a simplification of politics—two parties plus Golkar (technically not a political party) and the military.

Although Indonesia possesses the full apparatus of a military dictatorship, the regime has actually permitted considerable freedom of expression, notably in the press. But until 1972, Mr. Suharto and his immediate family were

Indonesian President Suharto is received at the Elysée Palace by President Pompidou.

spared any direct criticism. This immunity was breached in 1972 when Mrs. Suharto sponsored a controversial $25,000,000 cultural and amusement park, "Indonesia in Miniature," to be constructed in Jakarta. The plan aroused suspicions of repetition of the corruption and diversion of public funds which characterized many of former President Sukarno's pet prestige projects. Student demonstrations, newspaper criticism and a parliamentary investigation ensued. Finally, President Suharto was provoked into an uncharacteristically heated defense of the project and condemnation of its critics. But he also gave assurances that no public funds would be involved and the financing would remain strictly private.

Although apparently committed to the eventual conversion of government to a democratic civilian form, Suharto strongly defended the military's exercise of nonmilitary functions for the present and immediate future. The armed forces served, he argued, as an essential dynamic and stabilizing factor at this stage in Indonesia's development. At the same time he led an effort to "revitalize" the armed forces by "retiring" 36 generals and attempting to inculcate in the young military generation the revolutionary "spirit of 1945," when the revolt against Dutch colonialism began.

Indonesian foreign policy exhibited a strong preoccupation with national security. Despite the emerging detente between China and the United States, Jakarta's military leaders remained suspicious of Peking, which they accused of incessant subversive efforts in Indonesia, including an attempt to revive the outlawed Indonesian Communist party.

The growing Soviet naval presence, coupled with an apparent U.S. withdrawal from the region, was another source of concern. Indonesia proposed to cope with this situation by strengthening the region's capacity for self-defense. This might be done by encouraging military cooperation among the Association of Southeast Asian Nations (ASEAN)—Malaysia, Singapore, the Philippines, Thailand and Indonesia—and by fostering closer Indonesian relations with Japan, Australia and New Zealand. It was within this context that President Suharto visited Australia, New Zealand and the Philippines in 1972. For the same purpose, Indonesia agreed to cooperate with Malaysia on the tightening of security along the Borneo border and to take a joint stand against efforts by the great powers to internationalize the Straits of Malacca.

MARVIN C. OTT
Assistant Professor of Political Science
Mount Holyoke College

INDUSTRIAL PRODUCTION

Spurred by increased sales, industry enjoyed a year of strong economic revival in most parts of the world in 1972. Problems recently imposed by new pollution standards, stringent safety requirements, increased energy costs and price controls took a back seat to the welcome pickup in plant output and earnings.

The industrial recovery made its greatest progress in North America, but Europe and Japan also enjoyed increased plant operating rates. In a few less-developed countries, such as Argentina, Chile, the Philippines, Turkey and South Korea, high rates of inflation, often combined with political instability, stifled the business upturn.

In the United States the effects of President Nixon's New Economic Policy helped keep down inflation to about 3 percent, while the gross national product in real terms soared some 6 percent. Plant operating rates increased to more than 80 percent of capacity. Unemployment remained at the 5.5 percent level, but the year saw an extraordinary 2,500,000 gain in the total labor force.

Construction. Building, as opposed to most other industries, experienced a leveling off in 1972. The industry followed its classic contracyclical pattern, which contracts new housing as interest rates increase. Nevertheless, homebuilders offered an increasing variety of models. The high cost of single-family dwellings had boosted the demand for duplex, triplex and fourplex houses. For young couples and older persons townhouses and cooperative and condominium apartments, all economical in terms of both land and labor, became increasingly attractive. The trend was expected to continue.

In the United States residential housing peaked in February. New starts that month were at an annual rate of 2,700,000. In the following months the rate of new starts began to decline. For the complete year housing starts were some 2,300,000, a 10 percent gain over 1971. Contributing to the demand was a search for homes by the many men released from the military.

During the year, U.S. manufacturers shipped nearly 600,000 mobile homes, a 21 percent increase over 1971, to meet a burgeoning demand for vacation homes and to provide low-cost housing for persons with limited means. Some 5,000,000 Americans live in mobile homes, in permanent-type communities that provide utilities and other services.

Nonresidential construction chalked up a record year in new starts on hospitals, outpatient clinics, nursing homes and other medical-care facilities. Building in this sector received an impetus from the population shift to suburbia.

Construction of stores, warehouses and office buildings also was up in 1972, but new plant and school construction was off. Total U.S. nonresidential construction, according to

A continuing revolution in telecommunications and electronics created new wants for home stock market tickers (left) and calculators.

Marketline Division of Sonex, Inc.   Craig

U.S. Department of Commerce statistics, reached $39,500,000,000, some 5 percent over 1971.

With plant utilization nearing capacity, big gains were expected in industrial building— more than sufficient, in fact, to offset the drop in residential construction.

Chemicals and Plastics. Spurred by increased demand for plastics, synthetic fibers, fertilizers and inorganic materials, the chemical industry rebounded from a 1970–71 abyss. Processing plants, which had had substantial idle capacity for two years, operated more efficiently. The result was a strong boost in productivity. Stringent cost-cutting programs, combined with improved operating rates, enabled most chemical companies to show big improvements in profits.

A few chemicals, caught in short supply, zoomed up in price. One was benzene, a basic raw material for styrene. Another was DDT. For ecological reasons its use had been banned almost totally in the United States, and major producers in the United States and Europe had stopped producing it. Because it remains the best insecticide against mosquitoes, however, it is still needed to fight malaria in Africa. As a result, new manufacturing plants may be built in West Africa.

In the United States chemical shipments in 1972 reached about $56,800,000,000, some 9 percent above 1971. In real terms capital spending in the industry was down for the sixth consecutive year. But spending for environmental control exceeded $280,000,000. As a result of the Federal Water Pollution Control Act of 1972, spending on pollution-control devices was expected to continue to grow.

Food Processing. Increased use of convenience packaging, more automated production and demand for more nutritional foods and low-calorie foods were among trends in food processing in 1972. Food processors not only developed new pouches, more aluminum foil containers and new tetrahedron packages for the housewife, but also marketed labor-saving food packages for restaurants and institutions. The convenience packages for food-service operators were designed for easy storage as well as fast preparation.

Food additives continued to be under government scrutiny in the United States. Following the ban on cyclamates in 1969, formulators of diet foods and drinks turned to saccharin. In 1972 it appeared possible that the Food and Drug Administration would also ban the use of that sweetener. Thus chemical houses were searching for new artificial sweeteners. One possibility was a dipeptide consisting of two amino acids.

Increased leisure time created a boom in snack foods and soft drinks. U.S. consumption of both increased some 7 percent in the year—

Whether owing to fad or to consumer rejection of processed foods, health food stores proliferated.

Christa Armstrong from Rapho-Guillumette

to 26 gallons per capita. At the same time, candy manufacturers boosted their sales 7 percent—to about $2,160,000,000. Among the new products being test-marketed were boxes of frozen chocolates sold in supermarket freezers. Advantages include freshness, resistance to sticking and stability of color, aroma and flavor.

Overall, the U.S. food processing industry reported about a 5 percent increase in sales. The year was one in which beef, milk and other highly nutritional foods continued to increase their share of the market.

Iron and Steel. World steel production, which had dropped in 1971, enjoyed a substantial 8 percent gain in 1972. The renewed growth was due to increased demand for steel in the United States, Western Europe and Japan. Total production reached an estimated 628,000,000 metric tons.

The developing nations, which had not suffered the severe recession of the industrialized countries, continued their record-setting growth in steel. Their increasing output caused considerable concern among the old, established steel-producing countries. For example, South Korea during the first six months of 1972 exported four times as much steel to the United States as it had in the equivalent period in 1971. Mexico boosted its U.S.–bound steel by 50 percent. These new steel-exporting countries enjoyed the benefit of being exempt from the quota arrangements that limit West European and Japanese steel exports to the United States.

Steel producers in Japan and the other industrialized countries increased productivity by going to continuous casting, cold rolling and annealing. Nippon Kokan's system of welding coil ends together to avoid threading each coil individually was adopted in the United States by National Steel. A new bottom-blowing basic oxygen process, known as Q-BOP, was given its first large-scale test by U.S. steelmakers. The process originated in West Germany.

Most steel producers, however, had little need for new plant capacity. In Japan the Ministry of International Trade and Industries called for a two-year halt of steel expansion projects. In other industrialized countries steel companies stretched out their expansion plans.

In the United States domestic steel shipments reached some 92,000,000 net tons, a 6 percent increase. The gain was primarily in sheet and strip production for vehicles.

Machinery. Government efforts to stimulate the economy revived capital spending in most of the industrialized countries. In the United

Westinghouse

The countertop range, an innovation in kitchen ranges employing hidden coils and specially designed vessels, came of commercial age.

Scratch and smell children's books, olfactivated by flick of a fingernail, took buyers by storm.

The National Cash Register Company

The National Machine Tool Builders show, held in Chicago, featured a potpourri of inventions.

States liberalized depreciation rules and the tax investment credit boosted spending for plant and equipment to some $88,540,000,000, a 9 percent increase over 1971.

Because U.S. industry was operating at less than 75 percent of capacity at the start of the year, the new spending was primarily for modernization and replacement rather than for more capacity. Manufacturers sought equipment that would cut costs and boost productivity. Many companies invested in new equipment to reduce pollution and to meet the new safety and low-noise standards of the Occupational Safety and Health Act. Economists predicted another 11–12 percent increase in capital spending in 1973.

Leading the recovery was the machine-tool industry. New orders for metal-cutting and metal-forming tools exceeded $1,400,000,000, a 60 percent increase over 1971. Tool orders received a boost in September at the big International Machine Tool Show in Chicago. Highlighting the exhibition were new developments in low-cost numerically controlled machines and in minicomputers to guide machine tools. These computer numerical control (CNC) systems make it possible to operate a machine from a memory core rather than from tape.

Record-breaking vehicle sales, which in the United States reached 10,943,000 cars and 2,474,000 trucks, also helped boost machinery sales. General Motors placed orders for a tooling program to mass produce the Wankel rotary engine for use in its 1974 Vega cars.

Machine-tool builders in Europe, Japan and the United States also benefited from orders for equipment for the huge Kama River project in the U.S.S.R. Planned as the world's biggest truck plant, it is scheduled to produce 150,000 heavy duty trucks a year.

Nonferrous Metals. Demand from the construction, transportation, electrical distribution, packaging, steel and liquefied natural gas industries enabled nonferrous metal producers to make a comeback from the recession years of 1970–71. However, for most metals prices and profits remained low.

Aluminum producers reactivated the potlines that had been idled in 1971. Production climbed from 80 percent of capacity in 1971 to about 93 percent of capacity at the end of 1972. In the United States aluminum shipments established a record—10 percent over the 5,203,000 tons shipped in 1971.

Basic aluminum ingot prices remained at their 20-year low of about 20 cents per pound, but there was less discounting by the major producers. Reduced profits resulted in the postponement of big projects, such as the American Metal Climax, Inc., alumina mining complex in Kimberley, Australia. With little new capacity scheduled to go on stream in 1973 and 1974, price increases were indicated.

U.S. copper producers also hoped for a price increase to help absorb higher labor and capital equipment costs. A major problem was the expense of pollution-control devices needed by smelters to meet proposed sulphur dioxide emission limitations.

New copper developments on Bougainville island in the South Pacific and Freeport Minerals Co.'s huge Ertsberg project in Indonesia helped boost non-Communist copper production in 1972 some 10.2 percent to 6,694,500 tons. A further 5 percent increase was expected in 1973. Total U.S. consumption in 1972 was about 1,965,000 tons.

Political developments continued to affect the supply of copper. Of prime interest was Kennecott Copper's battle with the Chilean government for compensation for a 49 percent interest in the expropriated El Teniente mine. As part of their battle, Kennecott lawyers went to court in France, Holland and other countries where freighters attempted to unload copper mined at El Teniente. Chile, in turn, tried to sell more of its copper to China and other Communist countries. At stake were some 600,000 tons of the world's copper supply.

Lead producers, meanwhile, continued to suffer from the removal of that metal from gasoline, but they benefited from an increased use of lead for noise abatement and in batteries. Total U.S. lead consumption was up some 2.5 percent. New mines helped boost the supply about 14 percent, with the result that domestic prices dropped to $14.50 a pound.

U.S. zinc production was down some 8.5 percent—a consequence of the closing of smelters that could not meet pollution control standards. With demand up some 9.5 percent, imports surged.

Bell & Howell

The five-pound, briefcase microfilm reader is aimed at business, school and general trade.

Nickel consumption in the non-Communist countries reached about 900,000,000 pounds—a 9 percent increase over 1971. In September, Falconbridge Nickel Mines Ltd. increased the price of electrolytic nickel 20 cents to $1.53 a pound. Other producers immediately followed suit, stating that the increase was necessary to finance new production facilities.

STEPHEN W. KANN
Editor and Publisher, *Industrial World*

A new town rises below the Ertsberg copper deposit to house employees of the mining project.
Freeport Minerals Company

INSURANCE

The consumer movement, as had been its custom in recent years, continued to focus attention in 1972 on the need for reform in the insurance field. Automobile and health care insurance systems remained under public and legislative scrutiny in the United States. Moreover, nature forced Americans to reconsider an additional hazard of major proportions to the insuring public.

Flood Protection. Devastating floods in the vicinity of Rapid City, S.D., and in Pennsylvania and New York in June (*see* Meteorology) revived the question of insurance coverage for natural disasters. Although insurance could not have been expected to compensate for all of the destruction (estimated at $3,500,000,000 from tropical storm Agnes and $100,000,000 from the South Dakota rains), in both areas only limited flood protection was provided under the National Flood Insurance Program. Under this joint industry-government plan, coverage at relatively low rates was available up to $17,500 for single-family houses and $30,000 for small business firms. For some unexplained reason, however, neither the government nor the insurance industry had publicized effectively the program to those living in communities exposed to the hazard. For instance, only 29 policies had been issued in Rapid City—a community of 50,000—and only six of the policy holders had purchased the maximum coverage available. Similarly inadequate coverage resulted in economic destitution in Pennsylvania's Wyoming Valley. Consequently, Congress came under pressure to enact a broader flood control and protection law. As an interim step the government increased its subsidy under the existing program, thereby reducing premiums by 40 percent to stimulate purchases.

Health Care. Revisions in existing health care delivery and payments systems continued to preoccupy legislators in Washington in 1972 (*see* Health). Medical costs again had emerged as a major factor in the cost-of-living inflationary spiral, and ten bills relating to health care were simultaneously under Congressional scrutiny. Political and public discussions, however, centered on three proposals: (1) the Kennedy plan, (2) the Nixon plan and (3) the Medicredit plan, proposed by the American Medical Association.

The Kennedy plan envisaged essentially a national health insurance system, providing very comprehensive benefits to all Americans irrespective of income, administered and underwritten by the government and financed from general revenues as well as payroll tax assessments on employer and employee.

The Nixon plan also offered broad coverage and comprehensive benefits, but it relied on the private insurance industry to perform the underwriting and administrative functions. Benefits for the poor, near-poor and aged were to be financed by the government through an expansion of the Medicare and Medicaid programs. Benefits for all others were to be financed through a payroll-tax system under a shared contribution arrangement, with employers ultimately paying three-fourths of the cost. The plan would impose a deductible as well as a coinsurance payment on those covered by employers' group contracts.

The Medicredit plan would provide the least comprehensive benefits and retain the existing voluntary system of health coverage underwritten by private insurance companies. Medicare would continue to cover the aged, while the poor and near-poor would receive payment vouchers from the government. All others would finance their premiums from personal funds but would receive tax credits based on income levels. This latter feature would offer an indirect government subsidy to lower-income-bracket taxpayers and those burdened with heavy medical care outlays.

Auto Coverage. At the state level in 1972 legislators concentrated their attention on proposals for adoption of no-fault auto insurance laws. Some 37 states reviewed at least one of several versions of no-fault insurance. No-fault laws already were on the books in two other states—Florida and Massachusetts. Two states, New Jersey and Connecticut, enacted laws to become effective in 1973.

Although the trend toward no-fault as the basic approach to automobile insurance appeared to be irreversible, legislators voted against such proposals in all the other states involved, including such major ones as New York, Michigan, Colorado and California. Their rejections did not appear to imply dissatisfaction with the principle of no-fault as much as with specific aspects of the versions under consideration.

Automobile insurance reform also commanded the attention of legislators at the Federal level. The Nixon administration proposed that the Department of Transportation assist the states in developing model legislation that would ultimately be adopted by each state. In contrast to this state-by-state approach, the Hart-Magnuson bill, submitted in the Senate, called for a national uniform no-fault statute. The insurance industry opposed the bill, which was returned to committee for further study.

RAYMOND F. VALENTI
School of Management, Syracuse University

IRAN

The Shah of Iran's determination to play a major role in the affairs of the Persian Gulf, thereby ensuring neutralization of the region in the wake of the British forces' withdrawal, involved his country in conflict with several of its Arab neighbors. Iranian occupation of the strategic Abu Musa and Tunb islands in the Persian Gulf in December 1971 provoked criticism in the Arab press and incited protest marches in Qatar and Bahrain. A more serious dispute, however, developed with Iraq, with which Iran has long engaged in intermittent hostilities over their common Shatt al-Arab boundary north of the Gulf. In January-February 1972, Iraqi security forces expelled some 50,000 Iranians residing in various Iraqi cities; the government claimed that they had entered Iraq illegally, were paying no taxes and had been competing with native Iraqis for jobs. The expulsion imposed a severe hardship on the destitute refugees and strained Iranian welfare services to the limit.

Of potentially greater impact on Iranian foreign policy than the deportations, however, was Iraq's signing, in March, of a 15-year treaty of alliance with the U.S.S.R. Subsequently, in April, Iranian armored units crossed the border in force and clashed with Iraqi forces, causing heavy casualties. The forceful Iranian response to Iraq's foreign policy initiative was a visible reminder of Iran's military superiority and a warning to Iraq against seeking too close an involvement with the U.S.S.R.

Even while the border clashes were erupting, the Shah was shopping for more advanced weaponry for his 150,000-man army and air force in order to maintain Iran's military edge over its neighbors. President Nixon visited the country on May 30–31, assuring the monarch that he had full U.S. support and promising to expedite shipments of the Phantom jets and missiles he had requested.

The internal political scene remained mostly quiet. However, bomb explosions which occurred at a wreath-laying ceremony during the Nixon visit indicated that opposition to the Shah's autocratic rule still existed, although forced underground. The 32 deputies of the Mardom party, the only political opposition permitted to function in Iran, refused to vote on the budget when it was presented to the Majlis (parliament). However, approval of the budget, which at $7,300,000,000 was the largest in the nation's history, appeared to be assured as the oil-based Iranian economy continued to boom.

WILLIAM SPENCER
Professor of Middle Eastern History
The Florida State University

IRELAND, REPUBLIC OF

Two great issues—the decision as to whether to join the European Community (the Common Market) and the continuing crisis in Northern Ireland—dominated all others in the Republic of Ireland in 1972.

Economics and Europe. The Common Market question was put before the electorate in a referendum on May 10. Of the 71 percent of those eligible to vote who actually voted some

Survivors of the April 10 earthquake that claimed 5,000 Iranian lives gather in temporary shelters.

Hugues Vassal, Gamma

83 percent (1,041,890) favored entry, and 17 percent (211,891) opposed it. The referendum thus ratified by a 5 to 1 majority the Irish government's signature on Jan. 22 in Brussels of the treaty of accession.

At a European Community summit meeting held in Paris in October, Taoiseach (prime minister) John B. Lynch expressed satisfaction that an agreement, proposed by Britain, to make special provision from community funds for regional development had been reached. The agreement was particularly important because underdevelopment remains Ireland's major economic problem. Since 1952 development policy had contributed to the creation of 300 industrial enterprises representing an investment of $150,000,000, mostly in the south and west.

But demographic trends suggested that the republic's population would grow from 2,800,-000 in 1972 to 4,100,000 by 1986. And in view of the number of jobs currently expected to be available, and allowing for an unemployment rate of 4 percent, Ireland could not be expected to support a population of more than 3,500,000. Thus, unless the rate of development is increased very rapidly, at least 750,000 more Irish men and women will have to emigrate by 1986.

In spite of the country's daunting economic problems, however, the Irish budget in 1972 projected increased outlays for social welfare, retirement and old age and widows' pensions; provided for free public transport for all

Provisional IRA leader Sean MacStiofan, speaking June 13 in Londonderry, proposes a temporary cease-fire and peace talks with the British.

persons over 70; cut corporation taxes from 58 percent to 50 percent; and increased agricultural subsidies. The budget entailed a deficit of $82,500,000.

The Irish Question. The year started with the explosion by the Provisional Wing of the Irish Republican Army of a bomb in the center of Belfast which injured 62 persons. On Jan. 30, some 13 civilians were killed by gunfire in Londonderry as British troops stormed the predominantly Catholic Bogside area of the city. On Feb. 22 an IRA bomb blasted the headquarters of the Parachute Brigade of the British army in Aldershot, England, killing six civilians, five of them women, and a Catholic chaplain. In July a series of IRA bombings in Belfast killed 11 persons and injured 130. During the year some 70 individuals, both Catholic and Protestant, were the victims of apparently motiveless murders.

Behind the violence, however, a series of steps was taken on both sides leading toward at least an interim solution of the problem. With the province becoming virtually ungovernable, Britain suspended the local parliament at Stormont Castle, Belfast, at the end of March and imposed direct rule from Westminster. Subsequently the new minister for Northern Ireland, William Whitelaw, published a Green Paper—a government discussion paper—on possible future constitutional developments. The most important element in the paper was its acknowledgement that the future has to take account of "the Irish dimension."

In November, on the other hand, Mr. Lynch's government arrested the alleged chief of staff of the Provisional IRA, Sean MacStiofain. He was charged with being a member of an illegal organization. And on Dec. 7, in a referendum on proposed deletion from the Irish constitution of Article 44, which gives the Roman Catholic church a privileged standing in the Irish state, the Irish voted overwhelmingly (85 percent) to abolish the "special position."

A plebiscite in the North on the question of retaining or ending the British connection was promised for early in the New Year, to be followed after the inevitable outcome by firm British proposals for a new Ulster constitution. Thus, the scene apparently was being set for an "imposed accommodation," guaranteeing Protestants a link with Britain for as long as they want it but forging a new link also with the republic.

JOHN ALLAN MAY
Chief, London Bureau,
The Christian Science Monitor

The coffins of the 16 Puerto Rican victims of the May 30 Lydda Airport massacre are loaded aboard a U.S. Air Force plane for the return journey to their homeland. The Puerto Ricans had arrived in Israel on a pilgrimage to the Christian holy places.

ISRAEL

A new phase and one potentially more destructive than any previous stage in the extended Arab-Israeli conflict emerged in 1972 when the Palestinian guerrillas shifted their strategy from regional to global terrorism. Although such factors as the demonstrated effectiveness of Israeli security forces in dealing with internal subversion and of Israeli cross-border raids in circumventing the guerrillas made this tactical shift virtually inevitable, the implications of this new strategy came as a shock to world opinion. For the first time since the establishment of the state, Israeli citizens were exposed to violence abroad as well as at home.

An incident which provided a foretaste of future developments occurred on May 9 when commandos of the Black September Organization, a militant group founded after the September 1970 defeat of guerrillas by the Jordanian Army, hijacked a Belgian airliner to Lydda Airport near Tel Aviv. There the hijackers proceeded to hold the passengers hostage against the release of 100 of the estimated 3,000 Palestinians jailed in Israel. Israeli police disguised as mechanics stormed the plane and killed two of the hijackers; the other two, both women, were captured and later sentenced to life in prison.

Three weeks later, Lydda Airport was the scene of a second and more violent terrorist assault when Japanese members of a left-wing movement, the United Red party, suddenly opened fire on a group of persons congregating in the passenger terminal, killing 25 and injuring 78. The dead included members of a Puerto Rican charter flight on a pilgrimage to the Holy Land. The sole surviving terrorist said that the group's action was motivated by support for the Palestine cause, the success of which it viewed as a necessary step in the world revolution.

In September tragedy reached deep into the fabric of Israeli life as the Black Septembrists won international notoriety by murdering two and kidnapping nine members of the Israeli Olympic team in Munich. All the kidnapped athletes were subsequently killed in the course

Workers in the Israeli-occupied Gaza Strip prepare bricks to make housing for the Arab refugees.

of a shootout between the guerrillas and West German police forces. Shortly afterward, letter-bombs that had been mailed to Israeli diplomats abroad killed one diplomat and injured several others. These actions, coupled with the subsequent release of the three surviving Munich terrorists after their comrades hijacked a West German Lufthansa airliner, enraged Israeli public opinion and led to a resumption of retaliatory raids into Lebanon and Syria and of Israeli-Syrian aerial encounters.

Ironically the outbreak of global terrorism came at a time of internal peace for Israel, a condition which otherwise might well have fostered overtures to the elusive peace settlement with the Arabs. Terrorist incidents in the country continued to show a steady decline. As a consequence, all travel restrictions were abolished for Arabs living in the occupied territories and special permits annulled for residents of the Gaza Strip, most of whose citizens work in other sections of Israel. The first movie theater opened on the strip in 1972, and 1,200 new housing units were built there for Arab refugees. Elections for municipal councils were held in the occupied West Bank; 84 percent of the eligible voters participated despite a call by the Palestinian guerrilla leadership for a boycott of the elections.

The majority of candidates elected to the councils represented the emerging business and professional interests as opposed to the traditionally conservative Arab family leaders, most of whom were defeated. Several elected councillors spoke openly of cooperation with Israel and rejected Jordan King Hussein's suggestion of a federated Jordanian-Palestinian Arab kingdom.

Israel also achieved some measure of success with an experimental program designed to allow Arabs from neighboring nations to visit the country as tourists or to hold reunions with family members who are Israeli residents. The program, limited to the summer months, attracted in the neighborhood of 100,000 Arab visitors.

A by-product of Arab pressures on Israel was the break in diplomatic relations initiated by Uganda, the first non-Arab African country to take this course. Uganda's President Amin, following a visit to Libya, expelled Israel's 70-member military training mission and terminated several Israel-sponsored technical aid projects. About $15,000,000 in Israeli loan funds were affected by Amin's actions. Otherwise few major changes occurred in Israel's foreign relations. The United States remained Israel's staunchest ally, committing $300,000,000 for military aid in addition to the record $213,000,000 raised by the United Jewish Appeal (UJA).

Israel's population reached 3,160,000 in August. Despite an exit head tax imposed by the U.S.S.R. on Soviet Jews as reimbursement to the state for their academic education, some 25,000 Soviet Jews emigrated to Israel during the year.

Apart from foreign aid provided by the United States, West Germany and others, and despite an austerity budget for the 1972–73 fiscal year, the Israeli economy continued to expand. Production of the Avra jet aircraft and the ground-to-ground Gabriel missile, along with other military items, was sufficiently high for the government to begin taking orders for export. Loss of the Uganda aid program was compensated for by an expansion of aid to Ethiopia as a second Israeli-financed cotton project got under way. Israeli exports of industrial goods to the African kingdom reached a record total of $4,300,000.

WILLIAM SPENCER
Professor of Middle Eastern History
The Florida State University

In the Sinai desert Israel unveils a self-propelled M-107, a 175mm, U.S.-built artillery piece.

UPI

Partially or wholly closed throughout the year, Rome's Colosseum undergoes major repairs to arrest decay.

UPI

ITALY

Deep political, social and economic troubles beset Italy throughout most of 1972, leaving Italians sour and baffled. Politicians seemed equally moody and confused, and economists warned that the future looked bleak. Given two opportunities, voters nevertheless rejected appeals by Communists and neofascists to try something different, refusing at the same time to give traditional leaders a clear mandate.

The long-brewing political troubles boiled over on Jan. 15 when Premier Emilio Colombo resigned after 17 months in office. The ostensible reason was a decision by the small Republican party to withdraw from Colombo's coalition. But the real cause was disagreement among the coalition partners on how to cope with the problems facing the country.

After Colombo failed to form a new government, President Giovanni Leone turned to Giulio Andreotti, a bookish 53-year-old veteran of many political battles and a member of nearly every cabinet since World War II. Although he failed to reconstruct a coalition, Andreotti put together a minority government composed only of fellow Christian Democrats. It took office on Feb. 16—the 33rd government since World War II—and it lasted ten days. The Senate refused on Feb. 26 to accord it a vote of confidence, and Andreotti resigned.

President Leone then dissolved parliament and ordered new national elections on May 7–8. The ensuing campaign was bitterly fought among eight national parties, with law and order and the floundering economy emerging as chief issues. But the closest attention was focused on the prospects of the Communist party and a right-wing alliance of monarchists and the neofascist Italian Social Movement. Both blocs waged expensive and ambitious campaigns to exploit middle-class discontent with the Christian Democrats.

As it turned out, the right-wing alliance scored the biggest gains, capturing 8.7 percent of the total vote; it won 56 out of 630 seats in the Chamber of Deputies and 26 of the 315 elected seats in the Senate. The figures were almost twice the right-wing totals in the last national elections, in 1968. The Communists gained two seats in the Chamber and lost eight in the Senate, but the party retained its position as the second largest political bloc. The Christian Democrats won 267 seats in the Chamber, one up from 1968, and held their 135 seats in the Senate. The big loser was the extreme left-wing Socialist Party of Proletarian Unity, which lost all of its 23 Chamber seats.

The election over, Andreotti returned to the job of forming a government. He finally succeeded on June 24, but only by abandoning the center-left coalition formula preeminent since 1963. Instead, Andreotti served up a slightly more conservative concoction bringing the right-of-center Liberal party into the cabinet. The Liberals replaced the Socialist party, which lost favor with most Christian

Democrats after it pressed for closer cooperation with Communists. The Republicans refused to enter the cabinet but pledged their support in parliament. Andreotti and his 26-man government took the oath of office on June 26, and parliament endorsed it two weeks later.

Andreotti's government program emphasized reforms in education, family rights (including the abolition of dowries), public housing and the legal system. He pledged austerity combined with pump priming in order to get the economy moving. By the end of the year, however, much of the program remained unrealized.

One result of the election was an automatic one-year delay of a referendum on the 1970 divorce law that Roman Catholics and the Christian Democrats oppose on moral grounds. Thus the country and government gained time to mull over this most emotional of Italian issues.

Voters returned to the polls on Nov. 26–27 to elect 778 city and municipal councils, plus two provincial legislatures and two members of parliament. The elections concerned only about 4,000,000 voters, but in Rome the voting was viewed chiefly as a test of Andreotti's popularity and the ability of the extreme right to maintain its strong showing in May. The combination of monarchists and neofascists slipped a bit, as did the Communists, and the Christian Democrats lost both seats in parliament, leaving Andreotti with a majority of four in the Senate.

The Communist party changed leadership on March 17. Enrico Berlinguer, a chain-smoking Sardinian, moved from deputy secretary to general secretary, succeeding Luigi Longo as chief of the largest Communist party in the West. Actually, Berlinguer had been running the party for several years because of Longo's precarious health.

Economically, the combination of runaway prices and standstill production that Italians call "stagflation" persisted all year, and economists warned that the future looked gloomy. Most experts placed the blame fairly on politicians, labor leaders, big business and international monetary developments that caught the lira in the middle.

The bad news included a record budget deficit, a sizable decrease of foreign reserves, record unemployment, soaring inflation and near zero industrial production growth. Negotiations on contracts covering one out of every four workers touched off waves of nationwide strikes. Good news included a record $2,500,-000,000 in tourist earnings, a trade surplus of almost $700,000,000 and a fairly healthy balance of payments.

Foreign reserve holdings fell by $650,000,-000, to an overall total of $6,032,000,000, in the first six months of the year, and unemployment exceeded 1,000,000. The national economic growth rate was 1.5 percent in 1971, and even optimists put it at no more than 3.5 percent in 1972. At the same time, the cost of living rose 7 percent for the year ending Oct. 31.

The 1972 budget showed revenues of $22,-908,508,000 and expenditures of $26,996,604,-000. The deficit did not include losses by such state enterprises as the tobacco and salt monopolies, railroads, highways and the post office. Counting these agencies, the deficit reached a record $5,441,908,000.

Despite his austerity pledge, Andreotti agreed in the autumn to raise the salaries—doubling them in some cases—of 7,000 top civil servants. Under the new pay scale Andreotti's own pay increased from $15,000 to $40,000 a year. This, like the other raises, caused an uproar among taxpayers and economists, who said Andreotti should set an example.

To deal with soaring food prices, Rome authorities froze prices on Aug. 28 for 60 days, but more effective action had come earlier from the Bank of Italy, which cut the bank rate from 4½ percent to 4 percent in order to stimulate economic expansion.

Italy did not escape the politics of violence. The most sensational case was the murder of Giangiacomo Feltrinelli, a 45-year-old millionaire publisher who in 1957 introduced Boris Pasternak's *Dr. Zhivago* to the West. Police found Feltrinelli's body on March 15 on the outskirts of Milan, mutilated and surrounded by dynamite sticks beneath a damaged electricity pylon. It was the end of a life of riches and rebellion for a man who quit the Communist party in 1956 and thereafter embraced a variety of anarchist and extremist causes. Left-

GIULIO ANDREOTTI

Premier Giulio Andreotti, born in Rome on Jan. 14, 1919, was graduated from Rome University in 1940. Undersecretary in the De Gasperi and Pella governments, the Christian Democrat headed the ministries of finance, defense and commerce and industry in various governments. In late 1968 he became leader of his party in the Chamber of Deputies.

Michelangelo's "Pieta," damaged when a man vaulted a barrier and struck the Virgin's nose and left arm with a hammer, was removed from St. Peter's and ultimately almost perfectly restored.

and right-wingers accused each other of his murder, but authorities contended that they could not determine the circumstances of his death. Officials said only that he had died of injuries suffered in a premature explosion at the pylon.

An employee of the Libyan embassy, Abdel Weil Zuaiter, 38, was shot dead on Oct. 16 in Rome. Police called it a well-planned assassination. Al Fatah, the major Palestinian guerrilla organization, said in Beirut that the victim was its agent in Italy and proclaimed him a martyr slain by Israeli gunmen.

The biggest publishing event of 1972 was a 1,262-page report on the Mafia, eight years in the writing by a commission appointed by parliament. It produced almost no new information, despite government promises of full disclosures about prominent politicians who, it said, shielded organized crime.

Antonio Segni, 81, died in Rome on Dec. 1. During his political career, the former leader of the Christian Democrats served as agriculture minister, defense minister, foreign minister and president of Italy.

CHARLES W. BELL
Former Manager for Italy
United Press International

JAPAN

For Japan, 1972 was a year in which the man in the street asked himself who he was, and the country's new government pondered where the nation was headed. A series of bizarre, traumatic events had jarred the Japanese who, single-mindedly pursuing economic prosperity, thought of themselves as diligent, peace loving people, whereas they had a reputation abroad for being "economic animals."

Worse, a series of shocking incidents involving Japanese, coming one after another, caused a deep identity crisis and a search for direction. The sword-wielding militant students who hijacked a plane to North Korea, the anachronistic *seppuku* suicide of novelist Yukio Mishima in protest against the "pointlessness" of Japan's modern mass culture, the rude reception Emperor Hirohito received in some parts of Europe, the return after 28 years in the Guam jungle of Sgt. Shoichi Yokoi (who feared surrender would dishonor the Emperor), the kangaroo court killings of comrades by extremist young radicals of the United Red Army, the unsettling suicide of Nobel Prize winning novelist Yasunari Kawabata, and the *kamikaze* massacre of 25 innocent persons by three Japanese radicals at Israel's Lydda air-

port in May 1972, had filled the nation with shame.

For months newspaper and magazine articles, television round-table discussions and best-selling books raised critical questions of Japanese identity. "What is Japanese civilization?" "Who are the Japanese?" "Where is Japan headed?" One of the biggest postwar best-sellers, *The Japanese and the Jews,* had sold a remarkable 1,800,000 copies by the end of 1972, not because the Japanese were particularly interested in the Jews but because of what it revealed about themselves.

Okinawa. The year 1972 began auspiciously with a summit conference between Prime Minister Eisaku Sato and President Nixon at San Clemente, Calif., during which both national heads reaffirmed the necessity of maintaining cooperative relations to ensure peace and security in Asia. But for Sato the most important result of the meeting was that Okinawa would be returned "nuclear-free" to Japan on May 15, after 27 years of occupation.

After only a day's banner headlines the event passed quickly into history. In opposition to the number of U.S. bases remaining on the Ryukyu Island chain, Okinawa Governor Chyobo Yara boycotted the reversion-day ceremony attended by Emperor Hirohito, Prime Minister Sato and Vice-President Agnew. Okinawans themselves had mixed feel-ings, wanting at once to be free of foreign rule but also remembering that U.S. occupation had been generally benevolent, while as a prewar prefecture of Japan they had been economically neglected and discriminated against. There was also a fear among Okinawans that reversion might cause Japan to use its broadened defense perimeter as a pretext for a "revival of militarism," but that fear was unfounded as the country continued to rely basically on the U.S.-Japan Security Treaty. The anxieties about economic loss were heightened by an unfavorable dollar-yen exchange rate and consequent revaluation.

Politics. The promise to repossess Okinawa had kept Prime Minister Eisaku Sato in office for a record four terms. Following the reversion, pressure for his resignation began to mount. The Nixon "shocks" (various economic decisions and the trip to China, announced without first consulting Japan), which had destroyed Japanese confidence in Sato's ability to deal with the U.S. government, and opposition party pressure for a policy which would accommodate mainland China's desire for normalizing relations helped force Sato's resignation. But equally important was the pressure exacted within Sato's own party by powerful faction leaders who wanted to succeed him.

Sato's actual decision to step down did not come until June. A scramble for the succession

The new Parliamentary Library and Museum in Tokyo blends contemporary and traditional Japanese elements of architectural design.

Premier Sato (left) announces his retirement in June. The winner in a three-way party contest to succeed him, International Trade and Industry Minister Kakuei Tanaka, 54, is shown at right.

ensued. The key contenders for the office of Liberal Democratic party president who, as majority leader automatically becomes prime minister, were the 67-year-old Foreign Minister, Takeo Fukuda; 54-year-old International Trade and Industry Minister, Kakuei Tanaka; 54-year-old former Defense Minister, Yasuhiro Nakasone; and two former foreign ministers, 62-year-old Masayoshi Ohira and 63-year-old Takeo Miki. Although the favorite of Sato and the business community, Fukuda was not well regarded in Peking and therefore seemed likely, if designated premier, to slow down the process of Sino-Japanese normalization. Ohira, Nakasone and Miki agreed to step out of the race and support Tanaka at the July convention.

With the election of the ebullient, youthful Tanaka, Japan marked the end of an era of phlegmatic politics. The emergence of a down-to-earth maverick who, despite 25 years in public life, symbolized a fresh approach, foreshadowed a new crop of young politicians eager to seize power.

Tanaka lost no time making important decisions. His three major supporters were appointed to important posts: Ohira as foreign minister, Nakasone as minister of international trade and industry and Miki as deputy prime minister, a post previously unfilled.

Following his first cabinet meeting, Tanaka declared that on the domestic front he would

focus on such problems as pollution, housing and land reform without sacrificing Japan's economic growth, while in foreign affairs he would aim at normalizing diplomatic relations with China. In his first press conference, he stressed China again; declared that he considered the United States "like an older brother," inseparable from Japan; hoped to adjust U.S.-Japanese trade problems; and reasserted his strong support for continued maintenance of the U.S.-Japan Security Treaty.

KAKUEI TANAKA

Born to a farming family on May 4, 1918, and brought up in poverty, Kakuei Tanaka went to Tokyo at the age of 15 to win fame and fortune. Although he lacked formal schooling, he owned a construction company at 25. He was first elected to the Diet in 1947, and beginning in 1949 served in various cabinet posts until July 5, 1972, when he was elected leader of the ruling Liberal Democratic party and consequently premier.

Fulfilling a pre-election vow to visit Peking, Premier Tanaka shakes hands with Chairman Mao in September. Premier Chou is at left.

Finally, he pledged to try to avoid another yen revaluation and promised not to dissolve the House of Representatives and hold an election in 1972 (a promise that was not kept).

In his plan of reconstruction, to be coordinated by a newly-created agency, Tanaka envisaged a more livable society the gross national product of which, however, would continue to grow by 10 percent a year until it reached $1,000,000,000,000 in 1985. Tanaka would halt the further expansion of population and factories in the crowded "Tokaido" area that extends from Tokyo to Osaka and concentrates 32 percent of the nation's population in only one percent of its area. By means of punitive tax measures against industries refusing to move to less sparsely-populated areas and subsidies to those agreeing to do so, Tanaka hoped to create 25 new "cities of 250,000." The new cities would include industrial parks, recreation centers and academic, farming, forest and residential areas. Pollution was to be strictly controlled. Air, rail and road transport was to be vastly improved. Although the plan received considerable support, opponents charged that it would serve only to benefit land speculators and spread pollution.

As soon as Tanaka assumed office, Chinese Premier Chou En-lai (who had repeatedly charged Japan with pursuing a policy leading to military rearmament), performed an about-face and began sending Tanaka signals to the effect that China would welcome a Tanaka visit affording the two leaders an opportunity to discuss normalization of relations.

Tanaka and a party of 49 left Tokyo for Peking on Sept. 25, and after five days of lavish, televised ceremonial dinners, entertain-

ments by acrobats, conferences and a tiring walk through the Forbidden City, a joint communiqué was issued. It stated that Japan reproached itself for the "great troubles" it had inflicted "on the Chinese people through war" and that both nations had formally agreed to establish diplomatic relations, pledging to work for lasting friendship. In the process, Japan broke diplomatic relations with Taiwan.

The China issue out of the way, Tanaka enjoyed the pinnacle of popularity. An Asahi Shimbun poll showed that 62 percent of the adult population supported him, compared with 47 percent support for Eisaku Sato after the same period in office. Capitalizing on his popularity, Tanaka dissolved the Diet on Nov. 13th and called a national election of the lower house for Dec. 10th.

In the 1969 lower house election the LDP had been returned to power with 288 out of 486 seats, a healthy majority. At the time of dissolution, owing to a number of crossovers, the LDP held 297 seats and was confident of winning at least 280 in the election. In the surprising result, however, the LDP retained only 271 seats (with ten elected independents expected to switch over later). The tiny Communist party, shedding its image as a classical Marxist party bound to the Soviet Union and for the first time campaigning on such respectable domestic issues as traffic and pollution, increased its representatives from 14 to a record 38, thus entitling the Communists to sit in with the major parties on decisions regulating Diet business. The leading opposition Socialist party also increased its seats, from 90 to 118, while the Komeito dropped from 47 to 29 seats and the Democratic Socialist party from 31 to 19.

Within the LDP, Tanaka strengthened his hold by adding members to his faction, while the opposition Fukuda faction lost some seats. Assuring him, as it did, of at least two more years in office, perhaps five, Tanaka's reelection augured for a continuation of close relations with the United States, some independent stirrings in foreign affairs and probably a greater emphasis on domestic problems.

Foreign Relations. In 1972, Japan exhibited a rare degree of change from its previous postwar policy of almost complete dependence on Washington. Shortly after President Nixon returned from Peking, the Japanese government for the first time dispatched two foreign ministry officials to Hanoi to seek an improvement of relations with North Vietnam. This was followed by a month-long return visit by a top-level economic delegation from Hanoi. At the same time Tokyo extended recognition to Bangladesh (although the United States still re-

Tanaka, Chou and Japanese Foreign Minister Masayoshi Ohira (left) converse before signing a communiqué establishing diplomatic relations.

fused to do so). Later, following negotiations in Moscow, the Japanese and Mongolian governments announced that they had agreed to establish diplomatic relations.

The government also softened its attitude toward North Korea, ignoring South Korean protests, by issuing reentry permits to a group of resident Koreans, who had applied to visit Pyongyang for the celebration of Premier Kim Il Sung's 60th birthday and by permitting Kuno Chuji, a key Liberal Democratic party Diet member, to head a parliamentary delegation to Pyongyang to seek improved relations with North Korea. The delegation signed an agreement encompassing considerably expanded trade in the next five years and establishment of diplomatic relations.

In January, Soviet Foreign Minister Andrei Gromyko visited Japan for the first time in five and one-half years, to attend the second Japan-U.S.S.R. consultation meeting. Both nations agreed to open negotiations for a peace treaty, arrange for mutual visits by the two nations' leaders, continue regular ministerial conferences and vigorously pursue economic, cultural and scientific interchanges, as well as jointly develop resources and promote trade. During the year a number of missions discussed the feasibility of joint exploration of Siberian oil and gas resources. No headway was made, however, on a peace treaty or on visits by the leaders of the two governments, owing to Moscow's cool response to Japan's quest for reversion of its northern territories.

Economy. The strength of the Japanese family-nation—its hard-working, loyal labor force—and the resilience of the nation's economy proved themselves in a year during which Japan's currency had been revalued by nearly 17 percent in relation to the U.S. dollar and foreign pressures had forced the restriction of exports. Notwithstanding both developments, the economy grew by 9.5 percent and was slated to grow in 1973 by another 10.9 percent (real terms), according to government estimates. Gross national product reached an estimated all-time high of $310,000,000,000, and per capita income attained a record $2,340, according to government estimates.

Economic problems continued to dominate U.S.-Japan relations, with a mounting U.S.-Japanese trade deficit that had grown to an estimated $4,000,000,000 in 1972. Partially to overcome the deficit, President Nixon and Prime Minister Tanaka agreed on Sept. 1 that Japan would purchase about $1,100,000,000 worth of U.S. goods by 1974.

To avert pressure for another revaluation of the yen, the Japanese government announced on Oct. 1 a third series of "yen defense measures," basically designed to encourage imports and curb exports, but these had not gone into effect as the year ended. Both the United States and members of the European Economic community felt further measures to curb Japanese exports and liberalize trade and investments would be necessary to maintain an acceptable trade balance.

While trading firms began preparing for what they considered an inevitable second revaluation, by negotiating forward orders at a yen rate of around 280 to the dollar (compared with 300), the Tanaka government continued to insist that all efforts were being made to avoid another revaluation.

Domestic Affairs. Japan had its own minor *Pentagon Papers* case when several Foreign Ministry documents concerning compensation in connection with Okinawa's reversion were leaked by a Foreign Ministry secretary to a *Mainichi Shimbun* reporter. The documents showed that the Japanese government would actually compensate certain Okinawan landowners, although for public consumption it was to be announced that the United States would pay the claims. Inasmuch as the leak was first disclosed by the opposition Socialist party in the Diet, the government did not regard the issue as one concerning freedom of the press, but rather as a case of stealing government documents for political purposes. The secretary and reporter were awaiting trial at the year's end.

Pollution remained a key domestic issue, with Tokyo continuing to hold the dubious distinction of being the world's most polluted city. A series of historic court decisions awarded record sums to citizens whose health was damaged by industrial pollution. Meanwhile, Honda Motors became the first Japanese auto manufacturer to develop what it claimed was a virtually pollution-free engine.

The Japanese continued to oppose in public opinion polls any tendency to go nuclear. With considerable difficulty the government succeeded in passing its fourth five-year defense build-up program, which called for a total budget of more than $15,000,000,000, a 98 percent increase over the third five-year program. Under the new five-year build-up plan, by the end of 1976 the Ground Self Defense Forces would consist of 179,000 men, the Maritime Self Defense Force would be a fleet of ships aggregating 146,000 tons, and the Air Self Defense Force would be made up of 970 aircraft.

BERNARD KRISHER
Tokyo Bureau Chief, *Newsweek* magazine

Harrison Salisbury, "The New York Times"

A mosaic of well-drilled Koreans fills Pyongyang Stadium in a spectacle staged for guests in May.

KOREA

On July 4, 1972, North and South Korea startled the world and their own peoples with an historic joint communiqué announcing that they had held secret talks to reduce tension, enlarge contacts and "achieve peaceful unification." In implementing the joint communiqué's provisions, direct telephone communication was established between Seoul and Pyongyang, and a South-North Coordinating Committee met for the first time at Panmunjom on Oct. 12. Both governments ended propaganda broadcasts and other hostile acts directed against each other in mid-November.

These momentous actions, after a bloody civil war (1950–53) and more than two decades of hostility, subversion and vilification, were enthusiastically welcomed by Koreans. Both governments announced their intentions to begin serious discussions on mutual trade, cultural exchange and arms reduction. Prospects appeared good for further limited progress in 1973. However, "unification" was more a propaganda slogan, useful in legitimizing government moves and internal controls, than a realistic objective of the negotiations. Both states still competed diplomatically—South Korea and its allies defeated pro-North Korea resolutions at the United Nations in September

—and both sought popular support on the Korean peninsula at the other's expense. Antithetical patterns of economic development and fundamental differences of ideology and social system will preclude rapid unification. For example, the North-South Red Cross negotiations, begun in 1971, had so far failed to reach agreement on reuniting divided families or even on mail exchanges. Nevertheless, the two Korean states apparently had begun a dialogue directed toward peaceful accommodation. The price of détente may be authoritarian rule in both Koreas.

SOUTH KOREA, REPUBLIC OF (R.O.K.)

President Park Chung Hee, in a series of military and "legal" actions from October to December, removed the last vestiges of representative government, press freedom and civil liberties in South Korea. President Park declared martial law on Oct. 17 and suspended the constitution, banned all political activity and enforced stringent overt censorship. With opposition politicians under house arrest, dissenters terrorized into silence or hiding and all discussion or political activity forbidden under martial law, a national referendum on Nov. 21 approved a new constitution. According to R.O.K. officials, 91.1 percent of those eligible

voted, and 92.3 percent of the votes favored the change. The new constitution's major provisions are: sweeping powers for the president, including additional terms of office; emasculation of the National Assembly through presidential appointment of one-third of its members; formation of a National Council for Unification (NCU) empowered to elect the president (thus ending direct presidential elections in South Korea); and termination of certain guarantees of civil and political rights.

On Dec. 15 the 2,359 members of the NCU, many reportedly hand-picked by the government and all forbidden to campaign or discuss issues, were "elected" by a reported 70.3 percent of the voters, the lowest election turnout in South Korea's history. Eight days later the NCU elected President Park Chung Hee, who was unopposed, to a six-year term. On Dec. 27, President Park was inaugurated, South Korea's new constitution was promulgated and the fourth Republic of Korea was initiated.

Government leaders explained this blitzkrieg as necessary to defend South Korean interests at a time of shifting international alignments, a reference to the U.S.-China détente. A second justification was the desire to strengthen South Korea's unity for negotiations with the North. President Park defended his actions as the creation of a new form of "Korean democracy." He stated that representative government with civil liberties was unsuitable for the R.O.K. Independent observers added one more reason: the prolongation of President Park's personal rule, which would have ended in 1975 under the old constitution.

South Korea announced in September that its 38,000 troops in Vietnam would be withdrawn over a six month period starting in December. However, the withdrawal apparently was postponed, amid reports that the R.O.K. had agreed to retain troops in Vietnam, as a strategic reserve for the U.S. residual force, in return for the continued stationing of U.S. troops in the R.O.K. Wide scale atrocities committed by South Korean troops in Vietnam, and efforts by the U.S. government to conceal the incidents, were substantiated by the disclosure of secret U.S. government reports and the revelations of former U.S. officials. Despite this documentation and U.S. Congressional criticism, South Korean military leaders continued to deny that R.O.K. troops had committed atrocities.

NORTH KOREA (D.P.R.K.)

North Korea for the first time invited journalists from major U.S. newspapers to visit the Democratic People's Republic of Korea

(D.P.R.K.). Reporters from *The New York Times* and *The Washington Post* toured North Korea in May and June and wrote the first dispatches from Pyongyang since 1950. While severely restricted in their movements and contacts with ordinary North Korean citizens, the journalists' visits marked a major relaxation of North Korean entry restrictions and policy toward the United States. In interviews, Premier Kim Il Sung expressed hopes for better relations with the United States but insisted that U.S. troops should be withdrawn from South Korea and that Korean unification was purely a Korean matter.

North Korea's major diplomatic moves, aside from negotiations with the South, were directed at improving relations with Japan, which does not recognize the D.P.R.K. On Sept. 7, Deputy Premier Pak Sang Chul told Japanese reporters that the abrogation of the 1965 Japan-R.O.K. treaty was not necessary to improve relations with North Korea. Pak characterized previous Japanese policy as "unfriendly" and called for the establishment of diplomatic relations between the D.P.R.K. and Japan. As a spur to rapprochement, North Korea purchased two plants to produce polyester fiber and, in October, sent its first economic mission to Japan. Additional contracts for an integrated steel plant, an ethylene plant and lightweight steel rails followed in November and December. Japanese business leaders responded to North Korea's trade diplomacy by forming a trade promotion association and sending a high-level delegation to Pyongyang.

Japan relaxed its restrictions on North Korean visits to Japan and on travel from Japan of North Korean residents. The first "unofficial" agreement on cultural exchange between the two countries was signed in September. Premier Kim expressed satisfaction at the improved relations to a Japanese teachers' delegation in November. However, Japanese Premier Kakuei Tanaka said in the same month that Japan was not considering establishing diplomatic relations with North Korea at that time.

Domestically, North Korea also moved to "consolidate" political control and facilitate negotiations with the South by revising its constitution, which it did in October. On Dec. 28, the D.P.R.K. announced that Kim Il Sung had been elected president of North Korea, in addition to being premier. The step appeared to be related to similar moves in South Korea.

FRANK BALDWIN
Assistant Professor of Korean
Department of East Asian Languages & Cultures
Columbia University

LABOR

Economic revival affected organized labor in a variety of ways in 1972, accompanied as it was by mounting employment, rising production, ascending profits, wage increase pressures and distended inflation in most countries. The "stagflation" of 1971—a combination of economic stagnation and price inflation—was largely ended. Prosperity debouched, but inflation remained, forcing some of the countries—notably the United States and Britain—to take strong cooling off actions.

United States. Under Phase 2 of the Nixon administration stabilization regulations the inflationary fever in the United States subsided in 1972. The pace of wage increases slowed. Labor productivity rose. Strikes declined markedly. Employment increased more than 2,400,000 to 83,000,000. Unemployment receded to a 5.1 percent rate toward the year's end after staying stubbornly at the 5.5 percent rate for months.

On the other side of the coin, retail prices went up faster than the 2.5 percent to 3 percent rate set as a goal under the stabilization program. In consequence, the purchasing power of workers' earnings slipped in the closing months, while corporate profits escalated. This brought charges from organized labor that the program was being administered inequitably.

Labor had cooperated reluctantly with Phase 2, which began on November 14, 1971, after the expiration of a 90-day wage-price freeze. Labor's cooperation turned to opposition, however, after the U.S. Pay Board sliced away large union-negotiated wage increases in the aerospace and West Coast longshore industries.

In March, 1972, the AFL-CIO Executive Council withdrew its three members from the Pay Board. President Leonard Woodcock of the United Automobile Workers followed suit. The AFL-CIO declared it would no longer serve as "window dressing" for a system that imposed "unfair government control of wages for the benefit of business profits."

However, the fifth labor member, President Frank Fitzsimmons of the Teamsters, stayed on. President Nixon, insisting controls would be kept, reorganized the board from its tripartite composition to a seven-man public panel, made up of the existing five public members, plus Fitzsimmons and one industry member.

Thus, the board continued to function, and so did an autonomous tripartite Construction Industry Stabilization Committee, which administered controls in the construction field. Wages had soared in construction in 1971—by 15 percent to 20 percent—but the committee

slowly trimmed the pace. By the end of 1972 the committee claimed that increases had been reduced to about the stabilization guideline level. The actual figure was 6.6 percent.

Meanwhile, for the economy as a whole, the Labor Department reported that the rate of wage increases had been pared to less than the 5.5 percent guidepost. The Department put the average increase in major negotiated contracts at 7 percent, down from 11.6 percent in 1971. Smaller wage increases in the non-union sector and smaller deferred raises due in 1972 under previously-negotiated contracts brought down the overall average.

The stabilization job was made easier for the reconstituted Pay Board by the fact that far fewer major wage agreements were up for renegotiation in 1972 than in 1971. Such major agreements had involved 4,700,000 workers in 1971, but only 2,800,000 in 1972. This relative quiet on the bargaining front also contributed

Cesar Chavez, fighting head of the United Farm Workers Union, announces in February the first contract covering workers in the Southeast.

UPI

to a drastic decline in strikes. Man-days of idleness due to strikes fell by October to a 26-year low of 7/10 of a day for each 1,000 working days put in.

As the economy surged, the Labor Department reported that worker productivity—output per man-hour—rose approximately 4.2 percent in the private economy, substantially more than the long-range rise of about 3 percent a year. As a result, unit labor costs, after a long period of increases, rose only 1.6 percent for the entire year.

A dark spot in the brightening economic picture, however, was a faster rise in the Consumer Price Index than contemplated under the controls program. Toward year's end the index was moving up at a 3.5 percent annual rate, thwarting the administration's hope of slowing the rate to below 3 percent. Price Commission officials claimed the rise would have been greater without controls. Moreover, the inflation was less marked than that in most other countries.

To the surprise of many, President Nixon ended mandatory wage and price controls in all fields except food, health and construction on Jan. 11, 1973. Federal rent controls were also ended. Secretary of the Treasury Shultz announced that Phase 3 of the Nixon economic program would rely on "voluntary cooperation" with wage-price guidelines. Although the Federal Price Commission and Pay Board were abolished, the White House announced that Mr. Nixon would ask Congress to extend the Economic Stabilization Act, which gives the President authority to control wages and prices, until April 30, 1974.

In the otherwise quiet strike year of 1972 one of the longest stoppages occurred at a big General Motors assembly plant in Norwood, Ohio. Involving the touchy issue of alleged "speedup" on the assembly line, it was settled on a compromise basis in late September after 172 days. An earlier 22-day strike flared over the same issue at GM's Vega assembly plant in Lordstown, Ohio, described as the fastest assembly plant in the world.

After the Norwood stoppage the UAW turned to a new strategy in an effort to deal with the problem—that is, two or three-day strikes at various GM plants around the country. The new tactic also left the basic problem largely unresolved, but the UAW served notice that "humanizing" of the assembly line operation would constitute a major demand in general auto industry bargaining, coming up in 1973.

The four-day, 40-hour week, or variations thereof, continued to make progress, mostly in small nonunion plants and offices and in small units of larger companies. However, the 4-day week movement lost some of the glamour it had acquired in 1971.

One of the year's big developments on the labor scene was the decision of the AFL-CIO Executive Council, under the leadership of President George Meany, to abandon a policy of supporting the Democratic Presidential candidate, and to maintain neutrality in the race between President Nixon and Sen. George McGovern, the Democratic nominee. Meany said the decision reflected a division that already existed in labor's rank and file over McGovern's "neo-isolationism" and over left-wing or far-out elements that rallied to the McGovern banner.

The neutrality policy left individual affiliates free to pursue their own political courses. Leaders of about 35 affiliates formed a labor committee for McGovern, and a number of other leaders separately backed McGovern. On the other hand, heads of many building trades unions and also the Teamsters and a few other unions came out for Nixon, who won by a landslide. Inasmuch as labor did well in the Congressional races (Democrats gained two seats in the Senate and lost only 11 in the House despite the Nixon avalanche), Meany viewed the result as vindicating the AFL-CIO Executive Council's neutrality.

Prior to the campaign, Nixon made various gestures to woo labor—notably, shelving an administration bill in Congress to impose a form of compulsory arbitration in transportation disputes. After the election he made a further bow to labor by picking Peter J. Brennan, leader of the AFL-CIO Building Trades Councils in New York State, as his Secretary of Labor. Brennan, a "hard hat" symbol but a lifelong Democrat, had strongly supported Nixon for reelection.

Another dramatic event of the year in the labor field was the court-ordered, government administered election of officers of the United Mine Workers. A 1969 election won by the slate of incumbent President W. A. Boyle, a protégé of the late John L. Lewis, was set aside by a Federal court as marred by fraud and irregularities. Boyle's opponent in that election, Joseph A. Yablonski, a veteran UMW officer, later was brutally murdered, along with his wife and daughter. The killing sparked an uproar, which led to the conviction of the hired killers and to indictments of several subordinate UMW officials. Boyle strongly denied complicity and was not indicted. But subsequently he was convicted of other charges of illegally using union funds for political purposes.

The court order for a new election brought the most severe government monitoring of a union in U.S. history. Precautions included placing government-named overseers at UMW headquarters and at 30 district offices; regulation of the union's financial operations; and strict supervision of the union's official journal, which was required to give equal space to all candidates.

A rival slate known as the Miners for Democracy and made up of followers of the late Joseph Yablonski triumphed in the election, thus ushering in a new era for the buffeted UMW. The slate was led by Arnold R. Miller, a West Virginia coal miner disabled by black-lung disease. Miller had headed an association which successfully fought for legislation to make black lung a compensable hazard. He vowed to eradicate abuses in the union.

A trend toward union mergers continued in 1972. The United Papermakers and Paperworkers joined the Pulp, Sulphite and Paper Mill Workers to form a new 350,000-member United Paperworkers International Union. The Lithographers, Bookbinders and Photoengravers amalgamated into the Graphic Arts International Union, with which the Newspaper Guild also began merger discussions. The former District 50, once a "catchall" division of the United Mine Workers with members in many industries, merged with the United Steelworkers of America.

One of the year's historic collective agreements was reached between the United Transportation Union and the railroads, bringing final settlement of a 35-year dispute over the employment of firemen on diesel locomotives in road freight and yard service. The agreement

Labor Department monitors count ballots in a court ordered United Mine Workers election.

UPI

UMW challenger Arnold Miller awaits successful outcome of vote to unseat Tony Boyle.

UPI

assured retention of approximately 18,000 remaining firemen until they retire, die, are discharged for cause or are promoted to engineers. Also, the agreement specified that future engineers would come from the ranks of firemen, and that the railroads would set up programs to train firemen for engineers' posts.

Canada. Turbulence marked the labor landscape in Canada in 1972, and it was exacerbated by a combination of high unemployment and inflationary pressures.

The country experienced a series of major strikes, most of them prolonged—by longshoremen on the West Coast, dock workers in Quebec, woodworkers in British Columbia, municipal workers in greater Vancouver, Metro Toronto civic workers and 200,000 provincial hospital and civil service workers in Quebec.

The latter strike, in April, was the most tumultuous. Quebec passed legislation ordering an end to the strike, and court antistrike injunctions were issued. But three leaders of a labor common front in the province recommended defiance of the injunctions for which they were convicted of contempt and sentenced to one-year jail terms. Many lesser union officials also were convicted.

Jailing of the three leaders precipitated an outburst of protest strikes, some marked by violence, around the province. The strikes subsided after eight days. Late in the year most of the issues in the dispute—wages and working conditions—were settled by negotiation. Among the repercussions was a split in the French-oriented CNTU. Some of its major affiliates, charging ideological radicalization by a leadership committed to political "revolution" in the province, broke away and formed a rival Centrale des Syndicats Démocratiques (Congress of Democratic Trade Unions) committed to straight trade union objectives.

Meanwhile, throughout Canada, the international unions (those based in the United States) increasingly felt the hot breath of nationalism. Several big locals of the United Steelworkers Union broke away and formed a separate national union. Several other disaffiliations occurred, although two-thirds of Canadian unionists remained part of the internationals.

Canadian unemployment rose to 7.1 percent in September, one of the highest rates in a decade, fell to 6.6 percent in November, then mounted again in the winter months. Consumer prices rose more than 5 percent above those of a year earlier, sharply reducing the buying power of workers' wage increases, which averaged about 6.5 percent.

Japan. Emerging from a "mini-recession" Japan's economy achieved a 9.5 percent annual growth rate by the end of 1972. It had fallen to a little more than 5 percent in 1971.

The recession's aftermath, however, reduced the pace of wage increases won by unions during the annual "shunto," or spring wage offensive, to an average of about 15 percent, down from more than 16 percent in 1971. Rising labor productivity offset much of the wage increases, and the rise in the Consumer Price Index was held to approximately 5.5 percent.

Most strikes, as is customary, lasted only a few hours or a few days, but a few were longer, notably one by the Seamen's Union which dragged on for 91 days, the longest in the history of Japanese shipping. Also, the two leading unions on the Japan National Railways —Kokuro, the National Railway Workers Union, and Doryokusha, the union of Locomotive Engineers—staged several brief strikes over wages and operational changes, despite the law's prohibition of stoppages on the government-owned system. Thereupon, the JNR management imposed penalties on thousands of rail unionists, including pay cuts, suspensions, dismissals, warnings and reprimands. Later the two unions initiated "work to rule" slowdowns in protest over the firings and over arrests of some strikers accused of engaging in violence. In line with past practice the two unions compensated the penalized strikers for their financial losses.

Trends continued during the year toward raising the traditional 55-year retirement age, toward job switching and toward the five-day work week. The shift to a higher retirement age has been spurred by a tightening labor market and by the rising cost of large severance payments made to those retiring at 55. Unions negotiated extension of the compulsory retirement age to 60 in some industries. Another tradition, that of lifetime employment with the same firm, was also crumbling. More and more workers were shifting jobs, particularly those between the ages of 20 and 30.

Unemployment, which reached a high of 1.8 percent in March, dropped to a little more than 1 percent later in the year.

Latin America. Inflation ran wild in much of South America in 1972. In Chile, under Marxist President Salvador Allende, prices skyrocketed 99 percent between January and October, fueled by government resort to "printing press" money to pay its bills.

In August most of Chile's 136,000 storekeepers struck for a day to protest rising taxes, price curbs and threats to nationalize small business. In October small truck owners struck, partly for higher rates and partly to protest a

government move to establish a state trucking company in a southern province. The truck strike paralyzed shipments of many vital supplies, and the government declared a state of emergency. However, widespread sympathy strikes by taxi drivers, bus owners, construction men, civil engineers, bank employees, teachers and students and airline crews followed. These strikes were pictured as evidence of growing resistance, particularly in the middle classes, to Allende's efforts to push Chile along the path of socialism. After 27 days, the government yielded and the strikes ended.

In Brazil an inflation rate that was 90 percent a few years ago was trimmed to 15 percent by the nation's military regime, which also virtually outlawed strikes.

In Bolivia, after the government devalued the peso by two-thirds and imposed a series of other austerity measures, labor unrest broke out. Textile workers staged a 24-hour stoppage in November, barricading themselves inside their mills, demanding wage increases sufficient to compensate for the peso devaluation. The government, charging a leftist plot, sent troops to the factories and arrested 40 unionists. Thereafter, thousands of other workers staged protest strikes, which ended two days later in return for release of the arrested unionists and a government promise to negotiate on wage increases.

In Peru the military dictatorship sought to win over labor by authorizing worker councils to take over management of seized sugar plantations and by enacting one law designed to give workers a 25 percent share in industrial profits and another spelling out collective bargaining procedures, which culminate, however, in final decisions by the authorities.

In Argentina the Peronist-oriented General Confederation of Labor maintained a wary relationship with the military government. Strikes occurred frequently as inflation soared approximately 50 percent during the year. The Confederation led a drive to have Juan Peron, 77, nominated as a presidential candidate by the Justicialist party. Peron, one-time ruler of Argentina who spent years in Spanish exile, was allowed to return by the military but was ruled ineligible to run for president. Under labor's prodding the Justicialist party nonetheless nominated Peron, who, however, declined to run and retired from the scene. The party then named Hector Campora, Peron's personal representative, as its standard bearer, and the laborites then walked out of the nominating convention.

Europe. An inflation epidemic hit most of Western Europe in 1972, with retail price rises averaging more than 7 percent and cresting at 10 percent. Britain's Conservative government sought to meet the problem by imposing a wage-price freeze late in the year for at least 90 days. It did so against a backdrop of price rises of about 8 percent; an economic growth rate that fell to zero in some months; a million unemployed; wages escalating an average of more than 12 percent; and a widespread wave of strikes involving such basic industries as coal mining, railroads, longshoring, auto manufacturing and construction.

Italy, as it had been the year before, was hit by a wave of strikes throughout the year in virtually all branches of industry and government. Most strikes lasted only a day or two. Meanwhile, living costs rose at nearly a 7 percent rate; unemployment hit an estimated 8 percent; and industrial production rose by only a little more than 2 percent.

France enjoyed one of the continent's higher growth rates, its gross national product rising more than 5 percent in real terms (after subtracting the effects of a 6 percent inflation rate). Wages rose at about an 11 percent rate. In September the government announced a series of anti-inflationary measures, including restraints on credit and a reduction in the value added tax at the retail level. In November a wave of strikes for higher pay pockmarked France, bringing out rail workers, civil servants, postal workers, newspapermen, hospital workers, miners and many others, mostly for 24 to 48-hour periods.

In West Germany the labor front quieted in 1972. Unrest grew toward the year's end, however, as the rise in consumer prices approached 7 percent. Industrial production staged a slow comeback from a 1971 slump, but unit labor costs went up as the rate of productivity slipped. Unemployment stood below the 1 percent mark, and the number of imported foreign workers reached 2,300,000.

Most other countries of Western Europe found themselves beset with wage increases of 10 percent to 12 percent and price rises of 5 percent to 8 percent. Austria contended with a nationwide strike of doctors and dentists protesting moves to socialize the nation's health services, and Belgium was confronted with a two-day strike of 700,000 small retail businesses.

In Soviet Russia labor productivity lagged behind prescribed goals despite a drive by the government-dominated Soviet trade union apparatus to induce members to "increase and improve output."

RUBEN LEVIN
Editor and Manager, *Labor*

LAW

It became clear in 1972 that the law was in transition, but the changes were so subtle that it remained for the future to reveal what ultimate directions U.S. law would take. The changes were most apparent in the Supreme Court, where the impact of four nominees of President Nixon turned the Court toward a more conservative direction in some respects, while in some legal areas the Court continued the libertarian tradition that had distinguished the high tribunal under Chief Justice Earl Warren.

It was a Court that could rule, on the one hand, that law-abiding civilians who had been targets of Army surveillance had no right to go to court to stop the abuses, that grand juries could force journalists to disclose information told them in confidence and that a grand jury could interrogate Sen. Mike Gravel (D-Alaska) and his staff about their role in making public the top secret Pentagon Papers.

A death row inmate views an electric chair following Supreme Court ruling that capital punishment as currently enforced is unconstitutional.

UPI

On the other hand, it could unanimously declare unconstitutional government wiretapping of domestic radicals without court authority, could require free lawyers for poor defendants in all cases involving possible imprisonment and could outlaw capital punishment as it had been practiced in the United States for almost two centuries.

While the changes on the high court were murky, the reason for them was not. It was the presence of the four jurists appointed by President Nixon—Chief Justice Warren E. Burger and Justices Harry A. Blackmun, Lewis F. Powell, Jr., and William W. Rehnquist. President Nixon had said, when he appointed each of them, that he was naming "judicial conservatives" who would turn the Court from its recent liberal course. Justices Powell and Rehnquist did not join the Court until its 1971–72 term was half over. Yet before the term was over, it was evident that the President had succeeded to a remarkable degree in selecting conservatives who agreed with each other on the sensitive issues of the times.

Of the 70 cases in which all four participated, they all joined the same opinion in 45, for an astounding 64 percent record of togetherness. Usually they supported conservative answers to the questions at stake.

At the same time, the Court was also being further polarized by the gravitation of four other justices toward a position together on the philosophical left. William O. Douglas, William J. Brennan, Jr., and Thurgood Marshall had been there all along during the era of the Warren Court. But as the Nixon appointees coalesced on the right, Potter Stewart, a Republican appointee of President Eisenhower's, became increasingly liberal in his rulings. There were suggestions that he did this to prevent an unseemly rapid break with recent precedents, but the result was that he frequently joined the three liberal holdovers from the Warren Court.

The effect was to make Byron R. White, a colorless justice who had been overshadowed by the liberal pyrotechnics of the Warren Court, the swing man, who repeatedly determined which way the decisions of the Supreme Court would go. There were 19 cases in which the "Nixon four" joined together in 5 to 4 decisions. In eight of these, Justice White joined with them and gave their side a majority. In ten others he swung the other way, leaving the Nixon bloc in dissent. In only one did he join the liberal side to have another justice—Stewart—swing the case to the Nixon appointees' side.

This produced a Supreme Court that seemed, to the public, to be unpredictable and almost

MAJOR SUPREME COURT DECISIONS[1]

CHIEF JUSTICE: WARREN E. BURGER (1969)

ASSOCIATE JUSTICES

WILLIAM O. DOUGLAS (1939)
WILLIAM J. BRENNAN, JR. (1956)
POTTER STEWART (1958)

BYRON WHITE (1962)
THURGOOD MARSHALL (1967)
HARRY A. BLACKMUN (1970)

LEWIS F. POWELL, JR. (1972)
WILLIAM H. REHNQUIST (1972)

CASE	DATE	DECISION
GROPPI V. LESLIE	JAN. 13	In overturning the 1969 contempt citation against the Rev. James E. Groppi the court ruled that the Wisconsin Assembly had violated Groppi's right to due process. (The Assembly had waited two days after Groppi and his welfare-rights workers had disrupted a legislative session before voting a contempt sentence.) Vote 7–0 (Powell, Rehnquist not voting).
ALEXANDER V. LOUISIANA	APR. 3	Ruled that the burden of proof was on the state of Louisiana to show that its selection of grand jurors was not racially discriminating against Negroes. Vote 7–0 (Powell, Rehnquist not voting).
STANLEY V. ILLINOIS	APR. 3	Ruled that unwed fathers have the same right as unwed mothers to obtain custody of their children providing they are fit parents. Vote 5–2 (Burger, Blackmun dissenting; Powell, Rehnquist not voting).
COLE V. RICHARDSON	APR. 18	Upheld the constitutionality of a Massachusetts loyalty oath which requires public employees to swear that they are against the violent overthrow of the government. Vote 4–3 (Brennan, Douglas, Marshall dissenting; Powell, Rehnquist not voting).
WEBER V. AETNA CASUALTY AND SURETY CO.	APR. 24	Declared unconstitutional a Louisiana law permitting legitimate but not illegitimate children to receive workmen's compensation benefits because of the work-connected death of their parents. Vote 8–1 (Rehnquist dissenting).
DUKES V. WARDEN	MAY 15	Held that a defendant cannot withdraw a guilty plea as involuntary solely because of possible conflict of interest on the part of his counsel. Vote 7–2 (Douglas, Marshall dissenting).
NLRB V. BURNS INTERNATIONAL SECURITY SERVICES, INC.	MAY 15	Ruled that when a subcontractor takes over a prior subcontractor's work and hires a majority of the workers from the previous employer, the new employer must bargain with the existing union, although he is not bound by previous labor contracts. Vote 5–4 (Rehnquist, Burger, Brennan, Powell dissenting).
UNITED STATES V. BISWELL	MAY 15	Held that Federal agents have a right to search licensed weapons dealers even without a search warrant. Vote 8–1 (Douglas dissenting).
JACKSON V. INDIANA	JUNE 7	Ruled that persons judged mentally incompetent to stand trial must be committed to a civil institution within a reasonable time or released. Vote 7–0 (Powell, Rehnquist not voting).
ADAMS V. WILLIAMS	JUNE 12	Ruled that the "stop and frisk" law can be extended so that a policeman, following an anonymous tip, has the right to stop a suspect. Vote 6–3 (Douglas, Brennan, Marshall dissenting).
FLOOD V. KUHN	JUNE 19	Reaffirmed the ruling that professional baseball is exempt from antitrust laws; suggested that Congressional action is appropriate. Vote 5–3 (Douglas, Marshall, Brennan dissenting; Powell not voting).
WRIGHT V. CITY COUNCIL OF EMPORIA	JUNE 22	Struck down the effort of a predominantly white Southern city to secede from a black county school system. Vote 5–4 (Burger, Powell, Blackmun, Rehnquist dissenting). (This was the first non-unanimous decision in a school desegregation case.)
PETERS V. KIFF	JUNE 22	Ruled that a white defendant, as well as a Negro, can challenge a conviction if it can be shown that Negroes were excluded from the grand jury that indicted him. Vote 6–3 (Berger, Blackmun, Rehnquist dissenting).
MORRISSEY V. BREWER	JUNE 29	Held that persons on parole have the right to an informal hearing before they are returned to prison and must be informed in writing of the reason their parole is being revoked. Vote 8–1 (Douglas dissenting).

[1] Not discussed in Law article

On May 15 the Supreme Court ruled that Amish children are exempted from state compulsory secondary education laws. The Amish argued that children in secondary schools are taught worldly values which are in conflict with the Amish philosophy.

John Launois, Black Star

schizophrenic. The most astounding decision was *Furman v. Georgia,* a 5 to 4 decision in which the Court dramatically spared 600 condemned men and women on death rows across the country by declaring unconstitutional capital punishment laws that permit juries to impose the death penalty at their discretion against persons found guilty of capital offenses. The gist of the majority's ruling was that these laws are so rarely and so erratically invoked that their enforcement amounts to "cruel and unusual punishments," which are forbidden by the Constitution's Eighth Amendment. As a result, most capital punishment laws were invalidated, and it appeared that executions would become possible again only if laws were passed making death mandatory for certain crimes.

Almost as surprising was a unanimous decision in which the Court expanded the right to counsel by holding that no defendant could be jailed for any offense, no matter how minor, unless he had been represented by a lawyer at his trial (*Argersinger v. Hamlin*). For financially hard-pressed cities and states this came as a shock, as it meant a vast new demand for public defenders in misdemeanor courts. But it brought some solace to the legal profession, which had been told by the president of the

American Bar Association, Robert W. Meserve, that law schools would soon be churning out twice as many young lawyers each year as there were new jobs for lawyers.

Another surprise was the Court's 8 to 0 decision, with Justice Rehnquist abstaining, holding that the government may not wiretap radicals without court permission (*United States v. United States District Court for the Eastern District of Michigan*). The Nixon administration had placed much of its prestige behind its claim that it could constitutionally wiretap radicals that the attorney general considered a threat to the national security. But in a strong opinion by freshman Justice Lewis F. Powell, Jr., the court held that the Fourth Amendment's rule against searches without court warrants applied to the government's surveillance of alleged radicals. "We have as much or more to fear from the erosion of our sense of privacy and independence by the omnipresent electronic ear of the government," Justice Powell declared, "as we do from the likelihood that fomenters of domestic upheaval will modify our form of governing."

Other rulings also reflected continuity with the Warren Court's liberal traditions. In *Reed v. Reed,* the first Supreme Court ruling to strike down a law because of sex discrimination, the

Court unanimously overturned an Idaho statute that favored men over women as administrators of deceased persons' estates. In another decision (*Eisenstadt v. Baird*), the Court declared unconstitutional a Massachusetts law that barred anyone but doctors and pharmacists from distributing birth control devices. The Court also ruled that children of the Amish religious sect, which believes that formal education beyond the eighth grade is sinful, need not obey a state's compulsory school attendance law (*Wisconsin v. Yoder*). It also ruled that witnesses cannot be summoned to testify before grand juries on the basis of evidence obtained by illegal wiretapping (*Gelbard v. United States*). And it invalidated restrictive election laws in many states by striking down a Tennessee law that required a year's residence in the state before a person could vote. The Court hinted pointedly that any waiting period of more than thirty days was probably unconstitutional (*Dunn v. Blumstein*).

However, other decisions gave ample proof that the law was in transition, shifting away from some of the liberal doctrines of the Warren years.

Three 5 to 4 rulings in the last week of the 1971–72 term pointed the way. In one, the majority held that the Army's surveillance of civilian political activities was beyond the reach of the courts, because persons who were targets of the surveillance were said to lack legal standing to bring the issue into court (*Laird v. Tatum*). In another, the Court ruled that the First Amendment does not protect journalists from being compelled to tell grand juries the identities of confidential sources, or information given the newsmen in confidence (*Branzburg v. Hayes*). Finally, the Court held that

Congressional immunity did not excuse Sen. Mike Gravel and his aides from being compelled to tell a grand jury about their role in arranging for the publication in book form of the Pentagon Papers (*Gravel v. United States*).

In each of these, Justice Rehnquist provided the crucial fifth vote in favor of the Justice Department's positions, after having dealt with the subject matter at issue only months before, when he was an assistant attorney general in the Justice Department. This so outraged the government's opponents in the Army spying case and the Gravel case that they demanded rehearings without Justice Rehnquist—the first time in the Supreme Court's history that lawyers had sought to disqualify a justice on conflict of interest grounds. Justice Rehnquist refused in an unprecedented memorandum of explanation, saying that Justices have a strong "duty to sit" to resolve issues and that he had not been involved directly with the cases but only in varying degrees with the issues involved.

There were other harbingers of a swing to the right. The Court held, again 5 to 4, that criminal defendants in state courts could be convicted on less than unanimous jury verdicts (*Apodaca v. Oregon*). It ruled that the government could bar an alien intellectual from entering the United States to lecture on the ground that he was a Marxist (*U.S. Acting Attorney General v. Mandel*). It declared that privately owned shopping centers could bar political pamphleteers from the entire premises (*Tanner v. Lloyd Corporation*). It declared that private clubs holding state liquor licenses could bar Negroes as guests, and presumably also as members (*Moose Lodge v. Irvis*). Finally, it ruled that unindicted suspects were not entitled to counsel when they were placed

UPI

As the result of a 1972 Supreme Court decision, Sen. Mike Gravel (D-Alaska) is not exempt from interrogation by a grand jury concerning his role in releasing the Pentagon Papers.

in police lineups (*Kirby v. Illinois*), and that witnesses compelled to testify before grand juries could later be prosecuted for the crimes they were forced to disclose, so long as the evidence used against them was not obtained through their testimony (*Kastigar v. United States*).

The sense of contradiction and confusion was magnified by two further imponderables. Lewis Powell, the 65-year-old former Virginia lawyer and American Bar Association president, showed signs of independence and leadership during his early months on the Supreme Court that indicated that he might break the solidarity of the "Nixon Four" on some issues.

Running counter to this was the reelection of President Nixon, which raised the possibility that he could replace some of the Court's most liberal justices during his final four years in office. Justice Douglas seemed healthy at age 73, but he carried a pacemaker in his body to regulate his heartbeat. Justice Brennan was 66 and reportedly considering retirement, and Marshall, 64, had suffered a series of illnesses.

If events were to give President Nixon the opportunity to replace one or more of these with conservative justices, it could transform the Supreme Court in a way that could perhaps prove to be one of the most important and durable developments of the Nixon presidency.

As the Supreme Court became more conservative, the legal grassroots produced a series of developments that demonstrated a growing tendency to depart from doctrines of official orthodoxy. A jury in Harrisburg, Pa., refused to convict the Rev. Philip Berrigan and six others accused of conspiring to kidnap Presidential aide Henry A. Kissinger. Another jury, in California, deadlocked over murder charges leveled against Angela Davis, a black Communist said to have been involved in a murderous jail break attempt by California's imprisoned "Soledad Brothers." Abortion "on demand" had by 1973 become a reality in six jurisdictions—Alaska, California, the District of Columbia, Hawaii, New York and Washington. The legislatures of Oregon and Hawaii followed the recommendations of the National Commission on Obscenity and Pornography—which had been denounced as too permissive by President Nixon—and abolished the states' laws against pornography, so long as it is not shown to minors or thrust on unwilling adults. And Michigan's two communities of East Lansing and Ann Arbor became the first in the United States virtually to decriminalize both the possession and use of marijuana, called "pot." The two communities made history when they eliminated all prison penalties for smoking marijuana and left only the possibility of imposing nominal fines on its users.

FRED P. GRAHAM
Supreme Court Correspondent
CBS News

The members of the Supreme Court in 1972 were: (sitting l-r) Justices Stewart, Douglas, Burger, Brennan and White; (standing l-r) Powell, Marshall, Blackmun and Rehnquist. With four liberal and four conservative jurists on the bench, Byron White's vote was the deciding one in many cases.

Harris & Ewing from Photo Trends

Robert Wedgeworth (r), newly appointed executive director of the American Library Association, discusses the best seller "How to Read a Book" with its author Mortimer Adler (l) and Alex Ladenson, chief librarian of the Chicago Public library.

LIBRARIES

The circulation of photocopies of copyrighted works has long been a sensitive issue between libraries and publishers. Many publishers consider the practice as copyright infringement. Early in 1972, Williams and Wilkins brought a case against the National Institutes of Health and the National Library of Medicine to the U.S. Court of Claims. Court Commissioner James F. Davis concluded that the medical library, in making and providing photocopies of articles, had indeed infringed the publisher's copyright, and that the publisher was "entitled to recover reasonable and entire compensation for infringement of copyright." The report and recommendation will be reviewed by the entire court. Undoubtedly, the case will be appealed to the Supreme Court. The conflict is between social utility—the contribution of copyrighted works to scientific and scholarly research—and financial compensation to the copyright owner. The implications for libraries of all types, but particularly for public, academic, and research libraries, are far-reaching.

Faced with rising costs and reduced income, many libraries curtailed services. The San Francisco Public Library Commission, inhibited by a freeze on hiring new personnel, voted to close three branches, but vigorous public protest forced the branches to remain open. The New York Public Library reduced evening schedules in two important branches. For the third straight year, Cleveland anticipated a shortage of $200,000 in annual support, with resultant losses in personnel and hours of operation. Bookmobile service in one New York system was cut when the state reduced its support, and Vermont was phasing out bookmobiles completely, replacing them with mail service.

The Federal government continued its support of library services, but the budget for fiscal year 1973 envisaged sharp reductions from previous allocations. The amount allocated for public library services was reduced from $46,500,000 to $30,000,000, and no funds for public and academic library construction were included. On the other hand, provisions for medical libraries, the Library of Congress and library training were increased. In spite of declining revenues, however, the starting salaries for new librarians were not appreciably affected; typical beginning salaries were between $8,300 and $8,500, and trained librarians with professional experience could command an average salary of $9,800.

Censorship demands continued to plague many libraries, particularly school libraries.

The Board of Education in Ridgefield, Conn., claiming that parts of Mike Royko's *Boss: Richard J. Daley of Chicago* slandered law enforcement officials and downgraded police departments generally, ordered the book removed from a reading list. The Roselle, N.J., Board of Education removed John Kenneth Galbraith's *Affluent Society* and Robert Lekachman's *Age of Keynes* from its high school library. Both works were cited as examples of "permissive liberalism."

Kenneth H. Fagerhaugh was named director of libraries, Carnegie-Mellon University, Pittsburgh. Louis L. Martz succeeded Herman W. Liebert as director of the Beinecke Rare Book and Manuscript Library at Yale. Milton S. Byam became director of the new Martin Luther King Memorial Library in Washington, D.C. Douglas W. Bryant took over the directorship of Harvard University library. Richard M. Dougherty was appointed librarian at the University of California, Berkeley. W. David Laird was named University of Arizona librarian. Joseph M. Dagnese assumed the directorship of libraries at Purdue, and Stanley McElderry was appointed director of the library at the University of Chicago. Charles H. Stevens became the first executive director of the National Commission on Libraries and Information Science, and Clifford Currie, former executive director of the Canadian Library Association (CLA), was appointed librarian at the Ashmolean Museum, Oxford. Bernard McNamee, who had been librarian of Dawson College in Montreal, was named executive director of the CLA.

The University of Virginia received a gift of $350,000 from Arthur J. Morris for a new law library. The New York Public Library was granted $500,000 from the National Endowment for the Humanities on a matching basis, with the prospect of additional grants. The National Historical Publications Commission gave $35,135 to Cornell University Libraries to aid the program of listing all known manuscripts of the Marquis de Lafayette.

The Free Library of Philadelphia acquired the Edgar Allan Poe collection of Richard Gimbel. In addition to the manuscripts of *Murders in the Rue Morgue* and "The Raven," and a first edition *of Tamerlane,* the collection includes manuscripts, autograph letters and rare editions. The Library also received the Emerson Greenaway collection of early American children's books. The Rodgers and Hammerstein Archives of Recorded Sound, housed in Lincoln Center, New York City, received 263 tapes of radio broadcast interviews with major dance personalities, musicians, critics and composers. Austin Kelly III gave the Massachusetts Institute of Technology 30 rare books valued at $100,000, including a first edition of Thomas Paine's *Common Sense.* The personal and professional papers of Max Lincoln Schuster covering 44 years of publishing history and including 46,000 documents and a library of 30,000 volumes went to Columbia University. The University of Kansas received a Mencken collection from Mrs. Joseph A. Snyder, and Flannery O'Connor's personal library as well as manuscripts and correspondence with her literary agent went to Georgia College, Milledgeville.

LIBRARY ASSOCIATIONS

The American Library Association (ALA) appointed Robert Wedgeworth, age 35, as its executive director to succeed retiring David H. Clift. Wedgeworth has had a wide range of library experience and was engaged in doctoral study when he was appointed. He assumed the directorship at a time when the association faces a reduction in membership and serious financial problems.

The association held its mid-winter and annual meetings in Chicago. The June conference, under the presidency of Keith Doms, Philadelphia librarian, had as its theme "Media —Man, Material, Machine." Doms was succeeded by Katherine Laich, a member of the faculty of the University of Southern California and former assistant librarian of Los Angeles.

The International Federation of Library Associations (IFLA) held its annual meeting in Budapest in August-September. To tie in with UNESCO's designation of 1972 as International Book Year, the meeting emphasized the importance of reading in contemporary society. IFLA had been one of 41 international governmental agencies suspended by UNESCO because one of its members, the South African Library Association, was guilty of racial discrimination. As that association was unable or unwilling to change its policy it lost its IFLA affiliation; as a result, UNESCO was expected to reinstate IFLA.

The European Association of Research Libraries, organized in 1971 to bring the directors of major libraries together to stimulate research and explore problems of mutual concern, held its 1972 meeting in Bordeaux, France. Libraries of more than 20 nations are members. The association promises to be as effective as its American counterpart, the Association of Research Libraries.

LEON CARNOVSKY
Professor Emeritus, Graduate Library School
University of Chicago

LITERATURE

Because it is always entertaining to see the mighty reduced to rubble and the influential made to look like fools, no literary event in 1972 provoked as much excitement and explanation as did a book that was never published. Clifford Irving, the journeyman author of a book about a man who forged paintings, convinced McGraw-Hill and *Life* magazine that they should turn over to him $1,000,000 in return for the autobiography of the billionaire industrialist Howard Hughes. Hughes, a notorious recluse, had long been the subject of vulgar curiosity; according to Irving, this inaccessible man would reveal everything—but only to Irving. McGraw-Hill and *Life* devoured the bait and defended the enterprise long after its credibility had collapsed. In fact, the affair was a hoax, concocted by Irving and an assistant, and aided by Irving's wife. Much of the material that *Life* paid for so dearly was drawn from Time-Life's own files. The conspirators received brief terms in jail.

Two of the most influential figures in 20th-century literature died in 1972. The first, Edmund Wilson, a literary critic who dabbled in poetry, fiction and plays, was a vastly learned and idiosyncratic man who introduced American readers to such European writers as Proust and Joyce. For Wilson, literary criticism was both complex and comprehensive, involving "a history of man's ideas and imaginings in the setting of the conditions which have shaped them." The second, Ezra Pound, known first for his lyrical poems and graceful translations from many languages, and finally for the knotty and often incomprehensible poems in the *Cantos*, will be remembered as a mentor of greater writers: Yeats, Joyce, Frost and Eliot among them. In 1972, Pound was denied a medal by the American Academy of Arts and Sciences because of his anti-Semitism and wartime propaganda for fascist Italy—which resulted in his incarceration in an American asylum for 12 years and his subsequent exile to Italy, where he died.

The year also saw the publication of the first of a three-volume supplement and revision of the *Oxford English Dictionary*—a massive addendum to the 12 parent volumes which comprise what is incontestably the greatest (though somewhat dated) reference work relating to the English language.

Fiction. The trend in fiction in 1972 was toward sharp, witty novels about women's desperate

Santi Visalli, Photoreporters

Clifford Irving's super-hoax ended in July when, convicted, he met the press and went to jail.

lot—women as victims of men, of cultural conditioning, of their own neuroses. Cynthia Buchanan's *Maiden* proved light and funny; Norma Meacock's *Thinking Girl* more substantial, but the cleverest and most convincing was Alix Kates Shulman's *Memoirs of an Ex-Prom Queen*, the story of a pretty girl done in by her conception of what men want.

Martin Shulman

Alix Kates Shulman enriched the fiction of women's revolt with an acid confection about an ex-prom queen.

By far the best novel of the year is Alexander Solzhenitsyn's *August 1914,* a work comparable to Tolstoy's, which celebrates the spirit of Russia while investigating the collapse of the Romanov order. By concentrating on Russia's ordeal during the opening weeks of World War I, culminating in the disastrous defeat at Tannenberg, Solzhenitsyn manages to convey the sense of Russian society on the verge of collapse. Battle scenes have rarely been as well portrayed in fiction, but Solzhenitsyn's concern is principally for those who endure the confusion, frustration and uselessness of war.

Solzhenitsyn's realistic novels, which he uses as vehicles to record history, stand in sharp contrast to much of the most talented of recent fiction, which is anti-realistic in approach. In his novella *The Breast,* Philip Roth follows the tradition of Gogol and Kafka with a parable of a man who turns into a 6-foot, 155-pound female breast. The situation leads to some wit and even more desperation, but Roth's uncertainty of tone detracts from his effect.

More inventive and more successful is John Barth's *Chimera,* three related tales that take off from the story of Scheherazade and the myths of Perseus and Bellerophon. Extrapolating from the ancient stories, Barth plays wittily with words and time, digresses into metaphysical foolery, delights in the joys of living, loving, even of mortality. Even more substantial, if less likable, is Michel Tournier's *The Ogre,* a long and complex symbolical fable of an obsessive Frenchman who endures the excesses and perversities of World War II while searching for his destiny as a "beast of burden," a modern

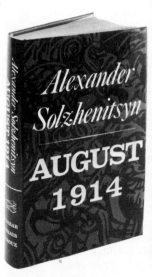

Nobelist Alexander Solzhenitsyn, shown (right) at memorial service for Alexander Tvardovsky in Moscow, awed critics with "August 1914," a novel about the fall of Imperial Russia.

Jorge Luis Borges' collection of stories "Doctor Brodie's Report" received an indifferent press.

St. Christopher who will be saved when he finds his master, his Christ, to bear.

The two best collections of short stories in 1972 were John Updike's *Museums and Women* and Donald Barthelme's *Sadness.* Updike is, most of the time, a realist who seems more at ease with short fiction than with novels. The stories in this collection are relaxed, graceful, often witty; over most of them hangs an elegant melancholy. Barthelme, by contrast, is a surrealist who relies on irony to reveal the banality of everyday life. His stories are very short, sometimes no more than fragments; when read with close attention, they reveal a mordant wit and an intriguing use of symbols.

Vladimir Nabokov and Jorge Luis Borges, the most distinguished living masters of fiction, each published two books during the year, one old and one new. Nabokov's *Glory* is one of his early novels now translated from the Russian, a pleasing if slight effort; *Transparent Things,* his first novel to be written in English since *Ada,* combines the familiar themes of his early work with the punning and elusive style of his recent books. The result is disappointing.

Borges' *A Universal History of Infamy,* first published in Argentina in 1935, contains brief stories that combine the economy, precise detail and fondness for violence and mystery that have brought Borges closer to the wellsprings

of narrative art than any other living writer. *Doctor Brodie's Report,* a collection of new stories, is simpler, seemingly more naive in approach; Borges says that he has now found his true style, but it is likely that he will be remembered for his more complex tales.

Biography. The year also saw the beginning of one impressive biography, the first volume of Cecil Woodham-Smith's *Queen Victoria,* the first to be based on family documents, and the conclusion of two others—the fifth volume of Leon Edel's *Henry James* and the fourth of James Thomas Flexner's *George Washington.* Edel's book, if overlong, is a truly literary biography—readable, perceptive of James' complexity, and in a Freudian way revisionist in its interpretation of James' life. Flexner's Washington is equally literary and scrupulous in its scholarship, though free of Freudian influence; in his pages, Washington emerges as an admirable but very human being—though some readers will be surprised by Flexner's stern views on Thomas Jefferson.

Other Nonfiction. Few inadvertent autobiographies are as entertaining as Dan H. Laurence's volumes of Bernard Shaw's *Collected Letters.* The second volume covers the years from 1898 to 1910, which saw many of Shaw's greatest plays—*Ceasar and Cleopatra, Man and Superman, Major Barbara* and *The Doctor's Dilemma* among them. Shaw's letters are better than the essays of lesser men. In them he courts actresses, lectures experts on their crafts, exhorts, insults, moralizes and aphorizes, insisting always on his own infallibility.

Elie Wiesel's *Souls on Fire* is an informal history of the great Hassidic Jewish masters about whom an oral tradition has developed. Anti-intellectuals, they insisted that "song is more precious than words, intention more important than formulas." A Jew, then, could come to God not only through adherence to the law, but through love of man. The masters themselves were often arrogant and argued with God, but they were witty and concerned with the suffering of their fellow Jews. Wiesel writes about them in part to keep their memory alive—which is for him a holy task.

Robert Craft's *Stravinsky: Chronicle of a Friendship* is a brilliant memoir of the 23 years Craft spent as an aide to the composer. One of the world's last great listeners, Craft recorded conversations between his master and such luminaries as Evelyn Waugh, W. H. Auden, T. S. Eliot and Aldous Huxley; he writes about Stravinsky with affection and admiration, and about the others with wit and sometimes malice. It is a long, entertaining and moving book.

Simone de Beauvoir, in *The Coming of Age,* examined at exhaustive length man's historical, literary and social attitudes toward old age—and found them depressing and dehumanizing. If De Beauvior's investigations are deficient in research among the old themselves, they are most impressive in many other disciplines; the book transcends its subject to touch on the nature of time, memory, the creative process and the organization and criticism of society.

In *The Best and the Brightest,* David Halberstam produced a staggeringly long and detailed study of the Presidents, Cabinet members and military men who led the United States into the Vietnam war. Beginning with the inauguration of President Kennedy (though looking back, at times, to Roosevelt) and ending with the advent of the Nixon administration, Halberstam analyzes, step by step, and with long digressions into the biographies of the participants, the way decisions are actually made in

David Halberstam rendered a telling account of U.S. warmaking in "The Best and the Brightest."

government and the assumptions and traditions of the men who make them. The result is an intelligent, critical and highly readable book, informed by a moral vision.

Poetry. The year saw the publication of what are probably the last collections of verse from two of America's best poets, both suicides—Sylvia Plath and John Berryman. The poems in *Winter Trees* date from the time of Plath's best collection, *Ariel.* They are, like most of her best work, extraordinarily condensed; the individual concrete images are sometimes better than the poems that contain them. Some reveal a bitter wit. Some are exclamatory; in some Plath is seen worrying about the deception she finds in the world. There is an occasional optimistic line ("The children leap in their cots"), and a few poems—for example, "Mystic"—show her at the height of her power, changing tones between stanzas as a musician changes keys. Her pessimism is often present: "Not this troublous/Wringing of hands," she writes, "this dark/Ceiling without a star."

Berryman's *Delusions, Etc.,* set in proof before he jumped from a bridge in Minneapolis, contains several hints of his desperate condition: "I faint for some soft & sudden way out," he writes in one poem, "as quiet as hemlock." And in another: "I don't feel this will change./I don't want any thing/or person, familiar or strange./I don't think I will sing/any more just now;/or ever." Although it is not clear whether Berryman regained his faith in God, some of the religious poems in this collection are quite effective, and one, commemorating the death of Dylan Thomas, is a masterpiece, one of the very best poems of our time.

The war in Vietnam produced two of the year's most effective books of verse. *Winning Hearts and Minds,* at first privately printed, is an anthology of war poems by veterans of Vietnam; taken together, they compose a striking indictment of the effects of the war—mechanized slaughter, the laceration of children, the impossibility of communicating what one really feels to the Vietnamese themselves. The poems are plain, blunt, unsophisticated, but terribly affecting. Michael Casey, whose work is included in this volume, published a collection of his own war verse, *Obscenities.* Casey writes with wit and an ear for soldiers' dialogue; each of his poems is a condensed short story. This, the most disparaged of all American wars, was a long time producing its own literature, but in the poems in these two volumes it may have found its first authentic literary voices.

PETER S. PRESCOTT
Book Review Editor, *Newsweek*

The 1972 Newbery Medal winner was "Mrs. Frisby and the Rats of NIMH," written by Robert C. O'Brien and illustrated by Zena Bernstein.

By permission of Atheneum Publishers

LITERATURE, JUVENILE

Only 2,150 new general trade books for children were announced for publication in the United States in 1972, a continuation of the downward trend in juvenile book production that began in 1969 with the cessation of Federally funded programs specifically for the purchase of books for school libraries. In his first administration, President Nixon vetoed two education appropriation bills, and inasmuch as education was not among the priorities included in his $30,000,000,000 revenue-sharing bill, the downward trend appeared unlikely to be reversed in his second administration. As 80–85 percent of the market for new children's books is in public school and public library purchasing, the buying power of any school and library funded by local, state or Federal tax revenues has a traceable effect on the sales of books for children and thus on the plans of the publishers who produce them.

The average price of new hardcover children's books in 1972 was more than $4.25. Moreover, printing, binding and distributing costs were rising and threatened to drive the price still higher. Children themselves, therefore, were considered unlikely to be able to buy hardcover books in quantity and were expected

to turn instead to the new juvenile paperbacks, the annual production of which had nearly doubled in five years—from 150 new paperback titles each year to more than 250. Four paperback book clubs dealt directly with classroom selection and sales—the only significant new factor in regular personal book buying by children in 50 years. However, the children's choices were restricted to the titles made available to them by the clubs, and children remained the readers without significant influence on publishers or distributors.

Adult interests are everywhere discernible in each year's new children's books. For instance, in the early 1960's adult concern for civil rights equality for blacks began a trend toward fuller, franker fiction and nonfiction accounts of the black experience, past and present, in the United States, and the number of good new titles reflecting this continuing social problem has continued to increase. By the end of the 1960's the concern had extended to other racial and ethnic minority groups and was swiftly reflected in every reading level among the books published for children.

Similarly, the feminist outcry against role stereotyping by sex, which had its widest publicity in 1970 and 1971, by 1972 already had effected a visible change in the picture books, fiction and biography being published for younger readers. Picture books showing boys and girls playing the same games became common, and their mothers were regularly pictured at other than household tasks. Juvenile novels depicting girls with career aspirations appeared in force, and biographies of outstanding women, always hitherto in short supply, could be found on almost every juvenile publisher's current list.

The exception to the rule that adult trends in literature dictate juvenile ones is to be found in the area of sex. Citizen groups across the United States, acting in strong opposition to sex education in the classroom, have made librarians and school teachers wary of using any book that might focus protests. While children's books themselves had attracted little attention by 1972, many adult books in junior high school and public library collections for minors had—with the result that court cases were brought for the books' removal.

Franker treatment of sex and sexuality nevertheless continues to characterize new novels for older children, such as June Jordan's *His Own Where* (out-of-wedlock pregnancy), Lynn Hall's *Sticks and Stones* (homosexuality) and Norma Klein's *Mom, the Wolf Man, and Me* (illegitimacy). Not the general value but the specific content in such books is the point at issue, and children's book specialists in library service and education are not in agreement about the validity of sex as a subject in children's books.

The prizes for children's books that continue to enjoy the most publicity are the Newbery and Caldecott Medals, awarded, respectively, by the American Library Association's Children's Services Division and the National Book Awards' children's book choice, sponsored by the Children's Book Council, Inc. Both 1972 award winners—shown in the accompanying table of recommended new juvenile titles— drew very little criticism from adult book selectors and proved popular with child readers, too.

LILLIAN N. GERHARDT
Editor in Chief, *School Library Journal*

NEWBERY MEDAL
Robert C. O'Brien, *Mrs. Frisby and the Rats of NIMH*

CALDECOTT MEDAL
Nonny Hogrogian, *One Fine Day*

NATIONAL BOOK AWARD
Donald Barthelme, *The Slightly Irregular Fire Engine*

FOR OLDER READERS
Leon Garfield, *The Ghost Downstairs*
Gail Graham, *Cross-Fire: a Vietnam Novel*
M. E. Kerr, *Dinkey Hocker Shoots Smack!*
Mildred Lee, *Fog*
Ursula K. Le Guin, *The Farthest Shore*
Julius Lester, *Long Journey Home: Stories from Black History*

FOR INTERMEDIATE READERS
Lloyd Alexander, illustrated by Lester Abrams, *The Four Donkeys*
Betsy C. Byars, *The House of Wings*
Eleanor Clymer, *Me and the Eggman*
Margaret Hodges, *When Hitler Stole Pink Rabbit*
Georgess McHargue, *The Impossible People*
Johanna Reiss, *The Upstairs Room*

FOR YOUNGEST READERS
Margaret Wise Brown, illustrated by the author, *The Runaway Bunny*
Amy Ehrlich, illustrated by Robert Andrew Parker, *Zeek Silver Moon*
Russell Hoban, illustrated by Lillian Hoban, *Egg Thoughts and Other Frances Songs*
Arnold Lobel, illustrated by the author, *Frog and Toad Together*
Arlene Mosel, illustrated by Blair Lent, *The Funny Little Woman*
Yuri Suhl, illustrated by Margot Zemach, *Simon Boom Gives a Wedding*
Judith Viorst, illustrated by Ray Cruz, *Alexander and the Terrible, Horrible, No Good, Very Bad Day*
Charlotte Zolotow, illustrated by William Pène du Bois, *William's Doll*

"The Slightly Irregular Fire Engine," written and illustrated by Donald Barthelme, won the National (children's) Book Award.

Reprinted with the permission of Farrar, Straus, Giroux

Nonny Hogrogian won her second Caldecott Medal for "One Fine Day." Inspired by an Armenian folktale, it is the story of a greedy fox.
The Macmillan Company

LUXEMBOURG

Luxembourg, with a political and economic weight in the EEC much greater than its population of 345,000 suggests, maintained its policy of diversifying its economy in order to lessen its dependence on steel. The country's generous fiscal policies continued to make finance and banking (with concentration on unit trusts, holding companies and the Eurodollar market) the fastest growing sector of the economy in terms of employment. There were no fewer than 2,780 holding companies in the grand duchy in 1972. They were attracted from all over the world by the absence of a capital gains tax for foreigners and a very small stamp duty.

The Social Christian–Liberal coalition was due to stay in office until elections scheduled for 1974. In September, Luxembourg's first and only woman minister, Madame Madeleine Frieden-Kinnen, was forced to resign following accusations that she had witnessed two young men, one of whom was a Catholic priest, swimming nude in an artificial lake. She was minister of family and youth affairs, social solidarity, public health and cultural affairs.

RICHARD NORTON-TAYLOR
Foreign Correspondent
The Guardian, Manchester and London

MALAYSIA

On balance, 1972 was a good year for Malaysia. The nation continued its remarkable political and economic recovery from the frightening race riots of May 1969. Indications of economic health included a fairly steady growth rate of the gross national product (GNP), declining unemployment, stable prices, diversification of exports, a growing balance-of-payments surplus, foreign currency reserves equivalent to more than 80 percent of Malaysian currency in circulation and a rising per-capita national income. This was achieved in the face of unfavorable market prices for Malaysia's two principal exports, rubber and tin. It made Malaysia highly attractive to foreign investors and earned it an expression of confidence from the World Bank, which pledged future loans of at least $150,000,000 annually.

The second five-year plan (1971–75) aims at a 6.5 percent annual growth of the GNP, a doubling of industrial production and the creation of 600,000 jobs. All of these objectives appear to be attainable. The plan also is designed to encourage Malays to escape the low-income sector of the economy by participating in commercial and industrial enterprise. Despite its focus on the Malays, the plan pledges an attack on poverty, irrespective of race, and seeks to reassure the Chinese and Indian communities that they will continue to have an opportunity to earn and retain a stake in the nation's prosperity. Indications were that the plan had been accepted by non-Malays.

Politically, the ruling Alliance party—composed of the United Malay Nationalist Organization, the Malayan Chinese Association (MCA) and the Malayan Indian Congress (MIC)—further strengthened its already pre-eminent position. The Alliance handily won

UPI

Malaysia's economy continued to improve in 1972. Particularly in the capital city of Kuala Lumpur (l), unemployment declined, prices became more stable and the per capita income began to increase.

two important by-elections, and there were also several defections from the opposition. These included two members of parliament from the Democratic Action party, who joined the MCA component of the alliance. The MIC, however, was riven by a leadership split. In Perak the Alliance entered a coalition government with an opposition party enjoying non-Malay support—thus repeating a pattern previously established in Sarawak and Penang.

In foreign policy, Malaysia continued to press its proposal for a neutralization of Southeast Asia guaranteed by the United States, the Soviet Union and China. Malaysia welcomed U.S. President Nixon's visit to Peking, but it had no immediate plans to extend diplomatic recognition to China. Contacts between the two countries were confined largely to trade, and China agreed to increase its already substantial purchases of Malaysian rubber, palm oil and timber. Malaysian delegations attended the Canton Trade Fair in April 1972. Distinguished visitors to Malaysia included Queen Elizabeth II, Prime Minister Lee Kuan Yew of Singapore, Prime Minister McMahon of Australia and the foreign minister of Bangladesh.

MARVIN C. OTT
Assistant Professor of Political Science
Mount Holyoke College

MALTA

On March 26, after nine months of intense bargaining, Malta and Britain signed a seven-year defense agreement, thereby ending a military, economic and political crisis in the Mediterranean.

The crisis had blown up in 1971 when Prime Minister Dom Mintoff, whose Labour party governs the island by one vote in parliament, claimed that Britain was paying too little for the right to maintain a military presence on Malta. He ordered Britain to raise its $13,000,000 annual defense payment to $78,000,000 or withdraw all troops by Dec. 31, 1971.

Mintoff twice extended the deadline for Britain's withdrawal while bargaining went on in Valetta (Malta's capital), Rome and London. Almost all of the 3,100 British troops had left by the time the new treaty was signed. Under its terms, Britain agreed to restore the 3,100-man force to the island and, along with its NATO partners, to pay Malta $36,400,000 yearly. The United States' share was $9,000,000. The treaty also stipulated that the Soviet Union and other members of the Warsaw Pact were barred from using the island's facilities. By mid-May the British troops were moving back on the island.

Alain Dejean, Gamma

Following a March agreement, 3,100 British troops were returned to the island of Malta.

The resolution of the defense agreement was a personal triumph for Mintoff, who was attempting to rescue Malta from serious financial difficulties. At the start of the year government figures had shown Malta floundering under a $132,600,000 trade deficit, with foreign debts totaling $28,600,000. Adding to the crisis was the fact that Malta has almost no industry or important minerals.

In the 1973 budget, anticipated revenue exceeded spending by about $10,000,000, but Mintoff estimated that the surplus would not be enough to solve the island's economic ills. He resorted therefore to foreign aid. In April, after returning from a trip to China, he announced that Peking had extended $42,600,000 in loans and aid. He also announced a $5,000,000 loan by the United States.

Domestically, Mintoff's quest for revenue entailed increasing taxes on a wide range of consumer goods. His 1973 budget also abolished special tax benefits for foreigners, who had been lured to Malta by low taxes and prices.

CHARLES W. BELL
Former Manager for Italy
United Press International

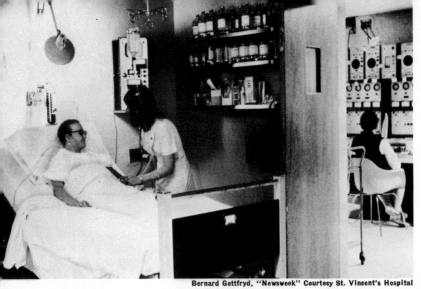

Hospital emergency units received additional attention in medical circles in 1972. Centers equipped with electrocardiograph monitors and coronary-care units can save the lives of patients with possibly fatal heart attacks.

MEDICINE

A 12-year-old girl named Collette and a 15-year-old boy named Colin made important medical news in 1972 by defying apparently hopeless prognoses. The girl suffered from cystic fibrosis, the boy from a growth hormone deficiency that once would have condemned him to be a midget.

Cystic Fibrosis. By all odds, Collette should have died in 1970 from the terminal stage of her disease, a hereditary ailment that fatally undermines the lungs and digestive system. Nevertheless, Collette was alive and apparently well at the end of 1972—one of a significant number of cystic fibrosis victims on both sides of the Atlantic whose lives have been spared by a new regimen of therapy.

Collette is one of 17 cystic fibrosis patients under the care of Dr. James Allan, a pediatrician in Macclesfield, England. Her illness was diagnosed when she was an infant, and her physicians estimated that she—and approximately 500 other British children condemned by the same diagnosis that year—would not survive her teens or early 20's.

When Collette was nine, Dr. Allan had her admitted to a local hospital, ostensibly for the last time because, in his words, "She was a physical wreck with advanced lung changes." She weighed 41 pounds. Her parents, exhausted and despairing, asked that the doctor "just let her die."

Dr. Allan's treatment involved both chemotherapy and, more importantly, a new look at diet and a switch of emphasis in trying to understand the causation of the disease. The diet, which represents ten years of research by Dr. Allan, consists of a beef serum extract, a particular type of glucose, certain fats in a specific form, a standard mineral mixture and vitamins. The beef extract has a precise composition of amino acids (the building blocks of protein), and this part of the diet is "tailored" to the patient's specific needs.

Its effect on Collette was dramatic. She left the hospital eight weeks later, and at the age of 12, in late 1972, she weighed more than 70 pounds and required little medical care.

In the meantime, Dr. Allan had presented a paper to a closed medical group in Manchester. In it, he discussed his work with Collette and his other patients, whose ages ranged from five months to 20 years. Dr. Helen Berry, assistant professor of research pediatrics at Cincinnati University, was persuaded. She and her colleagues subsequently used the diet, with some modifications, on more than 20 U.S. patients, aged two to eighteen years. At the end of 1972 her correspondence with Dr. Allan indicated results similar to his own plus a widespread interest in the diet in the United States.

The main point of scientific interest is Dr. Allan's contention that his findings produced a shift of emphasis from one organ of digestion to another—from the pancreas to the small intestine. Treatment has usually centered on the pancreas, but Dr. Allan believes the basic trouble may lie in the small intestine—that the failure of absorption and the fatal nutritional pattern may actually begin there.

Cancer. The fatal pattern of cancer in all its forms continued to resist the pressure of meticulous research around the world. Limited success or the promise of it, however, rewarded the efforts of some researchers.

The conservative approach of Drs. Roger Barnes and Abraham Ninan of Glendale, Calif., in the treatment of cancer of the prostate, a gland in the male reproductive system, appeared to have yielded good results. Their findings suggest that total removal of the gland may be unnecessary.

Barnes and Ninan initially had reviewed the histories of 136 patients who had been considered for radical treatment but who instead were given one milligram a day of a drug known as diethyl-stilbestrol. The patients underwent minor surgery to prevent obstruction of the urethra by the swelling gland, but nothing more radical.

More than half survived ten or more years and of 108 diagnosed 15 or more years previously, more than 30 were alive in late 1972—most of them in good health.

Meanwhile, in London, Dr. Kurt Hellman, continued to be enthusiastic about the potential of his discovery, drug ICRF-159. Dr. Hellman, head of the chemotherapy department at the Imperial Cancer Research Fund, and his colleagues have moved their research from mice to men, and the drug is now undergoing intensive clinical trials. Basically it is a strong antimitotic (it inhibits cell division). ICRF-159 also maximizes the effect of some other drugs, particularly those which synchronize cell division. It has also been shown to have an unusual antimetastatic effect—prevents spreading. Furthermore, evidence is accumulating that it may sensitize cells to radiotherapy.

Commenting on chemistry's international attack on cancer, Dr. Hellman said: "It is in a very exciting state at the moment. Many new avenues are opening up. . . . We are just beginning to see some of the light and logic in the way we treat cancer."

At the Medical Research Council unit in Newcastle General Hospital in northeast England an early warning test was developed. It was based on the detection in cancer patients of sensitized lymphocytes (white blood cells). This would not, in itself, give any clues as to the spread or site of the tumor, but it might reveal the presence of cancer cells perhaps seven or more years before there were obvious symptoms. If the initial research findings hold good, the test could lead to possible immunization against cancer.

Heart Disease. More than 1,000,000 Americans suffered heart attacks in 1972. In addition, the percentage of heart attacks among younger men (25–44 years) had increased 14 percent since 1950, and about 25 percent of those who died from coronaries in 1972 were under 65 years of age.

Several steps were taken during the year to counteract the trend. Across the United States,

A patient at a Peking hospital undergoes acupuncture. The instruction model (below, r), on exhibit at Peking's Museum of Chinese History, shows major points of acupuncture named for the governing organs.

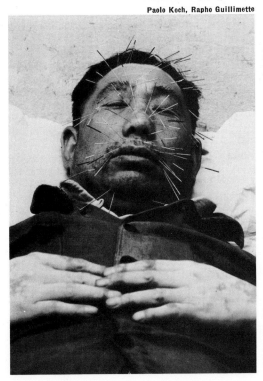 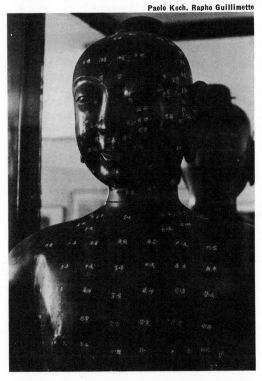

more and more hospital emergency units were being equipped with portable electrocardiograph monitors and coronary-care units to detect and treat the early stages of heart attacks. New surgical techniques—including the saphenous vein transplant and installation of a completely artificial heart, powered by atomic energy—and new drugs were also being studied. Furthermore, President Nixon signed a bill calling for a three-year, $1,300,000,000 program to fight heart and lung disease, and named Dr. John S. Millis, president and director of the National Fund for Medical Education, chairman of an 18-member President's Panel on Heart Disease.

Acupuncture. The ancient Chinese technique of acupuncture, a type of therapy based on the insertion of needles in various parts of the body, was under investigation in the United States and elsewhere in 1972. In fact several U.S. medical institutions, as well as the U.S. National Institutes of Health, were studying acupuncture as a possible anesthetic, therapeutic device and pain reliever.

Abortion. There was little doubt in the minds of gynecologists that many women were just beginning their demand for abortion, particularly in Britain. In fact abortion news continued to make headlines. Efforts to repeal New York State's liberal abortion law failed, and Connecticut's new anti-abortion law was undergoing examination in the courts. During 1971 there had been 262,807 abortions in New York State. The majority of the women were under 25 and more than 25 percent were under 20.

Harvey Karman, a Los Angeles psychologist, pioneered the two-minute, two instrument abortion: a plastic speculum and a cannula with suction being employed to remove the contents of the uterus during very early pregnancy.

Influenza. As winter and possible influenza time approached, there was hope that a new, live virus vaccine would be marketed in time for the next onslaught. It was formed from a genetically defective Asian flu virus of the 1965 type "mated" in the laboratory with the 1968 Hong Kong virus. The result, according to preliminary reports from clinical tests at the U.S. National Institute of Allergy and Infectious Diseases, was a live viral agent which, while protecting people against the latest type of influenza, did not damage their lungs.

Mentally Handicapped. In Britain there was a conference on the mentally handicapped—by the mentally handicapped. All the delegates were from hospitals, hostels or special home care centers and had a lot to say about their work, environments, pay, relations with each other and with the staff. Suggestions were well

articulated, and changes are likely to follow.

Dropsy. Doctors from the Indian Council of Medical Research at Hyderabad, India, were extremely concerned at what they described as a resurgence of epidemic dropsy in the Subcontinent. While recurrent epidemics of dropsy were reported as far back as 1878, no outbreak had been reported since the early 1950's. Consequently the disease was no longer considered a public health problem.

Authorities placed the blame for the resurgence on the contamination of edible oils—such as that made from sesame seeds. The contaminant, they said, was argemone oil, which is believed to cause the disease.

Diabetes. And how much remains to be learned about diabetes? Dr. Marvin Tile of St. Joseph's Hospital in Toronto, Canada, believes that some of the so-called typical slipped discs may be caused by diabetes in its latent stage. He had several patients in whom disc pain was the first sign of a diabetic state. Accordingly, he suggested to other doctors that they might consider a glucose tolerance test on some of their more puzzling disc patients—at least to discount the possibility of diabetes.

Mercury Poisoning. In Scotland, a lock of poet Robert Burns' hair rested in a Glasgow Laboratory helping medical scientists to chart part of the history of pollution. Using a technique known as activation analysis—irradiating the whole sample and separating its constituents—Dr. John Lenihan showed that Burns died with more than twice as much mercury in his hair as that found, on average, in today's human hair.

Did the poet die of mercury poisoning? If he did, the doctors of his time almost certainly killed him, as mercury was a common treatment for a variety of ailments. If he did not, what was the source of the mercury? Dr. Lenihan and his colleagues were still looking for the answer at the year's end.

Hormone Treatment. And finally, there was the story of Colin, who was born without pituitary growth hormone and became the first child in Britain to undergo continuous hormone treatment to enable him to grow normally. It appeared to be an unusual success story.

The treatment, at London's Great Ormond Street Hospital, started just after Colin's sixth birthday. In 1972 he was 15 and, on the basis of skeletal maturity estimation, is expected to reach an adult height of about five feet, five inches. His therapy—already longer than that of any child in the world—will continue throughout adolescence.

See also Drug Abuse; Health.

PETER BROCK
News Editor, *World Medicine*

METEOROLOGY

During 1972 the atmosphere served as a focus of both global and domestic efforts to preserve and improve the world environment.

International Meteorology. In June representatives of 113 nations met in Stockholm, Sweden, for the first United Nations Conference on the Human Environment. The delegates, among other actions, approved a plan to monitor changes in the atmosphere and proposed that studies be made, not only of human responsibility for such changes, but also of the influence of these variations on man. The conference also approved the establishment of a network of weather stations to determine the global extent of air pollution and its potential impact on the world's climate.

Intimately linked to these proposals was the existing World Weather Program, which had completed an initial four-year phase at the end of 1971. Plans for the period 1972–75, as coordinated by the World Meteorological Organization, included extension of existing weather-observing networks, establishment of a new generation of weather satellites equipped to make vertical temperature soundings of the atmosphere, improvement of methods of weather prediction by computer and increased meteorological aid to developing nations.

Air Pollution. A 20 percent increase in the carbon dioxide component of the earth's atmosphere by the year 2000 was predicted by Dr. Lester Machta of the National Oceanic and Atmospheric Administration's (NOAA) Air Resources Laboratory. Carbon dioxide is one of the normal constituents of the atmosphere, and when nature is in equilibrium, it is generated by animals and decaying plants at about the same rate as it is used by green plants during their growth processes. However, the massive burning of coal, gas and oil in recent years has upset this natural balance. The imbalance, in the absence of other influences, tends to raise the temperature of the lower atmosphere. Thus, the increase in carbon dioxide content predicted by Dr. Machta might exert a significant effect on the global climate in future years.

For the more immediate future, Dr. Freeman Hall of NOAA's Wave Propagation Laboratory has developed a device that can provide continuous measurement of temperature inversions, those layers of warm air which trap and concentrate air pollutants. By using a special instrument that emits high-frequency sound waves vertically into the lower atmosphere and then records the "echo" returned by the temperature inversion, observers can determine the height and intensity of the warm air mass. Because the measurements can be continuously monitored, scientists believe the technique can help to provide better warnings of potentially critical atmospheric conditions so that steps can be taken to curb the emission of polluting material.

Weather Modification. During the summer an experiment was conducted over eastern Colorado in an attempt to suppress lightning strokes, which cause 70 percent of the forest fires in the western United States. The study was directed by Dr. Heinz Kasemir of NOAA's Atmospheric Physics and Chemistry Laboratory. Thunderstorms were "seeded" from aircraft with aluminized strips which tend to make the air conduct an electrical current more readily, thus avoiding the massive build-up of electric charge that produces the lightning stroke. While some foresters contend that such lightning-caused fires are necessary to preserve the ecological balance, others point out the desirability of deferring such fires during hazardous weather conditions to periods when they can be more easily controlled.

On Nov. 1 a Federal law went into effect requiring all weather modification activities in the United States to be reported to the secretary of commerce. The purpose of the new law is to create a source of weather modification information, and to help avoid scientific and geographic duplication of effort.

Severe Weather Warnings. Spurred by the flash floods of hurricane Camille, which caused the deaths of more than 150 persons in Virginia in 1969, the National Weather Service began installing a new flood warning system in 1972. The system consists of a water-level sensor located upstream on a river and an alarm signal situated downstream in a firehouse, police station or other continuously-manned emergency center. When the alarm is triggered by rising water, the public is warned by emergency radio and television broadcasts and police or civil defense sirens, according to a prearranged community plan. One such system was installed during the year at Wheeling, W. Va., and others are planned for critical river locations in Maine, New Jersey, Virginia, the Carolinas and Ohio.

In June the National Weather Service, together with other public safety organizations, joined in a campaign to urge the use of cables anchored in concrete to prevent damage to mobile homes by severe winds. Because mobile homes are considerably lighter than most conventional houses, gusts from even severe thunderstorms can overturn them, inflicting injury or even death on those inside. Experts believe that proper "tie-down" cables would prevent 50 percent to 70 percent of such casualties.

Extensive rains took 250 lives in the Philippines in August. In the town of Bay, children innocently enjoy the disastrous flooding.

Weather Highlights. The year began with generally fair weather prevailing over most of the United States, but by the end of the first week heavy snow had fallen over the Pacific Northwest and the northern Rockies. Strong winds accompanied the storm along the east slopes of the Rockies, and on Jan. 11–12 gales in the Boulder, Colo., region caused damage in excess of $1,000,000. As the disturbance moved eastward, snow spread over the Mississippi and Ohio valleys to the eastern seaboard. Cold weather followed in the wake of the storm, with temperatures dropping to a record −53° F. at Moose Lake, Minn., on Jan. 15. Heavy rains during the third week of the month caused damaging floods in western Washington and Oregon. Cold wintry weather prevailed over most of Canada, and an unusual outbreak of sub-freezing temperatures in faraway Iran near the end of the month stranded thousands of travelers and caused 14 deaths.

February began with a major storm that spread heavy snow over much of the eastern third of the United States. Deep drifts blocked highways over the Appalachian mountains, and helicopters supplied food to and evacuated injured persons from remote areas. By contrast, in southern California, Los Angeles recorded no precipitation whatever during the month, making it the driest February in 73 years. On the night of Feb. 26 heavy rains in West Virginia burst a coal slag dam on Buffalo Creek; hundreds of persons were reported drowned or missing, and many homes were destroyed. Elsewhere, snowstorms and strong winds battered much of Italy on the 19th, causing an avalanche that destroyed the village of Champorcher near the French border. An Indian Ocean cyclone (hurricane) caused more than 50 deaths in the Malagasy Republic.

In March heavy rains fell along the northern Pacific coast of the United States, but central and southern California, Arizona and most of Nevada remained dry. Thunderstorms spawned a series of tornadoes in the Mississippi Valley, and a trailer park at Ozark, Ala., was wiped out during the first week of the month. Unseasonably warm weather, which produced ex-

tensive melting of snow, caused flooding in North Dakota. In Canada, Pacific storms brought heavy rains to western British Columbia.

A late winter storm produced heavy snow in the northern Great Plains during the first week of April. Snow drifts and icy highways stalled automobile traffic and closed schools in the Dakotas, Minnesota and Wisconsin. On April 5 a rare tornado struck Vancouver, Wash., killing six persons and causing damage estimated at $6,000,000. In the middle of the month a storm over the Southwest drove 60 mile-per-hour winds over the desert areas of California and Arizona, while blizzards raged in Nevada, Utah, Colorado and Wyoming.

May was a rainy month in the eastern United States, but drought conditions persisted in California and much of the Southwest. A cloudburst north of New Braunfels, Tex., on the night of May 11 caused a flash flood that drowned 25 persons and resulted in damage exceeding $15,000,000. Tornadoes and severe thunderstorms occurred in the Dakotas, Minnesota and Iowa on the 24th, and baseball-sized hailstones fell in Mississippi on the 25th. Generally seasonable weather, however, prevailed over Canada. In Chile antarctic storms during the first week of the month left more than 15,000 persons homeless as floods devastated much of the southern part of the country.

In June two disastrous storms occurred in the United States. On June 10 a flash flood in the Rapid City area of North Dakota killed 235 persons and caused damage estimated at more than $100,000,000. On June 17 heavy rains again sent floodwaters surging through the area, adding to the damage and resulting in one additional death. During the period June 19–24 hurricane Agnes deposited heavy rains on the eastern United States, causing severe flooding in northern Virginia, Pennsylvania and New York. The death toll was 122, and property damage totaled $3,500,000,000. On the night of June 7 heavy rains in the Caucasus Mountains unleashed floods in Tbilisi, U.S.S.R., leaving thousands of citizens homeless, while torrential rains in the British crown colony of Hong Kong in mid-June resulted in the deaths of more than 100 persons and the destruction of thousands of homes.

Typical summer weather prevailed over the United States in July and August. During the third week of July the eastern third of the nation suffered a prolonged heat spell, accompanied by severe air pollution, but showers and thunderstorms alleviated the problem by the end of the month. Southern California, which had not had rainfall since early spring, experienced welcome showers in August. Elsewhere, the Philippine island of Luzon was declared a disaster area on July 13 as typhoon and monsoon rains brought death to 250 persons and left more than 800,000 homeless. Japan also suffered from the rains, which resulted in a death toll there estimated at 300. On Aug. 11 a rare tornado killed two persons and injured more than 100 in the Netherlands, and during the last week of the month heavy rains in South Korea caused more than 300 deaths and millions of dollars in damage.

During the first week of September tropical storm Carrie moved northward off the U.S. East Coast, drenching New England with more than ten inches of rain. Frost began to appear in the northern United States by mid-month, and snow was reported in southern Canada and the Cascade mountains of the United States as the month ended. In the western Pacific typhoon Helen struck Japan on the weekend of Sept. 15–17, causing more than 50 deaths, destroying more than 100 buildings and sinking several fishing vessels.

October brought typical fall weather to the United States. Snow fell in Montana early in the month, and sub-freezing temperatures were common from the northern Great Plains eastward to New England by mid-month. Heavy rains fell in Arizona and New Mexico on the 5th and 6th, and rain and strong winds lashed the northern Pacific Coast during the last week of the month. Elsewhere, typhoon Bebe swept the Fiji Islands on Oct. 25, leaving 13 persons dead and 3,000 homeless, and near the end of the month heavy rains caused severe losses to the Yugoslavian wheat crop.

November was unusually stormy in the United States. A severe downpour (with snow upstate) drenched New York City on the 8th, crippling air and highway traffic. During the second week of the month a major storm system swept eastward from the Pacific coast, through the Rockies and Great Plains to the East Coast. Snow and rain, accompanied by gale winds, blocked highways, flooded low-lying areas and caused millions of dollars in damage along the entire path of the storm. Unusually high waves flooded beach areas of the Great Lakes, and the year-long drought in California was ended. During the same period, western Europe suffered one of the most severe storms of the century. Winds of 125 miles per hour were recorded, and at least 64 persons in seven countries died as a result.

JACK C. THOMPSON
Professor of Meteorology
California State University, San Jose

President Echeverria shuns remoteness and mingles with the masses at the National Anthropology Museum to celebrate Women's Day.

MEXICO

While the Mexican economy had boomed during the late 1960's, it was less buoyant in 1972. The gross national product in 1971 had increased by only 4 percent, well below the 7 percent annual growth rate of the 1960's, and 1972 was not much better. The government claimed to be favorable to capital, but in fact, President Luis Echeverria represented a relatively leftist group within the Partido Revolucionario Institucional (PRI). The government announced the nationalization of Telefonos de Mexico.

Dissidence and repression were rife. Peasants in Acapulco seethed with resentment over the government's failure to compensate them for land taken to make way for real estate developments. Mexican guerrilla leader Genary Vasquez Rojas was killed, allegedly when his car crashed west of Mexico City. Part of the

unrest in Mexico was stimulated by an idealized concept of Aztec society, similar to the cult of Tupac Amaru (Tupamaros) in South America or Aztlan among the Chicanos of the United States. A small group of fanatics was working toward the destruction of the republic and the restoration of the Aztec empire. A guerrilla leader wrote from the state of Guerrero to *Siempre* magazine, saying the struggle would continue. Unrest was evident at several universities. At the University of Sinaloa in Culiacan one student was killed and 100 arrested. A Mexican Boeing 727 airliner was hijacked to Havana by a group claiming to represent an underground Mexican guerrilla movement.

The official PRI has a stranglehold on Mexican politics; it has elected all of Mexico's 29 state governors, all of the 60 senators and all of the 178 directly elected members of the lower

house of Congress. (Minority parties are given a small, fixed number of seats.) It was, therefore, a shock when the city of Tampico elected a member of the Popular Socialist party, a Marxist group, mayor. Disturbed by the obvious lack of popular support for the PRI, President Echeverria vowed to revive the revolutionary principles of men like Emiliano Zapata; he subsequently doubled the amount to be spent on agricultural projects. Following the President's lead, the annual assembly of the PRI attempted to pose a genuinely revolutionary party and denounced "the imperialist threat."

The year marked the centennial of the death of Benito Juarez, the symbol of militant liberalism and socialism. In order to stress the PRI's claim to be heir to the Juarez tradition, the government proclaimed 1972 the "Year of Juarez." President Echeverria traveled repeatedly throughout the countryside in an effort to bring the government's message to the people. In the mountain village of Guelatao (near Oaxaca), where Juarez was born, he delivered titles to more than 1,000,000 acres of land to communal farmers. The government also announced a plan to double-track the railroad from Salina Cruz to Coatzacoalcos to permit the rapid transit of containerized goods from the Pacific to the Atlantic. The hope was that this would revitalize the entire Tehuantepec Isthmus area.

In other parts of the country similar activities were under way. The National Commission for Arid Zones (CONZA) was active in attempts to develop the northern deserts, where the rural poor live in abject poverty. A series of fiscal incentives was used to stimulate the establishment of industries outside of the Mexico City, Guadalajara and Monterrey areas. The government made a special effort to develop Baja California and the west. A major steel plant was planned at the mouth of the Balsas River, some 11 miles from the iron ore deposits at Las Truchas in the state of Michoacan.

As part of its plan to win popular support the government increased taxes on the highest incomes from 32 percent to more than 40 percent. It proposed to liberalize the constitution by reforming certain articles. A new agency, the National Housing Fund (FONAVI), was created to carry out public housing schemes.

A cause of deep unrest in Mexico was rapid population growth, resulting in economic pressures and unemployment. A World Bank population study predicted that by the year 2000 the country's inhabitants, about 53,000,000 in 1972, might number a staggering 130,000,000. The Mexican government had hitherto been openly scornful of control schemes, but in the light of the evidence, it changed its attitude and announced a program of family planning.

President Echeverria visited the United States in June, and the results were regarded as positive but not impressive. The U.S. Department of Commerce opened a trade center in Mexico City to promote U.S. exports. However, in order not to antagonize Mexican producers, only such products as the Mexicans themselves do not manufacture are to be shown. At the same time there were signs that Mexico would be less cordial to U.S. investments. In view of the fact that the country already had a negative trade balance with the United States, there was resentment over the application to Mexico by the Nixon administration of the 10 percent surtax on imports. There was also resentment over the smuggling of Mexican art treasures into the United States, and the government implemented strict controls to halt the outflow.

Although formal ties with Cuba were maintained, there was no cordiality in the relations, as Castro was suspected of being behind Mexican unrest. One indication of coolness was Cuba's closing of *Prensa Latina*, the Cuban news service in Mexico City; the Mexican government had steadfastly refused to allow a Cuban national to serve as manager. However, a Cuban trade mission did effect an agreement for direct bilateral trade. Following the expulsion from Mexico of five Soviet embassy officials in 1971, relations with the U.S.S.R. remained cool; the Soviets, too, were thought to be encouraging revolutionary leaders.

Mexican trade with Japan grew steadily. Japan became Mexico's second-largest customer and fourth-largest supplier. The government encouraged trade with Japan in order to reduce its deficit and its dependence on the United States. President Echeverria visited Japan in March, and hundreds of Mexican and Japanese businessmen crossed the Pacific. Japanese investment was especially heavy on the west coast of Mexico. The two countries signed an air agreement providing for Aeromexico and Japanese Airlines to fly between Mexico City and Tokyo, with stopovers in the United States or Canada.

The so-called Estrada Doctrine requires that Mexico recognize all de facto governments; it has been disregarded notoriously in the cases of Franco Spain and Communist China. Nevertheless, following the Nixon visit to Peking, Mexico broke with Taiwan and recognized the mainland. It even tried to promote trade with China and sent a commercial mission to the Canton Trade Fair, which resulted in the sale

A Mayan stone carving offers Tokyo residents a vivid glimpse of Mexico's rich cultural heritage.

of $1,500,000 worth of cotton. China bought several hundred Mexican-made automobiles. However, there was resentment that Peking failed to respond adequately to Mexican overtures.

RONALD HILTON
Executive Director
California Institute of International Studies

MONGOLIAN PEOPLE'S REPUBLIC

Some important shifts in the political leadership of the People's Republic of Mongolia occurred in 1972. For the most part they involved state positions, a result of changes made in the Mongolian People's Revolutionary Party (MPRP) at its congress in November 1971. Many of the changes were dictated by a need to deal with the country's pressing industrial and agricultural problems. Some shifts, however, occurred because of the death on May 20 of the president of the People's Republic, Jamsrangiyn Sambuu.

When the People's Great Hural (Mongolia's parliament) met in June, no one was named to fill the presidential vacancy. It is assumed that in time the presidency will be filled by Premier Yumjaagiyn Tsedenbal. Meanwhile, Tsedenbal's close colleague Sonomyn Luvsan was named to a newly-created post of first vice president and thus serves as acting president. Four other important changes, involving the

Council of Ministers, were made during the June session. Dunjmaagiyn Dorjgotov, former ambassador to Warsaw, was named minister of trade and procurement. Deputy Chairman of the Council and Acting Minister of Culture Tsevegjavyn Puntsagnorov was delegated to represent Mongolia at the United Nations. Professor Dondogiyn Tsevegmid, chairman of the People's Great Hural and rector of the state university, was named to replace Puntsagnorov, and, finally, Sereeteriyn Purevjav obtained the chairmanship of the State Committee for Information, Radio and Television, an important propaganda post.

At the root of these changes were troubling economic considerations. Mongolia, in its fifth five-year plan, had a recent history of heavy livestock losses and failure of factories to fulfill their goals. Although the country hopes to increase its industrialization, the details of the current five-year plan (1971–1975) that became available showed that agriculture continues to be emphasized. A total of $475,000,-000 is to be invested in the agricultural sector during the plan period, while only $300,000,-000 is earmarked for industrial development. Only mining appeared to be receiving special attention. The country expects mining to grow by 150 percent during the present plan period and minerals to become an increasingly important export item.

ARTHUR C. MILLER
Senior Editor, *The Asia Letter*

MOTION PICTURES

The year 1972 witnessed the complete recovery of the American motion picture industry from the "Graduate-Easy Rider" syndrome that had, at the decade's beginning, caused a rash of wildly executed films aimed at duplicating the bonanzas reaped by *Graduate* director Mike Nichols and by Dennis Hopper and Peter Fonda with their cheaply made motorcycle epic. Exuding the somewhat gamey aroma of the young, these films were characterized by an emphasis on youth-in-rebellion, sex, nudity, foul language, drugs and bizarre and intrusive camera work. And although few of them made any significant money, the influence they represented survived another year in a second series that changed the "now" of the first to "then."

This group, usually reflecting the recollections of older men, also concentrated on adolescent agony, sex, nudity and four-letter words—for example, *Red Sky at Morning, Summer of '42, The Go-Between* (a British import) and Mr. Nichols' *Carnal Knowledge.* But the rebellion motif, with its concomitant clamor, was replaced by nostalgia, the films appealing as much to the middle-aged as to the under-30 crowd. They were thus better patronized and, in the case of at least two—Peter Bogdanovich's *Last Picture Show* and Italian director Vittorio De Sica's *Garden of the Finzi Continis*—they achieved a degree of artistry acknowledged in the 1971 Academy Awards.

By the time the awards were made, in the spring of 1972, another trend clearly was in the making. *The Godfather,* biggest grosser since the mawkishly contrived *Love Story,* contained a minimum of sex and nudity. Moreover, the technique employed by director Francis Ford Coppola and Mario Puzo, who adapted the screenplay from his best-selling novel, was so conventional that it seemed old-fashioned.

To underscore the shift in public interest, reissues of *The Graduate* and *Easy Rider* failed to provoke a stampede to the box office, and two separately made productions by the creators of the latter—Hopper's *Last Movie* and Fonda's *Hired Hand*—died ingloriously. Admittedly, Stanley Kubrick's *Clockwork Orange* and Sam Peckinpah's *Straw Dogs* (both released in late 1971) seemed to indicate a still-large audience for youth-slanted erotic material flamboyantly treated. But the real focus of both—like that of *The Godfather* and the Academy Award-winning *French Connection* of the previous year—was violence. And it was violence, combined in many cases with nudity and explicit sex, that in 1972 supplanted youth, both "now" and "then," as the industry's most saleable commodity.

The public's hunger for violence could be discerned in its response not only to such big-budget items as *The Godfather, Straw Dogs,* and *Clockwork Orange,* but also to low-budget horror epics and an increasing number of productions intended for the burgeoning black market. Two of the latter—*Slaughter,* starring James Brown, and *Super Fly*—occupied prominent places (the latter, third from the top) on *Variety*'s weekly list of the 50 top-grossing films.

Super Fly, a jazzy but tedious examination of the vicissitudes of a Harlem cocaine-pusher, was made without benefit of either name actor or notable investment on the part of its allegedly all-black backers. Thus the hordes storming the doors wherever it appeared (actually breaking down one in New York) are certain to be taken into consideration by all fat-cat producers and bring about a deluge of similar atrocities in the future.

The *Variety* list on which this film placed third, with an 11-week take exceeding $4,500,-000, was headed by *The New Centurions,* a fictional inquiry into the activities of the Los Angeles Police Department whose only claim to critical attention was its total waste of the talents of Stacy Keach and George C. Scott, its two stars. Nevertheless, although violence underlay every moment, the film did not, like so many other releases of the same period, descend to the level of appealing to the incipient sadism of its audiences.

Such deliberate arousal of the audience's bloodlust lay behind the extraordinary success of *Dirty Harry* (released in late 1971), *Straw Dogs* and numerous black-slanted films, in which hideous examples of white brutality invariably evoked screams for the offender's scalp.

Directed by Don Siegel from a screenplay by the Fink brothers (H. J. and R. M.), *Dirty Harry* concerned a pathological killer who threatens to shoot (from San Francisco skyscrapers) one person a day until the city pays him an enormous ransom. He selects his victims from women, priests, blacks and children and is so thoroughly repulsive that when Clint Eastwood, in the role of a tough cop, finally has him spread out on the ground with a gun ready to blow his head "clean off," dozens in the audience on at least one occasion rose to their feet and roared, "Shoot!"

One, of course, expects such shenanigans in a vehicle for Mr. Eastwood, whose initial popularity derived from a series of Italian-made ("spaghetti") Westerns and for whom

violence has become a stock-in-trade. Sam Peckinpah, who directed *Straw Dogs,* however, is another matter. A director of unusual imagination and skill, he decided several years ago to provide patrons of his movie *The Wild Bunch* with the ultimate in artistically rendered bloodbaths. And in *Straw Dogs* he went, if possible, even farther.

The story revolves around the disintegrating relationship of a mild-mannered mathematician and his sexually provocative wife in an English village roughly equivalent to Dogpatch, Ky. The couple soon becomes the object of a game of sexual humiliation conducted by a gang of rustic toughs, reminiscent of Earthquake McGoon and the Scraggs. Throughout the preliminaries everything possible is done to whet the audience's longing for the tormentors' destruction, which is then graphically effected in a prolonged climax, dripping with gore. That Peckinpah does not need to resort to such devices to demonstrate his abilities is indicated by *Junior Bonner,* which amounted to a touching and cinematically exciting portrait of an unsuccessful rodeo contestant, engagingly played by Steve McQueen. Although containing a barroom brawl and plenty of action in the rodeo sequences, it was essentially nonviolent, which probably accounts for the fact it did not do nearly so well financially as *Straw Dogs.*

A film that did, Kubrick's brilliant *Clockwork Orange,* was also nonviolent in philosophy, although it abounded with violence, made bearable by the fact that the director treated it in a stylized manner. Indeed, so stylized was Kubrick's adaptation of Anthony Burgess' futurist novel about youth gangs terrorizing the inhabitants of London that the spectator had difficulty finding a basis for personal identification. Its cleverest device was a classical music score that, serving as a contrast to the characters' horrible cruelty, projected a simultaneous image of man at his most sublime.

Despite its tendency to alienate, rather than emotionally involve, *Clockwork Orange* (probably because of its X-rating) was a hit—but nothing like *The Godfather,* whose grosses by the last week of October approached $43,000,-000. Such was doubtless due in part to the built-in audience represented by the millions who had devoured the book, but it was a good movie in its own right.

The straight narrative film has suffered in recent years, owing to the inclination of directors to use plot as simply an excuse to show off their techniques (for example, Bernardo Bertolucci's *Conformist*). In *The Godfather,* however, Coppola demonstrated what a splendid story-telling medium the motion picture can be. The atmosphere of the 1940's was faithfully rendered in the tasteful low-key photography; and, although obliged to omit much of the background meat that gave his novel such full-bodied flavor, Puzo's screenplay managed to include all the significant characters and events in the gang war among New York's five Mafia families. Even the violence seemed necessary. The casting, like the direction, was appropriate, and the acting—particularly that of Marlon Brando in the title role—was above reproach.

The result was a film that reduced such prior classics of the genre as *Little Caesar* and *Public Enemy* to the status of caricatures. But although *The Godfather* may well be the best gangster movie ever made—and certainly one whose influence can already be seen in releases like *The Valachi Papers*—it was not the best film of the year.

Of equal artistic and social importance were Lonne Elder's and Martin Ritt's *Sounder* (notable for its treatment of the problems of a black family living in the South during the Depression), John Huston's *Fat City,* Bob Fosse's *Cabaret* and David Newman's and Robert Benton's *Bad Company.* Of journalistic importance was Marcel Ophuls' *The Sorrow and the Pity,* concerning French collaboration during the Nazi occupation.

Fat City was especially significant, not only because of its all-round excellence but also because it reestablished Huston, who had slipped noticeably over the last few years, as one of the country's foremost directors. The film tells the fragmented story of an aging boxer and his pathetic efforts to make a comeback after a long layoff in skidrow flophouses and bars. The plot is episodic, consisting of various inconclusive encounters between the boxer, sensitively portrayed by Stacy Keach, and denizens of his subworld—punchy fight managers, female lushes and a 19-year-old boy (Jeff Bridges), whom the hero treats alternately as rival and son. The screenplay, adapted from his novel of the same name by Leonard Gardner, was flawless in its authenticity and simplicity. But the triumph was one of direction.

In a long introductory sequence, shot without a word of dialogue, Huston communicates the lassitude and futility that, arising from a lifetime of failure, has corroded the soul of his protagonist, with such clarity the rest of the film seems almost unnecessary. And this same visual, as opposed to verbal, articulation characterizes every scene. It is hard to recall a recent work in which the camera has been so

"The Godfather," starring Marlon Brando and directed by Francis Ford Coppola, was rated as "the best gangster movie ever made."

Sidney Poitier and Harry Belafonte appear together in "Buck and the Preacher," a post–Civil War Western about a black trail guide who protects black homesteaders.

© 1972 Paramount Pictures Corp.

James Earl Jones is "The Man," the first black to become president.

© 1972 Columbia Pictures

Blythe Danner, Howard Da Silva and William Daniels perform in the movie version of the hit musical "1776."

© 1972 Metro-Goldwyn-Mayer Inc.

Richard Roundtree is the black detective John Shaft in Gordon Park's "Shaft's Big Score." The story centers on $250,000 hidden in a coffin in New York City's Harlem.

"Young Winston," written and produced by Carl Foreman, features Simon Ward as Winston and Robert Shaw as Lord Randolph Churchill.

In Depression-desperate Berlin of the 1930's, "life is a cabaret" for nightclub performers Liza Minnelli and Joel Grey.

eloquent and, at the same time, so unobtrusive. Compared to its masterful use here, all the frenzied zooming, intercutting and stop-action hokus-pokus of the younger directors seem mere gibberish.

An example in which such devices were put to good use is *Cabaret*. As in the Broadway musical from which it was adapted, the theatrical framework for this story, of a young Englishman's loss of innocence through traumatic contact with a tawdry nightclub singer, is a Berlin cabaret during Hitler's rise to power. The social corruption implicit in the political events is expressed both in the triangular relationship of the three principal characters and the songs delivered from the stage of the cabaret. By intercutting between these pointedly obscene sequences and action occurring elsewhere, director Fosse and scriptwriter Jay Allen effected a visual counterpoint and an inspired blending of method and matter that, as much as the stunning performances of Liza Minnelli and Joel Grey, were responsible for the film's popularity with critics and public.

Bad Company, a product of the same writing team responsible for the 1967 wonder *Bonnie*

For a few moments in "Play It Again, Sam," Woody Allen sees himself as Humphrey Bogart.

and Clyde, attained its principal distinction from the way Newman and Benton (the latter directing) combined their talents with that of cinematographer Gordon Willis to create the feeling and vernacular of a long-dead past. The story is of a mama's boy who, fleeing West to escape conscription during the Civil War, falls in with a band of fellow draft-dodgers and develops into a hardened criminal. A question the film raises but does not answer is whether this development represents a growth or deterioration in character. Barry Brown is perfect as the boy, and Jeff Bridges (his nemesis) again proves, as he did in *Fat City* and *The Last Picture Show,* that he has the makings of a fine actor.

The year also saw releases of a number of films of lesser stature but by no means without merit, among them Michael Ritchie's *The Candidate,* a dramatically unfocused but socially important study of political image-making, particularly appropriate to a presidential election year, and Milton Katselas' *Butterflies Are Free,* adapted from the Broadway play about a blind youth's love for the girl next door. While telling a difficult story with humor and insight, it functioned mainly as a vehicle for the talents of newcomer Edward Albert and Goldie Hawn. Also of interest, not so much for their merit as for the identity of their directors, were Roman Polanski's *Macbeth* and Alfred Hitchcock's *Frenzy,* both of which capitalized on the general trend toward violence.

Almost every year has its monument to bad taste. In 1968 it was *Candy,* in 1970, *Myra Breckenridge,* and in 1972, *Portnoy's Complaint,* which, considered from any angle, was a disaster. Alternative examples might be found in Alan Abel's *Is There Sex after Death?,* Woody Allen's comic takeoff on Dr. David Reuben's *Everything You've Always Wanted To Know about Sex, but Were Afraid to Ask* and an X-rated animated cartoon based on Robert Crump's strip "Felix the Cat." Unlike *Portnoy,* their frank treatment of obscene subject matter was accomplished with some wit and imagination. They were, therefore, infinitely more bearable.

All things considered, 1972 was a year in which sex gave way to violence. The trend did not necessarily constitute a step forward, but the fact that John Huston—who directed *Candy* and played a prominent role in *Myra Breckenridge*—chose to bestow his talents on a project like *Fat City* may.

R. H. GARDNER
Drama and Film Critic
The Baltimore Sun

A brilliant production of "Carmen," starring Marilyn Horne, opened the Met's 1972–73 season.

MUSIC, CLASSICAL

When the Metropolitan Opera opened its 1972–73 season on Sept. 19 with Bizet's *Carmen,* it was unexpectedly an occasion for mourning as well as joyful celebration. Goeran Gentele's tragic death in an auto accident in Sardinia in July was perhaps the single most devastating event to affect the music world during the entire year. After 22 years of autocratic and increasingly conservative rule by Rudolf Bing, the Swedish director's plans for the Met had created much anticipatory excitement in musical circles everywhere, and—for the first time in years—even in the house itself. For one thing, virtually annual disputes with the Met's thirteen unions, with resultant strikes or delays in the season's openings, had suddenly given way to an almost euphoric atmosphere in labor relations under Mr. Gentele's firm but diplomatic touch. Moreover, Gentele had broken ground by selecting as the musical director Rafael Kubelik, who in turn appointed to the Met's conducting staff the brilliant young American, James Levine. These decisions, along with a number of interesting plans for specific opera productions in the forthcoming years, had at last raised hopes for the "old Met" and opera in general. These were temporarily dashed by Gentele's untimely death.

Nevertheless, the season's opening was also an occasion for rejoicing. With Leonard Bernstein in the pit and a team of directors (led by Bodo Igesz) bent on preserving in detail Gentele's own directorial ideas about *Carmen,* the performance was, according to *The New York Times,* "brilliant, daring and provocative" —an appropriate memorial to what was to have been the beginning of the Gentele era. Schuyler Chapin, the equivalent of a "career diplomat"

Schuyler Chapin bows head as Met Board Chairman Lowell Wadmond eulogizes Goeran Gentele.

Cincinnati's 95-year-old Music Hall, home of the Cincinnati Symphony for 77 years, embraced opera as well in 1972 following a $6,000,000, three-year renovation. The city's Summer Opera will present a four-week season in the auditorium each summer.

in music, with experience in management, television and recording as well as five years as a vice president of Lincoln Center, was appointed acting director of the Met with express instructions to carry out Gentele's plans.

Meanwhile, hard on the heels of the Met opening, symphony orchestras around the United States were gearing up for their new seasons. Across the plaza at Lincoln Center, Pierre Boulez and the New York Philharmonic inaugurated a season featuring the works of Haydn and Stravinsky, a counterpart to the previous season's Liszt-Berg "festival," which had been received with mixed feelings by Philharmonic audiences. Contemporary music, particularly by Americans, was still virtually nonexistent on Philharmonic programs, undoubtedly a result of Boulez' own unjustified disdain for American composers. A token concession was offered by "segregating" new music in a special downtown Greenwich Village chamber music series under Boulez' direction. But this rather feeble gesture was hardly designed to bring new young audiences to the Philharmonic's regular home. Nor did Boulez' selection of European guest conductors, such as Michael Gielen and Bruno Maderna, to conduct (primarily) European contemporary music inspire much confidence among the comparable home-grown product.

Elsewhere, other orchestras were looking forward to seasons with newly or recently appointed music directors: Lorin Maazel in Cleveland, Seiji Ozawa in San Francisco and Boston, Michael Tilson Thomas in Buffalo and Lawrence Foster in Houston.

Curiously, the much-talked-about crisis of the American symphony orchestra did not materialize, at least not in the form and to the extent predicted by such gloom-and-doom prophets as Leonard Bernstein and Lukas Foss. If orchestras faced a crisis, it was not so much in the realm of economics as in the area of musical direction. Contrary to general opinion, conductorial talent abounds. But a conductor is not necessarily a "music director." And orchestras were finding it increasingly difficult—in an era of jet-age travel and high-powered contractual manipulations emanating from entrepreneurial management offices in New York—to retain conductors on an exclusive basis. An alarming number of "music directors" are so in name only, dividing their energies between two, and in some cases as many as four or five, orchestras—often with debilitating effect on the caliber and growth of the organizations involved. However, at least one hopeful factor resides in the emergence and greater acceptance of black conductors, such as Henry Lewis and James DePriest.

Composers were still faring relatively well in 1972. Never were more commissions given, grants awarded or festivals, conferences and symposia of contemporary music organized.

Much of this energy—particularly in university circles—was directed to the benefit of the young composer. Even Washington's Kennedy Center for the Performing Arts staged a week-long festival of "avant-garde" music. But the most significant event of the year was undoubtedly the 20th anniversary of the modestly-sized, but enormously effective Fromm Foundation, newly headquartered at Harvard University. Through its support not only of composers directly, but indirectly of artists and organizations devoted to new music, the Fromm Foundation has proven itself to be unique in the field.

Opera, too, was flourishing, as a result of a massive trend of decentralization, away from New York and other metropolitan centers. Regional operas, supported energetically by private sources and foundations, were holding their own rather well, both artistically and financially. In 1972 one was as likely to encounter an excellent *Rosenkavalier* in Portland, Oregon, as at the Met or the New York City Opera. Not only in Sante Fe, but in Seattle, Minneapolis, San Francisco, Kansas City, Tanglewood and Augusta (and in a temporarily revitalized Central City, Colorado) one could hear adventurous, often ambitiously produced new operas as well as staples of the operatic repertory in high quality performances. As a significant by-product of this decentralization, there were signs on the operatic horizon that at least some of the public had had its fill of the domination of opera by "super stars": Birgit Nilsson, John Sutherland, Beverly Sills, Marilyn Horne and a few others.

Recording of classical music, as in recent years, was curtailed, with many companies content to reissue still another round of "Greatest Hits." Happily, the trend of recent years to explore the enormous riches of renaissance and baroque music continued unabated. With men like Charles McKerras, Nikolaus Harnoncourt and Raymond Leppard and companies like Nonesuch in the forefront, many of the pre-Bach treasures buried for centuries on library shelves were finally being brought to light and to the public's consciousness.

GUNTHER SCHULLER
President, New England Conservatory

In the second of a projected three-work cycle of Donizetti "Tudor" operas, the New York City Opera presented Beverly Sills, center, as Maria Stuarda.

Pierre Boulez, New York

MUSICAL CHAIRS

Perhaps owing to the extraordinary durability of 20th century symphony orchestra conductors in general—several of the most prominent have remained active into their 80's and 90's—younger conductors have had to wait, often impatiently, for major positions in both Europe and America. In an unprecedented shakeup of the U.S. musical establishment in the early 1970's, however, most of the major orchestras have experienced a change of command practically overnight, with the result that a seemingly entire new generation of conductors and musical directors has come of age. Only Eugene Ormandy, in Philadelphia, among the titans of the old school, remained in command of a metropolitan U.S. orchestra of the front rank. Shown here are several of the new conductors, most of them typically neither native born nor trained, who have recently captured the most coveted prizes.

Seiji Ozawa, Boston

Los Angeles Philharmonic

Houston Symphony Orchestra

Zubin Mehta, Los Angeles

Lawrence Foster, Houston

Lorin Maazel, Cleveland

Georg Solti, Chicago

The Cleveland Orchestra

Chicago Symphony Orchestra

Mick Jagger and the Rolling Stones toured 30 North American cities in 1972. Their double-record album "Exile on Main Street" was high on the top-ten charts.

MUSIC, POPULAR

No one trend dominated popular music in 1972. Rock concerts continued to attract huge audiences, although critics generally acknowledged a decline in the quality of the music itself.

Rock. The event of the year was the Rolling Stones' first North American tour since 1969; playing in 30 cities during the early summer, the group grossed between $3,000,000 and $4,000,000 and attracted front page publicity from coast to coast. At the same time, their double-record album *Exile On Main Street* was a number-one best seller.

Other widely heralded events were Elvis Presley's first live New York concert, at Madison Square Garden in June, and Neil Diamond's two-week solo engagement at New York's Winter Garden Theater in October. Two androgynously attired British rock stars, Marc Bolan (with his hard-rock group T. Rex) and David Bowie, made highly publicized American tours but failed to generate the same hysteria in the States that they did at home. In the live performances of these and other stars there was an increasing emphasis on theatricality—elaborate costuming, makeup and stage business. The most notorious and one of the most popular acts was the Alice Cooper band, whose life performances featured transvestism, mock execution and the (male) lead singer, Alice, twining a live boa constrictor around his neck. Their album *School's Out* was one of the year's biggest sellers. Many critics viewed such goings-on as signifying the terminal decadence of the rock culture.

Growing nostalgia for the early days of rock 'n' roll was another significant trend. Many radio stations boosted their ratings by altering their formats to play only old hit records from the 1950's and 1960's. Countless "oldies" were reissued, singly and in anthologies. Promoter Richard Nader made a fortune with his touring "rock 'n' roll revivals," featuring such legendary performers of the 1950's as Little Richard, Chuck Berry and Bill Haley and the Comets. In 1972, Nader produced 55 such revivals. After a three-month run in an off-

Broadway theater the year's most popular musical comedy, *Grease,* billed as "A New 50's Rock 'n' Roll Musical," began a long, profitable run on Broadway.

The general feeling that rock had reached its peak and was declining achieved definitive expression in one of the year's top hits, **Don McLean's** "American Pie," an 8-minute folk-rock allegory tracing the 20-year history of the big beat up to "the day the music died." Probably the year's biggest hit single, however, was "Alone Again (Naturally)," a pleasant narrative ballad sung by Gilbert O'Sullivan, a 25-year-old Irish former postal clerk discovered by Gordon Mills, the producer who had made Tom Jones and Engelbert Humperdinck tremendous stars.

Other number one hits of more than passing distinction were Harry Nilsson's "Without You," Roberta Flack's "The First Time Ever I Saw Your Face" and Bill Withers' "Lean On Me." The biggest stars among the pre-teen set continued to be the Osmond Brothers, the Jackson Five, David Cassidy, the Carpenters and Three Dog Night. Two of the Jackson Five, Michael and Jermaine, also had hits as soloists. Donny Osmond, of the Osmond Brothers, was the reigning pre-teen idol. Three Dog Night was probably the year's most successful touring band.

Recordings. The long playing album continued to be the most important marketing unit of the recording industry, with discs outselling tapes five-to-one. Late in 1971 the first "quadro-

Richard Howard, Camera 5

The most popular singles of the year were Roberta Flack's "The First Time Ever I Saw Your Face," "American Pie," by Don McLean (below, 1) and Gilbert O'Sullivan's "Alone Again (Naturally)."

United Artists   Photo Trends

phonic" (four channel) records were released. Two competing systems for home quadrophonic sound reproduction were introduced on the consumer market in 1972, one by Columbia and the other by RCA. By the end of the year it was not clear which one would eventually be adopted as standard by the record industry. Nor was it certain that the consumer could be induced to invest his money in four loudspeakers instead of two.

Of the year's artistic achievements in recorded popular music probably the most impressive were the many fine albums made by singer-songwriter-instrumentalists. The best of these were by Paul Simon (formerly of the team Simon and Garfunkel), who released a brilliant solo album, *Paul Simon,* for Columbia; and Randy Newman, whose *Sail Away* album for Reprise was a dazzling tour-de-force of musical eclecticism and verbal irony. Other important records in the singer-songwriter category were released by Eric Andersen, Van Morrison, Neil Young, Jackson Browne, David Ackles, Loudon Wainwright III, Judee Sill, John Prine, Joni Mitchell and Leon Russell.

After several disappointing records, Elton John's excellent album *Honky Chateau* reestablished him as one of the most creative figures in pop music. Another British rocker, gravel-voiced Rod Stewart, received even more acclaim for his witty and earthy *Never a Dull Moment* album.

The most popular "soul" artists of the year were Al Green (an excellent balladeer who bore a close stylistic resemblance to the late Otis Redding), Roberta Flack, Donny Hathaway and Sly and the Family Stone. Aretha Franklin, "the queen of soul," released a magnificent gospel album, *Amazing Grace,* that did not achieve quite the commercial success it deserved.

In country music the most popular singers were Charlie Pride, Lynn Anderson, Tammy Wynette, Loretta Lynn, Sonny James and Merle Haggard.

Curtis Mayfield's score for the black adventure movie *Super Fly* was probably the year's most popular soundtrack album.

Jazz. The year also saw a resurgence of interest in jazz. The Newport Jazz Festival, founded in 1954 and closed in 1971 after incidences of gate crashing and vandalism, found a new home in New York City. The festival's 45 events, encompassing all styles and eras of jazz, drew a total attendance of about 100,000 fans.

Several ambitious attempts to fuse jazz and rock also were made. The most influential figures involved in this fusion were Miles Davis, the great jazz trumpeter, and John McLaughlin, who was hailed as the most important guitarist since Eric Clapton and Jimi Hendrix. With his Mahavishnu Orchestra, McLaughlin released one of the year's finest records, a passionately mystical masterpiece, *The Inner Mounting Flame.*

I Sing the Body Electric, another rock-jazz synthesis, by the group Weather Report, also received critical praise. While both of these albums had only moderate success, the driving, less cerebral jazz-tinted rock of the band Chicago reached new heights of popularity. Their fourth and fifth albums topped the charts within a few weeks of their release.

STEPHEN HOLDEN
Contributor, *Rolling Stone*

To the delight of 100,000 jazz fans, the Newport Jazz Festival, which had been canceled in 1971, moved to New York City in 1972.

NETHERLANDS, THE

The Dutch faced more problems in 1972 than their two Benelux partners. With the cost-of-living index rising at an annual rate of more than 6 percent, the Netherlands had the worst inflation problem in the European Economic Community. Rising costs constituted a major issue in the Nov. 29 elections and will be one of the main concerns of any new coalition government. Shortly before the vote the Dutch government already had introduced a price control system.

The elections were held three years early because the two members of the Democratic Socialist party (DS'70) resigned during the summer over budgetary policies. (Before resigning the two ministers had proposed an immediate wage-price freeze and a reduction in defense spending to cut inflation.) The four other parties in the government, the Catholic, Liberal, Anti-Revolutionary and Christian Historical (the two last-named both Calvinist), continued as a minority government. With the voting age reduced for the first time to 18, left-of-center parties registered a slight gain in the elections.

By the end of the year no new government had yet been formed, and Premier Barend W. Biesheuvel continued in office in a caretaker capacity. Because of the proliferation of parties, however, a centrist coalition government seemed the most likely prospect.

Of all western European countries, the Netherlands has the reputation of being the most tolerant. A rightist Dutch government in 1972 proposed legislation making the possession and use of soft drugs in private a civil rather than a criminal offense. In another demonstration of tolerance, the country—the most densely populated in western Europe—had quickly and successfully absorbed 300,000 Indo-Dutch after Indonesian independence.

The greater the surprise, then, when—in August—clashes between Dutch and Turkish immigrants broke out in Rotterdam. Several stabbings were reported, and more than 40 persons were arrested. More than 5,000 Turks were living in the city, and the root cause of the problem was overcrowding. The immediate reason for the clashes was the eviction by a Turkish immigrant from his newly bought house of a Dutch tenant and her three children. The mayor of Rotterdam, Mr. Thomassen subsequently asked the government to give him greater powers to control the housing situation in order to limit the influx of Turkish laborers.

RICHARD NORTON-TAYLOR
Foreign Correspondent
The Guardian, Manchester and London

NEW ZEALAND

Reflecting a change in political mood rather than sharp disagreement on specific issues, New Zealanders voted the Labour party into office in November in the country's biggest electoral landslide in nearly 40 years. Labour won 55 of the 87 seats in the House of Representatives to give 49-year-old Norman Eric Kirk the prime ministership and end 12 years of National party rule.

During the election campaign, Labour had pledged an end to the military draft; a broad-based tax incentive plan to encourage savings; a freeze on government service charges, including postage; the creation of regional development councils; the lowering of the voting age to 18; and creation of a ministry of sport and recreation.

The incoming prime minister promised to review the government's economic stabilization measures. In foreign affairs Kirk foreshadowed numerous changes, including a "phasing out" from the Southeast Asia Treaty Organization. SEATO, he said, should be replaced by an organization that would bring countries together rather than separating them on SEATO lines. Kirk also promised new initiatives toward diplomatic recognition of China and against nuclear testing in the Pacific.

The election came at the close of a year of generally noncontentious and minor legislative activity. The outgoing government appeared to have run out of ideas. In February, John R. Marshall had taken over the prime ministership when Sir Keith Holyoake stepped down (he became minister for foreign affairs).

In the economic sphere, 1972 was a year of general recovery, although inflationary pressures were barely contained. The pace of business activity rose slowly, improving after the budget (presented in mid-year) provided a 16 percent increase in government spending and gave further stimulus through a combination of tax cuts and social security benefits. In the second half of the year interest rates were eased. Building activity increased, and farm, personal and company incomes were higher. Manufacturing activity also expanded.

The New Zealand dollar was revalued slightly upward early in the year, when a fixed exchange rate pegged to the U.S. dollar rather than to the pound sterling was introduced.

Further changes in trade patterns are to follow Britain's admission to the European Economic Community. Preferential tariff treatment for British goods will be phased out over a three-year period beginning in mid-1974.

R. M. YOUNGER
Free-lance Writer

NOBEL PRIZES

Keystone

RODNEY R. PORTER

Fabian Bachrach

GERALD M. EDELMAN

The 1972 Nobel Prizes were presented in Stockholm on Dec. 10 to eight Americans, two Britons and a West German. Each prize was valued at approximately $100,000. For the first time since 1967, the five-man committee of the Norwegian Parliament withheld the Peace Prize.

Rodney R. Porter, 55-year-old professor of biochemistry at Oxford University and Gerald M. Edelman, a 43-year-old molecular biologist at Rockefeller University in New York City, shared the award for physiology and medicine. The British and American scientists were cited for independent research on the chemical structure of antibodies (the group of blood proteins which have a major part in the body's defense against disease). In 1959 both men presented the first results of their investigations leading to a clarification of the nature of antibodies.

PHYSICS

University of Illinois at Urbana

JOHN BARDEEN

Keystone

LEON N. COOPER

University of Pennsylvania

JOHN ROBERT SCHRIEFFER

The physics prize was shared by John Bardeen, 64-year-old professor of electrical engineering and physics at the University of Illinois at Urbana, Leon N. Cooper, 42-year-old professor of physics at Brown University in Providence, R.I., and John Robert Schrieffer, 41-year-old professor of physics at the University of Pennsylvania in Philadelphia. Jointly the physicists had developed a theory of superconductivity (the property of certain metals and alloys, including lead and tin, whose electrical resistance disappears at a temperature just above absolute zero, $-273°C$.). Following announcement of the award, Dr. Erik Rudberg, secretary of the Swedish Royal Academy of Scientists, pointed out that the "application of superconductivity is important not only for scientific instruments, but also for accelerators and motors." (Dr. Bardeen is the first to win two Nobels in the same category.)

CHEMISTRY

CHRISTIAN B. ANFINSEN

STANFORD MOORE

WILLIAM HOWARD STEIN

For "fundamental contributions to enzyme chemistry," Christian Boehmer Anfinsen, 56, Stanford Moore, 59, and William Howard Stein, 61, shared the chemistry award. Since 1950, Dr. Anfinsen has worked as a biochemist at the U.S. National Institutes of Health. Drs. Moore and Stein have been associated with the Rockefeller University for more than 30 years and are the university's 11th and 12th Nobel laureates. The three Americans were honored for their work "with the same enzyme, ribonuclease." According to an Academy statement, "Anfinsen's investigation has provided the answer to an important question concerning the way in which the active enzyme is formed in living cells. Moore and Stein have elucidated important principles related to the biological activity of the enzyme. These properties we generally associate with the concept of life and with living organisms."

MEMORIAL (ECONOMICS)

LITERATURE

SIR JOHN HICKS

KENNETH J. ARROW

HEINRICH BÖLL

Since its establishment in 1969 by the Swedish National Bank, the Nobel Memorial Prize for economics had been won only by Americans. By sharing the 1972 honor with Kenneth J. Arrow, Sir John Hicks, retired Oxford professor, broke this tradition. The 68-year-old Briton and the 51-year-old Harvard professor were cited for "their pioneering contributions to general economic equilibrium theory." According to the equilibrium theory, which is basic to investment, trade and price structure, active forces cancel each other and produce a state of balance.

A 54-year-old West German novelist, short-story writer and playwright, Heinrich Böll, won the literature prize. He was honored for "his writing, which through its combination of a broad perspective on his time and a sensitive skill in characterization has contributed to a renewal of German literature."

Lars Korvald, leader of Norway's Christian People's party, was named premier in October.

NORWAY

The question of membership in the European Economic Community (EEC), the most hotly debated issue of 1972 in Norway, was resolved by a plebiscite in which the Norwegian people rejected membership. Norway had been conducting negotiations with the EEC for about ten years, and early in the year it was thought that eventual Norwegian entry was assured, especially in view of the fact that all the major political parties—except the Center party (Agrarians)—had, together with the press and big industry, strongly supported membership. Opposition to Norway's entry, however, had built up gradually, concentrating in the ranks of farmers and fishermen, conservationists, environmentalists and left-wing radicals. The political parties had agreed to be guided by the result of the plebiscite, and the final decision was left to the voters on Sept. 25. Surprisingly, the adverse vote was 1,049,272, while only 906,985 voted for EEC membership.

The Labor cabinet headed by Trygve Bratteli, in power since 1970, had announced prior to the vote that it would step down if the electorate rejected its policy at the polls. The cabinet resigned in the week following the plebiscite and in mid-October was succeeded by a coalition cabinet headed by Lars Korvald of the Christian People's party. The new cabinet consisted of representatives of the Center, Liberal and Christian People's parties.

The 1,100th anniversary of the founding of the Norwegian kingdom was celebrated in June. Historians generally hold that the Battle of Hafrs Fjord, in which King Harald Fairhair subdued the last resistance to his efforts to unite all parts of the Norwegian realm, took place in 872 A.D. King Olav V and huge crowds paid tribute to the memory of Harald Fairhair at Hafrs Fjord, an inlet near Stavanger, and also at the site of his memorial and assumed burial mound near Haugesund.

The potential production of natural oil and gas from the North Sea floor continued to figure large in the nation's future economic picture. Three areas, known as Ekofisk, Tor and Frigg, all within Norway's sector of the North Sea, were found to be commercially exploitable following test drillings and various oil strikes. In June, the government created the Norwegian Oil Company, with an initial capital investment of approximately $825,000.

ERIK J. FRIIS
Editor, *The American-Scandinavian Review*

OCEANIA

A sharp divergence in policy and outlook between the English-speaking island nations and territories of the South Pacific and the French-controlled territories became apparent in 1972. The English-speaking group showed greater unity of purpose than ever before, accentuating regional cooperation in economic as well as political matters.

In Papua New Guinea the decolonizing process advanced rapidly with the confirmation by Australia that self-government in all spheres except foreign affairs and defense would become effective in the territory in 1973. By contrast, moves toward a greater degree of autonomy in French Polynesia and New Caledonia were brought to a halt, and in New Hebrides, the British-French condominium, the French spokesman scotched British suggestions designed to foster progress toward independent status for the island group.

South Pacific Forum and South Pacific Conference. At the South Pacific Forum, which met in Canberra, Australia, in February, the leaders of Fiji, Nauru, the Cook Islands, Western Samoa and Tonga expressed keen concern over France's plans to conduct nuclear tests in the atmosphere above the South Pacific; however, despite the forum's formal protest (with backing from New Zealand and Australia), France carried out its mid-year test series.

Economic development for Oceania was a dominant theme at the February meeting, and the group agreed to set up a bureau of economic cooperation to advance joint action on economic matters of mutual interest. Headquartered in Suva, Fiji, the new bureau immediately

began gathering basic data on production, consumption and distribution patterns in the individual island countries.

Soon after the bureau was established, Australia and New Zealand stepped up their commitments of financial aid to South Pacific territories, with Fiji as the principal beneficiary. Australia pledged $18,000,000 for South Pacific economic development projects and expert and technical assistance programs through 1975.

Meanwhile, island farmers were switching to new crops as a result of an increased demand for market garden produce and livestock products (all attributable to the demands of tourists and the improved local diet) and of weakened demand for some traditional export crops, including copra.

In September, at the South Pacific Conference (the annual meeting of seven Pacific island countries and five metropolitan powers with Pacific dependencies), France withheld support from a proposal to increase the South Pacific Commission's operating budget. In the absence of full agreement on its future role, the commission, after 25 years as Oceania's advisory and consultative body in the fields of economic and social welfare, appeared to be waning in influence.

Political Developments. After concerted behind-the-scenes efforts directed from Paris to dampen local moves toward autonomy, French Polynesia and New Caledonia in September elections returned status-quo territorial assemblies. Essentially the voters' choice lay between those candidates seeking a greater degree of local authority and those who considered the territories to be inalienably French. In New Caledonia the autonomists barely held ground with an unchanged 17 seats against 16 op-posed, while in French Polynesia they lost five seats and thus relinquished their dominant position.

Following general elections in Papua New Guinea, the Pangu party (pledged to press for immediate self-government) was able to form a governing coalition with splinter parties and independents, and the party's leader, Michael Somare, became chief minister. A greater share of administrative responsibility was accepted by the new ministry, and plans were drawn up to facilitate the rapid transfer of power.

In Fiji, the government of Prime Minister Ratu Sir Kamisese Mara was returned to power in April elections against a background of economic difficulties arising from steep inflation. The status quo also was preserved by election results in the Cook Islands.

The Western Pacific High Commission (created by Britain a century ago) relinquished control over the Gilbert and Ellice Islands, and the colony became responsible directly to London, with a governor of its own. The 56,000 islanders live on three dozen atolls with a total area of only 380 square miles. The land currently supports the growing of little but coconuts and pandanus trees—but the colony hopes to expand copra output and stimulate tourism.

Pace of Change. In New Hebrides the stream of registration by foreign companies (largely Australian and U.S. firms) continued as the island took on the role of a "tax haven."

Papua New Guinea's chief administrative and commercial center, Port Moresby (population 60,000, two thirds of whom are New Guineans), was elevated to the status of a city, with Oala Oala-Rarua its first lord mayor.

R. M. YOUNGER
Free-Lance Writer

Gamma

Despite formal protest from the leaders of the nations of Oceania, France conducted a series of nuclear tests in the atmosphere at mid-year.

OCEANOGRAPHY

Reinforced by mounting concern for the future of the terrestrial environment, several large scale research programs designed to expand man's knowledge of the ocean and its resources were initiated or continued in 1972.

Oceanic Circulation. Measurements taken with moored instruments in the last few years contributed to the planning for project MODE (Mid Ocean Dynamics Experiment). The Anglo-American undertaking seeks to determine the significance of oceanic motion with a time scale of a few weeks and space scales of a few hundred kilometers in the large central ocean areas. The experiment involves three U.S. oceanographic ships and one British research vessel, a fixed array of current meters and temperature recording instruments moored to 16 different positions on the sea bottom and a variety of other moored, free-floating and airborne instruments.

By mapping current and temperature, the oceanographers hope to prepare the first equivalent of a weather map of the ocean and, hence, to begin to understand the dynamic processes involved. Previous interpretations of oceanic motion had assumed that the mid-ocean regions were quiescent, having only a small mean flow, and that most of the circulation existed in large peripheral current systems, such as the Gulf Stream and the Kuroshio Current, located near the continental boundaries of the ocean. However, preliminary use of monitoring devices in mid-ocean indicated that oscillatory, or episodic, flow occurred there. Delineation of this pattern in more detail is the purpose of the MODE experiments. The results could significantly enlarge understanding of the ocean's influence on climate and of the ability of the ocean to cope with various pollutants.

Geochemical Studies. A similar international program was underway in 1972 to provide information on how the ocean mixes over long periods of time and over vast distances. Known as GEOSECS (Geochemical Ocean Sections Study), the program involves a survey along north-south tracks in the major areas of the ocean. Each cruise plan follows the approximate known trajectory of the bottom water currents. The U.S. contribution includes major survey work in the Atlantic, Indian, Pacific and Antarctic oceans. Complementary programs are contemplated by West Germany and Japan; other nations will add supplementary data.

The Atlantic Ocean survey began in July 1972 and was to continue until March 1973. Some 120 stations were projected along the main survey route—each station designed to make a vertical profile on the basis of 50 samples measuring about 30 liters each. Alternate stations were also equipped to take very large samples of 1,000 liters each at about 18 to 20 different depths in order to provide for measurement of trace constituents and low concentration radioisotopes. The vertical spacing of the samples was to be determined by continuous on-station recording of temperature, salinity and dissolved oxygen.

"The major objective of GEOSECS is to understand the origin and circulation of deep water in the ocean," said Dr. Derek Spencer of the Woods Hole Oceanographic Institution, just prior to the departure of the Atlantic Ocean expedition. "We have to be able to predict how fast any waste material introduced into the ocean will disperse, and where it will go. In another area, people in fisheries would like much more information on the cycling of nutrients—nitrates, phosphates and silicates—nutrients which eventually feed fish. What happens if ocean circulation changes? In an area off the West Coast, the sardine fishery recently dried up. Why? Was this overfishing or was there perhaps some small undetected change in circulation? Any information we can get would be helpful in a number of such instances. These could be some of the benefits coming from GEOSECS even though our major purpose is to learn about the origin and time scale of ocean mixing."

The GEOSECS program represents a major portion of U.S. participation in IDOE (International Decade of Ocean Exploration—1970–80).

Ocean Food Resources. In an effort to answer questions relating to the food resources of the ocean, the National Marine Fisheries Service undertook an integrated research program called MARMAP (Marine Resources Monitoring Assessment and Prediction Program). In addition to gathering information on the food resources of the ocean, particularly over the continental shelf and slope, the program is developing tools and techniques for understanding the processes which control the size of fish populations.

Several nations are cooperating in MARMAP projects. Agreements were concluded calling for cooperative collecting by U.S. and Japanese scientists and for experimental sampling by scientists from Thailand and Singapore. Five countries—Canada, France, the U.S.S.R., the United States and West Germany—took part in a joint study to determine the size of the herring spawning stocks in the Northwest Atlantic. Using as their measure estimates of small herring larvae off the New England coast, the research vessels employed standard sampling

Oceanographers from the research project MARMAP gather samples and obtain quantitative measurements of oceanic food resources (I). Later, scientists analyze graphs (below) of data obtained by various instruments in order to determine the factors which govern fluctuations in marine populations.

equipment and reporting methods. They found, among other things, that the offshore herring population is six times greater than the inshore population.

MARMAP data will be used as a basis for negotiating international fishing quotas. Kenneth Sherman, field director of the project, noted: "Systematic monitoring of marine populations and their environment is as vital . . . for maintaining viable resources as the continuous monitoring of atmospheric events is to the forecasters of tomorrow's weather."

Other Programs. The Deep Sea Drilling Program's (DSDP) research vessel *Glomar Challenger* continued to supply new data about deposits on and beneath the sea floor. Interpretation of such data has radically changed scientific understanding of geological processes.

Aerial reconnaissance methods for monitoring inshore pollution of the ocean environment developed rapidly in 1972. New infrared satellite photography was used to check oceanic and estuarine areas. In addition, attempts were made to evaluate the productivity of ocean areas by satellite. Such techniques may make possible future control and better exploitation of fisheries.

DAVID A. MCGILL
Professor, Ocean Science
U.S. Coast Guard Academy

PAKISTAN

For Pakistan, 1972 was a year of trauma. Adjustment to the debacle of 1971, when East Pakistan with more than half the national population was lost, came hard. Psychological, social, economic and political strains rocked the new Pakistan—the old West Pakistan. Stresses increased as the months passed with no settlement of war issues, with Indian troops still occupying more than 5,000 square miles of Pakistani territory and with approximately 90,000 Pakistani prisoners of war still in Indian hands. It was a year in which Pakistan could say at least that it survived.

As the year began, Pakistanis still could not believe that what—from their perspective—had started in March 1971 as an effort to put down dissidence and rebellion in East Pakistan had ended in December with a humiliating defeat by India, the capture of all Pakistani forces in the east and the creation of the independent state of Bangladesh out of the former East Pakistan. They could hardly believe that their forces on the western front had failed to prevent Indian troops from seizing pockets of territory in the Punjab and Sind and from pushing new salients into the 1949 ceasefire line in Kashmir.

As a consequence of the two-week war in December the 1947 Pakistani dream of a nation composed of all the Muslim-majority regions of the Indian subcontinent was dead. Pakistani national morale lay shattered. The first task, clearly, was to pull the country together and look to the future rather than the past. Ataturk had done this in the Turkish heartland after the dissolution of the Ottoman empire. Could Pakistan similarly bring new confidence out of disaster?

In late 1971 the process had begun with a change of leadership. The youthful but experienced Zulfikar Ali Bhutto, civilian leader of the principal political party in West Pakistan, assumed the presidency of the country with military and political backing. His predecessor, Gen. Yahya Khan, who had presided over the 1971 disasters, was arrested. Bhutto promised a return to the democratic processes that Pakistan had last experienced in 1958, although for the time being he governed under the martial law ordinances already in force.

Two fundamental questions faced the new Pakistan administration. One was what settlement of war issues a defeated Pakistan could obtain from India and Bangladesh. The other, even more central to Pakistan's survival, was how to build a new sense of nationhood.

Presumably to ease the path of conciliation after the war, Bhutto promptly released from West Pakistani detention the Bangladesh leader, Sheikh Mujibur Rahman, whom Pakistani troops had arrested the preceding March in Dacca on the first night of the ill-fated attempt to put down Bengali dissidence. This gesture brought meager results, however. By the end of 1972, Pakistan had reached no settlement with Bangladesh, which insisted on diplomatic recognition as a precondition of any substantive discussions and which declared its intention of trying some hundreds of the Pakistani prisoners on charges of war crimes.

Nor did the efforts made by Pakistan and India to settle their bilateral war issues proceed rapidly. After disputes and delays, President Bhutto and Indian Prime Minister Indira Gandhi met without preconditions in late June. The six-part "Simla agreement" they signed seemed to point the way toward the first general agreement in years between Pakistan and India. Subsequent disputes over interpretation and difficulties in drawing a "line of control" in Kashmir stalled implementation, however. The first significant breakthroughs came in December when President Bhutto released the 617 Indian prisoners that Pakistani

President Bhutto arrives in Peking to sign a border pact cementing Sino-Pakistani relations.

Camera Press from Pictorial

President Bhutto visits the U.S.S.R. which supported India during its conflict with Pakistan.

Sheik Zayed of Abu Dhabi welcomes President Bhutto, in quest of Arab support for Pakistan.

forces had captured on the western front, and India reciprocated. Agreement was then reached on a control line in Kashmir, following which Indian and Pakistani troops withdrew from the others' territory that each had seized in the 1971 war. Other issues remained unsettled, however.

While negotiating with India, President Bhutto also moved energetically to restore Pakistan's position in world affairs and to influence attitudes of the wider international community. Immediately on assuming power, he received the shah of Iran and visited the king of Afghanistan. Later he went to Peking to consolidate Pakistan's relations with China, visited Moscow to adjust relations with the Soviet Union and traveled to Islamic and particularly Arab states in search of wider support. In an effort to deter other countries from precipitate recognition of Bangladesh, his government broke relations with several that took that step. Pakistan also left the Commonwealth when Britain, Australia and other Commonwealth members recognized Bangladesh, and quit SEATO, the Southeast Asia Treaty Organization, after the reaffirmation of Pakistan's links with China. However, when such major powers as the Soviet Union and Britain established diplomatic relations with Bangla-

desh, Pakistan stopped attempting to prevent others from doing the same. In addition, Bhutto expressed his desire to strengthen relations with the United States.

Meanwhile, the Pakistani president faced internal contradictions in many ways more severe than his difficulties with India and Bangladesh. Of the four provinces of the old West Pakistan, only the Punjab and Sind were under his Pakistan People's party control. In the Northwest Frontier Province and in Baluchistan influential elements among the Pathan and Baluchi inhabitants resisted central government supremacy much as Bengalis had done in 1971. Their politicians even talked of separate statehoods. Political demonstrations in these provinces, police strikes in several major cities, student activism and serious language riots, especially in Sind, seemed to jeopardize the integrity of what remained of Pakistan.

Nevertheless, by the autumn of 1972, President Bhutto seemed to have invoked a fairly broad national consensus on maintaining the unity of the new Pakistan. He achieved agreements with the opposition parties, first on the temporary distribution of governmental powers and later on the projected form of a new constitution. As a special gesture he brought the beginnings of democratic forms to the pre-

viously feudal establishments of the mountainous regions of Gilgit and Baltistan.

How far political unity could hold would depend somewhat, it became evident, on developments on the economic front. The war had not only left large numbers of prisoners in Indian hands but had made refugees of hundreds of thousands of West Pakistanis whose homes were in areas occupied by Indian troops. Food production was dislocated. The patterns of trade with east Bengal that had evolved during the years when both wings were part of Pakistan had come to an abrupt end, with the results that several industries in West Pakistan lost substantial markets and that imports from the eastern wing to which West Pakistanis had become accustomed were no longer available. Government accounts and foreign exchange balances were also disrupted. Confidence sagged badly, as a result both of these difficulties and of opposition to Bhutto's initial populist economic policy. Later, Pakistanis began to feel hope for economic improvement in the longer run. By the usual measures, Pakistan's ratio of resources to population was comparatively favorable.

Taken as a whole, 1972 was a harrowing year for Pakistan. As it moved toward its end, however, drafters were at work on a new constitution, and progress became visible in some other key areas as well. For the future, Pakistanis concluded that, if appropriate settlements of war-related issues could be achieved with India, their country, even though truncated, could make its way with a new sense of purpose and direction.

PHILLIPS TALBOT
President, The Asia Society

PARAGUAY

Latin America's longest-ruling dictator, 60-year-old Gen. Alfredo Stroessner, announced in October that he would run again in Paraguay's 1973 elections. If he wins, as expected, he will remain president until 1978. He has been in power uninterruptedly since 1954.

During 1972, however, his 18-year-old regime showed new signs of strain in its established way of life. It bowed, under pressure from U.S. President Nixon's drive against narcotics, to the extradition of the extremely well-connected Joseph Auguste Ricord, indicted by a New York grand jury on charges of being "Monsieur André," the mysterious chief of an international smuggling ring dealing in drugs out of easy-going, landlocked Paraguay. The U.S. government officially denied press allegations that the French-born Argentine citizen had for years enjoyed the protection of top figures in the Stroessner regime, themselves implicated in the narcotics traffic. The fact remained, however, that prior to the August ruling of Paraguay's supreme court, Washington sent an undersecretary of state to Asuncion to meet the president.

The Roman Catholic Church clashed with the regime after the latter expelled two Jesuit priests, dubbed "subversives," in February and May. The priests had worked, with full approval of their bishops, to organize poor peasants. In the capital university students protested against the detention without trial, and of many years' duration, of political opponents of the regime.

RICHARD WIGG
Latin-American Correspondent
The Times, London

J. P. Laffont, Gamma

Paraguay responded to U.S. diplomatic pressure by permitting the extradition of French-born Auguste Ricord (left), an alleged mastermind of international drug traffic who was indicted by a N.Y. grand jury.

PARKS:
YELLOWSTONE CENTENNIAL

To most Americans national parks mean something enduring in an age of change—something good, something alive and beautiful. They also represent something distinctly American, an idea that took form in the vast reaches of the 19th century frontier and subsequently reached around the globe. Throughout the world the National Parks Centennial Year commemorated the fact that it all began at Yellowstone. How did it happen?

The men who made the first detailed exploration of the Yellowstone plateau in 1870 were men of the frontier, and, as such, they recognized the commercial potential of the spectacular tract they had explored. They also recognized, however, that they had surveyed an irreplaceable work of nature, and in consequence they took the unprecedented step of urging that the area be set aside under national protection for the use of the public in perpetuity.

They were Yellowstone's original sponsors, and in less than two years they convinced a nation. On March 1, 1872, President Ulysses S. Grant signed into law a bill setting aside 2,000,000 acres of Wyoming and Montana wilderness "as a public park or pleasuring ground for the benefit and enjoyment of the people."

Although the cornerstone of what was to become a national park system embracing tens of millions of acres had been laid, the survival and growth of that system nevertheless were by no means assured. For Yellowstone itself initially lacked the funds needed merely to maintain it. The first superintendent received no salary and was expected to pay his own expenses. Poachers and souvenir hunters threatened to destroy the wildlife and unique thermal formations. In the case of Yellowstone the U.S. Cavalry ultimately came to the rescue, administering the park from 1889 until the National Park Service was established in the Department of the Interior in 1916. In the meantime, other cherished areas had been added piecemeal to the system, which eventually grew to more than 280 parks.

Congress, meanwhile, had also authorized a separate system of national monuments, to preserve both natural and historical treasures. In the years following the creation of the National Park Service many landmarks, military

The world's first national park preserve, Yellowstone, marked its centenary in 1972, its splendor nearly undisturbed from time immemorial.

George A. Grant, National Park Service

Encompassing an area of incomparably dramatic thermal springs, Yellowstone was immediately understood by surveyors to be unique. The Mammoth Hot Springs, steam perpetually rising from its boiling cauldron, is one of dozens preserved in the park.

Old Faithful, to millions the symbol of Yellowstone Park, is the world's most famous geyser.

camps, battlefield sites and other historic monuments—administered by a host of different Federal agencies—were consolidated under the service. The agency also assumed responsibility for administering most national recreation areas, usually associated with the oceans, lakes, rivers and impounded waters of hydroelectric dams.

In the summer of 1971 the National Park Service opened still another kind of park— Wolf Trap Farm Park for the Performing Arts—a cultural oasis devoted to annual summer seasons of music and theater in the wooded Washington suburb of Vienna, Va.

The centennial celebration began officially with a banquet in Washington on March 1. In his proclamation designating 1972 as the National Parks Centennial Year, President Nixon noted that Yellowstone has "inspired more than 100 nations to set aside over 1,200 national parks and reserves." In honor of the occasion he signed legislation creating the National Parks Centennial Commission, a body authorized by Congress to oversee centennial activities. Edmund B. Thornton was appointed head of the 15-member group, on which I was privileged to serve.

At the outset the commission decided that the centennial should be more than a celebration, that it provided an opportunity for the nation to assess its National Park System and parks policy and to accelerate the planning needed to ensure that national parks continue their unique service.

To this end, the commission empowered the Conservation Foundation of Washington, D.C., to conduct a national parks symposium from April 13 to 15 at Yosemite National Park in California. There, representatives of a broad cross-section of the country discussed the challenges to national parks and proposed possible new ways of meeting them.

The findings of the symposium were presented at the major event of the centennial—the Second World Conference on National Parks, held at Yellowstone and Grand Teton National Parks during Sept. 18–27. Cosponsored by the Centennial Commission and the International Union for Conservation of Nature and Natural Resources, the event drew some 500 delegates from almost 100 countries.

Throughout the year almost every area in the National Park System held a special centennial observance of its own. Local events ranged from a series of summer seminars at Rocky Mountain National Park in Colorado through the centennial and tricentennial commemoration at Castillo de San Marcos National Monument (a 17th century fort in Florida) to a goat roast at Navajo National Monument in Arizona.

The consensus at all of the centennial gatherings was that the national parks face problems—of too many people, too many automobiles, too much litter and just plain human conflict. However, many of those concerned shared my conviction that the abiding spirit which created Yellowstone National Park 100 years ago will be equal to future tasks.

ROGERS C. B. MORTON
U.S. Secretary of the Interior

Culver Pictures

The original north entrance bore the statutory words "for the benefit . . . of the people."

Not the least of Yellowstone's enthusiasts, Theodore Roosevelt paid a state visit as President.

Culver Pictures

Undisturbed wilderness, least known but perhaps most beguiling of Yellowstone's charms, is aplenty.

Jonathan Blair, National Park Service

Following a 20-year absence, Charles Chaplin returned to the United States April 2. Two weeks later the 82-year-old comedian was awarded a special Oscar for the "humor and humanity" he has brought to so many motion pictures.

J.-P. Laffont, Gamma

PEOPLE

UPI

In June the U.S. Supreme Court declined to overturn the civil contempt conviction of Earl Caldwell. The court ruled that newsmen must testify before grand juries concerning information obtained confidentially. "The New York Times'" reporter had refused to testify before such a jury in a 1970 Black Panther case.

Margaret Truman Daniel ended the year by leading her family and the nation in mourning the death of her father, Harry S. Truman. Her intimate, "warm-hearted" biography of the nation's 33d president had been published only a few weeks earlier.

UPI

Marina Whitman, professor of economics at the University of Pittsburgh and a member of the Price Commission, was the first woman appointed to the Council of Economic Advisers.

Alfred Lunt, 79, and Lynn Fontanne, 85, celebrated their 50th wedding anniversary in May. Subsequently, ANTA presented the theatrical couple with its first National Artist award.

On Dec. 20, the Rev. Philip Berrigan (center) was released from a Danbury (Conn.) prison after serving 39 months for antiwar activities. He was met by the Rev. Daniel Berrigan (r), who had been released earlier, and 300 sympathizers.

Meyer Lansky was arrested by FBI agents in Miami on Nov. 7 and charged with income-tax evasion and racketeering. The reputed financial genius of the U.S. underworld had sought asylum in several foreign countries after having been denied citizenship in Israel.

A "lovely party": Edith Evans (l), Peggy Ashcroft (holding glass) and Agatha Christie (r) joined to mark the 90th birthday of Dame Sybil Thorndike. Of the event, Dame Sybil said: "I don't feel 90 in my head but I feel 180 in my body. It's such a bally nuisance."

Don Carl Steffen, Rapho Guillumette

Columnist Jack Anderson published documents proving that the administration supported Pakistan in its 1971 war with India and a memo linking the settlement of an ITT antitrust case with an ITT contribution to the GOP convention.

UPI

Yvonne Braithwaite Burke, 40-year-old California assemblywoman, served as cochairman of the 1972 Democratic convention and was elected to the U.S. House of Representatives in November.

"New York Daily News" Photo

Motion-picture producer Alfred Hitchcock released "Frenzy" and was awarded a Doctor of Humane Letters degree by Columbia University in 1972. The honorary degree's citation said: "You have explored and exorcised the guilts and fears of your characters and your audiences with a unique blend of macabre humor and meditative humanity."

John P. Davies, Jr., whose foreign-service career ended in the aftermath of China's Communist revolution, reviews Sino-American relations after World War II in "Dragon by the Tail."

Charles O. Finley, owner and general manager of the Oakland Athletics, was the club's main fan as the A's won the World Series. He also purchased pro hockey and basketball teams.

Musician and writer Robert Craft (r) discussed his association with the late Igor Stravinsky (l) in "Stravinsky: The Chronicle of a Friendship, 1948–1971."

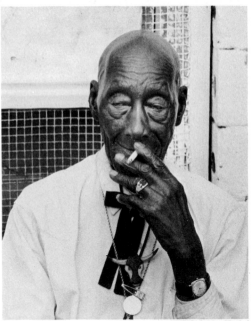

Charlie Smith turned 130 and refused to visit his native Liberia. The oldest living American does not believe men have walked on the moon, although he watched the Apollo 17 launch.

Benjamin L. Hooks, 47-year-old Baptist minister, Memphis lawyer and criminal court justice, became the first black to serve on the seven-member Federal Communications Commission.

The Rev. Dr. Nathan Scott, Jr. (r) presented the Rev. Theodore Hesburgh, president of Notre Dame University, with the first Reinhold Niebuhr Award. Later, at the request of President Nixon, Hesburgh resigned as chairman of the Commission on Civil Rights.

PERU

Although moderating its pace, Peru's ruling junta, which seized power in 1968, continued in 1972 to pursue its goals of social reform, international independence and state domination of the economy.

Headed by Gen. Juan Velasco Alvarado, the "revolutionary government," which attempts to avoid the pitfalls of both capitalism and Communism, continued a sweeping agrarian reform under which 8,000,000 acres of farmland and 1,300,000 head of cattle have been distributed. It also spurred the formation of "industrial communities," through which workers share in the ownership and management of various firms.

Internationally, Peru maintained its policy of forging diplomatic and economic links with nations of different ideological hues. In February the government exchanged ambassadors with mainland China, and in July the reestablishment of diplomatic relations with Cuba was announced—just seven months after Premier Castro's cordial visit to Lima. Although unsuccessful, Peru—which increasingly views itself as a leader among Latin American states—led the fight in the Organization of American States to have economic and diplomatic sanctions against the Havana regime lifted. Similarly, it continued to champion the principle of national sovereignty over coastal waters within a 200 mile limit.

Expropriations tightened the government's grip on the economy. In July, for example, the generals-turned-politicians took over the National Telephone Company, formerly a European-owned firm, which handles long distance calls in Peru.

Ecological changes caused the flight from Peru's waters of *anchoveta,* the raw material from which fishmeal is made, dealing a severe blow to an industry which employs 30,000 Peruvians and generates one-third of the nation's export earnings. The decline bankrupted several small fishmeal producers and injured bankers who had extended credit to businesses in the sector. While exports of cotton, sugar and wool also dropped, mining production rose 5 percent between January and July, prompting the finance ministry to estimate a 7.5 percent rise in GNP for the year—an overly optimistic forecast in light of a 500,000 ton decrease in fishmeal production by August. Low levels of private investment plagued the economy as domestic and foreign capitalists viewed with apprehension the creation of more "industrial communities."

A bright spot appeared on the economic horizon as foreign petroleum companies, which had avoided Peru after the expropriation without compensation of Standard Oil's International Petroleum Corporation in 1968, signed contracts to explore for deposits in the eastern jungles. These agreements required the foreign firms to share 50 percent or more of the oil produced instead of paying taxes or royalties—two items which in the past had triggered disputes. The finance ministry also took heart at the willingness of a pool of U.S., Canadian and European banks to extend credits and reschedule debt payments totaling $111,500,000, thereby brightening Peru's fiscal and balance of payments prospects for the next year.

In his Oct. 3, 1972, anniversary speech to the nation, Velasco stated that "our patience to tolerate the work of the enemies who are undermining the revolution is reaching its end." Thus, the government will intensify efforts to exile captured guerrillas, expel dissident priests and sanction hostile newspapers. These measures, all of which were undertaken in 1972, were justified on the ground that a strong hand is needed to guide the social and economic transformations of a regime which in four years has done more for the country than all previous governments combined.

Because the generals lack a political vehicle with which to handle disputes—elections were suspended, the congress closed and parties intimidated in 1968—a "national system of support for social mobilization" has been advanced to assure "participation of an organized people" in the Peruvian revolution, perhaps through a corporate state based on the "industrial communities" and a new labor confederation.

GEORGE W. GRAYSON
Associate Professor of Government
College of William and Mary

PHILIPPINE REPUBLIC

The worst rains and flooding in the country's history struck the Philippines in mid-1972. In September, however, this natural disaster was overshadowed by the imposition of martial law by President Ferdinand Marcos.

Politics. The more than usually bloody 1971 election campaign, in which nine persons were killed and 96 wounded at a Liberal Party rally, was followed in 1972 by what seemed to be a mounting wave of politically related acts of violence. The climax was reached on Sept. 22 with an unsuccessful attempt to assassinate Defense Secretary Juan Ponce Enrile.

The attack on the defense secretary was followed within hours by the imposition of martial law by President Marcos. Political opponents of Marcos were subsequently detained

for alleged support of the country's growing Communist movement. Those arrested included Liberal Sen. Benigno Acquino, Jr., widely regarded as a possible successor to Marcos. Newspapers and broadcasting stations were closed down, and many journalists were jailed.

President Marcos' action came at a time when an elected constitutional convention was deliberating whether to make the Philippine government parliamentary rather than presidential. Such a move was favored by Marcos, who could then remain as the country's leader, but it was not expected that a popular referendum scheduled for 1973 would approve the change. The imposition of martial law had been publicly predicted by critics of the president, who claimed that he would not relinquish the office.

Insurgents. President Marcos justified his takeover as a defense against a threat to the nation. The Maoist "New Peoples Army" was becoming bolder in its attacks (and allegedly receiving arms from abroad), while several leading opposition politicians and journalists were accused of having given encouragement to the Communists. Even Phillippine intelligence estimates, however, placed the number of regular Communist guerrillas at no more than 1,200 persons, a group augmented by 8,500 to 10,000 other insurgents.

The declaration of martial law had the effect of markedly restricting, at least temporarily, the escalating clashes between Muslims and Christians on the southern island of Mindanao.

Floods. Nearly five weeks of almost continuous monsoon rains in mid-1972 left 430 Filipinos dead, nearly 750,000 persons homeless and property destruction in the hundreds of millions of dollars.

Economy. Partly as a result of the devastating floods, the economic situation had deteriorated in the months before martial law was established. Inflation, however, had been taking its toll for a much longer period and by mid-year had reached an annual rate of 18 percent. Rice and fish, in which the nation is still not self-sufficient, were in shorter supply than usual, and sugar and corn as well as rice were apparently being held back by hoarders.

President Marcos made several bold economic moves after proclaiming martial law. He sought to control, and even reduce, prices and succeeded in forcing hoarded foodstuffs into the open market. The country's two steel mills were nationalized, and utility companies and airlines were taken over by the government. In a move as much political as economic, Marcos also ordered the redistribution of nearly 4,000,000 acres of farmland to former

Photos UPI

On live TV, a man draws a knife and stabs Mrs. Imelda Marcos, wife of the Philippine president. She recovered. Guards shot the assailant dead.

tenant farmers. Government help, however, would be needed to provide the capital before the farmers could take advantage of the decree.

Foreign Relations. Relations with the United States continued to dominate Filipino foreign policy. In August the Philippine Supreme Court ruled that U.S. citizens could not hold land acquired since independence (1946). After the proclamation of martial law, however, President Marcos, in his bid for U.S. support and investment (which totaled between $2,000,000 and $3,000,000 in 1972), announced that U.S. citizens could continue to hold land, even after the Laurel-Langley Treaty expires in 1974.

RICHARD BUTWELL
Chairman, Department of Political Science
State University of New York
College at Brockport

Kodak's pocket Instamatic cameras were a major 1972 innovation. Their size, weight and ease of use appealed to the amateur photographer.

PHOTOGRAPHY

One of every five Americans—about 42,000,-000 in all—possessed some sort of photographic equipment in 1972. With every indicator pointing toward a future in which amateur photography would attain the dimensions of a folk art, manufacturers of equipment appeared to be embarking on a new round of competition to provide the market with more sophisticated tools.

Moreover, the increasing interest among amateurs in recording the experiences of their daily lives was reinforced by a marked trend among professionals. The documentary photograph—the printed record of an actual person, event or condition—clearly was the priority of the serious photographer, a fact which was revealed in an increased number of photo exhibits throughout the United States during the year.

New Equipment. In the field of advanced cameras, Japanese based manufacturers were taking over where the Germans left off. Japan's rapidly accelerating production activity resulted in growing East-West amalgamation. And, with the introduction by Kodak and Polaroid of new camera and film systems, the amateur photo field saw signs of a coming revolution.

The sluggishness of the West German photo industry was evident as early as Jan. 1, 1972 —the official closing date of the New York offices of the Camera Industries of West Germany. The once mighty Zeiss manufacturer had seen the demise of most of its photographic operations. As 1972 drew to a close, only Leitz and Rollei manufacturers remained as the bulwarks of the West German photo industry.

To strengthen their respective economic conditions, two German companies made alliances with two Japanese corporations. The Germans wanted the benefit of the Japanese manufacturers' ability to produce quality photo equipment on a mass scale; the Japanese sought the technical expertise of the German manufacturers.

In the area of photo repair cooperation was burgeoning. A group of Japanese manufacturing representatives visited the National Camera Repair training center in Denver, Colo. A U.S. based association of photo technologists pushed for easier and cheaper repair service for the increasingly popular Japanese produced automatic cameras.

Much of the year's new equipment was introduced at Photokina, the international show held every other fall in Cologne, West Germany. (Rumors placed the 1974 show in Japan.) Olympus, a growing Japanese manufacturer, introduced a new 35mm camera, lens and accessories system as a contender against the Nikon and Canon systems. New models of old favorites made by Leitz and Rollei had been presented earlier in the year. Also at Photokina, a group of Japanese manufacturers hopped on the automatic bandwagon with excellent electronic-exposure-system cameras.

Other technical equipment news included the introduction of increasingly computerized flash units and the increased marketing of a variety of color products geared to encouraging at-home color processing.

In the amateur field, Kodak came out with a pocket Instamatic camera, the first major change in the Instamatic line since its introduction in 1962. Everything about it—size, weight, ease of use, automatic exposure sys-

Documentary photo exhibits enjoyed increasing popularity in 1972. A show of Chinese photographs at the Metropolitan Museum of Art in New York City was a particular favorite.

Bhupendra Karia © ICP

tem—is aimed at encouraging the non-camera buff to carry one. The initial campaign was obviously successful. By summer, just four months after its introduction, the millionth unit was in production.

Polaroid introduced a new instant-print camera in the fall. Tentatively named the SX-70, this completely automatic camera (even to film advancement) represents the first major change in Polaroid cameras since the first one, an in-camera processing system, went on sale. The most striking feature of the new camera is its film, which develops outside the camera in full view of the photographer. The brilliant color prints, sheathed in unscratchable plastic, are the end result of an ecology-conscious, garbage-free process which eliminates the chemical laden throwaway that was an integral part of Polaroid's old processing system.

Polaroid was planning to make its own film for the SX-70. Plants were being built in the

This moving photograph of a dead man and his mourners was part of a successful W. Eugene Smith exhibit which toured Japan during 1972.

Photograph by W. Eugene Smith/ICP

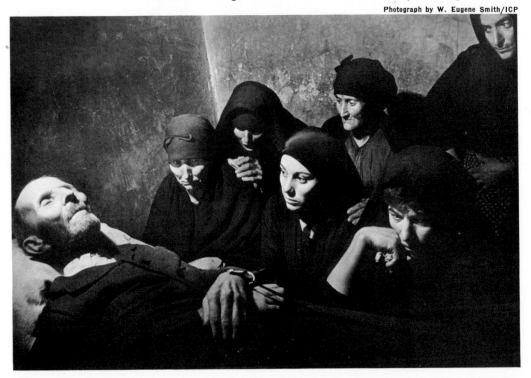

Boston (Mass.) area to handle the complete assemblage of the components and production of the entire film package, work that had been subcontracted previously.

In addition to presenting its new Instamatic, Kodak decided to enter the instant-photography field which had been Polaroid's monopoly. The company plans to make film for use in older Polaroid models and to manufacture its own in-camera processing system by the mid-1970's.

Photo Exhibits. For the first time, New York City's Whitney Museum of American Art opened its doors to photography. David Douglas Duncan's 21-year retrospective "One Generation of War and Peace"—a collection of the *Life* photographer's prints from Korea in the early 1950's to Vietnam in the late 1960's to Bali in 1971—was followed by the group exhibit "Executive Order 9066." The latter was a record of the internment of 110,000 Japanese-Americans in the United States during World War II.

The Metropolitan Museum of Art held two important photo exhibits: a 20-year retrospective of the work of Edward Weston, well known for his photographs of Mexico in the 1920's and of Western U.S. landscapes in the 1930's, and a show devoted to photos of China. Two other New York City galleries had shows on China—a reflection of the increased interest in that country spurred by President Nixon's visit in February.

The most characteristic attitude of the 1972 photographer was concern—with people and how they live. The trend was revealed in several group shows. A traveling exhibit, organized by the International Fund for Concerned Photography, included the work of more than 80 photographers who had covered everything from poverty to war, hippies to politics. And in Washington, D.C., a group exhibit of the work of "Documerica" photographers showed the first works from the federally sponsored project, organized in 1972 to document the effects of pollution on the U.S. environment. Concern was also evident in the works of nine photojournalists whose Vietnam war photos were exhibited at the Brooklyn Museum in New York City.

Photojournalists on the U.S. West Coast were particularly active. Three different groups published these alternate-form works: a datebook titled *Winds of Change, 1972,* a book called *America in Crisis* and a third book titled *Shots: Photographs from the Underground Press.* All three publications, which were distributed as paperbacks and sold for less than $5.00, were the works of highly partisan, little known photographers who considered themselves "participants" in, rather than observers of, the American scene. They had specialized in photographing the antiwar movement, blacks and the urban condition.

In the fall, an exhibit of more than a dozen essays on various American lifestyles opened in New York City in conjunction with the publication of *America: Photographic Statements,* published by *Camera35.* The new style annual departed from the traditional nonthematic collection of a few photos by many photographers to extended statements by a handful of photographers each with a viewpoint. The annual also included essays by women photographers, whose work was being published more frequently than before.

BARBARA L. LOBRON
Senior Editor, *Camera35*

The Concerned Photographer/ICP

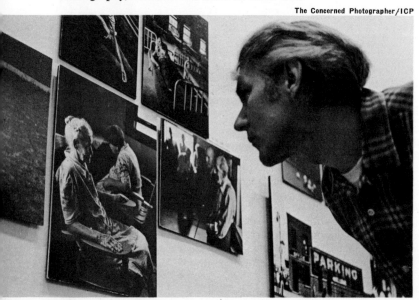

With concern for people and how they live a major photo trend, the International Fund for Concerned Photography organized traveling exhibits.

PHYSICAL SCIENCES

Relativity Test. One of the strangest predictions of general relativity theory is that under special circumstances time will contract. Ever since Albert Einstein published his theory more than fifty years ago, experimenters have been wondering how to test this so-called clock paradox, and in 1972 two physicists finally succeeded in doing so.

Relativity theory implies that a clock moving at high speed would run more slowly than an identical clock remaining at rest. Presumably, a boy or girl taking a trip to a nearby star in a spacecraft that traveled at close to the speed of light could return to earth as a young adult, though over 50 years might have elapsed on earth. But his or her playmates would be wrinkled and gray with age, because time would have moved more rapidly for them.

At speeds that man ordinarily attains, the contraction of time is very slight and difficult to measure. But the accuracy of atomic clocks, which keep time according to the vibrations of certain atoms, has been so improved recently that they can now measure time within the range of a few nanoseconds (billionths of a second). Four such clocks were used in a simple experiment conducted by J. C. Hafele of Washington University and Richard E. Keating of the U.S. Naval Observatory. They took the clocks on two round-the-world airplane trips—one eastward, the other westward.

Owing to the additional velocity supplied by the rotation of the earth itself, the airborne clocks behaved differently on the two flights. Compared with standard clocks at the Naval Observatory, they lost an average of 59 nanoseconds during the eastward trip and gained an average of 273 nanoseconds flying westward. Both figures agreed closely with those predicted by relativity theory.

Pollution Controls. As they have since 1970, chemists and physicists continued to work on preserving and improving man's environment. D. Challinor of the Smithsonian Institution released preliminary figures that measured the absorption of sunlight by polluted air. Considerably less ultraviolet light reaches ground level at Washington, D.C., than in the neighboring community of Rockville, Md., where the air is less badly polluted by automobile exhaust fumes. Previous reports by the Smithsonian showed that the amounts of solar radiation now reaching Washington are significantly less than the levels recorded in 1907 and 1919, when air pollution was only a minor problem. For future comparisons, measurements are now being made of incident sunlight in Jerusalem, Point Barrow (Alaska), Rock-

Radiation Biology Lab, Smithsonian Institution

Recordings of the incidence of ultraviolet light provide a measure of pollution intensity at this instrument's site in Rockville, Md.

ville and Washington. The Smithsonian investigators want to be able to follow trends in pollution and also to evaluate any possible environmental effects of the English-French supersonic transport planes.

A variety of solutions for automotive exhaust problems was proposed in 1972. Roger J. Schoeppel reported that he and his colleagues at Oklahoma State University had converted four gasoline engines so that they could run on pure hydrogen gas. The obvious advantage of using hydrogen as a fuel is that the exhaust would then consist almost entirely of water vapor. A hybrid automobile that can run on gasoline in the country and hydrogen in the city has been designed by R. H. Wiswall, Jr., and J. J. Reilly of Brookhaven National Laboratory, Long Island. Still a third new approach to this problem is the Boston Reformed Fuel Car, which contains a small unit that pretreats gasoline, converting it into hydrogen and carbon dioxide, as explained by Harold Sorenson of International Materials Corporation, Boston. In a more conventional approach to auto pollution control, a team of Bell Telephone Laboratory scientists developed a much cheaper material to replace the platinum catalysts that had been contemplated for 1976-model cars in order to meet the new strict Federal clean-air requirements.

A flock of new ways to dispose of solid and liquid wastes is being developed. Old automobile tires, after they have been shredded, can be further degraded by a fungus, according to Walter J. Nickerson of Rutgers Institute of Microbiology. If the resulting powder is then

The fuel reformer in the trunk of a prototype automobile converts standard gasoline to carbon dioxide and hydrogen in a preliminary step. The hydrogen-carbon dioxide mixture can then be used as a relatively nonpolluting fuel in a conventional engine.

plowed into sandy or clayed soils, it will improve soil consistency so that rainwater will penetrate at just about the right rate.

Several scientists have recently urged a careful study of one of the commonest methods of disposing of wastes—by dumping or pumping them into deep wells. The U.S. Geological Survey is currently trying to determine the long-term effects of this method under different conditions and in different locations. The chief worry is that materials injected into wells may seep out and pollute the vast underground lakes that supply well water to many communities, especially in the Southwestern states. In other cases, wells have been known to rupture; one such well spewed 150,000 gallons of paper mill wastes into Lake Erie. Another danger from waste disposal by this method was pointed up when the Geological Survey's Earthquake Research Center determined that a succession of minor earthquakes near Denver was almost certainly caused by the Army Corps of Engineers' practice of pumping poisonous wastes into a well two miles deep.

Chemical Innovations. Chemists continued to augment the flow of promising new products. They have determined that the natural properties of wool yarn can be greatly enhanced by exposing the material to a gas discharge similar to that in a neon light. Two U.S. Department of Agriculture scientists, Merle M. Millard and Kay Sue Lee, reported that the discharge alone reduced wool shrinkage from 45 percent to only about 3 percent in a standard wash test. The same gas discharge can be used to graft small amounts of certain chemicals onto the wool fibers to make them mothproof, fire-resistant and oil-repellant.

Chemists at the Du Pont company have produced a fiber that has the strength of stainless steel wire but only one-sixth the weight. Its characteristics suit it for use in helicopter rotor blades, reinforced paneling and many other products.

The development of an experimental "surgical glue" was announced by the Walter Reed Army Medical Center in Washington. The new adhesive is a liquid that solidifies into a tough, sterile, plastic film that stops bleeding almost instantly. Tests under combat conditions in Vietnam and in several civilian operations show that the glue works well and produces no ill effects.

New Physical Tools. The world's mightiest scientific instrument, a proton accelerator at Batavia, Ill., began operating at close to its designed maximum of 200,000,000,000 electron volts which later technical innovations doubled to 400,000,000,000 electron volts, with a potential existing for a further increase in power. It almost immediately started to yield new information about basic physics. This hollow ring is equipped with magnets and other electronic gear that whip circling protons (hydrogen nuclei) to almost the speed of light, at which point they have energies of 300,000,-000,000 electron volts.

One interesting finding from experiments is that the increase in the number of assorted particles produced by collisions between protons is not so large as the increase in the energy of the protons—at least in going from 28,000,-000,000 up to 300,000,000,000 electron volts. Physicists had had some reason to believe from results of prior cosmic-ray experiments, that at such high energies the number of particles produced might not total much more than the number observed at somewhat lower energies. However, there is a definite increase, but not in direct proportion to the energy increase.

One prospect is that the new accelerator will generate a particular heavy nuclear particle, the intermediate boson, that has been predicted by theorists but never observed. If this particle can be found, it will help to unify theories that link electromagnetic forces with the so-called weak interactions, such as those that influence radioactive decay of nuclei.

Recent findings also encouraged physicists to construct much more powerful electron microscopes. Some theorists had said that at energies exceeding about 1,000,000 volts the electron beam, which serves the same purpose as light in an ordinary microscope, would severely damage whatever specimen was being examined. Now experiments by Gareth Thomas and Robert Glaeser of the University of California show that electron beams ranging in energy up to a level of 2,500,000 volts are actually less damaging to biological specimens than those in the lower energy ranges. The high-energy beams seem to pass through the specimen before they have a chance to inflict serious damage. It now seems likely that a 5,000,000 volt electron microscope will produce clear pictures of DNA and RNA molecules, viruses, cell membranes and other extremely small biological entities that are vital to life.

Applied Physics. In 1972 physicists also unveiled some innovations in more mundane machines that may change the lives of millions of people. One is a miniature hearing aid, developed at the Callier Hearing and Speech Center in Dallas. Its main feature is a tiny magnet, weighing little more than one-hundredth of a gram, that can be permanently attached to a projection on the eardrum. Linked electronically to a comparably small microphone that is inserted in the ear, this magnet makes the eardrum vibrate. This eliminates the annoying "squeal" that ordinary hearing aids sometimes generate.

The variety and usefulness of lasers (instruments that emit exquisitely focused beams of light) continued to increase. Sturdy lasers, made of a semiconductor material, have been induced to emit visible orange light, and two groups of experimenters now believe that they can create lasers that emit X rays.

The distance between the earth and the moon has been measured with a greater degree of accuracy than ever before by bouncing laser beams off three reflectors left on the moon by the Apollo 11, 14 and 15 missions. Bursts of red laser light are aimed at the reflectors from the McDonald Observatory in Texas, and the time it takes them to return to earth (somewhat more than two seconds) is then carefully measured. With present equipment astronomers estimate that they are measuring the earth–moon distance to an accuracy of within six inches, which is sufficiently precise to yield new information about the observed wobbling of the moon on its axis.

James L. Flanagan of Bell Telephone Laboratories demonstrated two computerized talking machines. They, or their successors, will help people obtain travel information, medical data and other information without stepping out of the house. The person would simply pick up the phone, dial the appropriate source of information—a library, for instance —and be greeted by a synthetic voice saying: "This is a computer speaking." The caller could then ask his questions, which would be interpreted by the talking machine and changed into a computer code. The computer would look up the information and relay it to the caller in its synthetic voice. Although this way of communicating may at present seem like far-out science fiction, many scientists are confident that such a service will be available at reasonable cost within their lifetimes.

Some projects presently under investigation may well produce no practical results for a century or more, yet they fascinate scientists who like to dream about the future and what they can do to shape it. Richard C. Arnold of Argonne National Laboratory near Chicago recently described how he transmitted Morse code with a stream of subatomic particles called muons. Generated by an accelerator, the muons passed through a five-foot wall before being picked up by a "listening post" set about 150 meters away. In time, says Arnold, muon beams may become as good a way for broadcasting voice and television signals as microwave relays and transmitter satellites.

The question of where to build power-generating plants has provoked a great deal of controversy in recent years. More electric power is in demand, yet any proposal to build a new plant meets with the objections of conservationists who fear pollution by smoke or waste heat, or in the case of nuclear reactors, the chance of a disastrous runaway reaction. What is perhaps the ultimate solution to this dilemma was proposed at an American Chemical Society meeting by a group of researchers from the Georgia Institute of Technology. Their suggestion is to place a compact nuclear power plant in orbit around the earth. It could be remotely controlled from earth and its radioactive waste products could be safely shot off into another orbit around the sun.

GEORGE A. W. BOEHM
Free-lance Science Writer

Security is tight as Poles line streets of Warsaw to welcome U.S. President Richard Nixon.

POLAND

In late May 1972, Poland and West Germany finally ratified the treaty, originally signed in December 1970, normalizing relations between them. They simultaneously established diplomatic relations. After long debate and some persistent opposition in the Federal Republic, the two states renounced the threat and use of force in their mutual relations, agreed to "proceed from" their current joint border and not to attempt to change it unilaterally and reaffirmed the inalienable right of self-determination for all peoples. The Poles quickly announced that the long-disputed Oder-Neisse frontier had been recognized as final and inviolable in international law.

In late June the Vatican demonstrated its de facto recognition of full Polish sovereignty over the former German territories by announcing the appointment of six resident Polish bishops to the area and reorganizing diocesan boundaries within it. In a conciliatory move on its part the regime of Edward Gierek abolished a ten-year-old law requiring the church to maintain inventories of its property for governmental inspections and tax purposes, and restored extensive properties in the western lands to church ownership. In November the Roman Catholic primate of Poland, Stefan Cardinal Wyszynski, traveled to Rome for talks aimed at reestablishing formal relations between Poland and the Vatican.

Domestically, the Gierek regime sought to strengthen its political support and to continue to improve the economic conditions that had provoked workers' riots in 1970. In elections for the *Sejum* (parliament) at the start of the year the Polish electorate overwhelmingly chose the "preferred" candidates of the "Front of National Unity," replacing almost two-thirds of the members of the previous body. Subsequent structural and personnel changes in the new government were designed to streamline it and increase its flexibility, and to emphasize such long-neglected areas as science and technology, ecology and social problems.

Mieczyslaw Moczar, once considered a top rival to Gierek, lost his last power base when he was removed as chairman of the large veterans' organization ZBoWiD. After 17 months of revision the draft program of the new five-year plan (1971–1975) for the socio-economic development of Poland was adopted. In November, following President Nixon's mid-year visit to Warsaw, the first trip by an American president to Poland, the United States and Poland signed a series of agreements expected to triple trade between the two countries over the next several years. A new consular and trade pact was also signed by Poland with Yugoslavia.

JOSEPH F. ZACEK
Professor of History
State University of New York at Albany

POPULATION

Interest in the growth and distribution of human populations continued to increase in 1972. The U.S. Commission on Population Growth and the American Future issued an intelligent and bold report, arguing that population touches many areas of American life and that population policies ought therefore to be included in governmental policy-making and planning. The Club of Rome, a private group of wealthy industrialists and international intellectuals, issued a report entitled *The Limits of Growth,* in which elaborate computer models purported to show that the world is doomed if either population or industrial output continues to grow much longer. And all over the industrialized world, fertility continued to drop sharply, prompting some European experts to worry over too low fertility.

By far the most impressive intellectual and political development of the year was the report of the Commission on Population Growth and the American Future. Chaired by John D. Rockefeller III and with a professional staff directed by Charles F. Westoff, the body had commissioned more than 100 research papers on all areas relating to population by the country's finest researchers. After two years of deliberation the commission concluded:

1. ". . . every country always has a population problem, in the sense of achieving a proper balance between size, growth, and distribution on the one hand, and, on the other, the quality of life to which every person . . . aspires," and that

2. while population growth has not caused most of our social problems, there "is hardly any social problem confronting this nation whose solution would be easier if our population were larger."

3. Population growth is clearly not the sole cause of environmental decay, as has been claimed by some analysts. Attention must be paid more to how we do things—our way of life—than to how many people are doing these things. Nonetheless, it remains true that "increasing numbers press us to adopt new technologies before we know what we are doing. . . . Slower population growth will not eliminate this situation, but it will reduce the urgency, the 'crash program' character of much that we do."

4. "The nation has nothing to fear from a gradual approach to population stabilization." Indeed, a reduction in the rate of population growth would bring important economic benefits if the United States develops policies to take advantage of "the opportunities for social and economic improvement that slower population growth would provide."

5. The many state laws restricting access to contraceptive information and supplies, sterilization, and abortion should be modified to allow all Americans to avoid unwanted births.

6. "Recognizing that our population cannot grow indefinitely, and appreciating the advantages of moving now toward the stabilization of population, the Commission recommends that the nation welcome and plan for a stabilized population."

Publication of the Club of Rome report *Limits of Growth* was accompanied by a high-powered public relations effort, but was followed by acid criticism from most scientific reviewers. A major source of criticism was the failure of the authors (Donella H. Meadows, Dennis L. Meadows, Jorgen Randers, William W. Behrens III) to provide any information on the assumptions and methodology of their calculations. *Limits of Growth* presented only the final output in the form of spaghetti-like computer graphs, but as with all such computer simulations the results were entirely dependent on the accuracy of the models used and assumptions made. Under such circumstances many scientists concluded, perhaps unfairly, that the highly promoted report was an exercise in propaganda rather than science. Recognizing this reaction, the authors published their data, methods and assumptions.

Meanwhile, for reasons totally unrelated to the reports of the Commission and the Club of Rome, fertility in industrialized countries has been dropping rapidly since the mid-1960's. The most recent preliminary data indicate that U.S. fertility has undergone the sharpest decline in its history, and is currently at record low levels very near to replacement (the level required for each reproducing generation merely to replace itself, leading eventually to zero population growth). Fertility in Europe and other industrialized countries is also declining rapidly, prompting some (particularly French) experts at the Second European Population Conference, held in Strasbourg, France, in September 1971, to express concern about "stagnation" and "decline." Such talk has not been heard since the low fertility of the 1930's, but by now most experts realize that fertility averaging "replacement" over the long term is an appropriate goal for most countries and that short-term drops below replacement are not a cause for serious concern.

MICHAEL S. TEITELBAUM
Office of Population Research, Princeton

PORTUGAL

In a colorful ceremony in April in Rio de Janeiro, the president of Portugal, Adm. Americo Thomas, handed over to the Brazilian head of state, Emilio Medici, a box containing the bones of the man who founded Brazil as an independent and sovereign state 150 years ago.

That ceremony was intended to symbolize Portugal's contribution to the history and culture of Brazil on the occasion of the 150th anniversary of the independence of the South American country. The presentation of the bones of Emperor Dom Pedro IV of Portugal and I of Brazil, carried out on the banks of the Ipiranga River near São Paulo, where the Emperor had first declared the freedom of the new country, marked the beginning of a new era in Portuguese-Brazilian relations.

In June, almost 50 years after it was imposed, formal press censorship was abolished in Portugal and its overseas territories. In practice, however, the board of censors still functions with the same responsibilities but under a different name. The old designation of Comissão de Censura has been replaced by the Comissão de Exame Previo (Prior Review Board).

Under the newly formulated law, modeled on the one in effect in Spain, nothing has really changed, although newspapers, magazines and other publications no longer print the phrase honored by half a century of use, "Passed by the Board of Censors." The government, in fact, prohibited further publication of the phrase, claiming that the Board of Censors no longer exists.

A few opposition newspapers did, however, try to append the phrase "Passed by the Prior Review Board" to their publications, but they stopped after receiving a stern warning from authorities that they could be heavily fined and face legal action if they continued. The government obviously was anxious to avoid reminding readers that censorship still exists in their country.

In July the members of the National Assembly (parliament) reelected Thomas, the only candidate for the position, to a third term as president, with a seven-year mandate. President Thomas was first elected in 1958 by universal suffrage, but later his candidacy—proposed by the late dictator Premier Antonio Salazar—was challenged by Air Force Gen. Humberto Delgado. General Delgado was assassinated mysteriously just across the border in southwestern Spain in 1964, and the Portuguese constitution was later amended so that in future the president would be elected directly by members of the National Assembly.

Also in July, after nearly three years of hard negotiations, Portugal and the European Economic Community (EEC) signed an accord in Brussels granting Portugal preferential treatment in its trade with the enlarged EEC as of Jan. 1, 1973. A founding member of the European Free Trade Union (EFTA), Portugal will retain its ties with EFTA countries even after it enters an association with the Common Market. This will enable Portugal to maintain close relations with two huge economic blocks and thereby with the whole of Western Europe.

True, such traditional Portuguese exports as textiles and agricultural products will encounter difficulties in penetrating the markets of Common Market countries because of the duties that are to be charged under the agreement; but ultimately Portugal has everything to gain and nothing to lose through its progressive association with the EEC. The pact is considered in Lisbon as a first step toward eventual full-fledged membership in the EEC for Portugal within the next 10 or 15 years.

W. CEMLYN-JONES
Foreign Correspondent in Spain
The Guardian and *Observer*, London

Adm. Americo Thomas, first elected president in 1958, was reelected to a third term in July.

Casa de Portugal

POSTAL SERVICE, U.S.

In 1972 the U.S. Postal Service, an independent agency of the U.S. government since July 1, 1971, encountered various problems, partly owing to the novelty of the system and partly

A postal employee monitors the operation of an electronic reader, which optically scans the city, state and zip code of an address in order to consign a piece of mail to its proper bin. Up to 36,000 pieces per hour may be sorted by this method.

to the inherent weaknesses in the underlying philosophy that the application of private business methods to a public service would produce immediate satisfactory results.

In its first full year the Postal Service earned a gross income of $9,354,000,000 while expending $9,529,000,000. Its total delivery of 87,200,000,000 pieces of mail in 1972 barely kept pace with the previous total of 87,100,000,000. By the end of fiscal year 1972 the total number of postal employees had dropped to 680,663 from 728,911 a year earlier, while the number of individual post offices totaled 31,722, just under the 31,957 offices operative in fiscal 1971.

Although a number of significant changes in the handling of the mail was instituted, the work force was reduced and business work-measurement methods were introduced in the Postal Service, the volume of complaints about deficient service continued to grow. The complainants ranged from the housewife who received an invitation to an event too late to attend it, to the U.S. Senator who calculated that the Pony Express had delivered the mail faster in 1884 than it was being delivered in 1972. Postal rates were increased during the year with the approval of the Postal Rate Commission, an independent agency. Nevertheless, promised improvements in postal services were late in appearing.

Signs of public dissatisfaction with the Postal Service appeared almost immediately. Large mailers experimented with novel methods of making mass mailings. The privately-owned, unsubsidized United Parcel Service delivered more parcels in 1972 than the subsidized Postal Service and managed to realize a profit while doing it. The postal unions, whose work patterns have been altered drastically and whose members all too frequently have received the bulk of the complaints, have, in fact, encouraged expansion, rather than contraction, of services. Local postmasters, untrained in collective bargaining, have tended to refer all personnel and work-practice grievances to top management for resolution. Unsettled labor grievances would thus exacerbate local personnel relationships and further decrease postal efficiency. On-going talks among the separate letter carriers, postal workers and communications workers unions could, if a proposed merger were achieved, ultimately produce the largest single union affiliated with the AFL-CIO.

Some of the changes recently initiated in the service, however, had started to show positive results. Inefficient practices were being weeded out; the prospect of profit-loss balance in postal operations was starting to come into view; special services for special problems were being developed at a profit. Some progress also had been made in adapting the model of collective bargaining employed in the private sector to the Postal Service. Management was increasing its in-service training programs, and the albatross of political patronage was being unwound from the neck of the Postal Service, thus permitting more managers to rise from the ranks. More than 800 post offices were modernized, while plans were announced to upgrade another 10,000 and build 2,000 new buildings at a cost of $1,000,000,000. Central bulk-mail facilities were being established as an improvement over the previous system, and new approaches to speeding up first class mail delivery also were being investigated.

HARVEY L. FRIEDMAN, Director
Labor Relations and Research Center
University of Massachusetts, Amherst

PRISONS

U.S. prisons experienced another year of violence and turmoil as the soul-searching aftermath of the Attica crisis subsided. Plagued by overcrowding, inadequate facilities and programs, increasing racial antagonism and the continuing spread of political militancy among inmates, pressures continued to build in institutions already recognized as crucibles of tension and conflict.

The expanded use of probation, parole and other alternatives to incarceration has resulted in a rapid increase in the percentage of violence-prone inmates and a decrease in the number of nonviolent inmates who normally had a stabilizing effect on overall inmate populations. This trend has tended to increase the level of violence within the institutions, both of inmate against staff and inmate against inmate.

Because of problems created or aggravated by overcrowding, the Florida Corrections director, in an unprecedented move, ordered his institutions not to accept new inmates. While there was some question about the legality of this action, it drew the support of the state attorney general and other state officials who recognized the riot potential which could be heightened by further overcrowding of the prisons.

Inmate Protest and Violence. Many American prisons and jails again reached the boiling point, and some erupted as the nation's correctional apparatus encountered growing pressures both from within and without.

For example, a convicted murderer attempting a desperate escape from the Massachusetts Norwalk Prison Colony, shot and killed a correctional officer, a civilian employee and the convict's wife, who had smuggled two handguns into him. Thwarted in his attempt, the would-be escapee then killed himself. Prison unrest in Massachusetts also resulted in an inmate strike at Concord, a volatile sit-in at the women's institution at Framingham and a full-blown riot at Walpole State Prison.

A wave of prison riots swept over Maryland institutions where rioters caused more than $2,000,000 in damages at the Maryland State Penitentiary, Patuxent Institution and the House of Correction. Work stoppages and rioting also occurred at the Baltimore City Jail. Hostages taken in several disturbances were released unharmed after personal intervention by the governor.

Anxiety and unrest were also manifest in a variety of peaceful protests, strikes and less violent and destructive incidents in U.S. prisons. Strikes occurred at the Arizona State Prison, the Federal Correctional Institution at Marion, Ill., and the District of Columbia's Lorton Reformatory.

Less than a month after the five-day Lorton strike, armed prisoners at this institution seized 10 hostages, including the corrections director, and demanded their freedom. After two days of rioting and fitful and tense negotiations, a settlement was reached in the U.S. District Court. The hostages were freed after officials agreed to institute reforms, expedite court action and review cases of rebel inmates, and assured the prisoners that there would be no reprisals.

The increasing level of violence within institutions and particularly the growing number of attacks on prison staffs have created a dilemma for correctional administrators, who must recognize the legitimate fears and concerns of personnel while assuring that the institutions function as efficient, productive vehicles of prisoner rehabilitation. Correctional officers in many states have demanded that they be allowed to carry guns while off duty in order to protect themselves against released prisoners harboring grudges. Within the institutions officers complain of a collapse of routine security and discipline, interference by the courts and other outside groups which hamper their efforts to oversee the prisons and lax security which permits infiltration of weapons and drugs.

Of greatest concern to the officers is the growing risk of physical violence. Some feel that the threat of personal danger has been increased by the 1972 Supreme Court decision abolishing the death penalty as it is currently administered. The Court's ruling, they maintain, eliminated the final deterrent to physical violence within the prisons.

The deepening conflict between, on the one hand, efforts to develop and implement improved rehabilitation programs and, on the other, the concern of both the general public and prison employees over the spread of crime and increased danger to personal safety, presents an impediment to needed change in the correctional system.

Collectivization of Personnel and Inmates. During 1972, the trend toward unionization of both correctional employees and of inmates gathered momentum. Correctional employee unions staged a variety of strikes, job actions and "sick-outs" to bring their grievances to the attention of the public and legislators.

The formation of the first prisoners' union in the country—by inmates of Green Haven Correctional Facility at Stormville, N.Y.—occurred in 1972. Supported by a Federal

grant, the organization asked for recognition as the exclusive bargaining agent for the inmates of the Green Haven institution. The organization, called the Prisoners Labor Union at Green Haven, will seek to negotiate with prison authorities on wages, hours and work rules for inmates. The state court upheld the right of the inmates to organize, and similar prisoner organizations have emerged in California, Massachusetts, Maine, Rhode Island and a number of localities in the Midwest.

After its first full year of operation, officials at the Washington State Penitentiary were impressed with the apparent success of the Walla Walla experiment in inmate self-government. The experiment involves a resident government council, elected by the prisoners. The program includes liberalized approaches to dress, visitation, temporary leaves, telephone and mail use and participatory, or collaborative, management of the institution by staff and inmates.

Rights of the Confined. Civil rights activists continued the national movement to expand the rights of prisoners and bring about changes in the prison system through litigation. Challenges to the system by inmate lawsuits alleged that constitutional rights are violated by arbitrary and unauthorized rules and unchecked discretion of prison and parole officials. Increasingly the courts are subjecting prisons to greater scrutiny based on recognition of the fact that a prisoner does not lose all of his civil rights when he is incarcerated.

Growing activism on the part of the courts in the area of rights of the confined and the flood of prisoner litigation which has resulted from this new approach have spurred several states to seek alternative methods for resolving inmate complaints and grievances. In the city of Philadelphia and the states of New York, South Carolina and California "ombudsmen" have been appointed to make unbiased evaluation of prisoner complaints and to see that remedial action is taken on those that merit such action. In Maryland a five-member Inmate Grievance Commission was created to hear a growing number of prisoner grievances. Anticipating court decisions, several states, including Pennsylvania, Florida, Kansas and Illinois, established a "Bill of Rights" for inmates of state prisons.

Reflecting a growing concern over the need for uniform policy guidelines, the Association of State Correctional Administrators developed, and urged the states and the Federal government to adopt, their model code of prison rules, changing the system of appeals from disciplinary action, liberalizing privileges and providing access to news media by inmates.

Findings and Recommendations. In its report to the nation based on a one-year study of the riot at Attica State Prison, the McKay Commission found "no justification for the clearly indiscriminate firing" by the assault force of state troopers and warned that the Attica tragedy could be repeated in other institutions across the United States unless changes are made more rapidly in the correctional system.

Citing the fact that few changes were instituted during the ensuing year, the Commission included the following unanimous recommendations in its 518-page report on the riot:

Prisoners should retain all of their rights as citizens except that of liberty of person, including their rights to be adequately paid for work, to receive and send letters, express political views, practice or ignore religion and be protected against summary punishment.

Prisons should no longer be "shrouded from public view," but should permit free circulation of literature, regular visits by outsiders and controlled trips outside by prisoners.

Community groups and outside professionals should be allowed to participate regularly in prison life.

Guards should be paid well and trained in order to make them sensitive to and able to understand and deal with "the new breed of inmates from the urban ghettos and to understand and control the racism within themselves."

The "unfair" parole system must be changed to include clear standards for grant or denial of parole.

The major conferences on the problems of the correctional system recommended:

Prisons should be smaller, more humane and more manageable and should be located in the communities where the inmates live.

Concerted efforts should be made to reduce the isolation of institutions and prisoners from constructive community ties and influences.

Inmates should receive more practical and realistic training in preparation for release.

The use of halfway houses and pre-release centers located in the community should be expanded.

E. PRESTON SHARP and W. DONALD POINTER
American Correctional Association

PRIZES AND AWARDS
ART, ARCHITECTURE, DANCE AND MUSIC
American Institute of Architects Awards
Critics' Medal: WOLF VON ECKARDT, architecture critic, *The Washington Post*
Gold Medal: PIETRO BELLUSCHI, Thomas Jefferson Professor of Architecture, University of Virginia
American Institute of Graphic Arts Medal: MILTON GLASER, cofounder and partner, Push Pin Studios, Inc., New York City
National Academy of Recording Arts and Sciences Awards (Grammy Awards)
Album of the year: TAPESTRY, Carole King
Album of the year (classical): HOROWITZ PLAYS RACHMANINOFF
Jazz performance (big band): NEW ORLEANS SUITE, Duke Ellington
Jazz performance (group): THE BILL EVANS ALBUM, Bill Evans Trio
Jazz performance (soloist): THE BILL EVANS ALBUM, Bill Evans
New artist of the year: CARLY SIMON
Opera recording: VERDI: AIDA, Erich Leinsdorf conducting the London Symphony
Pop vocal performance (duo, group or chorus): THE CARPENTERS
Pop vocal performance (female): TAPESTRY, Carole King
Pop vocal performance (male): YOU'VE GOT A FRIEND, James Taylor
National Institute of Arts and Letters Awards
Arnold W. Brunner Memorial Prize in Architecture ($1,000): RICHARD MEIER
Awards in art ($3,000 each): RICHARD AAKRE, painter, VARUJAN BOGHOSIAN, sculptor, LOWRY BURGESS, painter, MARY FRANK, sculptor, MAUD GATEWOOD, painter, HERMAN ROSE, painter, ANTON VAN DALEN, painter
Awards in music for creative work in musical composition ($3,000 each): EARLE BROWN, JOHN EATON, JOHN HARBISON, WILLIAM OVERTON SMITH
Charles E. Ives Award ($10,000): HAROLD FARBERMAN, conductor
Charles E. Ives Scholarships ($3,500 each): THOMAS JANSON, ROBERT KRUPNIK, MICHAEL SEYFRIT
Marjorie Peabody Waite Award ($1,500): VITTORIO RIETI, composer
Richard and Hinda Rosenthal Foundation Award for painting ($2,000): BARKLEY L. HENDRICKS
Royal Institute of British Architects Gold Medal: LOUIS I. KAHN, U.S. architect

JOURNALISM
National Magazine Awards
Fiction: MADEMOISELLE, for the "consistent high quality of its fiction over many years, including the steadfast encouragement of new writers"
Public service: PHILADELPHIA MAGAZINE, for "The River Pirates," a "courageous demonstration that a magazine, depending for its existence on a narrow constituency, can engage in searching and comprehensive investigation of conditions affecting a three-state area"
Reporting excellence: THE ATLANTIC MONTHLY and ROSS TERRILL (contributing editor), for "The 800,000,000: Report from China"
Specialized journalism: ARCHITECTURAL RECORD, for its December 1971 issue devoted to a single subject "New Life for Old Buildings"
Visual excellence: ESQUIRE, for "its bold innovation in visual concepts, specifically the use of neo-surrealism to illustrate fiction, nonfiction editorial comment, and features such as humor and fashion"
Overseas Press Club Awards
Asia award for best article or report on the area in any medium: JOHN RICH, NBC News, for China reports
Book on foreign affairs: ANTHONY AUSTIN, *The President's War*
Business news reporting from abroad in any medium ($500): LEONARD SILK, *The New York Times,* for "The International Money Crisis"
Cartoon on foreign affairs ($250): DON WRIGHT, *The Miami News,* for "We survived the war. It was the winding down that got us."
Daily-newspaper or wire-service interpretation of foreign events: ROBERT S. ELEGANT, *Los Angeles Times,* for European and Asian articles
Daily-newspaper or wire-service photographic reporting from abroad: THE NEW YORK TIMES, for general excellence
Daily-newspaper or wire-service reporting from abroad: SYDNEY SCHANBERG, *The New York Times,* for coverage of the India-Pakistan war and its aftermath
George Polk Memorial Award "for best reporting in any medium requiring exceptional courage and enterprise abroad" ($500): NICHOLAS W. STROH, *The Evening Star,* Washington, D.C., missing and presumed dead in Uganda
Latin America award for best article or report on the area in any medium: JONATHAN KAPSTEIN, *Business Week,* for "Booming Brazil Finds a Key to Growth"
Magazine interpretation of foreign affairs: GORDON L. WILLIAMS and JOHN L. COBBS, *Business Week,* for "The Deadlock Over the Dollar"
Magazine reporting from abroad: ARNAUD de BORCHGRAVE, *Newsweek,* for "Interviews with Sadat and Meir"
"Out of category" award: NEIL SHEEHAN and THE NEW YORK TIMES, for series on the Pentagon Papers
Photographic interpretation of foreign affairs in a magazine or book: FRANK FISCHBECK, *Life,* for photo essay on contemporary China
Radio documentary: JOHN RICH, NBC News, for "Return to Peking"
Radio interpretation of foreign affairs: NBC NEWS, for "A World Reflection: How They

See Us," James Quigley (producer), Wilson Hall (anchorman)

Radio spot news reporting from abroad: CBS NEWS, for reports on India-Pakistan war

Robert Capa Gold Medal "for superlative still photography requiring exceptional courage and enterprise abroad": LARRY BURROWS, *Life,* killed on assignment in Laos

Television documentary on foreign affairs: GEORGE WATSON (correspondent) and ERNEST PENDRELL (producer), ABC News, for "Terror in Northern Ireland"

Television interpretation of foreign affairs: JOHN HART and CBS NEWS TEAM, for "The Two-Week War: Whose Victory?"

Television spot news reporting from abroad: PHIL BRADY, *NBC Nightly News,* for reports from Vietnam and on the India-Pakistan war and the birth of Bangladesh

White House Correspondents Association Awards

Merriam Smith Memorial Fund Award "for excellence in presidential news coverage": CARROLL KILPATRICK, *The Washington Post*

Raymond Clapper Memorial Award ($1,000): JAMES R. POLK, *The Evening Star,* Washington, D.C., for series on concealed campaign contributions

Worth Bingham Prize ($1,000): FRANK WRIGHT, *The Minneapolis Tribune,* for series on dairy organizations and campaign contributions

LITERATURE

American Library Association Awards

Grolier Award for "exceptional achievements in stimulating reading and providing school and public library service to children" ($1,000): RONALD W. MCCRACKEN, school librarian Keswick Public School, Keswick, Ontario

John Newbery Medal for the "most distinguished contribution to American literature for children": ROBERT C. O'BRIEN, *Mrs. Frisby and the Rats of NIMH*

Randolph J. Caldecott Medal for the "most distinguished American picture book": NONNY HOGROGIAN, *One Fine Day*

Bancroft Prizes for "books of exceptional merit and distinction in American history, American diplomacy and the international relations of the United States" ($4,000 each): CARL N. DEGLER, *Neither Black Nor White: Slavery and Race Relations in Brazil and the United States;* ROBERT MIDDLEKAUFF, *The Mathers: Three Generations of Puritan Intellectuals, 1596–1728;* SAMUEL ELIOT MORISON, *The European Discovery of America: The Northern Voyages*

Canada Council's Governor General's Literary Awards ($2,500 each)

English fiction: MORDECAI RICHLER, *St. Urbain's Horseman*

English nonfiction: PIERRE BERTON, *The Last Spike,* a second volume history of the Canadian Pacific Railway

English poetry and drama: JOHN GLASSCO, *Selected Poems*

French fiction: GÉRARD BESSETTE, *Le cycle*

French nonfiction: GÉRARD FORTIN, *La fin d'un règne,* a collection of essays

French poetry and drama: PAUL-MARIE LAPOINTE, *Le réel absolu,* a book of poetry

Goncourt Prize: JEAN CORRIERE, *L'Espervier de Maheux*

Mystery Writers of America (Edgars)

Mystery novel: FREDERICK FORSYTH, *Day of the Jackal*

First mystery novel: A. H. Z. CARR, *Finding Maubee*

True-crime book: SANDOR FRANKEL, *Beyond A Reasonable Doubt*

Mystery short story: ROBERT L. FISH, *Moonlight Gardener*

Juvenile Mystery: JOAN AIKEN, *Nightfall*

National Book Awards ($1,000 each)

Arts and letters: CHARLES ROSEN, *The Classical Style: Haydn, Mozart, Beethoven*

Biography: JOSEPH P. LASH, *Eleanor and Franklin*

Children's book: DONALD BARTHELME, *The Slightly Irregular Fire Engine or The Hithering Thithering Djinn*

Contemporary affairs: STEWART BRAND, *The Last Whole Earth Catalog: Access to Tools*

Fiction: FLANNERY O'CONNOR, *Flannery O'Connor: The Complete Stories*

History: ALLAN NEVINS, Ordeal of the Union series volumes VII and VIII

Philosophy and religion: MARTIN E. MARTY, *Righteous Empire: The Protestant Experience in America*

Poetry: HOWARD MOSS, *Selected Poems:* FRANK O'HARA, *The Collected Poems of Frank O'Hara*

Science: GEORGE L. SMALL, *The Blue Whale*

Translation: AUSTRYN WAINHOUSE, *Chance and Necessity: An Essay on the Natural Philosophy of Modern Biology* by Jacques Monod

National Institute of Arts and Letters Awards

Awards in literature ($3,000 each): HARRY CREWS, novelist; PETER DAVISON, poet; PAULA FOX, novelist; PENELOPE GILLIATT, novelist and critic; PAULINE HANSON, poet; MICHAEL S. HARPER, poet; ISRAEL HOROVITZ, playwright; WALTER KERR, critic; GILBERT ROGIN, fiction writer and editor; ANN STANFORD, poet

Gold Medal for history: HENRY STEELE COMMAGER

Gold Medal for the novel: EUDORA WELTY

E. M. Forster ($5,000): FRANK TUOHY, fiction writer

Loines Award for Poetry ($2,500): WILLIAM JAY SMITH

Morton Dauwen Zabel Award ($2,500): DONALD BARTHELME, fiction writer

Richard and Hinda Rosenthal Foundation Award ($2,000): THOMAS MCGUANE, *The Bushwhacked Piano*

National Medal for Literature "for the excellence of his total contribution to the world of letters" ($5,000): LEWIS MUMFORD

Poetry Society of America Awards

Alice Fay di Castagnola Award for a "Work in

"The French Connection" won five Oscars in 1972, including best actor (Gene Hackman at bottom of stairs), direction and picture.

progress in poetry or subject related to poetry" ($3,500 shared): ERICA JONG, New York City; MYRA SKLAREW, Bethesda, Md.
Shelley Memorial Award to an American poet in need ($1,800): GALWAY KINNELL, N.Y.C.

MOTION PICTURES
Academy of Motion Picture Arts and Sciences Awards (Oscars)
Actor: GENE HACKMAN, *The French Connection*
Actor (supporting role): BEN JOHNSON, *The Last Picture Show*
Actress: JANE FONDA, *Klute*
Actress (supporting): CLORIS LEACHMAN, *The Last Picture Show*
Direction: WILLIAM FRIEDKIN, *The French Connection*
Film editing: *The French Connection*
Foreign-language film: THE GARDEN OF THE FINZI CONTINIS, Vittorio De Sica, Italy
Picture: THE FRENCH CONNECTON
Song: THEME FROM SHAFT, music and lyrics by Isaac Hayes
Song score: FIDDLER ON THE ROOF, adapted by John Williams
Writing (screenplay); ERNEST TIDYMAN, *The French Connection*

Writing (story and screenplay—not previously published or produced): THE HOSPITAL, Paddy Chayefsky
Special award for "humor and humanity": CHARLES CHAPLIN

Cannes International Film Festival Awards
Actor: JEAN YANNE, *We Will Not Grow Old Together*, France
Actress: SUSANNAH YORK, *Images*, England
Director: MIKLOS JANESCO, *Red Palm*, Hungary
Grand Prize: THE MATTEI AFFAIR, Francesco Rosi, Italy; THE WORKING CLASS GOES TO PARADISE, Elio Petri, Italy
Special prize: OPERATION X-70 (an animated cartoon), Raoul Servais, Belgium

PULITZER PRIZES
Journalism ($1,000 each except for public-service gold medal)
Commentary: MIKE ROYKO, *Chicago Daily News*
Criticism, FRANK PETER, JR., music critic, *St. Louis Post-Dispatch*
Editorial cartooning: JEFFREY K. MacNELLY, *Richmond News Letter*
Editorial writing: JOHN STROHMEYER, *Bethlehem* (Pa.) *Globe-Times*, for editorial campaign to reduce racial tensions in Bethlehem

Surrounded by members of his family, Lewis Mumford accepted the National Medal for Literature in New York in December.

"Brian's Song," a television movie starring James Caan as Brian Piccolo, was voted an Emmy as the best program of the year.

Feature photography: DAVE KENNERLY, United Press International, for Vietnam war photos

General local reporting: RICHARD COOPER and JOHN MACHACEK, *Rochester* (N.Y.) *Times-Union,* for coverage of the Attica prison riot

International reporting: PETER R. KANN, *The Wall Street Journal,* for coverage of India-Pakistan war

National reporting: JACK ANDERSON, syndicated columnist, for reporting of U.S. policy decision-making during India-Pakistan war

Public service: THE NEW YORK TIMES, for publishing Pentagon Papers

Special local reporting: TIMOTHY LELAND, GERARD M. O'NEILL, STEPHEN A. KURKJIAN and ANN DeSANTIS, *The Boston Globe,* for exposure of widespread corruption in Somerville, Mass.

Spot news photography: HORST FAAS and MICHEL LAURENT, The Associated Press, for "Death in Dacca" (picture series)

Letters and Music ($1,000 each)

Biography: ELEANOR AND FRANKLIN by Joseph P. Lash

Drama: no award

Fiction: ANGLE OF REPOSE by Wallace E. Stegner

General nonfiction: STILWELL AND THE AMERICAN EXPERIENCE IN CHINA, 1911–1945 by Barbara W. Tuchman

History: NEITHER BLACK NOR WHITE by Carl N. Degler

Music: WINDOWS by Jacob Druckman

Poetry: COLLECTED POEMS by James Wright

SCIENCE

Albert Lasker Medical Research Awards ($2,000 each)

Administration ($5,000): C. GORDON ZUBROD, director of division of cancer treatment, National Cancer Institute

Burkitt's Lymphoma: DENIS BURKITT, Medical Research Council, London; JOSEPH H. BURCHENAL, Memorial Hospital, New York City; JOHN L. ZIEGLER, National Cancer Institute; V. ANOMAH NGU, Centre of Health Sciences, Cameroun

Choriocarcinoma: MIN CHIU LI, Nassau Hospital, N.Y.; ROY HERTZ, New York Medical College, Valhalla, N.Y.

Hodgkin's Disease: PAUL CARBONE, National Cancer Institute; VINCENT T. DeVITA, JR., National Cancer Institute; EMIL FREI 3d, Children's Cancer Research Foundation, Boston

Lymphatic Leukemia: EMIL FREI 3d, EMIL J. FREIREICH, University of Texas; JAMES F. HOLLAND, Roswell Park Memorial Institute, Buffalo, N.Y.; DONALD PINKEL, St. Jude Children's Research Hospital, Memphis

Skin Cancer: EDMUND KLEIN, Roswell Park Memorial Institute; EUGENE J. VAN SCHOTT, Temple University

American Cancer Society

National Award: HENRY S. KAPLAN, Stanford University

Distinguished Service Award: MURRAY M. COPELAND, University of Texas

American Chemical Society's Arthur C. Cope Award for outstanding contributions to organic chemistry ($40,000 shared): ROBERT B. WOODWARD, Harvard University; ROALD HOFFMANN, Cornell University

American Heart Association's Research Achievement Award: EUGENE BRAUNWALD; Harvard Medical School

Atomic Energy Commission's Enrico Fermi Award ($25,000): STAFFORD L. WARREN, University of California, Los Angeles; SHIELDS WARREN, Harvard University

Institute of Life Prize ($50,000): RENÉ DUBOS, Rockefeller University

Louisa Gross Horowitz Prize for "outstanding research in biology" ($25,000): STEPHEN W. KUFFLER, Harvard Medical School

National Academy of Science Awards Hartley Public Service Medal: LEONARD CARMICHAEL, National Geographic Society

Arthur L. Day Prize ($10,000): HATTEN S. YODER, JR., Carnegie Institution

Agassiz Medal ($1,000): SEIYA UYEDA, University of Tokyo

Henryk Artowski Medal ($5,000): FRANCIS S. JOHNSON, University of Texas

James Craig Watson Medal ($2,000): ANDRE DEPIT, National Aeronautics and Space Administration

U.S. Steel Foundation Award in Molecular Biology ($5,000): HOWARD M. TEMIN, University of Wisconsin

TELEVISION AND RADIO
George Foster Peabody Awards
Broadcast news: JOHN RICH, NBC Radio and Television

Radio education: WHA, Madison, Wis., *Wisconsin on the Move*

Radio promotion of international understanding: VOICE OF AMERICA, Washington, D.C.

Radio public service: NBC-RADIO, New York, *Second Sunday*

Radio special awards: WCCO-RADIO, Minneapolis, Minn., *The Heart of the Matter;* ARTHUR GODFREY, CBS-Radio, New York

Radio youth or children's programs: WWVA, Wheeling, W. Va., *Junior Town Meeting of the Air*

Television education: WQED, Pittsburgh, Pa., *The Turned-on Crisis*

Television entertainment: NBC-TV, New York, dramatic programming; CBS-TV, New York, *The American Revolution: 1770–1783, A Conversation with Lord North;* ABC-TV, New York, and WILLIAM BLINN, "Brian's Song," *The Movie of the Week*

Television promotion of international understanding: UNITED NATIONS TELEVISION, New York, *United Nations Day Concert with Pablo Casals*

Television public service: NBC-TV, New York, *This Child is Rated X: An NBC News White Paper on Juvenile Delinquency*

Television special award: GEORGE HEINEMANN, NBC-TV, New York

Television special education: MISSISSIPPI AUTHORITY FOR EDUCATIONAL TELEVISION, Jackson, Miss., and WILLIAM SMITH, executive director

Television youth or children's programs: ABC-TV NEWS, *Make A Wish*

Special award: FRANK STANTON, CBS, New York

National Academy of Television Arts and Sciences Awards (Emmy Awards)

Actor–comedy series: CARROLL O'CONNOR, *All in the Family,* CBS

Actor–dramatic series: PETER FALK, "Columbo," *NBC Mystery Movie,* NBC

Actor–single performance: KEITH MITCHELL, "Catherine Howard," *The Six Wives of Henry VIII,* CBS

Actor–supporting performance in comedy: EDWARD ASNER, *The Mary Tyler Moore Show,* CBS

Actor–supporting performance in drama: JACK WARDEN, "Brian's Song," *The Movie of the Week,* ABC

Actress–comedy series: JEAN STAPLETON, *All in the Family,* CBS

Actress–dramatic series: GLENDA JACKSON, *Elizabeth R,* Masterpiece Theatre, PBS

Actress–single performance: GLENDA JACKSON, "Shadow in the Sun," *Elizabeth R,* PBS

Actress–supporting performance in comedy: VALERIE HARPER, *The Mary Tyler Moore Show,* CBS; SALLY STRUTHERS, *All in the Family,* CBS

Actress–supporting performance in drama: JENNY AGUTTER, "The Snow Goose," *Hallmark Hall of Fame,* NBC

Children's programming: SESAME STREET, PBS

Comedy series: ALL IN THE FAMILY, CBS

Daytime drama: THE DOCTORS, NBC

Documentary programming

Dealing with artistic, historical or cultural subjects: HOLLYWOOD: THE DREAM FACTORY, *The Monday Night Special,* ABC; A SOUND OF DOLPHINS, *The Undersea World of Jacques Cousteau,* ABC; THE UNSINKABLE SEA OTTER, *The Undersea World of Jacques Cousteau,* ABC

Dealing with events or matters of current significance: A NIGHT IN JAIL, A DAY IN COURT, *CBS Reports,* CBS; THIS CHILD IS RATED X: AN NBC NEWS WHITE PAPER ON JUVENILE JUSTICE, NBC

Individual contributions: LOUIS J. HAZAM (writer), *Venice Be Damned!;* ROBERT NORTHSHIELD (writer), *Suffer the Little Children—An NBC News White Paper on Northern Ireland,* NBC

Dramatic series: ELIZABETH R, Masterpiece Theatre, PBS

Magazine–type programs

Individual contributions: MIKE WALLACE, *60 Minutes,* CBS

Programs, program segments or series: CHRONOLOG, NBC; THE GREAT AMERICAN DREAM MACHINE, PBS

New series: ELIZABETH R, PBS

Performer–music or variety: HARVEY KORMAN, *The Carol Burnett Show,* CBS

Single program–drama or comedy: BRIAN'S SONG, *The Movie of the Week,* ABC

Single program–variety or musical

Classical music: BEETHOVEN'S BIRTHDAY: A CELEBRATION IN VIENNA WITH LEONARD BERNSTEIN, CBS

Variety and popular music: JACK LEMMON IN 'S WONDERFUL, 'S MARVELOUS, 'S GERSHWIN, Bell System Family Theatre, NBC

Special events—program achievements: THE CHINA TRIP, ABC; JUNE 30, 1971, A DAY FOR HISTORY: THE SUPREME COURT AND THE PENTAGON PAPERS, NBC; A RIDE ON THE MOON: THE FLIGHT OF APOLLO 15, CBS

Sports–creative programming: ABC'S WIDE WORLD OF SPORTS, ABC

Trustees award: BILL LAWRENCE (posthumous), FRANK STANTON

Variety–musical series: THE CAROL BURNETT SHOW, CBS

Variety–talk series: THE DICK CAVETT SHOW, ABC

THEATER

Antoinette Perry Awards of the American Theater Wing (Tony Awards)

Actor (play): CLIFF GORMAN, *Lenny*

Actor (supporting in a play): VINCENT GARDENIA, *The Prisoner of Second Avenue*

Actor (musical): PHIL SILVERS, *A Funny Thing Happened on Way to the Forum*

Actor (supporting in a musical): LARRY BLYDEN, *A Funny Thing Happened on the Way to the Forum*

Actress (play): SADA THOMPSON, *Twigs*

Actress (supporting in a play): ELIZABETH WILSON, *Sticks and Bones*

Actress (musical): ALXIS SMITH, *Follies*

Actress (supporting in a musical): LINDA HOPKINS, *Inner City*

Choreographer: MICHAEL BENNETT, *Follies*

Costume designer: FLORENCE KLOTZ, *Follies*

Director (play): MIKE NICHOLS, *The Prisoner of Second Avenue*

Director (musical): HAROLD PRINCE and MICHAEL BENNETT, *Follies*

Lighting designer: THARON MUSSER, *Follies*

Musical: TWO GENTLEMEN OF VERONA, Joseph Papp, producer

Musical book: TWO GENTLEMEN OF VERONA by John Guare and Mel Shapiro

Play: STICKS AND BONES by David Rabe, Joseph Papp, producer

Scenic designer: BORIS ARONSON, *Follies*

Score: FOLLIES, music and lyrics by Stephen Sondheim

New York Drama Critics Awards

Foreign play: THE SCREENS by Jean Genet

Musical: TWO GENTLEMEN OF VERONA

Play: THAT CHAMPIONSHIP SEASON by Jason Miller

Village Voice Off-Broadway Awards (Obies)

Best theater piece ($500): THE OPEN THEATRE, for *The Mutation Show*

Distinguished performance: SALOMO BEY, *Love Me, Love My Children;* MAURICE BLANC, *The Celebration: Jooz/Guns/Movies/The Abyss;* ALEX BRADFORD, *Don't Bother Me, I Can't Cope;* MARILYN CHRIS, *Kaddish;* RON FABER, *And They Put Handcuffs on Flowers;* JEANNE HEPPLE, *The Reliquary of Mr. and Mrs. Potterfield;* DANNY SEWELL, *The Homecoming;* MARILYN SOKOL, *The Beggar's Opera;* KATHLEEN WIDDOES, *The Beggar's Opera;* ELIZABETH WILSON, *Sticks and Bones,* ED ZANG, *The Reliquary of Mr. and Mrs. Potterfield*

UNITED STATES AND WORLD SCENE

Four Freedoms Foundation Award for distinguished service in behalf of the four freedoms: FRANK E. FITZSIMMONS, president of the International Brotherhood of Teamsters

National Institute of Social Sciences Gold Medals for "distinguished service to humanity": HENRY A. KISSINGER, presidential adviser; MRS. LAURANCE ROCKEFELLER, member of National Board, Y.W.C.A.; GEORGE BUSH, U.S. representative to UN; ARCHBISHOP FULTON J. SHEEN, former Roman Catholic Auxiliary Bishop, New York

Presidential Medal of Freedom for significant contributions to the "quality of American life": LILA and DEWITT WALLACE, founders of the *Reader's Digest;* JOHN PAUL VAN, presidential adviser on the Indochina War

Rockefeller Public Service Awards for "outstanding service to the Government of the United States and to the American people" ($10,000 each): Administration: VERNON D. ACREE, commissioner of customs, U.S. Department of the Treasury

Human Resource Development and Protection: SAMUEL C. ADAMS, JR., assistant administrator for Africa, Agency for International Development

Intergovernment Operations: BARBARA M. WHITE, special assistant to the director, U.S. Information Agency

Professional Accomplishment and Leadership: WALLACE P. ROWE, chief, laboratory of viral diseases, National Institute of Allergy and Infectious Diseases, Department of Health, Education and Welfare; LAURENCE N. WOODWORTH, Chief of Staff, Joint Commission on Internal Revenue Taxation

Norman Cousins introduced "World," a review "of ideas, the arts and the human condition."

PUBLISHING

While new titles and sales of books turned slightly downward in 1972, magazine and newspaper publishing showed definite signs of prosperity during the year, despite a chorus of alarms about the threat posed to periodicals by projected steep increases in postal rates in the next few years.

Book publishing experienced a year of further consolidation in which some observers saw the means of eventual recovery. The number of magazines increased, as several newcomers entered the field—among them *World*, founded by Norman Cousins, former editor of the *Saturday Review*.

The newspaper industry recorded gains in both advertising and circulation revenues. Although three major U.S. newspapers disappeared from the scene, the larger newspaper groups continued to enlarge their operations and their profits. Arthur Ochs Sulzberger, publisher of *The New York Times*, called for more automation to counteract increasing operational costs. Papers across the United States continued to turn to offset printing and computerized operations.

Books. President Nixon proclaimed 1972 International Book Year. Clifford and Edith Irving, accordingly, made book writing an international topic with a widely publicized Howard Hughes autobiography hoax. The Irvings eventually admitted the autobiographical material was a forgery and began prison terms after accepting some $750,000 from McGraw-Hill for the book. Grove Press published a sequel by Irving on *What Really Happened?* McGraw-Hill had similar problems with *The Memoirs of Chief Red Fox*. Out-of-court settlement followed the disclosure that some of the book's contents had been lifted from another book.

The bible of the book publishing industry, *Publishers Weekly*, celebrated its centennial in 1972. Launched in 1872 by Frederick Leypoldt, the magazine provides the industry with vital statistics and news coverage. It noted that 25,526 new books were published in 1971, up from 24,288 in 1970. New editions also were up, from 11,783 to 12,166. Although the number of books increased in 1971, this trend failed to continue in 1972. In the first six months, declines were reported both in new books and new editions.

"The year 1972 was a time less of innovation than of consolidation in the book industry—a period in which the industry was bearing up remarkably well in a recession economy—perhaps recovering somewhat," *Publishers Weekly* reported. Dollar sales continued beyond the $3,000,000,000 mark. The Department of Commerce predicted that sales would reach $4,500,000,000 by 1980.

The book clubs continued to produce best sellers. The Book-of-the-Month Club, with some 1,250,000 members, had sales approaching $45,000,000. The *Reader's Digest* Condensed Books continued to account for some 10,000,000 volumes annually and revenues of $40,000,000 to $45,000,000. The Literary Guild and its associated clubs sold from $70,-000,000 to $80,000,000 in books in 1971, according to a study in *Publishers Weekly*.

Herbert S. Bailey, Jr., president of the Association of American University Presses, noted

some problems facing publishers. Many, especially the university presses, experienced a retrenchment policy. The result, however, was better books. The pollution cleanup added some costs to paper, while computers were used more to control inventories.

Magazines. In the magazine field the better known publications continued to dominate in circulation, but newcomers shared the limelight in 1972. Norman Cousins founded *World*, with 75,000 charter subscribers and a staff composed largely of former *Saturday Review* colleagues. Meanwhile, the *Saturday Review* continued to grow, approaching 800,000 circulation.

Time, Inc. introduced a new publication, *Money*, late in the year. Hugh Hefner's *Playboy* increased its circulation to 6,600,000 and its founder branched out with *Oui* with an international approach. *Playboy* added a German-language edition.

Time's ad revenue for 1971 passed the $100,000,000 mark for the first time; the trend continued with $55,000,000 for the first half of 1972. Also for the first time it surpassed the long-time leader, *Life*. Meanwhile, *Life*, which had announced an increase in its number of ad pages and curtailed circulation to 5,500,000 (tenth place), ceased publication with a Dec. 29 year-end double issue.

Postal rate hikes continued to upset many publishers. Kent Rhodes, *Reader's Digest* executive vice-president, said "the rates as proposed cannot be justified." Other publishers concurred while many experimented with deliveries by other than the Federal postal service. *Time* warned that many of the 10,000 publications involved would be in jeopardy if the full 150 percent proposed hike in rates took effect over the next five years.

With a circulation of 1,300,000, *Ebony* continued its leadership among the publications produced for black readers. Several newcomers joined it—among them, *Encore, Black Enterprise, Black Sports, Relevant* and *Essence*.

Ms., founded by Gloria Steinem, became the most talked about magazine for the women's liberation movement. Similar magazines were started, although some experienced short careers. These included *Up From Under, Off Our Backs, New Woman, Progressive Woman* and *You*. Pamela Howard wrote that "At least awareness has been generated (by these magazines) and that's what we in the movement are working for—awareness and acceptance of the new woman."

Publicity obviously was *Cosmopolitan*'s goal when it splashed a near-nude spread of Burt Reynolds for its readers. The rush for copies helped to hike *Cosmo*'s newsstand sales.

Reader's Digest celebrated its 50th birthday and retained its position as the world's circulation leader. A slight gain placed the U.S. edition over 18,235,000, plus more than 11,000,000 in the overseas editions. *TV Guide* pushed closer to the top, passing 17,600,000 weekly.

Better Homes & Gardens also celebrated its 50th birthday and passed 8,060,000 in circulation. *Family Circle* and *Woman's Day*, two magazines that depend 100 percent on newsstand and supermarket sales, were in the 7,800,000 bracket. *National Geographic* inched up to 7,670,000, while *McCall's* kept its lead over *Ladies' Home Journal*, 7,500,000 to

The 89-year-old Newark (N.J.) "Evening News" went to press for the final time on Aug. 31, 1972.

7,031,000. *Playboy* and *Life* completed the top ten.

The New Yorker continued number 1 among consumer magazines in ad pages, with 1,685 for the first half of 1972, up 4 percent over 1971. *Newsweek* replaced *Business Week* in the runner-up position.

New publications tended to be specialized. Magazine Publishers Association, Inc., reported that during the 1962–1971 decade some 753 magazines were founded, while only 160 were sold, merged or discontinued.

In Canada, *Time, Reader's Digest,* and *Chatelaine* dominated the magazine market, carrying more than 75 percent of the advertising money spent in the first half of 1972.

Newspapers. The year was one of contrasts in the newspaper industry. Three large newspapers died. The *Boston Herald-Traveler* was taken over by the *Record-American* on June 19; the *Washington News* merged with the *Evening Star* on July 12; and the Newark (N.J.) *Evening News* ceased publication on August 31.

At the same time, the Los Angeles Times Mirror Co. reported 1971 revenues of $566,-085,000 and profits of nearly $35,000,000. And Paul Miller, "the Rochester acquirer," continued to expand his Gannett newspaper group. The Nashville *Banner* and the El Paso *Times* joined the group, which by mid-1972 totaled 52 dailies and 14 weeklies.

The American Newspaper Publishers Association reported that education, income and population trends favor the expansion of newspapers for the next decade. Daily circulation figures passed 62,000,000, and Sunday editions approached 50,000,000. Readers spent some $3,000,000,000 for copies in 1971, with the trend upward for 1972 as more papers adopted a 15 cent daily rate. Advertisers added another $6,200,000,000 to the publishers' income. This helped to pay the industry's 370,000 employees and to buy the more than 5,000,000 tons of newsprint used during the first half of 1972. Recycled paper was introduced by some publishers, and Canadian paper mills were cutting costs by trimming the variety of shades.

Weekly newspapers also gained. Although the total, 7,567, represented a slight drop, the circulation of 30,495,921 was up 1,000,000 over 1970.

The *Chicago Tribune* went public and thus revealed its financial record. The firm owns the *Tribune* and *Today* in Chicago, the New York *Daily News* and five Florida Newspapers. It earned profits of $13,500,000 on revenues of $478,900,000 in 1971.

The U.S. Supreme Court held, 5–4, that "constitutional guarantees of freedom of speech and freedom of the press are not abridged when newsmen are required to testify before grand juries, state or Federal." Publishers warned about "growing, insidious infiltration of secrecy" by the government.

Jack Anderson won his first Pulitzer Prize for his attacks on the Nixon administration and its handling of the India-Pakistan war. He became better known to American readers for his attack on the ITT affairs and his charges, later retracted, against Sen. Thomas Eagleton (D-Mo.). *Newsweek* called Anderson "a muckraker with a mission." More than 700 outlets carried his column. Anderson feels that the first amendment gives newsmen "the right and the duty" to pry into government secrets.

Minority employment in the journalism field increased, although less than 1 percent of professional news staffs were black. Some black newsmen .on *The Washington Post* protested and called for more of their race in key employment. An increase of minority students in the nation's schools of journalism was seen as one solution to the problem.

The Newspaper Guild invited criticism by endorsing Democratic Presidential candidate George McGovern. Many Guild members voiced their individual opposition to the action.

The Newspaper Preservation Act of 1970 was upheld in its first court test. In San Francisco the Bay Guardian Co. sued the *Examiner* and *Chronicle*. Harrison Salisbury of *The New York Times* and John Chancellor of NBC News turned to *Playboy* to debate "The News Media." The Twentieth Century Fund noted that "new and potentially corrosive frictions" have arisen between government and media, threatening the free flow of information.

Gabriel Gilbert, publisher of Quebec's *Le Soleil*, became the president of the Canadian Press national news agency. The Canadian News Hall of Fame admitted its first woman, giving posthumous recognition to E. Cora Hind of the *Winnipeg Free Press*.

Canadian dailies grew, with 1,505,757 combined circulation of 21 morning dailies, 3,098-922 for 94 afternoon dailies, and more than 2,000,000 for the 16 weekend newspapers.

Canadian publishers rejected the idea of a national press council but voiced support for improved editorial quality. Local press councils were established in Alberta, Ontario and Quebec.

See also Literature; Postal Service; Prizes and Awards.

WILLIAM H. TAFT
Professor of Journalism
University of Missouri

An overflowing crowd at the Notre Dame convocation manifests the extent to which the charismatic movement has permeated Catholicism.

RELIGION

While most religious worshipers looked to their churches and temples for continuity and tradition in 1972, organized religion generally underwent a year of dynamic change. Events ushered onto the scene a new spiritual leader of the Eastern Orthodox Church, new chief rabbis of Israel's two principal Jewish communities, both progress and regress in ecumenical affairs and an explosion of Pentecostal activity.

Pentecostal Movement. Pentecostalism, a form of religious expression previously restricted largely to bodies on the fringes of traditional Christianity, conclusively swept into the life of most established churches in the United States in 1972 in what was clearly the most significant development on the religious scene. Once-staid Roman Catholics, Presbyterians, Lutherans and Episcopalians stood at the forefront of the burgeoning neo-Pentecostal movement—or "charismatic" movement, as they often preferred to call it, hearkening back to the Greek term for a spiritual gift. Many of the new Pentecostals reported ecstatic experiences which they identified as being "baptized in the Holy Spirit," and some at the height of worship uttered strings of consonants and vowel sounds which they described as "speaking in tongues."

Because the charismatic movement depended largely on spontaneity and little on organization, no precise estimate as to how many regular churchgoers had been touched by it could be made. There were, however, some indicators of its growth. The annual summer gathering of Catholic charismatics on the campus of Notre Dame University, a meeting that attracted only a few hundred when it first convened in 1968, counted 11,500 participants in 1972.

Moreover, members of the Catholic hierarchy, who had reacted to the Catholic Pentecostals' first stirrings with considerable wariness, began to accommodate themselves to the movement—partly no doubt as a consequence of repeated assurances by Catholic Pentecostal enthusiasts of their fidelity to the traditions of their church and to the authority of the bishops. The Catholic bishop of Rockford, Ill., approved the formation of the nation's first official Catholic Pentecostal congregation, the Community of the Holy Spirit, in St. Charles, Ill. Auxiliary Bishop Joseph C. McKinney of Grand Rapids, Mich., speaking at the Notre Dame meeting, declared: "It is Jesus who saves, and we need to be saved."

Later in the year the unofficial First International Lutheran Conference on the Holy Spirit convened in Minneapolis, attracting another large body of participants, mainly Lutheran but including numerous clergy and lay persons of other churches, both Protestant and Catholic. However, the leaders of the three principal U.S. Lutheran bodies were conspicuously absent.

The Pentecostal explosion was not limited to North America. Pentecostal bodies were said to be the fastest growing religious institutions in Latin America. Presbyterian evangelist Mel Tari asserted that the enormous number of conversions to Christianity among Indonesians—700,000 since 1965, he said—was a consequence of the "tremendous working of the Holy Spirit." The Very Rev. Lord MacLeod of

Religious News Service Photo

Demetrios I was elected Ecumenical Patriarch of Eastern Orthodox Christians in July.

Fuinary, a former moderator of the Church of Scotland and one of the elder statesmen of social activist Christianity, assessed the surge of Pentecostalism as an "astonishing supradenominational outburst" and urged that Christian pacifists, of whom he is one, make common cause with the new movement.

Jesus People. The psychological dynamic of the Pentecostal movement bore a close resemblance to that underlying the so-called "Jesus People," an unorganized movement of young people galvanized by a simplistic and often fundamentalist reading of the New Testament into seeking to recreate the life-styles of the first Christian communities. The Jesus People were less in evidence in 1972 than in the years immediately preceding it, although the Campus Crusade for Christ, an old-line, well-financed evangelical effort to preach to young people, attracted 85,000 to Dallas for "Explo '72." Many of the participants were authentic Jesus People, but many were simply members of high school-age Sunday school classes.

One of the best-known and most controversial Jesus People groups, the Children of God, moved most of its members out of the United States to Europe and Latin America, according to James Johnston, a Dallas lawyer. The group, whose founder, David Berg, is a former Christian and Missionary Alliance minister, takes literally Jesus' mandate to his followers to leave parents and family and follow him. Members adopt new biblical names when they join the Children, and generally sever all ties with their families. This practice, and the conviction of some parents that their children were being held under duress, gave rise to several lawsuits.

Eastern Orthodox Church. One of the most notable religious leaders who died during the years was Patriarch Athenagoras I, the ecumenical patriarch of Constantinople and spiritual leader of the world's Eastern Orthodox Christians. The 86-year-old patriarch had a determined enthusiasm for Christian unity that sometimes incurred harsh criticism from coreligionists who felt he should cultivate a greater regard for the purity of Orthodox doctrine.

The Turkish government moved rapidly to block the election of potential successors it feared might perpetuate the Athenagoras tradition. Archbishop Iakovos of New York was even denied entrance to Turkey to attend Athenagoras' funeral, and Metropolitan Meliton of Chalcedon, another contender for the patriarchal seat, was formally listed as unacceptable to the Turkish government. After some deliberation the holy synod of the patriarchate elected the little-known Metropolitan Demetrios as the new patriarch and enthroned him as Demetrios I.

Ecumenism. Death also claimed Lord Fisher of Lambeth, who as Geoffrey Francis Fisher served as Archbishop of Canterbury from 1945 to 1961. One of Lord Fisher's main endeavors in his later years was advocating the defeat of the proposal to unite the Church of England with the English Methodist Church. For a second time, the plan failed to win ratification by the Anglicans in 1972.

If Anglican-Methodist unification stumbled in England, proposals to reunite divided Christendom inched forward on other fronts. The small Presbyterian Church of England and the many congregations of the even smaller Congregational Union of England merged to form the United Reform Church. Scottish Christians were presented a plan that proposed the merger of the Church of Scotland (Presbyterian) with the United Free Church of Scotland, the Episcopal Church of Scotland, the Methodist Synod, the Congregational Union and the Churches of Christ. However, parts of the proposal encountered immediate opposition. At the Church of Scotland's annual general assembly the Rev. A. F. Lamont inveighed against the plan's proposed office of superintendent as a plan to introduce bishops to the kirk.

Church union won final approval in Sri Lanka (Ceylon) by the governments of the Methodists, Baptists, Anglicans, Presbyterians

and the diocese of Jaffna of the Church of South India. But the participation of the Anglican diocese of Colombo was delayed at least temporarily by a lawsuit filed by three laymen. Church union schemes in New Zealand and Australia also moved ahead, but Canadian efforts to unite the United Church of Canada, the Anglican Church of Canada and the Canadian Christian Church (Disciples of Christ) persisted only amid predictions of doom.

In the United States the nine-denomination Consultation on Church Union (COCU), an effort to negotiate a united church that would have some 25,000,000 members, encountered grave difficulties. Responding to a request for official comment on the proposed plan of union, the executive council of the United Church of Christ asked sharply, "To what extent has the COCU process been one that belongs to another day?" It suggested that the Consultation needed to make a "candid reassessment of itself and its prospects." Later in the year, when the matter of continuing participation in the Consultation came before the general assembly of the United Presbyterian Church the commissioners (delegates) voted decisively to withdraw the 12-year effort. Whether the United Presbyterians would return and what impact their withdrawal would have on other participants remained to be seen.

During a visit to Britain, Jan Cardinal Willebrands, the Dutch prelate who is the chief Vatican expert on ecumenical affairs, openly predicted the coming of Roman Catholic-Anglican structural unity and predicted that Anglicans would retain their distinctive traditions in the reunion of the communions. (Late in 1971 the two churches had published a memorandum detailing an agreement on the doctrine of the eucharist.)

Still to be gauged, however, was the Roman Catholic reaction to the growing possibility that Anglicans would break with nearly 2,000 years of Catholic tradition and admit women to the priesthood. Late in 1971 the Anglican bishop of Hong Kong had ordained two women priests. In 1972 several independent Anglican provinces, including the Episcopal bishops of the United States, approved the idea of women priests in principle, although no such ordinations were conducted.

Judaism. The attention of Jews throughout the world was commanded during the year by the sudden—and largely unexpected—increase of desire among the estimated 3,000,000 Jews of the Soviet Union to emigrate to Israel. What, as recently as 1970, had been a trickle of emigrants from the U.S.S.R. to Israel swelled to a tide in the early months of 1972, reaching an annual rate of 30,000. These emigrants, who had battled and demonstrated their way through miles of red tape to win their exit permits, made up only a small part of those who had applied, and it was estimated that the formal applicants were in turn only a fraction of those who secretly wished to go. Zionist-minded Soviet Jews and their American and Western European supporters discovered the potency of the telephone as a weapon as they kept the non-Communist world informed of each step of their campaign for exit visas through telephone dispatches. Soviet authorities reacted by canceling the telephone service of known activists.

In August the Soviet government abruptly proclaimed a new and heavy tax—reaching as high as $35,000 in the case of one individual—purportedly designed to reimburse the Soviet government for the cost of providing higher education to those Jews with university degrees who wished to emigrate. At the year's end the status of the emigration education tax remained uncertain.

In Israel itself there were indications of an easing of the inflexible grasp that ultra-Orthodox Jewish groups had exercised over religious affairs. The nation's two aged and unbending chief rabbis, Ashkenazi Rabbi Isser Y. Unterman, 86, and Sephardic Rabbi Yitzhak Nissim, 76, were voted out of office by younger men. The new leader of Israel's Sephardic (Oriental) Jews was Rabbi Ovadia

Rabbi Goren is expected to display flexibility as the new leader of Israel's Ashkenazi Jews.

Yosef, 51. At the head of the Ashkenazi (European) Jewish community was Rabbi Shlomo Goren, 55, a former chief chaplain of the Israeli army. While both new chief rabbis were clearly Orthodox in their religious commitment, Rabbi Goren is noted for his exceptional skill in finding precedent in Jewish tradition to ease the more extreme and awkward requirements of the halacha, the Orthodox code that prescribes for virtually every detail of life.

Third World Developments. The decade of the 1960's was marked by the rapid phasing out of European and North American missionary direction of Christian groups in Africa, Asia and Latin America, and a number of theologians and church historians suggested that the most imaginative Christian thought and work was to be found among "third world" churchmen. The member churches of the World Council of Churches confirmed the trend in August by electing a third-world clergyman, the Rev. Dr. Philip A. Potter, a native of the British West Indies island of Dominica, as general secretary of the organization. He succeeded the Rev. Dr. Eugene Carson Blake. In the United States the National Council of Churches elected the Rev. W. Sterling Cary, a black minister of the United Church of Christ, to a three-year term as president.

Churches continued to play a central role in the struggle of blacks to break the hegemony still exercised by whites in southern Africa. The South African government expelled the

second Anglican bishop who attempted to exercise jurisdiction in Namibia (South West Africa). The deportee, the Irish-born Rt. Rev. Colin O'Brien Winter, lost his residence permit after he spoke out in defense of workers of the Ovambo tribe who mounted an unprecedented and successful strike against government-sponsored contract labor policies.

In some countries continuing steps toward de-Westernization exacted a toll on Christian customs that are taken for granted elsewhere. In Zaire, which has a substantial Christian population, President Mobutu decreed an outright ban on Christian names and required all citizens to assume new African appellations. In Sri Lanka a new constitution in effect established Buddhism as the state religion. The nation had already eliminated the traditional seven-day week in favor of a calendar based on Buddhist holidays that are determined by the phases of the moon.

The favored place accorded Buddhism in Sri Lanka was seen to represent another advance in the great revival Buddhism has enjoyed in the 20th century, and particularly in the post–World War II years. During 1972 an assembly of the World Fellowship of Buddhists attracted delegates from 50 nations. Princess Poon Pisma Diskul of Thailand is the organization's president.

Religious sects arising from Eastern spiritual traditions continued to win increasing numbers of adherents among the American young. Among the best-known of these groups were the Hare Krishna—chanting mendicants of the International Society for Krishna Consciousness, whose shaven heads, saffron–colored robes and outstretched palms were a familiar sight on the streets of most major American cities; the devotees of Yogi Bhajan's 3HO (Healthy-Happy-Holy Organization) Foundation; and the disciples of Guru Maharaji Ji, who staged a midsummer festival near Boulder, Colo., that attracted thousands of participants.

Another rapidly expanding group in the United States and elsewhere, the Nichiren Shoshu sect of Buddhism, dedicated a vast new temple headquarters at the foot of Japan's Mount Fuji in October. The sect had expanded enormously in Japan in the previous 25 years, especially among the poor and disadvantaged. According to authorities of Sokagakkai, the group's lay movement, the new $158,000,000 High Sanctuary of the Daisekiji is the world's largest religious edifice, exceeding St. Peter's Basilica in Vatican City in height, width and floor space.

WILLIAM R. MACKAYE
Religion Editor, *The Washington Post*

Dr. P. A. Potter is the first "third world" churchman to head the World Council of Churches.

RUMANIA

In 1972, Rumania continued its courtship of various socialist and capitalist states in an attempt to gain political and economic backing for its autonomous stance in the Soviet sphere.

When the Rumanian Communist party met in July, Party Leader and President Nicolae Ceausescu called for improved relations among socialist states and especially for broader Soviet-Rumanian cooperation, based on the principles of national sovereignty and mutual non-interference in internal affairs. Also conciliatory were the new "treaties of friendship and mutual assistance" signed with Hungary and East Germany. A meeting between Ceausescu and Israeli Premier Golda Meir in May seemed to imply that Rumania might help mediate the Israeli-Arab dispute. Similarly, Ceausescu's four-week visit to eight African nations indicated Rumania's determination to be a leading spokesman for small and medium-sized states in world politics.

On the economic front, Ceausescu was confirmed as head of a new Supreme Council for Economic Development charged with completing the current five-year plan before the 1975 deadline. In June the European Economic Community postponed a decision on Rumania's request to be granted trade preferences as a "developing nation." On the other hand, in July, U.S. Secretary of State William Rogers signed a consular agreement to promote normal travel and commercial contacts between the two countries and announced that the United States would extend the credit facilities of the Export-Import Bank to Rumania for the purchase of U.S. equipment.

The most impressive political-economic achievement of the year was the formal inauguration in May of the Rumanian-Yugoslav hydroelectric and navigation project at the Iron Gates gorge on the Danube. Built jointly over seven years at a cost of $450,000,000, it ranks among the five largest such projects in the world and is the biggest joint venture to date by any two socialist countries.

JOSEPH F. ZACEK
Professor of History
State University of New York, Albany

SINGAPORE

Under the firm direction of Prime Minister Lee Kuan Yew and his People's Action Party (PAP), Singapore in 1972 continued to enjoy political stability combined with rapid economic growth.

At the beginning of the year there were some signs of growing political discontent among the Chinese-educated bulk of the electorate. Grievances included restrictions on wage increases (in force since 1968) despite economic gains, the confiscation of land set aside for a Chinese cemetery and the more notable emphasis on English-language education by a government bent upon rapid modernization. Various actions subsequently taken by the government could be interpreted as an attempt to halt any erosion of political support caused by these issues. There was a general 8 percent wage increase, plus bonuses, and a campaign against such "unwanted by-products of the western way of life" as hippies, drugs and long hair. (Visitors to Singapore were required to conform in this regard.) The enduring political strength of the PAP was clearly demonstrated by its sweep of all 65 seats in the Sept. 2 parliamentary elections.

The robust health of the economy allowed a projected increase of 10.9 percent in government revenue over fiscal 1971. The gross national product (GNP) rose about 10 percent in 1971, one of the highest growth rates in the world. In addition, foreign exchange reserves equaled the entire value of Singapore currency in circulation, the balance of payments was favorable and there was nearly full employment. The principal dark spot in this otherwise bright picture was a declining rate of growth in the trade sector (which comprised one-third of the GNP). Reasons for this decline were many: pursuit of direct trade policies by neighboring states, a depressed world market for natural rubber, the diminishing U.S. military presence in Vietnam and the general uncertainty of the international monetary situation.

In foreign policy, Singapore indicated qualified endorsement of Malaysia's proposal for the neutralization of Southeast Asia, while voicing reservations concerning an Indonesian-Malaysian initiative to prevent the internationalization of the Straits of Malacca. Lee Kuan Yew made an official visit to Malaysia during the year—his first since Singapore left the federation in 1965. During the visit the remaining issues arising from the dissolution of Malaysia-Singapore Airlines and the distribution of the residual assets of the colonial Currency Board of Malaya and British Borneo were finally resolved. The Prime Minister also visited Indonesia during the year. Visitors to Singapore in 1972 included Queen Elizabeth II and Prime Minister William McMahon of Australia. Special U.S. presidential envoy John B. Connally met with Singapore's leaders in June.

MARVIN C. OTT
Assistant Professor of Political Science
Mount Holyoke College

SOCIAL SECURITY

Social Security was initiated during the New Deal as a modest program that aimed to give support to the retired, the disabled and the widows and children of deceased workers. By 1972, Social Security has become a mighty social and economic engine, providing benefits to 28,000,000 Americans, involving 96,000,000 workers and their employers in tax payments and providing almost 25 percent of all tax revenues collected by the Federal government. During the year the 92nd Congress provided even more fuel for this engine.

To begin with, on June 30 the Democratic Congress voted to increase Social Security benefits by a massive 20 percent. The increase was passed over objections by the Republican administration, which had wanted a more modest increase. Congress also voted for higher taxes to help pay for the benefit increase and also decided that beginning in 1975, Social Security benefits would automatically rise if the cost of living went up. This last decision was unprecedented in the history of the program.

To most people, Social Security means benefits to retired workers. In 1972, 17,700,000 retired workers and their dependents enjoyed Social Security benefits, which helped reduce the number of aged persons living in poverty. But Social Security also directed cash payments to dependents of deceased workers, of whom there were 6,900,000, mostly widows and young children, and to disabled persons, 3,100,000 of whom were, with their dependents, on Social Security.

The Social Security program is financed through payroll taxes that fall equally on employer and employee. In 1972 there was some discussion that the tax system was regressive, that the burden of these taxes rests on poor and low income workers. The talk centered on proposals that some Social Security funds come from general treasury revenues, but such suggestions got little attention from Congress or the Executive Branch.

Then, late in the session, Congress took a further look at Social Security and enacted another far-reaching bill.

The new law included a further raise in Social Security payroll taxes. The 5.2 percent rate paid by employees and employers in 1972 was increased to 5.85 percent beginning in 1973. Moreover, the wage base on which taxes are paid was increased from $9,000 in 1972 to $10,800 in 1973 and to $12,000 from 1974 through 1977. This means that workers earning at least these wages will pay $631.80 in Social Security taxes in 1973 (compared with $468 in 1972) and will pay $702 a year from 1974 through 1977. Employers will pay equal amounts. Thus, to an increasing degree, Social Security taxes have become a greater burden to low and some middle income taxpayers than have the Federal income taxes.

At the same time, Social Security old age minimum benefits were generally increased so that a low-wage earner who is under Social Security for 30 years will get at least $170 a month in benefits. For a low-income "30-year" couple, the minimum monthly benefit will be $255. In 1972 the lowest Social Security benefit paid was $84.50 a month. Attempts in Congress to boost the minimum benefit to $100 a month were unsuccessful.

Retired persons on Social Security will be permitted to earn $2,100 a year without losing benefits. This loss of benefits had long been a source of complaint among those who argued that a worker is entitled to all his old-age benefits regardless of income earned after retirement.

Beginning in 1974, the Federal government will take over from the states the welfare system for the blind, disabled and aged. The minimum income was set at $130 per month for a single person without other income and at $195 for a couple. Up to $20 a month in Social Security payments and $65 in earnings would be disregarded in determining whether beneficiaries have other income that would reduce their payments. Previously, each state had its own system and rules of eligibility for welfare payments to the aged, blind, and disabled. Benefits ranged from $70 a month in some states for an individual to as much as $350 a couple in other states. Under the new Federal system states will be entitled to boost payments over the U.S. minimum.

Social Security benefits for widows and widowers were increased from 82.5 percent of a deceased spouse's entitlement to 100 percent. As a result, about 3,800,000 persons will receive higher payments.

In addition to tying the level of Social Security to the cost of living, Congress decided to tie the wage base to the cost of living. Thus, while the base on which taxes are paid remains at $12,000 through 1977, in succeeding years, if the cost of living rises, the base rate can be boosted by the Executive Branch. These potential increases, coupled with rising tax rates, undoubtedly will fan the debate over Social Security—its costs, its benefits and the question of whether it imposes to heavy a burden for poor and low income Americans.

ROBERT W. DIETSCH
Business-Economics Editor
Scripps-Howard Newspapers

SPACE

Space activity in 1972 was highlighted by the fifth and sixth landings of men on the moon—the last two missions of the U.S. Apollo program—and by the launch of a U.S. deep-space probe designed to investigate the planet Jupiter and later to become the first man-made device to escape the solar system.

Apollo Program. The first of the year's two manned space flights, Apollo 16, was launched on April 16 from Kennedy Space Center, Florida. On board were spacecraft commander John W. Young, lunar-module pilot Charles M. Duke and command-module pilot Thomas K. Mattingly II. The spacecraft swept into orbit around the moon on April 19, and on the following day Young and Duke descended in the lunar-module *Orion* to a moon-landing in an area known as Cayley Plains. Mattingly remained in orbit in the command-module *Casper*.

The landing site was located in the moon's southern highlands some 60 miles from the great crater Descartes; it was an area believed to be covered with volcanic rocks from some of the most violent eruptions in the moon's history, but the two moonwalkers found surprisingly few such rocks.

One of the first tasks for Young and Duke was the deployment of an ALSEP (Apollo Lunar Science Experiments Package), a collection of instruments to report data to earth after the astronauts' departure. Then, in their four-wheeled, electric-powered lunar-roving vehicle, Young and Duke made three traverses, collecting soil and rock specimens and photographing the area. On one trip the rover was able to climb 1,000 feet up the side of a mountain; on another the astronauts toured a field of giant boulders, some of them 60 feet tall. The three trips yielded a total of 245 pounds of lunar rocks, surface soil and subsurface cores, about 50 pounds more than originally planned. Durations of the three traverses were 7 hours 11 minutes on April 21, 7 hours 23 minutes on April 22, 5 hours 40 minutes on April 23, for a total surface exploration time of 20 hours 14 minutes. The distance covered was about 18.5 miles.

On April 23, Young and Duke blasted off from the moon in the ascent stage of *Orion* and docked with the waiting Mattingly in the command module two hours later. After a day in lunar orbit, during which the lunar module was jettisoned, the command module broke out

With the Dec. 19 splashdown of Apollo 17, some 350 miles southeast of American Samoa, the U.S. Apollo program came to an end.

NASA

U.S. LUNAR AND MANNED ORBITAL FLIGHTS

ASTRONAUT	PROGRAM	DATE	NO. OF CIRCUITS	FLIGHT TIME
Glenn	Mercury-Atlas 5	Feb. 20, 1962	3	4 hrs. 55 mins.
Carpenter	Mercury-Atlas 7	May 24, 1962	3	4 hrs. 56 mins.
Schirra	Mercury-Atlas 8	Oct. 3, 1962	6	9 hrs. 13 mins.
Cooper	Mercury-Atlas 9	May 15–16, 1963	22	34 hrs. 20 mins.
Grissom Young	Gemini 3	March 23, 1965	3	4 hrs. 54 mins.
McDivitt White	Gemini 4	June 3–7, 1965	66	97 hrs. 59 mins.
Cooper Conrad	Gemini 5	Aug. 21–29, 1965	120	190 hrs. 56 mins.
Schirra Stafford	Gemini 6	Dec. 15–16, 1965	16	25 hrs. 51 mins.
Borman Lovell	Gemini 7	Dec. 4–18, 1965	206	330 hrs. 35 mins.
Armstrong Scott	Gemini 8	March 16, 1966	6½	10 hrs. 42 mins.
Stafford Cernan	Gemini 9	June 3–6, 1966	47	72 hrs. 21 mins.
Young Collins	Gemini 10	July 18–21, 1966	46	70 hrs. 47 mins.
Conrad Gordon	Gemini 11	Sept. 12–15, 1966	47	71 hrs. 17 mins.
Lovell Aldrin	Gemini 12	Nov. 11–15, 1966	63	94 hrs. 33 mins.
Schirra Eisele Cunningham	Apollo 7	Oct. 11–22, 1968	163	260 hrs. 12 mins.
Anders Borman Lovell	Apollo 8	Dec. 21–27, 1968	1¾ earth orbits 10 lunar orbits	147 hrs.
McDivitt Scott Schweickart	Apollo 9	March 3–13, 1969	151 earth orbits	241 hrs. 1 min.
Cernan Stafford Young	Apollo 10	May 18–26, 1969	1½ earth orbits 31 lunar orbits	192 hrs. 3 mins.

			TIME ON MOON	
Armstrong Aldrin Collins	Apollo 11	July 16–24, 1969	21 hrs. 36¼ mins.	195 hrs. 18 mins.
Bean Conrad Gordon	Apollo 12	Nov. 14–24, 1969	31½ hrs.	244 hrs. 36 mins.
Lovell Haise Swigert	Apollo 13	Apr. 11–17, 1970	2 earth orbits 1 swing around moon	142 hrs. 54 mins.
Shepard Mitchell Roosa	Apollo 14	Jan. 31–Feb. 9, 1971	33½ hrs.	215 hrs. 34 mins.
Irwin Scott Worden	Apollo 15	July 26–Aug. 7, 1971	66 hrs. 5 mins.	294 hrs. 12 mins.
Young Duke Mattingly	Apollo 16	April 16–27, 1972	71 hrs. 2 mins.	265 hrs. 51 mins.
Cernan Evans Schmitt	Apollo 17	Dec. 7–19, 1972	74 hrs. 59 mins.	301 hrs. 52 mins.

"I'll miss all those Apollo chaps."

UPI

Geologist Jack Schmitt studies a split lunar boulder.

of the moon's gravity and started the return to earth. On April 27, after a mission of 11 days, one hour and 51 minutes, *Casper* splashed down in the Pacific Ocean 1,519 miles south of Honolulu, only one mile from the recovery carrier, *Ticonderoga*.

Apollo 17, the final mission of the program, was launched early in the morning of Dec 7. Its crew was composed of spacecraft commander Eugene A. Cernan; Harrison (Jack) Schmitt, pilot of the lunar module *Challenger* and the first trained scientist (geologist) to fly an Apollo mission; and Ronald Evans, pilot of the command module *America*.

Apollo 17 entered lunar orbit on Dec. 10, and on the following day *Challenger* descended to the moon, carrying Cernan and Schmitt. The landing site was a 6-mile-wide valley near the large Littrow Crater and surrounded by the mile-high-plus Taurus Mountains. Scientists believed that in this area the moon had experienced its most recent volcanic activity, which may have taken place anywhere from 100,000,000 to 3,000,000,000 years ago. In other parts of the Taurus-Littrow site they expected to find rock samples dating back as far as 4,000,000,000 years.

A major finding by Apollo 17, perhaps the most important of the scientific phase of the entire program, was the discovery of a band of dirt colored bright orange around the rim of a crater. Studied on the spot by geologist Schmitt, this orange band was regarded as the first concrete evidence that the moon has a volcanic history, a theory long held but not absolutely confirmed by previous missions.

From the orbiting command module, Evans was able to spot volcanic domes on the dark side of the moon; again, there had been no prior evidence of backside volcanic activity.

Using the electric lunar rover, Cernan and Schmitt made three lunar traverses, traveling 19.9 miles, the longest distance covered by any Apollo moon tourists. Their pattern of exploration was similar to that of Apollo 16: deployment of another instrument package, extensive photography, core drilling and visual inspection of a variety of moon features, such as the massifs (mountains), craters and boulder fields. They brought back to the lunar module 258 pounds of rock, soil and core samples, again a record. This brought to 841 pounds the grand total of samples acquired by six Apollo moonwalking teams.

Cernan and Schmitt spent a record 22 hours 5 minutes exploring the surface on their three rover trips. After more than three days on the surface, *Challenger*'s ascent stage lifted off the moon on Dec. 14 and returned to dock with *America*. After two additional days in lunar orbit for visual and photographic study of the moon, *America* was thrust out of the moon's gravity field to start the earthward journey. On Dec. 19, it splashed down in the Pacific some 350 miles southeast of American Samoa, four miles from the *Ticonderoga*, which was again the recovery carrier.

NASA officials described the final mission as the best in terms of potential scientific gain. In addition to the records already mentioned, Apollo 17 set a number of new marks for the program. The duration—12 days, 13 hours, 52

THE SPACE COOPERATION AGREEMENT

By James C. Fletcher
Administrator, National Aeronautics and Space Administration

By their Agreement Concerning Cooperation in the Exploration and Use of Outer Space for Peaceful Purposes, signed at the Moscow summit meeting on May 24, 1972, President Nixon and Premier Kosygin committed the United States and the Soviet Union to three objectives: (1) to fulfill the National Aeronautics and Space Administration/Soviet Academy of Sciences agreement of January 1971 on space science and applications; (2) to develop compatible rendezvous and docking systems for future generations of manned spacecraft; and (3) to conduct a joint experimental flight during 1975 to test such compatible systems.

The NASA/Soviet Academy agreement of January 1971 provides for cooperation in several major areas of space research—meteorology, study of the natural environment, space science (including near-earth space, the moon and the planets), and space biology and medicine. Considerable progress has been made since 1971. A joint working group is designing experiments to advance the techniques of space meteorology and has begun exchanging meteorological data from sounding rocket networks in the eastern and western hemispheres. Another joint working group is defining coordinated experiments in remote sensing of the environment. Other working groups have exchanged findings of special interest obtained from U.S. and Soviet probes of Mars, held working sessions on the exploration of the outer planets, and exchanged lunar samples as well as highly detailed data and results of biomedical experience in the Soyuz/Salyut and Apollo programs.

Discussions of possible compatible rendezvous and docking systems began in October 1970, when experts from NASA and the Soviet Academy provided for the definition of design requirements for future spacecraft. In January 1971, Dr. George M. Low, then acting administrator of NASA, suggested an early rendezvous and docking test mission using existing spacecraft. In June 1971, both sides agreed to study the technical and economic implications of test missions. In December 1971, joint working groups concluded that a test mission was desirable. This conclusion, combined with agreement on management and operational principles to apply in the test mission, opened the way for the 1972 summit accord.

The systems which must be compatible include radio communications, radio guidance and optical tracking for rendezvous, docking aids and targets, equipment for crew transfer, and the docking system itself. For the latter, both parties have agreed on a universal androgynous system which will dispense with the probe-and-drogue devices which have been used in both the U.S. and Soviet programs.

As the test mission is now planned, a Soviet Soyuz spacecraft will be launched first. About seven and one-half hours later, the United States will launch an Apollo spacecraft from the Kennedy Space Center. The two spacecraft will dock approximately one day after Apollo lift-off. They will remain docked for about two days while crewmen exchange visits and conduct joint activities.

The summit space agreement promises substantial benefits. If compatible rendezvous and docking capability is successfully demonstrated, both countries will have increased their chances of rescuing astronauts in distress without commensurate increases in the costs of a standby rescue capability. A successful test mission would point the way to joint activities by the United States and the Soviet Union in space once future systems, incorporating compatible docking arrangements, are flying. In the larger scheme of things, the joint test mission, an intricate and complex goal which depends on the skill and good faith of both countries, should contribute to mutual confidence and trust. If United States and Soviet spacemen can meet in orbit before the eyes of the entire world, attitudes, viewpoints, and expectations should improve among men everywhere.

minutes—was the longest of any Apollo mission, as was distance covered—1,486,000 miles. Total time on the lunar surface—74 hours, 59 minutes—topped by almost four hours the previous record, held by Young and Duke of Apollo 16. Astronaut Evans also set a record time in lunar orbit—six days, three hours.

Future U.S. Programs. Apollo 17 ended U.S. lunar exploration for a period estimated to be at least 20 years. NASA's major program in coming years will be the manned space shuttle, a combination orbiting laboratory and delivery vehicle to become operational at the end of the 1970's. In 1972, the space agency was making final preparations for an interim manned space program, the Skylab earth-orbiting long-duration laboratory. Skylab, to be visited by three separate astronaut teams starting in the spring of 1973, was to focus on extensive biomedical, astronomical and earth resources survey investigations.

Another interim manned program was formalized in 1972 when, on May 24, President Nixon and Soviet Premier Kosygin signed an agreement for joint U.S.–U.S.S.R. cooperation in a number of areas of space research. The highlight of the cooperative program was to be an experimental mission in which a U.S. Apollo and a Soviet Soyuz will dock in orbit and crew members of both nations will visit each other's spacecraft. The venture was tentatively scheduled for July 1975.

Pioneer 10. The most important unmanned space mission of the year was the March 2 launch by NASA of Pioneer 10, a 550-pound spacecraft intended to make a fly-by of Jupiter and to continue beyond the solar system. Pioneer 10 carried 60 pounds of instruments for 11 types of experiments. The spacecraft was to report data on the composition of interplanetary space during the 21-month trip to Jupiter, send additional data on the environment of Jupiter and its satellite Io, then continue to transmit interplanetary information until it passes the orbit of Uranus, more than 2,000,000,000 miles distant.

The fastest-moving of all spacecraft, with 1972 speeds ranging up to more than 75,000 miles per hour, Pioneer 10 crossed the orbit of Mars on May 25, thereby entering a space realm never before explored. On July 15, the deep-space probe entered the Asteroid Belt, a 50,000,000-mile-thick ring of space debris

Astronauts prepare for NASA's next manned space program, Skylab. Charles Conrad (l, top photo) will command Skylab one, which is scheduled to last 28 days in the spring of 1973.

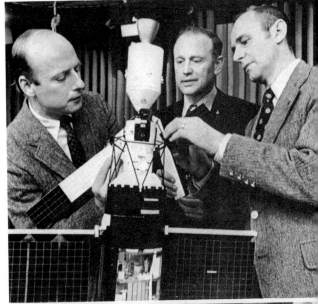

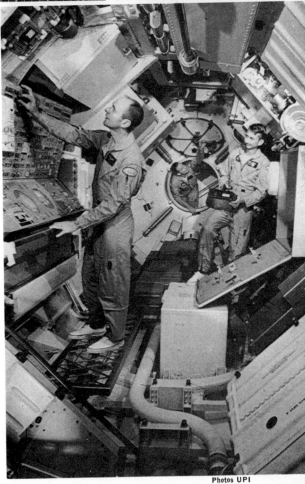

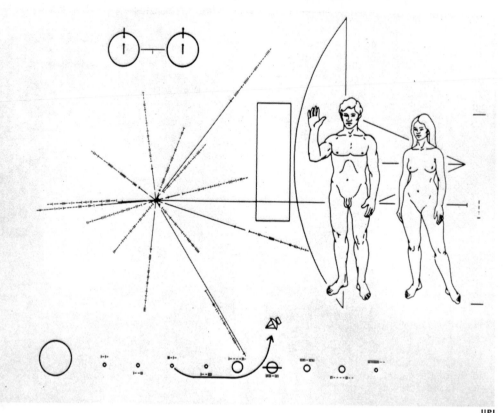

A Pioneer 10 diagram will explain to any future interceptor when, where and by whom the craft was launched. The radiating lines (l) and symbols (top) are a universal clock, the figure (behind the people) is the craft and the circles (bottom) are the planets ranging outward from the sun.

orbiting between Mars and Jupiter, containing rubble ranging from dust particles to asteroids as large as Alaska.

By year-end, Pioneer 10 was more than half-way through the Asteroid belt, which it was expected to clear by February 1973; all instruments were functioning. The flight plan called for its closest approach to Jupiter—about 87,-000 miles—on Dec. 3, 1973. The spacecraft was to reach Uranus in about 7½ years and the orbit of Pluto, the most distant planet in the solar system, in about 15 years. After that, its velocity would thrust the probe beyond the influence of solar gravity into interstellar space.

Mariner 9. Mariner 9, another U.S. interplanetary probe, launched in 1971, continued to operate in Martian orbit throughout most of 1972. After reaching Mars on Nov. 13, 1971, the spacecraft remained active through 698 orbits until Oct. 27, 1972, when the mission was concluded. During its 11-plus months of operation, Mariner 9 returned a wealth of instrumental data together with 7,329 photographs of the Martian surface. Among the major findings were indications that Mars may once have had free-flowing water and that the planet is geologically active, with volcanic mountains larger than any on earth.

NASA enjoyed a perfect launch record during the year, scoring 20 successes in as many attempts, including 17 earth satellites.

Scientific Satellites. In the U.S. scientific spacecraft category, the most important launch was that of Orbiting Astronomical Observatory-3, actually the fourth (and last) of this series (one failed in the launch phase). At 4,900 pounds the heaviest nonmilitary unmanned spacecraft ever orbited, OAO-3 was launched Aug. 21 from Cape Kennedy. It was designed to study the composition of interstellar gas, ultraviolet radiation and X-ray emissions from pulsars.

Other scientific satellites included Explorer 46, a meteoroid technology satellite launched Aug. 13 from NASA's Wallops Island, Va., station; Explorer 47, the ninth in NASA's Interplanetary Monitoring Platform series, launched Sept. 25 from Cape Kennedy; and Explorer 48, a satellite devoted exclusively to the study of

gamma rays, launched Nov. 16 from the Italian-operated San Marco launch platform in the Indian Ocean off Kenya.

Applications Spacecraft. In the applications category, NASA launched for the global communications satellite network three additional spacecraft of the high-capacity Intelsat IV type, bringing to five the number of Intelsat IVs in service. NASA also launched, for the National Oceanic and Atmospheric Administration, two more weather satellites. The second, known by NASA as the Improved Tiros Operational Satellite-D and by NOAA as NOAA-2, marked a milestone in meteorological satellite development. Launched Oct. 15, it was the first operational satellite capable of taking atmospheric data readings. Unlike all earlier satellites, which used video systems, NOAA-2 relies entirely on scanning radiometers for imagery. Its greater imaging capability coupled with its potential for vertical readings marks a major step toward longer-range weather forecasts. Launched piggyback with NOAA-2 was a small secondary payload, Oscar-6, designed for communications relay in the amateur radio bands.

Another advance in weather-satellite research was Nimbus 5, launched Dec. 11. Like NOAA-2, Nimbus 5 makes vertical soundings of the atmosphere, but it has the added capability of taking such readings through cloud cover. A battery of six advanced sensors makes possible the most precise measurements yet of the oceans, the atmosphere and the earth's surface. Nimbus 5 is an experimental forerunner of future NOAA operational satellites.

Another applications spacecraft, launched July 23, was ERTS-1, the first Earth Resources Technology Satellite, designed to study from space earth's crop, water, mineral and other resources (*see* Environment.) The 1,965-pound ERTS-1 is an experimental satellite, a first step toward a future operational system of vast economic potential. By yearend, data from ERTS-1 already were being utilized in hydrology, topography, land-use inventory and geological surveys. Preliminary results were described as excellent.

Joint Projects and Military Space Activity. NASA's remaining launches of the year were in support of foreign or joint U.S.–foreign projects. They included: HEOS A-2 (Highly Eccentric Orbit Satellite), launched Jan. 31, a satellite built by member countries of the European Space Research Organization (ESRO) to study interplanetary physics and the high latitude magnetosphere; TD-1A, launched March 11, another ESRO project, an astronomical research satellite described as the largest and most complex spacecraft ever built

in Western Europe; ANIK-1 (also known as Telesat-1), launched Nov. 9, a Canadian domestic comsat to be operated by Telesat Canada; ESRO IV, launched Nov. 21, a scientific satellite carrying a number of European experiments for the exploration of the polar ionosphere; and Aeros, launched Dec. 16, a West German-built upper atmosphere investigator.

U.S. military space activity continued at a rate of slightly more than one launch per month, a decline from the two-a-month rate of 1971 and three-a-month in 1970. Details of the military systems were classified, but the effort focused, as in the preceding year, on advanced development and operational use of spacecraft for reconnaissance, communications monitoring and early warning of attack by space detection of missile launches.

Soviet Program. The Soviet Union's space program was conducted at a launch rate approximately equal to that of 1971, averaging more than six launches per month. There were, however, no Soviet spectaculars. The U.S.S.R. flew no manned missions; the "stand-down" in effect since the tragic loss of three cosmonauts aboard Soyuz 11 in June 1971 continued throughout 1972.

The eighth in the Soviet series of Venera probes made a successful landing on the surface of Venus on July 22, reporting data throughout the descent and for some time after landing, as had previous Veneras. The U.S.S.R. launched three additional weather satellites—Meteors 11, 12 and 13—designed to monitor cloud formations under both day and night conditions. The Soviets also launched five additional Molniya spacecraft in the Orbita comsat network, which extends from Eastern Europe to the Far East. Three more Intercosmos satellites were launched, the sixth, seventh and eighth of their type. Intercosmos is a scientific program designed to give Soviet-bloc nations lacking their own space capability an opportunity to conduct experiments.

The remaining missions—67 satellites—were grouped in the Cosmos category. Cosmos is a catchall grouping that includes scientific experiments, advanced technology experiments and a variety of military projects like those being conducted by the United States. Of particular interest was Cosmos 521, launched Sept. 29, believed by some Western experts to be a new and advanced test vehicle in the Soviet program to develop a space interceptor capable of destroying other nations' military spacecraft.

JAMES J. HAGGERTY
Author, *Apollo Lunar Landing*

SPAIN

Generalissimo Francisco Franco-Bahamonde celebrated his 80th birthday on Dec. 4, 1972, in his 34th year as dictator of Spain, a tenure that makes him Spain's longest-ruling leader and one of the most durable surviving chiefs of state in the world. Although Franco had thus kept his promise, in his own words, "to remain at the helm of the ship of state as long as God gives me life and clarity of judgment," there were increasing signs during the year that the stability of his regime was being threatened from many quarters.

The threats to the old *caudillo's* power came not only from such outlawed movements as the Basque and Catalan separatist and left-wing opposition organizations, but also from members of his own establishment, now nervously jockeying for future positions. Generalissimo Franco's health was officially reported to be good for a man of his age. But there was growing speculation that his physical and mental powers were failing. Minor medical problems forced him to cancel some official engagements in May, although he nevertheless took the salute at the annual parade celebrating his victory over the Spanish Republic in 1939. Standing beside him at the time was the 34-year-old Prince Juan Carlos, who has been nominated by Franco as his heir and future king of Spain.

Political Dissension. In 1972 the old dictator seemed finally to have lost his skill at uniting divergent elements within his government because the split between the extreme right and the moderate section of the so-called National Movement had become increasingly apparent in the twilight of the Franco era. Franco designated the vice president, Adm. Luis Carrero Blanco, as the man who will assume the duties of prime minister (a post which Franco had reserved to himself together with that of chief of state) when he disappears from the scene. The nomination of the 69-year-old admiral, a loyal but reactionary officer, upset and confused the "technocrat" cabinet ministers appointed in 1969, who are closely associated with the powerful Roman Catholic organization *Opus Dei*. The aim of the *Opus Dei* "technocrats" has been to bring Spain fully into Europe as a member of the European Economic Community (EEC). However, the Spanish foreign minister, Sr. Gregorio Lopez Bravo, apparently has failed to improve the Spanish government's image in the Western democratic nations, partly because the "hawks" in the Franco establishment are in the ascendancy and are not prepared to change the political structure of the country in order to appease liberal democratic principles.

Even such conservative national elements as the members of the legal profession com-

Gen. Franco attends the wedding of his granddaughter Maria del Carmen and Alfonso de Borbon, a grandson of Spain's last king, Alfonso XIII.

Keystone

Keystone

Franco has named Vice-President Luis Carrero Blanco to succeed him as prime minister.

plained throughout the year about gradual erosion of the few remaining rights of Spanish citizens. University professors joined the protesters when the government instituted a political purge of faculty members throughout the country. Mounting discontent among students —only a small minority of whom are left-wing revolutionaries—over the need for not only academic but also political reform led to disturbances which virtually paralyzed most Spanish universities.

Equally disturbed by the rightist trend was an increasing number of the clergy and the Roman Catholic hierarchy. The hierarchy has made it unmistakably clear that it wants a complete separation of church and state, and a termination of the concordat between Madrid and the Vatican, which still grants special privileges to both the Spanish government and the Church in Spain. The cardinal archbishop of Madrid, Msgr. Vicente Enrique y Tarancon, is in the camp of Generalissimo Franco's nonviolent, but still outlawed, democratic opposition. Some of the younger clergy, most notably the worker priests, who actively support their parishioners' often illegal demonstrations in favor of social justice and free trade unions, and the Basque priests, who defiantly cooperate with the left-wing freedom fighters in the northern provinces, have come into open conflict with the Madrid government. Surprisingly, their bishops usually supported them.

A virtual civil war in the Basque provinces of northern Spain escalated during the year, despite an all-out attempt by Generalissimo Franco's security forces to stamp out the separatist movement. Basque nationalism is led by the Euzkadi Ta Askatasuna (E.T.A.), or Basque Homeland and Liberty Movement, made up of young guerrilla fighters, predominantly leftists, pledged to achieve independence for the Basques by force. Late in the year, France adopted a policy of cooperation with the Franco regime in order to suppress the Basque independence movement, which has overflowed into French territory.

Labor Unrest. Another sign of wear in the fabric of the 34-year-old regime was the complete lack of confidence in the obligatory state-run *Sindicato* trade-union structure, and the related upsurge of opposition shown by such outlawed organizations as the Marxist-oriented Workers' Commissions. One of the most violent clashes between militant left-wing workers and the regime occurred in Generalissimo Franco's birthplace of El Ferrol in northwestern Spain in March. Striking workers from the state-controlled Bazan shipyards defied back-to-work orders and virtually seized control of the town for 24 hours before massive armed police reinforcements arrived for a bloody confrontation in which at least two rebel workers were shot dead and more than 30 seriously wounded. Political motives, as well as the rapidly rising cost of living, precipitated most of the strikes, which erupted in various parts of Spain, particularly in Barcelona and Vigo.

Foreign Policy. Major foreign policy developments in Spain in 1972 included the signing of the first formal trade pact with the Soviet Union in continuation of a policy of increased commerce with Communist countries. Special concessions to Maghreb nations were signed in an attempt to preserve Spanish control over the phosphate-rich Spanish Sahara colonial territory and maintain friendly relations with the troubled regime of King Hassan II of Morocco. The Spanish foreign ministry continued to pursue a cautious policy on its long-outstanding claim for sovereignty over the British colony of Gibraltar, in the hope of gaining British support for Spain's ambition to join the EEC.

W. CEMLYN-JONES
Foreign Correspondent in Spain
The Guardian and *Observer*, London

SPORTS

Commercialization of Professional Sports

Once upon a time, sports were sports and when fans described them everybody knew what they were saying. In those days strikes were what the umpire yelled when batters missed the ball; courts were what basketball players played on; and arguments were disputes between players, not lawyers.

The 1972 sports year opened with lawsuits between the National and American Basketball Associations over stars' jumping from one league to the other. It ended with the possibility of a strike in 1973 by the National Football League Players Association. In the meantime, there had occurred a strike by major league baseball players. Even amateur sports were awry, with unrest at the Olympic Games caused by threatened boycotts, controversial decisions by officials and by killings.

The word used most frequently to describe professional sports during 1972 was commercialization. The athletes themselves, those gridiron and diamond heroes who have always represented everything wholesome in America, came under attack from an unexpected quarter —the fans. Athletes were called greedy, selfish and pampered. Fans reportedly were even toying with boycotting games as a means to show their disapproval of athletes' behavior.

Many questions were raised, and as many went unanswered as fans forgot their ire when the action on the field became hotter than their tempers had been. But the questions remained. Is the athlete playing for love of the sport or purely for money? Have his worth and importance been grossly exaggerated? Does anyone really need sports?

Indeed, did anyone really miss baseball during the strike? Would anyone suffer lasting damage if autumn Sundays were not spent watching football? Critics observed that sports were crucial neither to national defense nor to the economy, nor did they deserve so much attention as war in Indochina or poverty in the ghetto.

On the other hand, the athletes behaved as if they regarded themselves as essential cogs in the machine. During the baseball strike both players and owners asked the President himself to intercede. He declined.

In relation to the U.S. economy, sports are not big business. The combined net income of professional football, baseball, basketball and hockey could not hold a candle to the budget General Motors allocates for model changes each year. Judging from the events of 1972, critics said, the only aspect of sports that was truly big was the size of players' heads—that and the exorbitance of their demands.

Many sports executives felt that an end must come to the skyrocketing player salaries, or else the increase would have to be passed along to the fans in terms of higher prices. But would the fans pay more for their tickets? For parking? For concessions? With talent spreading itself thinner in every sport because of expansion, would the fans be willing to pay more and get less?

No one ventured a final answer, although many observers believed that the issue was headed toward a confrontation between owners and athletes, with salaries eventually leveling off. On the other hand, players' unions were stronger and better organized than ever before. Players could start their own leagues because they alone possess what the fans want—proficiency on the field—and the owners could not go out and replace them with untrained labor.

The possibility of a player take-over seemed real, especially considering the ease with which a professional league can be formed. Apparently all it takes is a group of wealthy men with the time and inclination to buy up players eager to have their bank accounts padded. The World Hockey Association is following this formula, luring stars away from the National Hockey League.

The year 1972 was a disturbed one for sports. The principal losers seemed to be in the stands, not on the field.

BOB BROEG
Sports Editor
St. Louis Post-Dispatch

Auto Racing

George Follmer, driving a Roger Penske Porsche, ended the five-year domination by McLaren cars in the rich Can-Am road-racing series. Follmer captured five of the nine events and became the first non-McLaren driver to win the Can-Am point title.

Follmer's victory capped a banner year for Penske, who also watched Mark Donohue, in a Penske-prepared McLaren, finish first in the Indianapolis 500-mile race.

For the second straight year the rewards of the United States Auto Club's Triple Crown were split three ways. Donohue took the 500.

Bobby Unser (6) takes an early lead in the Indianapolis 500. Mark Donohue, driving a Penske-prepared McLaren, won the race and $218,768.

Joe Leonard was the Pocono (Pa.) 500-mile race winner, and Roger McCluskey beat the field in the Ontario 500-mile race.

Leonard, a former motorcycle champion, blended three circuit victories with consistently high finishes to nail his second consecutive national driving crown.

A new name appeared in the Grand Prix spotlight. Emerson Fittipaldi, a 25-year-old from Brazil, won five Formula One races and became the youngest man ever to win the world driving championship. Scotland's Jackie Stewart, bidding for a second straight title, won four races, but missed two events because of a stomach ailment.

Two championship racers were killed—Jo Bonnier, at Le Mans, and Jim Malloy, while practicing for the Indianapolis 500.

BOB COLLINS
Sports Editor, *The Indianapolis Star*

AUTO RACING

World Champion: Emerson Fittipaldi, Brazil
USAC: Joe Leonard, U.S.
Can-Am: George Follmer, U.S.
NASCAR: Richard Petty, U.S.

GRAND PRIX WINNERS
Argentinan Grand Prix: Jackie Stewart, Scotland
South African Grand Prix: Dennis Hulme, New Zealand
Spanish Grand Prix: Emerson Fittipaldi, Brazil
Monaco Grand Prix: Jean-Pierre Beltoise, France

Belgian Grand Prix: Emerson Fittipaldi
French Grand Prix: Jackie Stewart
British Grand Prix: Emerson Fittipaldi
German Grand Prix: Jacky Ickx, Belgium
Austrian Grand Prix: Emerson Fittipaldi
Italian Grand Prix: Emerson Fittipaldi
Canadian Grand Prix: Jackie Stewart
United States Grand Prix: Jackie Stewart
Singapore Grand Prix: Jackie Stewart

USAC TRIPLE CROWN
Indianapolis 500: Mark Donohue
Pocono 500: Joe Leonard
Ontario 500: Roger McCluskey

Baseball

The 1972 baseball season began with a players' strike and ended with exciting play-offs and a seven-game World Series. In the latter the Oakland Athletics defeated the Cincinnati Reds.

The players' refusal to take the field following spring training until the clubowners agreed to added payments to the pension funds reduced the schedules in both major leagues. In all, 86 games were missed, but the greatest damage was the fan apathy provoked by the strike. Attendance dropped in both leagues, to a total of 26,974,713.

The Athletics won the game's top honors in a year in which their 1971 star, Cy Young Award winner Vida Blue, won merely six games and lost ten. Blue refused to join the team until several weeks after the season opened, and only after Commissioner Bowie Kuhn intervened in his salary dispute with clubowner Charles O. Finley. Against his original demand for a $90,000 salary, Blue settled for $63,000, of which Finley said $50,000 was base pay.

After three years as American League champions the Baltimore Orioles failed even to win the Eastern Division title, which went to the Detroit Tigers. Surprising late-season rushes by the Boston Red Sox and New York Yankees made it a four-club race. In fact, it went down to the next-to-last day. Woodie Fayman of the Tigers turned in a 3–1 victory over the Red Sox, who lost the pennant by one-half game. In a hectic five-game play-off series, in which Bert Campaneris was banished and fined for throwing his bat at Detroit Tiger pitcher Lerrin LaGrow, the A's triumphed on the last day. Blue Moon Odom and relief pitcher Vida Blue combined to turn in a 2–1 victory over the Tigers. Gene Tenace, who singled across the decisive run in the Athletics' pennant victory, was also the star of the World Series.

The Reds won the National League pennant in the last inning of the fifth game on a wild pitch by Pittsburgh reliever Bob Moose. Earlier in the same inning, Johnny Bench added to the dramatics of the play-offs by tying the score for the Reds with a lead-off homer.

Tenace hit two home runs in the first World Series game to launch the A's toward victory. The Reds fought off early defeat by winning the fifth and sixth games, but in the seventh they were held to four hits by Manager Dick Williams' manipulation of four Oakland pitchers. Tenace drove in two of the A's three runs in their decisive 3–2 victory in the seventh game. The series was uniformly a low-scoring affair, with Mike Epstein of the A's going hitless in 16 times at bat.

BASEBALL

AMERICAN LEAGUE Final Standings	WON	LOST	PER CENT	GAMES BEHIND
Eastern Division				
Detroit	86	70	.551	...
Boston	85	70	.548	½
Baltimore	80	74	.519	5
New York	79	76	.510	6½
Cleveland	₁72	84	.462	14
Milwaukee	65	91	.417	21
Western Division				
Oakland	93	62	.600	...
Chicago	87	67	.565	5½
Minnesota	77	77	.500	15½
Kansas City	76	78	.494	16½
California	75	80	.484	18
Texas	54	100	.351	38½

Oakland defeated Detroit in play-offs
Batting Champion: Rod Carew (.318) Minnesota
Cy Young Award: Gaylord Perry (24–16) Cleveland
Home-Run Leader: Dick Allen (37) Chicago
Manager of the Year: Chuck Tanner, Chicago
Most Valuable Player: Dick Allen
Runs Batted in: Dick Allen (113)
Rookie of the Year: Carlton Fisk, Boston

NATIONAL LEAGUE Final Standings	WON	LOST	PER CENT	GAMES BEHIND
Eastern Division				
Pittsburgh	96	59	.619	...
Chicago	85	70	.548	11
New York	83	73	.532	13½
St. Louis	75	81	.481	21½
Montreal	70	86	.449	26½
Philadelphia	59	97	.378	37½
Western Division				
Cincinnati	95	59	.617	...
Houston	84	69	.549	10½
Los Angeles	85	70	.548	10½
Atlanta	70	84	.455	25
San Francisco	69	86	.445	26½
San Diego	58	95	.379	36½

Cincinnati defeated Pittsburgh in play-offs
Batting Champion: Billy Williams (.333) Chicago
Cy Young Award: Steve Carlton (27–10) Philadelphia
Home-Run Leader: Johnny Bench (40) Cincinnati
Manager of the Year: George Anderson, Cincinnati
Most Valuable Player: Johnny Bench
Runs Batted In: Johnny Bench (125)
Rookie of the Year: Jon Matlack, New York
All-Star Game: National 4, American 3
World Series: Oakland Athletics

MINOR LEAGUES

American Association: Evansville
Eastern League: West Haven
International: Tidewater
Pacific Coast: Albuquerque

The star of the 1972 World Series was Gene Tenace of the Oakland Athletics. The 26-year-old catcher drove in nine of the A's 16 runs and batted .348.

On Sept. 30, Roberto Clemente of the Pittsburgh Pirates became the 11th player in baseball history to get 3,000 hits. The year ended with the star outfielder being killed in the crash of a cargo plane off Puerto Rico. He was delivering relief supplies to victims of the Nicaraguan earthquake.

The National League All Stars defeated the American League All Stars, 4 to 3, in Atlanta in July. Joe Morgan of the Reds singled home the winning run in a ten-inning game previously highlighted by two-run homers by Hank Aaron of Atlanta and Cookie Rojas of Kansas City. Aaron's homers during the 1972 season were a running story and added up to 34, for a lifetime total of 673, only 41 shy of the career record of 714 held by Babe Ruth.

Early in the season Willie Mays was sent from the San Francisco Giants to the New York Mets, returning him to the city where he first earned fame. The deal was made with the approval of Mays, whose future security was underwritten by Mrs. Joan Payson, owner of the Mets and a long-time admirer of the aging star. Mays played only part time but said he would be back as a player in 1973.

The one franchise switch of the season, one which saw the former Washington Senators operate in Arlington, Texas, proved a disaster from both attendance and competitive standpoints. Despite the novelty of major league baseball in that area of the state, the Rangers drew only 662,974, barely 7,000 more than in Washington in 1971. They were so hopelessly out-distanced that Ted Williams resigned after a four-year fling as major league manager.

Sadness overtook baseball in April, October and December. Early in April, with the players' strike in progress, the nation was shocked by the sudden death of the respected Gil Hodges, manager of the Mets and former star of the Brooklyn and Los Angeles Dodgers. On Oct. 24, Jackie Robinson died of a heart attack following months of declining health. A teammate of Gil Hodges, Robinson was the first black to play professional baseball outside of the all-Negro leagues. As the year ended, Roberto Clemente, the star outfielder of the Pittsburgh Pirates, was killed when a cargo plane crashed after take-off from San Juan (Puerto Rico) International Airport. Clemente, who had a lifetime batting average of .317 (highest among active players), was personally delivering relief supplies to victims of the Nicaragua earthquake (*see also* Deaths).

The majors saw 11 managerial changes during the year. At Kansas City, Bob Lemon was succeeded by Jack McKeon. At Minnesota, Bill Rigney gave way to Frank Quilici. Dave Bristol was released by Milwaukee in May and replaced by Del Crandall. Bobby Winkles succeeded California Angels manager Del Rice. Whitey Herzog took over for the Rangers.

In the National League, coach Yogi Berra succeeded the late Gil Hodges. Leo Durocher made news by accepting the post of manager of the Astros after being fired by the Cubs. He replaced Harry Walker. Whitey Lockman succeeded Durocher with the Cubs. Luman Harris was replaced as Atlanta manager after the All Star game by Eddie Matthews. Frank Lucchesi was succeeded at Philadelphia by Paul Owens, and Don Zimmer replaced Preston Gomez early in the year at San Diego.

The year's pitching star was, without dispute, Steve Carlton, of the Phillies. Pitching for a last-place club, he led the league in innings pitched, strikeouts, earned-run average, complete games and victories. He compiled an amazing 27–10 record.

SHIRLEY POVICH
Sports Editor, *The Washington Post*

UPI

Pitching for a last place club, the Philadelphia Phillies, Steve Carlton compiled a 27–10 won-lost record. For the accomplishment, he was presented with the Cy Young Award.

Basketball

Los Angeles was the city of basketball champions in 1972. UCLA won the National Collegiate Athletic Association (NCAA) tournament for the sixth consecutive year and the eighth in nine years. After several times falling just short, the Los Angeles Lakers swept through the National Basketball Association play-offs. Maryland won the collegiate National Invitation Tournament (NIT), and the Indiana Pacers regained the American Basketball Association title.

COLLEGE SEASON

NCAA. Coach John Wooden's Bruins of UCLA finished the 1971–72 campaign with a streak of 45 straight victories over two seasons. Their last win was an 81–76 triumph over formidable Florida State in the NCAA tournament finals at the Los Angeles Sports Arena.

This championship edition of UCLA was led by a 7-foot sophomore, Bill Walton, who was named college basketball's player of the year. He scored 57 points in the two games of the finals, took down 41 rebounds and intimidated the opposition with excellent defense, including a variety of blocked shots.

UCLA reached the final game by whipping Louisville, 96–77, while Florida State held off North Carolina, 79–75. When Florida State concentrated on stopping Walton in the championship game, another sophomore, Keith (Silk) Wilkes, only 18 years old, broke loose for 23 points.

The Bruins led the college polls from preseason to post-season. The team that rated second throughout most of the year, Marquette University, lost its 6-foot 11-inch junior center, Jim Chones, to the New York Nets of the American Basketball Association. Late in the season, Chones signed a pro contract for the 1972–73 season. Without Chones, Al McGuire's Warriors fell from the undefeated ranks by losing to Kentucky in the regionals.

BASKETBALL

COLLEGE
Conference Winners
- **Atlantic Coast:** North Carolina
- **Big Eight:** Kansas State
- **Big Ten:** Minnesota
- **Ivy League:** Penn
- **Pacific Eight:** UCLA
- **Southeastern:** Kentucky
- **Southern:** East Carolina
- **Southwest:** Texas
- **West Coast Athletic:** San Francisco
- **Western Athletic:** Brigham Young
- **Yankee:** Rhode Island

PROFESSIONAL
National Basketball Association
Eastern Conference Final Standings
Atlantic Division

	W	L	Pct.
Boston	56	26	.683
New York	48	34	.585
Philadelphia	30	52	.366
Buffalo	22	60	.268

Central Division

Baltimore	38	44	.463
Atlanta	36	46	.439
Cincinnati	30	52	.378
Cleveland	23	59	.280

Western Conference Final Standings
Midwest Division

Milwaukee	63	19	.768
Chicago	57	25	.695
Phoenix	49	33	.598
Detroit	26	56	.317

Pacific Division

Los Angeles	69	13	.841
Golden State	51	31	.622
Seattle	47	35	.573
Houston	34	48	.415
Portland	18	64	.220

American Basketball Association
Final Standings
Eastern Division

Kentucky	68	16	.810
Virginia	45	39	.536
New York	44	40	.524
Floridians	36	48	.429
Carolina	35	49	.417
Pittsburgh	25	59	.298

Western Division

Utah	60	24	.714
Indiana	47	37	.560
Dallas	42	42	.500
Denver	34	50	.405
Memphis	26	58	.310

ABA All-Star Game: East 142, West 115
ABA Coach of the Year: Tom Nissalke, Dallas
ABA Most Valuable Player: Artis Gilmore, Kentucky
ABA Rookie of the Year: Artis Gilmore
NBA All-Star Game: West 112, East 110
NBA Coach of the Year: Bill Sharman, Los Angeles
NBA Most Valuable Player: Kareem Abdul-Jabbar, Milwaukee
NBA Rookie of the Year: Sidney Wicks, Portland

NIT. For the second straight year the Atlantic Coast Conference (ACC) provided the NIT champion. The 1971 titlist, North Carolina, defeated Maryland for the ACC crown and the right to compete in the NCAA tournament. As consolation, Maryland, coached by Lefty Driesell and led by 6-foot 11-inch sophomore Tom McMillen, went to Madison Square Garden to play in the NIT. Maryland went on to defeat Niagara in the final, 100–69. Oral Roberts University, with Richie Fuqua and his 35-foot swishers, provided the tournament's fan appeal, but the Oklahomans lacked defense, and that undid them.

PROFESSIONAL SEASON

NBA. The title may have been the first for the Lakers since they left Minneapolis, but it was nothing new for coach Bill Sharman. He had guided the Utah Stars to the 1971 American Basketball Association championship, and during the 1950's and early 1960's was prominent as a player on the perennial NBA championship teams of the Boston Celtics.

The play-offs provided personal vindication for Wilt Chamberlain, the 7-foot 1-inch center of the Lakers. He played some of his best basketball as the Lakers beat the Chicago Bulls in four straight games, took four out of six from the defending champion Milwaukee Bucks and then won four out of five from the New York Knickerbockers, who had beaten the Lakers in the 1970 finals. Chamberlain played the championship game with what was later determined to be a broken right wrist. He made 24 points and got 29 rebounds at the Los Angeles Forum to finish off the Knicks.

The series was a David and Goliath affair, for the Knicks were without their regular center, Willis Reed, who was sidelined for most of the season with a variety of ailments. The Knicks, therefore, lacked the height to combat Chamberlain. Nevertheless, they got in the first punch, leveling the Lakers, 114–92, by shooting 72 percent from the field in the first half of the first game. Dave DeBusschere, New York's premier rebounding forward, suffered a hip injury in the second game, and the Lakers went the rest of the way without incident. The fourth game went into overtime as Chamberlain came as close as he ever has in 13 NBA seasons to fouling out.

The Lakers' biggest test had been in the semifinals against Milwaukee, but the Bucks'

Bill Walton (with ball), a 7-foot sophomore, led UCLA to its sixth consecutive NCAA title. He was named college basketball's player of the year.
UCLA

Wilt Chamberlain (13) dominated the 1972 play-offs as Los Angeles won its first NBA crown. In the play-offs the Lakers defeated the Chicago Bulls, the Milwaukee Bucks and the New York Knicks.

Oscar Robertson was hampered by an abdominal muscle strain. Kareem Abdul-Jabbar, who as Lew Alcindor led the Bucks to the 1971 title, could not quite handle the Lakers without Robertson's help, especially with Chamberlain playing in such an inspired way.

Although the Lakers' all-pro guard, Jerry West, finally played on a pro-championship team, he was not so big a factor in the play-offs as might have been expected. He had some wretched shooting luck. Gail Goodrich, Happy Hairston, Jim McMillian and, of course, Chamberlain, took up the slack.

During the regular season, the Lakers had set two records—best win percentage for a season (.841) and most consecutive victories (33). With a record of 69 wins and 13 defeats, they broke the 68–13 (.840) mark set by the Philadelphia Warriors in 1966–67, when Chamberlain was a member of that team. By winning 33 straight games, the Lakers bettered the mark of 20 set a year earlier by the Bucks. Oddly, the Bucks were the ones who ended the Los Angeles streak in a nationally televised game from Milwaukee.

ABA. The New York Nets were the surprise of the ABA, but they were outmatched by Slick Leonard's Pacers in the play-off finals. Indiana won the championship play-offs in six games, taking the last gasp game on May 20 by a 108–105 score.

Lou Carnesecca's Nets had surprised the Kentucky Colonels and Virginia Squires in earlier series. Indiana beat the Denver Rockets and dethroned the Utah Stars along the way.

The league's leading scorer, Charlie Scott, jumped to the NBA's Phoenix Suns late in the season, as the war between the two pro leagues —and the war with the colleges—slowly escalated.

CHUCK JOHNSON
Sports Editor, *The Milwaukee Journal*

Boxing

Muhammad Ali traveled the globe in 1972, but none of the opponents he met in the ring was named Joe Frazier, world heavyweight boxing champion and the only man ever to administer a professional beating to the boxer who was baptized Cassius Clay.

Ali, weighing a flabby 226, pounded Mac Foster, a former U.S. marine who was rated as the number three contender for the crown, for 15 rounds in Tokyo. He repeated his previous victory over Jerry Quarry in a bout halted by the referee in the seventh round at Las Vegas, Nev. After the loss, Quarry announced his retirement from the ring. Ali stopped Al (Blue) Lewis of Detroit in 11 rounds before an Irish audience in Dublin, but for the second time, George Chuvalo, the durable Canadian, went the route with the 30-year-old former champion. On that occasion the distance was only 12 rounds, and the site was Vancouver, B.C.

Ali used only his left hand to prove his superiority over aging Gregorio Peralta in the Barcelona, Spain, bullring and drew boos from the 10,000 spectators who had paid as much as $30 a seat. Actually, the fight was an exhibition without a referee or judges, although Ali proclaimed the bout as a championship fight on his arrival.

Ali closed his global gyrations in late August by meeting 37-year-old Floyd Patterson in New York's Madison Square Garden, where a throng of 17,378 paid $512,361 to see what all knew would happen—another defeat in the 20-year-fight career of Patterson. Ali had humiliated the same opponent in November 1965 in Las Vegas, and in 1972 only the setting was new. It was a dreary affair until the sixth round, when Ali showed his old form and opened a cut over Patterson's left eye. In the seventh, Ali concentrated on the wound but could not put Patterson down. When the bell for the eighth round sounded, Patterson refused to come out, and the referee raised Ali's right hand in victory.

During the busy summer Ali had slimmed down to 217 pounds and had improved his footwork.

Although Frazier spent much of the year in his native South Carolina, he registered a fourth round knockout over Terry Daniels on Jan. 15 in New Orleans and late in year agreed to meet George Foreman on Jan. 22, 1973, in Kingston, Jamaica. Earlier Frazier had knocked out Ron Stander in Omaha, Neb.

Frazier seemed confused by Stander's awkwardness in the opening round, but by the middle of the second the Iowan's face was cut near the nose and his head bobbing on the champion's uppercuts. Stander suffered additional facial cuts in the third but dashed out of his corner at the start of the fourth as if he intended to get in as many blows as possible before the inevitable end. Frazier dealt heavy punishment to Stander's head the rest of the round, and when it was over, the bout was stopped.

In a press conference the next day, Frazier announced plans for an extended Carolina vacation—"I'll just sit and stay there until somebody comes down with a check for $3,-500,000 to fight Clay."

While the champion and the contender were pursuing different routes to a probable return match, George Foreman was gaining stature steadily as an opponent for either of them. He had won an Olympic gold medal in the 1968 games at Mexico and had finished his first 36 pro fights without a defeat. Thirty-one of the triumphs came by knockouts.

Bob Foster, the World Boxing Council's light-heavyweight champion, also had a busy summer. His two major bouts were a second-round knockout of Vincente Rondon of Venezuela, who entered the Miami Beach ring as the World Boxing Association's world champion of the 175-pound class, and a knockout over Mike Quarry in a title fight that headed the Los Vegas card on which Ali stopped Jerry Quarry. Jerry said it was watching the beating brother Mike took from Foster that caused him to retire.

Ali knocked out light-heavyweight champion Foster in November in Nevada.

Possibly the most furious fight of the year was the June 26 one in Madison Square Garden in which Roberto Duran, a graduate of Panama street fighting, dethroned Ken Buchanan of Scotland as the king of the lightweights. The 21-year old Duran was declared the winner when Buchanan was knocked down by what he contended was a foul blow after the bell had sounded ending the 13th round and refused to come out for the 14th round.

Referee John LoBianco insisted that the blow was legal and that Buchanan had taken such a beating from Duran that he was unable to continue. Only after the tumultuous brawl was over was it discovered that in the excitement none of the three judges had scored the final round.

Rocky Graziano, middleweight champion in the late 1940's, and Sandy Saddler, featherweight king in the 1950's, were elected to the Boxing Hall of Fame.

Nat Fleischer, regarded by many as boxing's outstanding authority, died on June 25, 1972.

HAROLD (SPIKE) CLAASSEN
Free-lance Sportswriter

Larry Brown of the Washington Redskins became the third runner in pro-football history to gain 4,000 yards in his first four years in the NFL. He was named the year's most valuable player.

UPI

Football

The 1972 season was an historic one for professional football. The Miami Dolphins, a seven-year-old expansion team, completed the regular season and the playoffs without a defeat. The Dolphins' perfect season was capped with a 14–7 Super Bowl win over the slightly favored Washington Redskins. In the college ranks, the Southern California Trojans also finished their regular season without a loss and went on to defeat Ohio State in the Rose Bowl by a score of 42–17.

PROFESSIONAL SEASON

Although many football fans and analysts charged that an easy playing schedule helped the Dolphins obtain their unblemished regular season mark, the Miami team completely justified its laurels with victories in the two play-off games and in Super Bowl VII, in which Miami played nearly perfect football.

Super Bowl VII was played on Jan. 14, 1973, in 84-degree heat in the Los Angeles Coliseum before a record crowd of 81,706 spectators. Miami scored its first touchdown shortly before the first quarter ended on a Bob Griese pass to Howard Twilley. Its second touchdown came

when Jim Kiick went over the goal line from the one yard line late in the second quarter. Meanwhile, the Miami no-name defense, which had allowed the fewest number of points of any team during the regular season, was completely stopping the Washington Redskins, led by Larry Brown, the National Football League's most valuable player.

Two long second-half Redskins' drives ended in a missed field goal by Curt Knight and an intercepted pass by Miami's Jake Scott in the end zone. Scott, who made another vital interception for the Dolphins, was named the game's outstanding player. The Redskins' only score came on a rather unusual play. A long field goal attempt by Miami's Garo Yepremian was blocked and caught by the Cyprus-born place kicker himself. Instead of holding on to the ball and accepting the down, Yepremian threw a pass aimlessly that was caught by Washington's Mike Bass who ran it back for a touchdown.

Miami had earned its right to participate in the Super Bowl game by defeating the Cleveland Browns and the Pittsburgh Steelers in the play-offs. Miami came from behind in both games to win in the final quarter. In the Pittsburgh game the Dolphins' quarterback, Bob

The Miami Dolphins completely dominated Super Bowl VII as they capped an undefeated season with a 14–7 win over the Redskins.

Griese, who was out most of the season with a dislocated ankle, came off the bench to replace his back-up man, Earl Morrall, and led the team to victory. Griese also did an excellent job of quarterbacking throughout the Super Bowl.

Washington's road to the championship game, its first in 30 years, was a somewhat easier one. On Dec. 24 the pride of the nation's capital topped the Green Bay Packers, 16–3, and a week later George Allen's team of veterans defeated the Dallas Cowboys, the incumbent champions, 26–3. Washington's game against Dallas was highlighted by two touchdown passes by quarterback Billy Kilmer. Sonny Jurgensen, the regular Washington quarterback, had been lost for the entire season through injury.

COLLEGE SEASON

In an important season-end game against Notre Dame, Southern California's sophomore tailback Anthony (A.D.) Davis scored six touchdowns as the USC Trojans won their 11th consecutive game. The same day, Auburn scored a 17–16 upset over previously undefeated Alabama, and coach John McKay's Trojans became the only major undefeated college team in the nation. Subsequently, the Trojans were awarded the MacArthur Bowl, which is presented annually to the nation's number one team.

In the 59th Rose Bowl game, played before 106,869 fans, Southern California easily defeated the Ohio State Buckeyes. Following a 7–7 tie at halftime, the Trojans scored three touchdowns in the third quarter and two in the fourth. Fullback Sam Cunningham scored four of USC's touchdowns, a Rose Bowl record, and was named the game's outstanding player.

The Nebraska Cornhuskers humiliated the fighting Irish of Notre Dame in the 39th annual Orange Bowl game, 40–6. Heisman Trophy winner Johnny Rodgers of Nebraska scored four touchdowns and passed for another. After

Rose Bowl Game: Sam Cunningham (with ball) scored a record four touchdowns as he led the USC Trojans to a 42–17 win over the Ohio State Buckeyes.

Johnny Rodgers of the University of Nebraska gleefully accepted the 1972 Heisman Trophy on Dec. 5.

the game coach Bob Devaney, who had led the Cornhuskers to the nation's number-one spot the previous two seasons, retired.

In other New Year's Day action, seventh-ranked Texas defeated fourth-ranked Alabama, 17–13, in the Cotton Bowl, and Oklahoma was victorious over Penn State in the Sugar Bowl game at New Orleans.

There was some question as to whether Johnny Rodgers' off-the-field conduct would prevent him from winning the Heisman Trophy, awarded to the nation's outstanding collegiate player. Rodgers had been convicted of robbing $90 from a gasoline station during his freshman year in college and later had been arrested on suspicion of possessing marijuana. Despite his legal problems, Rodgers received 301 of a possible 934 first-place votes and received the coveted trophy. Having gained a total of 5,586 yards in three years (plus 244 yards in the 1973 Orange Bowl), the all-purpose back was the greatest offensive collegiate player in history.

For the first time in 21 years college freshmen were permitted to play varsity football. To the surprise of many, the frosh did very well.

BOB BROEG
Sports Editor, *St. Louis Post-Dispatch*

FOOTBALL

COLLEGE

Conference Winners

Atlantic Coast: North Carolina
Big Eight: Oklahoma
Big Ten: Ohio State-Michigan (tie)
Ivy League: Dartmouth
Mid-American: Kent State
Missouri Valley: Louisville-West Texas-Drake (tie)
Pacific Coast A.A.: San Diego
Southeastern: Alabama
Southern: East Carolina
Southwest: Texas
Western Atlantic: Arizona State
Yankee: Massachusetts

Bowl Games

Astro-Bluebonnet Bowl: Tennessee 24, LSU 17
Cotton Bowl: Texas 17, Alabama 13
Gator Bowl: Auburn 24, Colorado 3
Orange Bowl: Nebraska 40, Notre Dame 6
Rose Bowl: Southern California 42, Ohio State 17
Sugar Bowl: Oklahoma 14, Penn State 0
Sun Bowl: North Carolina 32, Texas Tech 28

PROFESSIONAL

National Football League Final Standings

American Football Conference

Eastern Division	WON	LOST	TIED	PER CENT
Miami	14	0	0	1.000
N.Y. Jets	7	7	0	.500
Baltimore	5	9	0	.357
Buffalo	4	9	1	.321
New England	3	11	0	.214
Central Division				
Pittsburgh	11	3	0	.786
*Cleveland	10	4	0	.714
Cincinnati	8	6	0	.571
Houston	1	13	0	.071
Western Division				
Oakland	10	3	1	.750
Kansas City	8	6	0	.571
Denver	5	9	0	.357
San Diego	4	9	1	.321

* Qualified for play-offs

National Football Conference

Eastern Division	WON	LOST	TIED	PER CENT
Washington	11	3	0	.786
*Dallas	10	4	0	.714
N.Y. Giants	8	6	0	.571
St. Louis	4	9	1	.321
Philadelphia	2	11	1	.179
Central Division				
Green Bay	10	4	0	.714
Detroit	8	5	1	.607
Minnesota	7	7	0	.500
Chicago	4	9	1	.321
Western Division				
San Francisco	8	5	1	.607
Atlanta	7	7	0	.500
Los Angeles	6	7	1	.464
New Orleans	2	11	1	.179

The Play-offs

Semifinals
Miami 20, Cleveland 14
Pittsburgh 13, Oakland 7

Washington 16, Green Bay 3
Dallas 30, San Francisco 28

Finals
Miami 21, Pittsburgh 17

Washington 26, Dallas 3

Super Bowl
Miami 14

Washington 7

Canada's Grey Cup: Hamilton Tiger-Cats

Golf

What started out as the year in which most links addicts predicted that Jack Nicklaus would become the first person to win the fabled grand slam of professional golf came to a grinding halt with a spectacular Lee Trevino chip shot on the next to last hole at Muirfield, Scotland.

The modern grand slam consists of the Masters at Augusta, Ga., the United States Open, the British Open and the U.S. PGA. The grand slam of the past had included the U.S. and British amateurs instead of the Masters and the PGA. It was won only once, by the late Bobby Jones in 1930. No one ever has won the modern slam.

Nicklaus played well as he led in every round of the Masters, April 6–9, and finished with a 3-stroke victory margin. It was his fourth Masters. Nicklaus alone conquered both the horrible weather and the awesome Pebble Beach layout near Carmel, Calif., for his third Open crown. Again, he never surrendered the lead and again he finished three strokes in front. In both tournaments, Bruce Crampton of Australia was second.

The two victories brought Nicklaus' career record of major titles to 13—the same number won by his idol, Bobby Jones. But then came the British Open at Muirfield, where Trevino retained the title by a single stroke and the PGA where Gary Player of Johannesburg, South Africa, annexed the laurels for a second time.

It was on the 16th hole of the final round of the British Open that Nicklaus, making a furious last-day charge after a trio of lackluster

Jack Nicklaus waves to the gallery after winning his fourth Masters' title at Augusta.

GOLF	
MEN	
American Golf Classic: Bert Yancey	
British Amateur: Trevor Homer	
British Open: Lee Trevino	
Canadian Open: Gay Brewer	
Kemper Open: Doug Sanders	
Masters: Jack Nicklaus	
Pacific Masters: Gay Brewer	
Professional Match Play: Jack Nicklaus	
Tournament of Champions: Bobby Mitchell	
U.S. Amateur: Vinny Giles	
U.S. Open: Jack Nicklaus	
U.S. PGA: Gary Player	
World Series of Golf: Gary Player	
WOMEN	
British Women's Amateur: Michele Walker	
U.S. Amateur: Mary Ann Budke	
U.S. Open: Mrs. Susie Maxwell Berning	
U.S. PGA: Kathy Ahern	
TEAM	
Curtis Cup (Women): U.S.	
World Cup (Men): Taiwan	

rounds, saw his grand slam dream go awry when he missed a 4-foot putt for a bogey. That dropped him one stroke behind Trevino, the Mexican joy-boy from Texas who was defending champion.

Trevino was in the twosome directly behind Nicklaus and successfully parred the 16th hole, but on the next he sent his approach into knee-high rough to the right of the green and some 30 feet from the flag. After making several flippant remarks to the gallery, Trevino dumped the ball into the hole for the needed par.

It was different at the U.S. PGA, played at Oakland Hills near Detroit, Mich. Nicklaus began the week in the hospital with an infected finger on his right hand and finished it in a tie for 13th place, six shots behind Gary Player, the meticulous Johannesburg rancher who took the $45,000 first place check to the South African veldt.

It was Player's 15th triumph in the United States. Player had gone over par on the 14th and 15th and sliced his tee shot on 16 into the rough behind a huge tree and near a small lake. He could not see the green but discovered that a chair on the hillock that barred his view was in direct line with the flag. With a 9-iron he dropped the ball 4 feet from the pin for a par and victory.

Although frustrated in his grand slam attempt, Nicklaus became the first golfer to win more than $300,000 in a single season and passed Arnold Palmer as the greatest winner of prize money in a career.

HAROLD (SPIKE) CLAASSEN
Free-lance Sportswriter

Horse Racing

Riva Ridge, Secretariat, Susan's Girl and La Prevoyante were the biggest names in horse racing in 1972, a year in which the sport conformed with the trend of the times. It was a year of youth. Riva Ridge and Susan's Girl were three-year-olds and Secretariat and La Prevoyante were two-year-olds. There seemed to be few talented older handicap horses.

Another three-year-old colt was also in the limelight. Key to the Mint, owned by Rokeby Stable, won the Derby Trial, Travers, Withers, Brooklyn Handicap and Whitney, beating older horses in the last two races.

Both Riva Ridge and Secretariat are owned by the Meadow Stable and trained by Lucien Laurin. Riva Ridge, winner of seven of nine races and $503,263 as a two-year-old, found the path leading to horse-of-the-year recognition as a three-year-old rather bumpy.

A son of First Landing out of the Bold Ruler mare Iberia, Riva Ridge was beaten in the Everglades at Hialeah Park, then came back to win the Blue Grass Stakes at Keeneland, the Kentucky Derby, Belmont Stakes and Hollywood Derby. These wins boosted his earnings to nearly $1,000,000. However, a sloppy track and bad racing luck nullified his chances of winning the Triple Crown. He finished fourth to Bee Bee Bee in the Preakness at Pimlico.

Some experts predicted that Secretariat would emulate Riva Ridge's success as a three-year-old, if not exceed it. Secretariat followed in Riva Ridge's footsteps, winning the Futurity Stakes at Belmont as had Riva Ridge in 1971. Previously, the beautifully made son of Bold Ruler had won the Sanford and the Hopeful Stakes convincingly.

Mrs. John Tweedy, who operates Meadow Stable for her ailing father, Christopher T.

Chenery, got the colt Secretariat on the toss of a coin. She sent Somethingroyal to Kentucky to be bred to Bold Ruler, whose connections chose a filly. This left Mrs. Tweedy with whatever resulted from the second mating of Bold Ruler and Somethingroyal.

La Prevoyante, a two-year-old filly, ripped off 12 straight wins with ridiculous ease. La Prevoyante, the beautifully streamlined daughter of Buckpasser out of the Neartic mare Artic Dancer, won most of her races in Canada but scored handily in the Matron Stakes at Belmont Park.

As the field lined up for the running of the Beldame Handicap at Belmont Park on Sept. 9, Fred W. Hooper, owner of Susan's Girl, told his wife: "I've always thought the Kentucky Derby was the greatest race to win—and I have won one—but I'd rather win this race than any race I know. This is the greatest bunch of fillies and mares I've ever seen." The nine fillies and mares, three-years-old and up, had won 59 stake races and earned a total of $2,922,867.

Hooper had his wish. Susan's Girl registered her ninth stakes victory as a three-year-old, beating Summer Guest by a length. Chou Croute, a four-year-old, was another length back in third place. The win boosted the earnings of the daughter of Quadrangle to $503,162.

Two Kentucky Derby winners were decided during the year. Riva Ridge won the uncontested one before a record racing crowd of 130,564 at Churchill Downs, beating No Le Hace by three and one quarter lengths. The throng set a record for betting on one race—$2,885,325 on the Derby itself—and $7,164,717 on a racing card.

The Kentucky Court of Appeals handed down a decision a week before Riva Ridge's victory giving Forward Pass, runner-up in the 1968 derby, the winner's purse. The appellate court reversed a decision of the Franklin Circuit Court that awarded the purse to winner Dancer's Image. Tests had revealed that Dancer's Image had traces of a forbidden drug in his system.

It was a good year and bad one for yearling sales. Keeneland averaged $37,101 per head—$5,000 more than 1971. Saratoga averaged $28,930, off five percent.

DEAN EAGLE
Sports Editor
The Courier-Journal, Louisville, Ky.

HORSE RACING

Kentucky Derby: Riva Ridge
Preakness: Bee Bee Bee
Belmont Stakes: Riva Ridge
Santa Anita Derby: Solar Salute
Wood Memorial: Upper Case
Louisiana Derby: No Le Hace
Florida Derby: Upper Case
Santa Anita Handicap: Triple Bend
Flamingo Stakes: Hold Your Peace
American Derby: Dubassoff
Hollywood Gold Cup: Quack
Suburban Handicap: Hitchcock
California Derby: Quack
Hopeful Stakes: Secretariat
Spinaway: La Prevoyante
Gazelle Handicap: Susan's Girl
Jockey Club Gold Cup: Autobiography

Ice Hockey

In the spring of 1971, after Montreal had won the Stanley Cup in Chicago, the team went through Customs on its return to Canada. "Are

Before a record crowd of 130,564, Riva Ridge won the 98th running of the Kentucky Derby.

you bringing back anything you didn't have when you went to Chicago?" captain Jean Beliveau was asked. "Just the Stanley Cup," said Beliveau. "You don't have to declare that," said the inspector. "It's Canadian property." He could have said "Canadiens' property" because the Montreal Canadiens had won it so often. But 1972 was a different story.

The Boston Bruins, who were favored to win the Cup before the play-offs started, were relieved when the New York Rangers eliminated the Montreal team in six games in the quarter-finals. The great Beliveau had retired at the end of the 1970–71 season, and the Canadiens missed his leadership. In the final event, Boston faced New York.

If there was a surprise during the season's regular play, it was the way 69-year-old King Clancy, who in February replaced ailing coach Johnny McLellan of the slumping Toronto Maple Leafs, rallied the Leafs and led them to a berth in the play-offs. But that was where the miracle ended. They were hardly in a class

with the powerful Bruins, who disposed of them in five games.

In the quarter-finals in the West Division, the Chicago Black Hawks did the expected by sweeping their series against the Pittsburgh Penguins. But there was a surprise in the division's other series as the St. Louis Blues upset the favored Minnesota North Stars. This hard-fought series went the limit, and was not decided until the Blues scored the winning goal in sudden-death overtime in the seventh game. The fans were so numbed by the disappointing ending that they had to be herded out of the North Stars' rink.

The surviving teams in the East Division then met the survivors in the West. This change in play-off format ensured that the two best teams would meet in the final series, thereby minimizing the chances of an anticlimax.

It came as a shock, therefore, that the New York Rangers knocked off the Chicago Black Hawks in four straight games. The Rangers

Bobby Orr (4) led the Boston Bruins to victory in the 1972 Stanley Cup and was awarded the Conn Smythe Trophy as the "most valuable player" in the play-offs.

Ken Regan, Camera5

outscored the Hawks, 17 to 9, and even their most rabid supporters were stunned by the ease with which they smothered the firepower of Bobby Hull, the Hawks' big gun. The other semifinal series was a romp for the Boston Bruins over the St. Louis Blues, who did not belong on the same ice with Boston. This also was a four-game series, with the Bruins outscoring the Blues by the margin of 28 to 8.

The stage was set for the final series—a showdown between those two great rivals, Boston and New York. "We have to start hitting them right off the bat," said coach Tom Johnson of the Bruins. "That's our style of hockey, and it's the reason we win games. When we lose, it's because we stop hitting." The Rangers, a well coached and disciplined team, play positional hockey and depend on a strong defense and pinpoint passing to win.

The Rangers had been hampered all season by injuries to key players, but nearly all of them were ready for the big test. When they lost the first two games in Boston Garden by one-goal margins, a question asked by Jean Beliveau back in March came to mind. "The Rangers have done a remarkable job of picking up the slack caused by injuries," he said. "But can they keep it up all through the play-offs?" The teams now switched to Madison Square Garden for the next two games, and the Rangers won the first one rather easily. But the Bruins resumed their hitting in the next encounter and took a 3–1 lead in games.

The teams returned to Boston for a fifth game. The Rangers, who by then had lost through injuries the services of Jim Neilson, Ab Demarco and Ron Stewart, somehow rallied their shattered forces and managed to force a sixth game in New York. On that occasion, however, Gerry Cheevers, the Bruins' netminder, settled the issue. The Rangers lost the game, 3–0, and the series, 4–2. They had

ICE HOCKEY

COLLEGE

NCAA Championship: Boston University

PROFESSIONAL—National Hockey League

All-Star Game: East 3, West 2

Final Standings

	W	L	T	Pct.
East Division				
Boston	54	13	11	119
New York	48	17	13	109
Montreal	46	16	16	108
Toronto	33	31	14	80
Detroit	33	35	10	76
Buffalo	16	43	19	51
Vancouver	20	50	8	48
West Division				
Chicago	46	17	15	107
Minnesota	37	29	12	86
St. Louis	28	39	11	67
Pittsburgh	26	38	14	66
Philadelphia	26	38	14	66
California	21	39	18	60
Los Angeles	20	49	9	49

Stanley Cup: Boston Bruins

Ross Trophy (scoring): Phil Esposito, Boston

Calder Trophy (rookie): Ken Dryden, Montreal

Vezina Trophy (goalie): Tony Esposito, Gary Smith, Chicago

Hart Trophy (most valuable player): Bobby Orr, Boston

Lady Byng Trophy (sportsmanship): Jean Ratelle, New York

Norris Trophy (defense): Bobby Orr

Conn Smythe Trophy (play-off performance): Bobby Orr

WORLD CHAMPIONSHIP: Czechoslovakia

managed to contain Phil Esposito, the league's leading scorer, throughout the series, but they could not stop the spectacular Bobby Orr, who won the Conn Smythe Trophy as the "most valuable player" in the play-offs.

DINK CARROLL
Sports Columnist, *The Gazette,* Montreal

Soccer

In Brussels in June, West Germany, managed by its former outstanding forward Helmut Schoen, defeated the stolid and predictable U.S.S.R. team to become European Champions for the first time. Some fans recognized West Germany as the best soccer team since the Hungarians of the early 1950's.

Ajax of Amsterdam, managed by Stefan Kovacs of Rumania, won the European Champions Cup, symbolic of victory in the national league titles, for the second consecutive year. The heavily defensive tactics of Internazionale of Milan and England proved to be old-fashioned and crude as both were knocked out of the European championship competition. England lost to West Germany before a home crowd of 100,000 and millions of television viewers.

Excessive roughness by the players plagued the sport. Fearing violence, Ajax refused to meet Nacional of Uruguay in Intercontinental Cup competition. Eventually, Panathinaikos of Greece, managed by Ferenc Puskas of Hungary, were persuaded to play. The game between Nacional, the eventual winner, and the Greek team became so rough that there were fears that the tournament would have to be canceled. Following the match, several players were suspended, one for life.

The Rangers of Glasgow, who won the European Cup Winners Cup, were barred from competition for two years (reduced on appeal to one season) when their supporters rioted at the end of the final in Barcelona. And in Germany, investigations continued into allegations of bribery and player corruption.

By remaining undefeated in 33 matches, Brazil surpassed Hungary's 1953 record for most consecutive victories. In England, Leeds United won the FA Cup for the first time; Derby County became League Champions for the first time; and Stoke City won the Football League Cup—the team's first trophy in its 79-year history.

Johann Cruyff of Ajax was named European footballer of the year and Pele of Santos scored his 1,000th goal in a July exhibition match in Toronto. The game had to be stopped after friendly Canadians swarmed onto the field.

ALBERT BARHAM
National Soccer Correspondent
The Guardian, Manchester

SOCCER

European Championship: West Germany

African Cup of Nations: Congo

Brazilian Independence Cup: Brazil

Intercontinental Cup: Nacional (Uruguay)

European Champions Cup: Ajax (Amsterdam)

South American Championship: Independente

European Cup Winners Cup: Rangers (Glasgow)

European Union of Football Federations Cup: Tottenham Hotspur (London)

European Youth Championship: England

South American Youth Championship: Paraguay

Swimming

Mark Spitz was the name in swimming in 1972, even before the Olympic Games began in Munich in August.

The mustachioed dental student from Carmichael, Calif., started the year by winning the Sullivan Award, given annually to the nation's top amateur athlete. Early in August he gave a preview of his Olympic performance by setting three world records in the U.S. Olympic Trials in Chicago. Spitz first swam the 200 butterfly in 2:01.53, snapping West German Hans Fassnacht's mark of 2:03.3. Then he bettered his own mark of 54.68 in the 100-meter butterfly with a 54.66 timing. And finally he cracked his own pending mark in the 100-meter freestyle with a 51.47 clocking.

Several American marks were lowered in events at the U.S. Military Academy, West Point, in March as Indiana University—anchored by Spitz—edged USC, 390–371, for a record-tying fifth straight national collegiate championship.

And 13 world records were set at the U.S. Olympic trials. Included were those by Gary Hall in the 400-meter individual medley (4:30.81); John Hencken in the 200-meter breaststroke (2:22.79); Mitch Ivey in the 200-meter backstroke (2:04.82); Rick DeMont in the 1,500-meter freestyle (15:52.97); Melissa Belote in the 200-meter backstroke (2:20.64); Jo Harshbarger in the 800-meter freestyle (8:53.83) and Karen Moe in the 200-meter butterfly (2:16.62).

Record setter Mayumi Aoki of Japan swam the 100-meter butterfly in 1:03.9 to lower Alice Jones' record of 1:04.1, and Roland Matthes of East Germany posted a new mark in the 100-meter backstroke.

A familiar name, Susie Atwood, was the star of the National AAU Short Course meet, winning three individual events, and an even more familiar name, Debbie Meyer, retired from the sport.

See also Olympic Games.

DWIGHT CHAPIN
Sportswriter, *Los Angeles Times*

Tennis

The outstanding players and personalities of the 1972 tennis season were Stan Smith of California and Ilie Nastase of Rumania. Smith won the singles title at Wimbledon in July and almost singlehandedly retained the Davis Cup for the United States in a hair-raising final in Bucharest in October. Nastase won the U.S. Open title at Forest Hills as well as the circuit prize in the Grand Prix.

Add to the list of focal characters the names of "the old ladies" of world tennis—Mrs. Billie Jean King, the 28-year-old U.S. superstar who won at Wimbledon and Forest Hills, and Mrs. Margaret Court, 30, of Australia—and you have summed up the 1972 tennis scene. After giving birth to a son, Mrs. Court dominated Britain's Dewar Cup circuit in the fall.

The greatest match of the year was played between Smith and Nastase at Wimbledon. Smith is the personification of the American college boy—towering more than six feet, boyishly blond and relentlessly demanding of the skills of both himself and his opponent. Nastase, gleefully and affectionately nicknamed "Nasty," is the player long anticipated by Europe to counter the massive Australian-American domination of the game.

TENNIS

Davis Cup: United States
Dewar Cup Men: Ilie Nastase, Rumania
Dewar Cup Women: Margaret Court, Australia
Federation Cup: (women): South Africa
Wightman Cup: United States
World Championship Tournament: Ken Rosewall, Australia

Wimbledon Champions
Men: Stan Smith, United States
Women: Billie Jean King, United States
Men's Doubles: Bob Hewitt (South Africa) and Frew McMillan (South Africa)
Women's Doubles: Billie Jean King and Betty Stove (Netherlands)

U.S. Open Champions
Men: Ilie Nastase
Women: Billie Jean King
Men's Doubles: Cliff Drysdale (South Africa) and Roger Taylor (Britain)
Women's Doubles: Betty Stove and Françoise Durr (France)

U.S. Clay Court Champions
Men: Bob Hewitt
Women: Chris Evert, United States

U.S. Indoor Champions
Men: Stan Smith
Women: Virginia Wade, Britain

Other Open Champions
Australian Men: Ken Rosewall
Australian Women: Virginia Wade
Canadian Men: Ilie Nastase
Canadian Women: Evonne Goolagong, Australia
French Men: Andres Gimeno, Spain
French Women: Billie Jean King
Italian Men: Manuel Orantes, Spain
Italian Women: Linda Tuero, United States

Chris Evert, an attractive 17-year-old who "loves tennis," played very well as the U.S. team defeated Britain for the Wightman Cup.

Al Satterwhite, Camera5

Nastase's greatest weakness at Wimbledon was his uncertain temperament—in striking contrast to Smith's very sportsmanlike cool. Nastase had the superior skill, but the question remained could he control his emotions? When the match stood at one set all, Nastase appeared to be looking for an alibi to lose. Throughout several games he had protested vehemently that his rackets were strung too tightly. Fortunately, however, he mastered himself, and the last three sets were contested as narrowly as possible, with Smith just edging out the Rumanian at the very end.

In Bucharest in October, Smith and his teammates—Tom Gorman, Eric van Dillen and Harold Solomon—were plunged into the vortex of the most controversial Davis Cup final ever. The partisanship of the Rumanian fans was so intense that some U.S. officials charged that, if the U.S. team won, it could not get off the court alive. However, on the final day, when Smith appeared in the stands after defeating Ion Tiriac in five sets and sewing up the U.S. victory, he received thunderous applause.

Smith had crushed Nastase, who reacted badly to the partisan atmosphere, and after Tiriac had beaten Gorman in a match marked by extremely blatant gamesmanship, Smith turned the tables by combining with van Dillan

Russ Adams

Ilie Nastase, a lieutenant in the Rumanian Army, won the men's singles title at Forest Hills and the circuit prize in the Grand Prix.

to annihilate Tiriac and Nastase. Smith then went on to defeat Tiriac in the final singles match.

Following an April agreement between Allan Heyman of the International Lawn Tennis Federation and Lamar Hunt of World Cham-

pionship Tennis, peace reigned in men's professional tennis. However, the future of professional women's tennis remained cloudy. A circuit led by Mrs. Gladys Helldman went on its own.

Among young players, Chris Evert of Florida helped the U.S. team to victory over Britain in the Wightman Cup contest, and Jimmy Connors and Bob Lutz, both of the United States, and Buster Mottram of England showed promise as future stars to be reckoned with.

JOHN BALLANTINE
Lawn Tennis Correspondent
The Sunday Times, London

Track and Field

The pole vault provided track and field's major news of 1972.

Outdoor Season. When the outdoor season began, Chris Papanicolaou of Greece held the pole vault record—18-0¼. But in 1972, Kjell Isaksson of Sweden soared over 18-1, then went 18-2. Subsequently he and American Bob Seagren both cleared 18-4¼ in the same meet. Then it was Seagren's turn. The former USC vaulter with the movie star good looks went a record-setting 18-5¾ in the U.S. Olympic Trials at Eugene, Ore.

Two world records were tied in the trials—Dave Wottle running 1:44.3 in the 800 meters, Eddie Hart and Rey Robinson clocking 9.9 in the 100 meters.

Janis Lusis of the Soviet Union threw the javelin 307-9 to better the 304-1½ standard set by Finland's Jorma Kinnunen. Another Finn, Lasse Viren, ran 8:14 to break Belgian Emile Puttemans' 2-mile record of 8:17.8. UCLA's Bruins were an easy winner over USC's Trojans for the national collegiate title.

Indoor Season. Records were set by several Americans—Rod Milburn in the 120-yard high hurdles (13.4); Cliff Branch in the 100-yard dash (9.3); Mark Winzenreid in the 1,000-yard run (2:05.1); Al Feuerbach in the shot put (69-4¾) and Herb Washington in the 60-yard dash (5.8).

Among U.S. women, new marks were established by Patty Johnson, in the 50-yard hurdles (6.4), and Kathy Gibbons, in the 1,000-yard run (2:34.8).

USC won the NCAA indoor championship, but the Trojans' record-breaking run of 1:20.7 in the 880-yard relay was not official because Donald Quarrie of Jamaica was on the team.

See also Olympic Games.

DWIGHT CHAPIN
Sportswriter, *Los Angeles Times*

In the Bermuda Race, 178 boats battled a cold front, Hurricane Agnes and a tropical depression. The British sloop "Noryema" was the overall champion of the event.

Yachting

The 1972 racing season featured exciting moments and interesting results.

The overall surprise winner of the Southern Ocean Racing Circuit, a series of six long-distance ocean races off Florida and the Bahamas, was Class D *Condor*, a four-year-old Redline 41 owned by Hill Blackett of Chicago. The significance of her victory was that she was a family cruiser-racer with mostly old sails and borrowed equipment. *Condor* outperformed some of the finest racing machines ever designed for such events.

The Bermuda Race, which began on June 16 off Newport, R.I., produced some of the tensest moments of the racing season. The 178-boat fleet was buffeted by the fringes of a cold front, Hurricane Agnes and a powerful tropical depression. Some veterans equalled the weather conditions to that of the 1960 storm that lashed the fleet. Surprisingly, for the first time in the 66-year history of this prestigious event, the United States lost the top overall prize. It was won by the 48-foot British sloop *Noryema*, owned by Ron Amey of Britian and sailed by Ted Hicks.

Immediately following the Bermuda Race, a record 48-boat fleet sailed from Bermuda for Bayona, Spain, on the Transatlantic Race. The race was a long slow one with hardly any wind for long periods. Richard S. Nye's *Carina* was first overall and first in Class B.

Frank Zurn, sailing his new 61-foot Mc-Curdy & Rhodes-designed *Kahili II*, took the Bayview-Mackinac Race and the Chicago-Mackinac Race.

In early September, Bayview Yacht Club returned the Canada's Cup to the United States in one of the closest match races ever. Llwyd Ecclestone's *Dynamite*, a 39-foot Ted Hood design sailing out of Bayview YC, took the Cup from the Royal Canadian Yacht Club's defender *Mirage*, a 40-foot Cuthbertson & Cassian design sailed by Gordon Fisher. And so, the Canada's Cup returned to U.S. soil where it had been for 54 of its 77 years.

Powerboat Racing. Before the Hennessy Classic of Feb. 26, Sandy Satullo of Fairview Park, Ohio, was considered a rookie. Satullo not only beat the 40-boat fleet with his 36-foot Cigarette *Copper Kettle*, but he also averaged 73.78 m.p.h., one-half mile per hour below the offshore record of 74.3 set by Don Aronow in Italy. Satullo went on to win the 200-mile Sam Griffith Memorial Race at Ft. Lauderdale, the Bahamas 500 and the Hennessy Grand Prix, out of Point Pleasant, N.J.

See also Olympic Games.

DIANE DURYEA
Yachting Magazine

SPORTS
Summary of Winners Not Included on Pages 374–95

ARCHERY—Free-Style World Champions
  Men: John C. Williams, Cranesville, Pa.
  Women: Maureen Bechdoldt, Loveland, Ohio
BADMINTON—U.S. Open Champions
  Men: Sture Johnsson, Sweden
  Women: Eva Twedberg, Sweden
BOWLING—American Bowling Congress
  Champions
  All-events (classic): Teata Semiz, River Edge, N.J.
  All-events (regular): Mac Lowry, Seattle
  Singles (classic): Teata Semiz
  Singles (regular): Bill Pointer, Pontiac, Mich.
  Doubles (classic): Carmen Salvino, Chicago;
  Barry Asher, Costa Mesa, Calif.
  Doubles (regular): Jerry Nutt–Bill Stanfield, Grand Rapids, Mich.
  Team (classic): Basch Advertising, New York City
  Team (regular): Hamm's Beer, Minneapolis
CANOEING—U.S. Champions
  Canoe Singles (500-meters): Roland Muhlen, Newport Beach, Calif.
  Canoe Singles (1,000-meters): Roland Muhlen
  Kayak Singles (500-meters): John Van Cleave, Newport Beach, Calif.
  Kayak Singles (1,000-meters): Pete Weigand, Newport Beach, Calif.
CASTING—U.S. Inland Champions
  Grand All-Round: Steve Rajeff, San Francisco
  All-Distance: Zack Willson, Delaware, Ohio
CURLING
  U.S.: Grafton, North Dakota
  World: Canada
CYCLING
  Senior Amateur Bicycle League Champion: John Howard, Springfield, Mo.
  Tour de France: Eddy Merckx, Belgium
DOGS—Best-in-Show Winners
  International: Ch. Joanne-Chen's Maya Dancer, Maltese
  Westminster: Ch. Chinoe's Adamant James, English Springer Spaniel
FENCING—U.S. Champions
  Epée: James Melcher, New York
  Foil: Joseph B. Freeman, Philadelphia
  Saber: Alex Orban, New York
GYMNASTICS—U.S. National AAU Champions
  All-Round: Makoto Sakamoto, Oregon
  Team: New York A.C.
HANDBALL—U.S. Handball Association 4-Wall
  Champions
  Singles: Fred Lewis, Miami Beach
  Doubles: Kent Fusselman, Warren, Ohio; Al Drews, Cleveland
HORSESHOE PITCHING—World Champions
  Men: Elmer Hohl, Wellesley, Ont.
  Women: Ruth Hangen, Buffalo, N.Y.
ICE SKATING—World Champions
  Men's Figure: Ondrej Nepela, Czechoslovakia
  Women's Figure: Beatrix Schuba, Austria
  Men's Speed: Ard Schenk, Netherlands

  Women's Speed: Atje Keulen-Deelstra, Netherlands
JUDO—U.S. National AAU
  Open: Johnny Watts, Sacramento, Calif.
LACROSSE
  Club: Carlings L.C., Baltimore
  Intercollegiate Assoc.: Hobart
MOTORCYCLING
  U.S. Grand Champion: Mark Brelsford, Los Altos, Calif.
PARACHUTING
  Overall: Clayton Schoelpple, Hartwood, Va.
POLO
  National Open: Milwaukee
ROWING
  Intercollegiate R.A.: Pennsylvania
RUGBY
  Commonwealth Cup: Washington R.C.
  Rugby League: St. Helens
  Rugby Union: Wales
SKIING
  World Cup Champions
    Men: Gustavo Thoeni, Italy
    Women: Annamarie Proell, Austria
  U.S. National Alpine Champions
    Men's Slalom: Terry Palmer, Kearsarge, N.H.
    Women's Slalom: Marilyn Cochran, Richmond, Vt.
    Men's Giant Slalom: Jim Hunter, Calgary, Alta.
    Women's Giant Slalom: Sandy Poulsen, Olympic Valley, Calif.
SOFTBALL
  Amateur Softball Assoc. Champions
    Fast Pitch: Raybestos Cardinals, Stratford, Conn.
    Slow Pitch: Jiffy Club, Louisville, Ky.
  World Champion: Canada
SQUASH TENNIS
  Open: Pedro Bacallao, New York
  U.S. Pedro Bacallao
SURFING—U.S. Champions
  Men: Dale Dobson, San Diego, Calif.
  Women: Mary Setterholm, Corona Del Mar, Calif.
TABLE TENNIS—U.S. Open Champions
  Men's Singles: Dal Joon Lee, Cleveland
  Women's Singles: Wendy Hicks, Santa Barbara, Calif.
VOLLEYBALL—U.S. Volleyball Assoc. Champions
  Collegiate: Santa Monica
  Open: Chart House, San Diego, Calif.
WATER POLO—U.S. Champions
  AAU: Concord (Calif.) Dolphins
WATER SKIING—U.S. Champions
  Overall: Mike Suyderhoud, Petaluma, Calif.
  Women's Overall: Liz Allan Shetter, Winter Park, Fla.
WRESTLING
  Outstanding Wrestler: Wayne Wells, Oklahoma City
  Team: Mayor Daley Youth Foundation

At Independence Hall in Philadelphia on Oct. 20, President Nixon signed the revenue-sharing bill into law. Houston Mayor Louie Welch (l), Vice-President Spiro Agnew and New York Governor Nelson Rockefeller attended the ceremony.

UPI

STATES, U.S.

On Oct. 20, 1972, President Nixon appeared at Independence Hall in Philadelphia to acknowledge the applause of scores of state governors and mayors and to sign a measure that could mean a new lease on life for localities. The bill was the revenue sharing act of 1972, which granted the states and cities an initial $5,300,000,000 in Federal tax money in 1972 and which will provide them with $30,200,000,000 during the five-year life of the act.

In 1972 virtually all 50 states faced a common chronic problem: they lacked revenues while at the same time local taxpayers were demanding greater services and property tax relief. In the 1972 fiscal year the U.S. Commerce Department estimated that spending by state governments exceeded revenues by $1,600,000,000. State income from all sources (prior to revenue sharing) totaled $97,200,-000,000, up 9.3 percent from fiscal 1971. But spending totaled $98,800,000,000, up 16.2 percent. The largest expenditure by the state governments was $35,100,000,000 for education. Spending on public welfare came to $16,300,000,000, some 23.3 percent more than in fiscal 1971. Highway spending totaled $14,800,000,000, and spending on hospitals, $4,600,000,000.

Caught in this financial vise, governors lobbied vigorously for passage of the revenue sharing bill, one of the major planks in President Nixon's domestic program. Essentially the measure is designed to help state and local governments finance public services with Federal money, with no strings attached to the outlays, on the theory that the Federal government can raise money more easily than state governments. Proponents noted that the Federal government collects much of its money through the graduated income tax, which automatically goes up as the economy expands and prospers. Sales and property taxes, on which states rely heavily, do not rise accordingly.

The revenue sharing bill was debated for two years before the Democratically-controlled 92d Congress passed the measure. At the Independence Hall signing, President Nixon said he hoped the revenue sharing money would not only provide better public services but also "stop the alarming escalation" of state and local taxes.

Even before the U.S. Treasury mailed out the first revenue sharing checks in December, there was discussion of what the states would do with the money. The consensus was that some states would use the no-strings Federal funds to trim taxes—mostly property taxes—and others would use the money, as intended, to build new public facilities, expanded public transit systems and additional recreational facilities.

For example, Wisconsin's Gov. Patrick J. Lucey (D) said he would commit his state's

$133,900,000 of first-year revenue sharing to property tax relief, and he urged Wisconsin cities to do the same. But in McCook, Neb. (pop. 8,500), officials were planning to use the city's $100,000 on 25 civic projects, ranging from a new fire station to more parks. New York City, which got about $247,000,000 (state and local government in New York State received $591,000,000 overall), budgeted the windfall to keep subway fares at 35 cents and help pay higher salaries for policemen, firemen and sanitation workers.

The revenue sharing money is distributed by a complex set of formulas that takes into consideration population, the amount of urbanization, the extent of poverty and local tax effort.

That some states intended to use revenue sharing monies to reduce property taxes was understandable. Property taxes have risen steeply in recent years and come under political and judicial attack. Critics charge that the property tax is levied unfairly and even unconstitutionally. According to Tax Foundation Inc., in 1969–70 the per capita property tax averaged $168 for the entire country but varied greatly from state to state. In Alabama the per capita average was $39, in California $262, in Connecticut $238, in Kentucky $69, in Massachusetts $250, in New Jersey $242, in Pennsylvania $119 and in South Carolina $60.

In the 1972 political campaign, both Presidential candidates had pledged fiscal and monetary moves to further ease property tax burdens.

ROBERT W. DIETSCH
Business-Economics Editor
Scripps-Howard Newspapers

Alabama. Gov. George C. Wallace (D), campaigning for the Democratic Presidential nomination, was shot May 15 in Laurel, Md. The assault left him paralyzed from the waist down. The would-be assassin was captured. ● Elizabeth Andrews (D) was elected to Congress April 4 to fill the seat vacated by the death of her husband, George W. Andrews. She did not seek reelection. ● A constitutional amendment establishing a classification system for assessing property taxes was approved by the electorate May 30. ● Young black mayors took office in Prichard and Tuskegee in October. ● In the Nov. 7 elections, Sen. John J. Sparkman (D) soundly defeated Republican challenger Winton M. Blount, a former U.S. postmaster general.

Alaska. The commander of a Soviet fishing fleet and two ships' captains were brought to court in Anchorage Jan. 22, charged with violating U.S. fishing regulations. Their ships had briefly resisted seizure. ● The U.S. Department of the Interior conceded March 20 that any method of moving North Shore oil would threaten the environment. It insisted, however, that the oil was "important [for] national security," and construction of a pipeline was approved May 11. Lengthy court battles were expected before work could begin. ● Democrats lost control of the state senate and had their majority in the house reduced to two seats in the Nov. 7 elections. Sen. Ted Stevens (R) and Rep. Nick Begich (D), the latter missing in an airplane crash since Oct. 16, were reelected.

Arizona. Former Sen. Carl T. Hayden (D) died Jan. 25 at the age of 94. ● The legislature, by approving several reorganization measures re-

UPI

In vain, rescue craft searched for the Cessna 310 missing in Alaska since Oct. 16 with Representatives Hale Boggs (D-La.) and Nick Begich (D-Alaska) aboard.

Californians marched in support of legalizing marijuana. A proposal to legalize the drug was defeated by the state's voters, Nov. 7.

quested by Gov. Jack Williams (R), endorsed a major overhaul of the state government. A new farm labor law, providing for a state board to supervise organization of farm labor unions and arbitrate disputes, was also enacted. ● Flooding of the San Francisco and Gila rivers in late October killed eight persons and caused property damage of more than $5,000,000. ● In the Nov. 7 elections, Republicans retained control of the state legislature and won the seat added to the state's Congressional delegation as a result of the 1970 census. All incumbent Congressmen were reelected.

Arkansas. A black youth was elected president of the student government at the University of Arkansas Feb. 16. The 12,000-student institution at Fayetteville has about 350 registered blacks. ● Gov. Dale L. Bumpers (D) was returned to the governor's mansion Nov. 7 by

the handsome margin of 76 percent. Sen. John L. McClellan (D) easily won reelection to the Senate. The distribution of Congressional seats remained the same—three Democratic and one Republican.

California. The state supreme court ruled Feb. 18 that the death penalty was cruel and unusual punishment, violating the state constitution. The U.S. Supreme Court later refused the state's appeal. ● Legislation lowering the age of majority to 18 years was enacted March 3. ● Black militant Angela Y. Davis was acquitted June 4 of all charges stemming from the 1970 shoot-out at a Marin County courthouse in which a judge and three other persons were killed. ● A jet crashed into an ice-cream parlor in Sacramento Sept. 22, killing 22 persons, including many children. ● The Nov. 7 elections saw the state's Congressional delegation en-

Financial and environmental considerations led Colorado voters to defeat a proposal to develop Denver as the site of the 1976 Winter Olympic Games.

larged to 43, owing to the 1970 census results. Voters favored restoration of capital punishment and approved prohibition of school busing. They rejected qualified legalization of marijuana as well as restrictions on pornography.

Colorado. A former army paratrooper was seized Jan. 20 near Sterling, shortly after he parachuted with $50,000 in extortion money from a plane he had hijacked. ● Some 70 persons were arrested in Boulder May 9, when 1,000 war protesters blocked intersections. ● Sen. Gordon L. Allott (R) lost his bid Nov. 7 for a fourth term in the Senate; the victor was Floyd K. Haskell, an apostate Republican. The state's fifth seat in the U.S. House of Representatives, mandated by the results of the 1970 census, was captured by the Republicans, who also retained control of the state legislature. The voters withheld funds for the 1976 Winter Olympics, all but eliminating Denver as a site of the games. A proposal to outlaw property taxes as a source of school funds was defeated.

Connecticut. A Federal court ruled the state's abortion law unconstitutional April 18. The legislature subsequently passed a new, stringent act, banning abortions even in cases of rape or incest. The new law was struck down by the same court Sept. 20. ● More than 40 persons were arrested April 26, as they tried to block-

ade the Groton submarine base in protest against the Indochina war. ● The legislature lowered the legal age of majority to 18 years. It rejected the 27th amendment (women's rights) to the U.S. Constitution. ● Republicans won control of both houses of the state legislature Nov. 7.

Delaware. The state legislature ratified the 27th amendment to the U.S. Constitution March 23. Several other antidiscrimination measures were enacted. ● The new Delaware Museum of Natural History was opened in Greenville May 13. ● The National Wildlife Federation named Gov. Russell W. Peterson (R) "conservationist of the year" for sponsoring the state's coastal zoning law. The 1971 act outlaws new industries that would hinder public use of Delaware's coastline beaches. On Nov. 7, however, Governor Peterson lost his reelection bid to Democratic challenger Sherman W. Tribbitt. ● Joseph R. Biden, Jr., a 30-year-old lawyer, unexpectedly defeated Sen. J. Caleb Boggs (R). Rep. Pierre S. du Pont 4th (R) was reelected to Congress. ● Shortly before Christmas the wife and baby daughter of Senator-elect Biden were killed in an auto accident. Two Biden sons were seriously injured.

Florida. Some 1,000 antiwar students from the University of Florida at Gainesville battled police on U.S. Highway 441 May 9–10; nearly

400 were arrested. Hundreds of students also protested at Tampa and Tallahassee. ● Hurricane Agnes claimed 12 lives in its rampage over the coastal panhandle June 20. Property damage was estimated at $25,000,000. ● The state supreme court ordered Sept. 9 that 40 convicts, previously under death sentences, be resentenced to life imprisonment. ● All the state's incumbent Congressmen won reelection Nov. 7. Of the three new Congressional seats given to Florida because of population gains, two were won by Democrats, one by a Republican. Democrats retained control of the legislature. The voters approved bonds for purchase of threatened shoreline and other recreational lands.

Georgia. The state General Assembly approved a sweeping government reorganization plan that will consolidate some 65 agencies into 25 independent units. The assembly also granted full adult status to 18-year-olds, effective July 1. ● State Rep. Sam Nunn (D) was the winner Nov. 7 in the senatorial race. He defeated Fletcher Thompson, who gave up his Congressional seat in order to run. Thompson's place was filled by the Rev. Andrew W. Young, a former aide to Dr. Martin Luther King, Jr. He was the first black Southerner to win a seat in Congress since 1870.

Hawaii. Hawaii became the first state March 22 to ratify the 27th amendment to the U.S. Constitution. ● A bill creating a Transportation Control Commission that will make annual recommendations on the maximum number of automotive vehicles permitted on each island was signed into law May 25. ● A new penal code, effective Jan. 1, 1973, was enacted by the legislature. A liberal divorce law, providing for "dissolution of marriage" without fault laid to either party, also was passed. ● The state voted Republican in the Presidential elections, but the two Democratic Congressmen were reelected.

Idaho. The state legislature ratified the 27th amendment to the U.S. Constitution. It lowered the age of legal majority to 18 years, but established the drinking age as 19. The legislature also repealed the state's new criminal code, in effect since Jan. 1, replacing it with the old code. ● A disastrous fire in the Sunshine silver mine, near Kellogg, took the lives of 91 miners in early May. ● Rep. James A. McClure (R) was the winner in the Senatorial race Nov. 7. The Congressional seat vacated by him was won by Steven D. Symms (R), while Rep. Orval Hansen (R) was reelected. Republicans retained control of the state legislature.

Illinois. Some 2,000 war-protesting students rioted in Champaign-Urbana May 9, breaking windows and looting. Other war protesters blocked expressways in Chicago and Evanston. ● The Lincoln Home in Springfield, formerly a state memorial, was made a national historic site. ● Dan Walker (D) narrowly won the governorship from incumbent Richard B. Ogilvie on Nov. 7. Sen. Charles H. Percy (R) was reelected by a wide margin. Republicans won 14 out of the state's 24 Congressional seats. On Dec. 8. Rep. George W. Collins (D) was killed in an airplane crash. ● A Federal court of appeals Nov. 21 voided the convictions of five of the "Chicago Seven" on charges stemming from riots during the 1968 Democratic National Convention.

Indiana. Gov. Edgar D. Whitcomb (R) vetoed a bill that would have lowered the age for entering contracts and drinking alcohol to 18 years. ● A new $11,300,000 Musical Arts Center was opened May 15 at Indiana University, Bloomington. ● Trying to halt the eutrophication of the state's rivers and lakes, the legislature prohibited, effective Jan. 1, 1973, the sale of any detergents containing phosphorus. ● Dr. Otis R. Bowen (R) defeated former Gov. Matthew E. Welsh in the gubernatorial race Nov. 7. The Rev. William H. Hudnut 3d (R) ousted Rep. Andrew Jacobs, Jr., from his four-term Congressional seat.

Iowa. The state legislature, meeting Jan. 10 to March 24, created a state Department of Environmental Quality; established by law the office of ombudsman, previously operating under an executive order; lowered the age of majority to 19 years; and ratified the 27th amendment to the U.S. Constitution. ● Gov. Robert D. Ray (R) won an easy reelection victory Nov. 7. Sen. Jack R. Miller lost his two-term seat to Democratic challenger Richard Clark, a political unknown. The state lost one Congressional seat due to reapportionment; the six remaining ones were equally distributed between the two parties.

Kansas. During its session, ending March 22, the state legislature ratified the 27th amendment to the U.S. Constitution, lowered the age of majority to 18 years and enacted a new penal reform law, to become effective in 1974. ● Gov. Robert B. Docking (D) won a landslide endorsement Nov. 7 for his fourth term, a record. Sen. James B. Pearson (R) did even better, wining 72 percent of the vote for his third term. All incumbent Congressmen were reelected.

Kentucky. The state legislature, adjourning March 17, abolished sales tax on groceries, created a board of ethics for legislatures, passed a consumer protection bill, adopted a new penal code (effective July, 1974) and raised workmen's compensation benefits. A special session June 8–15 created a state department of environmental protection and approved the 27th amendment to the U.S. Constitution. ● Sen. John Sherman Cooper (R) did not seek reelection Nov. 7. In his place, Kentuckians chose state Sen. Walter Huddleston (D), who defeated former Gov. Louie B. Nunn for the seat. The party division in the state's Congressional delegation remained the same—five Democrats and two Republicans.

Louisiana. Rep. Edwin W. Edwards (D) was elected governor of Louisiana Feb. 1; he took office in May. ● Students at Louisiana State University in Baton Rouge elected their first black student body president March 7. ● Sen. Allen J. Ellender (D) died July 27 at the age of 81. A three-way race to fill his seat was won Nov. 7 by former State Sen. J. Bennett Johnston, Jr. (D). Republicans won a single seat in the eight-man Congressional delegation. ● A memorial service was held for Rep. Hale Boggs (D), missing since Oct. 16 in an Alaskan airplane crash. ● Two young blacks were killed Nov. 16 during a confrontation between students and police on the campus of Southern University, Baton Rouge.

Maine. In a special session Jan. 24–March 10 the state legislature approved the creation of 11 new executive agencies. It also lowered the legal age of majority to 18 years. ● Some 1,250,000 chickens were destroyed in Maine after a high concentration of polychlorinated biphenyl was found in some of them. ● Clamming and other shellfish harvesting were banned for several weeks when toxic red algae were spotted off the coast Sept. 14. ● Sen. Margaret Chase Smith (R), long considered invincible, was defeated for reelection Nov. 7 by William D. Hathaway, a four-term Congressman. The House seat vacated by the latter was won by William S. Cohen (R), mayor of Bangor.

Maryland. Strip mining on state-owned land was prohibited by the legislature on April. ● Antiwar demonstrations, begun April 17 on the University of Maryland campus at College Park, culminated in two days of fighting between state police and some 2,000 students. ● Gov. George C. Wallace of Alabama, campaigning for the Democratic presidential nomination, survived an assassination attempt in Laurel on May 15. Wallace handily won the state presidential primary the next day. ● Republicans gained one seat in Congress in the

About 400 persons gathered at Louisiana's Capitol for a memorial service for two students killed in a confrontation with police.

UPI

Nov. 7 elections, for a total of four; Democrats also hold four seats. Voters approved a state-run lottery based on horse races. They rejected indirect state grants to parochial schools.

Massachusetts. The U.S. Supreme Court March 22 ruled unconstitutional the 93-year-old state law prohibiting distribution of contraceptive devices to unmarried persons. ● Some 1,000 persons were arrested April 21–May 11 in antiwar demonstrations. Among the arrested was Amherst College President John W. Ward. ● A wet, cool spring caused the worst growing season in memory. Estimates of crop losses were as high as $80,000,000. ● Toxic algae, seen off the coast Sept. 14, resulted in a temporary ban on shellfish. Some two dozen people suffered poisoning. ● On Sept. 26 it was announced that full-time lawyers' offices would be set up within the state prisons to handle legal matters for inmates. ● Massachusetts was the only state in the union to give the majority of its presidential votes to Sen. George McGovern Nov. 7. Incumbent Edward W. Brooke (R) won an easy reelection to the Senate. Democrats won eight Congressional seats and Republicans three; one was taken by an independent. Voters refused to put their flat-rate income tax on a graduated scale.

Michigan. Gun-firing plainclothesmen on March 9 broke into an apartment where four Detroit sheriff's deputies were playing cards, killed one and wounded the others. All the deputies were black. ● Army recruiting offices at the University of Michigan were vandalized April 21. A march through Ann Arbor by 1,500 students was dispersed by club-wielding police. ● The state's voters abolished the 137-year-old constitutional ban on lotteries May 16. ● Sen. Robert P. Griffin (R) won reelection Nov. 7, and 18 out of 19 Congressional races were won by incumbents. The party line-up remained the same—12 Republicans, 7 Democrats. A plan to limit property taxes as a source of school funds was voted down, and so was a constitutional amendment to drop the ban on graduation of tax rates. Liberalized abortions were rejected.

Minnesota. Some 25 students and three policemen were injured, and 30 arrests were made May 10, as thousands of antiwar students battled police on the University of Minnesota campus. The next day, Gov. Wendell R. Anderson (D) activated the National Guard. ● An ombudsman for correction, supposed to investigate complaints by inmates and parolees, assumed office July 10. ● Sen. Walter F. Mon-

dale (D) easily won a mandate for his second term Nov. 7. All the state's incumbent Congressmen were reelected.

Mississippi. The legislature, meeting from Jan. 4 to May 4, approved a $600,000,000 highway

U.S. GOVERNORS

STATE	GOVERNOR	TERM EXPIRES
ALABAMA	George C. Wallace (D)	Jan. 1975
ALASKA	William A. Egan (D)	Dec. 1974
ARIZONA	Jack Williams (R)	Jan. 1975
ARKANSAS	Dale Bumpers (D)ʳ	Jan. 1975
CALIFORNIA	Ronald Reagan (R)	Jan. 1975
COLORADO	John A. Love (R)	Jan. 1975
CONNECTICUT	Thomas J. Meskill (R)	Jan. 1975
DELAWARE	Sherman W. Tribbitt (D)ᵉ	Jan. 1977
FLORIDA	Reubin Askew (D)	Jan. 1975
GEORGIA	Jimmy Carter (D)	Jan. 1975
HAWAII	John A. Burns (D)	Dec. 1974
IDAHO	Cecil Andrus (D)	Jan. 1975
ILLINOIS	Daniel Walker (D)ᵉ	Jan. 1977
INDIANA	Otis R. Bowen (R)ᵉ	Jan. 1977
IOWA	Robert D. Ray (R)ʳ	Jan. 1975
KANSAS	Robert Docking (D)ʳ	Jan. 1975
KENTUCKY	Wendell Ford (D)	Dec. 1975
LOUISIANA	Edwin W. Edwards (D)ᵉ	May 1976
MAINE	Kenneth M. Curtis (D)	Jan. 1975
MARYLAND	Marvin Mandel (D)	Jan. 1975
MASSACHUSETTS	Francis W. Sargent (R)	Jan. 1975
MICHIGAN	William G. Milliken (R)	Jan. 1975
MINNESOTA	Wendell R. Anderson (D)	Jan. 1975
MISSISSIPPI	William L. Waller (D)	Jan. 1976
MISSOURI	Christopher S. Bond (R)ᵉ	Jan. 1977
MONTANA	Thomas L. Judge (D)ᵉ	Jan. 1977
NEBRASKA	J. J. Exon (D)	Jan. 1975
NEVADA	D. N. O'Callaghan (D)	Jan. 1975
NEW HAMPSHIRE	Meldrim Thomson, Jr. (R)ᵉ	Jan. 1975
NEW JERSEY	William T. Cahill (R)	Jan. 1974
NEW MEXICO	Bruce King (D)	Jan. 1975
NEW YORK	Nelson A. Rockefeller (R)	Jan. 1975
NORTH CAROLINA	James E. Holshouser, Jr. (R)ᵉ	Jan. 1977
NORTH DAKOTA	Arthur A. Link (D)ᵉ	Jan. 1977
OHIO	John J. Gilligan (D)	Jan. 1975
OKLAHOMA	David Hall (D)	Jan. 1975
OREGON	Tom McCall (R)	Jan. 1975
PENNSYLVANIA	Milton J. Shapp (D)	Jan. 1975
RHODE ISLAND	Philip W. Noel (D)ᵉ	Jan. 1975
SOUTH CAROLINA	John C. West (D)	Jan. 1975
SOUTH DAKOTA	Richard F. Kneip (D)ʳ	Jan. 1975
TENNESSEE	Winfield Dunn (R)	Jan. 1975
TEXAS	Dolph Briscoe (D)ᵉ	Jan. 1975
UTAH	Calvin L. Rampton (D)ʳ	Jan. 1977
VERMONT	Thomas P. Salmon (D)ᵉ	Jan. 1975
VIRGINIA	Linwood Holton (R)	Jan. 1974
WASHINGTON	Daniel J. Evans (R)ʳ	Jan. 1977
WEST VIRGINIA	Arch A. Moore, Jr. (R)ʳ	Jan. 1977
WISCONSIN	Patrick J. Lucey (D)	Jan. 1975
WYOMING	Stanley K. Hathaway (R)	Jan. 1975

ᵉ Newly elected in 1972
ʳ Reelected in 1972

construction program. ● An all-white jury March 21 rejected all claims to damages by relatives of victims in the 1970 police shootings at Jackson State College, where two black students were killed and 12 wounded. ● Sen. James O. Eastland (D) was reelected Nov. 7. Two of the state's five Congressional seats were won by Republicans.

Missouri. The Cincinnati Royals basketball team shifted its franchise to Kansas City, Mo., at the end of the 1971–72 season. ● The state legislature, which adjourned April 30, raised the gasoline tax, authorized free textbooks to pupils in nonpublic schools, passed anti-air pollution and clean water bills and extended unemployment compensation. ● The gubernatorial race Nov. 7 was won by 33-year-old State Auditor Christopher S. Bond (R). Nine Democrats and one Republican were elected to Congress. ● The U.S. government sued the state Nov. 14 for violating wage controls by raising judges' salaries up to 52 percent.

Montana. Work was ordered halted on a Safeguard missile site at Malmstrom Air Force Base May 27, a day after the signing of a U.S.-Soviet arms limitations agreement. ● A new state constitution, to replace—on July 1, 1973—the one from 1889, was narrowly approved by the voters June 6. The new charter enlarges citizens' rights and makes government more responsible to the people. Its passage was contested in court on the grounds that it had gained only a plurality and not a majority; the passage was upheld. The electorate also endorsed legalization of gambling. ● Sen. Lee Metcalf (D) won reelection Nov. 7 in a tight race. Both Congressmen were also reelected. The governorship was won by Lt. Gov. Thomas L. Judge (D). Control of the state legislature remained divided.

Nebraska. The state legislature enacted a court reform law that establishes a system of county courts, abolishing all justice-of-the-peace and police-magistrate courts. The age of majority was lowered to 19 years. ● Gov. J. James Exon (D) vetoed legislation providing for the state to assume two-thirds of the costs of all public schools. ● Some 16 constitutional amendments were approved by the voters May 9. ● Sen. Carl T. Curtis (R) won a fourth term Nov. 7. The three incumbent Congressmen, all Republicans, were reelected.

Nevada. A TWA jetliner at Las Vegas' airport was severely damaged by a bomb explosion in its cockpit Mar. 6. ● A welfare fund crisis in Clark County was solved by release of $160,-000 from the legislative interim contingency fund. ● A 22-year-old Vietnam veteran was arrested near Reno June 3, only hours after he parachuted with $200,000 in ransom money from a hijacked airliner. ● The Atomic Energy Commission conducted several underground nuclear tests at its regular test site. ● Democrats lost the state's Congressional seat Nov. 7 to David Towell, a Minden realtor, but in turn won full control of the state legislature.

New Hampshire. The General Court rejected March 2 the second attempt by Gov. Walter R. Peterson (R) to legislate an income tax. ● The 27th amendment to the U.S. Constitution was ratified. ● Toxic red algae, spotted off the coast Sept. 14, caused a temporary ban on shellfish. Several persons suffered seafood poisoning. ● Sen. Thomas J. McIntyre (D) won reelection Nov. 7, and so did both the Republican Congressmen. Meldrim Thomson, Jr. (R), won a three-way race for the gubernatorial office.

New Jersey. The state's first noise-control law—and the first such state-wide law in the country—was signed by Gov. William T. Cahill (R) Jan. 24. ● Former Newark Mayor Hugh J. Addonizio was refused appeal of his conviction and ten-year jail term by the U.S. Supreme Court Feb. 22. He was imprisoned March 6. ● The age of majority was lowered to 18 years May 18. ● The state legislature rejected Governor Cahill's proposal for a state income tax July 17. ● State Assemblyman Sylvio J. Failla (D) was shot to death Sept. 16, an apparent victim of robbers. ● The state minimum wage was raised from $1.50 to $1.75 per hour Oct. 9. ● Secretary of State Paul J. Sherwin (R) and two codefendants were convicted of a kickback conspiracy Oct 28. ● Sen. Clifford P. Case (R) won reelection Nov. 7. Eight Democrats and seven Republicans were picked for Congress. The voters withheld authorization of bonds for $650,000,000 intended mostly for new highways. ● A new daily 50-cent lottery with a top prize of $2,500 was begun Nov. 29.

New Mexico. A new drug control law, enacted by the legislature, provides for reduced penalties for marijuana users while those convicted of selling face stiffer sentences. ● The age of majority was lowered to 18 years. ● More than 35 war protesters were arrested May 10 at Kirtland Air Force Base, Albuquerque. ● Nine persons were killed in an air crash at Albuquerque May 19. ● Pete V. Domenici (R) won the Senatorial seat vacated by the retirement of Sen. Clinton P. Anderson (D). The two incumbent Congressmen (D and R) were reelected.

New York Deputy Attorney General Maurice Nadjari (center) announced the indictments of corrupt Queens detectives.

New York. A Federal court Jan. 11 ruled unconstitutional the 1971 state law providing for subsidies to parochial schools. Gov. Nelson A. Rockefeller (R) vowed that he would find other means to aid the schools. A new law, granting indirect aid, was signed by him May 22. It was struck down by a Federal court Oct. 2. ● An aircraft hijacker was shot to death in Poughkeepsie Jan. 27. Two days later another hijacker was shot and captured at Kennedy International Airport. ● Five high school students were killed and 45 injured March 24, when a train hit a school bus at Congers. ● Governor Rockefeller May 13 vetoed a bill that would have voided the state's two-year-old liberal abortion law and restored the old law. ● Fourteen counties in southern New York were severely affected by hurricane Agnes June 22. ● Rep. William F. Ryan (D) died Sept. 17 at 50. ● Governor Rockefeller named a special prosecutor Sept. 19 to handle all cases of corruption involving policemen, prosecutors and judges in New York City. ● A $1,150,000,000 bond sale for environmental purposes was approved.

North Carolina. The age of majority was lowered to 18 years. ● A 22-year-old rifleman fired into a throng at a shopping center outside Raleigh May 29, killing three persons and wounding eight. The youth then shot himself

through the head. ● Five children were killed May 30, when a backyard bomb shelter in Valdese was blown up by a gas explosion. ● Sen. B. Everett Jordan was unseated in the Democratic primary June 3. Jesse A. Helms (R) won his seat Nov. 7. James E. Holshouser, Jr. (R), captured the gubernatorial office. A constitutional amendment, making environmental protection "a proper function of the state," was approved.

North Dakota. A proposed new constitution was rejected by the electorate April 28. In separate votes, proposals for a unicameral legislature, lowering the age of majority to 18 years and authorization of lotteries in the state also were defeated. ● Rep. Arthur A. Link (D) won the governorship Nov. 7. The now single Congressional seat was retained by Rep. Mark Andrews (R). A proposal to liberalize abortions was voted down.

Ohio. On April 10, Gov. John J. Gilligan (D) signed a strip-mining control bill which tightly curbs open-pit operations and requires thorough reclamation. ● A Federal Court declared unconstitutional a state program of reimbursement to parents who have children in nonpublic schools. The ruling was upheld Oct. 10 by the U.S. Supreme Court. ● Democrats won a majority in the state House of Representatives Nov. 7. A proposal to repeal the 10-months-old state income tax was soundly defeated.

Oklahoma. The state House of Representatives rejected the 27th amendment to the U.S. Constitution March 28. The 52-day regular session of the legislature, ending March 31, was the shortest since statehood began in 1907. ● Sen. Fred R. Harris (D) did not seek reelection Nov. 7. In his place Oklahomans chose former Gov. Dewey F. Bartlett (R). Democrats gained one seat in the Congressional delegation, which now has five Democrats and one Republican. The voters refused to allow sale of alcohol by the drink.

Oregon. The U.S. Senate passed a bill March 14, establishing more than 30,000 acres of central Oregon coastline as the Oregon Dunes National Recreation Area. ● The Nov. 7 elections pitted former Sen. Wayne Morse (D) against incumbent Mark O. Hatfield in a Senatorial race won by the latter. All four incumbent Congressmen—two from each party—were reelected. Democrats won control of the state legislature. A proposal to eliminate property-tax financing of schools was rejected.

Pennsylvania. A weekly state lottery with a top prize of $50,000 began operations March 7. ● A state law that compensates parents for tuition paid to nonpublic schools was ruled unconstitutional April 6 by a Federal court. ● Four persons were killed and 43 injured April 16, when a bus crashed through a turnpike guardrail and overturned. ● The state supreme court observed its 250th anniversary May 23 with a session in Independence Hall. ● Gov. Milton J. Shapp (D) declared a state of extreme emergency June 22 after hurricane Agnes swept the state, leaving the capital, Harrisburg, isolated by flooded roads and destroyed bridges. In Wilkes-Barre the Susquehanna river overflowed its 38-foot dikes, causing enormous property damage.

Rhode Island. A new Department of Corrections, emphasizing rehabilitation of prisoners rather than punishment, began operations July 1. ● The legislature lowered the age of majority to 18 years and ratified the 27th amendment to the U.S. Constitution. ● Sen. Claiborne Pell (D) won reelection Nov. 7, defeating former Secretary of the Navy John H. Chaffee. The governorship was won by Philip W. Noel (D).

South Carolina. The state's black and white Methodist conferences, segregated since Civil War days, voted Jan. 27 to unite. ● Former Sen. and Gov. James F. Byrnes (D) died April 9 at the age of 92. ● A bill prohibiting sale of products made from any endangered species was passed July 22. ● Sen. Strom Thurmond (R) won reelection for his fourth term Nov. 7. Republicans gained one seat in the Congressional delegation—they now hold two out of six—and increased their strength in the state legislature.

South Dakota. More than 200 persons were killed June 10 when torrential rains and flash-flood waters surged through Rapid City, leaving a wide swath of destruction. ● Sen. Karl E. Mundt (R) did not seek reelection Nov. 7. His Senate seat was won by Rep. James G. Abourzek (D), whose Congressional seat in turn was captured by James Abdnor (R). Incumbent Gov. Richard F. Kneip (D) was reelected. Voters approved a ban on shooting mourning doves.

Tennessee. The state legislature ratified the 27th amendment to the U.S. Constitution April 4. Other measures approved by the session ending April 14 established new administrative departments of transportation, economic and community development and general services. A strip-mining control law was also enacted. ● A New-York-bound Greyhound bus collided with a trailer truck May 13 on a mountain

Torrential rains drenched Rapid City, S.D., June 10. More than 200 persons were killed and damage was estimated at $120,000,000.

Wide World

highway in Ben Station, killing both drivers and 12 other persons. ● Sen. Howard H. Baker (R) won reelection Nov. 7. Republicans also won five out of eight Congressional races—a gain of one seat in the state's delegation.

Texas. Rep. John Dowdy (D), convicted of receiving a $25,000 bribe to hinder a Federal investigation of a private firm, was sentenced Feb. 23 to 18 months in prison and a fine of $25,000. ● The speaker of the state House of Assembly, Gus Mutscher (D), and two of his aides, drew a five-year suspended prison term March 16 for their participation in a stock fraud scheme. ● Sen. John G. Tower (R) was reelected Nov. 7. Republicans gained one Congressional seat—for a total of four out of 24. Dolph Briscoe (D) won the gubernatorial race, and Democrats retained control of the state legislature. Two constitutional changes, easing property taxes of disabled veterans and old people, were endorsed.

Utah. Thousands of demonstrators marched in Salt Lake City April 24 to protest the Vietnam war. ● Joseph F. Smith, the tenth president of the Morman Church, died July 2 at the age of 95. ● Gov. Calvin L. Rampton (D) was elected Nov. 7 to become the first three-term governor in the state's history. Rep. Sherman P. Lloyd (R) was defeated by challenger Wayne Owens, while Rep. K. Gunn McKay (D) was easily reelected.

Vermont. The state supreme court ruled Jan. 14 that Vermont's 125-year-old statute on abortions was unconstitutional. ● A 1971 law authorizing aid to private schools was declared unconstitutional by a Federal court. ● Nonreturnable containers of beer, ale and soft drinks were banned, effective July 1, 1973. ● The state divorce law was liberalized, so that if both parties agree, a couple may get a divorce by living separately for six months. ● Thomas P. Salmon (D) won the governorship Nov. 7. Rep. Richard M. Mallary (R) was reelected, and Republicans retained their majority in the state legislature.

Virginia. Former Gov. John S. Battle (D) died April 9. ● Hurricane Agnes struck the state June 23, leaving 17 persons dead and 8,000 homeless. In Richmond two-story buildings were nearly submerged when the James River rose by 36 feet; drinking water was polluted. Gov. Linwood G. Holton (R) declared most of the state a disaster area. ● Sen William B. Spong, Jr. (D) lost his Senate seat to William L. Scott, a three-term Congressman. Virginians also

elected Republicans to seven out of ten Congressional seats—one more than previously.

Washington. The state legislature lowered the age of majority to 18 years. ● San Francisco Mayor Joseph L. Alioto and two former officials of Washington state were acquitted March 26 of wrongdoing in the splitting of $2,300,000 in legal fees. ● The state supreme court removed all constitutional limits on the duration of special sessions of the state's legislature. ● Democrats solidly won the Congressional elections Nov. 7, capturing all seven of the state's seats, while Gov. Daniel J. Evans (R) won an unprecedented third term. Voters agreed to state-sponsored lotteries but rejected greyhound racing with track betting. They approved the lowering of the ceiling of real-estate taxes.

West Virginia. Some 118 persons were killed in Logan County Feb. 16 when a coal refuse dam, impounding waste waters, gave way, causing the inundation of 14 mining communities. The site was immediately declared a major disaster area. The state legislature later appropriated $1,000,000 in relief to victims of the flood and enacted a Coal Refuse Disposal Control Act with an eye to ensuring human safety. ● Full adult status was given to 18-year-olds, effective June 11. ● Gov. Arch A. Moore (R), winning reelection Nov. 7, became the state's first chief executive to succeed himself. Sen. Jennings Randolph (D) and all four incumbent Democratic Congressmen also were returned to office.

Wisconsin. The age of majority was lowered to 18 years March 21. ● Four constitutional amendments were approved by the electorate April 4. ● Nine persons were killed April 4, when fire destroyed a boarding house in Rosencrans. ● Grades, transcripts and degrees were held up for 600 University of Wisconsin students on suspicion that their term papers had been bought from firms engaged in the sale of academic papers. ● Democrats won five and Republicans four Congressional seats Nov. 7. The state lost one as a result of the 1970 census.

Wyoming. The state and nation celebrated the centennial of Yellowstone National Park. Among those honored on the occasion was former Gov. Nellie Tayloe Ross (D), 94 years of age, the first woman to become a governor of a U.S. state. ● Sen. Clifford P. Hansen (R) and Rep. Teno Roncalio (D), the state's lone Congressman, were reelected Nov. 7. Republicans retained their majority in the state legislature.

King Gustav VI Adolf arrives aboard the royal sloop "Vasaorden" en route to a Stockholm City Hall ceremony celebrating his 90th birthday.

SWEDEN

In a speech on Feb. 2, Sweden's Prime Minister Olof Palme summarized his country's position vis-à-vis the European Communities and pointed out that: first, Sweden will continue to adhere to a firm and consistent alliance-free foreign policy; second, full membership in the European Economic Community (EEC) is not compatible with the line of action of Swedish foreign policy; and third, Sweden has a positive attitude toward European cooperation and seeks to attain, within the framework of the policy of neutrality, close cooperation with the EEC.

Having decided not to apply for full membership in the European Economic Community, Sweden, following protracted negotiations, signed a trade agreement with the EEC powers on July 22. Embodying a number of compromises, the agreement will, in effect, after a five-year transition period, open up a duty-free market of 300,000,000 potential customers for Swedish industrial exports. Swedish steel and paper producers particularly anticipated the expanded markets in which they would be able to sell their products at competitive prices.

In late February demonstrators in Stockholm and other Swedish cities protested rapidly rising food prices, which had soared almost 20 percent within the previous year. Housewives had initiated a boycott of milk and meat on Feb. 21 in response to the sharply accelerating cost of these items; milk prices had increased by one-half in two years, while the price of beef had risen by one-fourth within the previous two months. Such factors as substantive increases in the value-added tax, to an effective rate of 17.65 percent, and government-sponsored attempts to upgrade the incomes of farmers to the level of factory workers, contributed to the abrupt increase in food prices.

Another step toward income equalization was taken on May 31 when the Riksdag (parliament), having rejected the government's

original proposal further to increase the value-added tax, adopted instead a tax redistribution program. This approach entails income tax reductions for those on the lower and middle income levels, a 10 percent increase in child allowances and a doubling of the payroll tax paid by employers to 4 percent.

King Gustaf VI Adolf celebrated his 90th birthday on Nov. 11. The popular king, who in 1950 succeeded his father, Gustav V, to the throne, is the world's oldest reigning monarch.

Following a long period of deliberation, two royal commissions finally made public their reports and recommendations in 1972. The Commission on the Church-State Relationship suggested that the Lutheran Church be completely separated from the state and that the separation become fully effective by 1983. The other commission, appointed to propose a new Swedish constitution, presented a plan which would give the Riksdag increased powers, while all political power would be withdrawn from the crown. The proposed constitution would also give the nation the option of abolishing the monarchy, if the people so desired. However, no such changes are to take place during the reign of King Gustaf VI Adolf.

The widely heralded U.N. Conference on the Human Environment convened in Stockholm in early June. It was attended by 1,200 delegates from 114 nations.

(*See also* Environment).

ERIK J. FRIIS
Editor, *The American-Scandinavian Review*

SWITZERLAND

The most emotional issues of the year 1972 in Switzerland, ironic in a country so doggedly neutral, involved national defense, arms sales and military spending. Defense expenditures accounted for nearly one-fourth of a record 1973 budget. Swiss voters rejected a proposal that would have allowed arms sales only to

In December the Swiss Parliament voted to abolish 18 remaining squadrons of cavalry, thus eliminating an anachronism in the nuclear age.

Keystone

other neutral European countries, and decided instead to permit unlimited export of war materials. Arms sales, which in 1971 had totaled $65,000,000—an insignificant sum compared with those of the United States and Soviet Union—nevertheless drew domestic criticism. Opponents contended that any traffic in arms could jeopardize Switzerland's humanitarian traditions.

A months-long debate over the shape and size of the Swiss air force ended temporarily in September when Defense Minister Rudolf Gnägi announced that the government was postponing plans to buy 60 new jet fighter-bombers. The government decided to purchase instead 24 reconditioned British planes.

The problem of Jura autonomy persisted, with separatists demanding self-rule for their French language area within the canton of Berne. Isolated incidents of violence occurred before and after Berne voters said "no" on June 4 to a proposal to allow Jura schools to operate under French standards.

On June 27 the government announced that it was barring foreigners from purchasing Swiss real estate or securities. It subsequently ordered banks to charge an annual 8 percent penalty—a form of "negative interest"—on all foreign deposits.

The budget for 1973 exceeded $3,000,000,-000 for the first time and showed a deficit of $5,200,000. Military spending authorizations totaled $656,000,000, the largest single item in the budget. The outlay for social services ran a close second.

CHARLES W. BELL
Former Manager for Italy
United Press International

TAIWAN

In 1972, Chiang Kai-shek's government suffered a diplomatic setback when the President of the United States visited the People's Republic of China, whose territory is formally claimed by Taiwan.

Diplomacy. President Nixon's visit to Peking in February marked the end of an era for United States–Taiwan relations. For almost a quarter-century, Washington had supported Taipei's claim to all of China, and the Chinese Nationalists used American support and military assistance to maintain their separate existence.

A communiqué issued at the end of Nixon's trip shocked Taiwan even more than the original announcement that the U.S. leader would visit the People's Republic. In it the United States agreed to remove its forces and military installations from Taiwan. U.S. diplomats subsequently assured Taipei, however, that such a move would not begin until the Vietnam war had ended and would not be completed until the Taiwan question had been settled.

Nixon also agreed that there was only one China, that Taiwan was a part of China, and that the Taiwan question should be settled by "the Chinese themselves." Afterward, Washington assured Taipei that it would continue to recognize the Republic of China and would honor its defense obligations to it.

Later in the year, the visit of Japanese Premier Tanaka to Peking produced in Taipei only a little less disappointment and fear. Diplomatic relations between Japan and Taiwan were formally severed, and the ambassadors were recalled. Trade and other economic ties were not expected to be influenced initially.

Politics. There was speculation at the year's start that President Chiang Kai-shek, 84 years old, would not seek a sixth five-year term, and in February the Nationalist leader confirmed this. The following month, however, he allowed himself to be drafted.

Many Taiwanese believed that younger leadership would be necessary in order to compete with the Communists in the resolution of that difficult political situation. Chiang's activities as leader had declined during the year because of his age and health, and, despite the Generalissimo's reliance on his son, Vice President Chiang Ching-kuo, there clearly was a vacuum in the country's political leadership.

In March the ruling Kuomintang party's central committee called for parliamentary elections to add new members to the national legislature. In the Dec. 28 elections, the first since the flight from the mainland in the late 1940's, 89 additional seats in parliament and provincial and local offices were filled.

Economy. Taiwan's political problems did not hurt the country economically. The gross national product continued to rise and was expected to reach $7,000,000,000 by the year's end. Trade for the year totaled approximately $5,200,000,000, with a $222,000,000 trade surplus with the United States. External investment funds continued to flow into the country, although they were down $35,000,000 for the first six months of the year. As has been true since 1970, more than 90 percent of new investment was local. Foreign exchange reserves stood at about $1,500,000,000.

RICHARD BUTWELL
Chairman, Department of Political Science
State University of New York
College at Brockport

TAXATION

Tax reform became an important issue in the Democratic presidential primaries and thereafter in the U.S. presidential campaign of 1972. In the primaries, Gov. George Wallace of Alabama made it one of his most popular appeals, charging that wealthy individuals, corporations and foundations were not paying their fair share of taxes so that the little man had to pay more. Wallace explicitly coupled his demand for tax reform with a pledge that this would mean a tax cut for the average person.

Sen. George S. McGovern, Sen. Hubert H. Humphrey and other Democratic contenders soon embraced tax reform as a major theme in their primary campaigns. After he won his party's nomination, McGovern presented a detailed plan which he said would raise $22,000,-000,000 a year by closing a variety of tax loopholes. He pledged that much of this would be used to increase Federal school aid and finance education and thus permit a reduction of local property taxes, which finance education in most parts of the country. Judging by McGovern's overwhelming defeat, however, the issue appeared to have had little impact.

Nevertheless, promises given during the year made it certain that tax reform again would be closely examined during the 93rd Congress in 1973, just four years after a major law was enacted on the subject. Rep. Wilbur D. Mills (D-Ark.), the powerful chairman of the House Ways and Means Committee, which originates all revenue legislation, announced that tax reform would have top priority in his panel beginning in February 1973. Sen. Russell B. Long (D-La.), chairman of the tax-writing

Help—Or More Trouble?
Hesse in "St. Louis Globe Democrat"

Distributed by L.A. Times Syndicate

Senate Finance Committee, said his group also would be ready to act promptly on such legislation. And President Nixon declared that his administration would have some tax-reform proposals to submit to the new Congress soon after it convened. John D. Ehrlichman, the President's assistant for domestic affairs, disclosed after the election that these proposals would include recommendations for ways to reduce state and local property taxes.

There appeared, however, to be wide differences of opinion among the various speakers on the subject. Some cynical observers on Capitol Hill, noting the relatively modest changes enacted in the 1969 Tax Reform Act after a big public outcry against tax injustices, predicted the 1973 results also would be minimal. The administration did not reveal its plans. But aside from its desire to find a method to reduce the property-tax load, it was believed to be concentrating on simplification and not on big revenue gains.

Undersecretary of the Treasury Edwin S. Cohen, probably the administration's leading tax expert, said possibilities of increasing taxes on the rich had been much exaggerated. He warned that tax reform must not be used to end proper business incentives, which, he said, were essential to entice industry to create new jobs and modernize its plants so that it could hold prices down and compete in world markets.

McGovern's broad package called for taxing capital gains at the same rates as ordinary income (and not at one-half or less of the rates on earned income), reducing depletion allowances for oil and other minerals, taxing capital gains on inherited stocks and other property, repealing special tax breaks on real estate, reducing business depreciation deductions, disallowing excessive investment interest and discouraging state and local governments from selling tax-exempt bonds by offering them interest subsidies on taxable bonds.

In May 1972, Mills offered a sweeping proposal which he claimed would afford the best assurance that there be a searching review of all provisions in the tax code which give special treatment to any type of income. Under it, 54 such provisions would be repealed, 18 at a time, on Jan. 1 of 1974, 1975 and 1976. Congress then could decide which ones would be reenacted. The list included not only benefits often described as loopholes but also many items used by millions of taxpayers and considered by them to be entirely appropriate. In the latter category were the additional $750 personal exemptions for the aged and the blind, medical-expense deductions, home-mortgage

interest deductions, deductions of state and local taxes, the exclusion from gross income of scholarships and fellowships, and many more.

Senate Democratic Leader Mike Mansfield sponsored the Mills proposal in his house. But it received committee approval in neither the House nor the Senate. Many Senators and House members said there would not be a handful of votes for repeal of most of the items. Why eliminate them and then have to reenact them? they asked. However, Mills asserted that his Ways and Means Committee would proceed with its thorough review of tax-reform possibilities early in 1973 whether his proposal was accepted or not.

Some leading economists and political scientists contended that, because of the string of very large budget deficits during Nixon's first term and the prospect of steadily increasing outlays for defense, veterans benefits, pollution control and some social programs, a substantial Federal tax increase would be inevitable in 1973. The deficit for fiscal 1973 was officially estimated at about $25,000,000,000, but there were indications that it might exceed $30,000,-000,000. Early in 1972, the President showed interest in a value-added tax (VAT) as a new source of Federal revenue; the U.S. Treasury conducted studies on it. But many Democrats assailed VAT as a particularly obnoxious form of national sales tax, imposed as it is at each step in the process of producing a consumer item. Later, the administration let it be known that VAT no longer was being considered.

In fact, during and after the campaign, Nixon emphasized that he planned to ask for no new Federal taxes. However, a 468-page study made by the prestigious Brookings Institution in Washington, D.C., concluded in May that either a tax increase or a cutback in Federal programs, or both, would be inevitable if the government undertook any new high-priority initiatives in the next few years. The authors, headed by Charles L. Schultze, budget director under President Lyndon B. Johnson, maintained that defense outlays would increase in the years ahead and that total expenditures under existing and proposed programs would run $15,000,000,000 to $20,000,000,000 beyond revenues by 1975, even if the country achieved full employment prosperity. Revenues should balance outlays by 1977 if no new spending programs were introduced, the study said, but it added that nothing would be available to deal with emerging environmental, economic and social problems. The authors saw increases in individual and corporation income levies as the most promising revenue sources to meet Federal needs, although they recog-

nized that tax reform might make some contribution.

Public interest in tax reform was fueled during the year by charges that 106 persons with incomes of $200,000 or more paid no income taxes in 1970 and that leading corporations, such as McDonnell Douglas, Continental Oil and Aluminum Company of America, paid nothing in 1971, despite profits that in some cases exceeded $100,000,000. A Harris poll showed that 69 percent of those contacted sympathized with the idea of a taxpayers' revolt, and 82 percent felt the little man was bearing the biggest tax burden. One of the examples McGovern used in his campaign was this: "How can anyone defend the following real life case taken from the U.S. Treasury's own report: This American enjoyed an income of $2,300,000 from oil and gas, capital gains, and dividends and interest; he paid tax at less than half the 14-percent rate a working person pays on the first $1,000 earned."

Undersecretary Cohen countered with the assertion that, "In general, the rich pay Federal income taxes in large amounts." He argued that, while 106 persons with incomes of $200,000 or more paid no taxes in 1970, there were 15,200 others in this bracket who paid an average tax of $177,000 each for a total of $2,700,000,000. And the 106, he claimed, had substantial deductions for interest, charitable contributions, losses, fees for professional services and other legitimate reasons.

Senator Long said he believed that some people were paying too little taxes and that Congress could close in on them with a new tax-reform law. But he cautioned that the 1969 experience had made it clear there were limits to what could be done. Long said he thought there could be a boost in the inheritance tax, some provisions to tax capital gains on inherited property and further restrictions on the use of foundations as tax shelters.

Other lawmakers interested in tax reform declared that they would work to increase the revenue from the minimum tax included in the 1969 act; this is a levy that requires wealthy persons to pay some tax even though their income is sheltered in various tax preferences. The 1969 law also cut back on some of the benefits available to persons who make large charitable contributions, to foundations, to real estate investors, to tax-exempt groups which run businesses and to developers of oil and gas and other mineral properties.

JOSEPH W. HALL, JR.
Senate Staff
Washington Bureau
The Associated Press

"The Waltons," a new dramatic series, recalls the everyday lives and adventures of a closely knit family living in the Blue Ridge Mountains of Virginia in the 1930's.

Courtesy, CBS-TV

TELEVISION AND RADIO

Access to the medium was the motif in American television during 1972, marking an interesting change in the viewer-broadcaster relationship precisely in the 25th year of commercial television. The forms of access—public, political and producer, chiefly—seemed to grow out of the legal fact that the airwaves cannot be owned by licensed broadcasters because they are of the same air we breathe and therefore public. This, and the station licensee's obligation under the Communications Act of 1934 "to serve the public interest, convenience and necessity," suggested to many that they had rights in the medium that had never been exercised. In years past it had been assumed that the broadcaster controlled the sending and that the viewer possessed only take-it-or-leave-it rights, which is to say that he was powerless in the arrangement beyond switching off the set. In 1972, however, in order to preserve their valuable licenses, television and radio broadcasters yielded to special interest groups demanding representation in the program matter of both media.

Public Access to the Media. Certain minority groups, principally blacks and Mexican-Americans, who had felt shut out of the media because of their concentration on white middle class life, led the assault. Working through public interest law firms and access-minded organizations, such as the radio and television office of the United Church of Christ, they exacted pledges from individual stations both for larger minority hiring quotas and for schedules of programs on the air reflecting their life styles, attitudes and concerns.

The basic technique of those demanding greater access was either to challenge the station license with intent to take it over, a long and difficult course, or, more simply, to file with the Federal Communications Commission (FCC) a petition to deny the licensee a renewal of his right to operate the station for failing to serve adequately, or for ignoring, the needs of a significant part of his community.

Such petitions by pressure groups became common in 1972, and few major stations escaped one or more Petitions To Deny. The transfer of ownership from Triangle Publica-

tions to Capital Cities Broadcasting and from Time-Life to McGraw-Hill were but two cases in which the FCC approved the sales only after minorities petitioners were satisfied by written guarantees of more jobs and more specialized programming.

Meanwhile, several cable television systems opened public access channels, on which any citizen groups or individuals could televise their views or their talents as entertainers. In the access-anxious climate, commercial broadcasters were prompted to follow suit—in lesser ways, to be sure, such as vox pop programs or one-minute spots, but nevertheless to a significant degree. Also, numerous stations sought to establish better liaison with their communities through a newly designated television executive called the community affairs director or through on-the-air ombudsmen. Frequently, the new executive was a black or Chicano.

Local Initiative in Prime Time. Access of another, more official kind underwent a real test for the first time in 1972. The FCC had decreed in 1971 that network television programming be limited to only three hours per night in the peak viewing hours, releasing to local stations the nightly 7:30 P.M. half hour (or 6:30 P.M. in the Central Time Zone) under the "prime-time access rule." The decree was intended to provide both producer access to the medium for those who felt three networks were too few markets, and also station access to the choicest viewing time. The latter had been desired a decade ago by many stations that felt the networks, with their power, claimed too many hours of the broadcasting day; but by the time the rule came into being, most stations no longer desired the responsibility and the economic risk of creating programs of their own.

A partial test of the rule in late 1971 revealed that a majority of stations had avoided producing shows of their own for the 7:30 half hours but instead had filled them with programs syndicated on a market-to-market basis by independent production companies. By late 1972 the number of available syndicated series for the prime-time access periods had risen from 25 to 80. Experience proved that game show formats were both relatively inexpensive to produce and generally dependable for rating performance, and so a raft of old network hits were resurrected—*What's My Line?, The Price Is Right, Let's Make A Deal, Truth Or Consequences* and *I've Got A Secret.* Some producers went to Canada to produce dramatic and variety shows, because they could be done more cheaply there, and a number of syndicators imported shows from England. Hollywood, which was already suffering from an ailing

motion picture industry, chiefly suffered the effects of the prime-time access rule, as virtually all the network programs that had to be cut back had been produced there.

The networks and major film studios protested the FCC rule and pleaded for reconsideration, while the successful syndicators mounted an equally active lobby in support. But several FCC commissioners, and principally the chairman, Dean Burch, made known their disappointment with the quality of the programs that had been produced to satisfy the rules. They broadly hinted that the 1972 results might be the definitive test, leading to reconsideration and a possible rescinding of the rule in 1973. The access rule applied only to network-affiliated stations in the 50 largest markets in the country, and perhaps the most disheartening effect of it was that non-affiliated (or independent) stations in those cities were raiding the 7:30 audience with reruns of such old network shows as *I Dream of Jeannie, Hogan's Heroes,* and *Dick Van Dyke.*

Political Access and Government Intervention. Political access to the television medium was a particularly delicate matter in an election year, and a series of skirmishes erupted between the two parties over the uses to which they put their privileges. Specifically, several of President Nixon's speeches to the nation in prime time were held to be political, or in the nature of campaigning, by the Democratic National Committee, which sought equal time on the networks under the FCC's Fairness Doctrine to present an opposite view. On a few occasions, some of the networks obliged without benefit of FCC intervention, whereupon the Republicans demanded equivalent time, arguing that the President has the right to address the nation and that the Democrats, therefore, had gained access on false grounds and for strictly political purposes.

Government intervention in broadcast matters, which had been in high gear from the beginning of the Nixon administration, seemed to reach a peak in 1972. The Justice Department sued all three television networks for excessive program control. (Ten years previously the government had urged them to exercise more control.)

The White House Office of Telecommunications Policy also made much of the centralization of public broadcasting programming (leading to its decentralization) and recommended its withdrawal from news and public affairs programming, following charges that it held a liberal bias.

Subsequently President Nixon vetoed the Congressional funding bill to aid the Corpora-

tion for Public Broadcasting. His action led to the resignation of CPB's officers, who had been appointed by President Johnson, and to their replacement by President Nixon. Former Republican Congressman Thomas Curtis was named chairman and United States Information Agency official Henry Loomis appointed president. Critics charged that the administration was turning public broadcasting into "a domestic USIA" inasmuch as the outlet had been conceived as an independent, non-commercial system insulated from the influence of government.

President Nixon also took a public position on two other television issues. He sided with Hollywood craft unions in their complaint that the networks were showing too many reruns and therefore limiting the work opportunities for the film industry, and he came out against television blackouts of sports events (especially home football games) already sold out. As both positions were taken at the height of the election campaign, and on the face of it both seemed to correspond with the wishes of the average viewer (ergo, voter), they appeared to be politically motivated, and were not taken seriously within the industry.

Ratings and the Pleasure Principle. Culturally, the year was significant for the shattering of old puritanical television taboos that had given the medium's programs an antiseptic quality from the beginning. In an effort to reflect contemporary life and adapt to the changing mores of the times television programs adopted themes rejected by network censors only two or three years before: abortion, incest, menopause, homosexuality, venereal disease, lesbianism, adultery, wife-swapping and, to a slight degree, miscegenation. The general relaxation was in part an effect of sophisticated movies shown on television after their theatrical runs; to maintain a double standard, one for the movies and another for programs made expressly for television, had seemed absurd. The shift to racier subject matter also received impetus from the 1971 hit on CBS *All In The Family,* which went to the top of the Nielsen ratings in spite of or because of racial slurs, liberated dialogue and sacrilegious innuendo. Obedient to television's habit of imitating its hits, *All In The Family* spawned such other bold series as *Sanford and Son, Maude, Bridget Loves Bernie* and *M*A*S*H.*

Television's moral leniency in 1972 was in striking contrast to the same medium's sentimentality in 1969, when for all practical purposes a death in the family was invariably preferred to the more distressing contrivance of a divorce. The new wave brought in, among others, *Maude,* whose Auntie-Mame-like central character was four times married. *Anna and the King* introduced a principal character given to polygamy; *M*A*S*H* brimmed with sexual activity, and the first episode of *Bridget Loves Bernie* showed the young couple in bed apparently naked. All were scheduled early in the evening and were available to children. No serious outcry was heard from viewers.

History of sorts was made with the first television presentation of the movie *Love Story,*

"Maude" is a prime example of the racier situation comedy presented in 1972. It stars (l-r) Bill Macy, Beatrice Arthur (as Maude) and Adrienne Barbeau.

which not only scored the highest rating ever for a televised motion picture (playing on 27,410,000 home sets) but also retained on its soundtrack most of the arresting idiom of the original. For all the exposure the film received, the complaints were surprisingly few.

On radio across the country sex and sexual problems became a chief topic on talk shows, particularly during the morning hours when housewives primarily comprised the audience. Many stations established programs that dealt exclusively with the subject, and in New York and San Francisco radio also offered weekly "Gay Lib" radio shows dealing in frank discussions of homosexuality.

Competition and Technology. In television competition, ABC increased the number of its affiliated stations to more than 175 and thereby narrowed the edge held by its rivals, each with chains of about 200 stations. Making progress in news, sports and daytime programming and also proving stronger in prime time, mainly with movies and Monday night football games, ABC gave notice that it could no longer be written off as the third network, guaranteed to trail CBS and NBC. It made its mark as a network of equal stature with the others during August

with its superlative 16-day coverage of the Olympic Games from Munich and with its news coverage of the tragic political events that disrupted the Games.

Simultaneously cable television continued its march on the existing commercial system. The FCC, in its third reversal on the matter, finally instructed cable systems that they should originate their own programs. Investors showed faith in the future of cable, and the stocks of those companies rose. TelePrompTer, Cypress, Viacom, Cablecom General, All American Cablevision and General Electric were among the busiest in acquisition of new franchises and in essaying programming experiments. After years of isolated and generally unhappy tests, pay television was given the substantial beginnings of a brand new industry.

Mainly through two companies, Computer Cinema and Trans-World Communications (a subsidiary of Columbia Pictures), motion pictures found a new box office in hotel rooms, where they were offered, for pay, over closed-circuit television.

Video-cassettes, a magic word in 1970, made little exciting news in 1972 beyond the retreat of several companies from the market. The

UPI

On television, West German Chancellor Willy Brandt discusses the kidnapping and killing of members of the Israeli Olympic team by Arab terrorists. Satellite broadcasting, which increased considerably in 1972, made North Americans participants in the tragedy.

problems remained unsolved: the high price of the playing units and of the software (programs) for them, and the incompatibility of the various competing systems. The signs of progress were not in direct sales to the public but rather in increased use by certain industries, largely for training purposes, and by cable television.

Radio enjoyed a prosperous year, with audience levels and advertising revenues continuing their steady increase, but with an interesting difference, namely, the emergence of FM as a full-fledged competitor to AM. The effect of those additional stations' making a substantial claim on the audience was to fragment the listenership more than ever. For example, in Chicago, which used to be dominated by three or four AM stations, the listening had spread out over more than 30 stations, leaving none clearly dominant. In several cities, on the other hand, an FM station became the dominant one. Testifying to the potency of the once insignificant frequency modulation band was the sale of two FM stations by Kaiser Broadcasting for more than $5,000,000, a record price.

Contributing to the growth of FM was a boom in stereo equipment at the consumer level, which finally made FM's superior sound a competitive factor. Also important was the adoption of rock and sweet music formats, which served to dispel the longhair stigma that, many feel, retarded the growth of FM. While there were still some classical music stations, the range of programming has expanded on the FM dial, and the more moderate commercial policies compared with those of the heavily commercialized AM stations have contributed greatly to the gains in FM popularity. With 2,500 FM stations on the air in the United States, sales of FM and AM-FM combined sets appreciably surpassed the sale of AM-only sets in 1972.

Meanwhile, the world continued to shrink. The growth of satellite broadcasting carried the Tournament of Roses world wide from Pasadena, Miss Universe from Puerto Rico, the Nixon visits from Peking and Moscow, the Olympics from Sapporo and Munich, and the Apollo 16 and 17 lunar expeditions from the moon.

The U.S. exported television series in greater numbers than ever, but it also imported as never before. While the programs came chiefly from other English-speaking countries—mainly Britain, which provided, among others, *Vanity Fair, The Adventurers, The Protectors* and *U.F.O.*—there was a major foreign breakthrough when RAI-TV of Italy sold its *Leonardo da Vinci* series to CBS for a five-episode

National Educational Television

Susan Hampshire portrays Becky Sharp, and Dyson Lovell is her husband, Rawdon Crawley, in "Vanity Fair," imported from Britain.

summer run and the U.S.S.R.–produced *War and Peace* played on ABC in four installments. Both, of course, were exhibited in dubbed versions.

One other significant development in television was little noticed by the viewing public. The selection of one, and then a second, president for CBS Inc. from the ranks of big business rather than from broadcasting underscored the little-publicized but widespread Wall Street consciousness of the television industry. Career broadcasters were giving way to financiers and conglomerateurs, under the pressures of mounting costs, dwindling profits, government interference and new technologies on the horizon. As a company, CBS, which was built on broadcasting, was searching for new ways to diversify (such as its acquisition in 1972 of Steinway Pianos) as a hedge against drastic changes in the future that might hobble a corporation too narrowly based on television and radio.

See also Campaign Spending; feature article U.S. Election; Prizes and Awards.

LES BROWN
Television and Radio Editor, *Variety*

THAILAND

Largely owing to the United States' commitment to remove U.S. ground forces from Vietnam and its concomitant resort to increased air warfare following North Vietnam's invasion of the South in the spring, Thailand's role in the Indochina war increased dramatically in 1972.

The number of U.S. servicemen in Thailand rose to 48,000 (compared with 39,000 U.S. military personnel in Vietnam on Sept. 1 and approximately 27,000 on Dec. 1). Some 700 U.S. military aircraft were stationed in Thailand. Included were 150 planes that were transferred, together with 2,000 airmen, from Danang, South Vietnam, in order to meet President Nixon's Vietnam disengagement timetable.

Despite its greater involvement in the war, however, Thailand made its first public political contact with Communist China when a senior official accompanied a ping-pong team to Peking. Latent Thai fear of China and Communism nevertheless emerged late in the year, when the government expressed doubt that the Communists would "live up to" any Indochina peace settlement.

In domestic affairs, Thailand's premier, 61-year-old Field Marshal Thanom Kittikachorn, was given a second one-year extension beyond the normal date of military retirement on the ground that he was uniquely equipped to deal with the internal and external threat of Communism, which, however, did not immediately endanger the Thai state in 1972. Nonetheless, insurgent strength was up 15 percent over 1971; there were 4,000 rebels in the north, 2,000 in the northeast and about 800 in the south. Increased U.S. military spending gave a boost to Thailand's economy, which, while still impressive, expanded more slowly than in recent years.

RICHARD BUTWELL
Chairman, Department of Political Science
State University of New York
College at Brockport

THEATER

The healthiest sign in theater in 1972 was its increasing fragmentation. Artistically and commercially, Broadway remained a high-risk zone, but in direct contrast was the insurgence of institutional, noncommercial and regional theater. Gradually many of these estimable groups are infiltrating and invigorating the commercial theater. None has had such a salutory effect as Joseph Papp's Public Theater in New York.

While still keeping his operation off-Broadway, on Lafayette Street, and his free summer Shakespeare in Central Park, Papp has also become the leading Broadway producer. Jason Miller, a playwright and actor (he also appeared at the Public Theater in *Subject to Fits*), wrote a play called *That Championship Season*, which was optioned and subsequently rejected by a number of Broadway producers. Papp then produced the play at the Public, with a cast of lesser known actors directed by the promising young A. J. Antoon—giving it, as it turned out, the best imaginable production. The play, which is about a reunion 20 years later of a winning Pennsylvania high school basketball team, and deals with personal ambition, group cowardice and the hollowness of accepted American values, was greeted with encomiums by the critics. After a hasty miscount, *That Championship Season* was named best play by the New York Drama Critics Circle (who at first accidentally awarded the prize to another Papp protegee, David Rabe, for his *Sticks and Bones;* no Pulitzer Prize for theater was given in 1972).

After a sellout summer at the Public, Papp moved *Championship* uptown to Broadway, where it began a long, rewarding engagement. All the praise obscured the fact that the play, notwithstanding its outspoken language, was basically a traditional, naturalistic drama. However, it was exceedingly well acted, particularly by Paul Sorvino, beautifully staged by Antoon (with special credit to Santo Loquasto for his lifelike set) and perfectly aimed at its audience. Considering its low-cost production requirements and its easily identifiable emotions, the play was exactly right for Broadway.

Moreover, the New York critics gave their best musical award to another Papp invention, *Two Gentlemen of Verona* (with words by William Shakespeare), which began in Central Park and then moved to Broadway in the fall of 1971. Following that double play, Papp performed a triple. In the summer of 1972 he turned Antoon loose on *Much Ado About Nothing*. With all due respect to Shakespeare, Antoon converted the play into a Teddy Roosevelt-era salute to patriotism, optimism and romance—with beer-and-pretzel music by Peter Link and joyful performances by Sam Waterston and Kathleen Widdoes. Following an engagement in the park, *Much Ado* moved to Broadway, and then onto network television as a three-hour special. Unlike *Verona*, it was not strictly a musical; yet it was far from a straight play. For Papp, the Critics Circle may have to create a special category—best popularization of Shakespeare.

The critics also turned their backs on Broadway in choosing the best foreign play in the

Four former basketball teammates are reunited with their high-school coach in Jason Miller's powerful drama, "That Championship Season." A long, drunken night of revelations illuminates an underlying theme stressing the lasting impact of authority figures on the young.

Friedman-Abeles

1971–1972 season—Jean Genet's *The Screens*, a mammoth epic about the Algerian war which received its New York premiere in Brooklyn at the Chelsea Theater Center. The work is a difficult, diffuse one, impossible to do in commercial surroundings. The experimental Chelsea troupe also presented Allen Ginsberg's sensitive adaptation of his poem *Kaddish*, a personal account of the poet and his mad mother (stunningly portrayed by Marilyn Chris), and a freewheeling version of John Gay's *The Beggar's Opera*. Both works moved across the East River to off-Broadway.

In 1972, Broadway for a change was not filled with transplants from Britain. Simon Gray's *Butley* was one of the few to attract a mass audience in New York and that principally on the strength of Alan Bates' towering performance as a failed scholar, catastrophic lover and miserable yet extremely amusing human being. *Butley* was Gray's second play on Broadway during the year, his *Wild Child*, about a pair of petty thieves, having been a quick, and deserved, flop earlier in the season. Robert Bolt contributed *Vivat! Vivat Regina!*, still another play about Mary Queen of Scots and Queen Elizabeth (who rivaled Mary Lincoln as the stage heroine of the year), a stiff historical pageant that was justified by the bravura acting of Eileen Atkins as Queen Elizabeth. Off-Broadway there was Tom Stoppard's *The Real Inspector Hound*, a hilarious caricature of drama critics and Agatha Christie mysteries. Some of the more interesting new British plays were not produced in New York but in regional theater. David Storey's *The Changing Room* received its American pre-

Antoon's unique musical adaptation of "Much Ado About Nothing" opened in Central Park.

miere at the Long Wharf Theater in New Haven, and E. A. Whitehead's *The Foursome* was introduced at the Arena Stage in Washington.

The Spanish exile Arrabal himself directed the U.S. premiere of his horrifying outcry against injustice *And They Put Handcuffs on the Flowers*—a harrowing experience featuring a superb central performance by Ron Faber. The play was first presented off-off-Broadway, then moved off-Broadway for a long run. One

Friedman-Abeles

of Arrabal's favorite directors, Victor Garcia, mounted an innovative Spanish-language *Yerma* at the Brooklyn Academy of Music—placing that Spanish classic on a trampoline-filled stage.

Besides Jason Miller, Broadway was visited by Arthur Miller, and also by Paul Zindel and Neil Simon, and off-Broadway by Tennessee Williams. Arthur Miller's *The Creation of the World and Other Business* was an improvisational-style skit about the Bible, a diversion from the author's more serious work (one example of which, *The Crucible*, was revived nearby with moderate effectiveness by the Repertory Theater of Lincoln Center).

The Zindel, *The Secret Affairs of Mildred Wild*, which starred Maureen Stapleton as an aging movie fan, was an elaborate disappointment, and the Simon, *The Sunshine Boys*, about two old Vaudevillians returning briefly to former glory, was another case of Simon (with an assist from Alan Arkin as director). The Williams, *Small Craft Warnings*, was a slight and unresolved but touching little anecdote about derelicts in a California bar. Fulfilling a personal dream, Williams himself frequently appeared on stage in the part of an alcoholic doctor.

Subsequently, Broadway was introduced to Michael Weller, whose play *Moonchildren* was moved from the Arena Stage for a drastically abbreviated engagement. The play was unsatisfying, but the playwright is extremely talented, and the cast and the direction by Alan Schneider were superior. Gore Vidal's *An Evening with Richard Nixon and . . .* was an unconvincing political diatribe (although George S. Irving created a devastating portrait of Richard M.). Somewhat in the mold of Neil Simon was Bob Randall's *Six Rms Riv Vu*, a slim but appealing comedy about two unliberated, thirtyish people who find themselves on the far side of the generation gap. Jerry Orbach and Jane Alexander brought a touching reality to a contrived situation.

Elsewhere on Broadway, *Promenade All*, a multi-generation comedy by David Robison, was marked by versatile acting by Hume Cronyn, Eli Wallach and Anne Jackson, all of whom by turn played one another's parents and offspring. Melodrama was represented by the supernatural *Voices* and the sinister *Nightwatch* (both by Lucille Fletcher), each needless and farfetched. There were three plays about Mary Lincoln—*The Lincoln Mask* (Eva Marie Saint), *The Last of Mrs. Lincoln* (Julie Harris) and *Look Away* (Geraldine Page).

Beyond *That Championship Season*, Papp had scant success with new American plays, although he tried. John Ford Noonan's *Older*

People was a wheezy exercise about senility and sexuality. Alice Childress' *Wedding Band* was an old-fashioned story about interracial love. Two evenings of short black plays at the Public Theater served as showcases for promising black writers, actors and directors.

In the course of the year one new black playwright, J. E. Gaines (who is also an actor and director), had three full-length plays produced. His best was *What If It Had Turned Up Heads,* at the New Lafayette Theater. Actually the year was one in which black theater finally began to make inroads on the establishment, with black plays being staged on, off and off-off Broadway.

Musically the season was impoverished. *Sugar* was a disastrous recycling of the movie *Some Like It Hot,* only partially salvaged by Robert Morse's horseplay as a musician on the run from gangsters. *Pippin* was an overpraised attempt at a musical that was both historical and topical. In Roger O. Hirson's book, Pippin, son of Charlemagne, is seen as a misunderstood youth buffeted by adult expectations. The acting was good, the dances and direction by Bob Fosse loaded with ingenuity, but the book and music (by Stephen Schwartz) were undistinguished. Fosse, nevertheless, almost covered up the show's defects and preciosity.

Among other musical offerings, *Grease* was a raucous attempt to spoof the Elvis Presley era. Off-Broadway there were two revues representing the work of two master theater composers, Kurt Weill and Noel Coward. *Berlin to Broadway with Kurt Weill* had superior songs but was by far the inferior show, burdened as it was with a flatfooted narrative trivializing Weill's life and unblessed by singers with an ounce of Weill. *Oh Coward!,* on the other hand, was a small gem of a show—precise, witty and drily performed by a trio of Cowardians.

On Broadway there were two black musicals, *Don't Bother Me I Can't Cope,* an ebullient Gospel-style revue which introduced a talented young songwriter-singer, Micki Grant, and *Don't Play Us Cheap,* a down-home, folksy Harlem party, conceived, composed and staged by Melvin Van Peebles—a comedown from Van Peebles' *Ain't Supposed to Die a Natural Death,* but possessing some rousing songs. Off-Broadway, Don Goggin and Marvin Solley came up with a sprightly little contemporary review called *Hark!* The various *Hair* graduates were responsible for three musical disasters—the meandering *Dude,* the plot-heavy *Via Galactica,* a futuristic extravaganza about a garbageman in space (chosen to open the Uris theater), and the chaotic *Rainbow.*

The popular rock musical "Grease," set in 1959, evoked nostalgic recollections of the fifties.

During the 1972 season, Minneapolis' Tyrone Guthrie repertory company staged a successful revival of John Steinbeck's "Of Mice and Men," a moving drama of two transients in search of their roots in Depression-era America.

The year was also one for revivals of less than masterpieces. In New York, Phil Silvers brought back—too soon—*A Funny Thing Happened on the Way to the Forum,* and George Grizzard, Maureen Stapleton and Jason Robards revived *The Country Girl,* with more authority than it probably deserved. George Bernard Shaw's *Captain Brassbound's Conversion* lumbered briefly into town with a lovely Ingrid Bergman, while another glamorous lady, Melina Mercouri, tripped over *Lysistrata* in a catastrophic adaptation by director Michael Cacoyannis. Circle in the Square opened its new Broadway location with a revamping of Eugene O'Neill's *Mourning Becomes Electra,* starring Colleen Dewhurst and Pamela Payton-Wright.

Several other revivals contributed to an apparent Kurt Weill revival season. The Weill-Maxwell Anderson *Lost in the Stars* was forcefully sung by a New York cast headed by Brock Peters. The outstanding contribution to Weill's memory, however, was offered by the Yale Repertory Theater in New Haven, in a rediscovery of the Brecht-Weill *Happy End.*

The most notable revivals of the year were staged by New York's newest repertory company, the City Center Acting Company. This group, formerly known as the Juilliard Acting Company, was composed of members of the 1972 graduating class of the Drama Division at Juilliard. The artistic director, John Houseman, selected a challenging series of plays, which showed off the ensemble nature of his excellent company. The group presented Richard Brinsley Sheridan's *The School for Scandal,* Maxim Gorky's *The Lower Depths,* Thomas Middleton's rarely performed Jacobean tragedy *Women Beware Women,* Brendan Behan's *The Hostage,* and James Saunder's neglected, modern *Next Time I'll Sing to You.* The ambitious group misstepped only with Paul Shyre's adaptation of John Dos Passos' *U.S.A.*

The Repertory Theater of Lincoln Center also undertook classics, with mixed results—an adequate *Twelfth Night,* a dismal version of Edward Bond's *Narrow Road to the Deep North,* a respectable production of Arthur Miller's *The Crucible* and, most interestingly, the first American production of Gorky's *The Enemies*—marred, however, by serious miscasting, especially that of Joseph Wiseman, who gave a mannered performance in the role of an ineffectual alcoholic.

A more striking season took place downstairs at the Forum Theater. The audience was aroused by *The Ride Across Lake Constance,* by the controversial playwright Peter Handke. Black playwright Ed Bullins was outraged by what he considered a corruption of his play *The Duplex,* which was somewhat overstated but, contrary to the author's feelings, retained enough of Bullins' power and compassion to make it one of the stronger offerings at Lincoln Center. The Forum also featured David Wiltse's *Suggs,* a refreshing little play about an innocent's battle with the city, and ended 1972 with a Samuel Beckett festival, four plays by the 20th century genius (including one new play, *Not I*), acted by Jessica Tandy and Hume Cronyn.

As has often been the case, the primary excitement at Lincoln Center was offstage. The year closed with the simultaneous cancelling of the Forum season (after the Beckett festival) because of lack of money and the resignation of Jules Irving, for seven years the beleaguered artistic director of the company.

Among New York's other institutional theaters, the American Place Theater presented new plays by, among others, Jack Gelber, Robert Coover and Phillip Hayes Dean. The Negro Ensemble Company produced one of the season's finest American plays, Joseph A. Walker's *The River Niger,* directed by, and starring, Douglas Turner Ward.

Al Carmines, the resident composer, playwright, director and minister at the Judson Memorial Church, wrote and produced more musicals than anyone else in 1972. Two of his shows, *Wanted,* about the FBI's pursuit of heroic criminals, and *Joan,* his conversion of Joan of Arc into a bomb-throwing revolutionary, moved from Judson to off-Broadway. At Judson he also opened *The Making of Americans, Life of a Man* and *A Look at the Fifties,* with that last show his best, and New York's best, musical of the year—an intelligent, exuberant spoof of the 1950's.

One of the major theater events of 1972 was absolutely noncommercial. In August, Lincoln Center turned its open plaza into the Community/Street Theater Festival. Thirty-two companies from all over New York City and as far away as Wisconsin went to Lincoln Center with plays, musicals and statements of their own creation. They demonstrated that theater does not need its traditional trappings—not even money. "Theater belongs to the people" was the revolutionary cry that echoed during the two-week festival. A few of the groups floundered in the exposure, but many more—bursting with vitality and raw talent—proved that where there is life, there can be exciting drama.

See also Prizes and Awards.

MEL GUSSOW
Theater Critic, *The New York Times*

TRANSPORTATION

On the whole, 1972 was a better year for U.S. transportation than either of the two preceding years. Yet a year that began with considerable hope for important changes in Federal transport policy generated far more disappointment and frustration than constructive action. The post World War II period has been marked by numerous economic recessions which, though of modest proportions by comparison with previous experience, have put serious economic pressures on the U.S. transport system. Those that bottomed in 1954, 1958 and 1961 generated public concern and legislative recommendations. Then as in 1972, however, economic recovery relieved immediate pressures sufficiently to dull the urgency felt in the halls of Congress before any significant action was taken in the way of revision of Federal transport policy. The crisis atmosphere generated by the failure of Penn Central in June 1970 had substantially worn off and was not revived by the failure of Reading in late 1971 and of Lehigh and Hudson River and Erie-Lackawanna in 1972.

Traffic, Rates and Earnings. Traffic performance of the regulated carriers was unimpressive in 1972 and hardly commensurate with a rapid improvement in economic activity generally. Estimated rail ton miles for the first 34 weeks of the year rose 2.7 percent, and truck loadings showed a somewhat larger increase. Rail piggyback loadings rose more sharply, and it appeared possible that 1972 might prove to be a record year for that class of traffic. But mail carryings by both airlines and railroads declined significantly in 1972, reflecting a 50 percent drop in parcel post volume and continued shift of mail volume to contract truck operations. The traffic generated by economic growth apparently had gravitated very largely to exempt and private truck and water transport. Hence, the market share of regulated common and contract carriers probably continued to decline, and the long-run prospects of regulated carriers weakened.

Freight transport capacity was generally adequate. The winter wheat crop was handled with unusual freedom from car shortages, and rail carriers believed themselves well prepared to handle prospective volume in the fall. Major grain procurement by the U.S.S.R. in late summer, however, changed the picture virtually overnight. The supply of cars stockpiled in preparation for the fall harvest was quickly

The design of the Australian ship "Paralla" permits its lift trucks bearing cargo to roll on and off, thus markedly reducing cargo handling.

UPI

Soviet planes (above) were among the total of 150 planes, helicopters and gliders from 15 nations on display at the air show in Hannover.

The sleek design of the San Francisco rapid transit system cars typifies the modern engineering technology that pervades the new line.

absorbed by the movement of grain into export position. Unregulated barge rates increased rapidly as the supply of barge capacity tightened. Car shortages of some severity developed, with grain loadings running more than 20 percent above the prior year.

The year 1972 opened with temporary surcharges in effect on the railroads, further permanent rate increases under consideration and rate increase proposals in process in ten of the principal motor carrier rate bureaus. Intervention of the Price Commission resulted in a freeze on rate increases which was not lifted until March 25, when various rate increases were allowed to become effective.

On March 20 the Price Commission indicated its intention to delegate its authority in the regulated industries to the respective regulatory commissions. By fall, however, prolonged negotiations had resulted in only the Interstate Commerce Commission among the transport regulatory commissions having been certified to administer Price Commission guidelines. One rollback was ordered—in the case of New England motor carriers.

The impact of price controls not only restrained the amount of the increases approved, but also added to administrative complexity and increased the lag of rate increases after the events offered in justification—that is, wage and price increases. There was fundamental discord, therefore, between the price control program, which treats companies individually, and traditional transport regulation, which deals with rate levels for all carriers within broad territorial groupings. The Civil Aeronautics Board was compelled to deny United Airlines the 5 percent increase in freight rates which it approved for other principal airlines. United was able to meet Price Commission guidelines with a 4.5 percent increase, which thereupon was necessarily adopted by the other lines.

A rate war among ocean carriers on the North Atlantic was brought under control, and negotiations looking to consummation of a pooling agreement among container lines on that route were under way. Overtonnaging both of the Atlantic and Pacific trades, however, threatened continued pressure on ocean rates. The international air carriers had succeeded, in late 1971, in compromising longstanding differences over rates in the Atlantic market. With minor changes the agreed rates were approved in various proceedings before the Civil Aeronautics Board during the early part of 1972, the board operating for the first time under enlarged powers granted by Congress in respect of international rates. More competitive fare levels, increased charter activity by the certifi-

cated airlines and some clampdown on unlawful charter operations by supplemental carriers considerably relieved the heavy losses of tour and group passenger business experienced by certificated airlines in recent years.

Although traffic on major intercity transport modes continued to lag throughout most of 1971, rate increases in response to steep wage increases and price inflation generated an improvement in earnings. Class I regulated truckers realized $175,500,000 of net income in the first half of 1971, compared with $37,400,000 in the first half of 1970. Railroads realized $350,000,000 in ordinary income for 1971, compared with $229,000,000 in 1970 (their lowest net income since the Depression).

Railroads' 1971 income produced a rate of return on investment of 2.5 percent. Hence, railroads continued among the least profitable of all industries. The deficit of the roads in the Eastern United States declined from $273,-000,000 to $248,000,000—principally a reflection of an improvement in Penn Central's performance. Results for 1972 promised to be only slightly better.

Airlines experienced a turnaround in the last quarter of 1971 and earned $429,000,000 for the year, compared with a loss of $200,-000,000, in 1970. Some $17,000,000 of that, however, arose from a nonrecurring refund by the Federal government of sums deposited by the airlines on the abandoned Boeing supersonic commercial aircraft program.

Environmental Impact Enters Transportation. Pollution generated by the automobile, the disruption of urban areas and of the natural features of the countryside by highway construction and the danger of oil spills in the transport of petroleum over water were the environmental issues that received most public attention in the field of transportation. Substantial progress was made in the control of automotive emissions, and tighter Federal standards were still scheduled to apply in the 1975 model year. It remained unclear, however, whether prospective standards for air quality might not require restriction of automobile use in some congested urban areas.

Public attitudes continued to harden against transport facility development that disregards environmental impacts, and some portions of the Interstate Highway System in urban areas were held up on those grounds. Construction of the trans-Florida Canal likewise remained in abeyance, although the Warrior-Tombigbee project, for a ship canal-river passage from central United States to the Gulf of Mexico, cleared its final court test and was expected to proceed with dispatch.

Transportation Secretary John Volpe accepts the delivery of one of the first experimental safety cars. The front bumper will automatically extend one foot forward at speeds over 30 miles an hour to provide extra cushioning in the event of a collision.

New legislation tightened control over shippers of liquids and hazardous commodities. Environmental risks also led Delaware to prohibit potentially dangerous industrial development and to restrain expansion of petroleum refining capacity and deepwater terminals for supertankers throughout the country. The high rate of refinery operations and inadequate discoveries of new petroleum resources within the United States, both of which advanced the possibility of an early shortage of petroleum products paradoxically loomed at the very time that the first emission control devices were increasing automotive fuel consumption. Apparently inevitable increases in gasoline prices will in time tend to curb the growth in automobile use and reinforce the already quite pronounced trend toward smaller cars.

Controls directed particularly at sulfur emissions in stack gases continued to shift utility and industrial demand toward natural gas, in consequence of which more severe gas shortages were in prospect. The Federal Power Commission reconciled itself to approving higher well-head prices for natural gas, thus sacrificing the consumer interest it had long sought to protect in an effort to encourage more exploratory drilling. At the same time, the import of liquified natural gas appeared likely to expand substantially, with resulting higher costs and considerable stimulus to the shipbuilding industry. Applications already were in hand for shipbuilding subsidies for new tankers, and what would undoubtedly dismay the gas consumer could prove to be a boon to the shipbuilder and tankship operator.

No single transport project generated opposition equaling that directed against the Alaska pipeline, designed to deliver North Slope oil to ocean tankers. The objections remained largely unsatisfied. Pipelines carrying hot oil over permafrost were without precedent and the possible effects on a delicate environmental balance conjectural. In addition, the earthquake risk conjured fears of monumental oil spills. While construction was held up throughout the year, however, work was begun to improve design and minimize risk, at vastly increased prospective costs. Secretary of the Interior Rogers C. B. Morton after the most comprehensive study of environmental impact yet undertaken, approved the project on May 11. A Federal Court injunction, in force for 28 months, was subsequently dissolved, but environmentalists still sought means to prevent construction.

While the North Slope is a major oil find, it is miniscule in relation to expected increases in U.S. petroleum demand. Hence, the issue of deepwater ports to receive import petroleum in supertankers was certain to become more pressing, as no existing U.S. port can accommodate them.

Environmental considerations also intruded on the regulatory front. (The regulatory agencies are required to submit statements of environmental effects even in rate increase cases.) A court challenge to a temporary surcharge on

rail freight rates approved by the Interstate Commerce Commission led to a court finding that the commission's environmental statement was hopelessly inadequate and a requirement that the surcharge be lifted insofar as it applied to the movement of scrap materials and solid waste. In essence, the question was whether the rate structure did not encourage the extraction and use of primary materials, such as iron ore, and discourage the movement and use of alternative scrap materials.

While abandonment of light-traffic rail lines continued to be a means of improving the economic health of the rail industry, the contention that rail transport does less violence to the environment than highway transport was heard increasingly in abandonment proceedings. Much less horsepower is required to move freight by rail than by highway; hence, emissions are of less consequence.

The railroads also felt the impact of stricter regulation of sulfur emissions from coal burning. Low sulfur coals from Wyoming and Montana had been penetrating Midwest markets; in mid-1972 they found their way to generating stations in Kentucky and Texas. Burlington Northern was operating 40 trains of coal weekly, while loadings on Eastern lines were depressed by the displacement of West Virginia and Kentucky coals from some accustomed markets.

Appropriations and Legislative Proposals. Budgetary approvals for spending for transport purposes in fiscal 1973 differed only in minor respects from prior appropriation levels and administration requests. Nearly $4,900,000,000 was provided for the Federal-aid highway program, $230,000,000 for the urban mass transit program—plus $130,000,000 for the Washington Metropolitan Area Transit Authority—and $100,000,000 for airport development grants. More than $1,500,000,000 was provided for the Federal Aviation Administration for its regular programs of providing air traffic control, air navigation aids and other services to aviation. Subsidy provision for ocean ship operations and shipbuilding totaled about $500,000,000, while the regulatory agencies together were allotted $300,000,000. By contrast, the Federal Railroad Administration received $65,000,000, primarily for high speed ground transportation research.

The very modest appropriations for urban mass transit indicated clearly that the long-standing highway emphasis of Federal transport promotional programs had been only slightly dented. In April, however, Secretary of Transportation John Volpe forwarded to Congress draft bills that would effect major changes in the use of Federal-aid highway trust fund resources to finance new rural and urban transportation programs and improve highway safety efforts.

The proposed legislation would create a new urban transportation program with appropriations from the highway trust fund of $1,000,-000,000 in fiscal 1974 and $1,850,000,000 in fiscal 1975. Under the proposal, 40 percent of the amounts available would be allotted to the nation's Standard Metropolitan Statistical Areas in accordance with their respective proportions of total SMSA population; 40 percent would be allotted to the states, and 20 percent would be reserved for use at the discretion of the secretary of transportation. The Federal share of noninterstate projects, including mass transportation projects, would go from 50 percent to 70 percent in 1974.

In view of the obstacles encountered hitherto in urban transportation because most metropolitan areas are administered by a number of different local governments (some also spread across state boundaries), it was proposed that each SMSA form a consortium of the local governments within its area under standards enunciated in the proposed legislation. These consortia would plan and administer area-wide transport programs.

Although the Federal contribution to construction on the interstate system would continue at 90 percent, according to the proposals, the funds allotted to the system would be scaled down as diversion for urban and rural road improvements increased. Federal funding at 100 percent would be provided for certain highway safety programs conducted by the states and $185,000,000 provided initially for that purpose. Greatly increased Federal emphasis on highway safety was already in evidence and some results had been achieved, the annual number of highway deaths apparently having stabilized at 55,000.

In September, after intensive lobbying by the administration, the Senate acted favorably on the proposals—the first time either house of Congress had agreed to allow use of the highway trust fund for purposes other than road building. Efforts to dislodge companion legislation from the House Rules Committee, however, failed, and the proposals died there.

Meanwhile, in May, members of the House Transportation Committee complained of confusion arising from sharply conflicting statements by witnesses testifying on other Nixon administration transport bills. Confusion perhaps was understandable, not only because of divergent views among shippers, different carrier groups and spokesmen for the executive

branch but also because numerous conflicting bills, variously sponsored, were before the Congress. By September, 53 different bills concerning transportation were before Congress, most of them in both houses. Only five had been passed and sent to the President—all of them uncontroversial measures.

Two of the stymied bills had been introduced in Congress in late 1971 on behalf of the Department of Transportation—the proposed Transportation Assistance and Transportation Regulatory Modernization Acts. In January the President supported both proposals in his State of the Union Message. The bills, the result of

Push-button travel is envisioned by the designers of this electrically powered "people-mover." The four-to-six passenger capsule would be computer-programmed and could be guided electronically via a buried cable so as to deliver people non-stop to their desired destination.

The nation's first Personal Rapid Transit System will employ a vehicle (below) that can carry up to 21 passengers. The two campuses of West Virginia University will be connected by cars traveling 2.2 miles on concrete guideways.

The government is experimenting with this 10-passenger vehicle for conveying travelers around Dulles airport, near Washington. Riders can push buttons to select desired stops and a computer control center will guide the driverless car past any unwanted terminals.

policy studies under way in the department for years, represented further development of executive branch philosophy in evidence in successive administrations since World War II. A long delay had been encountered in submitting draft legislation because some features of the DOT proposals were controversial among agencies of the executive branch.

Most troublesome from the point of view of Congressional committees charged with handling the bills were certain features designed greatly to relax regulation of the rail, motor and water carriers subject to the Interstate Commerce Act. Under the proposal, carriers would be granted freedom to set rates within reasonable limits based on costs—a system similar in principle to that adopted for railroads in Canada in 1967. Suspension of rate increases before they become effective would be made more difficult, and rate bureaus would be forbidden to protest rate increases proposed by or on behalf of their member carriers.

The proposal also specified that carrier costs would be determined not by the Interstate

Commerce Commission, as in the past, but by the Department of Transportation. Moreover, rate bureaus which, under the Interstate Commerce Act as amended in 1948, allow carriers to determine rates jointly under prescribed procedures with antitrust immunity would have their scope cut back. Carriers might agree on joint rates (single charges for haulage over routes served by two or more carriers) and on the divisions of such rates, but not on rates that would apply to single-line traffic. Certificates of public convenience and necessity for entry into trucking and domestic water transportation would be made easier to secure by eliminating from consideration the effect of a new entry on the existing carriers serving a transport market.

Much else was included in the bills. However, neither carriers nor shippers appeared to desire greater intrusion of DOT into the regulatory process. Railroads sought greater rate freedom, whereas truck and water carriers vigorously opposed it. Shippers, as represented by the National Industrial Traffic League, also opposed these particular rate freedom measures.

Shippers and carriers, in short, were divided on the rate bureau proposals. Motor carriers opposed the modest changes in certificate requirements that would tend to ease entry into the trucking business, and the Interstate Commerce Commission, on the whole, opposed the entire plan for deregulation and offered a set of bills of its own designed to strengthen and improve regulatory performance. Apart from the executive branch of the government, principal support for the measures came from numerous academic economists, many of whom had advocated reduced regulation for years.

Accordingly, no action was foreseen on the DOT deregulation proposals. Moreover, compromise legislation, the proposed Surface Transport Act, showed little chance of enactment either. The bill originated in an agreement among the principal regulated carrier groups—rail, motor and water—and incorporated something of concern to each. Because it was a compromise among carrier groups whose interests often are in conflict, it avoided the more controversial issues, including deregulation.

A key feature of the bill was a loan guarantee program for $3,000,000,000, spread over five years, designed to assist financially weak carriers in providing track, signal systems and terminals. Separate legislation providing for a government guarantee of $2,000,000,000 for rail equipment obligations passed the Senate.

Both measures, however, were so hedged with restrictions with respect to dividend payout and corporate use of funds that it was doubtful the guarantee provisions would be used even if enacted. In addition, labor protective provisions had been attached in the meantime and proposals designed to expedite branch-line abandonment converted into additional hurdles. A part of the carrier-agreed program, prohibition of discriminatory tax assessment on carrier property, moved forward as a separate bill.

Some reform legislation seemed possible, but there was doubt that it would take a constructive form. Indeed, continued struggle with the same general range of transport issues for 25 years suggested that Congress still was unable to cope with the question of regulatory reform.

Meanwhile, the precarious condition of the railroads in the Northeast and revelations concerning some of the background of Penn Central's bankruptcy raised for the first time in 30 years a discernible movement urging a government take-over of some or all of the railroad system. Advocates observed that the railroads had already been relieved of a major part of their passenger service deficits by the creation of Amtrak (to provide intercity service) and by the action of various of the states, including those of the Northeast corridor, to pick up burdensome commuter losses. New equipment was also being publicly financed for several of the Chicago commuter services.

Although Penn Central's trustees had made progress in restoring service quality, rebuilding freight traffic and stemming the carrier's negative cash flow, critics pointed out that the problems to be corrected were of very long standing. Traffic of the Northeastern roads had been declining steadily since the end of World War II and was at its lowest level in more than 45 years. Rail traffic for the remainder of the country, on the other hand, stood 137 percent above the earlier level. It appeared, therefore, that a reduction of Eastern rail plant commensurate with the decline that had taken place in traffic was advisable. But neither railway labor nor some members of Congress were prepared to accept that solution.

Labor Developments. Both 1971 and 1972 were troubled years in transport labor relations. On July 1, 1971, the International Longshoremen's and Warehousemen's Union struck West Coast and Hawaiian ports, a stoppage that continued for 100 days until ended by a Taft-Hartley injunction on Oct. 6. Meanwhile, on Oct. 1, the International Longshoremen's Association had struck the East and Gulf coast ports. In late November, Taft-Hartley was resorted to in that strike also, with an injunction expiring on Feb. 14. The West Coast strike was resumed on Jan. 17, 1972, and ended Feb. 21 when an agreement was reached. East and Gulf coast

dockworkers continued to work after Feb. 14 in view of the imminence of a settlement.

While money issues were important in the negotiations, the question of labor displacement by containerized operations was a thorny issue in the East. Both agreements were, of course, subject to review by the Wage Control Board, and resumption of the strikes was threatened in the event of disallowance of any part of the agreements. Nevertheless, the first year increases were reduced.

Selective rail strikes called in 1971 by the United Transportation Union precipitated White House intervention and negotiations with a group of rail presidents in the place of the usual railroad bargaining conference. Meanwhile, a settlement had been reached in separate negotiations with the Chicago & Northwestern Railway. The UTU agreement, along with one reached earlier with the Brotherhood of Locomotive Engineers, may prove to be of historic importance. It opens the way for considerable relaxation of work rules which have grown increasingly anomalous in the light of the competitive pressures to which railroads are subject. Four states also repealed or modified their full crew laws, Arkansas by action of the voters in November.

In 1972 another constructive step brought the issue of firemen on diesel locomotives to a conclusion after 35 years of controversy. At least a tentative settlement was also reached with Penn Central on the crew consist issue, giving rise to the possibility that the trustees' objective of trimming train-service employees by some 5,000 might ultimately be attained through the route of attrition. By the summer of 1972 rail labor relations appeared to be in a more healthy and promising posture than at any time since the early 1930's.

The prolonged longshore strikes were exceedingly costly. Estimates of the losses to all parties, including agriculture and industry generally, ranged as high as $2,000,000,000. One noteworthy effect that may well prove long lasting was the diversion of considerable cargo to Canadian ports. Despite the advertised coastwise nature of the ILA settlement, cargo handling costs at East and Gulf coast ports are widely disparate, the range from low to high exceeding 100 percent. Notably high-cost ports face difficulties in maintaining their position in general cargo traffic.

Hijacking, Theft and Pilferage. Hijackings of commercial aircraft continued in 1972. Those for ransom received top billing. In one case force was used aboard an aircraft on the ground and, while successful in its object, resulted in the death of a passenger and injury to others. In all but one instance ransom payments by airlines were recovered, and a number of hijackers were apprehended.

Following a bomb explosion in a parked aircraft and another in the luggage compartment of a plane in flight—neither causing serious injury or death—stronger measures for the security of parked aircraft were instituted; search of carryon baggage became routine, and other steps were taken at the instance of Federal authorities. Not only were such precautions costly to the airlines and productive of delays. They could not be expected to be entirely effective. Renewed efforts to develop a more forceful international agreement for the return and trial of hijackers failed, however, in part because the issue of political asylum remained important. In the meantime, flight employees conducted a slowdown to protest insufficient action. The killing of an Eastern Airlines gate employee at Houston and the 29-hour ordeal of passengers on a Southern Airways flight in November rekindled concern. Negotiation with Cuba, via the Swiss embassy there, gave promise of some understanding on the future treatment of hijackers to Cuba.

New attention was focused on the growing toll of pilferage, theft and hijacking in freight transportation. The Senate Small Business Committee, which had been studying the problem since 1970, in its fourth report, issued in mid-1972, estimated the direct annual loss in truck transport at almost $1,000,000,000 a year. Annual rail losses and damage were set at $235,-000,000 for 1971, a ratio to gross freight revenues of 1.88 percent—compared with a loss of $123,000,000 and a ratio of 1.45 percent ten years earlier.

Improved security measures at some airports enjoyed considerable success. Helicopter surveillance of rail terminals in several major urban areas helped reduce both pilferage and vandalism. However, inadequate attention to security at terminals of all kinds remained a major factor in the rapid rise of freight loss.

Transportation Landmarks. For the first time in 65 years an entirely new rapid transit rail system was opened for service in the United States, on Sept. 11. Existing systems have been extended and improved during those years, but San Francisco's Bay Area Rapid Transit System was planned, engineered and constructed from the ground up, using the latest technology for automated two-rail passenger transport. Only one line was opened on that date—28 miles of a 75-mile system—but the whole was scheduled to be operational by mid-1973. Passengers were afforded speed and comfort unsurpassed in United States rapid transit history along with

abundant parking at suburban stations. Travel time from East Bay points into downtown San Francisco will be about a third that for motorists driving in peak hours over the congested Bay Bridge.

The project—decades in the making—was unveiled nearly 20 years after studies were begun and ten years after necessary bond issues were voted. It will be watched with inordinate interest for what it can show about the ability of high quality mass transit service to lure commuters away from automobiles. Scant success had been demonstrated elsewhere, although the Lindenwold line out of Philadelphia has attracted thousands of commuters to its trains, and the airport extension of Cleveland Transit has been more successful than anticipated. Toronto's subway is another success story, but the general trend away from transit to the automobile continues.

Transpo '72, held under DOT auspices near Dulles Airport outside Washington, D.C., from May 27 through June 4, although described as a great success, came under criticism for its cost in relation to its attendance and apparent results. It concentrated heavily on passenger transport, and especially on advanced concepts still in the developmental stage, ignoring almost entirely problems of freight movement. Concentration on developing technology, including linear induction propulsion, guided motor vehicles and various varieties of people movers, was considered by some observers as symptomatic of the American preoccupation with technological solutions whose application lies a decade and more away rather than with making the most of what is currently available.

The Department of Transportation celebrated its fifth birthday in April. Few planners anticipated any rapid change in U.S. transport policy when the department was instituted and given responsibility for many hitherto scattered transport functions. Many are critical of its performance. Yet much undeniably has been accomplished in broadening the view of transport taken by government, filling gaps in the research program, beginning to articulate broad policy approaches and altering the balance of emphasis in the government's promotional programs. Strong leadership has characterized the department since its beginnings.

Amtrak completed its first year of operations in May. With a skeleton service of intercity passenger trains substantially smaller than the railroads were operating when the corporation took over, Amtrak nevertheless had a loss of $147,700,000 in its first year. Only the fast services in the Northeast corridor operated on a profitable basis. Despite efforts to select the best of existing rail passenger equipment and to repair and upgrade it, Amtrak services encountered criticism, largely because of the high proportion of late trains and continuing equipment failures. Major additional funding was approved by the Congress so that significant improvement should become possible. International services were restored to Vancouver and Montreal, and sums were authorized for resumption of service to Mexico.

The long talked of "land bridge" became a reality during the year when through rail-ocean container services were instituted between the Far East and Gulf and Atlantic points via Pacific ports and between Pacific ports and Europe via New York. Exclusively rail container trains provide a five-day crossing of the United States in conjunction with ocean container lines on the several trade routes involved. Intermodal cooperation, in general, registered further advances.

For the first time a major U.S. railroad was sold to a corporation formed by officers and employees of the line. The Chicago & Northwestern, controlled by Northwest Industries, was transferred to Northwestern Employees Transportation Company under conditions approved by the Interstate Commerce Commission. The transaction was the largest, although not the first, spin-off of a railroad from a conglomerate organization.

Transportation facilities in much of the Northeast suffered severe damage when hurricane Agnes stalled over eastern New York State and Pennsylvania. Principal highway and rail routes were interrupted as rivers overflowed and bridges were carried away. Railroads suffered nearly $50,000,000 of damage to property and lost revenues, and the roads hardest hit were already in bankruptcy. Erie-Lackawanna was precipitated into trusteeship by the catastrophe, which seriously affected some 200 miles of its main line. Some of the minor lines damaged will not be restored.

Despite some notable successes, 1972 appeared to be another year of lost opportunity in transportation. Just as labor legislation designed to minimize the risk of transport strikes appeared to have a chance of passage, Presidential support was withdrawn. The differences among shipper and carrier groups which stand in the way of transport policy action were little moderated. Economic recovery again was the last, best hope for returning some semblance of health to the transport industries.

ERNEST W. WILLIAMS JR.
Professor of Transportation
Graduate School of Business
Columbia University

"Royal Viking Star," a luxury Norwegian cruise ship, made an inaugural sailing to the North Cape.

TRAVEL

While U.S. airlines appeared finally to be at the threshold of an era of mass, low cost travel that had already become a reality in Europe, ocean liners seemed destined in 1972 to become the future mode of luxury travel—and little else.

Charter. After stalling for almost two years, the U.S. Civil Aeronautics Board (CAB) in 1972 approved regulations permitting travel group charters (TGC), the chartering of airplanes by groups that exist only for travel purposes. Such charters may be sponsored by tour packagers and publicly advertised. The new regulations, which will be in effect on an experimental basis through 1975, superseded the old affinity rule which produced a chaotic charter travel situation.

An affinity group, as defined by the CAB, is an organization with a main purpose other than travel—for example, a church organization or a sports club. To participate in an affinity group charter, one must have been a member of the organization involved for at least six months. The group is not allowed to advertise publicly its charter flights (a regulation that was frequently flouted). Flying on such charters had been the only way most people could take advantage of the low charter airfares, which usually cost about half the price of the scheduled airline fares.

Charter organizers, nevertheless, customarily had placed blind advertisements in newspapers (for example, New York to London for $75) and waited for customer replies. With their tickets, passengers frequently were given predated membership cards. Despite poor service, crowded conditions, inedible food and the possibility of being stranded because of a periodic government crackdown, charter travel had an irresistible appeal to the public. It was inexpensive!

In announcing the TGC regulations on Sept. 27, the board declared: "There is an irresistible and understandable public demand for low cost air transportation, much of it on chartered services. This demand has up to now been met all too often by flouting existing charter rules. It is in the public's interest to promulgate new rules which will enable the customer's needs to be satisfied in a lawful manner."

Although the TGC regulations are simpler than the affinity rules—which are still on the books—they are conditional, too. TGC tours outside of North America and the Caribbean must be of at least ten days' duration, while within that area they must be of at least seven. This is to prevent competition with the popular eight-day winter Group Inclusive Tours (GIT) offered by scheduled airlines. One must book a TGC flight at least three months in advance and put down a 25 percent deposit (nonrefundable except in the case of death or serious illness). Legal action by scheduled airlines against the new rules was expected as 1972 ended.

From a high of 30 in 1947, the number of charter airlines had dropped to five in 1972—all professing to be operating in the red. The supplemental carriers have been hard hit by foreign competition (most of the illegal affinity

charter flights were on British and German airlines), increased charter activity by scheduled airlines and declining demand by the military for such service.

Charters enjoy the advantage over scheduled airlines of not having to fly unless the plane is full or almost full. Regular airlines must fly even if the plane is empty. The average occupancy on a scheduled transatlantic run is about 50 percent, and prices are fixed accordingly. The result is simple mathematics. Because a charter carries twice as many people, it can charge half the fare and still make a profit.

In Europe, where about 8,000,000 people yearly fly charters to vacation destinations, tour operators charter planes, rent hotels, hire sight-seeing buses and book entire restaurants. All together, they provide a very inexpensive vacation package. For example, an Englishman can fly from London to the Spanish island of Majorca for a four-day all inclusive vacation for about $40. In the United States such inclusive tour charters (ITC) must have at least three stopping points no less than 50 miles apart and last at least seven days. Moreover, the total cost must be at least 110 percent of the lowest fare of a scheduled air carrier operating on the same route.

Cruises. Economy and cost-cutting were not the trends in cruising in 1972. The year saw the much publicized around-the-world voyage of the liner *France,* a luxury cruise for which some passengers paid as much as $100,000.

In Norway the *Royal Viking Star* was launched, the first of a fleet of three sister ships intended to serve the U.S. cruise market on both coasts. The 21,500-ton ship carries 535 passengers in one class only—first. There are some 450 pieces of original modern Scandinavian artwork on the ship. The *Star*'s average daily rate is about $90.

The Cunard Line announced that it would spend more that $2,000,000 to renovate the *Queen Elizabeth 2.* And the German Atlantic Line introduced an "open bar" policy on its Caribbean cruises.

WILLIAM A. DAVIS
Travel Editor, *The Boston Globe*

Tourism Year of the Americas

Recognizing the economic and social benefits to be derived from tourism, the 23 member states of the Organization of American States (OAS) —comprising five islands in the Caribbean, all of Central America, Mexico, 11 countries in South America and the United States—officially proclaimed 1972 Tourism Year of the Americas. An accompanying program of activities was designed not only to increase tourism from other parts of the world to the Americas but also to promote a greater exchange of tourists among member countries.

A joint effort of the OAS and the International Union of Official Tourist Organizations (IUOTO), the program encouraged member states to combine efforts to project their own tourist images, and also that of the Americas as a whole, in international markets. It also stimulated efforts to develop home markets, facilitate international mobility and to promote better understanding among the peoples of the Western Hemisphere and of the world.

The activities included two round tables held in Europe in the early spring—one, in Madrid, at which development of promotional air fares was discussed, and one, in Rome, at which package tours and related bargains to attract the European market were reviewed.

In other events, the first Extraordinary Inter-American Travel Congress, held in Rio de Janeiro in August, reviewed the progress of the Tourism Year program, reported on resolutions adopted at the two European round tables and discussed ways to facilitate travel among the member states. And at a regional convention in Buenos Aires in November experts in the field of convention planning presented guidelines on ways to promote and administer conventions, which are an important source of tourist revenue.

Also in August, a major promotional campaign, employing a portable theater and multimedia slide presentation, was launched at the Pacific National Exhibition in Vancouver, B.C. The production subsequently toured major cities in the United States. Meanwhile, government tourist organizations in the member states prepared programs of developmental activities in cooperation with the private sector.

In his proclamation remarks, Galo Plaza, secretary general of the OAS, stated, "Travel is the expression of man's inherent curiosity to know other people and explore different lands and cultures . . . but . . . the people of this hemisphere still do not know the Americas. Many of them prefer to travel to other countries in spite of the fact that there is so much to see and admire in our countries. . . . No other region on earth can offer the variety, the color, the contrasts and the dynamism that are found in the Americas."

Tourism Year was the launching pad for an effort to change that state of affairs.

RICARDO ANZOLA-BETANCOURT
Director, Division of Tourism Development
Organization of American States

TURKEY

Urban terrorism, political bickering and parliament's failure to deal with acute social problems drove Premier Nihat Erim out of office on April 17, after 13 critical months. His resignation strengthened the indirect control of the government by military commanders. National elections, scheduled for 1973, promised to bring to a head one of the most dangerous crises since the death in 1938 of Mustafa Kemal Ataturk, the founder of modern Turkey.

The 60-year-old Erim, a scholarly lawyer with strong pro-Western leanings, stepped down after trying—initially with the benediction and sponsorship of the military—to restore social, political and economic health to the country. He had assumed office after the so-called "paper putsch" of March 1971— the written threat by military commanders to assume direct control unless Premier Suleyman Demirel resigned (which he did the same day). But Erim gradually lost the generals' favor, and his resignation, coming only hours after a historic state visit by Soviet President Nikolai V. Podgorny, was no surprise. His successor was Defense Minister Ferit Melen, who enjoyed the approval of the military.

A month of delicate negotiations between civilian politicians and the generals preceded Melen's emergence as head of an essentially nonpartisan coalition, the 39th government since Ataturk. At first, Suat Hayri Urguplu, a 69-year-old former premier and ambassador to the United States, had announced success in forming a 24-man coalition cabinet, but only a few hours later President Sunay rejected Urguplu on the ground that the military did not approve the makeup of his government. It took Melen another week to find men acceptable to the generals, and on June 5 parliament endorsed him and his avowed program of extensive reforms.

The new government was not without inner strains, and these came to the fore in November, when five cabinet members, all of them from the Republican People's party, resigned briefly, charging that the government was too conservative. Later, the five decided to remain in the government and quit their own party instead. A crisis was thereby averted. Earlier the Republican People's party had ousted Ismet Inonu, 88 years old, as leader after 33 years, choosing a younger man in his place.

In many ways, 1972 was even more bloody and violent than 1971, when terrorism resulted in the murder of an Israeli diplomat and the kidnaping of several U.S. servicemen stationed in Turkey. But a harsh crackdown on dissidents, marked by sporadic arbitrary arrests, armed clashes and martial-law decrees, had curbed much of the terrorism by mid-year. Authorities claimed to have crushed the Turkish People's Liberation Army, a left-wing organization responsible for a series of kidnapings and killings. Its leaders died on the gallows.

The security offensive had begun in January, when 84,000 troops cordoned off all Istanbul for a house-to-house search for terrorists. None was found, but a few days later police killed or captured seven prime guerrilla suspects in the city. The bloodiest day of the year, however, was March 30, when 500 troops raided a house northeast of Ankara after trying for hours to persuade 10 guerrillas to surrender three foreign NATO technicians they had kidnaped. All 13 men died in the ensuing battle.

More violence followed. An attempt was made to assassinate Gen. Kemalettin Eken, commander of the national police, and there were bombings and two airline hijackings. Authorities placed armed forces on the alert for the first time since a civil war threat on Cyprus in 1964. Major cities remained under martial law all year.

The production of opium remained a nagging problem. Under an agreement with Washington, all cultivation of poppies was banned in Turkey, effective Dec. 31, 1971, in return for $36,000,000 in grants to help farmers switch to less profitable crops. Subsequently, Premier Erim said he might approve a limited resumption of production because the ban was cutting too deeply into national income.

After Melen came into office, 100 members of parliament sent him a plea calling for renunciation of the agreement. They claimed the ban hurt the livelihood of 70,000 farmers. The problem was a sensitive one. On the one hand, Washington considers Turkey a main source of the heroin (the end product of opium) sold to American addicts. On the other hand, many Turks object to U.S. pressures to halt or interfere with their highly profitable crop.

Inflation continued to vex the economy, but large injections of foreign aid helped stabilize the situation (U.S. military aid for 1972 totaled $60,000,000, which was about one-half of what the Turkish military wanted.) Once again, Turks working overseas sent home more than $500,000,000 in valuable hard currency, and Commerce Minister Naim Talu disclosed at midyear that the foreign exchange reserves stood at $882,000,000, which he said exceeded the 1971 figure by 93 percent.

CHARLES W. BELL
Former Manager for Italy
United Press International

The U.S. Coast Guard escorted two Soviet fishing vessels to Adak Island, Alaska (above), and took their commander, in cap at left, into custody after they violated the 12-mile limit.

UNION OF SOVIET SOCIALIST REPUBLICS

In 1972 the Soviet Union moved vigorously to promote detente with the Western world while stiffening its stance toward China. At home, the economic managers coped unevenly with a poor grain harvest and failed to produce a promised breakthrough in consumer goods. Soviet industry as a whole suffered from a lag in labor productivity growth that continued to resist either exhortation of material incentives.

FOREIGN AFFAIRS

Detente with America. In foreign affairs the principal development was President Nixon's visit to Moscow (May 22–30). As a result of it the Soviet-American rivalry, which had been characterized by wide swings between brink-of-war hostility and periods of relative calm, settled into a formal mold of accommodation.

With an impressive set of agreements at the Moscow summit, the two superpowers accepted the principle of parity in strategic armaments, arranged for cooperation in the fields of commerce, science, technology, space and pollution control, and at the same time adopted a "Declaration of Principles" to guide their relationship "on the basis of peaceful coexistence."

The centerpiece of the Moscow accords was a treaty limiting deployment of antiballistic missiles (ABM) and a companion interim agreement on offensive strategic weapons. SALT I, as the ABM treaty was called, limits each power to two ABM deployment areas with 100 launchers each. No qualitative restrictions were imposed. The relatively simple content of the treaty was the product of no less than two and a half years of negotiation. Infinitely more complex was the question of offensive missiles, covered by the interim agreement, which is to last five years while the two sides attempt to devise a more permanent arrangement at SALT II, the second phase of the Strategic Arms Limitation Talks.

While Soviet commentators hailed both accords for fulfilling the requirements of "equal security," critics in the United States questioned the terms of the interim agreement,

which allowed the Soviets quantitative superiority in missiles and submarines. The Nixon administration maintained that for the time being U.S. qualitative superiority provided for an overall strategic balance.

As one authoritative observer viewed the arms control understanding, "Whatever detailed calculations may be constructed, neither superpower can consider itself to have any significant advantage over the other in terms of freedom to engage in nuclear war without incurring obliteration."

Next in importance in the Soviet-American rapprochement was a trade agreement signed in Washington on Oct. 18. It settled Moscow's lend-lease debt from World War II, included a White House promise to seek most-favored-nation status for the Soviet Union and called for a trebling of bilateral trade over a three-year period to an estimated $1,500,000,000.

In its wake, swarms of American businessmen converged on Moscow, eager to test the possibilities the treaty offered, although their expectations of profit verged on extravagance. As an indicator of the climate, the Soviets politely received the president of the New York Stock Exchange, an institution that had been a fixed target of *Pravda* editorialists and *Krokodil* cartoonists for half a century.

The biggest deal under discussion at year's end was a $45,000,000,000 contract to develop Siberia's natural gas resources for delivery to the United States, where an energy shortage was anticipated. The future pattern of Soviet-American trade was expected to be Soviet raw materials in exchange for American technology.

Less spectacular, but symbolic as "atmospherics," were agreements on joint medical research, a Soviet-American manned space effort in 1975, some 30 cooperative projects to monitor and protect the environment and a code of the sea to prevent incidents involving the two navies.

Nevertheless, competition between the two giants was not called off. Forces of the two alliances still confronted each other in the center of Europe, and an overlap of power persisted in some areas, such as the Middle East, with attendant dangers of friction. At the summit both countries pledged to "do their utmost to avoid military confrontations," and in December, Leonid I. Brezhnev, general secretary of the Soviet Communist party, authorized the beginning of talks on the reduction of forces in Central Europe, a reduction the Americans hoped would be balanced.

In the Soviet view, the summit was able to succeed because of President Nixon's "realism" —he responded "correctly" to the "contradictions" of American capitalism which impelled him to seek an understanding with Moscow. In brief, he needed the summit. This depiction

Presidents Podgorny and Nixon review the Soviet Guard of Honor upon the latter's arrival at Moscow's Vnukovo Airport on an official visit.

Tass from Sovfoto

of Nixon as the ardent suitor of an indifferent Brezhnev appeared somewhat threadbare when the President put the Soviet to the test 14 days before his arrival in Moscow by ordering the mining of the port of Haiphong. The low-key Soviet reaction to this unmistakable challenge clearly demonstrated that the Kremlin's stake in the summit was no less than Washington's.

The fact was that the Soviets felt they needed detente with the capitalist world for reasons which were quite their own. The leadership was heavily committed to improving the society's standard of living, particularly as measured by the availability of consumer goods. The consumer-oriented light industry sector had been chronically deprived to the benefit of an influential military-industrial complex in competition for allocated priorities. In the meantime, there had been a sharp rise in consumer expectations—partly encouraged by the authorities.

Heavy defense spending thus had been greatly responsible as a contributor to consumer goods shortages. Soviet defense expenditures, significantly increased in recent years, were roughly equal to those of the United States in 1972, although the nation's gross national product was about half as great and its population 10 percent larger. In other words, the burden of defense was more than twice as heavy for the Russian Ivan Ivanovich than for the American John Doe.

Revealed in the interaction of resource allocation-defense spending-detente was the paradox that increased arms outlays, which made parity and therefore SALT possible, could lead indirectly to a shift in resource employment aimed at a rising standard of living, as well as be an attraction for badly needed Western technology.

Friction with China. In the East, China posed a challenge to Soviet revolutionary purity and territorial integrity that showed no signs of abating. Moscow's response was a running fire of propaganda (attacking the Chinese for "great power chauvinism" and "institutional anti-Sovietism") which did not diminish with the return to Peking of the chief Soviet negotiator in the deadlocked border talks. Parallel to the verbal barrage, the Soviets pursued their military buildup on the frontier.

At the time of the border clashes in 1969 the Soviets had 21 divisions in the Far East; in 1971 there were 30. By the end of 1972 the number of divisions there had reached an estimated 44. Nor probably was Peking persuaded by a Soviet statement in October saying, "The U.S.S.R. has never threatened, is not threatening and is not going to threaten China." The troop deployments suggested the measure of Soviet concern about China, a concern that would provide an additional incentive to the Kremlin to seek an accommodation with the Western world.

Catering to 15,000 people daily, this well-stocked supermarket in Vladivostok, the largest in the Soviet Far East, appears distinctly Western.

Novosti from Sovfoto

Potential buyers view one of several different television models now available as a result of an increased emphasis on the production of consumer goods. The production of new television sets is actually slated to decrease slightly by 1975.

European Security. In Europe, the Soviet Union sought to draw the Western powers into closer economic and political ties with Moscow and directed its diplomacy toward blocking the formation of a cohesive political unit west of the Oder-Neisse. With the Nixon trump in their hand, Soviet diplomats obtained general consent for preparatory meetings on the vaguely defined Conference on European Security and Cooperation.

Seen from Moscow, the chief purposes of the conference appeared to be to gain Western recognition of the East German regime and de jure acknowledgment of Soviet hegemony in Eastern Europe. Western specialists conceded that a skillful Soviet diplomacy had made a marked advance toward the Kremlin's long-term objectives of removing the American military presence from the continent and of promoting the "Finlandization" of Western Europe.

Among the Warsaw Pact nations only Rumania dared challenge Soviet orthodoxy in foreign policy, but like the rest of Moscow's

A fully electric kitchen created by Novosibirsk designers comprises such modern equipment as an electric stove, air cleaner and dishwasher.

The construction of new housing on a massive scale to accommodate the Soviet Union's burgeoning population is strikingly apparent in Troporeva (above), a new residential district of Moscow, as well as in Bereznyaki, a new neighborhood on the left bank of the Dnieper in Kiev (left).

small allies, Bucharest scrupulously adhered to Moscow's strictures in its internal affairs.

Western analysts with deep suspicion of Moscow feared the Kremlin was preparing a great strategic move: first dividing and neutralizing the West to secure its rear while it dealt with China and afterward turning on a "Finlandized" Western Europe to draw the western part of the continent within Russia's sphere of influence.

What were Soviet intentions? And how should negotiations be affected by a perception of them? Most Western governments in 1972 appeared to accept the judgment of Henry A. Kissinger, written before he became President Nixon's foreign policy impresario: "It is not necessary to settle the question of the *real* intentions of the Communist leaders in the abstract. For we should be prepared to negotiate no matter what Communist motivations may be. Our responsibility is essentially the same whatever assessment we make of Communist purposes or trends."

A coordinated battery of threshers harvests a field of grain in the Tselinograd region of Kazakhstan. Much of the high-quality grain that was harvested, however, deteriorated from excess moisture. Heavy rains soaked the cut grain before it could be stored.

DOMESTIC AFFAIRS

Aside from one limited defeat suffered when President Anwar el-Sadat expelled the Soviet garrison from Egypt, management of Soviet foreign policy was generally successful in 1972. The handling of the domestic economy, however, was another matter.

Harvest Failure. A severe winter with inadequate snow cover caused a major kill of grain seedings in European Russia, and a summer drought stunted the reseeded wheat crop west of the Urals. The area affected by the drought stretched from the Black Sea to the White Sea and from the Dnieper to the Urals. Agriculture Minister Vladimir V. Matskevich described the weather as a "once-in-a-century" phenomenon. In a letter to Brezhnev a Volga farmer compared the harvest in his region to the famine year 1921. "The plants on all the acreage" of his 36,000-acre farm "wilted from the drought. *This year the collective farm reaped no harvest of grain.*"

The new farms east of the Urals, with their high-quality wheat, were counted on to compensate for the losses in the traditional Russian breadbasket. But the crop in the east ripened late, and steady autumn rains began to fall when the harvest began. Before harvesting had been completed, snow fell.

A note of panic crept into the normally sober official press when hints of mismanagement in the eastern harvest areas gave way to frank descriptions of chaos. Machinery was breaking down; crews were shorthanded and were declining to work overtime; and rail and truck transport was proving insufficient. In one instance a fleet of 11.5-ton trucks, badly needed to carry grain from the fields to the elevators, was unaccountably sent on a 720-mile errand to pick up a load of lumber.

General Secretary Brezhnev made a flying trip to the area in a last-ditch attempt to restore order, while *Pravda* called for a "mass political effort" to be concentrated on the harvest workers. Meanwhile, the grain was soaking wet and susceptible to rot. The authorities were unprepared. High-quality food grain was being brought to the elevators with a moisture content of 30–35 percent, and there were not enough drying facilities to bring the moisture down to an acceptable storing level of 14 percent before deterioration took hold. An enormous amount was spoiled; intended for bread, it was fit only for low-grade animal feed.

Thus, the Soviet Union was forced to go abroad and make massive grain purchases from the United States and Canada. Lesser amounts were bought from Australia, France and Sweden. The bill totaled more than $1,750,-000,000 in hard currency. News of the transactions was never published in the official press, although the word was spread through local party organizations to stem panic.

Farmers from as far as 150 miles away were coming to the well-stocked capital to buy bread sticks, macaroni and knapsacks full of bread loaves to take back to the countryside. Antihoarding posters appeared, and a save-the-bread campaign was launched with party backing, urging consumers to "conserve each crumb

Resembling primitive monoliths, giant cotton pyramids await collection at Uzbek "Samarkand" depot.

U.S.S.R. Minister of Culture Yekaterina Furtseva scrutinizes some of the equipment displayed in the U.S. Research and Development Exhibition in Moscow, a precursor of the accelerated technological exchanges planned between the United States and the Soviet Union.

of bread." Bread rations in Red Army mess halls were slashed.

Soviet officials hinted that the 1972 grain harvest would be about 167,000,000 metric tons, far short of the planned target of 190,-000,000. The official figure was to be published early in 1973. In the meantime, the best Western estimates were for a gross total of about 157,000,000 tons, and, considering the moisture level of the stored grain, about 120,-000,000 tons of usable grain.

Also hit by the drought were vegetable and potato crops. Potatoes were imported in quantity from Poland and East Germany as the price on the free farmers' markets rose to more than one ruble a kilo, treble the normal tariff.

Industrial Shortfalls. In industry, the special responsibility of Premier Aleksei N. Kosygin, performance was disappointing. Near the end of the second year of the ninth Five-Year Plan (1971–1975) there was no evidence that the promised shift from producer goods to consumer goods was taking place. Nor was there anything to suggest that Brezhnev's pledge of "saturating the market" with consumer items was being redeemed. "It is planned appreciably to increase the production of textiles, garments, shoes and knitted goods," the general secretary had declaimed to the 24th Party Congress in 1971. "In the case of such durables as TV sets, domestic refrigerators, radio receivers and washing machines, there is a real possibility of

Yugoslavia's Marshal Tito examines automated equipment at a Moscow bearing factory.

almost fully satisfying the needs of the population."

In a November 1972 issue, *Ekonomicheskaya Gazyeta* (Economic Gazette) scolded for shortfalls the ministries responsible for cotton fabrics, wool, flax, silk, knitwear, garments, shoes and refrigerators. Clothing and textile output was up only a shade more than 1 percent, and shoe production had managed to fall to 96 percent of its 1971 levels. The journal also complained about the chronically poor quality and limited selection of consumer goods.

Speaking at an expanded session of Gosplan (the state planning commission) on Sept. 30, Kosygin criticized the planners for inefficiency in the use of state funds and for waste in the use of materials. With additional claims on

A supervisor checks workers assembling intricate tape recorder circuitry at a Novosibirsk plant.
Novosti from Sovfoto

funds expected from agriculture in 1973, Kosygin told the Gosplan managers to prepare for some belt-tightening.

The Premier found too much unused industrial capacity, slow introduction of technology and "an excessive increase in unfinished (plant) construction." He noted with alarm that the worth of unfinished construction had risen from 24,500,000,000 rubles in 1961 to 70,000,000,000 rubles in 1972. (The ruble is worth $1.20 at the official exchange rate.) "Gosplan and the ministries," he said "should reduce the number of new plant sites in the 1973 plan."

Another problem raised by Kosygin in his speech was that of labor productivity, the targets of which, he said when he had unveiled the Five-Year Plan, "are of critical importance for our whole economic development program." Yet in the most recent summary available the growth in labor productivity was seen to be lagging. Targeted for a 6.1 percent increase in 1972, labor efficiency had improved by only 5.5 percent.

Otherwise, the planned goal for gross industrial production, a 6.9 percent increase for the year, appeared to be within reach as the managers revised the 1973 targets in light of the economic dislocation caused by the crop failure.

Politics. On the domestic political scene there was immobilism at the top and repression at the bottom. The leadership group around General Secretary Brezhnev remained virtually unchanged. Vasily P. Mzhavanadze, a candidate (nonvoting) member of the Politburo, was ousted as party first secretary in Georgia, and Politburo member Pyotr Y. Shelest was deprived of his power base in the Ukraine. Mzhavanadze was expected to lose his candidate member's seat as well for allowing widespread corruption in the Georgian Republic. Shelest, who was replaced as party leader in the Ukraine, apparently paid for his opposition to Brezhnev's pursuit of detente. Shelest appeared in danger of being eased off the Politburo at the next reshuffle.

Another victim of detente was cultural and ideological diversity, limited in any case. Accompanying the overtures to the West was a turning of the screw on literature and art. Arrests, trials and severe sentencing of political nonconformists, in the cases in which they were not forcibly exiled, testified to the regime's growing intolerance of competing views as it faced Western pressures to open frontiers to the free movement of people and ideas.

STEPHENS BROENING
Moscow Bureau, The Associated Press

UNITED KINGDOM

To adapt a quote from Shakespeare, 1972 demonstrated in Britain, as in some other countries, that there is a tide in the affairs of men which, breasted at the flood, leads governments to reverse their policies.

The year in Britain ended with a 90-day wage freeze and a period of price restraint. Prime Minister Edward Heath had declared as late as June that "Labour's compulsory wage freeze (1966) was a failure and we will not repeat it." With inflation rampant and wage levels 17.3 percent higher than a year before, in November he did repeat it.

Moreover, in March, Britain signed an agreement with its partners-to-be in the European Community (the Common Market) to fix narrow margins for permissible fluctuations in European exchange rates as a first step toward monetary union. On June 23 the pound sterling was abruptly cut adrift from the other European currencies and floated, as a temporary emergency measure.

Furthermore, government spending was to be cut and "lame duck" industries exposed to the invigorating wind of competition. By the end of the year, however, government expenditure was being increased very greatly, and many lame ducks were receiving first aid from the Treasury. Four yards owned by Upper Clyde Shipbuilders, which had been forced into bankruptcy in 1971 for want of further government subsidies, were given a new lease of life. Three of them were provided with $80,000,000 in government loans. One was taken over by the U.S. oil rig company Marathon Manufacturing. A major factor in the salvation of the yards was a "work-in" organized by two Communist shop-stewards, James Reid and James Airlie.

Ulster. In January the possibility of imposing direct rule of Northern Ireland from London was totally discounted. On March 30 direct rule was imposed.

Twelve months before, Mr. Heath had sent Ireland's Prime Minister John B. Lynch an angry telegram refusing him talks about the future of Northern Ireland, which, he reminded Mr. Lynch, constitutionally is a part of the United Kingdom. In November, Heath and Lynch had dinner together, after Lynch had addressed the Oxford (University) Union, and the subject of their table talk was the future of Northern Ireland.

In the meantime, Heath's Northern Ireland proconsul, William Whitelaw, had published a Green Paper—a government discussion paper —which for the first time conceded that the future of the province inevitably had to be

Syndication International from Photo Trends

Prime Minister Heath, visiting Northern Ireland for the first time since Britain assumed direct rule, stops at a Belfast memorial for the victims claimed by the violence in the North.

considered in "an Irish dimension." Visiting the North in November, Mr. Heath himself warned the Protestant majority that if attacks on the British army continued, or if unilateral independence was declared, the British would consider themselves released from their promise to continue the Union of the six counties of Ulster with Great Britain for so long as the majority there desires it.

A British trooper hovers over a predominantly Catholic area of Belfast, alert for any sign of violence on the first anniversary of internment.

Violence continued as an almost daily occurrence in Ulster. Severe bombings became the stock in trade of the Provisional Wing of the Irish Republican Army. In July the British army broke into the Catholic "no-go" areas, which had become sanctuaries for the "provos," and dismantled the barricades. This led to further violence. Meanwhile, a new militant Protestant group had been formed—the Ulster Defense Association. It also clashed with the army, which was in some danger of being caught in the middle of an ugly civil war.

The symptoms were appalling. But notwithstanding the violence, there was a certain inevitability about the steps taken both in Britain and in the Republic of Ireland leading toward an interim settlement at least on the government level.

Commonwealth and European Affairs. Far away in Rhodesia, where unilateral independence had been declared in 1965 by a "rebel" government led by Prime Minister Ian Smith, efforts toward a settlement were less successful. A royal commission headed by Lord Pearce reported that a majority of the black African population rejected the terms of a political settlement worked out between Mr. Smith and Foreign Secretary Sir Alec Douglas-Home. African support remained a necessary precondition for British recognition of Rhodesia's independence. Sanctions, imposed by the United Nations against Rhodesia and faithfully carried out by Britain, were continued.

In August, President Idi Amin of Uganda decided to expel all Asian residents of that country who had not taken Ugandan citizenship since independence (Oct. 9, 1962). Many of the Asians held British passports, a relic of the days when all residents of the British Empire could claim British citizenship. Although legislation had been passed in Westminster in 1962 and 1968 severely restricting the privileges conveyed by the ownership of such passports by non-nationals overseas, the British government accepted responsibility for the Ugandan Asians, and 27,000 were admitted into Britain.

In November, however, a reaction set in. The administration was defeated by a 35-vote majority in the House of Commons on an order to implement its new Immigration Act. Because the debate was on an "order" and not on the act itself, there was no question of the government's falling. But the vote did serve as a serious warning.

As it stood at the year's end, the law would allow a further 250,000 Asians in Africa, Malaysia, Singapore and India who do not hold local passports to claim the right to enter Britain in the event of local action to expel them, as in Uganda. While it had welcomed the Ugandans in a remarkably civilized and sympathetic spirit, in spite of vocal opposition led by Tory rebel Enoch Powell, the British public could by no means be counted on willingly to take in another quarter of a million.

There was, however, another important aspect to the government's November defeat in Parliament. It represented a reaction by many right-wing Conservatives to the painful realization that entering the European Community means giving Europeans privileges denied to the British-descended peoples of the "white" Commonwealth—mainly Australia, Canada and New Zealand. There is to be freedom of movement, and settlement, within the community for all community citizens equally.

Thus, the government was on notice that the Common Market issue was far from settled. On the vital second reading of the bill to join Europe in February, the government mustered a majority of only eight votes. On the third reading, in July, a mere formality, its majority still was only 17.

In the Labour party, Deputy Leader Roy Jenkins, a pro-European, resigned over the issue. Party Leader Harold Wilson, with some difficulty, edged Labour away from outright opposition to British entry and from a commitment to take Britain out if and when Labour should take over the reins of government. Instead, the party committed itself only to renegotiate the terms of entry, which is virtually an acknowledged impossibility.

A summit conference of community members was held in Paris in October. At the conference, Mr. Heath succeeded in obtaining a guarantee of community help for regions of high unemployment. Such help could, at least to some extent, counterbalance the very heavy payments that Britain seemed destined to make in the future toward financing the community's expensive common agricultural policy.

Britain officially entered Europe at midnight, Dec. 31. Very few people imagined that the historic event could be undone, or reversed. Whatever happens, it will remain the prime achievement of Edward Heath's term of office. However disquieting the defeat of his government on immigration and the commitment of the opposition Labour party to the renegotiation of the terms of entry, taken together with the need for emergency measures to float the pound and the return of considerable pressure on the British balance of payments, all tended to remind Europe that, as De Gaulle said, a Europe of nine inevitably will be very different from the Europe of six. The development of the Common Market is going to be changed by Britain's entry in ways which cannot be foreseen. Britain's strength will be welcomed, but its difficulties also will have to be accommodated.

Economy and Labor. On the home front, meanwhile, the year had witnessed a very sharp deterioration in labor relations. More workdays were lost because of strikes than in any year since before World War II.

There were two main reasons, although some observers would add a third in stressing the role of an increasingly militant Communist party: 1) the accelerating efforts of trade unions to break out of the standard-of-living strait-jacket imposed in 1968–69 by the Labour government, following its wage freeze; and 2) the introduction by the Heath administration of its new Industrial Relations Act, modeled to some extent on the U.S. Taft-Hartley law.

The upward wage curve had been brought down from a 13 percent per annum rise to 8.5

Asians, expelled from Uganda in August by President Amin, arrive in Britain to start a new life. Here, two refugee families await a train from Hertfordshire in cold, damp weather that provides a sharp contrast to that of their sunny homeland.

percent at the beginning of the year. But early in the year the nation's coal miners officially went on strike for the first time in 50 years (all intervening strikes had been local and unofficial), demanding pay increases averaging 25 percent. A court of inquiry under Lord Wilberforce subsequently awarded increases ranging from 15 percent to 30 percent according to the grade of skill involved—and thereby broke the wage dam. Meanwhile, the strike had introduced a wholly new kind of militant picketing into Britain. A "flying squad" of pickets, had actually confronted the police before major power stations.

The nationalized railways then suffered a prolonged "go-slow," in which, under the Industrial Relations Act, a ballot of members was required for the first time by the new Industrial Relations Court. The ballot backfired, so far as the government was concerned. The railwaymen voted 6 to 1 to support their leaders. A wage settlement eventually increased pay by about 13 percent.

The Industrial Relations Court then found itself involved in a docks dispute. The dispute was originally between members of the same union, the Transport and General Workers, over the "stuffing" or packing of containers at depots away from the docks. Five militant dockers who refused to recognize the new court were jailed for contempt. Immediately after they were freed (a decision of the House of Lords, acting as Britain's Supreme Court, having saved the face of the IRC) a national dock strike was called on July 27. The strike lasted until Aug. 16, seriously hurting the nation's exports.

In November the court ordered that funds belonging to the Engineering Union be sequestered, to pay a fine of $12,000 imposed on that union for contempt. The engineers had followed Trades Union Congress policy, which was not to recognize either the IRC or the Industrial Relations Commission.

This tangled web of trouble snared everybody when, in the early fall, Heath tried to get the TUC together with his government and the Confederation of British Industry to secure an agreed and voluntary incomes policy to reduce the dangerously rapid rate of increase of inflation in Britain. One of the TUC delegates was Hugh Scanlon, leader of the Engineers. Another was Jack Jones, Transport Union general secretary and in a titular sense the leader of the dockers.

In essence what Heath was offering the unions, before the talks broke down and the wage freeze was imposed, was a permanent place in the machinery for economic decision making. Regular machinery for government-TUC-CBI discussions, based on data produced by an economic model set up by a tripartite staff, was proposed.

Government. Heath's troubles were increased by the resignation in July of his deputy prime minister, Reginald Maudling, who as home secretary had previously instructed the police to investigate corruption charges stemming

Home Secretary Reginald Maudling resigned his position in July because of his previous involvement with a bankrupt architectural firm under police investigation for possible corruption.

Members of the royal family gather at Windsor Castle on the occasion of the 25th wedding anniversary of Queen Elizabeth and Prince Philip.

from a bankruptcy proceeding in which his own name had been mentioned. No allegation of corruption was made against Mr. Maudling, but in view of Britain's exacting standards of ethics for public officeholders, he was obliged to retire from the government while the inquiries were in progress.

Thereafter, Robert Carr took over as home secretary. Later Mr. Heath reshuffled the pack entirely. Secretary for Trade and Industry John Davies succeeded Geoffrey Rippon as secretary with responsibility for Europe. Peter Walker, who had been extremely successful as secretary for the environment, became responsible for trade and industry. Rippon succeeded to the environment post. A new minister for trade and consumer affairs was appointed and the numerical size of the cabinet increased from 18 to 19.

Foreign Affairs. In the area of foreign affairs a new cod war broke out with Iceland. That country in September declared (unilaterally) an extension of its fishery limits from 12 to 50 miles. Britain and West Germany took the case to the World Court, which ordered Iceland to desist pending an international settlement of the whole question of fishery limits. Iceland refused to recognize the court's right of jurisdiction in the matter. British deep-sea trawlers, which are very largely dependent on Icelandic waters for their cod catch (representing 20 percent of Britain's fish consumption), continued to fish within the new limit, and a number of clashes with Icelandic gunboats followed.

Malta, meanwhile, had ordered British naval and other forces to leave the island. However, the trouble was eventually patched up with a new agreement providing substantial economic aid for the Mediterranean island and denying the use of Malta's naval bases to Warsaw Pact navies.

Full diplomatic relations with the People's Republic of China were begun. The Chinese ordered three Concorde supersonic airliners from Britain and increased their order for medium-range Trident airliners to 20.

Royal Family. Queen Elizabeth II undertook highly successful tours in France, Yugoslavia and Southeast Asia during the year. On Nov. 20 she and the Duke of Edinburgh celebrated their silver wedding anniversary. Part of the celebration took the form of a "walkabout" among crowds in the inner City of London, the capital's oldest sector and now its financial hub, emphasizing the changing role of the monarchy in Britain. The throne now is less the source and guarantor of power, rank and privilege and more the sign and guarantee of the continuity of history and of civilized government.

The curtain fell on an earlier age of royalty when, on May 28, the Duke of Windsor died in Paris at the age of 77. The Duke had reigned as Edward VIII from Jan. 20, 1936, until he abdicated on Dec. 11 of that year in order to marry Mrs. Wallis Warfield Simpson. The burial in the royal burial ground at Windsor was private and was attended by both the Queen and the Duchess of Windsor.

JOHN ALLAN MAY
Chief, London Bureau
The Christian Science Monitor

UN Secretary-General Kurt Waldheim toured Communist China, Aug. 11–15. In his first year in office, the former Austrian foreign minister visited 25 countries.

United Nations

UNITED NATIONS

Despite the year's international dramatics—the Nixon trips to Peking and Moscow, agreement in the SALT talks, expansion of the Common Market, moves toward ending the Vietnam war, preparation for a European Security Conference—little of history's drama penetrated the United Nations in 1972.

The organization's first year under its fourth secretary-general—Kurt Waldheim of Austria—was devoted mainly to the perennial problems of the Middle East, Africa, colonialism and racism, and its economic and social work proceeded as usual under the specialized agencies and the UN Development Program. But the annual 13-week General Assembly session, while notably lacking in headline developments, did leave two indelible marks, one a victory for the concerted diplomacy of the United States, the other an unmistakable American defeat.

KURT WALDHEIM

Kurt Waldheim, the new secretary-general of the United Nations, was born on Dec. 21, 1918, near Vienna, Austria. He studied law and was trained as a diplomat. Entering the Austrian foreign service in 1945, he rose to be his country's ambassador to Canada (1956–1960), foreign minister (1968–1970) and chief representative to the United Nations (1964–68; 1970–71) before he was elected to head the world organization.

Opening in the penumbra of the massacre of Israeli athletes at the Munich Olympics, the indiscriminate shooting in the International airport at Lydda, Israel, and a rash of civil aircraft hijackings throughout the world, the session had been dubbed The Assembly of Terror even before it began in September. Behind the strengthened security measures that were in effect throughout the session, Secretary of State William P. Rogers appeared before the Assembly on Sept. 25 with a draft treaty against international terrorism and a resolution condemning global violence wherever it occurred. The item had been placed on the agenda by Waldheim after the incursion against the Israeli athletes at Munich.

The U.S. proposal, however, ran into strong opposition. The negative response came chiefly from Arab and African delegates, supported by the Communist countries. They feared that strong antiterrorist action by the United Nations would harm the national liberation movements they supported, chiefly those directed against Israel, Portugal and South Africa.

A substitute Western proposal, accepted as a compromise by the United States, called for the prestigious International Law Commission to draft an anti-terrorism treaty in the spring of 1973 for consideration at a plenipotentiary conference to be called during the 28th Assembly session. Neither it nor the original U.S. proposal ever came to a vote. Instead, by a 76–35 vote with 17 abstentions, the Assembly decided to create a 35-nation commission to make recommendations to its 1973 session, thus effectively shelving the issue of terrorism for a year.

The U.S. victory came on a touchy financial issue. Long before the Assembly met, the U.S. Congress had resolved to limit its UN appropriation to 25 percent of the assessed budget of the world organization, beginning Jan. 1, 1974. The budget—currently $226,000,000 in round figures—is assessed against the members on a sliding scale under which the United States has been paying 31.52 percent of the total, while 69 other countries have each been assessed only 0.04 percent of the costs.

Against predictable opposition, not the least of which came from the Soviet Union and its allies, which for years have refused to pay for UN costs of which they disapprove, U.S. Ambassador George Bush, with strong support in world capitals, began the battle to meet the Congressional fiat. Implicit in the U.S. campaign, but unspoken in debate, was a threat that Congress might decide to cut Washington's contributions to UN voluntary funds as well. Of these, the U.S. share usually is 40 percent of the total, on a basis of matching the combined contributions of other countries.

In the showdown vote the Assembly agreed to the U.S. demand to make the maximum assessment against any member 25 percent of the total budget. The vote was 81–27, with 22 abstentions, to reduce the assessments against the poorest countries from 0.04 percent to 0.02 percent each.

Despite the participation of one head of state—President Salvador Allende of Chile—six prime ministers or deputy premiers, 110 foreign ministers and about 3,000 other delegates who spoke in 500 meetings that examined more than 150 draft resolutions on a 101-item agenda, the 27th Assembly was an unspectacular session. But George Bush, who was recalled after 21 months as U.S. ambassador to be named by President Nixon as chairman of the Republican National Committee, did not find its dullness necessarily a bad sign. "Perhaps the lack of dramatics in the assembly hall may mean less confrontation upstairs," he said. Bush was to be replaced by John Scali, hitherto a presidential assistant.

Secretary-General Waldheim spent an active year. He instituted an austerity program which saved the financially-shaky organization some $4,000,000 and continued the traditional UN quiet diplomacy in such places as Burundi, newly-independent Bangladesh, the Middle East, Africa and even Vietnam.

Beginning with the United States a little more than three weeks after he assumed the post, the new Secretary-General visited 25 countries in his first year in office. He renewed his offer of good offices and maintained contact with the parties in the Vietnam war when peace talks bogged down late in the year although the Indochina conflict did not formally appear on any UN agenda.

Stanislaw Trepczynski, deputy foreign minister of Poland and the second Communist president of the General Assembly, referred to the Vietnam conflict in closing the session. "A new escalation of this war, so inhuman in all its aspects, jeopardizes the future of détente and carries the grave risk of increased tensions in international life," he said.

The world's other areas of belligerency were little more prominent than Vietnam in UN deliberations. The Security Council called on Israel in February to end military action it had undertaken against alleged Arab guerrilla bases in Lebanon. In September, however, it failed to act on Syrian and Lebanese complaints against Israel. At that time the United States used its veto—for the second time in history—to kill a resolution it considered one-sided.

The 15-nation Council fostered efforts to settle the future of South West Africa, the huge territory mandated to South Africa by the League of Nations, whose right to independence as Namibia has been proclaimed by the United Nations. Waldheim visited both South Africa and South West Africa, but subsequent negotiations conducted by his personal representative, Alfred Escher of Switzerland, were unproductive as the year ended.

On Dec. 15, John Scali, a presidential assistant, was named U.S. ambassador to the UN.

In the first meetings away from UN headquarters, the Security Council considered questions "relating to Africa" in Addis Ababa, Jan. 28–Feb. 5.

Twice the Council called on all countries to carry out full economic sanctions against the white-minority government of Rhodesia. U.S. action, authorized by Congress to buy Rhodesian chrome and other metals, was severely criticized.

Africa commanded major attention in many UN organs. The Security Council, meeting outside New York for the first time in 20 years, held a week's session in Ethiopia late in January. The Council condemned Portugal for violation of Senegal's frontiers from Portuguese Guinea and passed a number of resolutions against South Africa's policy of apartheid, or racial separation. Apartheid is under continuous scrutiny by a special Assembly committee, similar to the group that keeps watch on colonialism.

The People's Republic of China used its veto for the first time to block Security Council recommendation of membership for Bangladesh, formerly East Pakistan, which seceded from Pakistan in December 1971, with the active help of the Indian armed forces. Although the Assembly asked the Council to reconsider the application, China insisted that prisoners of war must be repatriated first in an Indo-Pakistani settlement.

Other highlights of the 91-day 1972 assembly session were the following:

* Approval by a vote of 86 to 7, with 31 abstentions, of a resolution reaffirming the guidelines for Middle East peace laid down by the Security Council on Nov. 22, 1967 (the so-called Resolution 242), and asking all countries to avoid action, including aid, that could constitute recognition of Israeli occupation of Arab territory. The United States voted no.

* Adoption of nine resolutions on disarmament, including the postponement of action on a Soviet demand for a World Disarmament Conference, by the creation of a committee to study the Soviet proposal. The United States, as Ambassador Bush put it, stood "in splendid isolation" against the conference idea in any form.

* Approval of a number of resolutions calling for complete nuclear disarmament, a halt to all nuclear weapons tests, prevention of proliferation of such arms, a pledge not to be the first to use them and a call for the renunciation of the use of force and the strengthening of international relations.

* Adoption of a series of measures reaffirming support for national liberation movements, calling for aid to victims of South African apartheid and demanding that Portugal negotiate with native leaders in its African territories.

* Agreement to convene a conference on the Law of the Sea in 1974 at Santiago, Chile, and to locate permanent headquarters in 1973 for the new international Environment Secretariat in Nairobi, Kenya, with Maurice Strong of Canada as executive director.

* Approval by consensus of resolutions declared "interdependent" urging reconsideration of the Bangladesh membership application and asking India and Pakistan to settle questions outstanding between them.

BRUCE W. MUNN
Chief UN Correspondent
United Press International

UNITED STATES

Any American President seeking reelection has certain advantages over his opponents. But seldom have the uses of incumbency been so amply or tellingly demonstrated as in 1972. Richard M. Nixon, the man who only ten years before had retired from politics after two defeats at the hands of the voters, dominated the year's news at home and many events abroad. He became the first President to visit Peking and the first to visit Moscow. He negotiated the first agreement limiting offensive and defensive nuclear arms. And four years after one of the narrowest victories for the Presidency in American history he won in 1972 a landslide reelection victory. His most bitter disappointment was the failure to end the Vietnam war, which he had believed would be possible in 1972.

The year began with the President conferring in San Clemente, Calif., with Premier Eisaku Sato of Japan in the last of a series of meetings with world leaders begun in late 1971 in preparation for the planned visits to the People's Republic of China and to the Soviet Union. At the meeting with the Japanese leader it was agreed that the United States would return Okinawa, held since the end of World War II, to Japanese rule on May 15. The two leaders also agreed to the installation of a hot line between Washington and Tokyo. However, it was clear that a number of issues were not resolved and that the Japanese continued to show resentment over the President's failure to notify them in advance in the summer of 1971 of his intention to impose import controls and to visit the Chinese mainland.

In domestic affairs, the President in his State of the Union message to Congress urged that 1972 be a "year of action" on his legislative proposals, including the principal reform recommendations he had made a year earlier and which had not been approved. He said that he had submitted more than 90 pieces of domestic legislation on which Congress had failed to act. In a call for higher defense spending, he sounded a theme that would be heard throughout the year's debates with the Democratic candidates. "We must maintain the strength necessary to deter war," Mr. Nixon

said. He claimed success for his Phase II economic programs, inaugurated in October 1971 to strengthen the economy, and pledged to free the economy again "when we achieve an end to the inflationary psychology which developed in the 1960's."

At a meeting with National Aeronautics and Space Administrator James C. Fletcher the President ordered work begun on a manned space shuttle. "The shuttle will revolutionize transportation into near space by routinizing it," he said. The new $5,000,000,000 program, opposed by many Democrats on the grounds that it takes money needed for social programs, is designed to create two flight test vehicles to blast off from earth, circle the earth for 30 days and return and land like airplanes.

UPI

On Jan. 20, President Nixon delivered his State of the Union address, calling for a "year of action" on 90 proposed bills.

With President Nixon spending more and more time at Camp David, the retreat's lack of press quarters posed increasing problems.

January also was the month for the formal launching of the Presidential campaign. On Jan. 4, Edmund S. Muskie of Maine announced his candidacy for the Democratic Presidential nomination. The less-well known junior Senator from South Dakota, George S. McGovern, had announced his candidacy months earlier. As the year began, few gave McGovern a chance of winning the nomination, and many believed that Muskie was almost the certain nominee of his party. He was ahead in the polls and far ahead in pledged support.

Shortly after Muskie announced, other Democrats entered the contest. They included Sen. Hubert H. Humphrey of Minnesota, the former Vice-President and the Democratic nominee in 1968; Gov. George C. Wallace of Alabama; Sen. Vance Hartke of Indiana; Sen. Henry M. Jackson of Washington; Rep. Wilbur D. Mills of Arkansas; and Rep. Shirley Chisholm of New York, the first black woman to campaign for the office. One Democratic leader said that he would not run. Sen. Edward M. Kennedy of Massachusetts filed an affidavit in his home state declaring that he would not be a candidate for President in 1972.

Three days after Muskie announced his candidacy, the President said in a letter to the New Hampshire secretary of state that he would seek a second term. Mr. Nixon said he sought reelection to "complete the work that we have begun." Two other Republicans announced that they would challenge the President for the nomination. Rep. John M. Ashbrook, a staunch conservative from Ohio, and Rep. Paul N. McCloskey, a liberal from California and opponent of the Vietnam war, entered the campaign for the GOP nomination. They and their supporters recognized that they had little chance of preventing the President's renomination, but they were representative of discontent in the party over the President's policies.

January also was a month in which two new justices joined the Supreme Court. Lewis F. Powell, Jr., and William H. Rehnquist became the third and fourth Nixon appointees to take seats on the high bench. A few days later, Federal District Judge Robert Merhige, Jr., propelled the already lively issue of busing to achieve racial balance in the schools into the Presidential debate when he ordered a merger of the Richmond, Va., city schools, which were

predominantly black, with two suburban counties, largely white, into a new metropolitan school district. Merhige said that it was "the only remedy promising immediate success" in the struggle to end an increasing pattern of segregated education.

Two months later, Federal District Judge Stephen J. Roth issued a similar ruling, declaring that "relief of segregation in the public schools of the city of Detroit cannot be accomplished within the corporate geographical limits of the city." Roth said it was his "duty" under the 1954 Supreme Court school desegregation ruling to "look beyond the limits of the school district for a solution." The busing orders became a major campaign issue.

The President meanwhile continued his Vietnam troop withdrawal program with the announcement on Jan. 13 that 70,000 additional troops would be withdrawn by May 1, when the ceiling would be 69,000. Later he fixed the ceiling for Dec. 1 at 27,000. He had begun the withdrawal of forces in the summer of 1969, when the ceiling was 549,500.

Toward the end of January the President surprised the nation by disclosing that Henry A. Kissinger, assistant to the President for national security affairs, had met 12 times in secret sessions with North Vietnamese leaders in Paris in an attempt to negotiate an end of the Vietnam war. The President charged that the Communists had broken off the negotiations. He said that the United States was prepared to resume them at any time and that he had submitted an eight-point plan to end the war. It called for the withdrawal of all U.S. and foreign troops from South Vietnam, Laos and Cambodia within six months; the return of prisoners of war; and new presidential elections in South Vietnam. President Nguyen Van Thieu agreed to resign one month before the balloting.

A week after the President's dramatic announcement, U.S. intelligence sources reported that the Vietnamese Communists were preparing a major offensive in South Vietnam to coincide with the President's visit to China in February. The implication was clear to experts that the Soviet Union would like to embarrass the President at that time and to disrupt his plans for a Sino-American rapprochement. Moscow had supplied the bulk of the equipment for the offensive. It did not take place, however, until a month after the President returned from his China visit, and while it did not disrupt Sino-American relations, it almost interrupted the U.S.-Soviet rapprochement.

Before the President left in February for China, he formally asked Congress to devalue the dollar by 7.89 percent by increasing the price of gold from $35 to $38 a fine ounce. He also accepted the resignations of Maurice H. Stans as secretary of commerce and John N. Mitchell as attorney general. They were succeeded, respectively, by Peter G. Peterson and Richard G. Kleindienst. Thereafter, Stans headed the finance committee for the President's reelection, and Mitchell became campaign director. Mitchell later resigned, however, declaring that his family needed him. He was succeeded by Clark MacGregor, a former Congressman from Minnesota and a White House aide. President Nixon also signed a new Federal election campaign bill requiring the reporting of funds and a limitation on campaign spending.

On Feb. 17, accompanied by Mrs. Nixon, the President departed for China. He said that he was "under no illusions that 20 years of hostility between the People's Republic of China and the United States are going to be swept away by one week of talks." But he said "we come in peace for all mankind."

On his first day in Peking, President Nixon held a "frank and serious" talk with Party Chairman Mao Tse-tung and then embarked on a series of lengthy conferences with Premier Chou En-lai. The President spent most of his time in working sessions, except for a visit to the Great Wall and the Ming Tombs and formal dinners and entertainment in the evenings. He also visited Hangchow and Shanghai. A joint communiqué recognized that differences existed between the two governments but emphasized their intention to work toward normalization of relations and for international peace. In a major concession, the United States accepted the Peking contention that Taiwan is "a part of China" and affirmed America's "ultimate objective" of withdrawing its military forces from Taiwan. The two governments also promised to increase trade and cultural exchanges and to maintain contact "through various channels." In a speech at a Shanghai banquet before departing for home, the President said: "This was the week that changed the world."

On his return to Washington, he modified that claim somewhat by asserting that "we made some necessary and important beginnings" which proved that two nations with "fundamental differences can learn to discuss those differences calmly, rationally and frankly, without compromising their principles. We did not bring home any magic formula which will make unnecessary the efforts of the American people to continue to maintain the strength so that we can continue to be free."

Back in Washington, President Nixon was confronted with charges that his administration had agreed to settle an antitrust case against International Telephone and Telegraph Co. and that ITT had pledged to underwrite a large part of the cost of the Republican National Convention scheduled for San Diego, Calif. Acting Attorney General Kleindienst vigorously denied the charges and asked that the Senate Judiciary Committee reopen its hearings on his nomination so that he could reply to the charges. The committee had unanimously approved his nomination, but the Senate had not acted. After lengthy hearings he was finally confirmed, but ITT continued to be a political issue in the campaign, and the convention was changed from San Diego to Miami Beech.

The Presidential race heated up in March in New Hampshire's opening primary, the President winning easily over McCloskey and Ashbrook. In the Democratic contest, Muskie, who had hoped to win with a strong lead in his neighboring state, won with only 46.4 percent of the vote. McGovern was second with 37 percent. In the ensuing Florida primary, Wallace won first place, with Humphrey, Jackson, Muskie and McGovern trailing in that order.

In a busing message, President Nixon urged Congress to order a moratorium on court-ordered busing to achieve racial balance in the schools. To counter a wave of skyjackings, he ordered the airlines to adopt stricter air and ground security measures, which, however, proved to be inadequate. The daring hijacking of airliners continued.

At the end of March attention again turned primarily to foreign problems when the Communists launched their biggest offensive in South Vietnam since the Tet offensive of 1968. As they made rapid gains across the demilitarized zone and elsewhere, the President ordered an increase in bombing attacks, but he went ahead with the withdrawal of American troops from the combat zone. On April 10, at a State Department ceremony at which more than 70 nations signed a treaty prohibiting the stockpiling of biological weapons, the President, in an obvious reference to the Soviet Union, said "a great responsibility particularly rests upon the great powers" not to encourage "directly or indirectly any other nation to use force or armed aggression against its neighbors." Soviet Ambassador Anatoly F. Dobrynin was at the head table with the President.

Many persons believed that President Nixon's sharp language had wrecked chances for the Moscow summit meeting scheduled for the following month. Nevertheless, two days after the Nixon statement, Secretary of Agriculture Earl L. Butz, ending a five-day visit to the Soviet Union during which he was bluntly told that Russia had experienced an extremely bad crop year, was invited to the Kremlin for a long meeting with Communist party leader Leonid I. Brezhnev. In the same week, U.S. bombers attacked Hanoi and Haiphong areas for the first time in four years. While the raids were in progress, the President spent two days on an official visit to Canada. He agreed with Prime Minister Pierre Trudeau on a major environmental program affecting the Great Lakes.

At the end of the month, with Soviet-American relations extremely uncertain, it was suddenly announced that Kissinger had visited Moscow for four days of secret talks with Brezhnev and other leaders. At the same time, talks began in Washington in another attempt to reach a settlement of a 25-year-old dispute on World War II debts the Soviet Union owed the United States for lend-lease shipments.

In Charlottesville, Va., former President Lyndon B. Johnson was admitted to a hospital after suffering a heart attack. Apollo 16 astronauts spent a record 71 hours and two minutes on the moon, with color television cameras recording their activities in one of the most dramatic broadcasts of recent years. In Pennsylvania, Democratic voters favored Humphrey, with Wallace second, McGovern third and Muskie fourth. In Massachusetts on the same day, McGovern won a clear majority, with Muskie a poor second with only 21.8 percent of the vote. Muskie thereupon announced his withdrawal from "active participation" in the primaries and released his delegates.

With the North Vietnamese making strong but less than spectacular gains in their offensive, the President on May 8 ordered the mining of North Vietnamese harbors. He said that "air and naval strikes against military targets in North Vietnam will continue." The announcements startled the nation and the world, and again there was the widespread belief that the Soviets would cancel the planned meeting with the President.

Also in May, Secretary of the Interior Rogers C. B. Morton announced that he would grant a permit for construction of the controversial trans-Alaska pipeline, to carry oil from the rich North Slope fields at the top of Alaska to an all-weather port in the south. He acknowledged that the pipeline, opposed by environmentalists, would involve "some environmental costs," but he said it was the fastest way to transport oil which "the United States vitally needs."

On May 15, Gov. George C. Wallace, while campaigning in Maryland, was seriously wounded by a would-be assassin's bullet as he moved through a crowd shaking hands. Arthur Herman Bremer, 21, of Milwaukee was arrested and later convicted and sentenced to 63 years in prison (later reduced to 53 years) for the attack. The Alabama governor was paralyzed from the waist down and forced to withdraw from active campaigning. Nevertheless, on the day after the shooting, Wallace won 51 percent of the vote in the Michigan Democratic primary, his first majority in a Northern state. McGovern was second with 27 percent, and Humphrey third with 16. Wallace also led in the Indiana primary, with Humphrey and McGovern trailing. The next day, John B. Connally, the only Democrat in the Nixon cabinet, resigned as secretary of the treasury and was succeeded by George P. Shultz, a former secretary of labor and at the time director of the Office of Management and Budget. Connally later headed the Democrats for Nixon organization in the campaign.

Despite the bitter dispute over Vietnam, Moscow signaled its interest in proceeding with the summit conference, and the President set out for the Soviet capital in late May, stopping briefly en route in Salzburg, Austria. The Moscow meeting proved to be another personal Nixon triumph, similar to the Chinese visit. After extensive discussions with Soviet officials, he and they agreed on a treaty limiting anti-ballistic defensive missile systems and on a five-year interim agreement limiting construction of offensive nuclear weapons. They agreed to begin in the late fall a second round of Strategic Arms Limitation Talks to replace the interim agreement with a treaty, and the meetings, called SALT II, began in Geneva in November.

In addition to the arms accord, the Moscow conference led to agreements on cooperation in the fields of environment, health, space, science and technology, in avoiding incidents at sea and in commercial relations. The two governments approved a 12-point statement governing their relationships. Extensive but secret talks were held on ways to end the Vietnam war. President Nixon invited the Soviet leaders to visit Washington at a later time.

Before returning to Washington, the President visited Iran and Poland for talks with government leaders. On his return home, he immediately addressed a joint session of Congress to report on his trip. "The foundation has been laid for a new relationship between

Apollo 17, the first space mission to be launched at night, went off at 12:35 A.M., Dec. 7.

Militant American Indians, demanding Congressional action on 20 proposals, occupied the Bureau of Indian Affairs in Washington, Nov. 2–8. During the occupation, damage, estimated at $2,280,000, was done to the buildings, its furniture and art work. Three BIA officials later lost "present authority for Indian affairs."

the two most powerful nations in the world," he said.

Partly as a result of the visits to China and Russia and partly because the Communist offensive was contained, Vietnam peace negotiations were resumed in Paris in the summer. Kissinger made another trip to Peking following the Moscow summit and resumed his secret trips to Paris for meetings with North Vietnam's Politburo member Le Duc Tho.

Meanwhile, the political campaign had intensified. McGovern, having won the Oregon, Rhode Island, New Jersey, New Mexico and, most important, the California primaries, was nominated on the first ballot at the Democratic National Convention in Miami Beach in July. He chose Sen. Thomas F. Eagleton of Missouri as his running mate. The AFL-CIO executive council, traditionally a bulwark of Democratic strength, voted not to endorse a Presidential candidate in 1972.

Shortly after the convention, moreover, it was disclosed that Eagleton had been hospitalized three times for treatment of mental depression. Although McGovern promised nevertheless to back Eagleton "1000 percent," under pressure from party leaders who saw the Eagleton matter becoming a major issue, he asked his running mate to leave the ticket. In his place, McGovern chose Sargent Shriver, former Peace Corps director and brother-in-law of the Kennedys. The Republicans dutifully renominated President Nixon and Vice-President Spiro T. Agnew. As he headed into the campaign, the President announced that the draft of young men for military service would end by July 1973. He continued to withdraw troops from Vietnam, but he failed to achieve his objective of ending the war before the campaign began.

McGovern, nominated by a deeply divided party, repeatedly tried to draw the President

LEGISLATION

Major bills passed by the Second Session of the 92d Congress and signed by the President

SUBJECT	PURPOSE
CAMPAIGN SPENDING	Imposes on candidates for Federal office limits on expenditures for advertising in all media; tightens requirements for reporting sources and expenditures of campaign funds. Signed Feb. 7. Public Law 92-225.
DRUG ABUSE	Authorizes over $1,000,000,000 for the creation of a Special Action Office for Drug Abuse Prevention which will coordinate Federal drug prevention programs. Signed March 21. Public Law 92-255.
SENIOR CITIZENS	Amends the Older Americans Act of 1965 to provide grants to states for the establishment, maintenance and expansion of low-cost meal projects, nutrition programs and opportunities for social contacts. Signed March 22. Public Law 92-258.
EQUAL EMPLOYMENT	Gives the Equal Employment Opportunity Commission authority to try cases in court. Signed March 25. Public Law 92-261.
ADDICT CARE	Authorizes the Attorney General to provide care for addicts on probation or released on parole. Signed May 11. Public Law 92-293.
SICKLE CELL ANEMIA	Authorizes expenditures of $115,000,000 over three years for research into a cure for this hereditary blood disorder that affects Negroes. Signed May 16. Public Law 92-294.
EDUCATION	Extends Federal aid programs to students and institutions of higher education; establishes the National Institute of Education to coordinate research; provides $2,000,000,000 to aid communities to desegregate grade and high schools; delays for 18 months court orders requiring busing to achieve desegregation. Signed June 23. Public Law 92-318.
UNEMPLOYMENT	Extends the Emergency Unemployment Compensation Act providing up to 13 weeks' additional unemployment compensation to workers in states where unemployment is high. Signed July 1. Public Law 92-329.
NATIONAL PARK SYSTEM	Establishes the San Francisco Bay National Wildlife Refuge to protect the wetlands complex. Signed July 1. Public Law 92-330.
SOCIAL SECURITY	Extends the $450,000,000,000 debt ceiling until Oct. 31, 1972, and provides a 20 percent increase in Social Security benefits, tying future benefits to the cost of living. Signed July 1. Public Law 92-336.
WATER POLLUTION	Authorizes $24,600,000,000 over three years for sewage treatment. President's veto overridden by both houses of Congress. Became law Oct. 18. Public Law 92-500.
REVENUE SHARING	Appropriates $30,200,000,000 in federal tax money for a five-year general revenue sharing program under which state and local governments are to receive funds without stipulations. Signed Oct. 20. Public Law 92-512.
PESTICIDES	Broadens the powers of the Environmental Protection Agency to regulate the use of pesticides and provides compensation for manufacturers whose products are banned. Signed Oct. 21. Public Law 92-516.
OCEAN DUMPING	Prohibits the dumping of hazardous materials into the ocean and regulates the dumping of other materials. Signed Oct. 23. Public Law 92-532.
PROTECTION OF DIPLOMATS	Makes it a Federal crime to harass, assault, kidnap or murder a foreign diplomat, his family or an official guest of the United States. Signed Oct. 24. Public Law 92-539.
VETERANS' BENEFITS	Increases education benefits for Vietnam-era veterans by $2,500,000,000 over five years. Signed Oct. 24. Public Law 92-540.
NOISE POLLUTION	Authorizes the Environmental Protection Agency to establish controls over noise from interstate trucks, buses, trains and other vehicles, including automobiles and motorcycles; calls for a nine-month study of possible regulations regarding airplane and airport noise. Signed Oct. 26. Public Law 92-574.
PRODUCT SAFETY	Creates an independent commission with authority to establish and enforce safety standards on thousands of consumer products. Signed Oct. 27. Public Law 92-583.
SOCIAL SECURITY	Raises the tax rate and the taxable wage scale for Social Security taxes; increases Social Security benefits and medicare and medicaid payments. Signed Oct. 30. Public Law 92-603.

The defendants in the Watergate case, including (l-r) Eugenio Martinez, Frank Sturgis, Virgilio Gonzalez, their attorney Henry Rothblatt and Bernard Barker, were arraigned on Sept. 19.

into debate. But Mr. Nixon was determined to remain above the battle. In late August he flew to Hawaii to confer with the new Japanese Premier, Kakuei Tanaka. On returning to Washington, he said that he would have to stay close to the White House while Congress struggled over key measures in its final days. The President made only infrequent campaign forays, but his effort to persuade the 92nd Congress to approve his programs was anything but successful. Of his six major reform proposals, only revenue sharing was approved. Mr. Nixon made much of this victory, claiming it was a major step in returning the power of government to state and local authorities. His welfare reform proposal was allowed to die in the Senate when neither he nor the Democratic leaders would compromise. Overriding a presidential veto, Congress enacted a $24,600,000,000 water pollution control bill, which the President maintained was too expensive. (Subsequently, the President ordered the Environmental Protection Agency to allocate to the states only $2,000,000,000 of the $5,000,000,000 authorized for pollution aid in fiscal 1973, and only $3,000,000,000 of the

$6,000,000,000 authorized for fiscal 1974.)

The Democrats had been handed a major issue at the beginning of the summer when five men, one of whom was security coordinator for the Committee to Re-elect the President, were arrested when they were discovered at night in the Democratic headquarters in the Watergate apartments in Washington. The men were later indicted, along with two former White House aides, on charges of conspiring to break into Democratic headquarters. Democrats claimed that there was a conspiracy to bug telephones and otherwise spy on their activities. There were other charges of corruption and political sabotage. Efforts were made to show that Presidential aides had spent large sums of money on political espionage and sabotage work.

The President denied that White House aides had engaged in unlawful activities, and the charges, while headline material in the newspapers, did not appear to make a great impact on the voters. From the day McGovern was nominated until the voters cast their ballots on Nov. 7, the public opinion polls showed the President far ahead.

Jean Westwood, McGovern's choice as chairman of the Democratic party, resigned Dec. 9.

On Oct. 26, Kissinger told a White House news conference following a bargaining session in Paris which had lasted nearly a week that "peace is at hand" in Indochina. He predicted that a cease-fire could be reached in one more secret session lasting "not more than three or four days." The session did not begin, however, until after the election, and the administration encountered severe opposition to its proposals from the Saigon government.

On Election Day the President won 49 states, losing only Massachusetts and the District of Columbia to McGovern. The electoral count was 521 to 17. The President won almost 61 percent of the popular vote. The Democrats however, picked up two Senate seats, to give them a majority of 57 to 43, and although the Republicans showed a net gain of 12 House seats, the Democrats retained control by a majority of 243 to 191 (one independent). Nevertheless, the President appeared to retain philosophical domination of the House through the coalition of Republicans and conservative Democrats which long had ruled the chamber.

On the day after the election, the White House announced that the President planned a major shake-up in his administration. He retained Secretary of State William P. Rogers, Secretary of Agriculture Earl L. Butz, Secretary of the Treasury George P. Shultz, Attorney General Richard G. Kleindienst and Secretary of the Interior Rogers C. B. Morton.

The President moved Elliot L. Richardson, secretary of health, education and welfare, to

UPI

© 1972, Roy Doty, "Newsweek"

President Nixon disclosed that in his second term he would concentrate administrative authority in the hands of eight principal assistants: George Shultz and Presidential Adviser Henry Kissinger, overall control; John Ehrlichman and H. R. Haldeman (White House assistants), White House machinery; Roy Ash (director of the Office of Management and Budget), management; Earl Butz, natural resources; Caspar Weinberger, human resources; and James Lynn, community development. The new Cabinet consists of:

State. William P. Rogers, retained as secretary of state, is the only original Nixon cabinet member continued in his original post. He was born in Norfolk, N.Y., on June 23, 1913. In 1947–50 he served as counsel to Senate investigating committees, and in 1953 he joined the Justice Department, becoming U.S. attorney general in 1957. Before becoming secretary of state in 1969, Rogers had had little diplomatic experience, but was known for his skill as a negotiator and for his knowledge of international law.

Treasury. George P. Shultz was appointed secretary of the treasury in May 1972. He was born in New York City on Dec. 13, 1920. While dean of the University of Chicago graduate school of business, Shultz served as adviser on fiscal policy and labor relations under Presidents Eisenhower and Kennedy. He became secretary of labor in 1969 and the following year was made first director of the Office of Management and Budget. He also serves as the administration's chief economic overseer.

Defense. Elliot L. Richardson, newly appointed secretary of defense, was secretary of health, education and welfare, a post he had held since 1970. He was born in Boston, Mass., on July 20, 1920. Educated at Harvard, Richardson served as a law clerk to Supreme Court Justice Felix Frankfurter. From 1957 he was successively assistant secretary for legislation in the Department of Health, Education and Welfare; U.S. attorney for Massachusetts; attorney general of that state; and U.S. undersecretary of state.

Justice. Richard G. Kleindienst, who became attorney general in July 1972, served as deputy under John M. Mitchell from January 1969. He was born near Winslow, Ariz., on Aug. 5, 1923, and, as an attorney there, managed several successful political campaigns, although he was defeated in his bid for governor in 1964. As deputy U.S. attorney general, Kleindienst supported the administration's emphasis on law and order. Alleged conflict of interest in Justice Department antitrust cases against ITT delayed his confirmation.

Interior. Rogers C. B. Morton will continue as secretary of the interior, a post he has held since Jan. 29, 1971. He was born in Louisville, Ky., on Sept. 19, 1914. In 1962 he was elected from Maryland to the U.S. Congress, in which he served on the Committee of Interior and Insular Affairs and the Ways and Means Committee. While his voting record on environmental issues was uneven, Morton, accepting his appointment, vowed to bring "the priority of our environment . . . into equity."

Agriculture. The President named Earl L. Butz secretary of agriculture in November 1971 in an effort to address his administration to serious economic problems on the farm. Born in Albion, Ind., on July 3, 1909, Butz was dean of the school of agriculture at Purdue University and vice-president of the Purdue Research Foundation. In 1954–57 he was assistant secretary of agriculture under Ezra Taft Benson. The Senate, resenting Butz' "agribusiness" connections, confirmed his appointment by a mere 51–44 vote.

Wide World

Commerce. Frederick B. Dent, a textile manufacturer from South Carolina, is Nixon's new appointee to the post of secretary of commerce. Born in Cape May, N.J., Dent transformed a small family-owned mill in Spartanburg, S.C., into a modern four-plant operation. As president of the mill from 1958, he was one of the few chief executives of a small company to sit on the prestigious Business Council. Dent was a leader in the textile industry's fight to impose import quotas.

UPI

Labor. Peter J. Brennan, president of New York's Building and Construction Trades Councils from 1957 and the man chiefly credited with bringing about Nixon's rapprochement with labor, was the President's choice as secretary of labor. In 1970, Brennan led a "hard hat" rally supporting the administration's Indochina policies. Born in New York City on May 24, 1918, he worked as a painter while in high school. After service in World War II he became a leader of a local painters' union.

Wide World

Health, Education and Welfare. Caspar W. Weinberger, director of the Office of Management and Budget and former Federal Trade Commission chairman, was named secretary of health, education and welfare. The secretary-designate is known as a fiscal conservative and tough administrator. Weinberger was born in San Francisco on Aug. 18, 1917. A lawyer, he served as California's finance director in 1968–69 and chairman of the state's Commission on State Government Organization and Economy.

UPI

Housing and Urban Development. James T. Lynn, former undersecretary of commerce, was named secretary of housing and urban development in December. Described as one of the wittiest men in the administration, Lynn served as general counsel to the Department of Commerce from 1969 until he became undersecretary there in 1971. In 1972 he was one of the chief architects of the U.S.-Soviet trade agreement. Lynn was born in Cleveland, Ohio, on April 27, 1927, and was a partner in a leading Cleveland law firm.

UPI

Transportation. A California oil company executive, Claude S. Brinegar, was nominated as the nation's third secretary of transportation. Brinegar was born on Dec. 16, 1926, in Rockport, Calif., and earned a doctorate in economics from Stanford University. With the Union Oil Company of California for 20 years, he became senior vice-president, a member of its board of directors and president of its gasoline division, Union 76. A man who "likes cars," Dr. Brinegar was also director of the Daytona (Fla.) Speedway.

UPI

Presidential adviser Henry Kissinger and North Vietnamese Politburo member Le Duc Tho (r) hold informal Vietnam talks on Nov. 16.

the post of secretary of defense. Caspar Weinberger, director of the Office of Management and Budget, succeeded Richardson as HEW secretary. Roy L. Ash, head of Litton Industries and an expert on governmental reorganization, succeeded Weinberger at OMB. Peter J. Brennan, 54-year-old president of the New York Building and Construction Trades Council, was brought in to be secretary of labor. Frederick B. Dent, a South Carolina textile manufacturer, was made secretary of commerce; Undersecretary of Commerce James T. Lynn was named secretary of housing and urban development; Claude S. Brinegar, a California oil executive, was appointed secretary of transportation.

As the year drew to a close, attention again focused on Vietnam, with high expectations that a cease-fire would be negotiated in Paris. In late November, Kissinger began what many believed would be the final round of talks with North Vietnamese Politburo member Le Duc Tho leading to a cease-fire. But after nearly two weeks, the effort failed. Kissinger returned to Washington and on Dec. 16 at a White House news conference reported that no agreement had been reached. He blamed the Communists for interjecting new issues. He said an agreement could be reached at any time Hanoi had the will to settle. The United States began bombing North Vietnam heavily once again. It was a dark moment for the President and a dark one for the country, which had been led to believe that peace was "at hand." But after twelve days of intensive bombing, the attacks were stopped and the two sides returned to the negotiating table in Paris. A settlement was announced three days after the President's second inaugural.

Despite the emphasis on Vietnam, the President increasingly turned his attention to the array of issues, largely economic, affecting America's relations with the European community. He focused on plans for a European security conference, on negotiations for reduction of NATO and Warsaw Pact forces in Central Europe and on SALT II negotiations with the Soviet Union. He promised to continue his efforts to bring about peace in the Middle East. He also planned to confer with European leaders prior to a meeting in Washington later in 1973 with Soviet Party Chairman Leonid Brezhnev.

See also Campaign Spending; China; Energy; Indochina War (p. 24); Law; Union of Soviet Socialist Republics; U.S. Elections (p. 10).

CARROLL KILPATRICK
White House Correspondent
The Washington Post

NINETY-THIRD CONGRESS: FIRST SESSION

SENATE

President Pro Tempore: James O. Eastland (D-Miss.)
Majority Leader: Mike Mansfield (D-Mont.)
Majority Whip: Robert C. Byrd (D-W. Va.)
Minority Leader: Hugh Scott (R-Pa.)
Minority Whip: Robert P. Griffin (R-Mich.)

Committee Chairmen
Aeronautical and Space Sciences: Frank E. Moss (D-Utah)
Agriculture and Forestry: Herman E. Talmadge (D-Ga.)
Appropriations: John L. McClellan (D-Ark.)
Armed Services: John C. Stennis (D-Miss.)
Banking, Housing and Urban Affairs: John Sparkman (D-Ala.)
Commerce: Warren G. Magnuson (D-Wash.)
District of Columbia: Thomas F. Eagleton (D-Mo.)
Finance: Russell B. Long (D-La.)
Foreign Relations: J. W. Fulbright (D-Ark.)
Government Operations: Sam J. Ervin, Jr. (D-N.C.)
Interior and Insular Affairs: Henry M. Jackson (D-Wash.)
Judiciary: James O. Eastland (D-Miss.)
Labor and Public Welfare: Harrison A. Williams, Jr. (D-N.J.)
Post Office and Civil Service: Gale W. McGee (D-Wyo.)
Public Works: Jennings Randolph (D-W. Va.)
Rules and Administration: Howard W. Cannon (D-Nev.)
Veterans' Affairs: Vance Hartke (D-Ind.)

HOUSE OF REPRESENTATIVES

Speaker of the House: Carl B. Albert (D-Okla.)
Majority Leader: Thomas P. O'Neil, Jr. (D-Mass.)
Majority Whip: John J. McFall (D-Calif.)
Minority Leader: Gerald R. Ford (R-Mich.)
Minority Whip: Leslie C. Arends (R-Ill.)

Committee Chairmen
Agriculture: W. R. Poage (D-Tex.)
Appropriations: George H. Mahon (D-Tex.)
Armed Services: F. Edward Hébert (D-La.)
Banking and Currency: Wright Patman (D-Tex.)
District of Columbia: C. C. Diggs, Jr. (D-Mich.)
Education and Labor: Carl D. Perkins (D-Ky.)
Foreign Affairs: Thomas E. Morgan (D-Pa.)
Government Operations: Chet Holifield (D-Calif.)
House Administration: Wayne L. Hays (D-Ohio)
Interior and Insular Affairs: James A. Haley (D-Fla.)
Internal Security: Richard H. Ichord (D-Mo.)
Interstate and Foreign Commerce: Harley O. Staggers (D-W. Va.)
Judiciary: Peter W. Rodino, Jr. (D-N.J.)
Merchant Marine and Fisheries: Leonor K. Sullivan (D-Mo.)
Post Office and Civil Service: Thaddeus J. Dulski (D-N.Y.)
Public Works: John A. Blatnik (D-Minn.)
Rules: Ray J. Madden (D-Ind.)
Science and Astronautics: Olin E. Teague (D-Tex.)
Standards of Official Conduct: C. M. Price (D-Ill.)
Veterans' Affairs: W. J. B. Dorn (D-S.C.)
Ways and Means: Wilbur D. Mills (D-Ark.)

SENATE

Alabama
John Sparkman (D)[r]
James B. Allen (D)

Alaska
Ted Stevens (R)[r]
Mike Gravel (D)

Arizona
Paul J. Fannin (R)
Barry M. Goldwater (R)

Arkansas
John L. McClellan (D)[r]
J. William Fulbright (D)

California
Alan Cranston (D)
John V. Tunney (D)

Colorado
Peter Dominick (R)
Floyd K. Haskell (D)[e]

Connecticut
Abraham A. Ribicoff (D)
Lowell P. Weicker, Jr. (R)

Delaware
William V. Roth, Jr. (R)
Joseph R. Biden, Jr. (D)[e]

Florida
Edward J. Gurney (R)
Lawton Chiles (D)

Georgia
Herman E. Talmadge (D)
Sam Nunn (D)[e]

Hawaii
Hiram L. Fong (R)
Daniel K. Inouye (D)

Idaho
Frank Church (D)
James A. McClure (R)[e]

Illinois
Charles H. Percy (R)[r]
Adlai E. Stevenson 3d (D)

Indiana
Vance Hartke (D)
Birch Bayh (D)

Iowa
Harold E. Hughes (D)
Richard Clark (D)[e]

Kansas
James B. Pearson (R)[r]
Robert J. Dole (R)

Kentucky
Marlow W. Cook (R)
Walter Huddleston (D)[e]

Louisiana
Russell B. Long (D)
J. Bennett Johnston, Jr. (D)[e]

Maine
Edmund S. Muskie (D)
William D. Hathaway (D)[e]

Maryland
Charles McC. Mathias, Jr. (R)
J. Glenn Beall, Jr. (R)

Massachusetts
Edward M. Kennedy (D)
Edward W. Brooke (R)[r]

Michigan
Philip A. Hart (D)
Robert P. Griffin (R)[r]

Minnesota
Walter F. Mondale (D)[r]
Hubert H. Humphrey (D)

Mississippi
James O. Eastland (D)[r]
John C. Stennis (D)

Missouri
Stuart Symington (D)
Thomas F. Eagleton (D)

Montana
Mike Mansfield (D)
Lee Metcalf (D)[r]

Nebraska
Roman L. Hruska (R)
Carl T. Curtis (R)[r]

Nevada
Alan Bible (D)
Howard W. Cannon (D)

New Hampshire
Norris Cotton (R)
Thomas J. McIntyre (D)[r]

New Jersey
Clifford P. Case (R)[r]
Harrison A. Williams, Jr. (D)

New Mexico
Joseph M. Montoya (D)
Pete V. Domenici (R)[e]

New York
Jacob K. Javits (R)
James L. Buckley (C-R)

North Carolina
Sam J. Ervin, Jr. (D)
Jesse A. Helms (R)[e]

North Dakota
Milton R. Young (R)
Quentin N. Burdick (D)

Ohio
William B. Saxbe (R)
Robert Taft, Jr. (R)

Oklahoma
Henry L. Bellmon (R)
Dewey F. Bartlett (R)[e]

Oregon
Mark O. Hatfield (R)[r]
Robert W. Packwood (R)

Pennsylvania
Hugh Scott (R)
Richard S. Schweiker (R)

Rhode Island
John O. Pastore (D)
Claiborne Pell (D)[r]

South Carolina
Strom Thurmond (R)[r]
Ernest F. Hollings (D)

South Dakota
George S. McGovern (D)
James Abourezk (D)[e]

Tennessee
Howard H. Baker, Jr. (R)[r]
William E. Brock 3d (R)

Texas
John G. Tower (R)[r]
Lloyd M. Bentsen, Jr. (D)

Utah
Wallace F. Bennett (R)
Frank E. Moss (D)

Vermont
George D. Aiken (R)
Robert T. Stafford (R)

Virginia
Harry F. Byrd, Jr. (I-D)
William L. Scott (R)[e]

Washington
Warren G. Magnuson (D)
Henry M. Jackson (D)

West Virginia
Jennings Randolph (D)[r]
Robert C. Byrd (D)

Wisconsin
William Proxmire (D)
Gaylord Nelson (D)

Wyoming
Gale W. McGee (D)
Clifford P. Hansen (R)[e]

[e] elected in 1972
[r] reelected in 1972
C=Conservative
I=Independent

House of Representatives

Alabama
1. Jack Edwards (R)
2. W. L. Dickinson (R)
3. William Nichols (D)
4. Tom Bevill (D)
5. Robert E. Jones (D)
6. J. H. Buchanan, Jr. (R)
7. Walter Flowers (D)

ALASKA
Vacant

ARIZONA
1. J. J. Rhodes (R)
2. M. K. Udall (D)
3. Sam Steiger (R)
4. J. B. Conlan (R)°

ARKANSAS
1. W. V. Alexander, Jr. (D)
2. Wilbur D. Mills (D)
3. J. P. Hammerschmidt (R)
4. Ray Thornton (D)°

CALIFORNIA
1. D. H. Clausen (R)
2. H. T. Johnson (D)
3. J. E. Moss (D)
4. R. L. Leggett (D)
5. Phillip Burton (D)
6. W. S. Mailliard (R)
7. R. V. Dellums (D)
8. F. H. Stark (D)°
9. Don Edwards (D)
10. C. S. Gubser (R)
11. Leo J. Ryan (D)°
12. B. L. Talcott (R)
13. C. M. Teague (R)
14. J. R. Waldie (D)
15. John J. McFall (D)
16. B. F. Sisk (D)
17. P. N. McCloskey, Jr. (R)
18. R. B. Mathias (R)
19. Chet Holifield (D)
20. C. J. Moorhead (R)°
21. A. F. Hawkins (D)
22. J. C. Corman (D)
23. D. M. Clawson (R)
24. J. H. Rousselot (R)
25. C. E. Wiggins (R)
26. T. M. Rees (D)
27. B. M. Goldwater, Jr. (R)
28. Alphonzo Bell (R)
29. G. E. Danielson (D)
30. E. R. Roybal (D)
31. C. H. Wilson (D)
32. Craig Hosmer (R)
33. J. L. Pettis (R)
34. R. T. Hanna (D)
35. G. M. Anderson (D)
36. W. M. Ketchum (R)°
37. Y. B. Burke (D)°
38. G. E. Brown, Jr. (D)°
39. A. J. Hinshaw (R)°
40. Bob Wilson (R)
41. L. Van Deerlin (D)
42. C. W. Burgener (R)°
43. V. V. Veysey (R)

COLORADO
1. P. Schroeder (D)°
2. D. G. Brotzman (R)
3. F. E. Evans (D)
4. J. T. Johnson (R)°
5. W. L. Armstorng (R)°

CONNECTICUT
1. W. R. Cotter (D)
2. R. H. Steele (R)
3. R. N. Giaimo (D)
4. S. B. McKinney (R)
5. R. A. Sarasin (R)°
6. Ella T. Grasso (D)

DELAWARE
P. S. du Pont 4th (R)

FLORIDA
1. R. L. F. Sikes (D)
2. Don Fuqua (D)
3. C. E. Bennett (D)
4. W. V. Chappell, Jr. (D)
5. W. D. Gunter, Jr. (D)°
6. C. W. Young (R)
7. Sam Gibbons (D)
8. J. A. Haley (D)
9. Lou Frey, Jr. (R)
10. L. A. Bafalis (R)°
11. P. G. Rogers (D)
12. J. H. Burke (R)
13. William Lehman (D)°
14. Claude D. Pepper (D)
15. D. B. Fascell (D)

GEORGIA
1. R. B. Ginn (D)°
2. M. Dawson Mathis (D)
3. J. T. Brinkley (D)
4. B. B. Blackburn (R)
5. Andrew Young (D)°
6. J. J. Flynt, Jr. (D)
7. J. W. Davis (D)
8. W. S. Stuckey, Jr. (D)
9. P. M. Landrum (D)
10. R. G. Stephens, Jr. (D)

HAWAII
1. S. M. Matsunaga (D)
2. Patsy T. Mink (D)

IDAHO
1. S. D. Symms (R)°
2. Orval Hansen (R)

ILLINOIS
1. R. H. Metcalfe (D)
2. M. F. Murphy (D)
3. R. P. Hanrahan (R)°
4. E. J. Derwinski (R)
5. J. C. Kluczynski (D)
6. H. R. Collier (R)
7. Vacant
8. D. Rostenkowski (D)
9. S. R. Yates (D)
10. S. H. Young (R)°
11. Frank Annunzio (D)
12. P. M. Crane (R)
13. Robert McClory (R)
14. J. N. Erlenborn (R)
15. L. C. Arends (R)
16. J. B. Anderson (R)
17. G. M. O'Brien (R)°
18. R. H. Michel (R)
19. T. F. Railsback (R)
20. Paul Findley (R)
21. E. R. Madigan (R)°
22. G. E. Shipley (D)
23. C. M. Price (D)
24. K. J. Gray (D)

INDIANA
1. R. J. Madden (D)
2. E. F. Landgrebe (R)
3. John Brademas (D)
4. J. E. Roush (D)
5. E. H. Hillis (R)
6. W. G. Bray (R)
7. J. T. Myers (R)
8. Roger H. Zion (R)
9. Lee H. Hamilton (D)
10. D. W. Dennis (R)
11. W. H. Hudnut 3d (R)°

IOWA
1. E. Mezvinsky (D)°
2. John C. Culver (D)
3. H. R. Gross (R)
4. Neal Smith (D)
5. W. J. Scherle (R)
6. Wiley Mayne (R)

KANSAS
1. K. G. Sebelius (R)
2. W. R. Roy (D)
3. Larry Winn, Jr. (R)
4. G. E. Shriver (R)
5. Joe Skubitz (R)

KENTUCKY
1. F. A. Stubblefield (D)
2. W. H. Natcher (D)
3. R. L. Mazzoli (D)
4. M. G. Snyder (R)
5. Tim Lee Carter (R)
6. J. B. Breckinridge (D)°
7. Carl D. Perkins (D)

LOUISIANA
1. F. E. Hébert (D)
2. Vacant
3. David C. Treen (R)°
4. J. D. Waggonner, Jr. (D)
5. Otto E. Passman (D)
6. J. R. Rarick (D)
7. John B. Breaux (D)°
8. Gillis W. Long (D)°

MAINE
1. Peter N. Kyros (D)
2. W. S. Cohen (R)°

MARYLAND
1. W. O. Mills (R)
2. C. D. Long (D)
3. P. S. Sarbanes (D)
4. M. S. Holt (R)°
5. L. J. Hogan (R)
6. G. E. Byron (D)
7. P. J. Mitchell (D)
8. Gilbert Gude (R)

MASSACHUSETTS
1. Silvio O. Conte (R)
2. E. P. Boland (D)
3. H. D. Donohue (D)
4. R. F. Drinan, S. J. (D)
5. Paul W. Cronin (R)°
6. M. J. Harrington (D)
7. T. H. Macdonald (D)
8. T. P. O'Neil, Jr. (D)
9. J. J. Moakley (I)°
10. M. M. Heckler (R)
11. James A. Burke (D)
12. Gerry E. Studds (D)°

MICHIGAN
1. J. Conyers, Jr. (D)
2. Marvin L. Esch (R)
3. Garry Brown (R)
4. E. Hutchinson (R)
5. Gerald R. Ford (R)
6. C. E. Chamberlain (R)
7. D. W. Riegle, Jr. (R)
8. James Harvey (R)
9. G. A. Vander Jagt (R)
10. E. A. Cederberg (R)
11. P. E. Ruppe (R)
12. J. G. O'Hara (D)
13. C. C. Diggs, Jr. (D)
14. L. N. Nedzi (D)
15. W. D. Ford (D)
16. J. D. Dingell (D)
17. M. W. Griffiths (D)
18. R. J. Huber (R)°
19. W. S. Broomfield (R)

MINNESOTA
1. Albert H. Quie (R)
2. Ancher Nelsen (R)
3. Bill Frenzel (R)
4. J. E. Karth (D)
5. D. M. Fraser (D)
6. J. M. Zwach (R)
7. Bob S. Bergland (D)
8. John A. Blatnik (D)

MISSISSIPPI
1. J. L. Whitten (D)
2. D. R. Bowen (D)°
3. G. V. Montgomery (D)
4. Thad Cochran (R)°
5. Trent Lott (R)°

MISSOURI
1. William L. Clay (D)
2. J. W. Symington (D)
3. L. K. Sullivan (D)
4. W. J. Randall (D)
5. Richard Bolling (D)

6. Jerry Litton (D)°
7. Gene Taylor (R)°
8. R. H. Ichord (D)
9. W. L. Hungate (D)
10. B. D. Burlison (D)

MONTANA
1. R. G. Shoup (R)
2. John Melcher (D)

NEBRASKA
1. Charles Thone (R)
2. J. Y. McCollister (R)
3. David T. Martin (R)

NEVADA
David Towell (R)°

NEW HAMPSHIRE
1. L. C. Wyman (R)
2. J. C. Cleveland (R)

NEW JERSEY
1. John E. Hunt (R)
2. C. W. Sandman, Jr. (R)
3. James J. Howard (D)
4. F. Thompson, Jr. (D)
5. P. H. B. Frelinghuysen (R)
6. E. B. Forsythe (R)
7. W. B. Widnall (R)
8. R. A. Roe (D)
9. Henry Helstoski (D)
10. P. W. Rodino, Jr. (D)
11. J. G. Minish (D)
12. M. J. Rinaldo (R)°
13. J. J. Maraziti (R)°
14. D. V. Daniels (D)
15. E. J. Patten (D)

NEW MEXICO
1. M. Lujan, Jr. (R)
2. H. L. Runnels (D)

NEW YORK
1. Otis G. Pike (D)
2. J. R. Grover, Jr. (R)
3. A. D. Roncallo (R)°
4. Norman F. Lent (R)
5. J. W. Wydler (R)
6. L. L. Wolff (D)
7. J. P. Addabbo (D)
8. B. S. Rosenthal (D)
9. J. J. Delaney (D)
10. Mario Biaggi (D)
11. F. J. Brasco (D)
12. S. A. Chisholm (D)
13. B. L. Podell (D)
14. J. J. Rooney (D)
15. Hugh L. Carey (D)
16. E. Holtzman (D)°
17. J. M. Murphy (D)
18. E. I. Koch (D)
19. C. B. Rangel (D)
20. Bella S. Abzug (D)
21. H. Badillo (D)
22. J. B. Bingham (D)
23. P. A. Peyser (R)
24. Ogden R. Reid (D)

25. H. Fish, Jr. (R)
26. B. A. Gilman (R)°
27. H. W. Robison (R)
28. S. S. Stratton (D)
29. C. J. King (R)
30. R. C. McEwen (R)
31. D. J. Mitchell (R)°
32. J. M. Hanley (D)
33. W. F. Walsh (R)°
34. Frank Horton (R)
35. B. B. Conable, Jr. (R)
36. H. P. Smith III (R)
37. T. J. Dulski (D)
38. J. F. Kemp (R)
39. J. F. Hastings (R)

NORTH CAROLINA
1. Walter B. Jones (D)
2. L. H. Fountain (D)
3. D. N. Henderson (D)
4. Ike F. Andrews (D)°
5. Wilmer D. Mizell (R)
6. L. R. Preyer (D)
7. C. G. Rose 3d (D)°
8. Earl B. Ruth (R)
9. J. G. Martin (R)°
10. J. T. Broyhill (R)
11. Roy A. Taylor (D)

NORTH DAKOTA
Mark Andrews (R)

OHIO
1. W. J. Keating (R)
2. D. D. Clancy (R)
3. C. W. Whalen, Jr. (R)
4. Tennyson Guyer (R)°
5. D. L. Latta (R)
6. W. H. Harsha (R)
7. C. J. Brown (R)
8. W. E. Powell (R)
9. T. L. Ashley (D)
10. C. E. Miller (R)
11. J. W. Stanton (R)
12. S. L. Devine (R)
13. C. A. Mosher (R)
14. J. F. Seiberling (D)
15. C. P. Wylie (R)
16. R. S. Regula (R)°
17. J. M. Ashbrook (R)
18. Wayne L. Hays (D)
19. C. J. Carney (D)
20. J. V. Stanton (D)
21. Louis Stokes (D)
22. C. A. Vanik (D)
23. W. E. Minshall (R)

OKLAHOMA
1. James R. Jones (D)°
2. C. R. McSpadden (D)°
3. Carl B. Albert (D)
4. Tom Steed (D)
5. John Jarman (D)
6. J. N. H. Camp (R)

OREGON
1. Wendell Wyatt (R)
2. Al Ullman (D)

3. Edith Green (D)
4. John Dellenback (R)

PENNSYLVANIA
1. W. A. Barrett (D)
2. R. N. C. Nix (D)
3. W. J. Green (D)
4. Joshua Eilberg (D)
5. John H. Ware 3d (R)
6. Gus Yatron (D)
7. L. G. Williams (R)
8. E. G. Beister, Jr. (R)
9. E. G. Shuster (R)°
10. J. M. McDade (R)
11. D. J. Flood (D)
12. J. P. Saylor (R)
13. L. Coughlin (R)
14. W. S. Moorhead (D)
15. F. B. Rooney (D)
16. E. D. Eshleman (R)
17. H. T. Schneebeli (R)
18. H. J. Heinz III (R)
19. G. A. Goodling (R)
20. J. M. Gaydos (D)
21. J. H. Dent (D)
22. T. E. Morgan (D)
23. A. W. Johnson (R)
24. J. P. Vigorito (D)
25. F. M. Clark (D)

RHODE ISLAND
1. F. J. St. Germain (D)
2. R. O. Tiernan (D)

SOUTH CAROLINA
1. M. J. Davis (D)
2. Floyd D. Spence (R)
3. W. J. B. Dorn (D)
4. J. R. Mann (D)
5. T. S. Gettys (D)
6. E. L. Young (R)°

SOUTH DAKOTA
1. F. E. Denholm (D)
2. James Abdnor (R)°

TENNESSEE
1. J. H. Quillen (R)
2. J. J. Duncan (R)
3. LaMar Baker (R)
4. Joe L. Evins (D)
5. Richard H. Fulton (D)
6. R. L. Beard, Jr. (R)°
7. Ed Jones (D)
8. D. H. Kuykendall (R)

TEXAS
1. Wright Patman (D)
2. Charles Wilson (D)°
3. J. M. Collins (R)
4. Ray Roberts (D)
5. Alan Steelman (R)°
6. O. E. Teague (D)
7. Bill Archer (R)
8. Bob Eckhardt (D)

9. Jack Brooks (D)
10. J. J. Pickle (D)
11. W. R. Poage (D)
12. James C. Wright, Jr. (D)
13. Robert D. Price (R)
14. John Young (D)
15. E. de la Garza (D)
16. R. C. White (R)
17. Omar Burleson (D)
18. B. C. Jordan (D)°
19. George H. Mahon (D)
20. H. B. Gonzalez (D)
21. O. C. Fisher (D)
22. Robert R. Casey (D)
23. A. Kazen, Jr. (D)
24. Dale Milford (D)°

UTAH
1. Gunn McKay (D)
2. Wayne Owens (D)°

VERMONT
R. W. Mallary (R)

VIRGINIA
1. T. N. Downing (D)
2. G. W. Whitehurst (R)
3. D. E. Satterfield III (D)
4. R. W. Daniel, Jr. (R)°
5. W. C. Daniel (D)
6. M. C. Butler (R)°
7. J. K. Robinson (R)
8. S. E. Parris (R)°
9. W. C. Wampler (R)
10. Joel T. Broyhill (R)

WASHINGTON
1. J. Hempelmann (D)°
2. Lloyd Meeds (D)
3. J. B. Hansen (D)
4. M. McCormack (D)
5. T. S. Foley (D)
6. F. V. Hicks (D)
7. Brock Adams (D)

WEST VIRGINIA
1. R. H. Mollohan (D)
2. H. O. Staggers (D)
3. John Slack (D)
4. Ken Hechler (D)

WISCONSIN
1. Les Aspin (D)
2. R. W. Kastenmeier (D)
3. V. W. Thomson (R)
4. C. J. Zablocki (D)
5. H. S. Reuss (D)
6. W. A. Steiger (R)
7. D. R. Obey (D)
8. H. V. Froehlich (R)°
9. G. R. Davis (R)

WYOMING
Teno Roncalio (D)

° newly elected in 1972; others reelected

URUGUAY

The Tupamaros, the urban guerrillas who for many years were synonymous with politically inspired terrorism in Latin America, suffered a series of spectacular and unexpected setbacks in 1972.

The turning point came in April, when President Juan Maria Bordaberry, a relatively little known landowner who had been a minister of agriculture before he assumed the presidency the month before, obtained congressional approval for an all-out "war" on the guerrillas by the country's 12,000-man armed forces. The declaration of a "state of internal war" was provoked by the divided guerrilla movement after the more militant wing had gone out into the streets of Montevideo and killed four government servants in one morning. With political liberties suspended, the army was able to round up quickly more than 1,000 guerrillas, or their suspected aides in many walks of life, and to liberate the kidnappers' longest-held victim in Montevideo. The waves of arrests broke up several newly organized rural-area columns of the Tupamaros, who take their name from Tupac Amaru, an 18th-century Indian leader put to death after spearheading a rebellion in Peru against the Spanish colonial authorities.

Disillusionment after four intense years of underground guerrilla life induced some top Tupamaro figures to collaborate with the army, providing vital information and persuading other guerrillas to give up. Arms caches and underground hideouts were discovered month after month, and on Sept. 1 the founder of the movement, Raul Sendic, was captured, seriously wounded.

Sendic, a 47-year-old former middle-class law student who started organizing rural sugar workers in 1962, had previously prophesied to Latin-American left-wing sympathizers that 1972 would show the Tupamaros emerging as a "real alternative" to the power of Uruguay's hitherto ruling class. Instead, President Bordaberry rapidly gained public support for his strong measures. This confirmed the November 1971 election result, which showed that a majority of Uruguayans rejected a violent solution to the country's grave economic crisis and its decline in living standards—the ills on which the guerrilla movement had fed.

On the other hand, the danger to Western-style democracy inherent in the "war" situation became evident in July when several hundred army officers publicly rebuked congress after legislators had expressed unease about mishandling by the services of suspects rounded up in military detention camps. Despite its successes, the government did not believe the guerrilla threat had been eliminated.

RICHARD WIGG
Latin-American Correspondent
The Times, London

VENEZUELA

Politics dominated the news in Venezuela in 1972 as the major political parties selected candidates for the 1973 presidential election. COPEI, the governing Christian Democrats, placed in nomination the name of Lorenzo Fernandez, a 43-year-old former interior minister who enjoyed the full support of incumbent chief executive Rafael Caldera but whose candidacy triggered a revolt by the party's young left-wingers. Democratic Action, the centrist party, which held the most seats in congress in 1972, chose as its standard-bearer Carlos Andres Perez, a 47-year-old former cabinet

Jubilant supporters of Juan Maria Bordaberry parade in downtown Montevideo to celebrate his election as president of Uruguay.

The recently completed Baralt traffic distributor in Caracas testifies to a degree of prosperity in oil-rich Venezuela. Cutbacks by foreign oil concerns nevertheless slowed the economy in 1972.

member who holds the anti-Communist, anti-Christian Democratic, anti-Perez Jimenez views that characterize the mainstream of his party, which hoped to gain backing from the Republican Democratic Union. The left-leaning New Force, a coalition composed of the Communists and the Electoral Movement of the People (MEP), named Jesus Angel Paz Galarraga, secretary-general of the MEP, while the Movement toward Socialism, a "revisionist" Marxist-oriented group, encouraged by poll results that showed that Federal District residents prefer socialism (48 percent) to capitalism (26 percent), advanced the candidacy of Jose Vicente Rangel. Perez appeared to be the early favorite in the contest, from which former dictator Perez Jimenez was expected to be excluded by the major parties.

The campaign was expected to center on economics because growth rates and employment levels have fallen as the production of oil, which accounts for 70 percent of the country's revenue, fell 18.6 percent during the first four months of 1972. The decline resulted from production cutbacks by major foreign petroleum companies in the wake of Venezuela's 1971 oil reversion law, which provides that the Venezuelan Petroleum Corporation, a state monopoly, will take over foreign holdings in about ten years. Despite threats to fine companies whose production does not reach officially designated levels, production was down, and both the U.S. oil companies and U.S. State Department officials emphasized that the United States will depend more in the future on Middle Eastern and Canadian suppliers.

The growing nationalism that has increased tensions between Caracas and Washington was seen in President Caldera's decision not to renew in July a reciprocal trade treaty first signed with the United States in 1939. Caldera's move was designed to belie the argument that his nation's projected entry into the Andean Common Market would give the United States preferred access to this vibrant trading bloc, which embraces Bolivia, Chile, Colombia, Peru and Ecuador. At the same time, Venezuela still hesitated to plunge into the icy waters of economic integration because its manufacturers feared that reduced tariffs would enable foreign products to compete too favorably with notoriously high-priced domestic goods.

As this Andean nation of 11,000,000 persons, fired by nationalism, slowly turned its face from North to South, it began desultory talks with Colombia aimed at settling a long-festering border dispute. Meanwhile, wary of Brazilian efforts to exert influence in Venezuela's backyard, the Caldera regime assumed a more conciliatory attitude toward Guyana, with which it has often clashed over boundaries.

While a mixture of petroleum, economic problems, nationalism and foreign entanglements had produced a heated electoral fight, the elections were expected to take place as scheduled. For the army appeared committed to the institutional system, and the guerrillas, led by Douglas Bravo, had focused their activities mainly in the outlying states of Falcon and Lara.

GEORGE W. GRAYSON
Associate Professor of Government
College of William and Mary

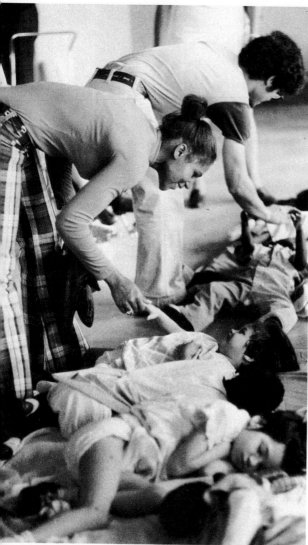

After completing training at Willowbrook State School in Staten Island, N. Y., welfare recipients join the school's staff as mental-therapy aides.

WELFARE

In 1972 the term "welfare" verged on obscenity in much of the United States. The idea of welfare—using taxpayers' money to help the indigent—had never seemed entirely consistent with the puritan ethic, and in recent years, and especially in 1972, the system experienced the most massive criticism it had known since becoming part of Federal law in 1935.

The main result of the criticism was that Congress again failed in 1972 to pass the reform "workfare" legislation requested (but not consistently supported) by President Nixon and actually tightened welfare rules and eligibility requirements. Many states did the same.

Broadly defined, "welfare" in the United States means government aid to the indigent, the handicapped and the disabled. The Social Security Act of 1935 contained the first major welfare legislation enacted on the Federal level, and it directed help to all three categories. The "poor law" sections of the Social Security Act established assistance for the aged and the blind and, most important, "Aid to Families with Dependent Children" (AFDC). The first two programs have virtually escaped criticism, while AFDC has become the target of increasing and roiling debate. Indeed, AFDC to many Americans alone constitutes the hated institution "welfare." The most compelling reason apparently is that the number of blind and handicapped receiving assistance has grown very little over the years.

Until recently the AFDC program also had escaped attention and criticism. The protests began when AFDC rolls mounted, to a point at which, of the 14,000,000 persons on "welfare," about 11,000,000 were on AFDC lists. In the mid-1960's, when the Johnson administration launched its "Great Society" programs and when welfare payments were boosted and eligibility rules somewhat relaxed, there were 4,400,000 AFDC recipients. The cost of the AFDC program subsequently rose from $1,600,000,000 to about $7,900,000,000 in 1972.

The AFDC program has been criticized for being too harsh in administration, too lax on eligibility and too costly. It was precisely for those reasons that President Nixon in 1969 proposed a sweeping reform program under which welfare administration would be taken away from the states and under which poor families, including those not on welfare, would receive an annual guaranteed income. The President proposed $2,400 as a minimum for a family of four; many welfare rights organizations asked $6,500. In any event, the proposals underwent intense and lengthy debate, with the result that the Democratic Congress consistently refused to enact any such legislation. Instead a number of restrictive Federal and state welfare bills with more stringent eligibility requirements was enacted.

For a variety of reasons the country seemed suddenly to have shaken off its liberal concern for the "deserving poor." The middle class increasingly began to view welfare clients as a class of unworthies and as persons whose very

poverty seemed to pose a moral affront to the American way of life. George Sternlieb, director of the Center for Urban Policy Research at Rutgers University, commented that "welfare people are now the closest thing to untouchables that this country has got."

By July 1972, Congress passed its own "workfare" bill, which required welfare recipients—if they were able-bodied and had no children under six years of age—to register for work and face a cutoff of benefits if they refused a job. As the year ended, the workfare idea continued to generate bitterness and confusion; whether it had succeeded in reducing welfare rolls and increasing employment remained very much in doubt.

For recipients, the law meant dealing with two bureaucracies—state employment services as well as state welfare agencies. For administrators, the concept intensified a long-standing antagonism between the welfare agencies, which are generally sympathetic toward the poor, and the relatively hostile employment officials.

The question whether the concept was realistic in a society in which more than five percent of the labor force was unemployed was very much a matter of conjecture. In New York State, for example, a report showed that only one percent of welfare recipients had obtained "workfare" employment lasting more than three months. Compounding the problem was the fact that while the economy recovered in 1972, the employment rate did not. During the year the number of AFDC clients continued to rise.

In 1971 and 1972 about 25 states reduced their outlays for welfare recipients. By the end of 1972 no fewer than 42 states were giving the poor less money than the sum they themselves certified as needed for human survival. Eligibility rules were tightened, not altogether without cause. For evidence showed that there were indeed some welfare clients who should never have been on AFDC rolls in the first place. Some states, including New York and Connecticut, tried to toughen their residency requirements, but in almost all cases these rules were struck down by the courts. One of the severest cutbacks was in the area of so-called "welfare frills," extra money for such things as carfare and education. An effort was also made to remove drug addicts from the welfare rolls.

The actual statistics about welfare recipients were seemingly lost in the reaction. Surveys show that despite popular notions most AFDC adults actually do want jobs, but are unable to get or hold employment because of health, presence of small children or lack of necessary training or job opportunities. Moreover, of the 3,000,000 families getting AFDC help, only one in 20 was headed by a man. The great majority of welfare recipients were women with dependent children and persons who were chronically ill or otherwise unfit for steady employment. Nevertheless, the growing consensus was that welfare had grown beyond its original purposes, and the time had come to think of alternatives.

Just what those alternatives might be, apart from enactment of a guaranteed annual income law, was not certain. One thing was clear: welfare would be debated throughout 1973.

ROBERT W. DIETSCH
Business-Economics Editor
Scripps-Howard Newspapers

WOMEN

Alice Paul, an 87-year-old suffragist, lives on Capitol Hill in a dilapidated 18th century structure that serves as the headquarters for the National Woman's Party which she founded. From this base of operation, she has been lobbying since 1920 to pressure Congress to pass a constitutional amendment guaranteeing the exercise of equal rights for women.

According to some reports, Miss Paul wrote the final version of the amendment that ultimately passed Congress on March 22, 1972. It states that "Equality of rights under the law shall not be denied by the United States or any state on account of sex."

When she received the word of its passage, Miss Paul celebrated the end of her 52-year crusade for constitutional equality with a cup of tea. Then she started to rally support for ratification by the 38 states still required for the amendment's final passage. By November, 21 states had ratified the amendment, and the League of Women Voters was predicting full ratification by May 1973.

Miss Paul's quiet diligence echoed the tone of the entire U.S. women's movement in 1972, a year which witnessed few of the sensational antics that marked the previous year's "women's lib" activities. On the contrary, the year was one in which American women made unostentatious but important strides toward more equal status in politics and under the law.

As the so-called "equal rights amendment" was being maneuvered through the Senate in the fall of 1971, the U.S. Supreme Court took an unprecedented step toward securing full equality for women. On Nov. 22, for the first time in history, the Court applied the "equal protection" clause of the Constitution's 14th amendment to the question of women's rights. In a unanimous 7–0 decision, the Court struck

down an existing Idaho law on the ground that it discriminated against women by specifically preferring a man over an equally qualified woman to administer an estate.

In the 1972 election year substantial numbers of women delegates attended both the Democratic and Republican National Conventions in Miami Beach, Fla. Since the 1968 conventions the Democrats had increased the delegate representation of women by 26.7 percent (to 39.7 percent); the Republicans, by 12.9 percent (to 29.9 percent). The National Women's Political Caucus attended both conventions with the stated goal of writing a strong women's rights plank, including the "right" to abortion, into both party platforms. This movement produced a bitter floor fight for the Democrats.

At 4:30 A.M. on July 12, the Democratic delegates defeated the abortion plank by a margin of only 466 votes—1569.80 to 1103.37. The fight had begun at 2 A.M., with feminist Gloria Steinem and Rep. Bella Abzug (D-NY) leading the pro-abortion faction. A dramatic floor fight ensued, ending with Steinem in tears and Abzug hurling accusations at actress Shirley MacLaine, who spoke out against the minority plank.

Some were shocked and others impressed by the fact that abortion had been discussed openly as a national political issue. Others saw the struggle as the first indication that idealistic feminists could fight within the political system, securing the support of a substantial minority of the electorate for their proposals.

When the Nov. 7 election was over, 14 women had been elected to the House of Representatives. (The highest number ever—20—served in the 1961–63 Congress.) However Sen. Margaret Chase Smith (R-Me.), the nation's only woman Senator and the ranking Republican on the powerful Senate Armed Services Committee, had been defeated, ending her 32-year Congressional career.

Meanwhile, a majority of American women told pollster Louis Harris in 1972 that they disapproved of the "women's lib" movement and were not themselves politically active, but that they did favor efforts to improve women's status in society and thought that the country would benefit if women played a more active role in politics.

Although some 32,000,000 women comprised 40 percent of the U.S. labor force, women still experienced difficulty trying to obtain credit or loans without the support of a husband. Testimony in June before the National Commission on Consumer Finance focused public attention on the nation's credit and financing policies as they affect women. Jorie Lueloff Friedman, an NBC newscaster in Chicago who earns a substantial salary of her own, cited as an example of such discrimination the fact that a store had rejected her charge account application because her new husband was "between jobs," having just lost an election for public office.

Meanwhile, outside the United States, feminists were also making progress, but few gains as substantive as those achieved in the United States were registered. In Spain the parliament voted to end parental control over women when they attained the age of 21. Until that July vote, Spanish women could not leave home without their parents' permission until the age of 25. A group of 300 "new feminists" in Norway, using a loophole in their country's balloting system, managed to elect female majorities to the city councils of more than 50 municipalities.

Women in South America and Africa also began to speak out against the doctrine of male supremacy. In May, 100 Brazilian women attended a feminist conference in Miguel Pereira, a small town whose top officials are all women. One educator attending the conference echoed the sentiments of many Latin American women when she noted, "We're against the machismo (male chauvinism) of the Latin American man, but Brazilian women are too feminine to act like a man and fight it."

A spring seminar at a Johannesburg (South Africa) university prompted one black welfare worker to remark, "The African woman is identifying herself with a worldwide revolt against male-dominated society." In 1971 the Black Sash, a civil rights organization, had petitioned South Africa's parliament on behalf of black women. However, leader Jean Sinclair stated, "This is no women's lib charter. It is the basic human rights African women in South Africa do not have."

In Britain, the London Stock Exchange and Oxford University indicated that they would henceforth accept applications from women. And in October it was reported that roving street gangs composed of women had begun to rob and beat Londoners at night. The viciousness of the so-called "bovver (for 'fighting') birds" prompted one judge to remark. "The girls are even tougher than the boys. It was once assumed that if a man and a woman committed a crime, the woman was under the domination of the man. I think that's rubbish from what I've seen."

JEANNETTE SMYTH
Reporter ("Style" Staff)
The Washington Post

"Ms." magazine takes its title from the indeterminate form of address preferred by many.

Gloria Steinem and Rep. Bella Abzug urged support for women's issues at the convention.

Rep. Shirley Chisholm was the first black woman ever to be put in nomination for the presidency.

YOUTH

For the youth movement the year 1972 was one of gradual clarification of confusing tendencies of past years rather than one of sudden surprises. Above all, to much of society the youth movement began to be less of a threat.

Industrial society, especially in the non-Communist West, has undergone in its temper and spirit a major shift, which began in the mid-1960's and accelerated to a fever pitch from mid-1969 to early 1971. This drift was one away from adherence to liberal thought; from enlightened, rational, optimistic faith in progress through good government, education and technology; and respect for mature adulthood. Youth turned toward a kind of neo-Romanticism, by no means unknown in the past, that emphasized feeling, was pessimistic of "progress," virtually condemned technology, was skeptical of rational principles and fascinated with youth as the measure of all things.

Conflict is particularly pronounced at the onset of a new intellectual period, and this is especially true in colleges and universities, which tend to vibrate with changes in advance of the rest of society. In the late 1960's, therefore, youth leaders were determined to stress their role and attitudes whether or not society as a whole was ready and able to digest what they said and did. In late 1971 and 1972, however, it became increasingly clear that much of society was absorbing and "legitimizing" youth culture so that youth no longer seemed so great a threat. Youth culture has permeated much of Western society as youthfulness has become one the highest of all standards.

In the 1950's and 1960's children and young people had been dressed somewhat like adults and had been expected to imitate the highest ideals of the older generation. In the period 1968–71 youth radically changed its appearance and life-style as a kind of self-assertion, and by 1972 many adults had begun to imitate youth. This could be seen, for example, in the clothing styles of men, which usually change less radically than those of women, and in the length of hair worn by respected men, including policemen. One automobile manufacturer even offered a car whose upholstery resembled blue jeans.

Youth has become less a particular age and more an attitude of mind as the entire period of youth has been extended in both directions. Children are maturing physiologically earlier. On the other hand, young people are staying longer in school, entering the full-time labor market at an older age, thereby remaining part of the youth scene longer. Adults over 30, who obviously wield a greater financial impact than younger citizens, were appealed to with advertisements that coupled images of youth with the "golden oldies," popular tunes of a generation past. The tone of youth seemed less offensive because youthfulness had become so widely accepted. For their part, young people no longer needed to shout to be noticed.

While by no means all young people are college students, much of this youth culture has been centered in colleges and universities. In 1971 and 1972 a less strident tone was manifest on campus. This change seemed to be attributable, first of all, to a much greater pragmatism among students, which some observers have mistakenly called apathy. Many young people grew suspicious of abstract ideologies and became aware that the extreme left bore a striking resemblance to the extreme right. They realized that protest confrontations had become counterproductive because most students resented their abrasive tone, because vast numbers of students and faculty had become "calloused" to them and because the belief in the moral obligation to renew a humane respect for personal dignity had reasserted itself.

College freshmen tended to ignore the ideological arguments of seniors regarding both campus matters and sociopolitical issues. As a result of their high school experiences students were less interested in the fiction of student governments and highly developed power structures and far more interested in the spirit of shared deliberation as the best way to achieve their ends. Instead of undertaking earthshaking projects, they increasingly sought a voice in policy-making on those issues that directly affected them. At some colleges they talked of developing student economic power as a lever. They attempted, for example, at some campuses to gain a major voice in the operation of the food service and dormitories, demanding that strict fiscal accountability be accorded them lest "profits" made at their expense be directed to nonrelated activities.

Students increasingly were concerned about the economic implications of their need to find employment during college and after graduation. They simply had less time for demonstrations.

There was another reason for the less strident tone on campus. Many of the "demands" of youth with regard to academic life had been met to some degree. On many campuses, the curriculum had been revised to permit greater flexibility and to develop interdisciplinary courses. Acadamic regulations had been eased to allow broader student options, to simplify procedures for modifications in programs of

Exuberant youths at a Dallas rally extend their arms in the "one way" sign of the Jesus Movement.

The pervasiveness of jeans as a form of attire for young people, both male and female, tends to blur previously clearcut class distinctions based on external appearance. Unusual designs are often embroidered on the jeans as an expression of individuality.

study and to liberalize grading systems. Students were, moreover, represented on most standing faculty committees and had a voice in the development of policy.

And students were no longer "imprisoned" in college, since attendance no longer served as an "escape" from military service. Students found it easier to transfer to different colleges. And there was a disappearance of the social stigma attached to dropping out and taking a leave from school, so that an individual might complete his education at his own pace.

Although ideological confrontation diminished, the neo-Romantic appeal remained broadly pervasive among youth. The turning away from reason and rational thought toward feeling continued, and also the drift from precision in the written and spoken work to nonverbal communication. The challenge became "How do you feel?" rather than "What do you think?" Movies gained a new interest, as some students made their own films, relying less on the spoken word and more on the evocation of emotion through audiovisual effects.

An interest in personal harmony was reinforced by the call of youth to a reverence for nature and a search for inner fulfillment. (Romanticism traditionally has stressed a worship of nature and viewed man as part of nature rather than as its master.) There was a corresponding interest in organic gardening and

natural foods, although this fascination seemed at times artificial. Similarly, significant numbers of young people could be found hitchhiking across the United States and Europe and camping both individually and in large gatherings devoted to rock music and religious experiences. During 1972 youth demonstrated an interest in religion (generally nondenominational), a fascination with astrology, demonology, yoga, Eastern religions and even Christianity.

One "tool" used for the stimulation of religious feelings and the search for self-knowledge was mild drugs. Youth were wary of drugs like LSD and heroin, but the youth culture spreading through broader segments of society carried with it extended use of marijuana as an escape from the monotony of the assembly line and the pressures of ever-accelerating social change. At the same time there was broadened interest in handicrafts—a rejection of technology, mass production and the "throw-away" philosophy of planned obsolescence in favor of the individual's search for self-fulfillment and retention of "humanity" in a "depersonalized" culture.

The broad acceptance of youth culture by young people also stimulated the evolution of mutual trust, a sense of generation cooperation and a search for "relevant" standards in an increasingly permissive environment. Young

people showed little interest in the study of history because the past seemed to belong to the older generation and appeared to be full of mistakes which had caused a "hangover" in the present. On the other hand, they showed great trust in each other, as exemplified by their willingness to pick up other young hitchhikers and share living accommodations with strangers. The generally easy mobility of youth was facilitated by new freedoms and changed responsibilities brought on by the easy availability of contraceptives. The basic questions, on which a moral decision would be based, were: "Will anyone else be hurt or used?" and "Can I handle the situation, especially if the relationship collapses?" This new tolerance extended to homosexual as well as to heterosexual relationships, but the tolerance had limits. It rejected theft from other young people as a violation of trust.

The activity of youth in the political arena was particularly interesting. Much was made early in 1972 of the possible impact of the youth vote, which potentially made up 14 percent of the U.S. electorate. Although there was early and overwhelming youth support for the presidential candidacy of Sen. George McGovern, polls of youth voting preferences showed disenchantment with him as the campaign ran its course. The election demonstrated that there was no monolithic youth vote that would automatically benefit left-of-center politicians. Young people behaved like other people. Some did not bother to vote, while others refused to be taken for granted and showed mature independence by ticket-splitting on election day. But youth culture had, nevertheless, a perceptible impact on the political climate as a persistent force pressing for peace in Indochina.

In spite of charges by some disappointed political figures that young people had become politically apathetic, and in spite of the fascination with self, youth retained a high degree of social consciousness. Many young people worked for reform of the criminal justice system, protection of the environment, improvement of the quality of life of minority groups in rural and urban poverty areas, the establishment of peace in Indochina and, in general, respect for the rights and needs of the dispossessed and downtrodden. While there was

Curt Gunther, Camera5

Newly enfranchised 18 to 21 year olds register to vote in the Presidential election. Concerted attempts to register new voters had a limited impact on the election, however, since only a relatively low percentage of the newly eligible voters did actually cast their ballots.

some hypocrisy in this humanitarianism and even a class gap between students and other young people, youth culture offered a needed stimulus to society as a whole to look carefully at its priorities.

EDGAR B. SCHICK
Vice President for Academic Affairs
and Dean, St. John Fisher College

YUGOSLAVIA

The year 1972 was one of shake-up in the government and party in Yugoslavia. A country-wide political crisis had been precipitated by the growth of nationalism and separatist feeling in Croatia.

After the shock of the previous year's outburst in Croatia, and its subsequent suppression by President Tito, the League of Communists of Yugoslavia (LCY), at its Belgrade conference of Jan. 25–27, blamed opportunism, statism and accumulation of power by a few individuals for the ideological crisis. The party presidium elected a new executive bureau, reducing its membership from 15 to 8, each republic and autonomous province having one representative. The LCY also banned the simultaneous occupancy of important government and party positions.

Later in the year, Tito moved to curb the Serbian party in order to reduce nationalism there and to reassert his power. In October, Marko Nikezic, the Serbian party chairman, was forced out, as was Mrs. Catinka Perovic, secretary of the Serbian Central Committee. They were accused of liberalism and defiance of central party authority. On Nov. 1, Mirko Tepavac, Yugoslavia's foreign minister, was ousted, and the next day, Koca Popovic resigned from the federal presidency in a personal protest. He was Serbia's most prominent politician and reputedly a liberal.

On the economic front, Tito called for an accelerated drive against "creeping capitalism" and "socialist multimillionaires." In this he encountered the opposition of economic pragmatists who see private enterprise as a job-creating stimulus to the economy. Simultaneously, the government attempted to stabilize prices through control measures. Production, exports and employment continued to grow, exceeding plans. But the government was unsuccessful in curbing consumption and leveling off budgetary and investment expenditures, and it had to introduce new restrictive measures. In May the Iron Gates hydroelectric and navigation project on the Danube, built jointly with Rumania, was formally inaugurated. It will provide 2,160,-000,000 kilowatt-hours annually.

Foreign affairs were marked by continued improvement in Yugoslav relations with other Communist countries. In June, Tito paid an official visit to the Soviet Union, seeking an expansion of Yugoslav-Soviet trade and underlining his hard-line position toward party moderates at home. (Yugoslavia needs raw materials and credits from the U.S.S.R. to set up metallurgical plants; it also seeks increased access to Soviet markets. Moscow wishes closer Yugoslav ties with the Eastern European trade bloc, Comecon.) Tito's visit to Warsaw the same month resulted in plans for further expansion of Yugoslav-Polish trade, which in 1971 had increased by 70 percent. A Yugoslav industrial exhibit in Peking further improved relations with China.

ISTVAN DEAK, Director
Institute on East Central Europe
Columbia University

ZOOS

Sino-American rapprochement in 1972 produced, among other things, the zoo story of the year—an exchange of two American musk-oxen for two Chinese pandas, a striking bargain for each country inasmuch as each acquired in domestic terms a unique commodity in return for a merely rare one. The pandas and musk-oxen were among a number of gifts exchanged during President Nixon's state visit to Peking in February.

Word of the exchange touched off a feverish competition among U.S. zoo officials for the honor of housing the pandas. Leading contenders were Chicago's Brookfield Zoo, which had acquired the country's first giant panda in 1937 and buried its last surviving one in 1953, and the Bronx Zoo in New York City, which had maintained four pandas in the period 1938–51. Tradition, however, favored the National Zoo in Washington, D.C., the repository since 1904 of all presidential animal gifts, and on March 13, President Nixon announced that the pair of pandas would, in fact, go to the zoo in the nation's capital.

On April 6, Dr. Theodore H. Reed, director of the National Zoo, and Day Mount of the U.S. Department of State flew to San Francisco to pick up the chosen musk-oxen, both of which had been raised from birth in the zoo there. Matilda, born in July 1970, stood 4½ feet high at the shoulders and weighed 400 pounds. Milton, a year younger, stood 2½ feet high at the shoulders and weighed 100 pounds. Milton, whose sniffles had delayed the departure for three weeks, had been raised in the children's zoo and was a great favorite with the young.

Hsing-Hsing, the male of the pair of giant pandas sent by China, grasps a bamboo shoot, a plant indigenous to their forested mountain habitat. A member of the raccoon family, the panda's striking markings render it undetectable against its natural background of snow and black rocks.

Smithsonian Institution

The pair were crated separately for their trip to Peking. Bales of alfalfa hay, a month's supply of goat's milk for Milton, sacks of feed and detailed instructions for the care and feeding of musk-oxen were loaded aboard a Military Airlift Command jet for the 28-hour flight with stops en route at Honolulu, Guam and Shanghai.

The plane landed in Peking on April 9, and five days later the giant pandas boarded the same plane for the return flight to Washington. Both Ling-Ling, a female, and Hsing-Hsing, a male, had been captured in the wilds of Szechuan Province. Ling-Ling was estimated to be about 18 months old, and Hsing-Hsing about a year. They, too, were crated separately, in metal containers painted with seven coats of green lacquer and bearing the message:

GIANT PANDAS
Presented from the Peking Revolutionary Committee, The People's Republic of China

At 7 A.M. on April 16 the precious cargo arrived at Andrews Air Force Base a few miles from the center of Washington. On arrival at the zoo the pandas were weighed, Ling-Ling tipping the scales at 136 pounds, and Hsing-Hsing at 74 pounds. Released into their separate cages, they explored the boundaries of their new, air-conditioned habitats and, apparently satisfied with the surroundings, curled up and slept until their breakfast of rice por-

A fleshy pad covering a long wristbone enables Ling-Ling, the female, to clutch her feeding dish in her forepaw. Herbivorous in the natural state, the zoo pandas are served meat as well as apples, carrots and their native bamboo shoots.

ridge and bamboo at 10. Four days later Mrs. Nixon officially accepted the gift in behalf of the people of the United States from Ting Hung, the head of Peking's Bureau of Public Service.

'The rarity of each gift was hardly a matter of conjecture. Aside from Ling-Ling and Hsing-Hsing, the only pandas outside China are a pair in a North Korean zoo and a pair, given to Japan in October, at Ueno Zoo. Moscow's An'-An' and London's Chi-Chi died earlier.

Because of the remoteness of their mountainous native habitat—the southern part of Kansu Province and the central and northern parts of Szechuan—very little is known about the panda's habits in the wild. They are solitary animals, pairing only in the breeding seasons of spring and fall.

The musk-ox, native only to the American Arctic tundra, was once abundant but is now exceedingly rare. It is protected by the governments of Canada and the United States, which has established a herd on Nunivak Island, Alaska. The animal, even in captivity, was unknown in China before Matilda and Milton arrived there.

SYBIL E. HAMLET
Public Information Officer
National Zoological Park
Washington, D.C.

Milton, the male of the pair of musk oxen sent to China by the United States, has a dense coat of long, woolly hair. Native to Arctic America, bands of musk oxen subsist on the tundra's sparse vegetation.

STATISTICAL SUMMARY

WORLD POPULATION

Total: 3.63 Billion

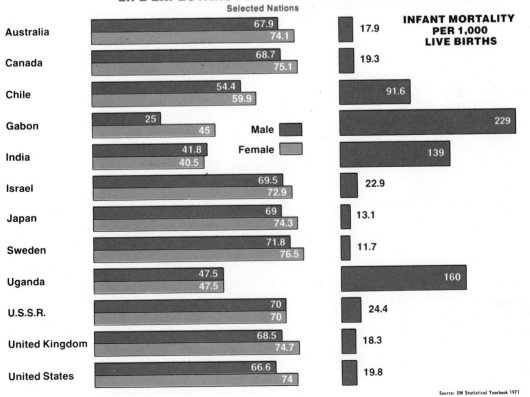

	% OF TOTAL		INCREASE PER YEAR
ASIA	**56.6%**	2.056 Billion	**2.3%**
EUROPE	**12.7%**	462 Million	**0.8%**
AFRICA	**9.5%**	344 Million	**2.6%**
LATIN AMERICA	**7.7%**	283 Million	**2.9%**
USSR	**6.7%**	243 Million	**1.0%**
NORTH AMERICA	**6.3%**	228 Million	**1.2%**
OCEANIA	**0.5%**	19.4 Million	**2.0%**

LIFE EXPECTANCY AND INFANT MORTALITY

Selected Nations

INFANT MORTALITY PER 1,000 LIVE BIRTHS

Male / Female

Nation	Male	Female	Infant Mortality
Australia	67.9	74.1	17.9
Canada	68.7	75.1	19.3
Chile	54.4	59.9	91.6
Gabon	25	45	229
India	41.8	40.5	139
Israel	69.5	72.9	22.9
Japan	69	74.3	13.1
Sweden	71.8	76.5	11.7
Uganda	47.5	47.5	160
U.S.S.R.	70	70	24.4
United Kingdom	68.5	74.7	18.3
United States	66.6	74	19.8

Source: UN Statistical Yearbook 1971

CANADIAN CENSUS

	1966	1971		1966	1971
Alberta	1,463,203	1,627,874	Ontario	6,960,870	7,703,106
British Columbia	1,873,674	2,184,621	Prince Edward Is.	108,535	111,641
Manitoba	963,066	988,247	Quebec	5,780,845	6,027,764
New Brunswick	616,788	634,557	Saskatchewan	955,344	926,242
Newfoundland	493,396	522,104	Yukon Territory	14,382	18,388
Northwest Territories	28,738	34,807	National Total	20,014,880	21,568,311
Nova Scotia	756,039	788,960			

1971 POPULATION OF INCORPORATED CITIES, TOWNS AND VILLAGES OF 5,000 OR MORE

City	Pop.	City	Pop.	City	Pop.
Acton, Ont.	5,031	Cobourg, Ont.	11,282	CMA	222,637
Ajax, Ont.	12,515	Collingwood, Ont.	9,775	Hamilton, Ont.:	
Alma, Que.	22,622	Corner Brook, Nfld.	26,309	City	309,173
Amherst, N.S.	9,966	Cornwall, Ont.	47,116	CMA	498,523
Amherstburg, Ont.	5,169	Côte-St-Luc, Que.	24,375	Hampstead, Que.	7,033
Amos, Que.	6,984	Courtenay, B.C.	7,152	Hanover, Ont.	5,063
Ancienne-Lorette, Que.	8,304	Courville, Que.	6,222	Hauterive, Que.	13,181
Anjou, Que.	33,886	Cowansville, Que.	11,920	Hawkesbury, Ont.	9,276
Antigonish, N.S.	5,489	Cranbrook, B.C.	12,000	Hespeler, Ont.	6,343
Arnprior, Ont.	6,016	Dalhousie, N.B.	6,255	Hull, Que.	63,580
Arvida, Que.	18,448	Dartmouth, N.S.	64,770	Huntsville, Ont.	9,784
Asbestos, Que.	9,749	Dauphin, Man.	8,891	Iberville, Que.	9,331
Aurora, Ont.	13,614	Dawson Creek, B.C.	11,885	Ingersoll, Ont.	7,783
Aylmer, Que.	7,198	Deep River, Ont.	5,671	Iroquois Falls, Ont.	7,271
Bagotville, Que.	6,041	Deux-Montagnes, Que.	8,631	Joliette, Que.	20,127
Baie-Comeau, Que.	12,109	Dolbeau, Que.	7,633	Jonquière, Que.	28,430
Barrie, Ont.	27,676	Dollard-des-Ormeaux, Que.	25,217	Kamloops, B.C.	26,168
Bathurst, N.B.	16,674	Donnacona, Que.	5,940	Kapuskasing, Ont.	12,834
Beaconsfield, Que.	19,389	Dorion, Que.	6,209	Kelowna, B.C.	19,412
Beauharnois, Que.	8,121	Dorval, Que.	20,469	Kenogami, Que.	10,970
Beauport, Que.	14,681	Drumheller, Alta.	5,446	Kenora, Ont.	10,952
Becancour, Que.	8,182	Drummondville, Que.	31,813	Kentville, N.S.	5,198
Belleville, Ont.	35,128	Drummondville-Sud, Que.	8,989	Kimberley, B.C.	7,641
Beloeil, Que.	12,274	Dryden, Ont.	6,939	Kingston, Ont.	59,047
Blainville, Que.	9,630	Dundas, Ont.	17,208	Kitchener, Ont.:	
Boucherville, Que.	19,997	Dunnville, Ont.	5,576	City	111,804
Bowmanville, Ont.	8,947	East Kildonan, Man.	30,152	CMA	226,846
Bracebridge, Ont.	6,903	Edmonton, Alta.:		Lachine, Que.	44,423
Brampton, Ont.	41,211	City	438,152	Lachute, Que.	11,813
Brandon, Man.	31,150	CMA	495,702	Lac-Mégantic, Que.	6,770
Brantford, Ont.	64,421	Edmundston, N.B.	12,365	Laflèche, Que.	15,113
Bridgewater, N.S.	5,231	Espanola, Ont.	6,045	La Prairie, Que.	8,309
Brockville, Ont.	19,765	Estevan, Sask.	9,150	La Salle, Que.	72,912
Brossard, Que.	23,452	Farnham, Que.	6,496	La Sarre, Que.	5,185
Buckingham, Que.	7,304	Fergus, Ont.	5,433	La Tuque, Que.	13,099
Burlington, Ont.	87,023	Flin Flon, Man. & Sask.	9,344	Lauzon, Que.	12,809
Calgary, Alta.		Fort Erie, Ont.	23,113	Laval, Que.	228,010
City	403,319	Fort Frances, Ont.	9,947	Leamington, Ont.	10,435
CMA[1]	403,319	Fort McMurray, Alta.	6,847	Le Moyne, Que.	8,194
Campbellton, N.B.	10,335	Fort St. John, B.C.	8,264	Lethbridge, Alta.	41,217
Camrose, Alta.	8,673	Fort Saskatchewan, Alta.	5,726	Lévis, Que.	16,597
Candiac, Que.	5,185	Fredericton, N.B.	24,254	Lincoln, Ont.	14,247
Cap-de-la-Madeleine, Que.	31,463	Galt, Ont.	38,897	Lindsay, Ont.	12,746
Carleton Place, Ont.	5,020	Gananoque, Ont.	5,212	Lloydminster, Sask. & Alta.	8,691
Chambly, Que.	11,469	Gandar, Nfld.	7,748	London, Ont.:	
Channel-Port aux		Gaspé, Que.	17,211	City	223,222
Basques, Nfld.	5,942	Gatineau, Que.	22,321	CMA	286,011
Charlesbourg, Que.	33,443	Georgetown, Ont.	17,053	Longueuil, Que.	97,590
Charlottetown, P.E.I.	19,133	Giffard, Que.	13,135	Loretteville, Que.	11,644
Charny, Que.	5,175	Glace Bay, N.S.	22,440	Magog, Que.	13,281
Chateauguay, Que.	15,797	Goderich, Ont.	6,813	Malartic, Que.	5,347
Chateauguay-Centre, Que.	17,942	Granby, Que.	34,385	Maniwaki, Que.	6,689
Chatham, N.B.	7,833	Grande Prairie, Alta.	13,079	Markham, Ont.	36,684
Chatham, Ont.	35,317	Grand Falls, Nfld.	7,677	Mascouche, Que.	8,812
Chibougamau, Que.	9,701	Grand Mère, Que.	17,137	Matane, Que.	11,841
Chicoutimi-Jonquière, Que.:		Gravenhurst, Ont.	7,133	Medicine Hat, Alta.	26,518
Chicotimi	33,893	Greenfield Park, Que.	15,348	Melville, Sask.	5,375
Jonquière	28,430	Grimsby, Ont.	15,770	Merritt, B.C.	5,289
CMA	133,703	Guelph, Ont.	60,087	Midland, Ont.	10,992
Chicotimi-Nord, Que.	14,086	Haileybury, Ont.	5,280	Milton, Ont.	7,018
Chilliwack, B.C.	9,135	Halifax, N.S.:		Mississauga, Ont.	156,070
Coaticook, Que.	6,569	City	122,035	Moncton, N.B.	47,891

Place	Population
Mont-Joli, Que.	6,698
Mont-Laurier, Que.	8,240
Montmagny, Que.	12,432
Montréal, Que.:	
City	1,214,352
CMA	2,743,208
Montréal-Est, Que.	5,076
Montréal-Nord, Que.	89,139
Montréal-Ouest, Que.	6,368
Mont-Royal, Que.	21,561
Mont-St-Hilaire, Que.	5,758
Moose Jaw, Sask.	31,854
Mount Pearl, Nfld.	7,211
Nanaimo, B.C.	14,948
Nashwaaksis, N.B.	7,353
Nelson, B.C.	9,400
Newcastle, N.B.	6,460
New Glasgow, N.S.	10,849
New Liskeard, Ont.	5,488
Newmarket, Ont.	18,941
New Waterford, N.S.	9,579
New Westminster, B.C.	42,835
Niagara Falls, Ont.	67,163
Niagara-on-the-Lake, Ont.	12,552
Noranda, Que.	10,741
North Battleford, Sask.	12,698
North Bay, Ont.	49,187
North Sydney, N.S.	8,604
North Vancouver, B.C.	31,847
N.-D.-des-Laurentides, Que.	5,080
Oakville, Ont.	61,483
Orangeville, Ont.	8,074
Orillia, Ont.	24,040
Oromocto, N.B.	11,427
Orsainville, Que.	12,520
Oshawa, Ont.	91,587
Ottawa-Hull, Ont.-Que.:	
Ottawa	302,341
Hull	63,580
CMA	602,510
Ontario (part)	453,280
Québec	149,230
Outremont, Que.	28,552
Owen Sound, Ont.	18,469
Paris, Ont.	6,483
Parry Sound, Ont.	5,842
Peace River, Alta.	5,039
Pelham, Ont.	9,997
Pembroke, Ont.	16,544
Penetanguishene, Ont.	5,497
Penticton, B.C.	18,146
Percé, Que.	5,617
Perth, Ont.	5,537
Petawawa, Ont.	5,784
Peterborough, Ont.	58,111
Pierrefonds, Que.	33,010
Pincourt, Que.	5,899
Plessisville, Que.	7,204
Pointe-aux-Trembles, Que.	35,567
Pointe-Claire, Que.	27,303
Pointe-Gatineau, Que.	15,640
Portage la Prairie, Man.	12,950
Port Alberni, B.C.	20,063
Port Alfred, Que.	9,228
Port Colborne, Ont.	21,420
Port Coquitlam, B.C.	19,560
Port Credit, Ont.	9,442
Port Hope, Ont.	8,872
Port Moody, B.C.	10,778
Prescott, Ont.	5,165
Preston, Ont.	16,723
Prince Albert, Sask.	28,464
Prince George, B.C.	33,101
Prince Rupert, B.C.	15,747
Québec, Que.:	
City	186,088
CMA	480,502
Quesnel, B.C.	6,252
Red Deer, Alta.	27,674
Regina, Sask.:	
City	139,469
CMA	140,734
Renfrew, Ont.	9,173
Repentigny, Que.	19,520
Richmond Hill, Ont.	32,384
Rimouski, Que.	26,887
Riverview Heights, N.B.	6,525
Rivière-du-Loup, Que.	12,760
Roberval, Que.	8,330
Rosemère, Que.	6,710
Rouyn, Que.	17,821
Roxboro, Que.	7,633
Ste-Agathe-des-Monts, Que.	5,532
St. Albert, Alta.	11,800
Ste-Anne-des-Monts, Que.	5,546
St-Antoine, Que.	5,831
St. Boniface, Man.	46,714
St-Bruno-de-Montarville, Que.	15,780
St. Catharines-Niagara, Ont.:	
St. Catharines	109,722
Niagara Falls	67,163
CMA	303,429
St-Eustache, Que.	9,479
Ste-Foy, Que.	68,385
St-Georges, Que.	7,554
St-Georges-Ouest, Que.	6,000
St-Hubert, Que.	21,741
St-Hyacinthe, Que.	24,562
St. James-Assiniboia, Man.	71,431
St-Jean, Que.	32,863
St-Jérôme, Que.	26,524
St. John's, Nfld.:	
City	88,102
CMA	131,814
St-Lambert, Que.	18,616
St-Laurent, Que.	62,955
St-Léonard, Que.	52,040
St-Pierre, Que.	6,801
St-Romuald-d'Etchemin, Que.	8,394
Ste-Scholastique, Que.	14,787
Ste-Thérèse, Que.	17,175
Ste-Thérèse-Ouest, Que.	7,278
St. Thomas, Ont.	25,545
St. Vital, Man.	32,963
Saint John, N.B.:	
City	89,039
CMA	106,744
Sarnia, Ont.	57,644
Saskatoon, Sask.:	
City	126,449
CMA	126,449
Sault Ste. Marie, Ont.	80,332
Selkirk, Man.	9,331
Sept-Îles, Que.	24,320
Shawinigan, Que.	27,792
Shawinigan-Sud, Que.	11,470
Sherbrooke, Que.	80,711
Sillery, Que.	13,932
Simcoe, Ont.	10,793
Smiths Falls, Ont.	9,585
Sorel, Que.	19,347
Springhill, N.S.	5,262
Steinbach, Man.	5,197
Stellarton, N.S.	5,357
Stephenville, Nfld.	7,770
Stoney Creek, Ont.	8,380
Stratford, Ont.	24,508
Strathroy, Ont.	6,592
Streetsville, Ont.	6,840
Sturgeon Falls, Ont.	6,662
Sudbury, Ont.:	
City	90,535
CMA	155,424
Summerside, P.E.I.	9,439
Swift Current, Sask.	15,415
Sydney, N.S.	33,230
Sydney Mines, N.S.	8,991
Tecumseh, Ont.	5,165
Terrebonne, Que.	9,212
The Pas, Man.	6,062
Thetford Mines, Que.	22,003
Thompson, Man.	19,001
Thorold, Ont.	15,065
Thunder Bay, Ont.:	
City	108,411
CMA	112,093
Tillsonburg, Ont.	6,,608
Timmins, Ont.	28,542
Toronto, Ont.:	
City	712,786
CMA	2,628,043
Tracy, Que.	11,842
Trail, B.C.	11,149
Transcona, Man.	22,490
Trenton, Ont.	14,589
Trois-Rivières, Que.	55,869
Trois-Rivières-Ouest, Que.	8,057
Truro, N.S.	13,047
Val-d'Or, Que.	17,421
Valleyfield, Que.	30,173
Vancouver, B.C.:	
City	426,256
CMA	1,082,352
Vanier, Ont.	22,477
Vanier, Que.	9,717
Vaughan, Ont.	15,873
Verdun, Que.	74,718
Vernon, B.C.	13,283
Victoria, B.C.:	
City	61,761
CMA	195,800
Victoriaville, Que.	22,047
Wabana, Nfld.	5,421
Wallaceburg, Ont.	10,550
Waterloo, Ont.	36,677
Welland, Ont.	44,397
West Kildonan, Man.	23,959
Westmount, Que.	23,606
Wetaskiwin, Alta.	6,267
Weyburn, Sask.	8,815
Whitby, Ont.	25,324
Whitchurch-Stouffville, Ont.	11,262
Whitehorse, Yukon	11,217
White Rock, B.C.	10,349
Windsor, Nfld.	6,644
Windsor, Ont.:	
City	203,300
CMA	258,643
Windsor, Que.	6,023
Winnipeg, Man.:	
City	246,246
CMA	540,262
Woodstock, Ont.	26,173
Yarmouth, N.S.	8,516
Yellowknife, N.W.T.	6,122
Yorkton, Sask.	13,430

1 CMA—Census Metropolitan Area

NATIONS OF THE WORLD

NAME & REGION	CAPITAL	AREA in sq. mi.	POPULA-TION in millions	G.N.P. millions of U.S. $	PER CAPITA INCOME in U.S. $	CONSUMER PRICE INDEX 1963=100
AFGHANISTAN, Cen. Asia	Kabul	250,000	17.9	1.6	57	
ALBANIA, S.E. Europe	Tirana	11,100	2.3	1,000		
ALGERIA, N. Africa	Algiers	919,593	15	4,660	251	103.5
ARGENTINA, S. America	Buenos Aires	1,072,158	25	31,400	914	512
AUSTRALIA, S.W. Pacific	Canberra	2,967,909	13	43,210	2,434	131.6
AUSTRIA, Cen. Europe	Vienna	32,374	7.5	16,756	1,728	134.1
BAHRAIN, Middle East	Manama	231	0.2			
BANGLADESH, S. Cen. Asia	Dacca	55,126	79.6			
BARBADOS, Caribbean	Bridgetown	166	0.3	160	399	
BELGIUM, W. Europe	Brussels	11,781	9.8	26,000	2,406	134.3
BHUTAN, Cen. Asia	Thimphu	18,000	0.9		54	
BOLIVIA, S. America	La Paz	424,163	4.9	1,060	180	151
BOTSWANA, S. Africa	Gaborone	231,804	0.7	66	97	
BRAZIL, S. America	Brásilia	3,286,478	95.408	40,100	341	1,268
BULGARIA, S.E. Europe	Sofia	42,823	8.7	9,360		
BURMA, S.E. Asia	Rangoon	261,789	29.1	3,500	75	
BURUNDI, E. Africa	Usumbura	10,747	3.8	230	44	118.2
CAMBODIA (KHMER REPUBLIC) S.E. Asia	Pnompenh	69,898	6.701	1,500	117	227
CAMEROUN, W. Africa	Yaoundé	183,569	5.836	1,060	120	107
CANADA, N. America	Ottawa	3,851,809	22.2	95,570	3,214	129.5
CENTRAL AFRICAN REPUBLIC, C. Africa	Bangui	240,535	1.6	200	58	
CEYLON (SRI LANKA) S. Asia	Colombo	25,332	13.2	1,920	150	130.4
CHAD, N. Cen. Africa	Fort-Lamy	495,754	3.9	195.3	90	150.8
CHILE, S. America	Santiago	292,259	10.2	7,050	613	718
CHINA, Far East	Peking	3,691,512	786.1	120,000	95	
COLOMBIA, S. America	Bogota	439,736	22.9	7,050	358	214
CONGO, W. Africa	Brazzaville	132,047	1.0	194	180	123.5
COSTA RICA, C. America	San Jose	19,575	1.9	921	501	119.8
CUBA, Caribbean	Havana	44,218	8.7	4,500		
CYPRUS, Middle East	Nicosia	3,572	0.6	540	802	
CZECHOSLOVAKIA, E. Cen. Europe	Prague	49,370	14.9	32,400		
DAHOMEY, W. Africa	Porto-Novo	43,483	2.8	218	71	
DENMARK, N.W. Europe	Copenhagen	16,629	5.0	17,300	2,875	153.9
DOMINICAN REPUBLIC, Caribbean	Santo Domingo	18,816	4.6	1,600	272	107.6
ECUADOR, S. America	Quito	109,483	6.5	1,500	247	136.6
EGYPT, N. Africa	Cairo	386,660	35.9	6,910	203	
EL SALVADOR, Cen. America	San Salvador	8,260	3.7	105	271	108.3

INDUSTRIAL PRODUCTION INDEX 1963=100	EXPORTS in millions of U.S. $	IMPORTS in millions of U.S. $	LITERACY RATE	ARMED FORCES	HEADS OF STATE AND GOVERNMENT (as of Jan. 15, 1973)
	86	75	10	84,000	Mohammad Zahir Shah, king Mohammed Musa Shafiq, prime minister
195	60	98	71.5	35,000	Enver Hoxha, Communist party secretary Mehmet Shehu, premier
	1,009	1,257	18.8	60,200	Houari Boumedienne, president
185	1,740	1,869	91.4	135,000	Alejandro Agustin Lanusse, president
144	5,072	4,633	99	88,110	Edward Gough Whitlam, prime minister Sir Paul Hasluck, governor general
162	3,169	4,189	99	43,000	Bruno Kreisky, chancellor Franz Jonas, president
			28.6	1,100	Isa bin Sulman al-Khalifa, head of government
					Abu Sayeed Choudhury, president Mujibur Rahman, prime minister
	39	118	98		Errol W. Barrow, prime minister Sir Winston Scott, governor general
140	12,392	12,856	98	90,200	Baudouin I, king Gaston Eyskens, premier
	92	84	5		Jigme Singye Wangchuk, king
	227	159	40	21,800	Hugo Banzer Suarez, president
			32.9		Sir Seretse Khama, president
117	3,904	3,696	61.1	198,000	Emilio Garrastazu Medici, president
237	2,182	2,119	90.2	146,000	Todor Zhivkov, Communist party secretary Stanko Todorov, premier
	127	135	· 57.7	148,000	Ne Win, prime minister
	19	30	23		Michel Micombero, president Albin Nyamoya, premier
	15	78	41	205,200	Lon Nol, president Hang Thun Hak, premier
	206	250	6	4,350	Ahmadou Ahidjo, president
159	17,573	15,458	98	84,000	Pierre Elliott Trudeau, prime minister Roland Michener, governor general
	31	34	2.1		Jean Bedel Bokassa, president
	327	334	75.3	12,500	William Gopallawa, president Sirimavo Bandaranaike, premier
	28	62	5.6	2,700	François Tombalbaye, president
	1,247	931	83.6	47,500	Salvador Allende Goossens, president
312	2,364	2,247		2,880,000	Mao Tse-tung, chairman Chou En-lai, premier
139	724	844	72.9	63,200	Misael Pastrana Borrero, president
	31	57	16.5	2,200	Marien Ngouabi, president
	225	350	84.3	None	Jose Figueres Ferrer, president
	1,043	1,300	77.9	108,000	Fidel Castro, premier Osvaldo Dorticos Torrado, president
153	115	263	75.9		Archbishop Makarios III, president
180	4,180	4,010	99	185,000	Gustav Husak, Communist party secretary Ludvik Svoboda, president Lubomir Strougal, premier
	42	76	4.6	2,250	Mathieu Kerekou, president
	3,691	4,615	100	43,400	Margrethe II, queen Anger Jorgensen, premier
	243	311	64.5	15,800	Joaquin Balaguer, president
	238	303	67.3	20,000	Guillermo Rodriguez Lara, president
136	789	890	26.3	325,000	Anwar el-Sadat, president Aziz Sidky, premier
	228	248	49	5,630	Arturo Amando Molina, president

485

NAME & REGION	CAPITAL	AREA in sq. mi.	POPULA-TION in millions	G.N.P. millions of U.S. $	PER CAPITA INCOME in U.S. $	CONSUMER PRICE INDEX 1963=100
EQUATORIAL GUINEA, W. Cen. Africa	Santa Isabel	10,830	0.3	76		
ETHIOPIA, N.E. Africa	Addis Ababa	471,777	26.2	2,550	44	143
FIJI, S. Pacific	Suva	7,055	0.6		238	
FINLAND, N.W. Europe	Helsinki	130,120	4.8	11,200	1,933	
FRANCE, W. Europe	Paris	211,207	51.9	170,000	2,606	138.1
GABON, W. Cen. Africa	Libreville	103,346	0.5	309	688	126.7
GAMBIA, W. Africa	Bathurst	4,361	0.4	46	79	
GERMAN DEMOCRATIC REPUBLIC, N. Cen. Europe	East Berlin	41,610	16.3	35,900		99
GERMANY, FEDERAL REPUBLIC OF, N. Cen. Europe	Bonn	95,743	59.2	210,000	2,698	126.7
GHANA, W. Africa	Accra	92,099	9.6	2,820	222	177
GREECE, S.E. Europe	Athens	50,944	9.0	10,200	891	121
GUATEMALA, Cen. America	Guatemala City	42,042	5.4	1,940	338	106.2
GUINEA, W. Africa	Conakry	94,926	4.1	717	95	
GUYANA, S. America	Georgetown	83,000	0.8	254	295	118.9
HAITI, Caribbean	Port-au-Prince	10,714	5.5	350	74	133.7
HONDURAS, Cen. America	Tegucigalpa	43,277	2.9	716	249	
HUNGARY, E. Europe	Budapest	35,919	10.4	15,600		
ICELAND, N. Atlantic	Reykjavik	39,768	0.2	482	2,155	249
INDIA, S. Cen. Asia	New Delhi	1,261,813	584.8	49,500	88	
INDONESIA, S.E. Asia	Jakarta	575,894	128.7	12,300	107	71,797
IRAN, Middle East	Tehran	636,294	30.2	12,100	341	118.6
IRAQ, Middle East	Baghdad	167,925	10.4	3,660	274	121
IRELAND, W. Europe	Dublin	27,136	3.0	7,200	1,248	157.9
ISRAEL, Middle East	Jerusalem	7,992	3.0	6,200	1,636	154.5
ITALY, W. Europe	Rome	116,303	54.5	103,600	1,587	134.4
IVORY COAST, W. Africa	Abidjan	124,503	4.5	1,574	309	131.4
JAMAICA, Caribbean	Kingston	4,232	2.1	1,178	545	
JAPAN, Far East	Tokyo	143,659	106.0	255,000	1,658	153.2
JORDAN, Middle East	Amman	37,738	2.5	810	280	
KENYA, E. Africa	Nairobi	224,959	11.6	1,650	130	114.9
KOREA, PEOPLE'S DEMOCRATIC REPUBLIC OF, Far East	Pyongyang	46,540	14.7	2,800		
KOREA, REPUBLIC OF, Far East	Seoul	38,922	33.7	8,100	241	205
KUWAIT, Middle East	Kuwait	6,178	0.8	3,565	3,880	
LAOS, S.E. Asia	Vientiane	91,429	3.1	250	61	302
LEBANON, Middle East	Beirut	4,015	3.0	1,610	487	109.4

INDUSTRIAL PRODUCTION INDEX 1963=100	EXPORTS in millions of U.S. $	IMPORTS in millions of U.S. $	LITERACY RATE	ARMED FORCES	HEADS OF STATE AND GOVERNMENT (as of Jan. 15, 1973)
				1,000	Francisco Macías Nguema, president
	126	189	5	44,570	Haile Selassie I, emperor
	68	128			Ratu Kamisese Mara, prime minister Sir Robert Foster, governor general
164	2,357	2,794	99	39,500	Urho K. Kekkonen, president Kalevi Sorsa, premier
160	20,420	21,137	100	500,600	Georges Pompidou, president Pierre Mesmer, premier
	121	80	12		Albert B. Bongo, president
	13	26	10		Sir Dauda K. Jawara, president
160	5,076	4,960	90	131,000	Erich Honecker, Communist party secretary Willi Stoph, premier
157	39,038	34,341	99	467,000	Willy Brandt, chancellor Gustav Heinemann, president
152	322	434	25	18,600	Ignatius K. Acheampong, head of government
217	662	2,098	82	157,000	George Papadopoulos, premier Constantine II, king (in exile)
145	290	297	30	13,200	Carlos Arana Osorio, president
			10	6,100	Sékou Touré, president Lansana Beavogui, premier
	138	132	86	2,200	Forbes Burnham, prime minister Arthur Chung, president
	47	60	10	5,500	Jean-Claude Duvalier, president
	188	194	48	5,725	Oswaldo Lopez Arellano, president
151	2,500	2,990	98	103,000	Janos Kadar, Communist party secretary Jeno Fock, premier
	150	221	100	None	Kristjan Eldjaran, president Olafur Johannesson, prime minister
143	2,051	2,406	29	960,000	Indira Ghandi, prime minister V. V. Giri, president
	1,242	1,173	60	317,000	Suharto, president
299	2,642	1,879	25	191,000	Mohammad Reza Pahlavi, shah Amir Abbas Hoveida, premier
	1,529	694	20	101,800	Ahmad Hassan al-Bakr, president
160	1,315	1,835	99	9,850	Eamon de Valera, president John M. Lynch, prime minister
228	915	1,786	90	300,000	Golda Meir, prime minister Zalman Shazar, president
146	15,111	15,968	93	427,600	Giovanni Leone, president Giulio Andreotti, premier
	456	399	20	3,500	Félix Houphouet-Boigny, president
	332	550	85		Michael N. Manley, prime minister Sir Clifford Campbell, governor general
270	24,019	19,772	98	260,000	Hirohito, emperor Kakuei Tanaka, prime minister
	32	215	30	69,250	Hussein I, king Ahmad al-Lawzi, premier
	219	515	25	6,730	Jomo Kenyatta, prime minister
267				402,500	Kim Il Sung, premier and president
433	1,068	2,394	90	634,750	Park Chung Hee, president Kim Jong Pil, premier
	2,406	650	50	9,200	Sabah al-Salim al-Sabah, head of state Jabir al-Ahmad al-Jabir, prime minister
	7	114	25	74,200	Savang Vatthana, king Souvanna Phouma, premier
	253	706	86	14,250	Suleiman Franjieh, president Saeb Salam, premier

NAME & REGION	CAPITAL	AREA in sq. mi.	POPULATION in millions	G.N.P. millions of U.S. $	PER CAPITA INCOME in U.S. $	CONSUMER PRICE INDEX 1963=100
LESOTHO, S. Africa	Maseru	11,720	1.1	94	82	
LIBERIA, W. Africa	Monrovia	43,000	1.2	282	181	124.3
LIBYA, N. Africa	Tripoli	679,360	2.0	3,170	1,305	134
LIECHTENSTEIN, W. Europe	Vaduz	61	0.021			
LUXEMBOURG, W. Europe	Luxembourg	999	0.4	1,000	2,162	129.3
MALAGASY REPUBLIC, S.E. Africa	Tananarive	226,657	7.3	887	124	123.2
MALAWI, S.E. Africa	Zomba	45,747	4.7	319	55	
MALAYSIA, S.E. Asia	Kuala Lumpur	128,430	11.4	4,360	302	107.2
MALDIVES, Indian Ocean	Male	115	0.110			
MALI, N.W. Africa	Bamako	478,765	5.3	278	71	
MALTA, Mediterranean	Valletta	122	0.325		635	116.4
MAURITANIA, W. Africa	Nouakchott	397,954	1.2	180	101	
MAURITIUS, Indian Ocean	Port Louis	720	0.9	189	222	120.7
MEXICO, N. America	Mexico City	761,602	54.3	32,000	632	130
MONACO, W. Europe	Monaco	0.4	0.024			
MONGOLIA, E. Cen. Asia	Ulan Bator	604,248	1.283	840		
MOROCCO, N. Africa	Rabat	172,997	16.8	3,450	186	115.3
NAURU, Pacific Ocean	Nauru	8	0.007	24		
NEPAL, S. Cen. Asia	Katmandu	54,362	11.8	885	57	128
NETHERLANDS, N.W. Europe	Amsterdam	15,770	13.3	39,870	2,156	151.7
NEW ZEALAND, S.W. Pacific	Wellington	103,736	3.0	7,470	2,004	150.1
NICARAGUA, Cen. America	Managua	50,193	2.2	880	387	131.2
NIGER, W. Africa	Niamey	489,190	4.1	360	78	125.8
NIGERIA, W. Africa	Lagos	356,668	58	9,900	71	159.1
NORWAY, N. Europe	Oslo	125,181	4	13,090	2,550	149
OMAN, S.W. Asia	Muscat	82,030	0.7		80	
PAKISTAN, S. Asia	Islamabad	310,403	66.9			143.7
PANAMA, Cen. America	Panama City	29,205	1.6	1,014	629	113.3
PARAGUAY, S. America	Asuncion	157,047	2.6	656	230	116
PERU, S. America	Lima	496,223	14.5	6,350	363	
PHILIPPINES, S.E. Asia	Quezon City	115,830	40.8	7,400	342	132.5
POLAND, E. Europe	Warsaw	120,724	33.7	45,300		109.3
PORTUGAL, W. Europe	Lisbon	35,553	9.7	6,250	610	163
QATAR, Middle East	Doha	8,500	0.1	280		
RHODESIA, E. Africa	Salisbury	150,333	5.4	1,440	252	121.5
RUMANIA, E. Europe	Bucharest	91,699	20.8	22,800		103
RWANDA, Cen. Africa	Kigali	10,169	3.8	233	32	
SAUDI ARABIA, Middle East	Riyadh	829,997	8.2	4,300	350	
SENEGAL, W. Africa	Dakar	75,750	4.1	745	190	118.5
SIERRA LEONE, W. Africa	Freetown	27,699	2.8	425	120	140.5

INDUSTRIAL PRODUCTION INDEX 1963=100	EXPORTS in millions of U.S. $	IMPORTS in millions of U.S. $	LITERACY RATE	ARMED FORCES	HEADS OF STATE AND GOVERNMENT (as of Jan. 15, 1973)
			40		Moshoeshoe II, king Leabua Jonathan, prime minister
	222	157	9	4,150	William R. Tolbert, president
	2,695	701	30	25,000	Muammar al-Qaddafi, president Abdul Salam Jallud, premier
				None	Francis Joseph II, prince
126			98	550	Jean, grand duke Pierre Werner, premier
	147	213	30	4,100	Gabriel Ramanantsoa, head of government
	72	109	5	1,100	Hastings K. Banda, president
	1,277	1,108	47	50,500	Abdul Halim Muazzam, paramount ruler Tun Abdul Racik, prime minister
					Ibrahim Nasir, president
	35	55	5	3,650	Moussa Traoré, president
145	45	156	22	None	Dom Mintoff, prime minister Sir Anthony J. Mamo, governor general
	91	57	5	1,400	Moktar O. Daddah, president
	65	83	60	None	Sir Seewoosagur Ramgoolam, prime minister
193	1,471	2,407	70	323,200	Luis Echeverria Alvarez, president
					Rainier III, prince
261			80	29,000	Yumzhagiyn Tsedenbai, Communist party secretary
131	501	698	15	53,500	Hassan II, king Ahmed Osman, premier
			99		Hammer DeRoburt, president
			6	20,000	Birendra Bir Bikram Shah Deva, king Kirti Nidhi Bista, prime minister
188	13,871	15,398	98	122,200	Juliana, queen
156	1,359	1,346	98	12,637	Norman Eric Kirk, prime minister Sir Denis Blundell, governor general
	183	210	50	7,100	Anastasio Somoza Debayle
	38	53	5	2,100	Hamani Diori, president
	1,811	1,510	25	274,000	Yakubu Gowon, head of government
150	2,563	4,083	99	35,900	Olav V, king Lars Korvald, prime minister
				6,000	Qabus ibn Said, sultan
	660	917		395,000	Zulfikar Ali Bhutto, president
	121	391	78	6,000	Omar Torrijos Herrerea, head of government
143	65	70	30	13,700	Alfredo Stroessner, president
	891	743	55	54,000	Juan Velasco Alverado, president
150	1,122	1,330	80	31,000	Ferdinand E. Marcos, president
193	3,872	4,038	98	274,000	Edward Gierek, Communist party secretary Piotr Jaroszewicz, premier
172	1,052	1,823	65	218,000	Marcello Caetano, premier Americo Thomaz, president
				1,800	Khalifa bin Hamad al-Thani, head of government
167	388	395		4,700	Ian D. Smith, prime minister Clifford Dupont, president
229	1,851	1,960	95	179,000	Nicolae Ceausescu, Communist party secretary Ion Gheorghe Maurer, premier
	22	33	10	2,750	Grégoire Kayibanda, president
	2,423	692	15	40,500	Faisal ibn Abdul Aziz, king
128	125	218	10	5,900	Léopold Senghor, president Abdou Diouf, prime minister
	97	113	10		Siaka P. Stevens, president Sorie I. Koroma, prime minister

NAME & REGION	CAPITAL	AREA in sq. mi.	POPULA- TION in millions	G.N.P. millions of U.S. $	PER CAPITA INCOME in U.S. $	CONSUMER PRICE INDEX 1963=100
SINGAPORE, S.E. Asia	Singapore	224	2.2	2,500	921	110.2
SOMALIA, E. Africa	Mogadishu	246,200	2.9	180	65	
SOUTH AFRICA, S. Africa	Pretoria Capetown	471,444	21.1	18,400	728	133.1
SPAIN, W. Europe	Madrid	194,884	33.9	37,100	889	167.9
SUDAN, N.E. Africa	Khartoum	967,497	16.8	1,830	104	
SWAZILAND, S. Africa	Mbabane	6,704	0.4	90	152	
SWEDEN, N. Europe	Stockholm	173,649	8.2	32,560	3,695	145
SWITZERLAND, W. Europe	Bern	15,941	6.4	24,500	2,895	134.6
SYRIA, Middle East	Damascus	71,498	6.6	1,800	244	126.5
TAIWAN, Far East	Taipei	13,885	14.3	6,100	364	124
TANZANIA, E. Africa	Dar es Salaam	364,898	14.0	1,300	91	130
THAILAND, S.E. Asia	Bangkok	198,456	38.6	6,600	169	119
TOGO, W. Africa	Lomé	21,622	2.0	267	79	119.6
TONGA, S.W. Pacific	Nuku'alofa	270	0.09			
TRINIDAD AND TOBAGO, Caribbean	Port of Spain	1,980	1.1	836	682	128.4
TUNISIA, N. Africa	Tunis	63,378	5.4	1,330	215	135.4
TURKEY, S.W. Asia	Ankara	301,381	37.6	13,400	362	156
UGANDA, E. Africa	Kampala	91,134	9.1	1,060	68	176
U.S.S.R., Eurasia	Moscow	8,649,512	248.0	536,000		98
UNITED ARAB EMIRATES, S.W. Asia	Abu Dhabi	32,278	0.2			
UNITED KINGDOM, W. Europe	London	94,216	56.6	130,000	1,993	148.1
UNITED STATES, N. America	Washington	3,615,123	209.2	1,164,000	4,274	132.3
UPPER VOLTA, W. Africa	Ouagadougou	105,869	5.6	305	45	
URUGUAY, S. America	Montevideo	68,536	3.0	2,400	773	2,876
VENEZUELA, S. America	Caracas	352,143	11.5	11,300	837	115
VIETNAM, DEMOCRATIC REPUBLIC OF, S.E. Asia	Hanoi	61,294	22.0			
VIETNAM, REPUBLIC OF, S.E. Asia	Saigon	67,108	18.7	4,700	181	698
WESTERN SAMOA, S.W. Pacific	Apia	1,097	0.143			120
YEMEN ARAB REPUBLIC, Middle East	Sana	75,290	6.1	460	50	
YEMEN, PEOPLE'S RE- PUBLIC OF, Middle East	Medina al-Shaab	112,000	1.4	140	166	
YUGOSLAVIA, S. Europe	Belgrade	98,766	21.0	12,600		286
ZAIRE, S. Cen. Africa	Kinshasa	905,566	18.3	1,900	65	400
ZAMBIA, Cen. Africa	Lusaka	290,585	4.6	1,500	375	146

all figures are latest annual figures available

INDUSTRIAL PRODUCTION INDEX 1963=100	EXPORTS in millions of U.S. $	IMPORTS in millions of U.S. $	LITERACY RATE	ARMED FORCES	HEADS OF STATE AND GOVERNMENT (as of Jan. 15, 1973)
	1,755	2,828	75	17,100	Lee Kuan Yew, prime minister Benjamin H. Shears, president
	35	63	5	13,500	Mohammad Siad Barre, head of government
	2,186	4,039		109,300	Balthazar J. Vorster, prime minister J. J. Fouché, president
213	2,938	4,936	92	301,000	Francisco Franco, head of government
	328	331	10	36,300	Gaafar al-Nimeiry, president
			25		Sobuza II, king Makhosini Dlamini, prime minister
151	7,478	7,091	99	750,000	Gustaf VI Adolf, king Olof Palme, prime minister
146	5,726	7,207	100	600,000	Roger Bonvin, president
171	195	438	40	111,750	Hafez al-Assad, president Abdel al-Rahman Khalafawi, premier
121			80	500,000	Chiang Kai-shek, president Chiang Ching-kuo, premier
	251	338	15	11,100	Julius K. Nyerere, president
	834	1,287	70	150,000	Bhumibol Adulyadej, king Thanom Kittikachorn, president
	49	70	10		Etienne Eyadema, president
					Taufa'ahau Tupou IV, king Prince Tu'ipelehake, prime minister
	519	656	80		Eric Williams, prime minister Sir Solomon Hochoy, governor general
133	216	342	25	24,000	Habib Bourguiba, president Hedi Nouira, prime minister
	677	1,088	55	449,000	Cevdet Sunay, president Ferit Melen, premier
	235	191	25	12,600	Idi Amin, president
189	31,000	31,700	98	3,375,000	Leonid I. Brezhnev, Communist party secretary Aleksei N. Kosygin, premier Nikolai V. Podgorny, president of presidium
				8,250	Zayd ben Sultan, president
125	22,353	23,944	99	372,331	Elizabeth II, queen Edward Heath, prime minister
140	42,770	45,459	98	2,391,000	Richard M. Nixon, president
	16	50	5		Sangoulé Lamizana, president Gérard Kango Ouedraogo, prime minister
121	206	222	91	15,800	Juan M. Bordaberry, president
127	3,127	1,931	90	33,500	Rafael Caldera, president
			65	513,250	Le Duan, Communist party secretary Ton Duc Thang, president Pham Van Dong, premier
216	4	255	50	503,000	Nguyen Van Thieu, president Tran Thien Khiem, premier
	6	13	90		Malietoa Tanumafili II, head of state Tupua Tamasese Lealofi IV prime minister
	13	143	15		Abdul Rahman al-Iryani, head of state Abdullah al-Hagri, premier
	105	158	10		Salem Ali Rubaya, head of state Ali Masir Mohammad, prime minister
186	1,837	3,298	80	229,000	Josip Broz, called Tito, president Dzemal Bijedic, premier
	781	533	58	50,000	Mobutu Sese Seko, president
127	679	553	15	5,700	Kenneth D. Kaunda, president

WORLD PRODUCTION OF MAJOR MINERALS[1]

Aluminum (Thousands of metric tons)

	1970	1971
United States	3,607.0	3,561.0
USSR[2]	1,100.0	1,180.0
Canada	972.0	1,002.0
Japan	733.0	893.0
Norway	529.8	529.0
West Germany	309.0	428.0
France	381.0	384.0
Australia	204.1	223.0
India	161.5	178.0
China	130.0	140.0
Spain	115.2	127.0
Italy	146.0	120.0
Netherlands	75.0	117.0
Greece	87.1	116.0
Ghana	113.4	111.0
Rumania	101.6	[2]110.0
Poland	98.9	100.0
Switzerland	91.6	94.0
Austria	89.8	91.0
Sweden	66.2	76.0
Hungary	66.2	67.0
Surinam	55.0	60.0
Cameroon	52.0	51.0
Total (est.)	9,645.0	10,250.0

Antimony (Metric tons)

	1970	1971
South Africa	17,370	14,246
China[2]	12,000	12,000
Bolivia	11,766	11,667
USSR[2]	6,700	6,900
Mexico	4,468	[2]3,200
Turkey	2,770	[2]2,800
Yugoslavia	2,900	[2]2,600
Thailand	2,357	2,294
Morocco	1,973	1,920
Italy	1,299	1,275
Australia	909	1,149
United States	1,025	930
Peru	599	[2]600
Czechoslovakia[2]	600	600
Austria	610	467
Total (est.)	68,841	63,747

Asbestos (Thousands of metric tons)

	1970	1971
Canada	1,507.4	1,482.9
USSR[2]	1,065.0	1,150.0
South Africa	287.4	319.3
China[2]	170.0	160.0
Italy	118.5	119.5
United States	113.7	118.7
Rhodesia[2]	80.0	80.0
Total (est.)	3,486.0	3,581.1

Barite (Thousands of metric tons)

	1970	1971
United States	774.9	748.4
West Germany	412.6	408.9
USSR[2]	284.9	299.4
Mexico	319.1	279.7
Italy	217.3	201.5
Ireland	[2]160.6	[2]160.6
China[2]	150.0	139.7
Peru	130.0	[2]129.7
Canada	133.6	124.3
North Korea[2]	120.0	120.0
Rumania[2]	116.5	116.1
France	105.0	[2]105.2
Greece	54.2	98.9
Spain	84.6	85.3
Morocco	84.8	84.5
Yugoslavia	79.7	79.9
India	71.9	61.6
Iran	60.2	[2]59.9
Japan	66.0	57.9
Poland[2]	50.0	55.3
Total (est.)	3,750.3	3,767.2

Bauxite (Thousands of metric tons)

	1970	1971
Jamaica	12,009.7	12,766.7
Australia	9,387.3	12,541.1
Surinam	5,341.4	[2]6,260.9
USSR[2]	4,267.4	4,470.6
Guyana[2]	4,144.5	3,817.3
France	3,051.2	3,115.2
Greece	2,278.0	3,087.8
Guinea	[2]2,641.7	[2]2,641.7
Hungary	2,021.9	2,090.0
United States	2,115.4	2,019.9
Yugoslavia	2,099.2	1,958.9
India	1,359.5	1,436.7
Dominican Rep.	1,066.9	1,311.7
Indonesia	1,229.4	1,237.5
Malaysia	1,139.0	977.4
Haiti	631.0	643.2
Sierra Leone	439.9	590.3
China[2]	497.9	548.7
Brazil	499.9	[2]499.9
Ghana	350.0	329.2
Total (est.)	57,163.0	62,975.8

Cement (Millions of metric tons)

	1970	1971
USSR[2]	95.20	100.30
United States	69.05	72.86
Cement (cont'd)		
Japan	57.19	53.75
West Germany	38.32	32.69
Italy	33.12	31.73
France	28.52	28.95
United Kingdom	17.05	17.90
Spain	16.54	16.99
India	13.54	14.89
Poland	12.18	13.08
China[2]	10.00	12.01
Brazil	9.00	9.80
Canada	7.21	8.65
Rumania	8.13	8.23
East Germany	7.99	[2]8.00
Turkey	6.37	7.54
Mexico	7.27	7.36
Czechoslovakia	7.40	7.27
Belgium	6.73	6.93
South Korea	5.82	6.87
South Africa	5.75	5.86
Total (est.)	571.96	590.22

Chromite (Thousands of metric tons)

	1970	1971
USSR[2]	1,750.0	1,800.0
South Africa	1,427.3	1,644.2
Turkey[2]	518.8	603.4
Albania	468.0	[2]600.0
Philippines	566.4	432.2
Rhodesia[2]	360.0	360.0
India	270.9	261.1
Iran[2]	200.0	200.0
Malagasy Rep.	[3]130.3	[2]140.0
Finland	120.5	112.0
Cyprus	33.3	40.6
Yugoslavia	40.6	34.3
Japan	33.0	31.6
Sudan	47.1	21.1
Total (est.)	6,049.0	6,357.4

Coal (Millions of metric tons)

	1970	1971
USSR	616.3	[2]633.9
United States	555.8	508.8
China[2]	382.8	410.0
East Germany	261.9	[2]266.1
West Germany	219.7	215.3
Poland	172.9	180.0
United Kingdom	138.2	[2]146.6
Czechoslovakia	109.8	113.0
India	77.2	72.8
Australia	73.4	72.3
South Africa	54.5	58.6
France	40.1	[2]35.0
Japan	39.7	33.6
Yugoslavia	28.4	30.9
North Korea	27.5	30.5
Hungary	27.8	27.4
Bulgaria	29.3	27.0
Total (est.)	2,809.4	2,821.7

Copper (mine) (Thousands of metric tons)

	1970	1971
United States	1,560.0	1,381.0
Chile	710.7	718.0
Canada	610.3	653.1
Zambia	684.1	652.0
USSR[2,4]	570.0	620.0
Zaïre	385.7	407.0
Peru	220.2	213.0
Philippines	160.3	208.3
Australia	157.8	177.0
South Africa	149.2	157.5
Japan	119.5	121.0
China[2]	100.0	100.0
Yugoslavia	90.8	94.4
Poland[2]	72.0	90.0
Mexico	61.0	63.2
Bulgaria	43.1	45.0
S. West Africa	31.4	32.0
Rhodesia	26.5	29.3
Finland	30.9	28.5
Sweden	26.3	27.5
Norway	19.9	22.5
Turkey	27.2	19.4
Cyprus	18.2	18.6
Uganda	19.2	17.1
Total (est.)	6,017.7	6,049.6

Diamonds (Thousands of carats)

	1970	1971
Zaïre	14,087	[2]13,700
USSR[2]	7,850	8,800
South Africa	8,112	7,031
Ghana	2,550	2,562
Angola	2,396	[2]2,167
Sierra Leone	1,955	1,935
S. West Africa	1,865	[2]1,900
Tanzania	708	[3]803
Liberia[3]	[3]812	739
Venezuela[2]	500	[2]500
Central African Republic	482	467
Total (est.)	42,586	42,189

Fluorspar (Thousands of metric tons)

	1970	1971
Mexico	978.5	1,181.0
Thailand	318.2	427.3
USSR[2]	408.2	417.3
Spain	341.7	399.9
France	290.3	299.4
Italy	289.3	291.0
China[2]	272.2	254.0
United States	244.2	247.0
United Kingdom	193.3	244.9
South Africa	173.0	239.0
Canada	124.1	72.6
Total (est.)	4,170.3	4,638.0

Gas (natural) (Billions of cubic feet)

	1970	1971
United States	23,786.5	24,104.0
USSR[2]	7,520.0	7,900.0
Canada	2,624.2	2,825.3
Venezuela	1,710.2	1,680.3
Netherlands	1,118.4	1,546.7
Iran	1,094.2	1,305.2
Rumania	875.4	935.3
Saudi Arabia	710.9	[2]915.0
Mexico	665.0	633.4
Libya	683.9	556.5
Total (est.)	46,454.5	49,014.3

Gold (Millions of troy ounces)

	1970	1971
South Africa	32.16	31.39
USSR[2]	6.50	6.70
Canada	2.40	2.24
United States	1.74	1.50
Ghana	0.70	0.70
Australia	0.62	0.67
Philippines	0.60	0.64
Rhodesia[2]	0.50	0.50
Japan	0.26	0.25
Colombia	0.22	0.19
Zaïre	0.18	0.18
Brazil	0.18	0.16
Mexico	0.20	0.15
Total (est.)	47.53	46.51

Graphite (Thousands of metric tons)

	1970	1971
USSR[2]	75.3	79.8
North Korea[2]	75.3	75.3
South Korea	59.5	72.5
Mexico	55.6	50.9
China[2]	30.0	30.0
Austria	27.7	21.4
Malagasy	19.9	20.1
West Germany	16.4	[2]17.2
Norway	10.4	8.3
Total (est.)	386.8	389.3

Gypsum (Thousands of metric tons)

	1970	1971
United States	8,560.2	9,448.3
Canada	5,723.1	6,168.9
France	6,088.2	5,111.5
USSR	[2]4,717.4	[2]4,717.4
Spain	4,228.0	[2]4,200.3
United Kingdom	4,275.5	4,173.0
Italy[2]	3,300.0	[2]3,501.7
Iran	2,100.0	[2]2,250.0
West Germany	1,473.0	1,593.3
Mexico	1,290.9	1,298.2
India	920.5	1,070.0
Australia	845.4	[2]919.8
Poland[2]	850.0	850.0
Austria	629.8	593.7
China[2]	550.0	550.0
Japan	538.8	535.9
Total (est.)	51,930.9	53,125.5

Iron Ore (Millions of metric tons)

	1970	1971
USSR	194.2	203.0
United States	91.2	82.1
Australia	51.2	62.1
France	56.8	55.9
China[2]	43.7	54.9
Canada	47.5	44.0
Brazil[2]	40.2	42.7
Sweden	31.8	33.3
India	31.4	32.3
Total (est.)	766.6	785.8

Iron (pig) excluding ferroalloys (Millions of metric tons)

	1970	1971
USSR	84.81	[2]88.30
United States	83.65	73.83
Japan	68.05	72.75
West Germany[5]	33.38	29.78
China[6]	22.00	27.00
France	18.74	17.90
United Kingdom	17.51	15.26
Belgium	10.84	10.40
Italy	8.33	8.54
Czechoslovakia[7]	7.55	7.96
Canada	8.24	7.88
Poland	6.85	[2]7.30
India	7.03	6.56
Australia	6.15	[2]6.13
Spain	4.17	4.83
Brazil	4.20	4.74

WORLD PRODUCTION OF MAJOR MINERALS[1] (Continued)

Iron (pig) (cont'd) (Millions of metric tons)

	1970	1971
Luxembourg	4.81	4.59
Rumania	4.21	4.38
South Africa	3.92	[2]4.01
Netherlands	3.59	3.76
Austria	2.96	2.85
Sweden	2.79	2.76
North Korea[2,6]	2.40	2.50
Mexico	2.26	2.36
East Germany	1.99	2.03
Total (est.)	431.81	430.12

Lead (smelter) (Thousands of metric tons)

	1970	1971
United States	604.8	589.7
USSR[2]	440.0	450.0
Australia	352.6	323.6
Japan	209.0	215.1
Canada	185.6	156.6
Mexico	150.3	136.1
France	119.9	108.3
Bulgaria	98.6	[2]99.8
China[2]	99.8	99.8
Yugoslavia	97.4	99.1
West Germany	112.4	94.9
Belgium	89.4	80.2
Spain	68.7	72.1
Peru	72.0	67.1
North Korea[2]	54.4	63.5
Poland	54.5	60.2
S. West Africa	70.1	58.8
Italy	54.3	48.4
Argentina	38.1	43.5
United Kingdom	43.8	38.6
Rumania[2]	36.3	36.3
Sweden	40.6	32.2
Zambia	27.3	27.7
East Germany[2]	24.5	23.6
Morocco	24.9	18.7
Total (est.)	3,286.1	3,168.1

Magnesium (Thousands of metric tons)

	1970	1971
United States	101.61	112.02
USSR[2]	49.90	51.71
Norway	35.34	36.46
Japan	10.34	9.69
Italy	7.58	[2]7.98
Canada	9.39	6.58
France	4.64	[2]4.72
Total (est.)	222.56	232.97

Manganese Ore (Thousands of metric tons)

	1970	1971
USSR[2]	6,841.1	6,985.3
South Africa	2,679.5	3,236.5
Brazil	1,878.8	2,601.8
Gabon	1,453.0	1,868.6
India	1,651.0	1,779.0
Australia	751.1	1,075.9
China[2]	997.9	997.9
Ghana	405.4	598.6
Zaïre	346.9	387.4
Japan	270.4	285.0
Mexico	273.9	266.9
Hungary	168.8	169.6
Rumania[2]	127.0	127.0
Morocco	112.4	101.5
Italy	50.1	30.6
Total (est.)	18,219.9	20,692.0

Mercury (Thousands of flasks)

	1970	1971
Spain	45.54	67.53
USSR[2]	48.00	50.00
Italy	44.38	42.67
Mexico	30.27	35.39
China[2]	20.00	20.00
Canada	24.40	[2]18.00
United States	27.30	17.63
Yugoslavia	15.46	15.56
Turkey	8.59	[2]9.50
Japan	5.17	[2]5.70
Philippines	4.65	5.02
Peru	3.13	[2]1.80
Total (est.)	283.82	305.72

Molybdenum (Thousands of metric tons)

	1970	1971
United States	50.5	49.7
Canada	15.3	12.8
USSR[2]	7.7	8.0
Chile	5.7	6.3
China[2]	1.5	[8]N.A.
Total (est.)	80.7	78.5

Nickel (Thousands of metric tons)

	1970	1971
Canada	277.5	266.7
USSR[2]	108.9	117.9
New Caledonia	105.4	102.3
Cuba[2]	35.2	36.3

Nickel (cont'd) (Thousands of metric tons)

	1970	1971
Australia	28.9	[2]30.8
Indonesia	18.0	27.0
United States	14.1	14.2
South Africa	11.6	12.8
Total (est.)	629.7	640.5

Petroleum, Crude (Millions of barrels)

	1970	1971
United States	3,517.5	3,453.9
USSR	2,594.6	2,778.3
Saudi Arabia	1,387.3	1,741.5
Iran	1,397.5	1,661.9
Venezuela	1,353.4	1,295.4
Kuwait	1,090.0	1,166.9
Libya	1,209.3	1,007.7
Iraq	569.7	624.3
Nigeria	395.8	558.4
Canada	461.2	495.7
Trucial States	283.5	386.7
Indonesia	311.6	325.7
Algeria	371.8	279.6
China[2]	146.0	186.2
Qatar	132.5	156.9
Mexico	156.5	155.9
Argentina	143.4	154.5
Oman	121.2	107.4
Total (est.)	16,689.6	17,563.2

Phosphate (Thousands of metric tons)

	1970	1971
United States	35,143	35,277
USSR (all forms)	20,808	21,650
Morocco	11,400	12,008
Tunisia	3,016	3,162
Nauru Island[3]	2,114	[2]2,087
South Africa	1,685	1,729
Togo	1,508	1,715
Senegal	1,129	1,545
China[2]	1,179	1,179
North Vietnam (all forms)[2]	1,048	1,143
Christmas Island[3]	1,072	1,089
Israel	1,161	765
UAR	584	[2]744
Jordan	1,200	650
Total (est.)	85,709	87,514

Potash[9] (Thousands of metric tons)

	1970	1971
USSR[2]	4,450	5,350
Canada	3,103	3,513
West Germany	2,645	2,915
East Germany	2,419	[2]2,449
United States	2,476	2,346
France	1,904	[2]1,905
Total (est.)	18,521	20,066

Pyrite[10] (Thousands of metric tons)

	1970	1971
USSR[2]	4,000	2,464
Spain	2,736	2,429
Japan	2,641	2,363
China[2]	2,000	2,000
Italy	1,568	1,518
Finland	963	861
Rumania[2]	807	840
Cyprus	930	781
Norway	747	781
South Africa	868	750
Sweden	575	663
West Germany	554	[2]554
North Korea[2]	500	500
Total (est.)	22,225	19,918

Salt (Millions of metric tons)

	1970	1971
United States	41.60	39.99
China[2]	15.97	14.97
USSR[2]	12.97	12.97
United Kingdom	9.19	[2]9.25
West Germany	10.45	8.41
France	5.48	6.55
India	5.59	5.79
Canada	4.86	4.84
Italy	4.37	[2]4.45
Mexico	4.15	4.36
Netherlands	2.87	3.17
Australia	3.07	[2]3.08
Poland	2.90	2.96
Rumania	2.26	[2]2.27
East Germany	2.18	[2]2.18
Total (est.)	145.50	142.67

Silver (Millions of troy ounces)

	1970	1971
Canada	44.25	45.95
United States	45.01	41.56
USSR[2]	38.00	39.00
Peru	39.84	38.40
Mexico	42.84	36.66
Australia	25.99	21.62
Japan	10.80	11.54
Bolivia	6.82	[2]6.80
Chile	2.39	5.36

Silver (cont'd) (Millions of troy ounces)

	1970	1971
East Germany[2]	4.80	5.00
Sweden	6.11	4.82
Honduras	3.82	3.64
South Africa	3.53	3.38
Yugoslavia	3.42	3.35
Ireland	2.17	[2]2.20
Argentina	2.05	[2]2.05
France	2.28	[2]2.00
Philippines	1.70	1.94
West Germany	1.77	1.80
Zaïre	1.71	1.80
Spain[2]	1.64	1.64
Total (est.)	303.90	294.71

Sulfur (elemental) (Millions of metric tons)

	1970	1971
United States (all forms)	8.67	8.75
Canada (recovered)	4.41	4.89
Poland (Frasch, ore)[2]	2.71	2.82
France (recovered)	1.73	1.81
USSR (all forms)[2]	1.60	1.70
Mexico (all forms)	1.38	1.27
Total (all forms) (est.)	22.10	22.88

Tin (mine) (Thousands of long tons)

	1970	1971
Malaysia	72.6	74.2
USSR[2]	27.0	28.0
Bolivia	28.9	27.4
Thailand	21.4	21.3
China[2]	20.0	20.0
Indonesia	18.8	19.4
Australia	9.4	9.4
Nigeria	7.8	7.0
Zaïre	6.3	[2]6.4
Total (est.)	229.4	229.5

Titanium (Thousands of metric tons)

(ilmenite)	1970	1971
Australia	889.9	814.8
Canada	766.3	775.3
Norway	579.0	641.6
United States	787.4	619.6
Malaysia[3]	192.5	156.0
Finland	151.0	139.5
Total (est.)	3,588.6	3,375.6
(rutile)		
Australia	368.1	366.7
Sierra Leone	44.1	5.2
Total (est.)	417.2	377.8

Tungsten[11] (Metric tons)

	1970	1971
China[2]	7,983	7,983
USSR[2]	6,713	6,985
United States	3,676	3,130
Thailand	711	2,508
North Korea[2]	2,140	2,140
South Korea	2,070	2,059
Bolivia	1,845	1,850
Canada	1,387	1,802
Australia	1,265	1,547
Brazil	1,156	1,398
Portugal	1,425	1,386
Peru	804	770
Japan	677	730
Total (est.)	33,581	36,618

Uranium Oxide (Metric tons)

	1970	1971
United States	11,583	11,709
South Africa	3,737	3,800
Canada	3,723	3,638
France	1,582	1,521
Gabon	377	545
Niger	38	506
Australia[2]	299	272
Total (est.)[12]	21,644	22,300

Zinc (smelter) (Thousands of metric tons)

	1970	1971
United States	796.3	695.3
USSR[2]	610.0	650.5
Japan	676.2	601.1
Canada	417.9	372.0
Australia	260.6	258.7
Poland	209.0	220.0
France	223.7	218.7
Belgium	241.2	206.8
Italy	142.1	138.9
West Germany	150.2	126.4
United Kingdom	146.6	116.5
China[2]	99.8	99.8
North Korea[2]	89.8	99.8
Spain	89.2	89.3
Mexico	80.7	77.9
Bulgaria	76.1	76.0
Total (est.)	4,879.5	4,611.0

[1] Output of countries not individually listed and estimates for other countries are included in world totals. [2] Estimated. [3] Exports. [4] Smelter production. [5] Includes blast furnace ferroalloys except ferromanganese and spiegeleisen. [6] Includes ferroalloys. [7] Includes blast furnace ferroalloys. [8] Not available. [9] Marketable in equivalent K_2O. [10] Gross weight. [11] Contained tungsten (W basis). [12] Excludes all socialist bloc countries.

BRIDGES, DAMS AND TUNNELS

WORLD BRIDGES UNDER CONSTRUCTION OR COMPLETED IN 1972

Name	Location	Type	Length (in ft.)	Date of compl.
Algyöi	Tisza R. near Széged, Hungary	Beam girder	1,608	1974
Bratislava	Danube at Bratislava, Czech.	Cable-stayed	1,416	1972
Brazo Largo	Parana R. at Brazo Largo, Arg.	Cable-stayed	3 mi.	
Burrard Inlet	Vancouver, Canada	Suspension	2,500[1]	
Caronte Viaduct	Etang de Berre, France	Inclined prop	984	
Dent	Dworshak Reservoir, Idaho	Suspension	1,550	1972
Düsseldorf	Rhine at Düsseldorf, W. Germany	Cable-stayed	1,936	
Eurasia	Bosporus at Istanbul, Turkey	Suspension	5,119	1973
Frieden Valley	West Germany	Girder	1,282	
George N. Wade	Susquehanna R. near Harrisburg, Pennsylvania	Girder	5,193	1973
Hooghly River	Calcutta, India	Cable-stayed	2,100	
Houston Ship Channel	Houston, Texas	Suspension	1,230	1973
Huccorgne Valley	Belgium	Cantilever	246	
Humber River	Hull, England	Suspension	4,580[1]	1976
Kingston	Glasgow, Scotland	Cantilever	880	
Köhlbrand	West Germany	Cable-stayed	1,706	
Leblanc-Papineau	Rivière des Prairies at Montreal, Canada	Cable-stayed	1,290	
Loire Estuary	St.-Nazaire, France	Cable-stayed	1,312[1]	
Ludwigshafen	Rhine at Ludwigshafen, W. Germany	Cable-stayed	1,420	
Makung-Yuweng	Taiwan archipelago	Girder	7,100	
Martigues	Near Marseilles, France	Box girder	2,867	1972
Mesopotamia	Parana R. at Corrientes, Arg.	Cable-stayed	5,469	1972
Milwaukee Harbor	Milwaukee, Wisconsin	Tied arch	600[2]	1974
Ohio River	Neville Island, Pennsylvania	Tied arch/girder	4,550	1976
Öland	Kalmarsund at Kalmar, Sweden	Prestressed concrete	19,882	1972
Padre Island	Intracoastal Canal at Corpus Christi, Texas	Prestressed concrete	400	
Rader Insel	Kiel Canal, West Germany	Box girder	4,910	
Rio-Niterói	Guanabara Bay at Rio de Janeiro, Brazil	Continuous box and plate girder	8.5 mi.	1974
Sagami Aqueduct	Sagami R., Japan	Steel arch	2,722	1973
San Diego Bay	San Diego, California	Box girder	1,880	
Santiago River	Guadalajara, Mexico	Inclined prop	984	
South Bonn	Rhine at Bonn, West Germany	Box girder	1,575	
Tennessee River	Near Decatur, Alabama	Plate girder	9,900	1973
Thames River	Near New London, Connecticut	Truss	6,300	1973
Tours	Loire R. at Tours, France	Continuous box and plate girder	1,938	
Uffington	Monongahela R. at Morgantown, West Virginia	Continuous deck truss	1,549	1973
Urato Bay	Kochi, Japan	Concrete box girder	3,000	1972
Yodo River	Osaka, Japan	Cable-stayed	709[1]	
Zarate	Parana R. at Zarate, Argentina	Cable-stayed	3 mi.	

[1] Center span only.
[2] Main arch only.

WORLD DAMS UNDER CONSTRUCTION

Name of Dam	Type	River and Basin	Country	Height Feet	Crest Length Feet	Volume (1,000 C.Y.)	Res. Cap. (1,000 A.F.)
Almendra	A	Tormes-Douro	Spain	649	13,438	3,267	2,025
Auburn	MA	N.F. American-Sacramento	U.S.A.	680	3,500	6,000	2,500

494

Balimela	E	Sileru	India	230	15,200	29,657	3,097
Beas	E	Beas-Indus	India	380	5,000	44,200	6,600
Cabora Basa	A	Zambezi	Portugal	550	994	589	129,389
Castaic	E	Castaic Cr.-Santa Clara	U.S.A.	340	5,200	44,000	350
Charvak	E	Chirchik-Syr Darya	U.S.S.R.	551	2,499	24,975	1,620
Chirkey	A	Sulak-Caspian Sea	U.S.S.R.	764	1,109	1,602	2,252
Cochiti	E	Rio Grande	U.S.A.	251	28,200	41,100	602
Dworshak	G	N.F. Clearwater-Columbia	U.S.A.	717	3,287	6,500	3,453
Emosson	A	Barberine	Switz.	590	1,736	1,400	182
Esmeralda	E	Bota	Colombia	754	919	14,126	661
Gokcekaya	A	Sakarya	Turkey	518	1,529	850	737
Gran Suarna	MA	Navia	Spain	499	1,150	882	567
Idikki	MA	Periyar	India	561	1,201	609	1,182
Ihla Solteria	EG	Parana-Rio de la Plata	Brazil	262	20,300	32,838	17,172
Inguri	A	Inguri	U.S.S.R.	892	2,198	4,967	891
Jaya Kwadi	E	Godavari	India	120	32,493	15,409	2,110
Kanev	E	Dnieper	U.S.S.R.	82	52,950	49,520	2,125
Kapchagay	E	Ili	U.S.S.R.	164	7,741	10,338	22,761
Keban	RG	Firat (Euphrates)	Turkey	679	3,598	19,600	25,110
Krasnoyarsk	G	Yenisei	U.S.S.R.	407	3,493	5,685	59,425
Las Portas	A	Camba	Spain	498	1,587	977	609
Marimbondo	E	Grande	Brazil	295	11,970	24,328	5,184
Mica	R	Columbia	Canada	800	2,600	42,000	20,000
Mratinje	A	Piva-Drina-Danube	Yugo.	722	853	1,019	749
Nagwado	A	Azur-Shinano	Japan	508	1,200	865	100
New Melones	R	Stanislaus-San Joaquin	U.S.A.	625	1,600	15,970	2,400
Nurek	E	Vakhsh	U.S.S.R.	1,017	2,390	70,806	8,424
Reza Shah Kabir	A	Karoun	Iran	656	1,247	......	......
Saratov	E	Volga-Caspian Sea	U.S.S.R.	131	4,130	19,034	10,854
Sayansk	A	Yenisei	U.S.S.R.	774	3,503	11,916	25,353
Tachien	A	Tachia	Taiwan	656	853	940	235
Tarbela	ER	Indus	Pakistan	470	9,000	186,000	11,100
Toktogul	A	Naryn-Syr Darya	U.S.S.R.	705	1,352	3,480	15,800
Ust-Ilim	EG	Angara	U.S.S.R.	344	11,695	17,090	48,100
Zeya	G	Zeya	U.S.S.R.	371	2,312	10,456	55,080

A—arch ER—earth, rockfill R—rockfill C.Y.—cubic yards
E—earthfill G—gravity RG—rockfill gravity A.F.—acre-feet
EG—earthfill gravity

WORLD TUNNELS UNDER CONSTRUCTION OR COMPLETED IN 1972

Name and Location	Type	Length	Remarks
Big Walker Mountain Tunnel, Interstate 77, southwest Virginia	highway	4,229 ft.	Completed in 1972.
East 63d St. Tunnel, New York City	railroad	3,500 ft.	Two levels—one for subway and one for rail—connecting boroughs of Queens and Manhattan.
Hong Kong	highway	5,280 ft.	First road connection between Kowloon on mainland and Hong Kong Island; completed in 1972.
Mersey River Tunnel, Liverpool, England	highway	8,200 ft.	Twin tunnel; to be completed in 1973.
Seikan Tunnel, under Tsugaru Strait, Japan	railroad	33 mi.	Will connect the main island of Honshu with northern island of Hokkaido; will be world's longest rail tunnel.
Straight Creek, Route 70, Colorado	highway	8,148 ft.	Pierces the Continental Divide in the Colorado Rocky Mountains; will be world's highest highway tunnel.
Trans Koolau, north of Honolulu, Hawaii	highway	4,400 ft.	Will carry Interstate H-3 through rugged Koolau Range.

ELECTRICITY PRODUCTION

COUNTRY	1971 PRODUCTION (Million KWH)
ALGERIA	162 (P)[1]
ARGENTINA	1,561 (P)
AUSTRALIA	4,974 (I + P)[2]
AUSTRIA	2,403 (I + P)
BELGIUM	2,766 (I + P)
BRAZIL	4,022 (I + P)
BULGARIA	1,751 (I + P)
BURMA	40 (P)
CAMBODIA	12 (P)
CAMEROUN	97 (P)
CANADA	17,919 (I + P)
CENTRAL AFRICAN REP.	4 (P)
CHAD	4 (P)
CHILE	694 (I + P)
COLOMBIA	674 (P)
CONGO (Brazzaville)	7 (P)
CYPRUS	47 (P)
CZECHO-SLOVAKIA	3,932 (I + P)
DAHOMEY	3 (P)*
DENMARK	1,433 (P)
EL SALVADOR	61 (P)
FINLAND	1,954 (I + P)
FRANCE	12,320 (I + P)
GABON	9 (P)
GERMANY, EAST	5,785 (I + P)
GERMANY, WEST	21,636 (I + P)
GHANA	245 (I + P)
GREECE	884 (P)
GUATEMALA	44 (P)
GUYANA	26 (I + P)
HONG KONG	408 (P)
HUNGARY	1,249 (I + P)
ICELAND	133 (P)
INDIA	4,910 (P)
IRAN	433 (P)
IRELAND	523 (P)
ISRAEL	637 (I + P)
ITALY	10,191 (I + P)
IVORY COAST	50 (P)
JAMAICA	69 (P)
JAPAN	31,593 (I + P)
KENYA	46 (P)
KUWAIT	220 (P)
LAOS	1 (P)
LEBANON	114 (P)
LUXEMBOURG	197 (I + P)
LIBERIA	24 (P)
LIBYA	35 (P)
MALAGASY REP.	16 (P)
MALAWI	12 (P)
MALAYSIA	308 (I + P)
MALI	4 (P)
MALTA	26 (P)
MAURITANIA	6 (P)
MAURITIUS	12 (I + P)
MEXICO	2,574 (I + P)
MOROCCO	174 (P)
MOZAMBIQUE	45 (I + P)
NETHERLANDS	3,742 (I + P)
NEW ZEALAND	1,222 (P)
NIGER	4 (P)
NIGERIA	151 (I + P)
NORWAY	5,223 (I + P)
PANAMA	58 (P)
PHILIPPINES	563(P)
POLAND	5,822 (I + P)
PORTUGAL	656 (I + P)
RUMANIA	3,275 (I + P)
SENEGAL	23 (P)
SINGAPORE	215 (P)
SOUTH AFRICA	4,393 (I + P)
SPAIN	4,993 (I + P)
SWEDEN	5,542 (I + P)
SWITZERLAND	2,732 (I + P)
SYRIA	60 (I + P)
THAILAND	415 (P)
TOGO	2 (P)
TRINIDAD & TOBAGO	102 (I + P)
TUNISIA	64 (P)
TURKEY	802 (I + P)
UGANDA	68 (P)
U.S.S.R.	66,666 (I + P)
UNITED KINGDOM	20,982 (I + P)
TANZANIA	35 (P)
UNITED STATES	143,126 (I + P)
UPPER VOLTA	3 (P)
VENEZUELA	1,053 (I + P)*
YUGOSLAVIA	2,452 (I + P)
ZAMBIA	97 (I + P)

[1] P: Gross production of electric energy for public use

[2] I + P: Total gross generation of electricity, including that by industrial establishments

* 1970 Data

Source: United Nations

MANUFACTURED GAS PRODUCTION

COUNTRY	1971 PRODUCTION (MILLION CU. M.)
ALGERIA	4.3 (A)[1]
AUSTRALIA	336 (A&B)
AUSTRIA	54.3 (A&B)
BELGIUM	248 (A&B)
BRAZIL	27.7 (A)
CANADA	215 (A&B)[1]
CEYLON	0.51 (A)[1]
CZECHOSLOVAKIA	615 (A&B)
DENMARK	32.2 (A)
FINLAND	4.25 (A)
FRANCE	230 (A&B)
GERMANY, EAST	373 (A&B)
GERMANY, WEST	1,569 (A&B)
GREECE	0.71 (A)
HONG KONG	5.07 (A)
HUNGARY	57.2 (A&B)
IRELAND	17.4 (A)
ITALY	243 (A&B)
JAPAN	265 (A&B)[1]
LUXEMBOURG	1.01 (A)[1]
NETHERLANDS	63 (A&B)
NEW ZEALAND	18.2 (A)
NORWAY	2.48 (A)
PANAMA	1.56 (A)
PHILIPPINES	1.86 (A)
POLAND	590 (A&B)[1]
PORTUGAL	10.40 (A)
RUMANIA	44.7 (B)
SINGAPORE	4.82 (A)
SPAIN	198 (A&B)
TUNISIA	1.47 (A)
UNITED KINGDOM	1,705 (A&B)[1]
UNITED STATES	2,029 (B)
YUGOSLAVIA	14.07 (A)

A gas produced by gasworks

B gas produced by cokeries

[1] - 1970 production

Source: United Nations

INDEX

A

Abdul-Jabbar, Kareem, U.S. basketball player 379
ABM (antiballistic missile) systems 180
Abortion 282, 296, 400, 472
Abrams, Creighton, U.S. gen. 55
Abu Dhabi 85
Abzug, Bella, U.S. rep. 473
Accession, Treaty of, Europe 50
Acheampong, Ignatius, leader, Ghanaian 50, 69
Acquino, Benigno, Jr., Philippines pol. 337
Acupuncture 295, 296
Advanced microorganism 114
Advertising 64–65
Aeros, satellite 371
Affluent Society, book 284
Afghanistan 65, 484–85
AFL-CIO, labor union 273
Africa 66–74
UN highlights 451–52
Agaronian, Ruban, Soviet violinist 133
Age of Keynes, book 284
Aging, theories of 115
Agnes, hurricane 299
Agnew, Spiro T., U.S. vice-pres. 11, 15, 20, 397
Agriculture 75–78
Afghanistan 65
Brazil 118
Chile 145
China 149
evolution of 81
India 249, 250
Mexico 301
Mongolian People's Rep. 302
U.S.S.R. 442–43
Aharoni, Yohanan, Israeli, archeologist 88
Aid to Families with Dependent Children (AFDC) 470–71
Airlines 423, 425, 433–34
Air Pollution 297
Alabama 398
Alaska 398
pipeline 209, 426, 456
Albania 78, 484–85
Alberta 135
Alcoholism 166
Al Fatah, Palestinian guerrilla org. 265
Algeria 85–86, 484–85
Algol, Star 103
Ali, Muhammad, U.S. boxer 382
Alice Cooper band, U.S. rock group 314
Allan, James, Brit. doctor 294
Allen, Woody, U.S. act. 308
Allende, Salvador, pres., Chile 145–46, 194
All in the Family, TV show 415
Alsop, Joseph, U.S. columnist 181
Aluminum production 256, 493
Ambassadors and envoys (list) to and from U.S. 79
American Basketball Association (ABA) 381

American Dance Marathon 169
American Library Association (ALA) 284
American Numismatic Association 241
American Revolution Bicentennial Commission 241
Amin, Idi, leader, Uganda 66, 68–69, 446
Amish people 280, 281
Amtrak, U.S. railroad 432
Anderson, Jack, U.S. columnist 333, 358
Andreotti, Giulio, premier, Italy 55, 263–64
Andres Perez, Carlos, Venezuelan pol. 468
And They Put Handcuffs on the Flowers, play 419
Anfinsen, Christian Boehmer, U.S. biochemist 319
ANIK-1 (Telsat-1), satellite 371
An Loc, S. Vietnam 25, 30
Anthropology 80–81
Antigua 140
Antoon, A. J., U.S. dir. 418
ANZUS treaty, Pacific area 106
Apartheid
Rhodesia 69–71
South Africa 71–74
United Nations 452
Apollo program, U.S. space 53, 365, 367, 369, 456, 457
Arab Emirates, United 85, 490–91
Arab-Israeli conflict 82–84, 261–62, 265
Arab Petroleum-Exporting Countries, Organization of (OAPEC) 86–87
Arab states 82–87
merger of Egypt and Libya 85
Aranda, Gabriel, Fr. jour. 222
Archeology 81, 88–89
Archery 396
Architecture 90–92
awards 350
Japan 266
Argentina 60, 93–95, 484–85
agriculture 77
labor 277
Arizona 398–99
Arkansas 399
Armed forces, U.S. 177–78
Arnold, Richard C., U.S. physicist 343
Arrabel, Spanish exile 419
Arrow, Kenneth J., U.S. econ. 319
Arts 96–101
prizes and awards 350
Ashbrook, John, U.S. cong. 15, 454, 456
Ashcroft, Peggy, Brit. act. 332
Association of Southeast Asian Nations (ASEAN) 252
Association of State Correctional Administrators 349
Astronomy 102–4
Athenagoras I, Eastern Orthodox patriarch 360
Atlantic Ocean, survey 322
Attica State Prison, N.Y. 349

Australia 61, 105–06, 484–85
South Pacific conferences 320, 321
Austria 106, 484–85
Automobiles 189, 256
insurance 258
pollution control 341–42
racing 374–75
safety cars 426
Avilov, Nikolai, Ukrainian athlete 44
Avoriaz, France 91
Awami League, Bangladesh 108, 112

B

Badminton 396
Baffin Island, Canadian national park 136
Bahamas, The 139
Bahrain 484–85
Balaguer, Joaquín, pres. Dominican Rep. 138
Balance of payments, U.S. 187–88, 192–93
Balanchine, George, U.S. choreographer 168–69
Ballet 168–69
Bandaranaike, Sirimavo, prime min., Ceylon 143
Bangladesh 50, 107–12, 247, 249, 324–26, 484–85
Banzer Suarez, Hugo, pres., Bolivia 60, 116
Barbados 484–85
Bardeen, John, U.S. physicist 318
Barnes, Roger, U.S. doctor 294–95
Barrett, David, Can. prem. 129, 135
Barth, John, U.S. author 286
Barthelme, Donald, U.S. author 287
Baseball 376–78
Basketball 379–81
Olympic games 40, 42, 45
Basque nationalism 373
Bates, Alan, Brit. act. 419
Bay, Philippines 298
Bay Area Rapid Transit System, San Francisco 431–32
Beard, Dita, ITT lobbyist 52
Beauvoir, Simone de, Fr. author 288
Bebe, typhoon 299
Begich, Nick, U.S. Rep. 59
Behavior, anthropology 80–81
Belafonte, Harry, U.S. act. 305
Belgium 50, 113, 484–85
Belladonna, Giorgio, Ital. bridge player 119
Belmont Stakes, horse race 388
Bennett, W. A. C., Can. pol. 129, 135
Berg, David, founder, Children of God 360
Berlin, Germany
East-West treaty 229–32
Berlinguer, Enrico, politician, Italy 64

Haile Selassie, emperor, Ethiopia 69
Haiphong, N. Vietnam 53
Haiti 138, 486–87
Halberstam, David, U.S. author 288
Hall, Freeman, U.S. meteorologist 297
Halstead, Bruce W., U.S. doctor 240
Handball 396
Harald Fairhair, king, Norway 320
Hare Krishna, religious sect 362
Harriman, W. Averell, U.S. states. 16
Hartke, Vance, U.S. sen. 454
Hassan II, king, Morocco 86, 87
Hawaii 401
Health 237–40
  insurance 258
Health Maintenance Organizations, U.S. 238
Hearing aids 343
Heart disease 295–96
Heath, Edward, prime minister, U.K. 60, 127, 445, 447–48
Helder Camara, Dom, Brazilian archbishop 117
Heldman, Gladys, tennis off. 394
Helen, typhoon 299
Hellman, Kurt, Brit. doctor 295
Henderson, Paul, Can. hockey player 128
Hennessy Classic, powerboat racing 395
Henning, Ann, U.S. athlete 39
HEOS A-2 (Highly Eccentric Orbit Satellite) 371
Heroin 184–85, 225
Herwig, Barbara, U.S. FBI assistant 216
Hesburgh, Theodore, U.S. college pres. 335
Hexachlorophene, disinfectant 239–40
Heyman, Allan, tennis off. 394
Hicks, Sir John, Brit. econ. 319
High Sanctuary of the Daisekiji, Japan 362
Highways 427
Hijacking 55, 261, 400, 431
Hitchcock, Alfred, U.S. film producer 333
Hockey, ice 128, 388–91
Hodges, Gil, U.S. athlete 378
Holum, Dianne, U.S. athlete 39
Holyoake, Sir Keith, prime min., N. Zealand 51, 317
Homestake gold mine, S.D. 103
Honduras 141, 486–87
Honecher, Erich, leader, E. Germany 229, 230–31, 234
Hong Kong 242
Hooks, Benjamin L., U.S. off. 335
Hoover, J. Edgar, U.S. off. 172, 216
Hormone treatment 296
Horse racing 388
Horseshoe pitching 396

Housing 243–45
Huang Yung-sheng, chief of staff, China 153
Hubble, Edwin, U.S. astronomer 102
Huebner, Robert, U.S. doctor 114
Hughes, Howard, U.S. industrialist 285
Humphrey, Hubert H., U.S. sen. 11, 15, 454, 457
Hungary 246, 486–87
Husak, Gustav, leader, Czechoslovakia 167
Hussein, king, Jordan 86
Hutus, Burundi tribe 66

I

Iakovos, Eastern Orthodox Archbishop 360
Iba, Henry, U.S. Olympic coach 40
ICBM (Intercontinental Ballistic Missile) 180
Ice hockey 128, 388–91
Iceland 246, 486–87
  Britain 449
  chess tournament 144
Ice skating 396
Idaho 401
Illinois 401
Immigration, Canada 126
Imports see Trade
Improved Tiros Operational Satellite-D 371
Income, United States 186, 187
India 52, 247–51, 486–87
  agriculture 77
  Bangladesh 110, 112
  Pakistan 324–25
Indiana 401
Indianapolis 500, auto race 375
Indians, American
  Washington sit-in 458
Indochina War 24–37, 178, 455, 456, 464
  armed forces, U.S. 177
  end-the-war legislation 219
  environmental destruction 207
  peace negotiations 457
  S. Korea 272
  Thailand 418
  UN views on 451
Indonesia 220, 251–52, 486–87
Industry 253–57
  Australia 105, 106
  Brazil 118
  Canada 126–28
  China 149, 151
  consumer affairs 186, 188–91
  crimes against 166
  energy consumption 202
  India 250
  United Kingdom 445
  U.S.S.R. 443–44
Inflation
  Chile 146
  France 223–25
  Latin America 276–77
  Netherlands 317

United States 186
  West Germany 232–33
Influenza 296
Insurance 258
Intelsat 371
Interest rates, U.S. 188
International Federation of Library Associations 284
International Machine Tool Show, Chicago 256
International Telephone and Telegraph Co.
  antitrust case, 146, 456
Iowa 401
Iran 259, 486–87
Iraq 53, 486–87
  petroleum production 55, 87
Ireland, Northern 50, 52, 260, 445–46
Ireland, Republic of 51, 259–60, 445–46, 486–87
Irish Republican Army (IRA) 51, 56, 260, 446
Iron and steel industry 128, 255
Irving, Clifford, U.S. author 285, 356
Irving, Jules, U.S. theater dir. 422
Israel 50, 55, 60, 219, 261–62, 486–87
  Olympic terrorism 38, 83, 84, 233
  Soviet emigrants 361
  Tel Beer-sheba dig 88–89
  Uganda expelled Israelis 68–69
  UN highlights 451, 452
Italy 263–65, 277, 486–87
Ivory Coast 486–87

J

Jablonski, Henryk, pres., Poland 52
Jackson, Henry M., U.S. senator 11, 180–81, 454
Jackson, Mahalia, U.S. singer 174
Jaffe, Jerome H., U.S. doctor 184
Jagger, Mick, Brit. singer 314
Jamaica 138, 486–87
James Associates, U.S. architects 91
Japan 265–70, 486–87
  agriculture 78
  China 58, 154
  iron and steel industry 255
  labor 276
  Mexico 301, 302
  Nichiren Shoshu sect 362
  Olympic games 38, 47
  United States 453
Jarring, Gunnar V., Swed. dip. 82
Javacheff, Christo, "Valley Curtain" 100
Jazz 316
Jenkins, Roy, Brit. labor leader 53
Jesus People, religious movement 360

Wolf Trap Farm Park for the Performing Arts, Va. 328
Women 471–72
  armed forces, U.S. 178
  crime arrests 163
  in literature 285, 288
  priesthood 361
Woodcock, Leonard, U.S. labor leader 52
Woodham-Smith, Cecil, British author 287
World Bank 221
World Council of Churches 362
World Fellowship of Buddhists 362
World Series 376
World Trade Center, New York City 156
Wottle, Dave, U.S. athlete 41
Wrestling 396

Wyoming 407

Y

Yachting 395
Yahya Khan, Agha Mohammad, former pres., Pakistan 50, 108, 110, 249, 324
Yellowstone National Park, U.S. 327–29
Yemen 490–91
  merger with Southern Yemen 59, 85
Yew, Lee Kuan, prime min., Singapore 363
Yosef, Ovadia, Sephardic chief rabbi 361–62
Young, John W., U.S. astronaut 53, 365

Youth 474–78
  crime arrests 163–64
  drug abuse 184–85
  Indochina War 36
  U.S. elections 19
Yugoslavia 478, 490–91
  Bulgaria 119
Yukon Territory 137

Z

Zaire 362, 490–91
Zambia 69, 490–91
Zayed of Abu Dhabi, Arab leader 325
Zinc production 257
Zindel, Paul, U.S. playwright 420
Zoos 478–80